I0876945

SIMMS

John Caldwell Guilds

The University of Arkansas Press
Fayetteville 1992

# SIMMS

## A Literary Life

Copyright © 1992 by John Caldwell Guilds

All rights reserved
Manufactured in the United States of America

99 98 97 96 95 5 4 3 2 1

First paperback printing 1995

*This book was designed by C. H. Russell using the Minion typeface.*

The paper used in this publication meets the minimum requirements of the American National Standard for Permanence of Paper for Printed Library Materials Z39.48-1984. ♾

*Library of Congress Cataloging-in-Publication Data*

Guilds, John Caldwell, 1924-
Simms: A literary life/John Caldwell Guilds.
p. cm.
Includes bibliographical references and index.
ISBN 1-55728-245-5 (cloth)
ISBN 1-55728-378-8 (paper)
1. Simms, William Gilmore, 1806-1870.
2. Authors, American—19th century—Biography.
I. Title
PS2853.G84 1992
818' . 309—dc20
[B] 91-35919
CIP

Portions of this book have appeared, in a different form, in publications by the author in the *Georgia Historical Quarterly,* the *Southern Literary Journal, Studies in Bibliography, South Carolina Journals and Journalists,* and *Stories and Tales,* vol. V of *The Writings of William Gilmore Simms: Centennial Edition,* and are reprinted by permission.

Frontispiece: Cameo brooch of William Gilmore Simms *(Given by Simms to his wife, Chevillette Roach Simms, in 1859; now in the possession of Mary Simms Oliphant Furman)*

To the memory of

*Mary C. Simms Oliphant*

*… all biography should be written* con amore. *… without violating the truth, and yet with some softening of its harsher effects.*

*Simms, 1867*

# Contents

## PART FOUR
## Against the Wind (1860–1870)



## Conclusion



## *Appendices*

# Preface

In 1988, in the introduction to *"Long Years of Neglect": The Work and Reputation of William Gilmore Simms,* I observed that sooner or later a reawakening of interest in Simms, one of America's most important writers of the nineteenth century, was bound to occur. As if confirming that Simms's "long years of neglect" were indeed coming to an end, the next two years saw the publication of two consequential scholarly works on Simms: in 1989 Mary Ann Wimsatt's *The Major Fiction of William Gilmore Simms,* the first book-length study of his fiction; and in 1990 James E. Kibler, Jr.'s, crucial edition of Simms's *Selected Poetry,* based on decades of research and study. The appearance in three years of three books focused on the *oeuvre* of William Gilmore Simms suggests that a gifted and compelling author is perhaps gradually reclaiming some of the distinction he held in the late 1850s during the peak of his literary production. At any rate, a reevaluation of Simms's literary significance is definitely in process. What has been most missing in Simms scholarship, and is also needed to fill a lacuna in American literary scholarship, is an up-to-date critical biography that permits the man and his works to speak for themselves. This I have attempted to write, and now, one hundred years after William Peterfield Trent's *William Gilmore Simms* (American Men of Letters Series, 1892), *Simms: A Literary Life* comes from the University of Arkansas Press.

The timing for a new biography is, I believe, fortunate. Not only does the distance of a century allow Simms to be seen in more objective perspective, but the current theoretical challenges to the canonization of American letters invite assessments of neglected or forgotten authors at the very time that Simms is coming back into print. *Simms: A Literary Life* examines the man's multifarious talents—literary, political, and social—as well as his personal relationships and his sometimes intense struggle with himself. Simms was a complicated person, marked by inconsistencies and contradictions, but with fervently held dreams of literary greatness for himself, his region, and his nation and an unfaltering commitment to the realization of those dreams. As biographer, I have benefited significantly from recent scholarship on Simms, some of which I have already cited. Particularly valuable has been Kibler's well-researched reappraisal of Simms the poet, whose achievement Kibler calls "impressive, almost staggeringly so, considering his neglect." In my work I have drawn from Simms's poems and from Kibler's annotations; yet I continue to believe that the uniqueness of Simms—and the basis for his claim to literary permanence—is to be found in his fiction, particularly in his novels, where his panoramic vision, unbridled imagination, and sweeping power are best displayed. My study has convinced me that Simms was in quintessence a novelist. As a professional man of letters, he studied and practiced every craft in his trade and excelled at most of them; he possessed unusual gifts not only in the short story and in poetry, but also in literary criticism and in letter writing. Nonetheless, his vision of an American literature by Americans found its fullest personal expression in the novel; and it is here, I believe, that his contribution is greatest.

The difficult task of writing Simms's biography has been eased by the generous help of many individuals and institutions. My largest debt is to the late Mary C. Simms Oliphant, the granddaughter of the novelist, who granted me access to the family archives and gave me, in innumerable interviews, letters, and open-ended "Simms sessions," the full benefit of her vast knowledge, wisdom, and passion for Simms. I am also greatly indebted to the scholar who introduced me not only to Simms but also to Mrs. Oliphant—the late Jay B. Hubbell, founding father of the serious teaching and study of American letters, whose encouragement sparked my early interest in Simms and whose guidance made meaningful my first research on Simms. Another scholar to whom I owe a great personal debt as well as the professional gratitude shared by all who study American literature is the late T. C. Duncan Eaves, my colleague at the University of Arkansas and the editor (with Mrs. Oliphant) of the impeccable *Letters of William Gilmore Simms.* Duncan's encyclopedic mind and sharp wit were a constant source of knowledge and insight into the intricate and paradoxical world of Simms. Those who gave freely of their time in the reading and criticism of the manuscript, much to the benefit of the writer, include Willard B. Gatewood, James B. Meriwether, James E. Kibler, Jr., Anne Blythe, Miriam J. Shillingsburg, Suzanne Maberry, and—most of all—Gertrud Bauer Pickar. I am indebted to graduate assistants Caroline Carvill, Neal Gibson, James P. Cantrell, and Caroline Collins for their help in preparing the manuscript in its various stages and would like to thank Deborah Bowen for compiling the index. I wish particularly to acknowledge the assistance of Mary Simms Oliphant Furman, great-granddaughter of Simms, who graciously gave of her time and made available most of the illustrations found in this book. Other colleagues, students, and friends who have contributed in one way or another to my research or to my understanding of Simms include Alester G. Furman III, Keen Butterworth, Patricia Stansell, Jonathan Steinberg, Margaret J. Yonce, Nell Nixon, Theresa Loftin, Ludwig Pfeiffer, Noel Polk, Ruth Taylor Todasco, Mary Ann Wimsatt, Stephen A. Meats, Rayburn S. Moore, Michael O'Brien, Mark Kaplanoff, David Moltke-Hansen, Harlan Greene, Nan Morrison, the late Charles S. Syndor, the late C. Hugh Holman, the late John R. Welsh, and the late James Brady Reece. In addition to Jay Hubbell, teachers at Duke whose learning and insight motivated my budding interest in Simms were Clarence Gohdes and the late Arlin Turner.

Heading the list of institutions that have lent financial and in-kind support are the University of Arkansas (to whose administration I am particularly indebted, especially Chancellor Daniel E. Ferritor, Vice Chancellor Donald O. Pederson, Dean Bernard L. Madison of Fulbright College of Arts and Sciences, and Prof. Keneth Kinnamon, chairman of the Department of English); Texas Technological College; the University of Houston; Clare Hall, Cambridge University; the University of Siegen; the American Philosophical Society; and Duke University. Libraries and archives where I have conducted research and have always received helpful and courteous assistance include the following: Alabama State Department of Archives and History; University of Arkansas; British Museum; Cambridge University; Colonial Williamsburg; Columbia University; College of Charleston; Charleston Library Society; Clemson University; Duke University; University of Georgia; Harvard University; University of Houston; Library of Congress; Long Island Historical Society; University of North Carolina; Southern Historical Collection, University of North Carolina; New York Public Library; The Public Record Office, Belfast; The Public Record Office, Larne; Queens University, Belfast; Rice University; South Carolina Department of Archives and History; South Carolina Historical Society; University of South Carolina; South Caroliniana Library, University of South Carolina; Stanford University;

The University of Texas, Austin; University of Virginia; The College of William and Mary; State Historical Society of Wisconsin; University of Wisconsin; and Yale University. Over and beyond even the highest expectations of courteous and efficient service were the special contributions made by Les Inabinet and Allen Stokes of the South Caroliniana Library; Mattie Russell of the Manuscripts Division, Duke University Library; Charles E. Lee, South Carolina Department of Archives and History; and John Harrison, University of Arkansas Library. In addition, I give a special word of thanks to Miller Williams for his sage counsel and to him and his staff at the University of Arkansas Press for their skill and dispatch in guiding the manuscript through the publication process.

Trudi, *Simms: A Literary Life* would be incomplete without you, and this preface is incomplete without an acknowledgment of your centrality in all I do.

JCG

*Woodlands Point, Cartwright Mountain*
*Mountainburg, Arkansas*

*… my ambition is such, that having fairly rid myself of one labour, I must necessarily go on to another. I cannot be content, if I would. The Alps may be passed but Rome's beyond them, and I shall not be satisfied short of a fine marble and permanent, not to say classically well-built residence in the Eternal City! So much for the love of fame, and human approbation, a terribly large development of which my head possesses.*

*Simms, 1834*

PART ONE

# The Formative Years
(1806–1832)

# 1 Ireland and Charleston

## *Background and Influences*

On Friday, April 18, 1806, the *Charleston Times* carried on its front page no fewer than twenty-six notices reflecting the bustling seaport's preoccupation with the going and coming of cargo ships both foreign and domestic. In 1806 Charleston was an important city, in essence "a center of the British Empire,"[1] with renown and influence disproportionate to its population of twenty-four thousand; it was, in many respects, the jewel in the South's crown, in much the same way that Boston was the jewel in New England's crown. Charleston clung to English tradition just as did Boston; and, like Boston, became the social, cultural, and intellectual center for its region, in the South's instance a vast, sparsely populated, predominantly agrarian land. The South Carolina low-country gentry visited Charleston to enjoy its social season, to transact business, and to participate in political discussion; and the talented young men came to establish themselves in the professions. In 1806 Charleston was a fashionable and relatively wealthy city proud of its heritage and complacent in its belief in the importance of its location, where, as reflected in the old saying, "the Ashley and Cooper rivers meet to form the Atlantic Ocean."[2] The notices and articles in the *Charleston Times* and the city's other daily newspaper, the *Charleston Courier*, were fairly typical on that Friday, April 18, 1806: they covered economics, politics, agriculture, business, the slave trade, and literature in routine fashion. Neither newspaper took note of the birth on the preceding day of a male infant named William Gilmore Simms, Jr. It is not surprising that announcement of this birth is missing; even if the *Courier* and the *Times* knew of the birth, which is unlikely, the arrival of a son to relatively obscure parents William Gilmore Simms, Sr., and Harriet Singleton Simms would not have been a newsworthy event. It is only with the hindsight of the historian that April 17, 1806, becomes memorable. But on that very day William Gilmore Simms, Jr., unobtrusively opened his eyes for the first time on the city to which his name is now inseparably linked as its chief literary figure. But in a real sense a book about the life of William Gilmore Simms must begin in Ireland, not Charleston.

Larne, Ireland, and Charleston, South Carolina, had little in common in the late eighteenth century other than being seaports in English-speaking nations with strong antipathies toward Great Britain and strong traditions in common with her. Yet Simms's biography provides a link. Shortly after the American Revolution William and Elisabeth (sometimes spelled "Elizabeth") Sims of Larne decided to leave the poverty and hardships of Ireland; seeking for their family better fortune in the new world, they first settled in upcountry South Carolina. Their elder son William moved shortly thereafter to Charleston, where William Simms (whose middle name was Gilmore and who added a second *m* to his father's spelling of the family name) eventually fathered a son by the same name. A connection between Larne and Charleston now existed. Today the two cities are associated as influences shaping the ancestry and destiny of William Gilmore Simms, correctly called by Jay B. Hubbell "the central figure in the literature of the Old South."[3]

Precious little is known of Simms's ancestry. No persons living in Larne today with the name "Simms" or "Sims" claim kinship with the American author. No extant passenger lists of ships leaving Belfast or Larne for North America in the late 1770s and 1780s include any Simmses or Simses.[4] But we do know that William and Elisabeth gave birth to four sons in Larne before departing for the United States: William (born 1762), James (born sometime in the 1760s), Matthew (born 1769), and Eli P. (born February 1, 1776); and that by the time of the first United States census in 1790 the family was listed as citizens of Lancaster District, South Carolina.[5] After a stay of unknown length with the family in Lancaster District, Matthew and Eli P. Sims moved to Tennessee and enjoyed prosperous lives there. Sons James and William remained much longer in South Carolina, not leaving the Palmetto state for Mississippi until relatively late in their adulthood. But whereas James for many years opted to continue living in the South Carolina piedmont, William soon migrated to the coastal city of Charleston, for by 1806 he was well established in business there, as a tavern keeper on King Street.[6]

Because the means of livelihood of the novelist's father has never before been specified other than that he was in the mercantile business, a close scrutiny of the evidence seems in order. The facts are as follows: a William Sims (either our subject's father or his grandfather) is listed, without occupation, in Charleston in the 1800 census;[7] the Charleston directory of 1803 lists "Sims, William, millwright, upper end of King-street," which seems to designate Simms's grandfather since he was by trade a millwright;[8] by 1806, however, not only is there a "Simms, William, tavern, 16 W. king street road" listing (already referred to), there is also again a listing of "Sims, William, millwright, 13 W. king street." This dual listing suggests that both father and son had moved to Charleston from Lancaster District, that the father continued his practice as a millwright at the 13 West King Street address, and that the son (i.e., the novelist's father) adopted the modified spelling "Simms" and went into business as operator of a tavern at 16 West King Street, very near his father's establishment. That the King Street place of business served as grocery as well as tavern is confirmed by the fact that the 1807 Charleston directory lists "Simms, William" under the heading "Grocers, and Licensed Retailers of Spirituous Liquors" and also contains the listing "Simms Wm. tavern & store 20 west king st. road."[9]

But much more important to this narrative is the knowledge that William G. Simms the tavern keeper and grocer succeeded in business to the extent that he could contemplate marriage. On Thursday, May 30, 1804, he wed Harriet Ann Augusta Singleton, daughter of John and Jane Miller Singleton[10] and granddaughter of Thomas Singleton, an old acquaintance of the groom's father and mother.[11] The bride, then nineteen, an attractive, gentle, and quiet young woman from a well-established family originally from Virginia, was much enamored of her forty-one or forty-two-year-old husband, who was "a large, admirably formed man, who in his vigor, was over 6 feet in height."[12] The *Charleston Times,* on Friday, June 1, 1804, took note of the wedding: "Married, last evening, by the Rev. Mr. Malcomson, Mr. William Simms, merchant, to Miss Harriet Singleton, both of this place,"[13] and the couple began their marriage with high hopes and expectations. The union rapidly produced offspring (and ultimately tragedy): first, a son named John Singleton, who was born sometime in 1805 and died in October 1806; second, another son, William Gilmore Simms, Jr., born April 17, 1806; and third, another son, James, who died in childbirth, along with his mother, on January 29, 1808. The strain and shock were too much for the husband and father, whose business failed almost simultaneously with the death of his wife and third child; and he became, almost overnight, it seems, a broken and embittered man, whose hair (according to his author-son more than fifty years later) "grew white in a week" (*PM*).

Thus, in fewer than four years the marriage of William and Harriet Simms, after an apparently auspicious beginning, was tragically ended: she and two of three children dead, he financially and emotionally bankrupt. The best pictures of Harriet Singleton Simms, who died before her twenty-third birthday, are painted in the words of the author himself. His account of her in his autobiographical notes written when he was fifty-eight reveals her gentle nature.

> My mother I never knew. She died when I was 21 months old. ... I have heard of my mother that she was handsome. She was young; her maiden name Harriet Ann Augusta Singleton. My grandmother used to think of her as the gentlest of creatures. She had a fine air for music, and sang without notes, solely, I believe, from the teachings of nature. There was a portrait of her which I remember, and had when I was a boy. It is lost. ... The portrait was painted by some obscure artist. I remember it as a feeble performance. It represented a fair young girl about 16 or 18, with her hair done up in a very artificial style, that was probably in vogue at the period. The eyes were sweet and expressive. The countenance and expression artless and girlish. The complexion, very fair. Like my father she was probably of sanguine temperament. I inherit my own temperament, which is almost purely sanguine from both my parents. My mother lies buried in St. Michael's churchyard, where her tombstone is still to be seen. (*PM*)

At his wife's death William Simms, calling Charleston "a place of tombs," deserted the city of his destruction and with it his young namesake son and sought better fortune in the Southwest, first in Tennessee, eventually in Mississippi. It is difficult to assess the psychological impact upon young William Gilmore Simms of having been left motherless and fatherless at age two. Though his father left him in the care of his maternal grandmother, Simms in effect became an orphan at the time of his earliest memories and the strong sense of alienation which permeated his adult life may have originated then. Years later Simms wrote revealingly of "the feeling of isolation in which I found myself at an early age—without father or mother, brother or indeed, kindred of any kind," as a result of which he "was always on the look out for opposition and hostility."[14]

On the other hand, Jane Miller Singleton Gates[15] did her best for her young grandson. Since she had lived near the Simmses on King Street even before her daughter's death, Jane Gates would have had many opportunities to help care for her small grandson even before the family tragedy; and, though a strict disciplinarian, she seems to have had a special touch with children. Perhaps the highest tribute Simms paid to his maternal grandmother was his recognition in later life that she was "a stern though affectionate parent" who "taught me the first great lesson without which we learn none—obedience" (*L,* I, 161). There can be little doubt that Jane Gates had a profound effect on young Simms in her role as surrogate mother, particularly in her imaginative storytelling ability. As a teen-aged girl during the Revolution Jane Miller had traveled with partisan spies in an open rowboat down the Cooper River into Charleston; her husband, John Singleton, had fought in the Revolution, and she knew at firsthand the heroic exploits of her wealthy father-in-law, Thomas Singleton, who, for his activities in the patriot cause, was arrested in 1780 by the British and sent on a prison ship to Florida. Jane Singleton Gates was a superstitious yet bookish person steeped in experience, history, literature, and the supernatural;[16] she fascinated her precocious grandson and sparked his interest in the glories of South Carolina, medieval France and Spain,[17] and ghosts of all kinds.

But it is nevertheless true that Mrs. Gates failed to give her ward (whether through shortsightedness or financial difficulties) the kind of educational opportunities he needed, nor did she provide him the strong emotional support a loving young mother might have given, deficiencies Simms noted in later life. In 1839, answering inquiries about factors shaping his career, Simms acknowledged that "My father left me when an infant to the care of an aged Grandmother" and that the "old lady" (whose "resources were small" and who was "one to economize them to the uttermost") had "wretchedly neglected" his education, which "accordingly was almost wholly nominal" (*L,* I, 161). In June 1841 Simms was even more candid concerning Jane Singleton Gates's niggardly ways; he complained that the "small maternal property" left him was "hoarded so religiously" by his grandmother "as to withhold the appropriations necessary to my education" (*L,* V, 357). But the statement by Simms which most tellingly reveals the impact of his orphanhood came in a letter of April 14, 1860, to fellow novelist John Esten Cooke, in which Simms explained that he lost his mother when only an infant: "I grew up without young associates. I grew *hard* in consequence, hard, perhaps, of manner; but with a heart craving love beyond all other possessions" (*L,* IV, 216).

Simms, then, grew up lamenting that as a child he had been deprived both of the loving care of his deceased mother and of the companionship of his deceased brothers. Try as she might, Jane Gates could not have filled that void, and disciplinarian that she was, could not have provided the reassuring warmth young Gilmore needed. Nevertheless, the bright and energetic boy was not neglected by his dutiful grandmother, who entered her young charge in the public schools of Charleston in 1812; and despite testimony to the contrary from the adult Simms, he seems to have obtained the rudiments of an education there. It is true, however, that most upper-class Charlestonians placed their sons in the hands of private tutors or enrolled them in prestigious private schools, and Simms's bitter thoughts later about his schooling perhaps may be attributed to his sense of alienation from the proud city's aristocracy as much as to the shortcomings of the schools themselves. But that the novelist did feel resentment about his grandmother's indifference to the quality of education he received as a child cannot be questioned. In the 1841 letter in which Simms first complained of Mrs. Gates's mismanagement of his inherited property left in her care, the writer frankly admitted that "the utmost" of his educational attainments "were those of a grammar school, irregularly attended."

In his "Personal Memorabilia" Simms was more specific in his criticism of "the common schools" which he entered when he was six: "... I was an example of their utter worthlessness," he wrote. "They taught me little or nothing. The teachers were generally worthless in morals and as ignorant as worthless." He commented on one "old Irishman" who "during one year taught me to spell, read tolerably, and write a pretty good hand." "He was the best," Simms ironically noted, "and he knew little. Not one of them could teach me arithmetic." Since there was, in Simms's words, "no supervision of the masters or commissioners worth a doit," in some cases the teachers "never came to the school for three days in the week." Such teachers, Simms observed, "we boys *then* thought ... the best. When they did come, they were in a hurry to get away." Under these conditions, the "boys did nothing. Never attempted to work out a rule in arithmetic, but put false proofs which were never discovered," for the master "knew as little as the boys." Simms concluded: "The whole system, when I was a boy, was worthless and scoundrelly" (*PM*).

Yet it has been noted that young Gilmore Simms was remarkably well read for his age, despite the deficiencies in his schooling. It perhaps would be more nearly accurate to say that Simms as a child was inquisitive enough and precocious enough to become a voracious reader and a facile writer despite inadequacies of his elementary schooling. Even the boyhood sickness, which produced frequent absences and brought about "almost the conviction with all that I could not be raised," had "its advantages," Simms recorded. "I got books, devoured them—books of all kinds without order or discrimination," and as a result, he asserted, "acquired a thousand times more that I could have done under the ordinary school advantages" (*L*, V, 357). Family tradition has it that as a boy he worked out an ingenious plan for reading late at night despite his grandmother's decree that the light in his room be out at dusk. By installing in his room a huge dry-goods box that effectively hid from her watchful eye the flicker of his burning candle, Gilmore managed to fulfill his thirst for reading and keep peace with his grandmother at the same time. The young scholar's initiative here anticipates the drive and inventiveness he was to demonstrate time and again throughout his long career. An earlier anecdote records the premature bookishness of Mrs. Gates's ward, who even before he could walk would crawl up to her bookcase and touch with delight the leather-bound volumes.[18] In Simms's own memory of his boyhood in Charleston, he was "a student, and an unsleeping one": "My reading was perhaps not less valuable because it was desultory," he recalled when he was thirty-three. "An inquiring, self-judging mind ... can never be hurt by reading mixed books, since it is always resolute to judge for itself, and very soon acquires a habit of discriminating. I soon emptied all the bookcases of my acquaintances" (*L*, I, 161). As for Simms's favorites as a boy, he was quoted by Paul Hamilton Hayne as having said, "I used to glow and shiver in turn over 'The Pilgrim's Progress,' and Moses' adventures in 'The Vicar of Wakefield' threw me into paroxysms of laughter."[19]

In the summer of 1816—when Gilmore was ten and had just completed his fourth year in school—an event occurred that was to have great impact upon his life. In leaving his son in Charleston in 1808 with his deceased wife's mother, the elder William Gilmore Simms had extracted a promise from Mrs. Gates that she would bring his son to him in the Southwest after he had established himself there. Eight years later the elder Simms called for his son to join him in the Mississippi territory. When Jane Gates refused either to take or send her ward to his father, William Simms dispatched his brother James to Charleston with legal authorization to get the ten-year-old from his maternal grandmother. According to family archives, James Simms accosted his nephew on the streets of Charleston, and only the frantic resistance of the boy, aided by Mrs. Gates, prevented his being, in effect, kidnapped. The shouts and shrieks of young Gilmore attracted the attention of neighbors, who rushed to his rescue. Foiled in this attempt, the elder William Gilmore Simms—still working through brother James—sought to get custody of his son by court order, and the case was tried before Judge Elihu Hall Bay. James and William Simms retained the services of Benjamin Cudworth Yancey, a distinguished Charleston attorney, to represent them in court; and in return Jane Gates retained John S. Richardson and Robert Y. Hayne, both also well-known members of the Charleston bar. But rather than decide the case himself, or have a jury decision, Judge Bay took a surprising action. He left the decision—whether Simms should go to Mississippi to join his father or to remain in Charleston with his grandmother—to the ten-year-old boy himself. Under these dramatic circumstances young Simms chose Mrs. Gates and Charleston[20]—and the pattern of his life was set.

The implications of the boy's decision were far-reaching, having a profound effect upon his life and his work. Opting as he did for Charleston, young Simms was turned toward the genteel professions, including the literary. Had he chosen the Southwest, he probably would have been directed away from the arts[21] and toward the practical, the political, the economic, with success assured him by his championing father. In later years Simms voiced regret, even resentment, about the decision forced upon him as a boy not mature enough to understand its ramifications. In a letter written twenty-three years later, Simms expressed bitterness about the episode: "At ten years of age, my answer was relied upon by the Judge, to make his decision. I declared my wish to remain with my Grandmother, and the rights of the father were set aside,—I think now improperly, and as I now believe, to my irretrievable injury in many respects. Had I gone with my father, I should have shown less feeling, but more world wisdom. ... I should then have recieved the additional education the want of which I often feel & shall continue to feel while I live" (*L*, I, 161). In choosing Charleston, he was rejecting his father. The events of the summer of 1816 left a scar on Simms's consciousness that never healed. A certain ambivalence was the inevitable result of this traumatic boyhood decision: ambivalence toward his father and, perhaps most of all, ambivalence toward Charleston—a love-hate dichotomy that lasted a lifetime. Simms committed himself to Charleston, and with it to the profession of letters, at an early age, and with that commitment he repudiated his father, whom he scarcely knew but whose image he honored—almost worshipped—with a son's dutiful love in which were mingled feelings of guilt. Simms's own words in his "Personal Memorabilia," written about 1864, offer insight into the author as well as his progenitor. If Simms romanticized his mother—he was particularly proud of her Virginia heritage—he seems to have idolized the hard manhood of his Irish-born father, as the following characterization attests:

> He was a large, admirably formed man, who in his vigor, was over 6 feet in height. When in 1825 I saw him last, he was a little bent with years, but was still vigorous, and had just come from a three months tour on horseback, into the wildest regions of the Southwest. He was then about 63. He was fair and florid; his hair white as cotton, and scarce a wrinkle on his face. His temperament was one of wonderful elasticity. He was full of fun and merriment, ready at quip and jibe, and joke, with a considerable fund of humour. He was not an edu-

cated man, according to the scholar's idea: but he was an endowed one—highly endowed, I think. [?] had read a good deal, as opportunity allowed and books—very rare in his days in our forage country—could be found: was observant, thoughtful, speculative, with a quick excursive fancy, eager temperament: large enthusiasm: freedom of language, and great force, occassionally [*sic*], of expression whenever his sympathies or feelings were touched; was clever at repartee, and wrote verses with great facility. When I was a boy, I remember to have been quite touched with some of his verses in his more melancholy moments, addressed to myself by his affections for me. His epigram, in impromptu, on Jackson, I have preserved.[22]

Vigorous in physique, he was brave and, from what I gathered from my grandmother, inclined to be prompt and passionate. I recall sundry matters vaguely in which he was the hero of the neighborhood. ... When a boy I was frequently thrilled by the accounts of his trials, dangers, privations, starvation, while on his Indian campaigns. For seven days, I remember, he wrote, he had been living on horse meat, the volunteers [in Jackson's troops] having to kill their horses for food. I am sure he never got a copper for his services—very sure I and mine have never got a copper.

When I was 12 years old, he paid us a brief visit in S. C. It was then that I knew him first. He was tender and affectionate. But even then I was impressed by a singular mixture of the gentle and strong. He was self-reliant—calm—sad even in his jesting—as if he jested in spite of his own heart; just as we may see that a wounded bird will still fly. He impressed me wonderfully with reverence, to which, indeed, I had been inclined from frequent hearing of him. (*PM*)

In the same autobiographical statement Simms directly linked an affinity for his father with a sometimes strongly felt antipathy toward Charleston:

My father was of Scotch-Irish stock, and came to Charleston from Ireland when a boy. He was a native of the little town of Larne. Several of his brothers also came out, whether before or after, I know not, and settled in the interior. One of them only did I know, my uncle James, who, of all the rest, was most intimately associated with my father. I may make some memoranda of him, for I remember him as a goodnatured old man. Very ugly, but always smiling, and always very kind to me. These other brothers were Mathew and Eli. There may have been another still: but I do not remember. James settled in the interior of S. C. in Lancaster district. They have descendants, but I have never seen one of them. My father I never saw to know until I was 12 years old when he visited me in Carolina. He had been a merchant in Charleston where he became a bankrupt, and about the same time, my mother, and my two brothers dying, he abandoned the City and State. My grandmother has a thousand times told me of that phenomenon in his case, which is reported of Marie Antoinette and the others—

> His hair grew white
> In a single night—?
>
> His, according to my grandmother, grew white in a week, and he fled the home of desolation. Twenty years after, when we were traveling together in the Southwest, he gave me in a brief remark, a proof of the intensity of his memory on this subject of his privation. When I declared my purpose of returning to Charleston,—where, by the way, I was already engaged to be married, he said to me abruptly—"Return to Charleston! Why should you return to Charleston, where you can never succeed in any profession, where you need, what you have not, friends, family and fortune: and without these, your whole life, unless some accident should favor you, will be a mere apprenticeship—a hopeless striving after bread. NO! Do not think of it. Stay here. Study your profession here. And pursue it, with the energy and talent which you possess, and I will guarantee you a fortune, and, in 10 years, a seat in Congress. Do not think of Charleston. Whatsoever your talents, they will there be poured out like water on the sands. Charleston! *I know it only as a place of tombs.*" Thirty odd years have passed, and I can now mournfully say the old man was right. All that I have has been turned to waste in Charleston which has never smiled on any of my labors,—which has steadily ignored my claims—which has disparaged me to the last—to which I owe no favors, having never received an office, or a compliment, or a dollar out of their hands: and, with the exception of some dozen of her citizens who have been kind to me, and some scores of her young men who have honored me with a loving sympathy, and something like reverence,—which has always treated me rather as a public enemy, to be sneered at, than as a dutiful son doing her honor. *And I too know it as a place of tombs.* I have buried six dear children within its soil! Great God! What is the sort of slavery which brings me hither? My father was right! (*PM*)

Simms's fervid and petulant defensiveness in this passage raises many questions. That he made no mention of the life-altering decision he was forced to make at age ten is particularly strange since his most vivid memory of his Uncle James must have revolved around the attempted kidnapping and the resulting court case. This omission is even more surprising in the light of his at-length discussion of his father's dire predictions about Charleston and his optimistic faith in the future of the wide-open Southwest. The absence of any reference to this traumatic event may well indicate that he had repressed it from his memory.

It is also of interest that one of the mature author's best-known stories displays, perhaps more revealingly than anything else Simms wrote, the lingering haunting effects of the traumatic choice he as a child was forced to make between father and grandmother. To achieve in "Grayling; or, 'Murder Will

Out'" the plausible air of reality so much admired by Poe, Simms uses the medium of "[m]y grandmother"—an "old lady who had been a resident of the seat of most frequent war in Carolina during the Revolution"[23]—to relate the intriguing tale of the Hamlet-like ghost. It is not without autobiographical significance that Simms's sympathy clearly lies with the "indignant ... old lady," who "in order to combat my father's ridicule," had been "tempted to relate for the fiftieth time" the ghost story, which the father scoffed at, using tedious, rationalistic arguments to account for its "superstitions" (p. 40). And is there no satire in the haughty expostulation of the father: "Now, my son ... as you have heard all that your grandmother has to say on this subject, I will proceed to show you what you have to believe, and what not" (pp. 40–41)? The concluding paragraph of "Grayling" is more than an ending to an imaginative piece of fiction:

> I heard my father with great patience to the end, though he seemed very tedious. He had taken a great deal of pains to destroy one of my greatest sources of pleasure. I need not add that I continued to believe in the ghost, and, with my grandmother, to reject the philosophy. It was more easy to believe the one than to comprehend the other. (p. 45)

In writing this passage Simms seems to recall ghosts of his boyhood mind. Does Grayling's rejection of his father's rationalism and acceptance of his grandmother's spiritualism not reflect the author's own early decision to reject Mississippi, business-politics, and father in favor of Charleston, imaginative literature, and grandmother? The conclusion of "Grayling" suggests that imbedded in Simms's psyche lay lingering resentment of a father figure, who—dominant and aloof (yet willing to leave him at his mother's death)—nonetheless expects obeisance and obedience. The paragraph stands as an almost involuntary artistic rendering of hostility toward patriarch deeply rooted in the writer's inner consciousness. It is unique in Simms, for nowhere else does the author allow even a peek at the latent resentment submerged in his justifiable pride in the manly character and heroic accomplishments of his father.

Simms's career unquestionably was affected by the events during his tenth year. But perhaps even more than his career, the mind of Simms was profoundly affected by his having been put in a position where he had to choose between surrogate mother and father, between Charleston and the Southwest, between the known and the unknown, between the near and the far, between the genteel and the virile. The sense of alienation and hostility, the sense of not being sufficiently appreciated that recur in Simms, particularly during times of stress, stem perhaps from resentment at having been forced as a child to make an adult decision. It is not surprising that Simms the writer many times second-guessed himself when he encountered difficulty in achieving recognition and fame in Charleston, thinking that he had erred and foolishly sacrificed himself, in not accepting his father's admonition to "go west, young man!" Simms wrote more than once of his early "consciousness ... that I could never be, in my native place, what I might be elsewhere"; he sensed a "hostility" to the "claims of my intellect," which "would never be anywhere more jealously resisted" than in the "proud, wealthy & insulated community ... in which I was born" (*L*, I, 164). Yet it is also possible that Simms's defensive posture toward his father—his glorification of his virtues and his denial of his shortcomings—was a cover for his own latent resentment that his blood father had deserted him as an infant, that he consequently never knew the sense of security provided by the presence of a strong father figure. That Simms as parent played the role of strong, kindly patriarch perhaps indicates his own determination that his children never suffer the void he had felt in his childhood. The ambivalence that Simms experienced toward his father—a mixture of resentment and pride, guilt and loyalty, insecurity and faith, coolness and love—projected itself onto his world view, including his attitude toward native city and state. In rejecting his father, Simms was choosing South Carolina and Charleston; his ambivalence toward Charleston—his love for it and his animosity toward it, particularly when he felt unappreciated—is cut from the same cloth as is his filial ambivalence toward his father. And all of this, as we shall see, is preserved in the nuances of his writings, with alternating rhythms of idealism, optimism, and melancholy.

William Gilmore Simms at age thirty-eight.
*(Portrait printed in 1844 by William Edward West; now in the possession of Mary Simms Oliphant Furman)*

Simms among contemporary American authors. (*From left to right:* Henry T. Tuckerman, Oliver Wendell Holmes, Simms [*seated, far left*], Fitz Greene Halleck, Nathaniel Hawthorne, Henry Wadsworth Longfellow, Nathaniel Parker Willis, William H. Prescott, Washington

Irving, James K. Paulding, Ralph Waldo Emerson, William Cullen Bryant, John P. Kennedy, James Fenimore Cooper, and George Bancroft; from the engraving in the possession of John C. Guilds)

Engraved portrait of Simms.
*(Based on an 1853 sketch by Henry Brintnell Bounetheau; courtesy of Mary Simms Oliphant Furman)*

Chevillette Roach at age eighteen after her engagement to Simms.
*(From a daguerreotype in the possession of Mrs. James C. Player; used with permission)*

Chevillette Roach Simms,
c. age twenty-eight.
*(From a photograph in the possession of Mary Simms Oliphant Furman)*

Nash Roach. Simms's austere father-in-law.
*(Courtesy of Mary Simms Oliphant Furman)*

"Lady Lyde."
Mary Eliza Donaldson,
wife of James Lawson.
*(Courtesy of*
*Mary Simms Oliphant Furman)*

James Lawson (1799–1880).
New York literary agent and
close friend of William
Gilmore Simms.
*(Courtesy of the children of*
*William Gilmore Simms*
*Oliphant)*

James Henry Hammond (1807–1864). Simms's "most intimate friend" and confidant for more than two decades. *(Courtesy of the South Caroliniana Library)*

Paul Hamilton Hayne (1830–1886). Simms's protégé and favorite among Charleston literati. *(Courtesy of the South Caroliniana Library)*

Evert Augustus Duyckinck (1816–1878). New York editor, critic, and correspondent. *(Courtesy of Mary Simms Oliphant Furman)*

Woodlands as rebuilt in the ruins of the last fire, 1865. *(Courtesy of Mary Simms Oliphant Furman)*

Geometrically constructed rendering of the restoration of Woodlands after the 1862 fire.
*(Rendering made in 1958 by R. E. Farmer, architect; used with permission)*

WILLIAM GILMORE SIMMS, LL.D.

William Gilmore Simms in 1843, shortly after being awarded an honorary degree by the University of Alabama. *(Courtesy of Mary Simms Oliphant Furman)*

ANNA AUGUSTA SINGLETON SIMMS
"Child of my youth . . .
Thou shall be near for weal or wo
Thy love a healing balm . . ."

Anna Augusta Simms Roach (1827–1898). "Shining sword in a rusty scabbard"; the first of Simms's thirteen children. *(From a miniature in the possession of Mrs. James C. Player; used with permission)*

Simms in his sixties after the Civil War.
*(Engraving in the possession of Juliet Caruana Eaves)*

Augusta's home, *front view*, on Society Street in which Simms died.
*(Courtesy of Mary Simms Oliphant Furman)*

Rear view (of the Society Street home) from the garden.
*(Courtesy of Mary Simms Oliphant Furman)*

Simms's original burial site in Magnolia Cemetery.
*(Photograph in the possession of Mary Simms Oliphant Furman)*

Monument to Simms in White Point Gardens on the battery in Charleston.
*(Copy of sketch by Oscar Wetherington, commissioned by the South Carolina National Bank; in the possession of John C. Guilds)*

Statue of Simms in White Point Gardens, executed by J. Q. A. Ward in 1879.
*(Photograph in the possession of Mary Simms Oliphant Furman)*

William Gilmore Simms in what is thought to be the last photograph taken of him.
*(Courtesy of Mrs. James C. Player, Simm's great-great-granddaughter)*

# II Education and Apprenticeship

The decision to remain in Charleston having been made, young Gilmore Simms—apparently with the support and assistance of Grandmother Gates—made plans to enter in the fall of 1816 one of the private schools then being operated within the buildings of the College of Charleston—the college itself lying "almost in a derelict state" ("virtually inactive") between 1813 and 1823.[1] His two years at the College (for him "little more than a grammar school")[2] were apparently rewarding, but it is tragic that the formal education of the bright, enterprising youth ended when he was twelve years old. Nevertheless, he profited immensely from his brief tenure in a "flourishing" grammar school taught by regular faculty members of the College of Charleston and conducted in college buildings, though not financially supported by the college's trustees. Simms read greedily in the classics and learned enough Latin, French, German, Italian, and Spanish to translate them into free-flowing English (*MCSO,* III, XII). He also began to dabble in science, fostering an interest which led him to consider briefly a career in medicine. Upon leaving the grammar school, the not-yet-thirteen-year-old Simms—with his practical-minded grandmother's encouragement—apprenticed himself in an apothecary shop in order to explore the options of a medical career.

But his scientific interests were soon dwarfed by his passion for literature, a passion abetted by the reading habits of Charlestonians and by the easy availability of good books at the Charleston Library Society, the city's well-stocked bookstores, and the private libraries of friends. Even before his adolescence

Gilmore Simms was familiar not only with Homer and Virgil but also with the early English Romantics, whose verses were frequently published in the pages of Charleston periodicals and read at the city's congenial literary gatherings. Simms's own early literary endeavors are vividly described in a letter to James Lawson on October 16, 1841:

> My impression is that I was about eight years old when I rhymed an address for my class to the schoolmaster, on the old text—
>
> "Pray master, pray master, be courteous & kind,
> To all the good fellows &c."
>
> The object was to solicit a longer term of holiday at Christmas than he contemplated; and the old address needed to be adapted to our particular case. I need not tell you that with my wonted independence I made an entirely new one. Of this stuff, I have scarcely any recollection. At the close of the war of 1815 I was somewhere between 8 & 9 and busied myself in versifying the events of the war. The battles of New Orleans—the affairs between the Hornet & Peacock—Constitution & Guerriére were all put into verse, and actually stitched into a little book which I devoted to this purpose. So early were my attempts at book making. Portions of this doggerel were destroyed within the last ten years. I think my first verses were put into the newspaper when I was fifteen. I remember some that were published with the figure (16) as a signature. From this period I became a regular contributor to the newspapers of all sort of doggerel. Prose, I did not attempt, until sometime later—except such prose as belonged to letter writing. ... At 14 I wrote a Tragedy called "The Female Assassin"—you may readily conjecture the sort of stuff which followed such a title. At 13 I wrote a poem on some Italian stories, in 4 or 6 cantos, called "The Ring"—portions of which my uncle has, I believe, to this day. I have in my possession now a Tragedy partly written when I was 17-18—founded on the apostacy of Count Julian (*L*, I, 285).[3]

A boy with such a strong literary bent was destined for the profession of letters, not of medicine, and young Simms gave up his apprenticeship as a pharmaceutical chemist and with it any aspirations of becoming a physician. As a youngster in Charleston Simms was the leader of a literary and dramatic group composed of eight or ten boys who came together to talk about what they were reading, to recite what they themselves were writing, and to stage dramatic scenes or perhaps to enact their own plays.[4] In addition to these enthusiastic juvenile gatherings, another major positive force in whetting the precocious young Simms's already sharp appetite for literature must have been Jane Gates's predilection for storytelling. One can imagine the effect upon Gilmore's already fertile imagination of his grandmother's stirring recital of the daring war actions of Thomas Singleton, her husband's father and a great hero of the Revolution. And it was of course she who initially told Gilmore of the exploits of his own father in murderous warfare against the Creeks under Andrew Jackson. Nor was Mrs. Gates's penchant for telling tales limited to stories of war; she also possessed a hoard of stories of the supernatural, at least one of which provided (as we have seen) the basis for "Grayling." Many others must have fascinated the receptive boy. Indeed, by his sixteenth birthday he had embarked upon a literary career and was by his own words already a published poet. Whatever her deficiencies in managing property and in providing high-quality education for her talented grandson, Jane Singleton Gates contributed to the store of literary material accumulating in the mind of young Gilmore, as he was called.

This store was greatly enhanced in 1824-25 when, with Mrs. Gates's blessing, the young novelist-to-be visited his father in the great Southwest. Apparently near the close of 1824 or at the beginning of 1825 Gilmore Simms, to reach the elder Simms, traveled from Charleston, in the words of William Stanley Hoole, "by stagecoach through Augusta to Milledgeville (Georgia) and Fort Mitchell to Montgomery (Alabama), then down the Alabama River to Selma and Mobile and up the Tombigbee to Demopolis and up the Black Warrior to Tuscaloosa. The last 160 miles westward from Tuscaloosa to Georgeville he made overland, via Columbus, Louisville and Koscuiskio (Mississippi)."[5] But Hoole (following William P. Trent's lead) is wrong in at least one detail: Georgeville as the site of the elder Simms's plantation and Simms's ultimate destination. Recent research by Miriam Shillingsburg has demonstrated that the Mississippi plantation of Simms's father was located near Columbia, a bustling town on the Pearl River and the seat of Marion County.[6]

At the plantation, the impressionable youth came to know his father really for the first time. According to Trent, "the active old man had [just] returned from a trip of three hundred miles into the heart of the Indian country," fascination enough for his novice son; but even more engrossing, for several months' duration the two Simmses rode together on horseback to various settlements on the frontier of Alabama and Mississippi, accepting graciously the peculiar hospitality of rough backwoodsmen and providing the Charleston youth the opportunity to posit in his memory eye-pictures that he would draw upon time and again in creating his Border Romances and other writings of the frontier. Once, when he and his father visited the Creek and Cherokee nations in Alabama, the younger Simms fell asleep and awoke to discover that "his head had been pillowed on a lonely grave" marked with a "rudely carved cross" (Trent, p. 15). Imagining the grave to be that of one of

De Soto's followers, the susceptive young writer-to-be never forgot the experience[7] and later used it for literary purposes. ("The Grave in the Forest" [1853] deals directly with the event, and his novel *Vasconselos* [1853] is concerned with De Soto's expedition.) Another work, a poem apparently composed on the spot and entitled simply "Written in Mississippi," records Simms's spontaneous attraction to the wilderness home of the Choctaw Nation, "where man has scarcely ever come. … Unchanged by love, unharm'd by hate."[8]

Probably it was also during this visit (which Simms at fifty-eight remembered occurring "[t]wenty years after" his father left Charleston) that the elder Simms had exhorted his son to forget Charleston, "where you can never succeed in any profession," and stay with him at his Mississippi plantation, where "I will guarantee you a fortune."[9] It is possible that Simms would indeed have preferred to remain with his father in the challenging and invigorating Southwest; but he had already made the commitment to seek his literary destiny in Charleston, and nothing had occurred since that momentous 1816 decision to dampen his enthusiasm for belles-lettres or to discourage his ambitions. On the contrary, by 1825 he was beginning to formulate specific plans about literature as a profession, rather than merely an avocation as it had been for the first eighteen years of his life. Simms's reflections in 1864 or 1865, colored by his perception of adversity encountered since his youth, do not—it seems safe to assume—accurately reflect his thinking at the earlier time. At any rate, Simms returned to Charleston, as scheduled, and although he brought from the Southwest a different perspective of our nation's destiny, he in no way had dropped his earlier ambitions. Indeed, he came back to the South Carolina seaboard with at least two new resolves.

In conjunction with his pursuit of a career in letters, he intended also to prepare himself for the practice of law, a profession consistent with his talent for oratory and for the spoken, as well as the written, word. Having dropped his medical ambitions, if not his interest in science, Simms in 1825 began the study of law in the office of Charles Rivers Carroll, a wealthy attorney with literary proclivities, who had earlier become acquainted with the young writer and remained his lifelong friend. Family legend has it that in addition to Carroll, the wealthy Charleston family of Henry Gourdin befriended Simms: they became so impressed with his ability as a juvenile that they offered to help send him to Europe for a proper education, an offer his pride would not allow him to accept. The same tradition purports also that Hugh Swinton Legaré, the noted classical scholar and lawyer who had recognized and encouraged Simms's poetic efforts as a juvenile,[10] had recommended Simms to Carroll, whom he also knew well, as a brilliant young Charlestonian with literary and political ideas close to Carroll's own. That Simms possessed a talent for law cannot be doubted, and under Carroll's able tutelage he made rapid progress with his legal reading.

But the study of law was only one of the resolutions of young Gilmore Simms upon his return to Charleston: the other being to leap headlong into his chosen profession. And leap into literary waters he did, but not with a resounding splash. When the *Southern Patriot* of June 9, 1825, announced that "a Society of Young Gentlemen" was planning to publish by subscription "a Weekly Literary Miscellany to be termed *The Album,*" probably few Charlestonians took note. Magazines and newspapers came and went in Charleston, and the appearance of a prospectus was hardly new to the citizens of the old city. Hardly a handful of readers could have known that nineteen-year-old William G. Simms, Jr., was included among the "young gentleman" editors; and the magazine attracted so little attention that its name was never mentioned by the Charleston press after the few encouraging comments inspired by the prospectus.

Nevertheless the *Album* was a bold, ambitious venture for Simms and his fellow fledgling editors. With the establishment of the small literary magazine, Simms had begun fulfilling what he must have projected for himself when he considered his options at his father's Mississippi plantation: a literary life in Carolina. With a start toward a career in law (which Simms knew from Carroll did not prohibit the practice of letters) and now with a start toward a career in literature, Simms had yet another interest. He had become enamored of Anna Malcolm Giles, two and a half years his junior, to whom, shortly after he began with the *Album,* he became engaged. Anna Malcolm, the daughter of Othniel J. Giles, who had at one time served as state coroner before going into business as a grocer on Market Street,[11] was from a respectable family no more socially prominent than Simms's, and the two young lovers must have felt comfortable with each other. In later life Simms intimated that nubile teen-aged Anna Giles had met the criteria for the "most sacred & vitally important selection in this life" in that she was "equally lovely in moral & physical respects."[12]

Before the couple were wed, however, the prospective bridegroom had not only become heavily involved with the *Album,* but within a year after his first visit to his father in Mississippi the young editor had made a second trip to the Southwest. The first issue of the *Album* appeared on Saturday, July 2, 1825,[13] and until recently it had been believed that the journal had died with its December 24, 1825, number. But in 1986 James Kibler (who has an extraordinary knack for turning up rare Simmsiana) reported discovering a unique second volume of the *Album* and with it some "biographical information ... of first importance," including Simms's first four published letters.[14] These "Letters from the West" (published in the *Album* for March 4, March 11, April 1, and May 20, 1826) reveal not only specific information about Simms's second trip within less than a year to Alabama, Mississippi, and Louisiana; but more important, the young editor's fascination with the crude, materialistic, yet picturesque frontier and his recognition of its literary appeal. Though his letters from New Orleans, Mobile, and Columbus, Mississippi, graphically reveal Simms's "disgust with materialism and greed on the frontier," they do not support the contention that "the theories of his [Simms's] mature work concerning American culture and the negative force the frontier had upon it were thus already formed at this early age."[15] (Simms's visionary views of the frontier, as will be demonstrated later, are too complicated and far-reaching to be so neatly categorized.) But the comic treatment of the Choctaw chief and the French dandy in Letter IV is, as Kibler points out, "Simms's first known use of backwoods humor ... nearly a decade before ... A. B. Longstreet's *Georgia Scenes* (1835), commonly accepted as the seminal work of the genre."[16] And of even more significance, perhaps, is the fact that Simms recorded in a "note book" material for further literary use—material he possibly used, for instance, in the composition of "Sharp Snaffles" during the last year of his life.[17]

After almost a year of existence, the *Album*—with the issue of the twenty-fifth number of the second volume (twenty-six issues were needed to round out the volume)—apparently ceased publication on June 24, 1826, without achieving either financial or critical success.[18] Nevertheless, the experience of serving as an editor was invaluable to young Gilmore Simms.[19] It gave him not only an organ for the publication of his own juvenilia (and one suspects that this was not a minor attraction), but also an opportunity to formulate policy for his future, larger-scale editorial ventures. Already he had learned to strike out boldly and fearlessly as a critic, and already he had initiated the theme that was to be the keynote of his career as a magazine editor: the advancement of Southern literature.

The student of American literature, however, is interested in the *Album* primarily because it contains some of the first published writings of an important literary figure. While most of Simms's contributions are no better than would be expected from the pen of an inexperienced young writer steeped in Scott and Byron, there is an occasional flash of vigor and gusto that anticipates the work of the mature Simms. Already apparent are his story-telling ability and his diffuse style. Although it is impossible to determine exactly how much of the *Album* is Simms's handiwork, since all contributions are either unsigned or signed by pseudonyms, he probably wrote considerably more than the seventy-six items ascribed to him[20]: sixty poems, four reviews, four letters, and eight works of fiction of varying length.

Although the poems by Simms in the *Album* are not distinguished poetry, they do represent the best to appear in the *Album,* and several of them ("The Captive," "The Miniature," "Shadows," "Come seek the ocean's depth with me," and "Ruins") anticipate some of his better later poems. The book reviews are notable chiefly for their independence and fair-mindedness; the young critic seems already to have realized that if his opinions were to be of value they must be independently formed, and that if his critical writings were to possess merit, they must attempt to analyze both virtues and defects, without compromising his own standards of excellence and without regard to the author's reputation or popularity. The letters are the earliest in what was to become a magnificent collection, perhaps the most impressive in nineteeth-century American literature.

But by far the most interesting of Simms's writings in the *Album* are the two novelettes published serially, "The Robber—an Eastern Tale" and "Moonshine." "The Robber," which runs to seven installments, appeared as the featured work of fiction in the opening numbers of the *Album:* it is a Gothic tale equipped with a villainous protagonist, an innocent heroine, gloomy caves with secret passages, a flesh-devouring ghoul, and fierce voracious birds. "The Robber" anticipates in a way "The Confessions of a Murderer," which in turn became the basis of *Martin Faber* (1833).[21] The second novelette, "Moonshine," appearing under the pseudonym "Triptolemus Twig," begins in the number before "The Robber" terminates, and continues through twelve more installments. Although the tale lacks unity, and its author changes his design after it is well under way, "Moonshine" is a forerunner of the first of Simms's "Revolutionary Romances," *The Partisan* (1835). "Moonshine" is laid in South Carolina just before the eruption of the Revolutionary War and, like the novel, has as one of its leading characters a Colonel Walton, who is a British sympathizer at the outbreak of the "rebellion" and the widowed father of the beautiful and charming heroine—Charlotte in "Moonshine," Katharine in *The Partisan.* In each case the heroine has a sympathetic maiden aunt and—more important—loves a partisan leader in General Marion's army. To carry the striking similarities even further, in both the story and the novel a decisive battle is fought near Colonel Walton's plantation.

Thus Simms was actively engaged in writing for the *Album* as well as in directing its editorial policy. Although for want of evidence one cannot say so definitely, the possibility exists that much of the *Album* was written by Simms.

Whatever the number, his contributions, though crude in themselves, prefigure some of his best poems and perhaps two of his major novels. Simms, the aspiring young author, was now published, albeit anonymously, had experienced disappointment without loss of face or ambition, and now was ready to commit his name, as well as his efforts, to literary creation.

William Gilmore Simms and Anna Malcolm Giles were wed on October 19, 1826. By this time Simms had almost finished reading for the bar examination (he was admitted to the Charleston bar on his twenty-first birthday) and had established himself as a hard-working and ambitious editor/writer soon to become a professional man of letters.

# III The Beginnings of a Career

Evidence of Simms's growing awareness of what it took to be a success in political-minded literary Charleston came during his busy tenure as editor of the *Album.* On August 16, 1825, Revolutionary War hero Gen. Charles Cotesworth Pinckney died in Charleston; and young Simms immediately began work on a eulogy of this highly honored and respected Carolinian with such alacrity that his *Monody, on the Death of Gen. Charles Cotesworth Pinckney* (published, incidentally, by Gray & Ellis, publishers of the *Album*) was ready in time to be favorably noticed by the *Charleston Courier* of September 14. Though the title page of *Monody* simply bore the inscription "by a South-Carolinian," the reviewer in the *Courier* stated that the "talent[ed] ... little poem" in heroic couplets had "proceeded from a hand not unknown to our readers," leaving little doubt that he knew its author. Since the *Courier* followed with an even more laudatory review in its September 25 issue, young Simms could hardly have missed the irony of the message: praise of great men wins recognition, laborious literary effort does not. Simms, it is not to be doubted, was sincere in his appreciation of Pinckney, but neither can it be doubted that the hard-working editor saw portrayal of national heroes as a profitable theme for future literary efforts. Simms's own valuation of *Monody* is perhaps indicated by his failure to mention it in his letters or include it in his various listings of his published writings.

His literary productiveness as editor of the *Album* left Simms with many completed works on hand and many more in progress. This store he put to good use. For his second volume of poetry, *Lyrical and Other Poems* (Charleston: Ellis & Neufville, 1827), which bears the date "Jan. 1, 1827" in its advertisement, but which he had begun assembling before September 1826,[1] Simms included no fewer than twenty poems that had first appeared anonymously or pseudonymously in the *Album,* and many others must already have been in whole or in part in manuscript form. In his introduction to *Lyrical and Other Poems*—published with his name on the title page for the first time—Simms acknowledged that "with few exceptions" he had written the selected poems "before my nineteenth year." Somewhat surprisingly, the slim volume was reviewed in the *New York Literary Gazette and American Athenaeum* for February 3, 1827; in a short, remarkably favorable notice (signed "FLORIO"), it ranked Simms "among the first of American Poets" and asserted: "The fire of true genius burns in his song, and its light is pure, warm and brilliant. We have read his poetry with unqualified pleasure, we like its very faults, for they are the bold generous faults of high genius, and lofty feelings" (III, 161–62). Such high praise from an unexpected source invites speculation whether Simms (who had used "Florio" as a favorite pseudonym in the *Album*) could possibly have arranged to review his own book: certainly the young author could have hoped for no better review *had* he written it himself.[2] Whatever the identity of "FLORIO," the notice of *Lyrical and Other Poems* under that name served Simms well. The *Charleston Courier* reprinted the "FLORIO" review in its issue of February 17, 1827, an action which seems to have prompted a review in the *Charleston Mercury* on February 27 and another follow-up critique in the *Courier* itself on June 2. In addition, the *U.S. Review and Literary Gazette,* recognizing many "blemishes" in the work of the novice, notwithstanding concluded that Simms possessed "no ordinary degree of poetical talent" (II [April 1827], 70–71). In truth, *Lyrical and Other Poems* was praised beyond its merits in these contemporary reviews; in later years Simms himself acknowledged that the collection "contained a great deal of very sorry stuff" which he nevertheless fancied "had something in them" (*L,* V, 356). But looked upon as a haphazard, yet earnest work by a highly talented nineteen-year-old poet unsure of his craft, the volume has flashes of brilliance and power that augured well for Simms's future artistic accomplishment.

By the time of his twenty-first birthday, then, William Gilmore Simms had accomplished several important things. He had become a member of the South Carolina bar; he was the author of two volumes of poetry; he had been editor of a literary journal and had published a substantial number of works in it; he was a married man, and his bride of six months, Anna Giles Simms, was pregnant with their first child. Furthermore, he was assembling a third book of poetry and planning to undertake another, more ambitious venture in editing a literary journal. Later in the year, 1827, he was appointed a magistrate for Charleston, culminating his study of law with Charles Rivers Carroll, although with time the legal profession would become decreasingly important in his life as he grew ever more committed to the literary and the political. On November 11, 1827, a daughter, who was to be the only offspring of William Gilmore and Anna Giles Simms, was born and subsequently christened Anna Augusta Singleton Simms in honor of her mother and her paternal grandmother. Both mother and daughter came through childbirth safely, but Anna Giles Simms was much enfeebled by the ordeal, and seems never to have regained good health. Nevertheless, the young couple, probably living in Summerville rather than Charleston to cut expenses, was happy in experiencing together the complexities of parenthood, and Simms's confidence that he had the ability to make it as a writer was rising.

Likely it was during the satisfying early period in Summerville that Simms the natural-born actor first displayed his talent for mimicry. Family records verify that Simms possessed a remarkable penchant for outrageous comic portrayal of four favorite characters: a backwoodsman, an Indian chief, a Yankee peddler or dandy, and a young Carolina low-country fop. As we shall see, Simms never outgrew his passion for mimetic characterizations and in later life occasionally offended sophisticated captive audiences with his brash impersonations. A particularly vivid anecdote involves the reminiscences of an eyewitness to an amusing dramatic performance of the youthful Simms in Summerville. It seems that in the opening presentation, Simms, who played the part of a Comanche chief, enacted his role as child-snatcher so fearsomely that the child-actor became terrified. As a result "the mother ... seated in audience ... let out a scream wildly, rushed up on the stage to grab, to rescue the child, and broke up the play."[3] Such light moments must have helped ease tensions for the hard-working young barrister-turned-writer, but for the most part he diligently pursued his newly chosen craft.

Even as he won appointment as a Charleston magistrate, probably through the influence of his mentor, Charles Rivers Carroll, young Simms completed putting together his third volume of poems, which he appropriately dedicated to Carroll. *Early Lays,* "by William G. Simms, Jun., Author of 'Lyrical and other Poems,'—'Monody on Pinckney,' & c.," was published in Charleston in August 1827 by A. E. Miller and was first reviewed by the *New York Courier* on September 20—a review which was reprinted in the *Charleston Courier* nine days later. That Simms was still drawing upon his stockpile of poems written earlier is made clear in his dedication—

> the present volume is principally compiled from a surplus ... left from the publication of "Lyrical and other Poems." In fact, the following pages present, mostly the effusions of a very early day; many of them preceding in composition those which constitute the first volume [*LOP*]; but few of them contemporaneous with, and still fewer subsequent to it.

The year 1827, then, was particularly eventful for the young husband-father-lawyer-poet, and he had plans of even greater scope. Almost exactly three years after the prospectus of the *Album* had appeared, the *Charleston Courier* of June 7, 1828, announced "Proposals for publishing by subscription, a Weekly Literary Gazette to be entitled 'The Tablet.'" Unlike the earlier one, however, the prospectus in the *Courier* was signed by name—by two of Charleston's literary figures: James Wright Simmons, Harvard-educated poet, playwright, and essayist, a man in his late thirties with experience both in belles-lettres and in business; and William Gilmore Simms, Jr., now the author of three modest volumes of verse but still only twenty-two years of age. Just how Simmons and Simms came together is not certain, but the possibility exists that Simmons was among the "Society of Young Gentlemen" who had assisted Simms in editing the *Album*. Indeed, James Kibler suggests "the possibility of continuity" between the *Album* (whose second volume bore the subtitle "Or, Charleston Literary Gazette") and the newly announced "Weekly Literary Gazette."[4] In any event, it is not surprising that Simms, as the most promising of Charleston's young writers, should have been known to another Charlestonian with literary ambitions.

One is struck by the similarity between the plans first proposed for "The Tablet" and those which had been announced for and carried out by the *Album*. "The Tablet," like the *Album*, was to be a weekly "literary Miscellany" of eight pages with an especial appeal to the "ladies" and with the express purpose of encouraging "native genius." Three weeks later, however, these plans were apparently abruptly cast aside; on June 27—the day the original prospectus ceased to appear in the *Courier*—Simms and Simmons ran an almost entirely new prospectus in the *City Gazette*, in which they announced their decision to make their magazine a monthly rather than a weekly. The second prospectus still called the proposed journal "'The Tablet;' [*sic*] or Southern Monthly Literary Gazette," and, despite its new format, the chief purpose remained unchanged: the encouragement of native genius—an aim the editors restated time and again, and a policy they would consistently follow. The first issue of the *Southern Literary Gazette* (the name under which the publication finally appeared) came forth in September 1828, amid a fanfare of local publicity.[5] Despite the consistently favorable reviews its opening numbers received, there was evidence that the young editors were experiencing financial difficulties, as intimated in the statement, "our patronage is too limited as yet to warrant a continuance of our plan [to publish a series of engravings]," which appeared in the November 1828 *Gazette*.[6] Perhaps the highest praise and strongest plea for the new monthly came in the *Charleston Courier* of March 2, 1829, which expressed "the earnest hope" that the Charleston public "liberally support a work of so much merit," particularly since even "the youthful town of Cincinnati" had its own monthly periodical. In addition to the thought that "it would be derogating, indeed, ... were we to permit ours to fall through," the *Courier* stressed "the spirit of Southern Literature" maintained in the "manly and candid" *Southern Literary Gazette*, and concluded: "... from the purest patriotism and justice, we cannot but yield it our support."

A magazine cannot live on praise alone, however, and after five numbers of the *Southern Literary Gazette* had appeared, the business-minded Simmons decided to let his partner continue the struggle alone. The two parted with no ill feelings; Simms, still only twenty-two, probably welcomed the opportunity to be acknowledged as the sole editor, and Simmons was gracious enough to make a public announcement of his withdrawal, at the same time expressing faith in his colleague. In his own statement Simms revealed confidence in his ability to make the magazine a success and announced a "*New Series* ... to be issued on superior paper in an improved form"[7]—that is, in the form of a semi-monthly. A new publisher, A. F. Cunningham, also stepped in at the beginning of Simms's sole editorship of the new series, and the *Southern Literary Gazette* appeared for another six months as a semi-monthly, apparently with no more security than the monthly. Finally, then, what seemed the prospectus for yet another magazine, the *Pleiades*, "a weekly literary gazette," was actually the death call for the semi-monthly *Southern Literary Gazette*, at least in its current form, for at the end of the "new series" Simms became editor of the weekly *Pleiades and Southern Literary Gazette*, apparently by prearrangement with the new publisher, James S. Burges. But, alas, the *Pleaides* died stillborn, apparently with a single issue which escaped all collectors for almost a century and a half.[8]

Thus the third attempt in less than a year to give the *Southern Literary Gazette* a new face (and new life) failed. The *Southern Literary Gazette* (for all three magazines are now so called) had gone full circle; first and last announced to be a weekly gazette, it appeared both monthly and semi-monthly but never actually weekly, because its first number under that standard was also its last.

In examining the *Southern Literary Gazette* for Simms's contributions, one quickly discovers that the editor of the *Gazette* was almost literally the author of the *Gazette,* as well. Some idea of how great a portion of the magazine was his own work can be gained from the fact that as many as 114 contributions (ninety-nine of which are certain, fifteen probable) in the two series (including the single *Pleiades* number) were written by this amazingly facile young man.[9] These 114 contributions embrace sixty-three poems, nineteen essays, and eighteen pieces of fiction.

Probably the outstanding poem in the *Southern Literary Gazette* is "The Lost Pleiad," sometimes considered one of the best in Simms's poetic career. It is the first printed version of the poem which appears in *Poems Descriptive, Dramatic, Legendary and Contemplative* (1853), although Simms expanded the work from forty-four to fifty-three lines and revised (and even rewrote) many individual lines. In nearly every case the revision improved the poem. "The Lost Pleiad" in any version stands far above the other poetry in the *Southern Literary Gazette,* most of which must be considered mediocre. One wonders if the success of "The Lost Pleiad" could have had any bearing on Simms's choice of *Pleiades* as the title for the new journal he agreed to edit for James S. Burges. The title (of both the poem and the magazine) perhaps suggests that the work was intended primarily for women readers.

The best of the other Simms poems in the *Southern Literary Gazette* are probably those he selected for the 1853 and the 1860 collections of his poetry, among which are "The Streamlet," "The Spring," "Fancy," "Morning in the Forest," "Lights of Hearts and Love," "Lines" (beginning "My life is in the yellow leaf"), "Concealed Character," "The Grave in the Forest," and a few of his songs and sonnets. Also worthy of comment is "Great Is the Yemassee," a poem included in the second of the "Chronicles of Ashley River" and the original of the highly effective "Mighty Is the Yemassee," which later appears in chapter 22 of *The Yemassee* (1835).

By far the most interesting piece in the *Southern Literary Gazette* is the "Confessions of a Murderer," the forerunner of *Martin Faber,* about which there was much controversy until its discovery in the long-missing twelfth number of the new series—the issue dated November 1, 1829. That discovery made possible the unequivocal validation of the 1837 claim by Simms (in indignantly denying having plagiarized F. M. Reynolds's "*Miserrimus*") that the origin of *Martin Faber* lay in one of his own early published writings:

> In conclusion, and to refer again to the supposed resemblance of "Martin Faber" to "Miserrimus," we may add, that the chief incidents of the former work were published in the *Southern Literary Gazette* ... about seven years ago.

> ... From the paper entitled, "Confessions of a Murderer," the work was subsequently elaborated—partly in 1829, partly in 1832, and finally revised for publication in 1833, when it appeared in its present form.[10]

In brief, although differences between the "Confessions of a Murderer" and *Martin Faber* are great enough that they should be considered separate stories, there can be no doubt that Simms used the early *Southern Literary Gazette* sketch as the germ for his first book of fiction. Though in rewriting, Simms altered his phrasing to such an extent that a collation list for the two texts is not possible,[11] they both employ language recognizably Simmsian in tone and character. Masculinity and verve are earmarks of Simms's style as much as verbosity and artificiality; and perhaps one of the appeals of the "Confessions of a Murderer" is its straightforward narrative style relatively unmarred by redundant and cumbersome rhetorical padding. The brief story is of interest for literary as well as bibliographical reasons in that it clearly suggests its author's skill and power of narration.[12]

Though the most interesting, "Confessions of a Murderer" is not the only one of Simms's tales and sketches in the *Southern Literary Gazette* to possess merit. The six "Chronicles of Ashley River," in which Simms depicted "one of those sad and grievous encounters between the whites and the savages of the western wilderness" (n.s., I, 176), anticipate his two novels of Indian warfare in colonial South Carolina, *The Yemassee* and *The Cassique of Kiawah.* Sgt. Rory M'Alister, a loquacious but manly Irishman with heavy brogue, and Redfoot, a cunning, intelligent Yemassee chief who speaks perfect English, are both well-conceived characters. The "Chronicles" are episodic and melodramatic but nevertheless display some of the writer's adeptness in storytelling.

In "Indian Sketch" (later revised, expanded, and retitled "Oakatibbe; or, The Choctaw Sampson") Simms made some revealing comments on the distorted contemporary portrayals of Indian character in novels and poems. "Nothing can be more amusing to one who is at all intimate with the Indian character," he wrote, "than the various pictures ... by the Poet and the novelist. Nothing more idle and extravagant." The white man's "ready and well-armed frontier" had exercised "such a powerful restraint" upon the Indian (whose "glory ... is the hunt and the battle field") that the latter has been "robbed" of all "pride, love of adventure and warlike enthusiasm," the "only romance" the native American "ever had in his character."[13] Already, then, Simms's interest in the Indian and his insistence upon realistic treatment of history had combined to make him highly critical of the romantically portrayed "savage."[14]

Another of the more interesting pieces of fiction in the *Southern Literary Gazette* is the sketch entitled "A Picture of the Sea." One wonders if Poe, who, as Sgt. Edgar A. Perry, was stationed at Fort Moultrie near Charleston in 1828, did not read this tale in the December number of the *Gazette.*[15] If so, certain passages in "A Picture of the Sea" may have given him the germ for his own "MS. Found in a Bottle," which in 1833 won the story contest conducted by the *Baltimore Saturday Visitor.* The similarities between these two supernatural tales of the sea are too striking to be ignored: both are narrated in the first person by a ship passenger who professes disbelief in superstition, but is awed by it; in both, a sudden furious storm strikes after the sea has taken on a mysterious foreboding appearance; in both, a huge ship manned by immortals (the "Flying Dutchman" theme) suddenly and unaccountably appears during the storm to crash down upon and sink the narrator's ship; in both, there are at first two survivors, one of whom is later killed; and in both, the sole survivor, who serves as narrator, faces certain death, a situation that presents a peculiar problem for the author. Simms got out of this difficulty in the conventional manner—by having the narrator awaken from a dream; Poe solved the problem much more artistically by putting to use the idea made explicit by his title. There is not a question of plagiarism, for even if Poe *had* seen Simms's story, he used his own genius to fashion a new tale from the mere framework supplied by Simms. "A Picture of the Sea" would be no discredit to any writer: the descriptions of the storm and of the frightening appearance of the phantom ship are vivid and terrifying; the grim struggle to death between the unheroic narrator and the other survivor over possession of a spar large enough to support only one of them is an early example of Simms's realism.[16]

Among the best of the other tales in the *Southern Literary Gazette* are "The Cypress Swamp," "The Fisherman—A Fact," and "Omens of War—A Recollection," all three signed with the pseudonym, "E." Simms incorporated some of "The Cypress Swamp"—which is in reality a mere descriptive sketch—into those scenes in *The Partisan* that have their setting in the South Carolina lowlands swamps.[17] "The Fisherman—A Fact" is a delightful story of a Southern gentleman's attempt to recover the fortune he has lost through folly and hard luck by fishing each day for a water-buried treasure, which he hopes to ensnare on his fishing hook. His strange actions convince his Negro assistants that he is the devil himself "'wid a big fishing line in 'e hand, ready for hook your poor spirit, 'fore 'e lef your body'" (n.s., I, 244). Humor and irony were not the young Simms's forte, but in this tale he handled both much better than he was wont to do. "Omens of War—A Recollection" is another early treatment by Simms of a Revolutionary War theme. It focuses on a veteran of the Revolution who in 1776 had seen a vision of approaching war similar to the phenomenon witnessed by the citizens of a little town in interior South Carolina sometime during "the summer of eighteen hundred and eleven, a short time before the declaration of the war with Great Britain" (n.s., I, 179).

Some of Simms's most significant remarks, however, appear in the piece entitled "Modern Criticism" (n.s., I, 173–74). In this essay he took a stand for "fair and impartial criticism," the benefits from which "can no more be doubted than the common advantages which result from education." For Simms, true criticism was "a liberal and humane art" aiming for "a just discernment of the real merits of authors" and avoiding "that blind and implicit veneration" which confounds "blemishes" and "beauties." The critical art, in short, "teaches us to admire and to blame with judgment, and not to follow the crowd blindly." Simms asserted that "to merit the high and distinguished title of critic," one must possess more than genius and reputation: "... something more is indispensably necessary to enable us to take our stand ... we ourselves must not regard the person writing, but the thing written ... we must divest ourselves of every kind of prejudice. ..." With these "requisites for a critic," Simms added, "we shall ... advance the literature of our country" and become "guardians of the portals of Fame's temple, not exactly forbidding unfledged genius to enter, but turning it back with all reasonable hopes for future success. ..."

Later in "Modern Criticism" Simms pointed out, however, that "with some few exceptions" the "critics of today" do not answer the definition for the simple reason that *"they are not totally unprejudiced."* In both the United States and Europe, Simms contended, "many books are reviewed before the reviewer has fully read the contents ... many times the book is merely used as the text for a *commentary*. ..." The critic who "lashes without mercy" when "his strictures should assume the form of friendly advice" particularly aroused Simms's contempt. Such a critic, he said, "is rather more bent upon displaying his peculiar skill, than improving the defects of the author. It is this shameful want of discrimination which has cast an indelible stain upon some of the foreign reviews of *everything American*. ..." This severe criticism, Simms summed up in conclusion, "so far from advancing the literature of a country, rather retards it, and sometimes *stunts* it in its growth." Although Simms was later to write much with regard to the functions of a critic, this essay penned at the age of twenty-three is one of the best expressions of his ideas on the subject, ideas that he consistently espoused throughout his career.

Naturally, most of the critical comments published in a journal devoted to the encouragement of national letters pertain to American writers. One of the early reviews deals with *Notions of the Americans* (1828), "another leaf" to Cooper's "brilliant laurel." Characteristically, Simms (for he doubtless was the reviewer) praised the book for its "method" and for its "style," but also pointed out a shortcoming: "Mr. Cooper is singularly, we had almost said, ludicrously minute in some of his descriptions. ... we are informed that you have 'egress from and ingress to the house, by its front and rear!' This is indeed new, and quite extraordinary." Simms later drew an interesting comparison between Irving (who "labored to conciliate") and Cooper (who "is far more likely to convince"). The manner of the "author of the 'Sketch Book,'" Simms wrote, has been "that of a well-bred man in a drawing-room"; on the other hand, Cooper's deportment "will challenge a handsome comparison" with that of Burns in observing and maintaining "admirable dignity and self-possession, when suddenly transferred from the plough to the society of the nobility and gentry." Simms concluded: "We believe, then, that these 'Notions' are likely to achieve much in behalf of the two countries; presenting, as they do, a *true* picture of the actual condition of these states in all their various relations ..." (I, 174, 177). Indeed it is Simms the critic who is best revealed in the pages of the *Southern Literary Gazette;* and despite his youth and inexperience, he emerges as a surprisingly sound and mature judge of literature. Yet for nearly a century his criticism has been almost completely overlooked.[18]

Of Simms's contributions to the *Southern Literary Gazette* it may be said that some are remarkably good—some "trash" by his own admission. Much of the material was later reworked and published in other magazines or in books. In general, the prose—whether fiction or criticism—is superior to the poetry, with the exception of a few individual poems. But before the reader comes to a settled conclusion on the merits of this highly productive young editor, he should remember Simms's own assessment: "As long as the Editor is compelled, as we have frequently been, to write one half of his book himself, one half of what he writes, must be trash" (n.s., I, 80).

Even before the demise of the *Southern Literary Gazette* Simms had managed to issue his fourth volume of poetry, a slim book entitled *The Vision of Cortes, Cain, and Other Poems,* published by James S. Burges in late July or early August 1829. Unlike *Lyrical and Other Poems* and *Early Lays,* the two books published in 1827, which were largely collections of previously published or much earlier written poems, *The Vision of Cortes* consists primarily of poetry written specifically for it, even though its best-known poem, "The Lost Pleiad," and at least five others appeared almost simultaneously in the

*Southern Literary Gazette.* But the two title poems appeared here for the first time: in the "advertisement" to *The Vision of Cortes, Cain, and Other Poems* (p. 6) Simms observes of "The Vision of Cortes" that only a fragment of an original version of "large dimensions" was being published; of "Cain" he noted plans to follow the first book with others if it were favorably received.[19] Simms's headnote to the section of sonnets indicates that these are the best of a group written earlier; the inferior ones had been committed "to the flames" during the author's twenty-first year.

James E. Kibler, Jr., has argued convincingly that Simms, though not a great poet, has been denied—largely through Trent's influence—his proper place in the history of American poetry. Kibler indicates that Simms was not "a 'belated' romantic," as Trent and others have seen him, "but was writing *before* our major romantics in America."[20] And in some of his "earliest poems composed from 1822 to 1830," Simms was "already evolving a philosophy" more aligned with Byron, Keats, and Wordsworth than "with Americans like Longfellow, Whittier, and ... Emerson."[21] In one respect, then, amateurish though he was, the early Simms was an innovator, even a pioneer, rather than the stereotyped, stale imitator portrayed by Trent; certainly his youthful efforts in *The Vision of Cortes* and the three prior volumes represent a phase in Simms's development essential to an understanding of his nature and standing as author.

In 1829, however, young Simms was still more interested in being an editor than in being a poet. When his second effort to establish a literary journal in Charleston failed in November, Simms was not long in deciding to direct his talent as editor into a more profitable channel. Forming a partnership with a printer named E. S. Duryea, he—unwisely, it seems—invested funds from his maternal inheritance in the *City Gazette,* a Charleston daily newspaper then up for sale. Simms served as editor of the *City Gazette* from January 1, 1830, until June 7, 1832—and those thirty months constituted for him one trying experience after another. His stand against the doctrine of Nullification made for him many personal and political enemies; on at least one occasion in 1831 only Duryea's prudence is said to have saved his partner from attack by an angry mob, to whom the young editor had defiantly shouted, "Cowards!"[22] Simms himself later summed up his ill-fated editorship of the *City Gazette:*

> It [the *Gazette*] had been declining in public estimation long before I purchased it and had got so low that when I—most imprudently—bought it, it must have been discontinued but for the sale and transfer into new hands. It resuscitated somewhat after it fell into my hands, and but for my taking ... the unpopular side of the question in Carolina, it must have succeeded. But all the

> sources of income which it derived from the Nullifiers, and which contributed fully one-half of its profits—were suddenly dried up, and at the close of a 2 1/2 years term of mental torture, I was only too happy to give it up. In that time, I had lost all the little maternal property which I had,—had incurred a heavy debt which I had no visible means of paying. (December 29, 1839; *L*, I, 162)

Simms was surprisingly candid in admitting his shortcomings as writer—and as human being—during his days with the *Gazette.* "Speaking without affectation," he wrote in 1839, "I must declare that my editorial writings were those of a crude, inexperienced boy—my prose style was not fixed & very cumbrous, unless where feelings were aroused, and then if my style was better, my matter was apt to be much worse." On the personal level Simms acknowledged being "rash & hasty, frequently violent and unjust," and he confessed to being "heartily sorry & repentant now" for many "sentiments and judgments which I then uttered" (*L*, I, 162). Although it is sometimes said that Simms's career as an author began with his disposal of the *City Gazette*;[23] his pen had been active long before he gave up the editorship.[24] While editing the *Gazette* and continuing to write in his spare time, Simms had not fully relinquished the practice of law, maintaining a law office in Charleston throughout the period. It may be indicative, however, of his declining interest in the legal profession that by 1831 he had given up his "Office of Attorney at Law" at a good central location on State Street (which he occupied in 1828 and 1829 shortly after opening practice); instead, the Charleston city directory for 1831 reveals that by that date his law office and his editorial office were combined in his residence in the Charleston Neck at "E side King, between Ann and Mary sts."[25] It is significant that the 1831 directory was the last in Charleston to list Simms as "attorney at law" or "magistrate" and that even that final legal listing was shared as follows: "Simms, W. G. *magistrate, and Editor of the City Gazette.*" Simms had recognized that his destiny was letters, not law.

In 1830 or 1831 an anonymous volume of poetry entitled *The Tri-Color; or, The Three Days of Blood, in Paris. With Some Other Pieces* appeared. While purportedly published in London by Wigfall & Davis in 1830, it was almost certainly printed in Charleston in early 1831 by James S. Burges, the publisher of *The Vision of Cortes.*[26] Why would Simms and Burges practice this deception (for evidence that it was a deception is overwhelming)? Of the several possible reasons, one has a significance beyond *The Tri-Color* for its revelation about British and American literary relationships. In the 1830s to have a book published in London was in itself a mark of prestige, and American reviewers, still highly dependent upon British literary taste,[27] were almost certain to be favorably impressed. In fact, as recently as 1952, A. S. Salley, believing *The Tri-Color* to have been published in London as stated on its title page, gave as evidence of the growing renown of young Gilmore Simms that "he must have had some European connections."[28] A second reason may be that Simms, who was taking a strong stand against Nullification as editor of the *City Gazette,* wanted to distance himself as far as possible from what may have been seen as self-serving political pronouncements in *The Tri-Color.* Simms himself wrote in 1831 to James Lawson of the "little volume hastily thrown off, & published *in our city* [italics mine], during my late visit to Louisiana & Mississippi," and noted, significantly: "I am not, nor do I wish to be known as its author, for a variety of reasons, none of which are of importance even to my friends" (*L,* I, 38). The fact that the title poem was first published in the *City Gazette* for September 24, 1830, may have added to Simms's desire for anonymity. Though an advertisement of *The Tri-Color* as "just received & for sale by S. Babcock" appeared in the *Charleston Courier* for April 27, 1831, there is no record that the little volume was reviewed in Charleston or elsewhere. Though one of the slightest of Simms's efforts, the work remains of interest to scholars primarily as a curious bibliographical phenomenon that focuses some light on American and British publishing at a time when no international copyright law existed and piracies and other deceptions on both sides of the Atlantic were common.

The years 1830–1832 were eventful for the young editor-poet for other, nonliterary reasons, the most devastating of which was the decimation of his family. The death of William Gilmore Simms, Sr., on March 28, 1830, in Mississippi probably occasioned the "late visit to Louisiana & Mississippi" Simms referred to in his 1831 letter to Lawson—a visit which took place between February and May, 1831. Simms's second journey to the Southwest is well chronicled in a series of ten travel letters entitled "Notes of a Small Tourist," published in the *Charleston City Gazette* between March 15 and May 17, 1831. While in Mississippi Simms evidently closed out some of the affairs of his deceased father, but no reference to his doing so appears either in the editorial correspondence he sent back to the *City Gazette* or in extant private letters or memorabilia written then or later. Perhaps one reason Simms delayed almost a year after his father's death to go to Mississippi to settle his estate was that Jane Gates, his maternal grandmother and surrogate mother, also died sometime in 1830, apparently shortly after the elder Simms. The loss within a few months of the only father and the only "mother" Gilmore Simms ever knew must have been a staggering emotional blow to the young writer. An even more upsetting loss was soon to follow, when on February 19, 1832, Anna

Malcolm Giles Simms, his fragile young wife (who had never fully recovered from the birth of their only child, Augusta), finally succumbed to incapacitating illness—leaving Simms with only his infant daughter.

A widower at twenty-six, who had experienced an amount of grief and disappointment unusual for so young a man, Simms was faced again with the decision of what to do with his life. It must have seemed to him as if everything he had undertaken in Charleston had gone awry. Perhaps, as Trent has suggested, it was only natural for him to look to the North in his efforts to win literary distinction. "Everything that he had tried at Charleston had failed, and now that his political principles were in disrepute, there was still less chance for future success … . He had already given up much that he might follow his literary bent, and come what would he was resolved to keep on as he had begun. But for a literary aspirant the North … was the proper field."[29] For a single parent with a dependent child, however, familial (and perhaps financial) problems had to be resolved before the literary father could leave home. The question concerning the disposition of four-year-old Augusta during Simms's first visit to the North in the summer of 1832 cannot be definitively answered; but, it is known that sometime during the year father and daughter moved again from Charleston to Summerville (where Simms owned a house), conceivably both to reduce living costs and to provide more playground space for Augusta; and it is probable that this change came in the spring after the death of Anna Giles Simms, providing the aspiring author opportunity to arrange for the safekeeping of his daughter even as he contemplated his exploratory trip to New York. Simms later gave the following account: "I left [Augusta] in the charge of a friend,[30] and, without any definite idea of what I was to do for the future, I went to the North." Though at the time, Simms professed, he had no "thought of writing novels," he carried in his trunk "the M.S.S. of parts of at least two which had been scribbled several years before" (*L*, I, 165).

At any rate, it is certain that by July 4, 1832, Simms was in Philadelphia en route to New York to visit his friend James Lawson,[31] with whom he had corresponded since sometime before 1830 but had never met personally. He apparently spent most of the summer in the North at work on various literary productions—and it was at this time that he must have become acquainted with William Cullen Bryant, Edwin Forrest, Prosper Wetmore, Willis Gaylord Clark, Fitzgreen Halleck, James Kirke Paulding, and William Holland. Simms enjoyed mingling with Lawson's literary friends immensely, and thereafter planned to travel annually to the North. The effect upon his already insatiable literary ambition must have been enormous, and for the first time at first hand he saw, through Lawson and his circle, that literary reputations were made in New York and the North, not in Charleston and the South. One can only speculate on the thoughts running through his mind in the late summer of 1832, but it is certain that he recalled both his father's admonition that he leave Charleston and his friend Lawson's invitation that he move to New York.

Pen pals James Lawson and William Gilmore Simms were immediately attracted to each other, and the summer of 1832 saw the beginning of an intimate friendship that grew stronger through the years. Lawson, a native Scotsman who had moved to New York in 1815, was like Simms interested in both business and literature, but unlike Simms he was able to combine the two in such a way as to achieve prosperity while still a young man. Seven years senior to Simms, Lawson possessed business experience and acumen the young Charlestonian lacked, and with New York as his base, he cultivated friendships with that great city's literati and moved in the best social circles. By the summer of 1832 Lawson also had a budding literary reputation, though not comparable to Simms's. He had published poems and sketches in the *Knickerbocker* and the *New York Literary Gazette and American Athenaeum,* and his play *Giordano* had been produced in Park Theater in 1828. His literary correspondence with Simms must have facilitated the serial publications of Lawson's *Tales and Sketches, by a Cosmopolite* (1830) in Simms's *City Gazette.* Like Simms, Lawson too was an editor. He edited the *New York Morning Courier* with John B. Skilman and James G. Brooks in the years 1827–1829, and upon giving up the *Morning Courier,* switched to the *Mercantile Advertiser,* which he co-edited with Amos Butler from 1829 to 1833.

But even more than by their mutual interests in editing and in all things literary, Lawson and Simms may have been brought together that summer of 1832 by the fact that both were eligible young bachelors. Though Lawson had never married and Simms was a widower, Lawson was much the more experienced in the protocol of high society courtship, to which he introduced the young Southerner with much pleasure, and to which Simms responded with the same enthusiasm as he had to the gallant Scotsman's literary acquaintances. It must have been reassuring to young Gilmore Simms to discover that the fashionable young women of New York found him attractive and his company enjoyable. Though at the time marriage was not on the mind of either Lawson or Simms for different reasons, they apparently spent four consecutive summers together courting a number of Manhattan's debutantes and thoroughly enjoying themselves. It is safe to say that Simms's first trip to the North was memorable for more reasons than simply that of fostering his already strong literary ambitions.

It was with Lawson that young Simms—probably following his friend's advice—made arrangements to have his next book published in New York—his first not to be issued from Charleston. Though *Atalantis. A Story of the Sea: In Three Parts* was published in October 1832 by the well-known New York publisher J. & J. Harper, Simms had begun working on its verses "when I was but eighteen" (*L*, II, 504) and had the manuscript almost ready for publication upon his arrival north. On July 17, 1832, Simms had written Lawson while stopping over in Philadelphia, en route to New York:

> I have on hand, and nearly in readiness for the Press, a dramatic poem, of some novelty in its plan and general construction. It is purely fanciful, and has no model in the language, unless I except something of the 'Comus' of Milton and a few scenes in the "Tempest" of Shakespeare. The characters are nearly all imaginative, and I have made free use of a dream of Plato's and one, too, not unfamiliar to the less visionary beings of a more modern period. ... This Poem I am desirous of giving to the Press, and would be glad ... to have you ascertain on what terms I can do so. I should not be unwilling to pay something in moderation, but would prefer publishing *it without any cost to myself*. ... I have the thing at heart, and, in Yankee phrase, value it some; and, if you can therefore oblige me in this respect, I shall be more than gratified. (*L*, I, 40–41)

It is worth noting that the stiffness and formality that characterize his early letters were gradually to be replaced by the easy informality and almost racy familiarity which earmark Simms's later correspondence with Lawson. Lawson responded favorably and effectively to the Charlestonian's request and played the major role in bringing the Harper brothers and Simms together. Simms later wrote, to Rufus W. Griswold, that he actually finished the preparation of *Atalantis* for the press in Hingham, Massachusetts,[32] a town he visited in September, after spending time in New York with Lawson. By October 25, 1832, Simms was back in Summerville, and his sixth volume of poetry was soon to reach him there—with a significant New York imprint on its title page,[33] to match the significant imprint that New York had made on the mind of the young author.

Even before his visit to New York—and even before he met face-to-face the persuasiveness of James Lawson—young Gilmore Simms, depressed by the death of his wife and the impending failure of the *City Gazette*, had on April 14, 1832, stated his intention of selling the *Gazette* and "leaving the state" (*L*, I, 47n). Such despondency, however, was understandable in one grieving, and may have been motivated more by an anxious desire to make a satisfactory sale of the *City Gazette* than by serious intent to leave South Carolina.[34] Yet after his return from his first visit to the North, Simms still pondered the idea of "expatriation." In a letter of November 25, 1832, to Lawson, Simms added that he now considered himself "rather a visitor in the state than a citizen" (*L*, I, 47).

At the end of 1832, then, hard-working William Gilmore Simms, still only twenty-six, already a father and widower, author of six books, and editor of three magazines or newspapers, was puzzled and discouraged. He could not have foreseen that 1833 would mark the beginning of a new literary thrust that would carry him to national eminence.

PART TWO

# The Making of an Author
(1833–1841)

# IV Ambitions and High Hopes

William Gilmore Simms's ambivalence toward his future is illustrated in a single paragraph from a letter of January 19, 1833, to his ever more intimate friend, James Lawson. "Things go wildly in this quarter," Simms wrote, "and I only linger in So. Caro. until something takes place. My uncle in Mississippi writes earnestly after me, and I shall only wait until the first of February is well over, when I shall probably bend my course to the stabling place of the Sun." Simms was ready, it would seem, to heed the earlier pleadings of his father, now echoed by his uncle as well, to leave South Carolina for Mississippi. His next sentence, however, reveals why he was never to forsake the city of his birth: "I have sent to the Harpers' the first volume of a novel, on which as yet I hear nothing" (*L*, I, 49). The implications of this statement are important. Simms has sent a partially completed *novel* to the Harper brothers—a novel, for the first time, after six consecutive volumes of poetry. Although there is some doubt about whether the reference is to *Martin Faber* or to *Guy Rivers,* both of which Simms was working on at the time and both of which were eventually published by Harpers, the thrust is nevertheless clear: Simms's "main work" (*L*, I, 45) is now the novel, not poetry as in the past. Ultimately, it was the publication of *Martin Faber* that changed a poet into a novelist. It was *Martin Faber* rather than *Guy Rivers* only because the former preceded the latter in publication by some nine or ten months—the difference between September 1833 and June–July 1834; either work alone could have changed Simms's life. At age twenty-six Gilmore Simms had found the genre for which his talents best suited him. Thereafter, although he never ceased writing poetry and experimenting with other literary forms, he was primarily a writer of fiction. The success of *Martin Faber* (to be followed quickly by *Guy Rivers*) catapulted the young Charlestonian into the public eye of literary America and spurred him into an amazingly fertile and imaginative decade in which he produced no fewer than twelve novels and two collections of short stories.

*Martin Faber*[1] was widely reviewed, both North and South, but perhaps nowhere more favorably than by Charles Fenno Hoffman in the *New York American* of September 28, 1833: "... we do not hesitate to say, that since Godwin carried that singular and impressive style, first introduced in modern fiction by our countryman Charles Brockden Brown, to such perfection in Caleb Williams, no work of that school has come under our notice which shows more power than the little tale before us." Hoffman concluded his generally favorable review: "... we express our unfeigned wish to hear soon again from the author of Martin Faber."

William P. Trent has the following to say about the strange sequence of events set off by Hoffman's review:

> On the Monday after "Martin Faber" was published, he [Simms] called on the Harpers, who referred to the criticism in the "American," and asked if he knew Hoffman. Receiving a prompt negative, they showed some surprise, which they explained by stating that a Doctor Langtree had said that Simms and Hoffman were bosom friends, which accounted for the favorable nature of the latter's criticism. On this slight provocation our warm-blooded author grew angry, and, after getting further proofs, proceeded, in company with his friend Randell Hunt, to call upon the talkative physician. Langtree (Samuel Daly Langtree, afterwards editor of the "Knickerbocker") rather evaded Simms's questions by answering that he had not read "Martin Faber." Whereupon Simms demanded a statement in writing of what had really been said. Langtree declining, the fiery author would have proceeded to violent measures, had not his friend Hunt interposed and induced Langtree to write his denial. When Langtree begged that the paper should be shown to the Harpers only, Simms declared that he would show it to anybody. He forthwith took it to Mr. Peabody, publisher of the "Knickerbocker," who had heard Langtree's remarks. Peabody, with an eye to business, advised him to publish the statement, as it would sell his book, to which Simms replied that he was a gentleman before he was an author. (*Simms*, pp. 79–80)

Whatever the merits of this episode and the record of it handed down by Trent (no record of it exists elsewhere, either in print or in Simms's private memorabilia), it does capture the great, perhaps excessive, concern of the hitherto unknown author for his personal and literary reputation. That at least two leading New York magazines also reviewed *Martin Faber* shows that Simms's talents were beginning to be recognized outside his native region. The *Knickerbocker* (then edited by Timothy Flint) noticed "obvious defects in the style" of *Martin Faber*, but called them "defects incident to youthful genius and talent" and concluded—"this story will excite and sustain interest, though we cannot but doubt the tendency of tales of such unmitigated horror" (II [October 1833], 317). The *American Monthly Magazine*, opening its review with the surmise that *Martin Faber* "is an attempt to beat *Miserrimus* on its own ground," also claimed to see much merit among many faults: "It is not without a moral although it is not a very obvious one,—that children should have their dispositions educated as well as have their heads stored. The book is faulty, but is is [*sic*] within an ace of being a very clever thing notwithstanding.—We suspect it to have been done in a hurry, and never to have undergone a cool revisal" (II, [October 1, 1833], 141).

In the "Advertisement to the Second Edition" in 1837 Simms successfully rebutted the charge that F. M. Reynolds's "*Miserrimus*" (London: Thomas Hookham, 1833) was the model for *Martin Faber* by pointing to the 1829 publication of the "Confessions of a Murderer" as its origin. One is struck by the accuracy of Simms's memory concerning the emergence of *Martin Faber* from the earlier and shorter "Confessions." If Simms wrote the preface for the second edition of *Martin Faber* in 1836, as seems probable, "about seven years ago" pinpoints the 1829 publication of the "Confessions of a Murderer." While the statement that "Confessions" filled "some eight or ten pages" in the *Southern Literary Gazette* is erroneous in its estimate of pages, Simms may have confused columns with pages ("Confessions" occupies eight columns on four two-column pages in *SLG*). The dates given for the "elaboration" of "Confessions" into a full-length *Martin Faber* are essentially correct,[2] and furthermore Simms is right in saying that the "sterner, darker features ... nearly all ... appear in the story as it was first given to the public"—that is, the character of William Harding and "the softening and gentler features" were added as "the fruit of an after labour." In brief, there can be no doubt that Simms used the early *SLG* sketch as the germ for his first book of fiction. This genesis is apparent in language as well as in plot, as, for instance, a comparison of the opening paragraph in the "Confessions" with the paragraph beginning, "My name is Martin Faber," in the 1833 *Martin Faber* (pp. 7–9) reveals.[3]

Trent gives a very full account of the "*Miserrimus*"—*Martin Faber*—"Confessions of a Murderer" controversy and quotes at length a statement by Simms said to be included among "certain 'Personal and Literary Memorials,' scribbled off by the young author on the fourth day of June, 1834, while he was smarting under the stupidity and malignity of some of his early critics" (*Simms*, p. 77). Although the notebook Simms labeled "Personal and Literary Memorials" now in the South Caroliniana Library does not contain the passage, Trent had material available to him that has since been lost, and the authenticity of the following quotation, said to be Simms's "own words," can most probably be accepted at face value:

> But, as I have said, the period of its publication was a period to me of bitter excitement. I had set out to produce an original book, and flattered myself to have succeeded; what, then, was my surprise to perceive, in several of the newspapers, notices, which, though in all respects highly favorable, yet charged the work with a glaring resemblance to 'Miserrimus,' a work then only recently put forth in England, which, until after this period, I had never read, and a few of the leaves only of which I had glanced over in the bookstore of Mr. Maltby at New Haven. The misfortune of 'Martin Faber' consisted in being about the same length with 'Miserrimus,' in being printed in similar form, with similar binding, and in comprising, like the work to which it bore so unhappy a resemblance, the adventures of a bad man. There was not a solitary incident, not a paragraph, alike in the two productions; and a vital difference between the two was notorious enough in the fact that the criminal in 'Miserrimus' was such, without any obvious or reasonable cause, while 'Martin Faber' from the first sets out with an endeavor to show how and why he became a criminal, and has a reason for his offenses. 'Miserrimus,' on the other hand, does his evil deeds wantonly, and simply because of a morbid perversity of mind, which could only have its sanction in insanity. They all praised, however, to a certain extent, some of them evidently without reading it. (pp. 77–78)

Poe, the greatest of Simms's Southern literary contemporaries, apparently did not review either the 1833 or 1837 editions of *Martin Faber* per se, but in later reviews of works by Simms he singled out the tale for special praise. For example, in his discussion of *The Damsel of Darien,* Poe mentioned parenthetically that *Martin Faber,* by then in its second edition, "well deserved a permanent success" (*Burton's Gentleman's Magazine,* V ([November 1839], 283); in his *Broadway Journal* review of *The Wigwam and the Cabin,* Poe placed *Martin Faber* among Simms's "best fiction" and said of its supposed resemblance to "*Miserrimus*"—"we perceive that the individual minds which originated the two stories have much in them of similarity—but as regards the narratives themselves, or even their tone, there is no resemblance whatever. 'Martin Faber' is the better work of the two" (II [October 4, 1845], 190). In a longer review of *The Wigwam and the Cabin* in *Godey's Lady's Book*

(XXXII [January 1846], 41–42), Poe devoted even more space to *Martin Faber* and its comparison with "*Miserrimus*":

> Mr. Simms, we believe, made his first, or nearly his first, appearance before an American audience with a small volume entitled "Martin Faber," an amplification of a much shorter fiction. He had some difficulty in getting it published, but the Harpers finally undertook it, and it did credit to their judgment. It was well received both by the public and the more discriminative few, although some of the critics objected that the story was an imitation of "Miserrimus," a very powerful fiction by the author of "Pickwick Abroad." The original tale, however—the germ of "Martin Faber"—was written long before the publication of "Miserrimus." But independently of this fact, there is not the slightest ground for the charge of imitation. The thesis and incidents of the two works are totally dissimilar;—the idea of resemblance arises only from the absolute identity of *effect* wrought by both. …
>
> … whatever may have been his [Simms's] early defects, or whatever are his present errors, there can be no doubt that from the very beginning he gave evidence of genius, and that of no common order. His "Martin Faber," in our opinion, is a more forcible story than its supposed prototype "Miserrimus." The difference in the American reception of the two is to be referred to the fact (we blush while recording it), that "Miserrimus" was understood to be the work of an Englishman, and "Martin Faber" was known to be the composition of an American as yet unaccredited in our Republic of Letters. The fiction of Mr. Simms gave indication, we repeat, of genius, and that of no common order. Had he been a Yankee, this genius would have been rendered *immediately* manifest to his countrymen, but unhappily (*perhaps*) he was a Southerner, and united the southern pride—the southern dislike to the making of bargains—with the southern supineness and general want of tact in all matters relating to the making of money. His book, therefore, depended entirely upon its own intrinsic value and resources, but with these it made its way in the end. The "intrinsic value" consisted first of a very vigorous imagination in the conception of the story; secondly, in artistic skill manifested in its conduct; thirdly, in general vigour, life, movement—the whole resulting in deep interest on the part of the reader. These high qualities Mr. Simms has carried with him in his subsequent books; and they are qualities which, above all others, the fresh and vigorous intellect of America should and does esteem. It may be said, upon the whole, that while there are several of our native writers who excel the author of "Martin Faber" at particular *points*, there is, nevertheless, not one who surpasses him in the aggregate of the higher excellences of fiction. We confidently expect him to do much for the lighter literature of his country. (pp. 41–42)

Though Poe's critical acumen has been universally acclaimed, this particular assessment has won few adherents, perhaps because Simms's strengths (so clearly seen by Poe) are not easily perceived by readers conditioned to take his work lightly. But "vigorous imagination," "artistic skill ... in conduct," and "vigour, life, movement" are the very qualities that distinguish Simms at his best—and Poe's judgment that "not one" of Simms's contemporaries "surpasses him in the aggregate of the higher excellences of fiction" should not—nay, can not—be cavalierly dismissed.

By and large, the second edition of *Martin Faber,* issued in two volumes in 1837, did not attract the wide critical notice of the first (but see the *Knickerbocker,* IX [May 1837], 528), nor did its reception have the same impact upon the author, who by 1837 had published four major novels, *Guy Rivers, The Yemassee, The Partisan,* and *Mellichampe.* Throughout his career Simms was fond of reciting the circumstances of the storm caused by the initial publication of *Martin Faber,* recitations which almost inevitably led to assessments of the book's merits. His long biographical letter to R. W. Griswold dated December 6, 1846, reads in part—

> the work which, in my literary career succeeded to the publication of "Atalantis," was "Martin Faber," a gloomy & passionate tale, which, assumed by certain *European* critics as well as American to have been provoked by the British tale "Miserrimus" was in fact expanded from a tale which I published ten years before in a Magazine in Charleston. ... "Martin Faber" belongs to the family of which Godwin's Caleb Williams is the best known model. But those who read the two works will fail to see any imitation on the part of the American author. (*L,* II, 223)

At this point Simms mentioned that he was enclosing a copy of Hoffman's review in the *New York American* "as a sample of the criticism which followed the publication of M. F." "All admitted the power & interest of the work," he added, "but some cavilled at the moral. The hero charges his crimes upon fate—an ordinary habit with such persons, & this is charged upon the author. He uses crime for his material, & in his case, as a young American beginner, the practice, unavoidable for any writer of fiction that ever lived, was supposed to be criminal." Later in the same letter Simms included *Martin Faber* (as well as "Carl Werner") among his several publications "marked chiefly by the characteristics of passion & imagination—by the free use in some cases of diablerie and all the machinery of superstition & by a prevailing presence of vehement individuality of tone & temper. They constitute, in all probability, the best specimens of my powers of creating & combining, to say nothing of a certain intensifying egotism, which marks all my writings written in the first person" (*L,* II, 224).

It is also significant that, when in 1868 Simms wrote to J. S. Redfield attempting to elicit his help in finding a publisher for a collection of "imaginative" short stories, the now veteran author recommended *Martin Faber* and "Carl Werner" as examples of his stories of "larger dimensions approximating the usual Dime-sized novellette ..." (*L*, V, 157). Forty years after outlining its essential plot in the "Confessions of a Murderer," Simms, then—in desperate financial straits, to be sure—was still hoping to resell *Martin Faber* in slightly refurbished format.

W. P. Trent gave short shrift to *Martin Faber:* "most readers of the present day would turn with loathing from the book; and few would read far enough to note the early appearance of a fault which was to mar all of Simms's future work,—careless inattention to details, consequent upon hurried writing" (*Simms*, p. 82); and scholars that have followed Trent have likewise given the book scant attention, harsh attention, or no attention at all.[4] Yet although *Martin Faber* contains many errors in style, structure, plot, and language, it is nevertheless a work of sufficient power and imagination to account for Poe's claim that it possesses "evidence of genius, and that of no common order." Its place as one of America's first fictional studies of the psychology of crime—its causes and effects—earns it a secure position in the history of our early literature. Crude and cumbersome as it is, *Martin Faber* has a narrative sweep and a sustained power of interest unusual in American literature in the 1830s.

The revisions which Simms made for the 1837 edition in many instances cannot be considered improvements, for they too frequently lengthen rather than compress, hardly an advantage to a work already verbose. But he did make at least two major revisions which seem to constitute important improvements. The seemingly unaccountable shift in point of view—from the first person to third person, which marred the final chapter of the 1833 version—was corrected in the 1837 edition, giving the book a consistent first-person narrator throughout. In addition, the site for William Harding's picture-hanging, psychological testing of Faber was changed from the village barbershop, in the 1833 edition, to the village art gallery in 1837. Although Trent scoffs at an author who gives a "stagnated" village "an art gallery, where exhibitions are held yearly with a hundred pictures lining the wall" (*Simms*, p. 82), the idea of an art gallery in a small village (capable also, it is to be remembered, of a fashionable wedding) is not so difficult to accept, perhaps, as the idea of the village's barbershop serving as the exhibition place for paintings. The important point, of course, is that Simms recognized the incongruity of having the painting hung in the barbershop and attempted to correct the error. It is quite possible, also, to defend the sharp shift in point of view in chapter 18 in the 1833 text, by choosing to look upon it as an artistic method of indicating the narrator's sudden, traumatic shift in identity, brought on by a rejection of self. And the modern reader should not overlook the fact that, in its depiction of sexual manipulation, *Martin Faber* seems well advanced for its time; in the seduction scene, for instance, Simms makes explicit that Faber succeeds with Emily Andrews by skillfully and industriously arousing "all the natural passions of her bosom" (chapter 5). In brief, there is life and vivacity in the work that augurs well for an author yet in his twenties. *Martin Faber,* like many other Simms stories and tales, warrants closer consideration.

But even before the publication of *Martin Faber*—and probably even before Simms knew definitely of its acceptance by Harpers—it was evident that he had not given up Charleston as the base of his literary operations. Before six months had passed in 1833—and less than a year after he relinquished the *City Gazette*—Simms had already issued the first number of a new Charleston publication: the *Cosmopolitan: An Occasional.*

When in May 1833 the *Cosmopolitan* was published as the anonymous work of "Three Bachelors," Simms was again making use of the traditional club mechanism. Though Trent was of the opinion that the *Cosmopolitan* was written entirely by Simms,[5] it was demonstrated later that at least three stories in it were from other hands.[6] This fact does not necessarily disprove that Simms was the *Cosmopolitan*'s only editor, but it gives more credence to the statement in the explanatory introduction to the first number: "There are three of us, and our college is limited to this number ..." (I, 7).

What, then, could be more logical than to assume that the "Three Bachelors" who conducted the *Cosmopolitan* were the three men who are known to have written for it—Simms, Charles Rivers Carroll, and Edward Carroll. That the Carroll brothers grew up in Charleston with Simms; that Simms studied law in the office of Charles Rivers Carroll, dedicated *Early Lays* and *Guy Rivers* to him, and named his youngest son for him; that both Charles Rivers Carroll and Edward Carroll were writers of some small note—all add weight to the conclusion that the *Cosmopolitan* is, as it claimed to be, the work of three authors.

*Authors* rather than *editors* is the correct term to use because, strictly speaking, the *Cosmopolitan* is not a magazine but a book—a collection of short stories and essays written by three men; no outside contributions were solicited, probably none were submitted, certainly none were accepted. Moreover, as its subtitle indicates, the *Cosmopolitan* was not a *periodical* issued at fixed points, but an *occasional* issued only at the whim of the authors.

In fact, the *Cosmopolitan* has much more in common, say, with Poe's projected volume of "Tales of the Folio Club" than with a magazine like the *Southern Review.* Like the "Folio Club" tales, the stories in the *Cosmopolitan* are supposedly related by the members of a small literary coterie who meet to discuss books and authors over a glass of good wine. This idea owes something perhaps to the *Serapionsbrüder* (1819–1821) of E. T. A. Hoffman[7] as well as to the more obvious sources—the *Spectator* and the "Noctes Ambrosianae" of *Blackwood's.*[8] Like the latter two titles—but unlike the "Tales of the Folio Club" and the *Serapionsbrüder* (not to mention other collections employing a framework similar to that of the *Canterbury Tales*)—the *Cosmopolitan* actually does represent the work of a small literary group or club. The members of the "club" (though fictitiously named) are real persons—not creations of the imagination of a single author.

Of course, the idea of such an occasional was not new to Charleston. Simms and other Charlestonians were familiar not only with *Salmagundi* and *Red Book* of Kennedy and Peter Hoffman Cruse, but also with James Gates Percival's *Clio No. 1,* which had been published in Charleston in 1822. The enormous popularity of Percival's work must have stuck in Simms's memory; perhaps he felt that an occasional mixture of wit and sentiment would appeal to Charleston's literary taste in 1833 as well as it had in 1822.

The opening number of the *Cosmopolitan*—issued sometime between May 10 and May 25, 1833—received a long and laudatory review in the *Charleston Courier* of the latter date. Lavishing high praise upon the authors for their "power of invention and grace of narration," the reviewer felt "no hesitation in commending this agreeable *melange* ... as worthy of public patronage. ..." At any rate, the *Cosmopolitan* obviously received more encouragement than Trent implies.[9] Apparently in response to public approbation of the first number, a second was issued late in July 1833 and elicited on July 27 enthusiastic approval from the *Courier,* which proclaimed "its literary execution ... highly creditable to Charleston" and its "talent and taste" richly deserving of "a liberal and stimulating patronage." The *Cosmopolitan*'s "ease and grace of composition," "fertility of invention," and "skill in the grouping of incident and general conduct of narrative and *denouement* of plot" were praised for evincing "a talent for novel writing, worthy of wider and more ambitious field."

Such favorable criticism in one of the leading contemporary newspapers seems thoroughly to discredit the tradition that Charleston was quick to discourage Simms's attempts in 1833. The *Cosmopolitan*'s apparent failure after its second appearance[10] can in no way be attributed to the hostility of Charleston critics: on the contrary, the *Courier* at least seems to have praised the new work indiscriminately in an effort to help the young authors win local backing.

Perhaps, too, the *Cosmopolitan* had already served the purpose for which it was intended. One suspects that Simms, with his previous editorial experiences still fresh in his memory, was somewhat reluctant to commit himself to the arduous task of putting together enough material to meet deadlines; but an "occasional"—to be written entirely by an editorial board of three—would provide him an organ for the publication of literary scraps perhaps already on hand, would entail little financial risk, and would eliminate most of the drudgery associated with issuing a periodical. Certainly Simms must have considered these factors when he and the Carrolls formed their literary alliance.

Although the approach was different, in the *Cosmopolitan* Simms was working toward the same end for which he had struggled in the *Album* and in the *Southern Literary Gazette:* the advancement of literature in his country, in his section, and more specifically, in his home state and town. And already as "Le Debut" makes clear, Simms saw the greatest threat to the creation of a healthy native literature in an overemphasis on politics. "Should the talents of our country—our city—only find an outlet," Simms queried, "… in the turbulent and temporary notoriety of a partisan harangue … ?" South Carolina, he asserted, "is literally overflowing with talent," but literature has "been neglected for the forum," and all its people "driven … into the wars of fierce and powerful disputation which have racked and wrung, not her alone, but our common country. …"

Consequently the *Cosmopolitan* scrupulously avoided all mention of politics.[11] Doubtless, Simms, who considered himself a martyr in the Nullification crisis, had had enough of political trouble; he had learned while directing the *City Gazette* that partisan editors not only make enemies and lose friends, but live no longer than do their causes. Now that the Nullification excitement had quieted, Simms as a sensible man was willing to maintain peace by steering clear of controversial issues. The fact that the first number of the *Cosmopolitan* was dedicated to Thomas Smith Grimké, who likewise had "boldly and passionately" opposed Nullification,[12] suggests, however, that Simms was still a Unionist, national in his political views—views which if expressed would have again embroiled him in political debate. It was in helping to encourage the literary talents of young Charlestonians that the authors of the *Cosmopolitan,* "as the pioneer for other and more experienced adventures" (I, 12–15), hoped to accomplish most in behalf of American literature.

Strangely enough, however, the stories in the *Cosmopolitan* do not serve as good examples of the use of American themes. Only four of the ten tales have pronouncedly American settings, and three of these are the work of the Carroll brothers: "The Outlaw's Daughter" and "Isabel of St. Augustine" by Edward; and "The White Horse: A Legend of Table Mountain," perhaps the best story in the collection, by Charles Rivers. The only other tale that makes use of a distinctly American theme is "An Old Time Story," which on the basis of internal evidence probably can be assigned to Simms. "An Old Time Story" is a rationalized ghost story in which the central character, Metapah, an insane Indian chief who is the last of his people, frightens the visitors to an Ashley River plantation by posing as the Grey Spirit. All in all, six other stories in the *Cosmopolitan* can be attributed to Simms, only two of which seem worthy of noting: "The Poet Chatelard," a romanticized treatment of the tragic love of young Chatelard for Mary Queen of Scots, in which Simms handles both the love scene and the death scene with unusual deftness; and "The Young Advocate," whose basic plot—the noble young lover must prove his worth before he wins the hand of the financially and socially superior heroine—may betray the writer's inner consciousness after his summer experiences with James Lawson in courting young women of wealth and social prominence in New York.

All told, there is little in the *Cosmopolitan* that adds to Simms's stature as author. With the possible exceptions of "An Old Time Story" and "The Poet Chatelard," the stories attributed to Simms are not counted among his best work. Yet as a literary experiment from which its conductors expected neither pay nor praise—and as a testing ground for aspiring young writers—the *Cosmopolitan* indeed served its purpose well. Simms sprang from the *Cosmopolitan* into a flurry of literary efforts, producing within the next two years three major works of fiction in addition to *Martin Faber,* then already in the publisher's hands.

During the summer of 1833 the young Southerner made his second pilgrimage to the North, where he made arrangements to publish a collection of some of his early previously published stories and sketches. Simms, however, seems to have exerted little effort in assembling *The Book of My Lady. A Melange,* which was then published in Philadelphia by Key & Biddle in November 1833 under the pseudonym "a Bachelor Knight." Though the December *Knickerbocker* reviewed the anthology flatteringly, the intent of *The Book of My Lady* as a potboiler designed for the growing market of women readers is best revealed in the reviewer's comment, "The ladies should all buy this book, or rather the gentlemen should all buy it for their respective favorites" (II, 483).[13] Simms himself did not deprecate the volume, which contained the most romantic and chivalric of his juvenile forays into prose and poetry. Writing to Lawson in late November 1833, he emphasized the importance of his modest effort, stating that "I do entertain the notion that its merit is very far from being inconsiderable. … the public will do themselves great unkindness if they do not find vast pleasure in its perusal." That the young writer may not have been altogether serious in extolling the virtues of *The Book of My Lady* is suggested by his closing comment to his New York friend, "So much for ego" (*L*, I, 53). Judged generously, *The Book of My Lady* reflects in Simms the puerility of an author still short of professional maturity.

Tragedy, not a stranger to the young widower, again lay in wait for him upon his return to South Carolina, where "the first intelligence that reached my sense on arriving in Charleston was—that my little girl & her grandmother, who were residing in Summerville, had had their residence burnt to the ground …" (Letter of November 27, 1833; *L*, I, 52–53). Simms reported that Augusta and Mrs. Giles "had lost everything, not excepting their wardrobe, and only saving the clothes on their backs—from some villainous indiscretion of the servants." The writer's personal losses included half of his winter wardrobe, "some 150 vols. of my books," and "a bundle of MSS. as the advertisements say—of little use to any but the owner." Resiliency characterized Simms young and old; and with the statement, "So much for my luck—the born curse still clinging to me," he rationalized: "Fortunately, I have grown philosophic. …" Forced to move Augusta (and perhaps Mrs. Giles) back to Charleston, Simms quickly closed the Summerville chapter of his life and was almost immediately back in literary harness again: "We are all now living in town and my novel hastens pretty rapidly" (*L*, I, 53), he reported almost cavalierly to Lawson.

The major share of Simms's energy in the fall of 1833 went into the writing of *Guy Rivers,* the first of the novels influenced by his trips to the Southwest, and the first in the series known as the Border Romances. On November 27, 1833, he wrote that "'Guy Rivers,' a story of the South, in two volumes, by the author of 'Martin Faber'—'Atalantis'—&c' is in rapid progress" (*L*, I, 53). Actually, Simms had been concentrating on *Guy Rivers* for more than a year, having remarked in November 1832 that "the first volume, in rough, is completed" (*L*, I, 45). By the end of December 1833 Simms had the work "finished—bating corrections," but reported to James Lawson that "it still remains in my hands." He then noted "a small blunder" in the advance notice of *Guy Rivers* in that the novel "does not relate in any degree to the late political difficulties in So. Carolina." Before closing his December 29, 1833, letter to his New York friend, the Charlestonian suggested the possibility "that you shall see me in New York before the winter is well over" if that season proved to be "the period most proper for … publication" (*L*, I, 55). Whether Simms got to the North during the winter months is unknown, but we do know that he was there by June 12, 1834, awaiting the publication of *Guy Rivers*, which occurred between that date and July 19. On the latter date, after reading the first reviews, Simms wrote from New Haven to the New Yorker: "Of course, the success of 'Guy' is not less grateful to me than to my friends; but you have not surely estimated only my strength of mind and character, when you suggest caution as to the manner in which I speak of its success and of my own. … As far as I have seen all the papers speak well of 'Guy'" (*L*, I, 59).

Among the most enthusiastic of the newspaper reviews were those in the *Charleston Courier* of July 19, 1834, and the *New York American*[14] of a few days earlier. The Charleston paper stated that "Mr. Simms has entered a new field … whose untrodden paths afford a large scope for his fine imaginative mind and he has used the materials … with a master's hand." The *American* proclaimed that "no American novel since the days when the appearance of Mr. Cooper's *Spy* created such a sensation … has excited half the interest that will attend the circulation of *Guy Rivers*. …" Perhaps the most significant magazine review of *Guy Rivers* was written by Henry William Herbert, editor of the *American Monthly Magazine*, for the July 1834 number of his journal. Herbert heaped praise on every aspect of the novel and, like the reviewer in the *American*, focused upon a comparison of the accomplishments of Cooper and Simms: "There is more acquaintance, displayed in these two volumes, with secret springs of human action," Herbert asserted, "than in all the novels Cooper ever has written, or will ever write. …" It is "in depicting character that the author of Guy Rivers is most happy," the reviewer continued; "… we unhesitatingly assign to Guy Rivers a high place in the scale of fiction … above every American novel that has met our eye. …" Herbert concluded that Cooper, "great as he is in graphic detail, could not have written Guy Rivers had he died for it …" (II, 295–304).

Even more than *Martin Faber*, then, *Guy Rivers: A Tale of Georgia* added luster to the growing reputation of William Gilmore Simms. Whereas *Martin Faber* was at best a short novel based largely upon an earlier short story, *Guy Rivers* represented, in Simms's own words, "the first of my regular novels."[15] Rather than springing from an earlier story, it was conceived from the beginning as a novel in two volumes; and for the first time Simms unloosened his verve and narrative power into the sustained creation of a distinctively American theme. It was with the publication of *Guy Rivers*, Simms was to write twenty years later, that he "commenced a professional career in literature which has been wholly unbroken since ..." (p. 7). With *Guy Rivers* Simms "abandoned the profession of the patriot and politician" and adopted his "first love," literature, as his "proper vocation" (pp. 9–10). *Martin Faber* had made Simms known to literary America for the first time, primarily as a promising young writer of fiction; *Guy Rivers* built upon that reputation and established him as one of the two major American novelists of his time, rivaled in popularity only by Cooper.

As its subtitle indicates, *Guy Rivers* (to quote the author) "is a tale of Georgia—a tale of the miners—of a frontier and wild people, and the events are precisely such as may occur among a people & in a region of that character" (*L*, I, 55).[16] It was this raw, fresh quality of *Guy Rivers* (a quality that was to mark the other Border Romances as well) that most offended Simms's first biographer, William P. Trent. Stating that Simms's series of novels "laid in nearly all the Southwestern States, are sometimes as rough in their construction as the people described were in their manners and customs," he noted: "All are marred by a slipshod style, by a repetition of incidents, and by the introduction of an unnecessary amount of the horrible and the revolting." Although he seemed to accept Simms's response to critics who objected to "the lavish oaths put in the mouths of his characters," noting that "he could not change for the better a backwoodsman's vocabulary," Trent charged that Simms "might have avoided, at least, introducing brutal murders not necessary to the action of the story," suggesting that "he might have remembered that a good artist is not called upon to exercise his powers upon subjects not proper to his art, simply because such subjects belong to the realm of the real and the natural." How much his own taste intruded upon his review can be seen in his summary:

> He [Simms] might have remembered that nobility is that quality of a romance which is essential to its permanence; and that the fact that he was describing accurately the life of a people whom he thoroughly understood would not alone preserve his work for the general reader. When all is said, one is forced to wish that Simms had written fewer or none of these stories, and that he had spent the time thus saved in polishing the really excellent historical romances. ... But he had to make a living, and the public liked sensational tales, so there is great excuse for him.[17]

This review is important because it clearly reveals the strong artistic and critical bias that permeates and negates Trent's assessment of Simms's frontier writing. It is not difficult for the modern reader or critic to see that what Trent considered Simms's most glaring faults might well be praised now as his main strengths: his ability to depict "accurately" the "real and the natural" life (and vocabulary) of Southern backwoodsmen "whom he thoroughly understood."

*Guy Rivers* is a powerful, if flawed novel. It reveals Simms's gusto in portraying the chase, the battle, the violence of the frontier: swift-moving, action-packed narrative flows from Simms's pen with ease and naturalness; it captures the reader's imagination and interest and holds them until Simms moves the action from the woods, hills, and caves to the drawing room, where stilted, pretentious language replaces the salty vernacular of the ruffian and backwoodsman. What vitality there is in characterization comes in the portraits of untutored frontiersmen like Mark Forrester. The plot is episodic rather than symphonic, and many narrative threads dangle loosely without context rather than intertwine into a closely woven carpet.

The hero and the heroine, Ralph and Edith Colleton, seldom rise above the cardboard artificiality of the Southern gentleman and gentlewoman either in their hackneyed speech or in their almost unbelievably heroic and unselfish actions. In one instance, however, Simms seems to question Edith's strict adherence to a principle of self-worth. When Guy Rivers offers to spare Ralph Colleton from death if Edith will agree to marry the outlaw, she unhesitatingly refuses: she is unwilling to adjust her concept of personal integrity and virtue even to save the life of the man she loves. In contrast, the other leading female character in *Guy Rivers,* Lucy Munro, who is also in love with Colleton, would have given herself to the outlaw, as Rivers himself points out, to save her lover from death. In this respect, Lucy Munro seems much more humanized, much more capable of love and concern, than the proudly inflexible heroine Edith. Perhaps the fact that Lucy is not the daughter of South Carolina aristocracy frees her from the rigid code of conduct and honor at the center of Southern chivalry. Her father had been a respectable man, but at his death Lucy became the ward of her uncle, Munro, a fellow criminal with Guy Rivers. Lucy, then, has an interestingly complicated background of a well-bred father on the one hand and an outlaw foster father on the other, and emerges as one of Simms's most believable heroines. She possesses ladylike reticence in going to Colleton's room at midnight to warn him of his danger, but once again her human concern outweighs her sense of protocol and she does go, despite her embarrassment, and helps him escape. She also makes a daring escape from Guy Rivers's fortress after she learns that her testimony may save Colleton from being falsely convicted of murder, though her confusion at having to reveal her presence in Colleton's room and at having to implicate her foster father in the crime renders her testimony useless. For the reader she is much more realistically conceived than most of Simms's inordinately lifeless ingenues. A possible flaw in Lucy Munro's characterization occurs, however, near the end of the novel. She has contended for Ralph Colleton's love, but has lost to Edith, to whom Colleton is betrothed. It seems inconsistent with Lucy's independence and free spirit, as previously drawn, that she would accept the invitation of Ralph and Edith Colleton that she come to live with them after their marriage.

Simms's portrait of the title character comes from a mixture of influences: the Gothic tradition that had also helped to produce *Martin Faber;* Simms's own experiences in the frontier Southwest, where he either saw, or heard about at firsthand, the leaders of a criminal gang who ruled with terror and horror; and a perverse desire on the author's part to create a well-educated lawyer-outlaw—with many of the traits of an aristocrat—who was corrupted as much by his resentment of his rejection by the gentry as by his own satanic nature and love of cruelty. Unfortunately, Simms fails to bring these diverse characteristics together into an artistic whole, and Guy Rivers comes through as a stiff, morose Byronic villain consumed with hate, too one-dimensional to be credible. Simms's attempt to humanize his criminal—and to offer insight into the psychology of crime—does not fully succeed because Rivers's attribution of his criminality to an undisciplined environment comes without sufficient build-up or development. Near the end of the novel the outlaw denounces his mother for having nurtured in him those qualities that led him to a life of crime: "... I charge it all upon her ... twenty years of crime and sorrow, and a life of hate, and probably a death of ignominy—all owing to the first ten years of my infant education, where the only teacher I knew was the woman who gave me birth!" (p. 454).

Although his judgment of *Guy Rivers* was too harsh, and was so, one might add, for self-serving reasons, Trent was nevertheless correct in attributing the novel's startling success with American readers and critics alike to Simms's discovery of a literary theme and a literary technique for which in 1834 America hungered. "Undiluted Americanism was what many readers were crying for, and they got it in 'Guy Rivers,'" Trent wrote; "excitement, sentimentality, bombast were what others were crying for, and they got all three in 'Guy Rivers.' What wonder, then, that the book was popular?"[18] But in patronizingly dismissing *Guy Rivers* as a vulgar popular novel unworthy of serious consideration, Trent reflects the condescending attitude spawned by a latent Victorian idealism that blinded him to any recognition of literary merit in the graphic portrayal of a squalid, untamed backwoods devoid of "nobility." In *Guy Rivers* for the first time in our literature the ugliness, the lawlessness, the brutality of the early nineteenth-century American frontier were fully exposed. Long before William Dean Howells, Simms perceived the necessity of replacing belles-lettres's "ideal grasshopper, ... the good old romantic card-board grasshopper" with a "real grasshopper ... simple, honest, and natural."[19] Simms's frontier, like Howells's grasshopper, is ugly and real—not ideal and uplifting; but it is deserving of belated recognition of its authenticity.

Flushed with the victory of *Guy Rivers* and more confident than ever of his ability to compete with all comers in the creation of stirring American themes, Simms was quick to follow his popular triumph with another major effort in the same genre. The first indication of Simms's thinking about a new novel came in his letter of July 19, 1834, to Lawson, long before the prolific South Carolinian knew the full extent of the critical acclaim of *Guy Rivers.* "I am doing nothing, but thinking much," Simms wrote, "and digesting the plan of an Indian tale—a story of an early settlement and of an old tribe in Carolina" (*L,* I, 61).[20] This first reference to *The Yemassee* was followed by another some three or four months later verifying that the new project was swiftly taking form. "My Yemassee gets on rapidly," Simms wrote in November 1834; though admitting that "the earlier chapters" were "only sketched" and could not be completed until "I have in *pro. per.* gone over the ground of the story, and become acquainted with its localities ..." he still planned "to have it ready for the publishers" by January (*L,* I, 63). Yet typical for Simms, even before completing the draft of *The Yemassee,* the ambitious young novelist was already visualizing "other plans" he was "anxious to get on with" (*L,* I, 63)—plans which doubtless included the first of his Revolutionary novels, *The Partisan,* since by late May 1835 he had completed and sent to the Harpers "some five chapters of a new work upon which I am going to be busy" (*L,* I, 68). Simms, in 1834–35, was consumed with literary fire, which blazed with remarkable intensity and even more remarkable volume.

With *The Yemassee,* Simms had once again managed to publish a groundbreaking new novel better than anything he had previously written, even while the accolades of his previous success were still echoing in his ears. *The Yemassee. A Romance of Carolina,* like *Martin Faber* and *Guy Rivers* before it, was published in New York by Harper—in late March or early April 1835. It was immediately hailed in the April number of the *Knickerbocker* as being superior to *Guy Rivers* and worthy of "high rank among our native fictions" (V, 341–43). Favorable reviews proliferated: the *Mercantile Advertiser and New York Advocate* of April 15 proclaimed "there is talent in every page of it, and it will not pass away and be forgotten"; the *New York Times* of the following day reviewed the book "with extreme delight," stating that Simms's reputation was now "permanently established" and that the large first printing had sold out in thirty hours; the *New York Commercial Advertiser*, the *New York Mirror*, and the *New Yorker* all highly favorably reviewed *The Yemassee* on April 18; five days later the *Baltimore American* stated that "*The Yemassee* establishes its author, Mr. Simms, among the first class of modern novelists"—all these critiques in well-known Northern papers or magazines within an eight-day period. No wonder that the first edition of twenty-five hundred copies sold out quickly, requiring two other printings before the end of the year. Simms, by his twenty-ninth birthday on April 17, 1835, had established for himself a literary reputation surpassed by no other contemporary American novelist.

*The Yemassee* was indeed Simms's best effort to date. While he retained all the advantages of the "new field" he had discovered—the Southern frontier—he also explored another of the "untrodden paths" to which his imaginative mind was attracted—the theme of the American Indian. By centering upon colonial South Carolina as his setting, Simms was able to utilize even more effectively than in *Guy Rivers* his great skill at depicting landscape, particularly that of his native state, which he much loved and with which he was thoroughly familiar. By concentrating upon the wars between the early white settlers and the Indian tribe indigenous to coastal Carolina, he was able, while using notably different locale, theme, and philosophy, to take advantage of the great interest aroused by Cooper's Leatherstocking novels. But Simms, as Vernon L. Parrington pointed out in his monumental *Main Currents of American Thought,* "did not follow Cooper's example and plunge into the wilderness," but instead focused upon the "frontier psychology" of "the squatter and settler," mimicking "their sordid prose." Simms crowded "a wealth of romantic material" into *The Yemassee*—"enough to serve Cooper for half a dozen tales" as Parrington observed—and though in so doing the young Southerner may have lost some of Cooper's "dramatic swiftness of movement," he gained an "abundance of accompanying action—the sense of cross purposes and many-sided activities, which *The Yemassee* so richly suggests." Compared to Cooper's Mohicans, Simms's Yemassees are much more complex human beings, with faults and virtues, much less the noble savage. In fact, nineteenth-century American literature produced no more realistic treatment of the American aborigines than did Simms in his novels *The Yemassee, Vasconselos,* and *The Cassique of Kiawah.* But as Parrington noted, it is idle to compare Simms with Cooper. Not only is Simms "incomparably the greater master of racy prose, as he is much the richer nature," but Simms was also "far too rich in his own right to live as a dependent on anyone, and certainly far too original to be an imitator."[21] While Simms consciously and sympathetically portrayed the Indians as credible human beings capable of corruption and destined for tragic defeat, he was also consciously creating a mythology about the Yemassee. In the 1853 preface to the Redfield edition of *The Yemassee* Simms, while contending that his "portraits ... are true to the Indian," confessed that he took "liberties" with "his mythology": "That portion of the story, which the reverend critics, with one exception, recognized as sober history, must be admitted to be a pure invention—one, however, based upon such facts and analogies as ... will not discredit the proprieties of the invention" (p. iv).

Simms was perhaps the first American writer to draw the distinction between *novel* and *romance,* as commonly observed in European literature—a distinction made notable in the United States by Hawthorne's famous statement in the preface to *The House of Seven Gables* in 1851. Though Simms was to make some modifications in the prefatory letter to the revised 1853 edition, he had already stated in the preface to the first edition (1835) of *The Yemassee:* "I have entitled this story a romance, and not a novel—the reader will permit me to insist upon the distinction." Rather than being restricted like the novel to the realistic representation of ordinary life, the *romance* (to Simms, and later to Hawthorne) gave the artist license to deploy legendary, imaginative, and poetic material usually associated with the medieval epic. In Hawthorne's words, the "legendary mist" of *The House of Seven Gables* has "a great deal more to do with the clouds overhead than with any portion of the actual soil of the County of Essex." Simms, on the other hand, contended that "Modern romance is the substitute which the people of today offer for the ancient epic. ... The modern romance is a poem in every sense of the word."[22] This epic concept of the romance, perhaps drawn from Simms's boyhood reading of Homer and Virgil, fit perfectly with the South Carolina author's discovery that the American reading public was attracted to heroic, dramatic, purposeful portrayals of national themes in their fiction. *The Yemassee,* then, was Simms's first attempt to write an American epic—the Great American Novel, as it were—dealing with American history in its initial savage form, the warfare between European settlers and Native Americans over the very land itself, and depicting an era fraught with the irreconcilable and competitive purposes, cultures, and philosophies of strikingly different peoples. The scope, the breadth, and the vision of *The Yemassee* are indeed epic, and the work has an energy and raw power unusual for American writing at that time. Despite flaws in structure, diction, and characterization, it effectively presents a view of America found nowhere else in our literature.

C. Hugh Holman has convincingly demonstrated that Simms was consciously influenced by Sir Walter Scott in creating this and other of his historical romances.[23] There can be little doubt of Simms's admiration for Scott. In "Modern Prose Fiction," an essay written earlier and finally published in the *Southern Quarterly Review* in 1849, Simms called Scott "more perfect, more complete and admirable than any writer of his age," partly because he combined "the peculiar powers of the *raconteur* with those of the poet, painter, and the analyst of events and character" better than any other writer.[24] The Scott formula of a dramatic encounter in which "the ancient rough and wild manners of a barbarous age are just becoming innovated upon" (*The Fortunes of Nigel*) is well represented in Simms's novel in the Yemassee war, a conflict between settler and savage; and the central love story, or aristocratic subplot, of Gabriel Harrison (Governor Craven) and Bess Matthews, seems to follow Scott's plot structure and his use of historical personages. But Simms's creative effort in *The Yemassee* owes little or nothing to Scott; it was inspired, perhaps most of all, by his three visits to the Southwest. During the first two he rode with his father throughout the Indian country, visited the Creek and Cherokee nations, and listened to the elder Simms's vivid stories of his own Indian experiences. During the third visit, undertaken to settle his father's estate in 1831, he evinced an even livelier interest in Indian affairs. Taking a seventeen-day journey on horseback through the Choctaw lands in Mississippi, Simms recorded with perception the startling changes that had taken place since his earlier visit. The most dramatic scene anywhere in Simms's work—the tomahawk murder by Matiwan of her own son, Occonestoga, undertaken to save him from ritualistic disgrace and humiliation—was probably inspired by the young writer's observation of a similar degradation of an Indian youth during his 1831 visit to Mobile, Alabama.

Certainly Simms's greatest achievement in *The Yemassee* is the creation of memorable characters like Sanutee, the sage chief of the Yemassees, and Matiwan, his wife, perhaps the most striking Indian woman in the literature of that day. Also worthy of recognition is the painstaking portrayal of the degeneration, by white man's alcohol, of the talented but weak and vain Occonestoga. Simms handles these Indian characters with unusual deftness and restraint, using direct characterization to allow them to reveal their dignity and their folly, their pain and their joy, in speech, manners, and action. The epic tradition that the fall of a worthy enemy is an event of tragic proportions—not an occasion for rejoicing—is preserved in Simms's skillful handling and the mood and tone of solemnity he conveys. The inevitability of the defeat of the Yemassee and the ascendancy of the white settlers evokes a sense of national tragedy in keeping with the epic dimension of the romance.

As the most forward-looking and realistic American novelist in his portrayal of the Indian, Simms also raised the question about the Native American's capability to adapt to the kind of civilization to which the white race aspired. In a heated debate with the Reverend Mr. Matthews, the young, untutored, but good-hearted stalwart Hugh Grayson states unequivocally his judgment that the inferior Indian can never live peacefully with the white settlers. "[I]t is utterly impossible that whites and Indians should ever live together and agree," Grayson proclaims. "The nature of things is against it, and the very difference between the two, that of colour, perceptible to our most ready sentinel, the sight, must always constitute them an inferior caste in our minds ..." (p. 291). The racial philosophy expressed by his characters—one based on the presumed superiority of the white race to the colored races, red or black—though disturbing to the modern reader because of its innate racism, nevertheless represents effectively and truthfully the thinking of Simms's day.

Similarly, though in 1835 the abolitionist movement was only beginning to inflame sectional feelings, Simms's concept that slavery under an enlightened owner was beneficial to the appreciative slave pervades the dialogue between Gabriel Harrison and Hector, the slave whom Harrison wishes to free for saving his life. Even though Harrison offers money, a house in Charleston, and freedom, because "You have saved my life, old fellow—you have fought for me like a friend, and I am now your friend, and not any longer your master," Hector is adamant in his rejection of the offer:

> I d——n to h——l, maussa, ef i guine to be free! ... I can't loss you company. ... 'Tis onpossible, maussa, and dere's no use for talk 'bout it. De ting ain't right: and enty I know wha' kind of thing freedom is wid black man? Ha! you make Hector free, he turn wuss more nor poor buckrah—he tief our of de shop he git drunk and lie in de ditch—den, if sick come, he roll, he toss in de wet grass of de stable. ... No, maussa—you and Dugdale berry good company for Hector. I tank God he so good—I no want any better. (437–38)

The passage is worth recording for two reasons: first, it reveals Simms's knowledge of, and ability to transcribe accurately, the Gullah dialect spoken by some low-country South Carolina blacks from colonial times to the present; second, it reflects Simms's philosophical assumption that the black race, more adaptable than the red, would benefit from its association with the white, to the advantage of both,[25] whereas—in Hugh Grayson's view at least—the inflexible red race could never live peacefully with the white.

In keeping with the historical record of the Yemassee War, Simms reveals that black slaves fought with the English settlers against both the Indians and the Spaniards. This fact is not surprising for two reasons: the supposition that the English practiced a "gentler form of treatment" that "won the affections of their serviles" (p. 374);[26] and the opposing reputation of the Spanish for cruelty to its plantation slaves in the Carribean—hence the concern lest Hector be captured and sold into slavery in Cuba (pp. 122, 127). What at first seems shocking, however—even though there is little reason to question the historical authenticity—is the unmerciful brutality of the blacks against the Indians.[27] Yet fear of being scalped—or worse, of being captured alive and sold for bounty to the Spaniards—was sufficient to arouse hate and vindictiveness in the slaves, who in addition could impress their masters with the ferocity of their zeal. No better evidence of the brutalizing effect of war can be given than Simms's revelation that red, black, and white[28] alike become inhumanly cruel when caught up in its passion.

As we have seen, Simms was so charged with creative fire, so eager to mine the rich literary vein he had struck almost by accident, that he was busy with the manuscript of *The Partisan* even while seeing *The Yemassee* through the press. By June 10, 1835, the indefatigable young man of letters informed Lawson: "I have sent some dozen chapters of my new novel to the Publishers. ... [It] will be ready & probably published by October" (*L*, I, 70–71). In late September or early October Simms went northward to confer with Harper to ensure that his first Revolutionary War novel was published on schedule, and, of course, to visit his good friend Lawson. The details are recorded in Lawson's letter to Robert Montgomery Bird: "Simms will sail homeward in ten days. ... His *Partisan* is finished—just finished—the last chapter today. The whole of the first volume (which I have read) & two thirds of the second are printed—" (*L*, I, 72n). *The Partisan: A Tale of the Revolution* (New York: Harper & Brothers, 1835), in two volumes, evidently was not issued until November, for Simms—back in South Carolina—seems not yet to have had a copy when he wrote Lawson on November 5, "I suppose the Partisan will be in your hands by the time that you recieve this letter" (*L*, I, 74).

The early reviews which appeared in the *Knickerbocker*, in New York, and in the *Southern Literary Journal*, in Charleston, must have pleased the author of *The Partisan*. The *Knickerbocker* in its December 1835 number called "[t]his latest production of the gifted Simms ... in many respects, the best" of all his works: "Mature, effective imagination, and fine descriptive powers are its prominent characteristics" (VI, 577). The *Southern Literary Journal* was even less restrained in its praise, calling *The Partisan* "decidedly the best historical American novel that has yet been given to the public" (I, 284–85) in a brief December notice and proclaiming in its full review the following month:

"Simms' success as a novelist is no longer problematical ... his name will hereafter be a sufficient guaranty to the recommendation of his works. ... Our state should, indeed, feel proud of him" (I, 347–58). Yet almost from the beginning the critical reception of *The Partisan* was less enthusiastic than Simms had hoped for—or expected—after the almost unstinted praise that had been heaped upon *The Yemassee.* His disappointment came not because the reviews were unfavorable—because the best of them were highly laudatory—but because he detected in them a certain condescension which, as he confided to Lawson, disturbed him.

One review which probably irked Simms more than he was willing to admit was written by his New York friend, Henry William Herbert, editor of the *American Monthly Magazine.* The critique begins with praise for Simms's earlier work and for Simms himself: "There is no author of whose abilities we deem more highly." Very quickly, however, Simms's latest work is damned: "From the title-page to the word *finis,* there are in every page the marks of carelessness and haste; in the matter as in the manner, in the sentiments as in the style, in the interest as in the incidents. The plot—if indeed that can be called a plot ... is crude and immature; the characters ... mere lifeless images. ..."[29] Simms also had Herbert in mind when he wrote complainingly to his confidant Lawson about "the insidious comparison of living & contemporary if not rival authors." Clarifying his view of the proper focus of criticism, he added: "Just criticism should be intrinsic, not comparative. ..." If "comparisons are made between Bird, Kennedy & myself," he continued, "it places the parties in an awkward predicament; God help us when our men of letters can only be judged when placed opposite each other in a cockpit" (*L,* I, 88).

But, most of all, in the same letter of April 29, 1836, Simms objected to what he felt was the condescending attitude of his critics toward his subject matter—the Southern lifestyle, its manners, its language, its personages. "The condescension is excruciating; and it amuses those who are conversant with our history," Simms asserted, "... to see the gross & complete ignorance of these cavilles upon [*The Partisan*]," a novel "most truly" based upon "the pecularities [*sic*] of our people, our climate, our customs. ..." Simms then pointed out that "In Carolina where the topic is well known,—the characters of our various classes &c, the work is more popular than anything I have yet written." Since *The Partisan* "has taken well here, whatever may be the estimate put on it elsewhere," Simms requested of Lawson: "Do when you write tell me the secret of all this hostility ..." (*L,* I, 88–89).

It is clear that the highly sensitive young Southerner even in 1836 was beginning to feel defensive about outsiders' perception of the "peculiarities" of his native region—a perception he felt was both patronizing and ill-informed. It is significant, perhaps, that in an earlier letter to Lawson, the novelist had defended Herbert's capacity as a critic. "I have seen Herbert's review ... and in many respects esteem it just," Simms wrote on April 15, 1836; "nor am I disposed to regard him with less warmth & good feeling than before." Simms maintained that Herbert "has erred" in objecting to his novel's "abruptness" and particularly to its "humour, simply because my individual taste does not seek it"; but, Simms confessed, "he is right in many other respects" (*L*, I, 85).

Edgar Allan Poe, reviewing *The Partisan* for the *Southern Literary Messenger* for January 1836, was equally as harsh as Herbert in his judgment of the book's overall merits:

> There is very little plot or connection in the book before us; and Mr. Simms has evidently aimed at neither. ... The cant of verbiage is bad enough—but the cant of laconism is equally bad. ... Of the numerous personages who figure in the book, some are really excellent—some horrible. The historical characters are, without exception, well drawn. ... The fictitious existences in "The Partisan" will not bear examination. Singleton is about as much of a non-entity as most other heroes. ... Porgy is a most insufferable bore ... a back-woods imitation of Sir Somebody Guloseton, the epicure, in one of Pelham's novels. ... Mr. Simms' English is bad—shockingly bad. ... Instances of bad taste—villainously bad taste—occur frequently in the book. ...

Yet Poe ended his commentary with a highly perceptive recognition of the talents of its author:

> In spite, however, of its manifest and manifold blunders and impertinences, "The Partisan" is no ordinary work. Its historical details are replete with interest. The concluding scenes are well drawn. Some passages descriptive of swamp scenery are exquisite. Mr. Simms has evidently the eye of a painter. Perhaps, in sober truth, he would succeed better in sketching a landscape than he has done in writing a novel. (II, 117–21)

There is no evidence that Simms saw and reacted immediately to Poe's *Southern Literary Messenger* review, but years later in 1845 Simms's response to a query from E. A. Duyckinck indicates his familiarity with the critique, but more significantly reveals his ability to separate personal feelings from literary judgment:

> Poe is no friend of mine, as I believe. He began by a very savage attack on one

> of my novels—the Partisan. I cannot say that he was much out in his estimate. In some respects, as a story for example—& in certain matters of taste & style, that was one of the very worst of the books I have ever written. Poe's critique, however, paid little heed to what was really good in the thing, and he did injustice to other portions which were not quite so good. Besides, he was rude & offensive & personal, in the manner of the thing. ... He knew, or might have known, that I was none of the miserable gang about town, who beg in the literary highway. I had no clique, mingled with none, begged no praise from any body, and made no conditions with the herd. He must have known what I was personally—might have known—& being just should not have been rude. ... I tell you all this to satisfy you of my sense of the varieties. I do not puff the man when I say I consider him a remarkable one. He has more real imaginative power than 99 in 100 of our poets & tale writers. His style is clear & correct, his conceptions bold & fanciful, his fancies vivid, and his taste generally good. His bolder effects are impaired by his fondness for detail & this hurts his criticism which is too frequently given to the analysis of the inferior points of style, making him somewhat regardless of the more noble features of the work. But, I repeat, he is a man of remarkable power, to whom I shall strive one day to do that justice which a great portion of our public seems desirous to withhold. (II, 42–43)

This fair-minded, discriminating estimate of a contemporary whom Simms considered unfriendly displays the acumen and the judiciousness that made Simms one of the more reliable literary critics in early nineteenth-century America, an aspect of his career that deserves greater attention.

Simms was correct in admitting that Poe "was [not] much out in his estimate" of *The Partisan,* overall, but—particularly with reference to Poe's finding Porgy "an insufferable bore"—the novelist was also correct in perceiving that the critic's "fondness for detail" and overemphasis on "analysis of the inferior points of style" occasionally made him overlook a work's "more noble features." A sufficient number of other contemporary critics agreed with Poe's low opinion of Porgy to cause Simms to exclaim to Lawson—"you have no idea how popular Porgy is with a large majority. He is actually the founder of a sect" (*L,* I, 82). The point is that Simms was conscious of his own strengths and weaknesses: despite justified criticism of the style, the structure, and the plot of *The Partisan,* Simms knew that in portraying the American Revolution as fought in South Carolina he had struck a rich vein of ore worth repeated mining. And despite what may have been unjustified criticism of Porgy, Simms recognized—from the beginning, it seems—that he had created an interesting, dynamic character that indeed was "the founder of a sect." In the words of Hugh W. Hetherington, Porgy was "the most adequate example of the ideal gentleman of the Southern Legend. The telling of the tale of Porgy was an important contribution to the formulation of that Legend or Myth."[30] Highly appreciative though he is, Hetherington seems not to perceive that Simms's inspired creation of Porgy depends upon his being the *antithesis,* and not the example, of Hetherington's Southern gentleman.[31] Porgy, like Simms, needs admirers; but also like Simms, what he needs first and most is understanding freed from stereotyping.

Though Porgy does not dominate *The Partisan* as he later does *Woodcraft,* the only Revolutionary Romance in which he is a central figure, he nevertheless plays an important minor role, revealing nearly all the characteristics that make him Simms's masterpiece. In *The Partisan* he is Lieutenant (not yet Captain) Porgy, who combines wit and bravery, corpulence and storytelling; he is a blustery, comic, lovable figure of a man who lends credibility and humanity to the Southern aristocratic tradition as does no other character in our literature. Compared to Lieutenant Porgy, philosophical but laughing and relaxed leader of guerillas, the other gentlemen characters seem wooden indeed—Major Singleton, the dauntless hero, and Colonel Walton, the more effectively drawn British sympathizer, not excluded. Katharine Walton, the colonel's spirited daughter who is Singleton's sweetheart, is more believable than most of Simms's heroines, displaying a spark of rebelliousness bordering on arrogance in rejecting her father's British friend as suitor. Simms later returns to Katharine Walton, giving her the main role in the novel which bears her name, and he of course retains Porgy, Singleton, and Colonel Walton for repeated appearances in later novels in the series.

In fact, Simms's intent to write the Revolutionary War saga in multivolumes—to continue the life stories of certain characters in later novels—accounts for some of the seemingly unresolved episodes and abrupt shifts in action in *The Partisan.* In a letter of April 1836, the young novelist called these apparent abortions in design "a necessary consequence of the plan, which contemplated a series, and reserved the futures of many of the persons for conclusion in a general sequel" (*L,* I, 85). Simms's assessment of *The Partisan* seems realistic and levelheaded, but his anticipation of its success made any less-than-laudatory comment devastating to him. "If the 'Partisan' has failed," Simms confided to Lawson on January 27, 1836, "it will throw me back greatly, and I seriously meditate, in that event, retiring from the field" and "retiring to the West" (*L,* I, 80).

Lawson probably knew his South Carolina friend well enough to recognize that Simms was simply giving vent to frustration and that he was too committed to literature and to Charleston ever to "retire from the field" or move away from South Carolina. Indeed, Lawson would have attached great significance to another comment by Simms in the same letter: "I have been busy upon a sequel to 'The Partisan' which I am pleased with. ... I have written some hundred pages or more & have forwarded two chapters to the *Harpers*."[32] Simms also confessed that he counted upon *The Partisan*'s success partly for financial reasons, because he was "thrown back greatly by the exigency of my situation, and with an income quite too precarious, as it depends on popular applause, to hope anything positively for the future" (*L*, I, 80). From their confidential and candid conferences in New York when they were bachelors together, Lawson was familiar not only with the courtly young South Carolinian's literary aspirations, but also with his ardor for other kinds of recognition, not the least of which called for a certain degree of financial solvency.

Despite his furious literary activity in these years, Simms found time for diversion not unusual for an eligible young bachelor. As we have seen, the idea of courting fashionable and wealthy young gentlewomen had been suggested to him by Lawson during their first summer together in New York in 1832. Simms had taken the suggestion and had immensely enjoyed the experience, never failing to ask Lawson to remember him to the "fair ladies of John Street";[33] and he brought back to Charleston with him his newfound delight in associating with women of society and substance. Thus it probably came as no surprise to Lawson that the handsome young novelist—after asking the Scotsman "pour votre affaire"—mentioned off-handedly in late 1833 "a strange report here that I am to be bound hand & foot & given o'er to the custody of some fair enslaver in our own parts." Despite "[a]ll I can say or do," Simms added, rumors abound that "a new maiden and a fresh, is forever taking the place of some sweet predecessor in my arms" (*L*, I, 53–54). Though Simms at the time denied any interest in matrimony with the memory of his first wife "haunting me still," his frequent, almost envious, references to Lawson's impending marriage to Mary Eliza Donaldson (whom Simms knew fondly as "Lady Lyde") belie his interest in the subject. A letter of November 5, 1835, removes all doubt; Simms jocularly wrote from Charleston to his New York friend: "I shall myself go for the Country as soon as the cold weather sets in. I have just parted with a certain fair one, who went this morning. Do you know I am fairly enamored. I shall certainly make love to her. ..." And, then, in closing, the young Southerner chided his older New York friend—"and who knows but I may beat you. Who knows but Mrs. S. may be a name before Mrs. L. It all depends on the weather" (*L*, I, 73).

The "certain fair one" was Chevillette Eliza Roach, a seventeen-year-old heiress to large twin plantations, Oak Grove and Woodlands, encompassing almost seven thousand acres on the rich banks of the Edisto River, near Orangeburg, some fifty miles from Charleston. The only daughter of wealthy landowner (and former factor of Charleston) Nash Roach, a literary-minded aristocrat of English descent, Chevillette must have met Simms through her father, who in addition to serving as plantation lord owned a Charleston town house in which he and his daughter lived during the summer months. At any rate, romance between the young heiress and the twenty-nine-year-old widower was not surprising, for both Chevillette Roach and Gilmore Simms were attractive persons with much to commend them as matrimonial prospects. In all Charleston, perhaps, there were in 1835 few more eligible than the daughter of Nash Roach and the author of *The Yemassee* and *The Partisan.*

The progress of Simms's courtship of Chevillette is best revealed through the author's correspondence with Lawson. The Southerner's jest that "Mrs. S. may be a name before Mrs. L" proved vain, for "Lady Lyde" Donaldson became Mrs. James Lawson late in 1835 or early in 1836. Simms wrote to congratulate "you & Mrs. L." on January 27, 1836, at which time he added: "for my own poor part, I fear I shall not soon be so fortunate." Admitting that he "was about to engage in a similar experiment (the love making) with yourself," Simms explained that he had been "thrown all aback by one or two inauspicious circumstances," the most significant being "a debt of an amount rather beyond my best ability to pay." When demand for payment was made, friends of Simms stepped in "to buy up the debt" which, as the writer related, only served to "substitut[e] one in its place ... much heavier." The action of his friends "transferred the outlay to the shoulders of those whom I would not have bear it." As a result, Simms despaired, "It is still beyond my present means of payment, but must & shall be paid ..." (*L*, I, 78). The despondent Simms recognized that any delay which might ensue from settling his debt might be disastrous to his marriage hopes.

However, Simms was equally determined "to marry no woman ... until I am perfectly independent of her resources, and her friends." This last obligation persuaded Simms "to forego the pleasant joys on which I had set my mind" rather than to "risk my independence, or the happiness & peace of a wife, by a marriage while my circumstances continue doubtful." In thus postponing if not relinquishing his hopes, Simms acknowledged, however, that he had "long since set upon a lady—fair, gentle, accomplished" he cherished to wed. Though "vain enough" to believe that his now "forborne" courtship had been "far from disagreeable," the young writer now feared "the misfortune, before I can improve or change my pecuniary condition, of seeing her taken away from beneath my eyes by some better prepared or less scrupulous adventurer" (*L*, I, 78).

Put in the context of his desire to marry Chevillette Roach, Simms's seemingly excessive concern about the success of *The Partisan* becomes understandable. By March 1836 Simms reported little progress to his newly married New York friend, but he seemed more hopeful: "My *affaire du coeur* stagnates. But as I revisit the country next week—it is highly probable something will come of it. If the washerwoman was unpaid by me, she must have some clothes of mine …" (*L*, I, 82). However it was that he arranged to pay the "washerwoman," Simms's visit to Oak Grove proved successful. On April 15, in a jubilant letter to Lawson apparently written at the plantation near Orangeburg, Simms excitedly proclaimed: "Ay di me alhama! Sympathize with me, *mon ami,* if you have tears prepare to shed them now!! I have been wooing—I have wooed and—have won. The Lady has smiled, and as much, perhaps, to rid herself of my importunacy as any thing else, has said 'Yes'" (*L*, I, 83). Although he noted, "you may congratulate me as soon as possible," Simms explained that the wedding would not take place "for sometime yet—certainly not before next winter, so you will see me, still a Bachelor in N. Y. next summer." Consequently, the newly betrothed Simms requested Lawson to "do me no small service by letting the fact be known, before I come on, to certain of your feminines who shall be nameless"—in so doing, he added, Lawson would give him "a fategiving benefit of future excruciation."

What type of person was the young woman who had won the heart of Charleston's outstanding man of letters? It is interesting to note how Simms himself described her. In writing Lawson from Charleston sometime in June 1836, the writer said happily but with more than a degree of objectivity:

> I see Chevillette daily, and our attachment seems to grow on both sides satisfactorily. You say truly when you speak of her as lovely. She is a creature of heart entirely—very fond, devoted, artless—of nice, unobtrusive, but ever active sensibilities, and the very personification of truth and amiability. She is pretty—very pretty—but some of her features are defective. They do not harmonize, yet her face, the *tout ensemble,* is remarkable for its general and sweet harmony. Her eyes are large and dark. Her hair dark, her forehead high. Her mouth well chiseled & sweet—her nose badly formed & rather large. Her face is a fine oval, rather pale as is the general case with the faces of our Carolina girls. Her head is narrow, and a fair one in the estimate of phrenologers. She is rather small in figure—but well & symmetrically made—with a bust, in our part of the world unusually fine. (*L*, I, 92–93)

It is indicative of the time and place—more than of the man—that the lover's description of his love stresses her physical attributes and her personality. Though Simms was certainly not blind to intellectual accomplishment of any kind, and though he immensely enjoyed, for instance, repartee and sparkling conversation, he never commented to Lawson (or, apparently to anyone else) on Chevillette's ability to articulate a point of view, develop an idea, analyze a situation, or appreciate a work of art.[34] But in 1836 those were not traits expected in a good wife—nor were they necessarily to be admired if they were found—and Simms's failure to comment to a male friend on his bride-to-be's cerebral qualities is not to be construed to imply that she possessed none; instead it is indicative of the view of women held in nineteenth-century America. The ideal wife was loyal, devoted, fair of face, sensitive and gracious, and physically well formed—attributes upon which Simms did comment admiringly (though well on this side of idolatry). Simms's romantic attachment to Chevillette's physical comeliness and amiable personality need not be questioned in recognizing that he was also attracted by the social and financial stature to be gained through marrying her. Simms of course had made no secret of his own financial situation in his letter to Lawson, nor did he attempt to conceal his pleasure that his standing—his way of life—would be improved after the marriage. In 1836 Simms, though a successful author, highly respected both North and South, nevertheless had not freed himself of financial obligation. Now with the most honorable of intentions, he sought to clear himself of debt before entering into marriage with "the only daughter—the only child—of a gentleman—a widower—a planter of our middle country, of moderate independence." Simms expressed these thoughts fully in his letter of May 27 to Lawson:

> ... to confess a truth, my dear L., I am and have been badly pushed for money. My books pay me but little,—my early patrimony has been exhausted in ridding me of the difficulties of an early monied involvement. ... Recently, a few of my friends have bought up my debts at a greatly reduced price, and these friends I must pay before I contract in marriage. Everything will depend upon the success of my books, and the generosity of my Publishers; for, though in marrying the lady to whom I am engaged, I should be at no sort of expense while living at the South, the case would be very materially altered if I wished to carry her with me to the North during the Summer, as my desire and my pursuits, alike, would render it necessary to do. Thus you have, in brief, the present situation of things. Happy when with her—happy even to extreme—I am yet desponding when I reflect how many contingencies yet rise as barriers before me. If the Partisan has sold well & been successful,—and this you must try and ascertain for me—and if I can get a good price for the work which I have in hand, I will be married early in the ensuing winter. (*L*, I, 90–91)

It is significant that, even amidst financial worries and preparations for marriage, the industrious Simms never ceased to think about, and work on, his next book—"the work … in hand" being *Mellichampe,* the second of the Revolutionary Romances, upon which he had been laboring since January, and which indeed was to be published by Harper in October before the marriage took place. It is also significant that Simms the lover did not lose sight of Simms the father during or after the courtship of Chevillette Roach. The only child of Simms's marriage to Anna Malcolm Giles, Anna Augusta, was now almost nine years old, and she had always been special to her father: he had dedicated to her *Martin Faber,* his first book of fiction. Named "Anna" for her mother and "Augusta" for her father's mother, Anna Augusta Simms (usually simply "Augusta") was a source of joy to her doting father, and in 1836 she was a vivacious, irresistible child filled with curiosity and wonder.[35] Perhaps thinking back to his own troubled early years, Simms wanted to give his young daughter every advantage he could possibly afford. His concern for the daughter of his first marriage during the months leading up to his second marriage is shown by his many references to her in his correspondence with James Lawson. For instance, in late January 1836 the South Carolina bachelor wrote to the newly married Lawson of his intentions of bringing his daughter north with him in the summer: "… tell Mrs. L. that I have already promised Augusta that she shall pay her a visit next summer" (*L,* I, 79). Apparently the Lawsons responded with a warm welcome to Simms's child, for in early March, the novelist wrote his New York friend, "Your kind proffer touching Augusta is grateful, and you have my thanks for Mrs. L. & yourself. I certainly think to bring her on with me, whatever disposition I may afterwards make of her Ladyship" (*L,* I, 82). As the summer after Simms's engagement to Chevillette Roach approached, the author reiterated his plan to bring Augusta with him and requested that Lawson "enquire for me where I can get boarding school accommodations for my daughter during the summer in or about N.Y. at moderate prices in a respectable sphere" (*L,* I, 89). The Lawsons—particularly Mrs. Lawson, the "Lady Lyde" of whom Simms was more than a bit enamored—opened their home at 15 Le Roy Place to both father and daughter during the summer months, a hospitality much appreciated by Simms and long remembered by Augusta, who became a lifetime friend of the genial New Yorkers.

Despite his concerns about his only child and his next novel—each kept him well occupied during those months in New York—Simms remained committed to his goal to marry Chevillette Roach as soon as his circumstances permitted.[36] Upon returning to Charleston in October 1836, he wrote to Lawson that "Mam'selle [Chevillette] is in good cheer & condition, and I am quite too happy, and have quite too much to do, at present, to write you a long letter" (*L,* I, 94). Among the things he and Chevillette had to do, apparently, was to plan their marriage, for on November 4, 1836, Simms wrote "dear Lawson": "I shall be married on or about the 15th. The day is not yet more especially appointed. I am anxious as you may suppose, and to the lady with whom it is left, I have declared myself 'toujours pret.' In a day or two after the event we go to the country, and enjoy our candy season in the woods of Orangeburgh" (*L*, I, 95–96). The marriage actually took place on Tuesday, November 16, 1836, two days after which the happy Simms proclaimed: "I am a married man, rich in the possession of a woman, gentle, sweet, good, and, in my eyes, very lovely in all respects. To make her happy is my present employment:—If I succeed, I am happy—very happy myself" (*L*, I, 97).

Thus, after almost five years as a widower and bachelor, Simms had entered upon a second marriage, a marriage that was to last, and grow more intimate, until Chevillette Simms's death in 1863. In the four years and nine months since the death of the first Mrs. Simms, Gilmore Simms had developed from an impoverished young writer striving to make himself known in his home city into a successful novelist with a steadily growing national reputation; from a writer who had yet to publish outside Charleston into a prolific man of letters who had published thirteen books, seven of them by Northern publishers, including five novels by the distinguished New York firm of Harpers. From being practically without financial resources, he had become a member of the gentleman-planter class, the perceived lord of Woodlands (for Nash Roach rapidly made the plantation available to his son-in-law and daughter for their permanent home), a magnificent estate of approximately four thousand acres, cared for by a "group of polite and happy slaves," approximately seventy in number.[37] There can be no question that Simms dearly loved Woodlands; he and Chevillette moved in upon their marriage and lived out their lives there. Woodlands was an inspiration for Simms—in poetry, in fiction, and in life; he knew every tree, every vine, every branch, every swamp on the plantation, and he exulted in its exquisite natural charm. It represented to him acceptance among the gentry of South Carolina, but it represented much more—it gave him a place of beauty, elegance, and dignity in which to spend his working days, fulfilling his ambition to be a great American author; he now had—as he had written to Lawson even before his marriage—the perfect combination for his tastes and his working habits—the autumn, winter, and spring at Woodlands; the summer months in New York keeping alive his literary associations. William Gilmore Simms's happiness with his situation in January 1837 was genuine—it went deep into his being—it permeated his consciousness—"he felt it to his bones," as family legend aptly put it (*MCSO*, I). For many men of lesser ambition, lesser drive, lesser energy the acquisition of Woodlands through a fortunate marriage to a wealthy and charming woman would have been reason to relax, to enjoy the comforts of plantation life in relative leisure. But for Simms the move to Woodlands represented an intensification of his already persistent efforts to make a name for himself in literature.

# V The Unquenchable Flame Burns On

What was it that motivated William Gilmore Simms to his greatest toil at just the time he seemingly had established himself for life financially and socially? Simms's own words provide the best answer. In writing to James Lawson in July 1834, the novelist candidly remarked that "my ambition is such, that having fairly rid myself of one labour, I must necessarily go on to another. *I cannot be content, if I would* [italics mine]" (*L*, I, 59). In another letter to Lawson in June 1835, Simms—after admitting that *The Yemassee* had been "certainly extravagantly" praised—confessed: "Perhaps, if the truth were known, I am still dissatisfied—I am not easily content. My achievements must go on—though upon the Alps, yet would I not slumber while Rome lay beyond them attainable, yet unattained—" (*L*, I, 71).[1] These passages give extraordinary insight into the makeup of William Gilmore Simms: his was a personality marked by a drive that kept him aggressively striving for more and more recognition, appreciation, and power; incapable of being completely fulfilled, he was incapable of being content. Long before the concept came into vogue, Simms was a "workaholic," relentlessly driven toward success, never satisfied to rest upon his laurels nor to enjoy a relaxed, leisurely existence. In yet another revealing passage, in a letter to Rufus W. Griswold in 1841, Simms declared dramatically: "Do not ... suppose me insensible to the sweet solicitings of fame. It has been the dream of my life, the unnamed inspiration of my boyhood—dearer than life, for which I take cheerfully to toil, and toil on, though I see not the reward" (*L*, V, 359). For such a man as Simms, then, his success in literature, in marriage, and in public esteem only whetted his insatiable appetite "cheerfully to toil on, and toil on" to the next summit of the Alps or the next Rome. He was fortunate in that his greatest joy in life was his work, unfortunate in that he could never believe that his work was sufficiently appreciated by his contemporaries. Simms's self-analysis was accurate: *I cannot be content, if I would.*

Even before his wedding date, we have observed, Simms had managed to complete the writing of *Mellichampe* and to see it published. His first mention of the new novel occurred in the letter of January 27, 1836, to James Lawson: "I have been busy upon a sequel to 'The Partisan' which I am pleased with. ... I have written some hundred pages or more & have forwarded two chapters to the Harpers." In his now intimate tone to Lawson, almost as an afterthought he confided, "... but I begin to distrust my own judgment dreadfully, and there is surely no worse sign than this" (*L*, I, 80). Throughout the rest of the winter and into the spring Simms kept working away on the novel he now called "a sort of continuation of, but not a sequel to the Partisan." At one time he considered dedicating *Mellichampe. A Legend of the Santee* to William Cullen Bryant, whom he had met at Lawson's in the summer of 1832. "By the way," he related to Lawson in April 1836, "I see that Bryant has come back from Italy. I have some thought of dedicating my next book to him. What do you think?" (*L*, I, 89). For whatever reason Simms did not dedicate *Mellichampe* to Bryant—or to anyone else, for that matter[2]—but when the book was published in late October, Simms, back in Charleston, wrote to Lawson requesting that he "[t]ell Fletcher Harper not to forget to send copies of Mellichampe to Bryant, Herbert & Leggett, with my respects" (*L*, I, 96).

*Mellichampe* is not one of Simms's better Revolutionary War novels, and consequently its failure to receive unmitigated praise from the press, Northern or Southern, is not surprising. Although there were no really harsh reviews and nearly all were polite and mildly favorable, they revealed lack of enthusiasm for the book. One exception is the critique written by an admiring fellow Charlestonian, Boston-born Caroline Gilman, editor of the *Southern Rose.* Gilman expressed admiration for Simms's characterization and inventiveness and called *Mellichampe* the most interesting of his works (V [November 26, 1836], 54). The noncommittal tone of most of the reviews[3] suggests respect for Simms, but reservations about the work at hand, and indeed the present-day reader cannot fault the literary critic of 1836–37 for finding *Mellichampe* a less than inspired effort.

Of special interest, however, is the long statement with which the author began the "advertisement" to the first edition of *Mellichampe* because it throws light upon the concept behind the Revolutionary series:

> The story which follows is rather an episode in the progress of the "Partisan," than a continuation of that romance. It has no necessary connection with the previous story, nor does it form any portion of that series originally contemplated by the author, with the view to an illustration of the several prominent periods in the history of the revolution in South Carolina; although it employs similar events, and disposes of some of the personages first introduced to the reader by that initial publication. The action of "Mellichampe" begins, it is true, where the "Partisan" left off; and the story opens by a resumption of one of the suspended threads of that narrative. Beyond this, there is no connection between the two works; and the reader will perceive that even this degree of affinity has been maintained simply to indicate that the stories belong to the same family, and to prevent the necessity of breaking ground anew. Much preliminary narrative has thus been avoided; and I have been enabled to … [plunge] at once into the bowels of my subject. The "Partisan" was projected as a sort of ground-plan, of sufficient extent to admit of the subsequent erection of any fabric upon it which the caprice of the author, or the quantity of his material, might seem to warrant and encourage. (p. 1)

*Mellichampe* has fewer loose ends than *The Partisan* partly because its design and structure are less complicated. One asset, Simms pointed out, is that in *Mellichampe* the author can "plung[e] at once" into the substance of subject; the opening action resumes "one of the suspended threads" of *The Partisan*—that is, the rescuing of Colonel Walton during the battle of Dorchester—and proceeds from that point. Unlike *The Partisan* and most of the other Revolutionary Romances, *Mellichampe* does not concentrate upon a major historical event, but rather portrays guerilla warfare, the swampland raids by Marion's partisans, whose depiction depends largely upon the author's imagination. But though his "Santee legend" is less "strictly historical" than *The Partisan,* Simms was quick to assert that *Mellichampe* "portrays truly the condition of the time." According to its author, the events "are all historical; and scarcely a page … is wanting in the evidence which must support the assertion" (p. 2).

Almost without question the most telling passages in *Mellichampe*—and some of the best in all of Simms's work—pit the cunning of two of the book's most interesting characters—the villainous "Goggle" Blonay and the roughhewn frontiersman, Bill Humphries, Singleton's aide—against each other. Blonay has been tracking Humphries for several days, hoping to surprise and murder him for having accidentally killed Blonay's mother in the closing raid in *The Partisan.* But the sagacious Humphries, more at home in the woods than his adversary, manages to outwit the wary "Goggle" and to trap him in the hollow cypress in which he has been hiding—Simms's ingenious "prison cypress tree" incident admired by Caroline Gilman for its inventiveness. Hardened partisan though he is, Humphries is unable to leave his enemy entrapped to die a slow, agonizing death. Thus Humphries returns, after a day's debate with his conscience, first to release the ungrateful Blonay, and then to refuse a challenge to duel because he knows that Blonay's crushed hand would render him impotent in battle. "You're from my own parish," Humphries tells "Goggle," who, even with death looking him in the eye, characteristically taunts his detested foe, "... and there's something to-night in the woods that softens me, and I can't be angry, I can't spill your blood" (pp. 405, 407). In this gripping episode Simms combines well-motivated characterization with his penchant for sensual, visual depiction of the lush Carolina low country.

Among the characters in *Mellichampe* introduced in *The Partisan* are Major Singleton, Colonel Walton, Katharine Walton, and Porgy, all of whom played larger roles in the earlier novel and were destined to figure prominently in later books as well. But the central protagonists in *Mellichampe* are Ernest Mellichampe, an aristocratic young planter who has lost the family estate to a Tory named Barsfield, and Janet Berkeley, another of Simms's beautiful but strong-willed heroines who has the patriotism and courage to defy her loyalist father. Barsfield, Mellichampe's foil both because he killed the latter's father and because he is rival suitor for Janet Berkeley's love, is a well-conceived enemy, whom Simms treats with unusual sympathy. For example, in a stirring scene with Janet, Barsfield explains that, wishing to remain neutral, he had become a Tory only after he had been tortured, then tarred and feathered by a band of Whigs under Mellichampe's father. "Can you wonder now, Miss Berkeley," Barsfield asks, "not that I am what I am, but that I am not worse? You can not. I were either more or less human to be other than I am" (p. 314). Young Mellichampe himself displays both strengths and weaknesses of character: he is hot-tempered and impulsive as well as manly and loyal, but he learns through Janet's tutelage that leadership requires more than bravado. In the end, of course, he succeeds in both avenging his father's death and winning the hand of Janet Berkeley.

Probably the most colorful character in *Mellichampe* is Thumbscrew Witherspoon, Mellichampe's salty-tongued, practical-minded scout, who teaches his young leader valuable lessons in temperance, verbal and actual. Accosted by Mellichampe for not having ambushed Barsfield when the hardy scout spotted him alone in the woods, Thumbscrew responds:

> My idee is, that fighting is the part of a beast-brute, and not for a true-born man, that has a respect for himself. … Soon as a man squints at me as if he was going to play beast with me, by the eternal splinters, I'll mount him, lick or no lick, and do my best, tooth, tusk, and grinders, to astonish him. But afore that, I'm peaceable as a pine stump, lying quiet in my own bush. …

Then he admonishes Mellichampe with fatherly concern and affection, "Hear to my words, Airnest, and don't be vexed now. Dang my buttons, you know, boy, I love you the same as if you was my own blood and bone, though I knows my place to you, and know you're come of better kin, and are better taught in book-larning; but, by God! Airnest, you hav'n't larned, in all your larning to love anybody better than I love you. …" With the patience and wisdom of nature, the philosophical scout continues:

> You're but young, yet, Airnest. … You haven't had a full trial yet, and you're only at the beginning. … Wait a little; and if you've had a little nonplush at the beginning, why, man, I tell you, larn from it—for it's a sort of lesson, which, if you larn it well, will make you so much the wiser to get on afterward … when you have a chance to turn your enemy upon his back. It a'n't revenge, but it's justice, and my lawful, natural right, that I fights for. … (pp. 34–37)

The contrast between Simms's effective use of dialect—whether the vernacular of the backwoodsman Thumbscrew Witherspoon or the Gullah of the slave Scipio—and the stilted dialogue of his heroes and heroines is so striking that the reader is puzzled. Why would an author capable of capturing the rhythms of the spoken word in dialect depart from reality in attributing artificial conversation to his aristocratic lovers? Ridgely offers the explanation that Simms's lovers "are not only exchanging protestations of their love: they are playing a complicated rhetorical game as well." According to Ridgely, the game of "beautiful sentiments" remained in vogue "longer in the South than in other parts of the country," and Simms's "picture of the South he knew" included "living people [who] actually could 'talk like a book'" (*Simms,* p. 74)—the kind of stereotyping that persists in popular notions of the South. However accounted for, the stiff dialogue between gentlemen and gentlewomen is one of the severest obstacles to the enjoyment of Simms's novels by the twentieth-century reader.

After the publication of *Mellichampe,* Simms temporarily dropped his favorite theme, portrayal of the heroic actions and rousing events of the American frontier, to turn his attention again to Europe. This diversion was probably influenced by the predilection of the day to ascribe greater significance to European topics than to those closer to home. Simms had written four consecutive full-length novels on historical developments in this country and seemingly had committed himself to the creation of "little American epics." But the newly married writer, now a member of the very South Carolina gentry by which he had felt rejected since boyhood, was encouraged by his new peers—among others, his father-in-law, Nash Roach—not to forsake the great literary traditions of Europe, to which they still looked, with something akin to awe, for cultural verification. These well-wishers, according to Trent, "could not bring themselves to believe that an author should waste his time on such trivial subjects as the legends and traditions of a country not two hundred years old. They urged him to try a more ancient and foreign and, therefore, more dignified theme" (*Simms,* p. 112). At any rate, whether Simms had simply exhausted his own exuberant energy and wanted a change of pace or whether he chose to follow the advice of others, early in 1837 he began a historical novel with a Spanish setting.[4] By the end of March he had completed "with the exception of the preface" the manuscript of *Pelayo: A Story of the Goth* and had it in the hands of the Harper brothers. "It is a much longer work than I had intended it to be," he said in a letter to Lawson, "and has cost me more time & thought than I had anticipated" (*L,* I, 99). By July Simms was asking Lawson about proofs; by September he was "turning into prose, the verse passages of Pelayo," (*L,* I, 116); by December he had received "the proof sheets of the dramatic portions of 'Pelayo'" (*L,* I, 122); and by the spring of 1838 *Pelayo* was published by Harpers in two volumes.

Unquestionably, Simms erred when he shifted from the American scenes and topics that he knew well to a Spanish scene and topic that he knew scarcely at all. *Pelayo* remains a derivative piece below the standards of an author of Simms's caliber. That *Pelayo* was generally favorably reviewed is attributable to the taste of the time and to the reputation of the author, not to the sagacity of the reviewers. Simms at first seemed unaware of his poor judgment in devoting his energy to a project that matched neither his ability nor his long-term interests. Other than a brief comment to Lawson in January 1839, "Some of the papers say that the first Edition of Pelayo is exhausted, and I have seen the laudatory notices of a few" (*L,* I, 138), he spoke relatively little of the work. The idea that Simms may have been dissatisfied with his Spanish romance is given substance by his omitting it years later from the Redfield collected edition of his works.

It is true that Simms nearly always had several projects simultaneously in progress; he seldom staked out an objective and worked it to completion without somewhere in the process beginning something else. Thus he was already at work on another American frontier novel even before *Pelayo* was through the press. The euphoria he experienced after marriage to Chevillette failed to sustain itself against the author's inbred discontentment and melancholy, and alternating moods of depression and optimism—lifelong traits—soon became dominant again. A falling out between Simms and his publishers, the Harper brothers, and the debilitating illness of his wife, pregnant with their first child, added to his despondency. The first hint of a break with the New York firm that had published seven of his works in a five-year span came in a November 1837 letter to James Lawson noting that Simms had heard neither from him nor the Harpers, and concluding: "I am in hopes to see them soon. If you have a moment's leisure do see the Harpers and ascertain the truth respecting them" (*L*, I, 118). The truth must not have been to Simms's liking, for the author began negotiating with the Philadelphia publishing house Carey & Hart about rights to his new American novel then in progress. The firm soon committed itself to publish *Richard Hurdis; or, The Avenger of Blood. A Tale of Alabama*, with only the date of publication at issue. On May 1, 1838, Simms wrote to Edward L. Carey: "I have no desire to press forward the publication of our books,[5] though dreadfully in want of some of the sixpences which a sanguine scribbler might look forward to secure from its rapid and extensive sale(?). ... As for publishing in August, it strikes me as scarcely late enough. Books with us sell better as the winter is coming on, and when our country merchants are just visiting the city. ..." In closing, Simms assured Carey of his confidence "in your better judgment in these matters" and adding: "Publish when you think best" (*L*, I, 130–31). The book came out in late August 1838.

Significantly, Simms's name did not appear on the title page of *Richard Hurdis* when the book was first published. The novelist, evidently wanting to test the reception of the work on its own merits, without benefit of his reputation, recognized that an anonymous book issued by a publisher unassociated with him would provide an excellent opportunity. Seventeen years later Simms shed light upon the anonymity of the first edition of *Richard Hurdis.* "I had my interest—ay, and my fun too—in the mystery with which the publication of the work was originally clothed," Simms wrote in the preface to the "new and revised" Redfield edition. He advised "the young beginner" to "cling to the anonymous in literature ... if you would hope for any honest judgments" (pp. 7–8). No doubt Simms was also drawing from personal experience when he commented, "... do not deceive yourself with the notion, that, by confiding to the persons nearest to you ... you can possibly derive any advantage from it. ... Your friends always find your own personality conflicting ... with your productions. They never separate *you* from your writings" (p. 8).

Simms must indeed have had his "fun" in reading the early reviews of *Richard Hurdis.* For instance, the *Knickerbocker* for October 1838, while objecting to the novel's "most hideous distortions of character," which were "enough to make a man sick of his humanity," nevertheless regarded *Richard Hurdis* as "a work of uncommon talent." Its author, "whoever he may be," instead of following "the beaten path" of other novelists, has "boldly struck out a way of his own," giving evidence that he "is capable of still better things" (XII, 367–69). Even more amusing—but hardly pleasing—must have been the review in the *Southern Literary Journal* for November 1838. The reviewer, concluding that "as a whole, the work is sadly deficient," disagreed with suggestions that the unknown novelist rivaled Simms: Simms, he felt, was clearly superior, and cited *The Yemassee*'s superiority to *Richard Hurdis* in power and style. Like the *Knickerbocker* reviewer, the *Southern Literary Journal*'s critic also objected to the novel's depiction of violence and depravity (n.s., IV, 332–49). Despite negative reviews, however, the novel proved popular with the reading public.

Whatever the assessment of his contemporaries, Simms, in writing *Richard Hurdis,* was ahead of his time, anticipating realism and naturalism. He was again treading the "untrodden paths" by which he had created a "new field" for himself; he was again on course, and on his way to increased literary fame. Vigorously defending the book in the advertisement to its second edition, Simms answered his critics' objections to the "sterner features" of *Richard Hurdis* by pointing out that "the general portraiture is not only a truthful one," but "the materials are really of historical character." *Richard Hurdis,* he asserted, "is a genuine chronicle of the border region where the scene is laid, and of the period when the date is fixed" (p. 10). Simms knew the region of Alabama in which the novel is set from his trips to the Southwest in 1824–25, 1826, and 1831, and the history of the John A. Murrell gang in the Mississippi valley was a matter of public record. In addition, the gang's exploits were highlighted in the tall tales of the Southwestern frontier which Simms had heard firsthand from his father and doubtlessly from others in the border states. In *Richard Hurdis* Simms was back on home ground that he knew well, and the novel has real power and movement, despite some clumsiness in syntax.

Though the theme and setting are familiar, in one important way *Richard Hurdis* is an experimental novel which attempts to deploy a new literary technique. In the 1855 preface Simms explicated his experiment in point of view:

> It will be seen that there is a peculiarity in the arrangement of the story. The hero tells, not only what he himself performed, but supplies the events, even as they occur, which he yet derives from the report of others. Though quite unusual, the plan is yet strictly within the proprieties of art. The reader can readily be made to comprehend that the hero writes after a lapse of time, in which he had supplied himself with the necessary details, filling up the gaps in his own experience. I have persuaded myself that something is gained by such process, in the more energetic, direct and dramatic character of the story; and the rapidity of the action is a necessary result, from the exclusion of all circuitous narration. (pp. 11–12)

This innovative plan to restrict viewpoint to a single person is not entirely successful because though it is Simms's intent that "hero and author [narrator] ... become identical," Simms at times allows an omniscient author to intrude upon the first-person narration. But it is nevertheless amazing that a thirty-two-year-old Southern novelist known for reckless power unconcerned with form should devise in 1838 a method of narration similar to the single vessel of consciousness technique that Henry James would perfect some four decades later. *Richard Hurdis* fits more into the realistic tradition than its predecessor, *Guy Rivers,* because of this limited point of view, and the process of having the story unfold only through Hurdis's eyes has the additional advantage of making the self-revealed Richard Hurdis one of Simms's most believable heroes. Hurdis is not the perfect gentleman; he reveals in his conversation that he is capable of jealousy, quick-temperedness, and bitterness. In conversation with his mother, for instance, Richard Hurdis gives vent to his feelings toward his older brother John and toward the girl both of them sought: "Has he not all? The favor of our grandmother gave him wealth, and with his wealth, and from his wealth comes the favor of Mary Easterby." When Mrs. Hurdis tells her son, "You do her wrong!," he retorts, "Do I, indeed? What! she takes him then for his better person ... and the ... manly qualities ... which I have not, but which he possesses in such plenty? Is it this that you would say, my mother?" (p. 19).

Hurdis later illustrates his tempestuous nature by his scornful treatment of Mary Easterby and by his fight with his brother, yet he also emerges as a courageous, honorable man who, like another title character, Mellichampe, must first learn self-discipline before he can assume the responsibilities of leadership. Hurdis's reflections on the untamed nature of the frontier, and on the characteristics of the people who inhabit it—views which probably echo the novelist's own—underscore the need for enlightened, strong-willed, adaptable pioneer leaders, who remain undeterred by hardship:

> The delicacies of society are most usually thrust from the sight of the pioneers; the nicer harmonies of the moral world become impaired ... and a rude indifference to the claims of one's fellow, must follow every breaking up of the old and stationary abodes. The wandering habits of our people are the great obstacles to their perfect civilization. These habits are encouraged by the cheapness of our public lands, and their constant exposure for sale. The morals not less than the manners of our people are diseased by the license of the wilderness; and the remoteness of the white settler from his former associates approximate him to the savage feebleness of the Indian, who has been subjugated and expelled simply because of his inferior morality. (p. 66)

The frontier for Simms thoroughly tests the character of a people. Those who are lured westward because of "the cheapness of our public lands," who leave behind the moral standards of society and attempt to carve a quick fortune in the wilderness, by exploiting fellow human beings as well as nature, succumb to the seductiveness of the challenge. Those who successfully meet the challenge are those hardy pioneers who maintain a healthy respect for human dignity and for the necessary rules of civilization; even in conquering the wilderness, they nurture and preserve its resources, rather than exploit and waste them. Such frontiersmen have a sense of responsibility for themselves, for the land they seek to cultivate, and for the nation to which they belong. They—not the former, more predominant kind of pioneer—must be the leaders of the western movement if our national destiny is to be fulfilled. This, indeed, is the theme of *Richard Hurdis,* and it is an underlying current in Simms's writing about the frontier[6]—whether it be Florida before the English settlement, South Carolina in colonial and Revolutionary times, or the border states of the Southwest during the slow push of civilization toward and beyond the Mississippi River. In the flowering of American literature this theme achieves great prominence, but is portrayed by no other writer as consistently or with such vision and vigor as Simms.

Despite his literary accomplishments in the 1830s, Simms was periodically sullen and sulky, almost bitter. Part of his moroseness in 1837 may have been caused by the pressure he felt from the gradual realization that his marriage to a frail young woman curtailed the freedom of movement to which he had become accustomed as a bachelor. Chevillette Simms gallantly tried to keep up with the fast tempo of her husband even while she carried his child; but during the summer after their marriage (when the Simmses—Gilmore, Chevillette, and Augusta—visited the Lawsons in New York) there is some indication that his wife's vulnerability to the adverse conditions of travel was a source of slight annoyance to Simms. The first hint appears in a letter of June 26, 1837, to "dear Lawson" which Simms wrote in Philadelphia while en route to New York: "Mrs. S. is rather an invalid & has suffered considerably at sea" (*L*, I, 102). Since Chevillette was some four months pregnant at the time, it is probable that her indisposition at sea was a natural consequence of her condition, but Simms's frequent references to her delicate health in his correspondence seem tinged with impatience. (It is indicative of the time, of course, that Simms never mentioned by name his wife's pregnancy even to an intimate friend as close as Lawson.) After a brief visit with the Lawsons in New York, the Simmses went on vacation to Great Barrington, Bryant's home town in the Berkshires of Massachusetts, where Simms reported to Lawson that "Madame was something fatigued with the stage traveling over a mountainous country; but she bore it better than I expected" (letter of July 12, 1837; *L*, I, 102). In Great Barrington Chevillette's condition was compounded by a severe cold that brought forth "a cough which has been distressing" and a "slight fever which kept her restless" (letter of July 20, 1837; *L*, I, 104). A week later, on July 26, 1837, Simms wrote his New York friend that "Mrs. S. has been suffering very much" from her cold "which brought on irritation, cough & finally fever" (*L*, I, 106). By August 30 Simms—perhaps wearied by Chevillette's sickness as well as fretting over the Harpers' coolness toward him[7]—complained to Lawson, "I am heartily tired of this region" (*L*, I, 113). In fact, even though Simms enjoyed renewing his friendship with Bryant,[8] his morale seemed to reach a particularly low ebb during his stay in Great Barrington: "I am doing nothing—literally nothing," he wrote Lawson. "I have had so many draw backs and disappointments this year, that I am dull and desponding" (*L*, I, 112) and again: "I lack my usual industry & elasticity" (*L*, I, 114).

It would be wrong, of course, to imply that Simms's increasing dissatisfaction and irritability were the product of his marriage; rather whatever stress he felt from his marital relationship was the result of his characteristic moodiness. The evolving picture, in Simms's thoughts of Chevillette, is the husband-lover merging with the patriarch. To his anguished mind Chevillette—almost like Augusta—had become an added responsibility; and that he administered the responsibility with dutiful compassion does not alter the fact that the ambitious, self-centered man of letters felt overburdened. In 1837 Chevillette Roach

Simms was a nervous nineteen-year-old wife about to bear her first child, and her husband worried about her condition almost as much as he did about his books and publishers. Back in Charleston, Simms wrote to Lawson on November 4 that "[m]y wife, as her time of trial approaches, gets more nervous & apprehensive, as is natural enough to many mothers" (*L*, I, 119). It is fitting that Virginia Singleton Simms was born on November 16, 1837, for as the proud father remarked in a letter to Lawson: "Give me joy. Madame was confined about 10 o'clock last night—the anniversary of her marriage. She gave birth to a fat and pretty daughter whose name will be Virginia Singleton. She, and her little one, in the familiar phrase, are doing quite as well as can be expected" (*L*, I, 119–20).[9] Mother and daughter continued "doing quite as well as can be expected" during the winter months spent at Woodlands, but Chevillette remained a source of concern to her husband, who wrote to James Lawson on March 28, 1838: "I am very much afraid that the health of my wife will not suffer me to travel with her next summer. She is yet very feeble, and now that we have two children [including Augusta], and one an infant, our movements even in the best state of health for both must necessarily be slow and tedious" (*L*, I, 128). Once more, the husband's annoyance at restrictions on his lifestyle seemed almost to outweigh his pleasure at his new family condition.

But Simms's relationship with his wife had its upside as well as its downside, its lightheartedness as well as its vexations. Simms seemed in particularly good spirits, for example, even after the debilitating experience at Great Barrington during Chevillette's pregnancy, when he wrote to Lawson of his wife's endearing anticipation of seeing Shakespearean drama in New York: "My wife is anxious to see [Edwin Forrest's] Othello & Lear. ... She, you must know is almost new to the theatrical world—has never seen the Lear, the Othello—few or none, indeed of the leading characters of the drama. Judge of her emotions, therefore, by anticipation!" (letter of September 19, 1837; *L*, I, 117). Such enthusiastic response to Chevillette's delight belies a lack of tenderness on the part of the novelist for his young wife. And because there can be no doubt of Simms's strong physical attraction to her, his paternal instincts toward her should not be overemphasized. And as Simms grew older, Chevillette—a bright, responsive woman who learned quickly—grew more and more into the role of an equal, thereby easing the strain of the marriage and providing comfort to her husband, whom she greatly admired and doted upon.

Chevillette Simms and "Lady Lyde" Lawson responded to each other almost as warmly as their husbands had to one another. In his letter of March

28, 1838, to Lawson, Simms enclosed a note from his wife to Mrs. Lawson which is of special interest since it is the only extant piece of her writing. The brief note shows Chevillette to be both articulate and sensitive:

> My dear Mrs. Lawson,
>
> I have been for some time meditating to write to you, but I have been such an invalid, almost ever since I left you that to take pen in hand, or indeed to do any thing that was not in itself unavoidable, I have found impossible. I left it to Mr. Simms to say so much in his letters to Mr. Lawson and I trust therefore that you have not thought me neglectful. You of course have heard about my little baby. I have a little girl like yourself, with dark eyes & hair, and your own experience will tell that this acquisition is another reason for my not writing. Even now she occupies pretty much all of my time, which as I now have the charge of the household upon me, is very much limited. I have also several female friends with me, and sincerely wish that you & your sister were among them. One is Augusta's teacher, Miss Kellogg,[10] a lady from the North whom you may remember to have seen when she called on me at your house. She will probably stay with us, until we return to town in the summer. Do give my love to Miss Caroline, & say to her that I shall be happy to hear from her at any time. Also remember me to your father & mother. Mr. Simms usually sends my respects to Mr. Lawson, but Mr. L. will be so good as to note that I now send them myself. I sincerely hope that you have all kept well, & that your dear little baby is as fat & hearty as ever. I only wish that you could bring her here & take a peep at mine, than which, nothing could be fatter. I trust that we shall have the pleasure—next winter at least of making the comparison. Excuse my short scrawl, for you must know, I am still too much of an invalid to write a long one.
>
> Affectionately yours
> Chevillette E. Simms
> (*L*, I, 129–30)

Tragedy, however, struck before Chevillette's wish to compare babies with the Lawsons could be fulfilled. Virginia Singleton Simms died on October 10, 1838, the first of nine children William Gilmore and Chevillette Simms were to lose during their marriage. Simms was visiting the Lawsons in New York at the time of his daughter's sudden and unexpected death, and the author's first psychic experience is reputed to have taken place at that time. According to both family oral tradition (*MCSO*, I) and the reminiscences about Simms written by Rosa Aldrich (who grew up as a neighbor and companion to the later Simms children), Simms was advised by a medium in New York of his baby's impending death. The Aldrich manuscript reads in part:

> He [Simms] told us a very remarkable experience during one of his visits to the Lawson family in Yonkers, N.Y., where he attended a seance of a Spirit medium with his friends. In his great amazement he had barely taken the seat offered him when the Medium said in a loud tone, and pointing to him—"Your baby is dying. You are needed in your home"—
>
> Had the communication been of a less serious nature he might have disregarded it, but instead he telegraphed for information, but before his dispatch was fairly started on its southward way a letter came telling him of the child's desperate illness. He departed on the earliest train but found the baby dead. It was actually dying at the moment the Medium announced the fact. He had left it in perfect health. Ever afterwards he was profoundly interested in this form of psychic phenomenon. ... (quoted in *L*, I, 136)

Despite some obvious inaccuracies[11] in the memoir, there is substantial evidence that Simms had an experience such as the one described; and in later years his conversations with James Henry Hammond over the question of psychic communication lend additional credibility to the oral and written memorabilia.

But certainly there can be no doubt that Virginia Singleton's death was a shock to the young mother and father. On November 5, 1838, Simms wrote Lawson that, despite "the sunshine & smooth water" of his "very short and very pleasant passage" from New York to Charleston, he found his "little dwelling" now completely "cheerless." "What a space is made by the departure of that little angel," he exclaimed. As for his "poor wife," Simms reported her "very feeble," in "bad spirits," and "troubled with a dry hacking cough, which depresses and annoys me not a little" (*L*, I, 137, 136). The loss of her first child afflicted the mother, who remained "a silent but constant mourner" for months, more than it did Simms, who explained that experiencing frequent deaths in his youth had "made me strong to endure" (*L*, I, 138).

It is important that we get this glimpse of Simms's domestic side to balance the portrait of the ebullient, vibrant, brash young writer compulsively committed to his craft and the advancement to the next "Rome" of his upwardly spiraling literary career. Though habitually volatile in his personal as well as his professional life, often mingling pessimism and optimism, buoyancy and despair, confidence and fear, Simms permitted none of this characteristic wavering to affect his work habits. He was capable of working most diligently even when he was complaining most stridently. Indeed, there is reason to believe that voicing his doubts and resentment was for Simms a form of catharsis, allowing him subsequently to burst forth with renewed energy.

The year 1838 saw the publication of yet another book of fiction: *Carl*

*Werner, An Imaginative Story; With other Tales of Imagination.* It was published in December in New York by George Adlard—another indication of the author's widening break with the Harper brothers. After its publication, Simms impatiently awaited news of its reception. He complained to Lawson in early January 1839: "Touching Carl Werner and the Poems [*Southern Passages and Pictures*] I lack all information. Whether they have been sold or not, been praised or blamed, is equally a thing unknown to me. The books have not yet reached our market" (*L*, I, 139); and for months he continued to query Lawson about the critical reception (and possible sales) of *Carl Werner* (see *L*, I, 141, 147, 149). The book actually received rather prompt and favorable attention. The *New York Mirror* of December 22, 1838, for instance, called *Carl Werner* "by far the most attractive [work] that has been given the public by Mr. Simms. There is more power and brilliancy, both of imagination and of language, in these brief romances, than we often find expended in a novel ..." (XVI, 207). The *New York Review* of January 1839 commented on *Carl Werner:* "We consider this work as among the most noticeable of the appearances of the current quarter. It is a production of no common order in the class of works to which it belongs" (VII, 267); and the *Boston Quarterly Review* of April 1839, though registering disapproval of the author's "free use of the supernatural" and his introduction of "a little more German diatribes than comports with our taste," nevertheless stated that the "Tales are written with considerable power, and contain many passages of great beauty" (II, 261).

One review, however, particularly irked Simms when he finally saw it. It had appeared in the *Knickerbocker* of January 1839 and reads in part:

> These volumes, by Mr. SIMMS, contain several tales, after the German school, and are well worth perusal. 'Carl Werner' and 'Conrad Weickhoff' please us better than the rest, though we doubt not that with some, the tales founded on Indian traditions may be greater favorites. In this collection, the author seems to us to have had in his eye, as respects style and subject, BULWER'S 'Pilgrims of the Rhine,' though he falls far below his model, in finish and effect. There is a peculiar manner, and a very careful elaboration, requisite to transfuse the German spirit into the English, and it is not a German castle nor a German heroine, that can insure a German Tale. A thorough study of the language, an appreciation of the beauties of the German poets and novelists, a knowledge of the superstitions of the people, and of the traditions to which they have given rise, through the medium of their native tongue; these are essential pre-requisites to the proper understanding of the character and peculiarities of the Germans. (XII, 80)

In a letter to Lawson, Simms claimed that the *Knickerbocker* had given "the performances of the most miserable pretenders" longer reviews and "larger commendation" than it had *Carl Werner* and other of his recent publications: "This, I do not complain of as a lack of friendship but as an act of injustice" (*L*, I, 156).

Even years later Simms continued to feel that *Carl Werner* never received its due, either in criticism or in sales; in writing to E. A. Duyckinck in June 1845 about the possibility of a volume "of a more imaginative character" to serve as a companion piece to *The Wigwam and the Cabin*, Simms grumbled about the untoward circumstances surrounding the publication of *Carl Werner*. "These were put forth at a most unfortunate season," he wrote, "during the money pressure, and just as the public mind had been made eager & selfish in consequence of the Cheap Literature passion. I made nothing by the venture. Adlard had no facilities, and books of Tales at $2. when similar collections were selling at 12 or 25/100 were not to be thought of." Simms then proposed that "A selection from these tales, with others not yet collected, would form a neat vol. for 37 or 50 and would, I think, sell. I am willing that you should propose these two volumes to W & P. [Wiley and Putnam] on terms the most favorable to them" (*L*, II, 66–67). As will be discussed later, Wiley and Putnam accepted *The Wigwam and the Cabin* but, like all the other publishers, rejected the idea of a collection of "Carl Werner" and other "moral imaginative" tales. Never quickly or easily discouraged, Simms reminded Duyckinck in August 1845 that *Carl Werner* "failed of circulation from the simple fact that it was an expensive book ... just ... when the great revolution in cheap literature had begun. I could wish that you would read these two volumes, which, it strikes me, contain as adequate proofs as I have ever shown, of the imaginative & inventive power" (*L*, II, 98). Similarly in an 1846 letter to R. W. Griswold, the persistent Simms classified "Carl Werner" among the "best specimens of my powers of creating & combining" (*L*, II, 224), and even as late as 1868 sought a new publisher for "Carl Werner," perhaps as a separate book (*L*, V, 157).

Consistent with the contemporary notices of *Carl Werner* which so displeased Simms has been the book's subsequent reception since his death. Devoting less than a paragraph to the "worthless" collection, Trent found it "hard to conceive" the object Simms "had in view, except to show that he had been reading translations from the German ..." (p. 115). The only twentieth-century scholar to give "Carl Werner" more than passing notice is J. Wesley Thomas, who includes it in his study of Simms's German sources, as a story in which "the German influence ... is largely confined to mood and style."[12]

As the title piece in a volume of tales which, according to Simms, "with, perhaps a single exception belong to the same moral imaginative class with the first," "Carl Werner, an Imaginative Story" in a sense stands at the head of this class of Simms's stories. Certainly it is not his best moral imaginative tale; but it illustrates best what Simms meant by the term. To Simms a moral imaginative tale is not simply, or even necessarily, a story exploiting the supernatural; it may well be, as in "Carl Werner," a "form of allegory" celebrating the "strifes between the rival moral principles of good and evil." (Apparently to make his allegory clearer, Simms once considered changing the subtitle of "Carl Werner" to "The Good & Evil Genii.")[13] The other "tales of imagination" included in *Carl Werner* are not memorable, with the exception of "Jocassee," one of his best Indian tales, which, in recognition of its value, Simms later included in *The Wigwam and the Cabin,* the collected edition of his short stories brought out in 1845.

Yet another volume by Simms appeared in 1838—a book which did nothing for his subsequent literary reputation and unfortunately placed him in the front lines of the North-South debate being waged over the issue of slavery. The slender volume was actually the reprint of an article that Simms had published in the November 1837 issue of the *Southern Literary Messenger,* ostensibly as a review of Harriet Martineau's *Society in America* (1837), but actually as an answer to her attack upon slavery. The essay, entitled "Miss Martineau on Slavery" in the *Messenger,* was brought out in Richmond by Thomas W. White as a separate publication with the title *Slavery in America, being a Brief Review of Miss Martineau on that subject* "By a South Carolinian." In it Simms voiced the patriarchal philosophy adopted by most intellectuals living in the seaboard South in the 1830s and 1840s:[14] *"He is a slave only, who is forced into a position below the claims of his intellect."* (p. 653). This essay—which was nothing more or less than an articulation of the point of view of the Southern planter class to which Simms now belonged—won enthusiastic applause from critics in the South, and even the *New York Mirror* of March 23, 1839, called it "an admirable critique" of Miss Martineau. While it does not belong to Simms's literary canon, as the author himself recognized, he did consider it "a very successful paper."[15]

The well-intentioned but misguided advice to Simms not to focus his talents on fiction dealing with the dramatic history of the South may have been responsible for three books he published in 1839 and 1840 which, like *Slavery in America,* did not further his standing as a major American novelist. The first of these, however, may well enhance his reputation as a poet: it is a volume of poetry entitled *Southern Passages and Pictures,* published in December 1838 (though the date on its title page is 1839) by George Adlard, the New York publisher of *Carl Werner.* The book was favorably reviewed by the New York press: the *New Yorker* for December 15, 1838, stated that with a few more writers like Simms "the romantic literature of our country will soon be near that high standard, to which we long to see it elevated" (VI, 205); the *New York Evening Post,* December 22, 1838, asserted that the poetry of Simms "in language, thought and versification, has a peculiar and characteristic manner. … He borrows … nothing from other writers" (p. 2); and the *New York Mirror,* reviewing *Southern Passages and Pictures* on the same day as the *Evening Post,* acclaimed Simms a master of blank verse: "His meter affords a good instance of the combination of melody and strength" (XVI, 207). A little later, the *Boston Quarterly Review* recognized the "genuinely poetical" romanticism of Simms, who "looks on nature with the eye of a poet, and sings from his own heart. He reminds us of Bryant, and endears us to the objects and scenes of his poems" (II [April 1839], 259–61).

It is significant that in *Southern Passages and Pictures*—and in his *The History of South Carolina* to be discussed below—Simms did not depart from familiar subject matter, though he chose a genre other than fiction. In Simms's time poetry was the most respected literary medium—not profitable but prestigious—and Simms never ceased looking upon himself as a poet. Indeed, it is in his poetry of Southern scenes and settings that Simms approaches artistic excellence. Usually a good self-critic, Simms recognized that *Southern Passages and Pictures* contained some of his "best *published* verses" (*L,* I, 362) and that "they denote a high order of thinking and a more decided originality than is common to American verse …" (*L,* I, 378). Later in life the volume became even more a favorite of the author; in June, 1851, he wrote that "'Southern Passages & Pictures' contain more passion than all the American Poets put together" (*L,* III, 127). Among the individual poems that stand out in this collection are "The Edge of the Swamp," "Taming the Wild Horse," "Summer Night Wind," "The Indian Village," "To the Breeze: After a Protracted Calm at Sea," "The Hunter at Calawassee," "The Prayer of the Lyre," "The Shaded Water," "Chuckwill's Widow, the Carolina Whippoorwill," and "The Slain Eagle." The scholar who has done the most work on Simms's poetry correctly states that "[t]his important book deserves none of the neglect which has marked its history," calling it "a prime candidate for reprinting in some Nineteenth Century American literature series."[16]

*The History of South Carolina* (published July 1840 in Charleston by S. Babcock and bearing Simms's name on the title page) reflects both the author's interest in the history of South Carolina and his love for his native state. Since South Carolina historical data substantially provide the basis for the Revolutionary Romances and other fiction, Simms's assuming the role of historian per se was not an abrupt departure from his use of history in writing fiction. Simms first mentioned that "I am now writing a History of S. Carolina, in one vol." in a letter of July 7, 1839, to James Lawson (*L*, I, 150), and explained to the New Yorker thirteen days later that the history was "intended for the use of schools and for the general reader" (*L*, I, 151). The book, which indeed was adopted for use in the public schools of South Carolina, was acclaimed by the *Charleston Mercury* of July 18, 1840, as "adding another leaf" to the "laurel chaplet" of "[o]ur distinguished fellow townsman": "Though modestly professing to fill the place of a mere compend for the use of schools, it is of far higher order. ..." It is probable that Simms looked upon the writing of the *History* primarily as a service to his state, but his concern about the education of thirteen-year-old Augusta may have provided another motive. The loving father gave her the benefit of a good private school in Great Barrington, where she could be with one of the daughters of William Cullen Bryant; however, he also wanted her while in Massachusetts to be able to read South Carolina history. It can be questioned whether compiling *The History of South Carolina* represented the best use of his time and energy at a crucial and hectic time in his literary career, but the research Simms did in preparation for the volume proved invaluable to him later when he resumed the Revolutionary War series in 1841, 1855–56, and 1867. For Simms history and literature were so entwined that knowledge of the one was frequently inspiration for the other.

The third volume published by Simms in the nineteen-month period in 1839–40 that represented a departure from his successful concentration upon fiction dealing with the Southern frontier was unmistakably a waste of his time. Simms began *The Damsel of Darien* during the early summer of 1838, swiftly dashing off "some 150 pages," only to report to Lawson on September 2, 1838, "& there it sticks" (*L*, I, 135). Seeming to lack a real taste for his task, he labored on and off at the "new novel" for at least a year,[17] before *The Damsel of Darien* was published, in September or October 1839 by yet a new publisher for Simms, the Philadelphia firm of Lea & Blanchard. A Spanish romance based upon the adventures of Balboa, it was such an uninspired effort that even Simms's steadfast friend, James Lawson, wrote a castigating review.

Lawson's critique, which appeared in the *Knickerbocker* of November 1839, temporarily aroused hard feelings on Simms's part. Lawson's main point, however, was valid:

> With all his power of description, his knowledge of human character, and his felicity of expression, Mr. Simms is often careless, and occasionally affected. ... That *The Damsel of Darien* was written in a hurried manner, we think the proofs are numerous. In fact, Mr. Simms writes so much, and publishes so

often, that it is next to impossible, with all his genius, that he can always avoid incorrectness of phrase, and tautology of expression. (XIV, 457–58)

Simms was apparently shocked by what he considered betrayal by an intimate friend, and the result was a partly serious, partly ironic, and partly sarcastic letter of December 29, 1839, written in cold polite anger. "I'll tell you what you can do, in the excess & zeal of your friendship," Simms began. "You can write a notice of my last and best book which damns its reputation & defeats its sale. This is an admirable trait of friendship; as if when you did not like the book, it was morally incumbent upon you to review it" (*L*, I, 153).

Concerning Lawson's assertion that *The Damsel of Darien* was flawed by redundancy and grammatical and stylistic errors, Simms responded defensively and revealingly: "Mere verbal correctness, good similes, and the simple exclusion of irrelevant matter do not constitute the only, or even the greater & more distinctive essentials of a novel or romance. Is nothing to be said of ... the creative faculty which makes the material to live, breathe, & burn. Is nothing to be said of that epic singleness of object which ... fixes the eye of the Hero & the reader, equally upon one great aim & purpose ..." (*L*, I, 154–55). Simms's belief that the discriminating literary critic must deal with "the larger topics" of a work as well as with its deficiencies in language and style is well stated here, but—in the words of J. V. Ridgely—"it is unfortunate that Simms chose one of his weakest books for such a spirited defense" (*Simms*, p. 41). Interestingly enough, *The Damsel of Darien* fared somewhat better with other critics than it did with Lawson. Although the reviewer with the *New York Mirror*, for instance, viewed the work as "the most ambitious and successful incursion into the realms of romance the author has yet made" (XVII [October 26, 1839], 143), most reviews could be classified as polite and respectful, rather than enthusiastic and laudatory.[18] For a second time Simms had attempted the kind of traditional European romance expected of him by some of his friends, and again his efforts failed to arouse the degree of excitement among critics and readers that had greeted his best writing with American themes and settings.

Although Simms was not yet ready to forsake the foreign romance forever, he did return to Southern frontier warfare for his next two novels, one a continuation of the Revolutionary Romance series set in South Carolina, the other an extension of the Border Romance series westward into Mississippi. Simms was at work on *The Kinsmen: or The Black Riders of Congaree* in January 1839, and long before completing it, began writing the sequel to *Richard Hurdis*, which he entitled *Border Beagles; A Tale of Mississippi.* Its first volume was complete by July 1839, and *Border Beagles*, though started later, was published in two volumes in September 1840 by Carey & Hart in Philadelphia; *The Kinsmen* was published, also in two volumes, in February 1841 by his other Philadelphia publisher, Lea & Blanchard.

Simms's initial reference, in July 1839, to the composition of *Border Beagles* reaffirms his writing habits: "The new work by the author of 'Richard Hurdis' is in press [Simms wrote]—*the second vol. being under way* [italics added]" (*L*, I, 151). Simms could (and did) write the first volume of a two-volume novel and send it to his publisher to be set in type, before he had written a substantial portion of the final volume. With such a practice, common in nineteenth-century American publishing, it is small wonder that Simms was susceptible to inconsistencies and redundancies, that his plots and structures do not neatly intermesh; the remarkable thing is that Simms's superb inventiveness, his great imaginative sweep, his gift at narration enabled him to put together readable, if imperfect works under circumstances of composition that would appall serious writers of the twentieth century.

It may be significant that *Border Beagles*'s title page indicates only that it is "By the author of 'Richard Hurdis.'" Simms's thinking on the advantages of anonymity[19] is known, but probably by this time few readers and fewer critics had any doubt as to the author of *Richard Hurdis*, and therefore it is questionable if Simms gained anything by omitting his name from the title page. At least one reviewer, in the *Knickerbocker* for October 1840, assuming that *Border Beagles* was by Simms, was puzzled that the novel was published without his name. The critique called Simms a "correct thinker, a close observer, and practised writer" capable of "unusual power and beauty" (XVI, 364). The *Ladies Companion* of the same date considered *Border Beagles* "decidedly an improvement" over *Richard Hurdis*, "containing more natural characters and greater fluency of style. The plot is well conceived, perspicuous and stirring in its arrangement and scything in its denouement" (XII, 306). It is interesting to speculate that Simms's experiment with publishing anonymously—or perhaps pseudonymously is the more accurate term—was depriving his steadily climbing reputation of some of its momentum.

*Border Beagles* ostensibly continues the Border Romance series at the point where *Richard Hurdis* leaves off—that is, with the pursuit of outlaw leader, Foster, who was still roaming free. The new novel suffers in comparison with its predecessor, however, in that Simms does not maintain the characterization of Foster at the same level of interest, and consequently the reader is not caught up in the plot leading to his capture. In *Richard Hurdis* Foster is a compelling character, believable in his unwavering commitment to the principles of success as a bandit, but given the name of Saxon—and given a lust for

Virginia Maitland—in *Border Beagles,* he becomes not so much the believer-exponent of outlawry as the unscrupulous rival of Harry Vernon. Vernon, who plays a role similar to that of Richard Hurdis but serves a quite different function, possesses most of the qualities of the Simmsian gentleman hero, with few interesting eccentricities to redeem him as a credible human being. As the novel begins, Vernon has been commissioned by the governor of Missisippi to track down Saxon (or Foster), but he seems more motivated by a desire for revenge upon the person who had betrayed a friend in matters of money and love. There is no dominant plot or theme to capture the reader's imagination and sustain it until the end. Perhaps reacting to the criticism that *Richard Hurdis* had been too realistic in its description of repulsive details, Simms toned downed the portrayal of violence in *Border Beagles* and attempted to substitute comedy for "dyed in blood"[20] narrative. As Simms matured as a writer, humor would become one of his stong points; and in *Border Beagles* the comic action is centered around an imaginatively conceived "humours" character, an actor from Mississippi named Tom Horsey. Simms apparently modeled him on James H. Caldwell, an early manager of Edwin Forrest in the South and Southwest, but the bombastic, stagestruck Horsey takes on an identity of his own as possibly the most amusing and entertaining character of all the Border Romances.

Other interesting figures in *Border Beagles* are Harry Vernon's frontiersmen associates, Wat Rawlins and Dick Jamison, whose racy, graphic speech provides welcome relief from the stilted dialogue of the well-bred gentlefolk. The blunt, outspoken character of Rawlins, a "tall backwoodsman, fully six feet in height, and solid and massive like a tower" (p. 165), is inherent in his colorful description of William Badger: "Billy Badger's a crumpy, stiff sort of a person—a raal, true-believing methodist, that preaches himself, when the parson don't come, and … makes a deuced sight the best prayer of any among them." Rawlins uses equally picturesque language in characterizing Badger's actions and motivations: "He'll give you a good supper, but you must swallow the long grace that goes before it; and, if one happens to be might hungry, it's a great trying of patience. … I do think if the house was a-fire, he'd sooner let it burn awhile than cut the prayer off in the middle" (pp. 170–71).

The speech of the crude, yet brave Alabamian, Jamison, likewise abounds in color. After cutting loose the bonds of the falsely accused Vernon in an effort to free him from jail, Jamison shouts at the overly excited constables: "Shut up, you yelping pugnose! … none of your d——d lies. … Look you, men, they had the gentleman corded up as if he had been a panther of the wilderness—roped his hands behind him—and he just out of a sick-bed. …

It's only they're sich blasted cowards, afraid of a sick man—afraid of any man." As if to clinch his rhetorical point, he sarcastically adds: "Dang my buttons, I'm almost ashamed I didn't borrow a pen-knife to do the business. This bowie-blade is a'most too big for such eternal small souls as they've got" (pp. 299–300). These passages from the speech of Rawlins and Jamison exemplify the realistic vernacular of Simms's backwoodsmen, and they contrast sharply with the biblical tones of the fiery frontier parson, William Badger.

Simms penned some gentle satire against the clergy in *Border Beagles* in his portrayal of Badger, the stern, deeply religious ruler of Zion Hill. Though not an ordained minister, William Badger misses no opportunity to preach a sermon, as Rawlins has already indicated, and his overwhelming religious zeal governs every aspect of his life. To Badger waste of words, levity in speech, and unmethodical living are sins; therefore, he speaks slowly, measuring his words, and walks slowly, measuring his steps. A good-hearted man, Badger is made human by his perpetual overestimation of his importance and his continuing desire to be the leader. He considers the attack on the Maitlands a personal affront to his efforts at Zion Hill. Unaware that his son Gideon is involved in criminal activities in the area, Badger is greatly offended when Vernon and Rawlins do not include him as leader of the forces to rout the outlaws.

Like the two earlier Border Romances, *Border Beagles* contains a character whose twisted physique and victimization by others make him a subject for Simms's keen interest in psychology.[21] It is noteworthy that Simms usually allows the character of malformed personages to be revealed either through their own actions or words or by what other characters say about them—not through authorial comment. Such is true of Richard Stillyards, an ugly, but muscularly elastic four-foot dwarf who is strikingly introduced when he suddenly swoops down upon Tom Horsey in the swamp, asking him such perplexing questions as "Who are you—can you bite? ... have you got teeth to bite, or are you nothing but a barking dog?" Seeing the grotesque little hunchback, the stage-struck Horsey is immediately reminded of Richard III and responds with surprise:

> "Teeth to bite—barking dog!—why, you talk as queerly as you look, my little Richard."
>
> "Richard! Why, who told you my name?"
>
> "What! your name is Richard, then?"
>
> "Yes, with a pair of scales to the end of it—you couldn't guess that, I reckon!"
>
> "No! I don't know what you mean."

> "I'll tell you—my name is Richard Stillyards, or Dick Stillyards—sometimes they call me Dick Still, and sometimes Dick Yards, and then it's only when I'm in the humor that I answer them. I always answer gentlemen when they call me by my right name." (p. 307)

Richard Stillyards' sly, hostile actions in *Border Beagles* are consistently motivated by greed, lust, or revenge. Even his "comical appearance" conveys evilness and dirtiness; Simms describes him as having ill-kept hair, beady eyes, and obscenely bowed legs. Richard spies upon Saxon because of the jewels and money given to him by Florence Marbois. Though he uses a respectful tone and calls her "ma'am," Stillyards without hesitation displays his audacious motive when Florence is deserted by Saxon: The dwarf makes a promise to Florence to betray Saxon to the regulators, but only if she submits to his sexual desires. Actually, he already intends to get revenge against Saxon for having pulled his ears "until the blood oozed out from the wound" (p. 382)—an unforgivable insult to Stillyards' dignity. When the bandit leader is finally captured, Stillyards takes vengeance by fiercely digging into the outlaw's ears "with his nails—which had been suffered to grow to an inordinate length" (p. 482). Simms makes it clear that neither heredity nor environment has been kind to Richard Stillyards, who displays the native cunning and ferocious instincts of a driven animal. Thus, though not Simms's best-sustained or most stirring novel, *Border Beagles* contains a rich variety of minor characters that emerged upon the American literary scene with a freshness and a vitality that mark the best of the realistic and humorous Southern and Southwestern sketches of Simms's time and later.

While probably no better work of art than *Border Beagles, The Kinsmen,* Simms's third novel in his Revolutionary Romances series, enjoyed greater contemporary popularity. As mentioned earlier, Simms conceived the plan for "a new South Carolina romance" in late 1838 or early 1839 (*L*, I, 139) and spent some sixteen months working upon it intermittently, before reporting to James Lawson in April 1840: "I have commenced & written a hundred pages or more of a new work, but there, for the present, I am disposed to stick" (*L*, I, 170–71). In late July the South Carolinian "spent a day" with Lea & Blanchard in Philadelphia working out arrangements for the publication of *The Kinsmen:* "... I have promised them the first vol. in the course of one month" (*L*, I, 178), a deadline later postponed until "the first of October" (*L*, I, 180). Even with the postponement, in August Simms, blaming "the heat of the weather," expressed fear that he would not "get through the work on hand" (*L*, I, 182). In the following months he continued to fret about "overaction of the brain" and lack of progress on the novel,[22] but by the beginning of the new year he had at last "finished my novel of 'The Kinsmen, or the Black Riders of Congaree.' It is now in press—the first vol. printed, and will be published in February" (*L*, I, 211–12). Again, slipshod publishing practices and work habits by both the author and his publishers are in evidence. In mid-February 1841, "a few days" before Lea & Blanchard published *The Kinsmen*, Simms confessed to James Lawson: "The typographical errors ... are numerous—I did not read the proofs" (*L*, I, 229).[23] Remembering Simms's sensitivity to the charge of hasty and sloppy composition made by his friend Lawson only the year before, one wonders how the novelist reacted to a similar charge from fellow South Carolinian James H. Hammond, who wrote him in March: "[*The Kinsmen*] seems to have been struck off hastily & therefore wants finish occasionally ... I wish you would write something—such as you could—with care & finish submitting to the drudgery of the 'labor limae' if only from time to time & keeping it by you to cap the column of your fame with" (*L*, I, 211–12n).[24]

Stylistic and typographical mistakes notwithstanding, *The Kinsmen*—which was retitled *The Scout* when it was republished by Redfield in 1854—met with wide and favorable response. The chorus of approbation was not unanimous, of course, and an early review in the *New York Mirror* for March 20, 1841, particularly displeased Simms: "The palates seem to crave ... sudden surprises, hair-breadth escapes, circumstantial murders, harrowing trials, and the like; in short, we must 'sup full of horrours.' To those who may be affected with this morbid taste, Mr. Simms' novel will prove acceptable" (XIX, 95). Gilmore Simms commented tersely to Lawson: "I see that [George Pope] Morris (Mirror) has abused the Kinsmen" (*L*, I, 248). The author did not need to respond in his own behalf, for the *Ladies Companion* came forth with a strongly worded commendation: "Mr. Simms already stands so high in the estimation of the reading public, that any commendation of ours is almost nugatory, yet we cannot refrain from expressing our conviction that the Kinsmen is, in many respects, superior to his preceding productions" (XIV [March 1841], 250); and the *Magnolia* for March called *The Kinsmen* the best novel written by Simms to date (III, 143–44). However, the review of most interest to present-day readers was written by Poe for *Graham's:* "A good novel is always welcome; and a good one from an American pen is doubly so. Since the publication of the Pathfinder, we have seen nothing equal to the Kinsmen" (XVIII [March 1841], 143).

The theme of brother against brother that had provided the fundamental plot for *Richard Hurdis* was in effect transferred by Simms from Alabama of the 1830s (and the Border Romances) to South Carolina of the 1780s in *The*

*Kinsmen* (and the Revolutionary Romances). In many ways it was a successful transfer, not only of the plot, but of the "dyed in blood" narrative technique as well—for the *Mirror* had been accurate in finding *The Kinsmen* replete with "sudden surprises, hair breadth escapes, circumstantial murders, harrowing trials, and the like." The tension between Clarence Conway, the good brother and partisan leader, and Edward Conway, the bad brother who secretly heads the Tory band of "Black Riders," is sufficient to maintain interest in what amounts to a civil war fought in South Carolina between Whigs seeking independence from Great Britain and Loyalists sympathetic to the crown. The rivalry between the two brothers (actually, half brothers) is further enhanced by the fact that each seeks the affection of Flora Middleton, one of Simms's more appealing heroines, a spunky paragon of virtue who philosophically sides with the patriots and, in the end, inevitably chooses the right brother.[25]

But a better reason why *The Kinsmen,* with all its faults, is a novel well worth reading is a male character who perhaps ranks second only to Porgy in all the Revolutionary Romances. John Bannister, better known as "Supple Jack," is not only a memorable creation in the author's tradition of noble backwoods scouts, but even more important, he gives voice in his own inimitable diction to the underlying theme in Simms's depiction of the Revolutionary conflict. In explaining why he felt no remorse after killing a British lieutenant, Bannister personifies the spirit of the revolution to a degree unmatched by any other Simmsian character: "... it made the gall bile up in me to see a man that I had never said a hard word to in all my life, come here, over the water, a matter, maybe, of a thousand miles, to force me at the p'int of the bagnet, to drink stamped tea. I never did drink the tea no how. For my own drinking, I wouldn't give one cup of coffee, well biled, for all the tea that was ever growed or planted." But, Supple Jack emphasizes, "'twas the freedom of the thing that I was argying for, and 'twas on the same argyment that I was willing to fight." Unwilling to "pay George the Third any more taxes," the wily frontiersman vehemently asserts—"for all his trying, he can't make me. Here he's sent his rigiments—rigiment after rigiment—and the queen sent her rigiment, and the prince of Wales his rigiment—I reckon we didn't tear the prince's rigiment all to flinders at Hanging Rock!—Well, then, there was the Royal Scotch and the Royal Irish, and the Dutch Hessians;—I suppose they didn't call them royal, 'cause they couldn't ax in English for what they wanted:—well, what was the good of it?—all these rigiments together, couldn't make poor Jack Bannister, a Congaree boatmen [*sic*], drink stamped tea or pay taxes. The rigiments, all I've named, and a hundred more, are gone like last autumn's dry leaves; and the only fighting that's a-going on now, worth to speak of, is American born 'gainst American born. Wateree facing Wateree—Congaree facing Congaree—Santee facing Santee—and cutting each other's throats ..." (pp. 140, 143). Ridgely is correct in pronouncing Bannister's "the authentic voice of the liberty-loving frontiersman," and in commending Simms's deft reproduction of its accents (*Simms*, p. 84). The Revolutionary War, particularly as fought in South Carolina, became a battle of "American born 'gainst American born"—brother against brother, Wateree against Wateree, Congaree against Congaree, Santee against Santee—the fiercest kind of infighting because the most personal and emotional—in seeming anticipation of conditions duplicated in the Civil War. Recognizing the strength of his creation, Simms changed the title in his revised edition from *The Kinsmen* to *The Scout,* thereby acknowledging that the exploits of scout Supple Jack Bannister constituted the dominant interest of the novel, rather than the conflict between the two half brothers, as originally intended.

While in the midst of getting *The Kinsmen* through the press, Simms wrote a short story which strikingly illustrates how far ahead of his times he was in the frank depiction not only of violence, but also of sex. Apparently having finished the story while in the North during the summer of 1840, Simms left the manuscript with James Lawson with instructions to locate a Northern publisher.[26] By September it became obvious that the story was proving difficult to place, and on September 28, 1840, the novelist wrote to Lawson, apparently in response to information given him by the New Yorker: "I cannot conceive what portions of the *Tale* can be offensive. It was written in haste, & never once read after being written. My blood is warm & impetuous, you know, and there may be a phrase or so, but I suspect nothing more, that will need amending." Simms requested Lawson to "read it, and let me know if you see anything & what" (*L*, I, 190–91).

Willis Gaylord Clark of the *Knickerbocker* turned the story down, after holding it for several months before considering it, much to Simms's ire.[27] But Simms persisted in his belief in the "warm & impetuous" though hastily written story, and at last found a publisher in P. C. Pendleton of the *Magnolia: or Southern Monthly*, a Savannah literary journal soon to move to Charleston (where Simms was to become its editor in July 1842). Published in three monthly installments beginning in May 1841, "Caloya; or, The Loves of the Driver," an account of the attempted seduction of a young Indian wife by a lustful black driver on a Georgia plantation, created an immediate furor.[28] A reader who termed himself "A Puritan" objected to "the low valley" of Simms's story, whether the author's intents were "wicked or charitable" (*Magnolia,* III [June 1841], 285–86). Pendleton, on the other hand, wrote a clear-minded defense of Simms,[29] and Simms himself came to Pendleton's and his own rescue in a "Letter to the Editor, by the Author of the 'Loves of the Driver'" in the August 1841 *Magnolia:* "I perceive that you have been censured for the publication ... of an article of mine, and no doubt you are quite as much astonished as myself. ... [I]t must be sufficiently clear ... that neither you nor I could have any deliberate purpose to put forth an immoral publication." Stating that he "certainly did not set out to write an immoral story," Simms recognized the crux of the problem: "It is a tale of low life—very low life—that is true"; but he defended his subject matter, stating that the "modes of life, passions, pursuits, capacities and interests" of all, including blacks and Indians, "are as legitimately the objects of the analyst, as those of the best bred people at the fashionable end of London. ..." Pointing out the parallel with *Othello,* "one of the most noble of all dramatic moralities," Simms affirmed: "The same passions are in exercise precisely—the same pursuit of lust;—passions the most demonic; lusts the least qualified and scrupulous." The author pounced upon the irony that "people in high life ... are to be justified, we suppose, in the exercise and indulgence of passions, which, however natural to red skins and black equally, are still not to be permitted them." Then, in a passage far ahead of its time, Simms spoke tellingly: "In this country we are very much the victims of what is plainly, but expressively called, 'mock modesty'. ... We are reluctant, in very nice society, to call things by their proper names. We dare not speak of legs, or thighs, in the presence of many very nice ladies. ..." It is appropriate only "to ask if the names of things and their qualities are falsely represented; if the truth is disguised, or blurred, or obliterated," Simms concluded, because "the end of the moralist is attained, if he takes care to speak the truth, the whole truth and nothing but the truth! In this, in fact, lies the whole secret of his art. *A writer is moral only in proportion to his truthfulness*" (*L.,* I, 254–59). This is an admirable exposition of the limits and responsibilities of art by a major writer known more for fiction than for literary criticism. It has sometimes been said of Simms that "[i]n taste and temperament [he] was a pronounced realist"[30] but that he had no theoretical perception of realism: this letter written in his own defense belies the latter half of that statement. Indeed, Simms had few peers among his contemporaries in the art and practice of criticism.

As highly productive as William Gilmore Simms had been during the four years since his marriage to Chevillette Roach, he nevertheless began feeling by 1841 that his literary efforts had gone largely unappreciated, particularly by fellow Southerners. "It is lamentable truth," he wrote in a moment of depression in February 1841, "that, up to this period, the Southern country is sadly deficient in most of those qualities which constitute and occasion desires [for a literary culture]." Then, giving his pessimism an economic turn, he went on to say, "*We have not one native professional author from the Potomac to the Sabine, who, if he relied on the South purely for his resources, would not, in half the number of months in the year, go without his porridge*" (*L*, I, 221). In a letter to Lawson on January 8, 1841, Simms had stated so bluntly his need for the "small sum of $3000" to avoid selling property "at an enormous sacrifice" that Lawson mistakenly thought the novelist was asking him to arrange a loan (*L*, I, 210–11; see also *L*, I, 228). Money was no doubt a genuine concern: Simms's second daughter—Mary Derrille—had been born (on September 6, 1839) with a club foot, adding not only anxiety but also medical costs to the family. When a third daughter, Agnes, came along on May 28, 1841, Simms confided in a letter to Lawson on the next day that "my mind and person are & have been, excessively occupied" with "family occurrences" (*L*, I, 249). Rather than ease his need for ready money, Simms's marriage into the proprietorship of the vast Woodlands estate had in fact increased his sense of responsibility, driving him to the limits of his endurance. Though now a proud and wealthy landowner, as well as "the most prominent novelist in the South,"[31] Simms had lost none of his need or capacity for hard work, and certainly none of his hunger for financial independence or literary fame.

Not surprisingly, Simms, later in the month in which he had complained of the South's lack of support for its writers, was once again at work on a novel. In February 1841 he mentioned "a story ... called 'The Blind Heart'" which he had "commenced ... in the winter" but had "stopped suddenly" (*L*, I, 234) after writing some 150 pages. This is the author's first reference to one of his most interesting novels, *Confession; or, The Blind Heart,* a work which successfully combines his interest in criminal psychology with his propensity for portraying violence in a Southern setting. By the end of May 1841 he had made no additional progress—"anxieties ... prevent me from doing anything at my desk"—and he fretted that he was "under ... engagement to Lea & Blanchard for another novel, which should be ready now" (*L*, I, 249). Less than three months later, however, Simms reported to Lawson that he had "just finished" the writing of *Confession:* "It is in two vols., written in the first person, on a new plan, and is now in the hands of the publishers" (*L*, I, 267). But there remain questions about the composition of *Confession,* with Simms himself giving seemingly contradictory information; for instance, though his first mention of *Confession* is of a new work "commenced ... in the winter," ten days later he stated that "though I have been turning over in my mind" the material for a story set "partly in my native city," as yet "I have addressed myself to no long work" (March 3, 1841; *L*, I, 236). The truth seems to be that Simms had written a "portion" of *Confession* ten years earlier—indeed, in a letter of September 10, 1841, to Lawson he commented, "I think [I] read [it] to you. You may recognize" (*L*, I, 278). In any case the author, in picking up the story again, considered it a "new work ... told in the first person ... an experiment & a dangerous one" (*L*, I, 278). This "new plan," this "dangerous ... experiment," with a discarded "early manuscript" of which "he had almost lost all recollection," possessed the author's "mind so warmly" that "the work grew to a size far exceeding his original purpose"—Simms's own statement in the 1856 introduction to the Redfield edition of *Confession*. It was "his own interest in ... psychological history" that led Simms to this pioneering novel of a paranoiac mind. What Simms was attempting, he clarified in this introduction, was a study of "the diseased development" of the "jealousy of self-esteem," a "form of monomania" of "far greater intensity than that which springs from mortified affections alone" (pp. 6, 7). He further explained that the "materials" for the story "are gathered from facts, in a domestic history," some of the events of which "occurred, ended, under [the author's] own observation" (p. 7).

*Confession* is a much better book than is generally acknowledged. It remained a favorite of Simms's throughout his lifetime, though it did not fare particularly well with critics contemporaneous with the author and has fared even less well with critics since his death. *Confession* actually came from the press in late October or early November 1841,[32] and the first published review—in the November *Ladies Companion*—anticipated the mixed reception the book was to receive: "... not one of the happiest efforts of Mr. Simms. The language ... is prolix and occasionally inflated, and the plot stretched out to unnecessary length; however, there is much that is excellent to balance against these defects, and in the present state of novel writing, it will, at least, rank with some which lay claims to greater favor" (XVI, 50). *Godey's*, for December 1841, succinctly commented on *Confession:* "An interesting and pathetic story with too strong an infusion of the appalling; but abounding in the talent characteristic of the author" (XXIII, 295). The most extended contemporary review—and the most favorable to *Confession*—appeared in the December number of *Graham's:*

> In general, Mr. Simms should be considered as one giving *indication*, rather than *proof* of high genius. ... So far, with slight exceptions, he has buried his fine talent in his themes. He should never have written "The Partisan," nor "The Yemassee," nor his late book (whose title we just now forget) about the first discovery of the Pacific. His genius does not lie in the outward so much as

> in the inner world. "Martin Faber" did him honor; and so do the present volumes. ... We welcome him home to his own proper field of exertion—the field of Godwin and Brown—the field of his own rich intellect and glowing *heart.* (XIX, 306)

Though mistaken in its cavalier dismissal of *The Partisan* and *The Yemassee* (both in Simms's "own proper field of execution" more so than *Confession*), this review—probably the work of Poe[33]—rightfully perceives the author's interest and ability "in the inner world," a view which Simms himself would not have disclaimed. Five years later Simms put *Confession*, along with *Martin Faber* among others, in a category of his writings "marked chiefly by the characteristics of passion & imagination." He further described these "several bretheren of the same order" in terms indicative of his favorable disposition toward them: "They constitute, in all probability, the best specimens of my powers of creating & combining, to say nothing of a certain intensifying egotism, which marks all my writings written in the first person" (*L*, II, 224). In Simms's mind these characteristics—first-person narrator, a hero who "charges his crimes upon fate," and "a prevailing presence of vehement individuality of tone & temper"—link *Confession* to *Richard Hurdis* as well as to *Martin Faber* (thereby accounting for the inclusion of the former among the Border Romances in the Redfield collected edition) but *Confession* ("in some respects ... one of my best [works]") apparently was his choice among these favorites.

With the notable exceptions of Donald Davidson and Lewis M. Bush, Simms scholars have found little to their liking in *Confession*, and in general have dismissed the work (and Simms's liking for it) curtly or have ignored it entirely. Trent set the tone with a particularly harsh, even hostile commentary: "It was because Simms's head had gone astray ... that he was tempted to write, within a year of each other, two such repulsive and uncalled-for stories as 'Confession' and 'Beauchampe.'"[34] Ridgely followed suit in saying that "rediscovery of old and useable material generally set the author's pen to scrambling but left his creative imagination idling. *Confession* ... is no exception."[35] Davidson, on the other hand, recognized the "clear merit" of *Confession* as the author's "strongest psychological novel" and included it among the dozen or so works that "form the massive body of Simms's real achievement."[36] Bush concentrated on similarities between Goethe's *Die Leiden des jungen Werthers* and *Confession* in his enlightening study and called needed attention to Simms's pioneering efforts to view crime as "the result of social pathological complexes, instead of innate perversions."[37]

*Confession* has certain similarities to *Othello* in that the hero, Edward

Clifford, a socially prominent young Charleston lawyer, is afflicted with a self-destructive, murderous jealousy that is all the more compelling because it is almost entirely hallucinatory. Clifford's "jealousy of self-esteem" stems both from his mortification that he is not capable of appreciating his beautiful wife Julia's artistic talents and from his well-founded suspicion that artistically inclined William Edgerton is attracted to Julia for sexual as well as intellectual reasons. Falsely convinced of Julia's infidelity when the love-stricken Edgerton visits her in Alabama after Clifford has moved her there from Charleston, Clifford challenges his rival to a duel, and in righteous indignation poisons Julia before going to slay Edgerton. But Edgerton has committed suicide and left behind a note taking full responsibility for his romantic attachment to Julia and affirming her lack of reciprocation. With both Julia and Edgerton now dead, Clifford recognizes the fatal flaw in his character and, for punishment, banishes himself to a life of "ATONEMENT!" on the "rich but barren" plains of Texas, "needing, imploring the vigorous hand of cultivation" (p. 398). It is significant, perhaps, that Clifford's only punishment for his crime is self-inflicted. Simms himself recognized, of *Confession* as well as of *Martin Faber,* that "some cavilled at the moral" (*L,* II, 224). But *Confession* deserves recognition for the power of its action and, most of all, for the forcefulness of its portrayal of monomaniacal destructiveness in a deluded egoist. With all its faults in style, structure, and motivation, *Confession* is a worthy forerunner to the psychological novel of the twentieth century.

At the close of 1841 Simms was well established as one of the truly important writers in American literature. He had perhaps not fully lived up to the extraordinary promise—to the predictions of literary greatness—that had greeted the publishing avalanche which had brought forth *Guy Rivers, The Yemassee,* and *The Partisan* within sixteen months in 1834–35; but at age thirty-five he was recognized throughout the United States as a novelist of solid accomplishment and even greater potential. Gilmore Simms, man of letters and gentleman planter, much envied and much admired, seemingly had a future as bright as his ambitions were lofty.

PART THREE

# Gentleman Planter

## *The Established Years*

## (1842–1859)

# VI The Lure of Politics and Diplomacy

Recent studies of the milieu of pre-Civil War Charleston reveal that the proud, aristocratic old seaport possessed a vitality in arts and letters, as well as in statesmanship and politics, that made it one of America's most stimulating cities of the time.[1] This much-needed correction to the picture of Old Charleston is helpful to the Simms biographer for it calls into question Trent's thesis that Simms was intellectually suffocated by the stultifying atmosphere of his native city. The new perception that Charleston had much greater interest "in the arts than the popular twentieth-century view has credited"[2] and the old perception that "the best South Carolinians [Charlestonians] disdained to read such things [as romances and novels]"[3] stand in direct contrast, but neither refutes the city's strong commitment to politics. Michael O'Brien and David Moltke-Hansen, among others, have demonstrated the fervor of literary interest in Old Charleston, but they also recognize that political interests ran even deeper and stronger. Both intellectual currents—the literary and the political—charged the imagination of the highly motivated young Gilmore Simms, and he responded to each with enthusiasm. Though primarily a literary man all his life, Simms was nevertheless public-spirited and civic-minded and was drawn toward politics by his fondness for debate, his knowledge of history and public affairs, and his desire for social standing. Indeed, Simms's remarkable correspondence was even more dominated by politics than by literature. The young lawyer-turned-novelist had an affinity for public discourse, a hunger for truth, and a tendency to examine issues firsthand. These qualities, together with his gift for oratory which attracted almost as much attention as did his writing talents,[4] led him to become an effective spokesman for his region. His penchant for politics was thus constantly pitted against his predilection for literature. Simms was committed to the profession of letters, and no one worked harder at his trade; yet no other major literary figure of his time strove as diligently as did he to be a knowledgeable and respected public servant. Literary eminence was his goal, but with characteristic ambivalence he also cherished the image of gentleman planter-turned-statesman.[5] Less energetic men than Simms might have been debilitated by an inability to decide what was most important in life and to concentrate upon it, but Simms was astute in directing energies simultaneously into widely divergent channels without appreciable loss of force. Indeed, it sometimes seems that he gained momentum by continually shifting focus from one project to another, thereby fueling his imagination anew and rekindling its fire. If Simms as a writer had concentrated upon one work at a time, he probably would have written a different set of books from the eighty-two credited to him, but he might not have written more or better books. The evidence suggests that his literary output did not suffer significantly because of his divergent interests. This chapter and the next deal specifically with two major, closely connected sub-careers—politics and magazines—in a seventeen-year period (1842–1859) during which Simms (also burdened with increased responsibilities at Woodlands) nevertheless produced more literary works than many less versatile authors complete in a lifetime. Such amazing productivity was encouraged and supported by Simms's perception that all his efforts—in politics, in editing, in public lecturing, in literature per se—were directed toward the intellectual betterment of his region and his nation. Thus, to Simms, diversion into politics or journalism was not entirely a departure from his chosen profession; to him politics, journalism, and novel writing were all cut from the same piece of cloth, were all means to the end of useful service and personal eminence.

As early as August 1841 Simms had toyed with the idea of going into politics. On August 16 of that year he wrote a long letter to James Henry Hammond indicating that under certain conditions he might accept the duty of public office. "I value that favorable opinion which makes you desirous that I should go into the Legislature," Simms wrote to the fellow South Carolinian who was his close neighbor in Barnwell District. "But circumstances do not permit this. I am not my own master. I am in debt. I have no leisure, & … lack the necessary spirit for politics." Simms expressed the opinion, however, that in a democracy "no man … has a right to withhold himself from the duties of state" when called upon. "But," he added, "the call should be *without* not from *within*. He should obey the voice of duty not of vanity ... *unless there is something to be done*, & he feels that *he alone can do it*" (*L*, I, 275–76).

A conflict with literature was not among reasons Simms gave for declining Hammond's suggestion that he run for the South Carolina legislature. Lack of time and lack of money were impediments to his entering politics, but nothing indicates that Simms considered the political innately incompatible with the literary. Indeed, when four months later he again broached the subject in a letter to Hammond, stating that "I am half inclined to comply with your ... [suggestion] to take the field as a Candidate for legislative honour," he added that "[t]here are several reasons why I should change my previous determination. Hitherto, the tasks of literary labor have given me sufficient occupation. Now, they do not. Their results are of such moderate importance that they do not require and will hardly justify the entire application of my mind. ... In the next place, my mind itself is of that energetic, impatient sort that it must have something to expend itself on ..." (*L*, I, 290). Simms later agreed to become a candidate and actually showed a taste for "electioneering" until the untimely death of Mary Derrille Simms, his youngest daughter, in April 1842, left him "almost wholly baffled and broken up" so that he could not "continue [to] campaign" (*L*, I, 304). But Simms had demonstrated a willingness to seek political office, and Hammond—who was rapidly becoming the author's chief confidant, replacing James Lawson—was determined to see his author friend in politics.

James Henry Hammond (1807–1864), whom Simms had known since the Nullification crisis (in which they had taken opposite sides), but with whom he had become friendly only since 1840, was a flamboyant elitist who rivaled Simms in wit and impetuosity and likewise burned with a passion for the intellectual. Hammond, having served a brief term in Congress (1835–1836), reentered politics to run successfully for the governorship of South Carolina (1842–1844) and later for the U.S. Senate (1857–1860). According to a daughter of Alfred Proctor Aldrich, Hammond—"the most intimate friend of both Mr. Simms and my father"—was "notedly handsome, and socially delightful":

> ... Hammond looked like a reincarnation of some Greek demigod. His cold and chiseled classic beauty; his statuesque form and stately poise were antique in impressiveness. He was perhaps the one man to whom Simms ever surrendered the floor in argument or conversation. They were foils to each other at every point. ("Simms' Circle," *L*, I, cxii)

At the time of Hammond's death in November 1864, Simms himself called

Hammond "my most confidential friend for near twenty five years," and noted: "Never were thoughts more intimate than his & mine. We had few or no secrets from each other—we took few steps in life without mutual consultation. ..." Recognizing "something kindred in our intellectual nature," Simms affirmed that "there was much, very much in common between us. Never did man more thoroughly appreciate his genius—its grasp—its subtlety—its superiority of aim. And most deeply did I sympathize with him, under that denial of his aim, and the exercise of his powers ..." (*L,* IV, 469–70).

Both Hammond and Simms were strong, outspoken men with common political and literary views, and—more important perhaps to their bonding—they shared a sense of alienation from the Southern society they both loved. Highly ambitious and strongly motivated, they goaded each other to higher achievement, one primarily in politics and the other in literature, but each with significant interests in both directions. Simms, it is safe to say, expanded Hammond's literary horizons just as Hammond sharpened the writer's political awareness. Their correspondence reveals that they addressed each other with remarkable candor on almost any subject, keeping nothing hidden. Their friendship was strong enough that neither hesitated to chide the other for poor taste or poor judgment when warranted. Hammond recognized Simms's talent as few of his close associates did and encouraged the writer to concentrate his efforts on a *magnum opus* rather than fritter away time, energy, and genius on ephemeral projects; but somewhat contradictorily, the well-meaning Hammond also was largely influential in persuading his literary friend that he had a bright future in politics.

This inducement toward the political was strengthened in December 1842 when Hammond's own ambitions were fulfilled with his election as governor. At the time Simms was fully committed to editing the *Magnolia: or Southern Appalachian;* but partly at Hammond's urging, he resigned as editor in June 1843 and was free to contemplate a career in politics. After his customary visit to the North during the late summer of 1843, Simms returned to Charleston knowing that fellow citizens would again attempt to persuade him to run for the South Carolina House of Representatives. They must have been at least partially convincing, for on or about March 26, 1844, Simms was writing back to his good friend Lawson in New York: "I have told them I am no candidate—that I will not canvass for votes, will in no wise electioneer—will neither treat not speechify—will not in short cross the road for their suffrages. If they elect me, I will do my duty as well as I can; but it will be at considerable personal sacrifices" (*L,* I, 410).

Reluctant candidate though he was—and despite the declaration that he would "in no wise electioneer"—Simms found himself "making stump speeches" (*L*, I, 419) in June and delivering a major oration in Aiken on the Fourth of July entitled *The Sources of American Independence.*[6] Hammond wrote in a playful lettter from the governor's mansion: "I am both amused & delighted at your electioneering troubles. You have only had a taste. Before the campaign is over you will be as sick of the troubled waters of politics as I am ..." (*L*, I, 418n). A different kind of letter was written to Simms by J. W. Harper (of Harper & Brothers), who flatly told the novelist that "the State legislature can confer no honour upon you—You are already above it" (*L*, I, 418n). Shortly after his Independence Day oration in Aiken, Simms informed Lawson: "My friends say there is no doubt of my election, but I doubt. ... The other Candidates are everywhere, every where busy, while I am at my desk, preferring my friends to my ambition ..." (*L*, I, 427).

Simms was probably correct in telling Lawson that "I know nothing myself, and almost care as little" about the outcome of the election (*L*, I, 427), because his trip North (from August 13 to October 28) coincided with election time and his letters during the period portray no anxiety about the results—indeed, they scarcely mention the election. But elected he was, in October while he was in New York, and though he was not overjoyed at his triumph, his temperament was such that he would have been sorely disappointed, even mortified, had he lost. Simms was too proud and too ambitious not to understand Harper's contention that he wasted himself in seeking small political office. "If it were for the Presidency, or even for Congress, I could most heartily wish you success—" Harper had added. Simms, then, must have looked upon election to the South Carolina legislature as a stepping stone, as a chance to demonstrate his powers of oratory and statesmanship, so that he might later, if he chose, be candidate for a major appointed or elected position. Such ambition reinforced his earnest desire to serve his fellow citizens with distinction; and Simms, a diligent and conscientious member of the state House of Representatives, performed well during his first session on two important committees, Federal Regulations and Publication of Proceedings.

The freshman legislator wrote Lawson from Columbia in late November 1844 that he was "beginning the duties with the drudgery of legislation," had listened to "a few stormy speeches," but "[a]s a prudent man and a young beginner, I shall keep quiet as long as possible" (*L*, I, 446). Knowing the fiery South Carolinian as well as he did, Lawson was hardly surprised to read in Simms's letter two weeks later: "I have not been a drowsy member, but placed on one of our most important committees (Federal Relations) have had to take the floor on two or three occasions. I felt nervous and awkward enough, but they tell me I got on very well, and with some fluency" (*L,* I, 448). Simms's special relationship with Governor Hammond assured his being intimately involved with the affairs of state.[7] In fact, perhaps one reason Hammond had promoted the novelist's candidacy for legislative position was to have Simms in Columbia for private discussions of political strategy. It is probable that the governor's opening "fiery & well written" message to the legislature—on the topic of the bank of the state of South Carolina and the annexation of Texas—was read and criticized by Simms before its delivery. In any event he worked in close consort with Hammond in seeing that the speech—really aimed at South Carolina's most powerful and influential politician, Calhoun—had maximum effect on fellow legislators. Reporting from the joint committee for Publication of Proceedings, Simms—obviously with advance knowledge of the content of the governor's oration—made the following resolution: "That while we look with hope to the action of the administration about to come into power in the Federal Government … we are yet reminded by the necessity of maintaining our own strict watch over those vital interests upon which the fortunes and the safety of the South depend …" (*L,* I, 446n). That Simms was Hammond's confidant and political advisor in an alignment against Calhoun is unmistakably clear. Having made the commitment to serve, Simms lent enthusiastic support to his friend's cause and influence so that Hammond rather than Calhoun would wield the most power in South Carolina politics. In allying himself with Hammond and the low country against Calhoun and the upcountry, however, at a crucial time in the history of the state, Simms risked alienating himself from the influential support of the South Carolina Piedmont. Such strong, perhaps politically short-sighted advocacy of Hammond's position may have damaged Simms's later efforts to secure a diplomatic post abroad, an appointment for which the author, with considerable bitterness, sensed a singular lack of enthusiasm on the part of the political leadership of the state as well as that of the nation.

Commitment and loyalty to Hammond, however, do not mean that politics dominated the life of William Gilmore Simms in the mid-1840s. He participated vigorously in the affairs of government in Columbia, but he explained to Lawson in 1845 that "circumstances compelled me … to take a more active part … than I had contemplated on taking my seat" (*L,* II, 9–10). A magnetic and powerful orator, with the skill of rhetoric and the sense of timing of an experienced writer of narrative, Simms (as Hammond had anticipated) knew how to move fellow South Carolinians as few other legislators could, and he immensely enjoyed his moments on the podium at the statehouse in Columbia. A critic as astute as Benjamin F. Perry was enthusiastic in his observations of Simms's debut in politics:

> William Gilmore Simms, the Poet and Novelist, next obtained the floor. I had never heard a speech from a Poet, and felt some anxiety for my friend Simms. As a talker he is unrivalled. ... I think he is one of the most interesting men in conversation I ever heard. As a writer and poet, he ranks with the most distinguished our country has ever produced. Whilst speaking his voice underwent such a change that I should not have recognized it. Poets can be embarrassed in a new field; but his speech was one which would not detract from his high reputation. He spoke fluently, and with great ease. He was in favor of a Southern Convention. In old times he, too, was a Union man ... and I am sure he still is. His conclusion was very beautiful: South Carolina had given him birth ... cradled him in his infancy ... she had a right to demand of him his life, his talents and his exertions ... and in death, he desired only to be received into her bosom. (*Greenville Mountaineer,* December 13, 1844)

Despite these highly favorable beginnings, Simms had no intention of devoting much of his life to South Carolina politics. Like many other literary men—Hawthorne, Melville, Cooper, Kennedy, Irving, Bryant, Lowell—Simms hoped ultimately to further his literary ambitions by securing a political appointment abroad.

As early as January 26, 1845, the novelist-turned-legislator revealed to Congressman Armistead Burt that what he really desired in the political realm was a diplomatic post: "I do not desire office for its own sake, but circumstances have never allowed me to travel out of the limits of our own country. Literature has only sufficed to enable me to live like a Gentleman at home, and ... I feel that I may ... declare my desire to see a little of the outer world. I should like to go to Europe, but it will please me to travel in other regions." After a brief summary of his "capacities" Simms closed with self-serving statements of his hopes and motivations in seeking an appointment abroad. "I am a genuine Southron, well hated by New England, hostile to the Tariff, Abolition &c, not to speak of a hundred other Yankee abominations," he observed. "Whether these are qualities to recommend me" to newly elected President James Polk "I know not," continued Simms, but "[t]hat they secure me the affections of all genuine Southrons I am very sure." Simms conjectured that as a literary man abroad, he might do his nation "a service apart from the performance of official duties" because he would "make a due record, & future elaborate use in fiction or in history" of "the traditions, the antiquities & the manners" of the host country. He then observed: "As for the pecuniary value of the berth, I care for it only so far as it will enable me with my little family to maintain the attitude of a Southern Gentleman in a foreign land" (*L*, II, 22–24).

Certainly the novelist's desire for a diplomatic assignment abroad was influenced by the fact that Woodlands—which enabled Simms "to maintain the attitude of a Southern Gentleman" at home, a matter of great importance to him[8]—did not provide the cash flow for foreign travel and other luxuries. In a letter to James Lawson on February 11, 1845, which closes with the statement "I shall pay off my last heavy debt ($1,000) in a few days & shall then feel more comfortable than I have done for many a day," Simms candidly discussed his prospects and his desires "for a foreign appointment." Admitting that his youth and political inexperience rendered "a controlling position" in Great Britain or France "out of the question," the South Carolinian nevertheless confessed his preference for "a position in Great Britain," or at least "in a literary & European neighbourhood." While "my modesty takes for granted that I cannot be the Ambassador," Simms noted that he was "yet unwilling to sink into one which is merely subordinate." He pointed to the office of consul as "one of usefulness & influence" which would interest him, "assuming ... that the compensation is adequate to my wants and appetites." Simms urged his New York friend (whose advice and assistance he obviously cherished) "to give me a frank and long letter ... in relation to these objects. And pray let it be as soon as possible, as my friends are anxious to know what will suit me best. We must decide on what we want before the inauguration" (*L*, II, 25–26).

That the subject weighed heavily on his mind is evidenced by the fact that two days later Simms broached it again in a letter to B. F. Perry, with the emphasis this time on a possible appointment to Mexico. Evidently, at this point Simms's strategy was to pursue almost every foreign possibility, attempting to match, however, each request with a potential benefactor knowledgeable about the desired country or post. After explaining "*sub rosa*" that he approved the movement "to present my name to the new President," Simms requested Perry "to sound [Waddy] Thompson [former minister to Mexico] as to the nature of [the] situation while in Mexico—how he relished that city & country and in how far it was agreeable & desirable to himself." Casting about in seeming frantic desperation, Simms then asked Perry for "some information" about appointments "to Italy—the Sicilies for example,—Rome &c." He admitted his "very ample ignorance of the advantages or disadvantages of almost every berth which might be found available"; and closed with an almost pathetic mixture of despair and hope: "I am very far from sanguine in my expectations. I have been no clamorer for Mr. Polk ... and simply took him for my man, as an alternative. I have no doubt that he is a worthy man, but very far from a great one. Still his choice of ministers & friends may be judicious, & I may be one of them!" (*L*, II, 32–33).

A fortnight later, on February 27, 1845, Simms—still obsessed with the hope of going abroad—wrote Perry that "Our S. C. delegation are pleased to urge my pretensions, and I fancy that they will find sympathy & support from others of the South." In an attempt to be realistic, however, Simms acknowledged that his "little part in politics of any kind" would scarcely "commend" him to Polk. "It is only as a Literary man," he granted, "one of the few whom the South asserts, that I can possibly hope to find any favor. And a claim like this is not often potential with a Western President" (*L*, II, 36–37).

About this time Simms apparently heard from Lawson that his chances for even a subordinate appointment to Great Britain were small, for in writing the New Yorker on February 27 to thank him "for the suggestions in your Letter," Simms stated that "[y]our opinions very generally coincide with my own" and that now "my first choice would be the Court of the Two Sicilies at Naples; next that of Sardinia at Turin, and thirdly the Kingdom of Portugal." Still holding out hope for the much-desired assignment, Simms asserted: "… I hear from every quarter of the South, that there is scarce any appointment that could be made from the South which would command more general approbation … than my own. Still, as you suggest, I put no faith in Presidents or Princes" (*L*, II, 38–39).

Lawson's cautioning proved prophetic, for the versatile South Carolina novelist was overlooked by the Polk administration in placing envoys abroad; and Simms—not surprised, but bitterly disappointed—wrote to James H. Hammond of his frustrated hopes for "one of those pleasant berths in Italy or elsewhere, where the salary is decent, and the duties nominal." "It would have been the most fortunate thing for me," he lamented, "just at this juncture, in a literary point of view to have stolen off to Europe, reposing on my oars for awhile, and preparing for the elaboration of other and more important tasks." The author expressed the fear that "a grand Carolina poem in my head, a tragedy and something more" might "God knows … now never see the light" (*L*, II, 45).

Rejection for the post which from "a literary point of view" was ideal particularly gnawed at Simms because he believed that "I have been sacrificed by some silly sophistications of my own friends." He explained in 1845 to Lawson: "Our delegation in Congress were pledged to me unanimously to present my claims to the President. But they took in dudgeon the ejection of Calhoun[9] from the Cabinet, and resolved to make no application in behalf of Carolina.

But for this I had every reason to hope for success" (*L*, II, 48). Later, still expressing bitterness at "How my own State has served me," he commented to Hammond: "I really think, putting my own views & wishes out of the question, that our delegates are a little too fastidious. They virtually say, because we cannot have all our rights, we will fling away those that we may secure. … These appointments … are rights which we claim in common with the rest. They are not favours" (*L*, II, 51). Though his great elasticity would enable him to bounce back, this defeat by default and his inbred sense of alienation and rejection combined in Simms to bring on unusually deep depression. The disappointment, together with financial worries, Simms confided to Lawson, threw him into "one of my fits of despondency": "Really, there is something very wretched in the condition & prospects of American literature, or I am one of the most luckless of our tribe." Simms's perception that he had been betrayed, or that he suffered injustice because he was a Southern writer, caused his greatest resentment. Because "the late administration had been distinguishing the literary men of the North"—and Simms named Irving, Everett, Walsh, Wheaton, Fay, and Bancroft as examples—it had seemed only fair, he surmised, "that the present, would perhaps like to distinguish … the only professional author of the South." The Southerner unbosomed himself to his Northern friend: "The disappointment dulls me, and coming with other things, the Season, want of money, and the gross prostration of our literature, leaves me, measurably *hors de combat.* 'Now could I drink black blood'" (*L*, II, 48–49).

One factor that affected Simms's possibility of securing an appointment abroad was the opposition of his father-in-law, an influence the author would have been reticent to discuss. But one of the more interesting anecdotes handed down by Simms's children as part of the oral history of the family involves a clash between Nash Roach and his son-in-law over the very issue. According to family tradition, the only unpleasant relationship between Roach and Simms revolved around the author's desire to obtain a diplomatic post, preferably in England, that would not only accord him the setting and the time conducive to writing, but would also allow him to reclaim for the family an English estate, the Willows, near Bristol, which was about to revert to the crown. With his aristocratic air, Roach, who did not wish to be separated from his daughter, made a remark to Simms which (according to the memory of his descendants) the author never forgot: "Mr. Simms, hasn't my daughter enough?" (*MCSO*, VIII). The story illustrates the highly formal, if friendly relationship between a father-in-law, who had bountifully provided for his daughter and who expected some deference from her husband, and a literary man, who—grateful for his good fortune in marriage—nevertheless had ambitions beyond the scope of patriarchal sympathy and understanding. Nash Roach's influence was powerful enough that his attitude, if known, could easily have worked against his son-in-law's chances for a prestigious foreign appointment. Roach's refusal to lend support coupled with the writer's controversial alignment with Hammond against Calhoun may well have dampened the fervor of some Southerners who otherwise would have championed Simms's cause as their own.

Albeit his desire for a post overseas overshadowed his pleasure in serving in the South Carolina legislature, Simms took umbrage at any suggestion that "I had any eye to a foreign mission when I consented to go to the Leg." (Simms to Hammond, April 10, 1845; *L*, II, 51). To demonstrate how much he valued a good foreign diplomatic assignment, Simms told Hammond half jokingly: "If the Mission to England is offered you, take it by all means, and—publish your novel in London!" In Simms's thinking, a legation abroad and literature went hand in hand.

By the time the South Carolina legislature went back into session, however, Simms's bouyancy had returned and November 1845 found the novelist again in Columbia "writing ... from my desk in the Hall of Representatives" (*L*, II, 120). In December he acknowledged that "Somehow, I have become quite a debater this Session & have found my hands full of business, and heard my voice, perhaps, too frequently for the ears of others" (*L*, II, 122). Nor had Simms dropped the idea of a foreign mission; Hammond in January 1846 wrote to the novelist: "Now as to your foreign longings. You know I have always approved that idea, with the hope it would give you the time & stimulate you to do something worthy of yourself. ... I don't remember who is Secretary of Legation at Paris. For a literary man that would be the most desirable post" (*L*, II, 140n). In a largely despondent letter to Lawson in February Simms could manage some enthusiasm only for the possibility of "an appointment abroad"; a subdued, yet still proud Simms stated that he would "have nothing less than a Charge-des-affaires, unless at one of the two Great Courts of St. James & St. *Cloud*," but he also admitted that he had "no idea what success will attend the inquiry" in his behalf by the South Carolina delegation and "other friends at work" (*L*, II, 140). But the hope that seemed to spring eternal in Simms was again disappointed.

Simms's resilience was twice to be tested in 1846: first, when despite strong efforts of friends like Hammond, nothing of consequence ever occurred with regard to a foreign appointment; and, second, when his bid for reelection to the South Carolina legislature was surprisingly unsuccessful. On the first of

October 1846 Simms stated in a letter to Lawson that he planned to make "a brief visit to my constituency," as he also had done "some three weeks ago," in preparation for the upcoming elections in South Carolina. "I do not know that this is necessary but it is proper," he added. "My friends tell me that there is no doubt of my reelection, though I have made few efforts to secure it, and would have withdrawn if I could" (*L*, II, 188). Simms was aware that "[t]here is a very strong opposition to me": "The cry is that I am a Northern man, that my affinities are with the North &c." (*L*, II, 191). It is possible, of course, that Simms's frequent visits to the North contributed to this perception, but his defeat at the polls can be more realistically attributed to internal politics. In the words of Jon L. Wakelyn, the chief student of Simms as a politician, the novelist "faced more opposition than he otherwise would have encountered" because a political ally of Simms, Alfred P. Aldrich, leader of the forces opposing Calhoun, faced "strong opposition for re-election" as Commissioner in Equity for Barnwell and Simms's "active work for him made the author equally unpopular."[10]

Simms nevertheless would no doubt have won the election if his friends and well-wishers had not stayed away from the polls, a fact which increased his resentment and his belief that he was not sufficiently appreciated. On October 19, 1846, he wrote to Benjamin F. Perry, "The conspirators have with great adroitness, and many falsehoods, succeeded in defeating my re-election" (*L*, II, 194). But chagrined as he was, Simms quickly recovered enough confidence in his political future to listen attentively when influential friends surrounded him with suggestions that he run for higher office. In a letter of October 23 to James Lawson he commented that though his defeat was personally "of no sort of importance," it had "caused quite a sensation as well out of the district as in it," resulting in the writer's finding himself "much more popular than I had ever fancied." As a consequence, Simms asserted, "already have I been applied to by leading men to consent that I shall go into the canvas for the next Congressional election." But, he added, "I have given them no encouragement" (*L*, II, 196).

Though once again Simms's willingness to listen to political blandishment came to no avail, he nevertheless continued to consider politics as perhaps the most viable alternative for a literary man who on the earnings of his pen alone found it difficult to live the life of a Southern gentleman. Woodlands, the pride of his existence, symbolized for him the kind of eminence he sought, but he confided to Lawson that "Mr. Roach's affairs do not prosper" and that "my worldly prosperity is by no means such as to make me desire to continue here" (*L*, II, 195–96). For the rest of the winter of 1846 Simms wrote long letters to South Carolina friends like Perry and Hammond analyzing the reasons for his lack of political success, with his most telling comment coming in a letter to Hammond: "... I should be tempted, repudiated as I am here, to clear out, and try my fortune wholly in literature either in the North or Europe. This defeat in Barnwell may hurt me elswhere—my pride at least. It was my boast that I had the sympathies of my people—that they believed in me and were grateful for my labors" (*L*, II, 208–9).

Characteristically, Simms alternated between being malcontent with the present and hopeful for the future, and once the prospect for a seat in Congress dimmed, he was rather easily persuaded to become a last-minute candidate for the lieutenant governorship of South Carolina. Writing to James Lawson in November 1846 that "the whole State is indignant at my defeat in the district," Simms revealed that "I am accordingly put in nomination for Lt. Gov. by friends [who] are desirous of relieving the State from the position which seems to have been assumed by the district" (*L*, II, 215). Despite strong editorial support from the *Greenville Mountaineer* and the *Columbia South Carolinian*,[11] Simms once again suffered defeat, losing to William A. Cain in a very close race. This marked his fourth political disappointment in rapid succession, and as is predictable, the moody novelist entered into even deeper despondency and began to question seriously his own assessment of his ability. In December 1846, shortly after learning of his loss at the polls, Simms candidly confessed to Hammond, "I am pretty well tired of a game in which it is so easy to be beaten." "I have almost come to persuade myself that my career has deluded nobody but myself," he added, "and that I should regard my recent defeats as a sufficient proof that I am not the person that I suppose myself & possess but few of the endowments upon which I had but too easily been satisfied to count" (*L*, II, 237).

In his response to Simms, Hammond pointedly advised his friend "to make choice of one walk in literature or politics if you prefer it—& devote your whole energies to some mighty work that will do to throw upon the waters—that can stem the rapid current of oblivion" (*L*, II, 247–48n). But despite his commitment to letters, despite his knowledge that his greatest talent, his greatest chance for fame, lay in literature, Simms could not fully heed his friend's advice. Perhaps it was simply a matter of ego, for the novelist had difficulty in accepting the idea that he had been found politically wanting; particularly in writing to acquaintances out of state Simms was likely to attribute his defeats to bad luck, the scheming machinations of his opponents, the overconfidence of friends who did not bother to vote, almost anything but his own lack of popularity. After analyzing the reasons for his loss for "Lt.

Gov. by one vote, & this with 9/10ths of the Legislature in my favor," for instance, Simms averred in a letter of January 1847 to James Lawson: "Nobody doubts but that I am one of the most popular men, at this moment, in the regards of the Legislature & people; and I have had applications numerously, before & since the election, to permit my friends to use my name for other offices" (*L*, II, 251). In communicating with fellow South Carolinians, however, Simms was likely to complain bitterly (or confess contritely, as the case may be) that he was anything but "popular" in his home state, in which (as he had written Hammond) he felt "repudiated" and embarrassed by lack of support. Thus once again the conflicting moods of hope and despair, optimism and pessimism, ebullience and bitterness find expression in Simms's correspondence.

Late in 1847, however, Simms's old desires for a diplomatic appointment abroad came alive yet again,[12] and for at least another decade Simms's name was bandied about whenever a choice political, semi-political, or cultural post became vacant. When Robert Barnwell Rhett announced his resignation from Congress in November 1847 Simms was rumored to be in line to succeed him.[13] In January 1848 Simms expressed to Hammond an interest in being named historiographer of South Carolina if such a position could be created by the legislature, as had been done in New York, Louisiana, Georgia, and other states.[14] Later that year, after campaigning vigorously and effectively for the election of Zachary Taylor as president, Simms was mentioned again for the ever-elusive overseas appointment;[15] in November 1849 the harried novelist was once more approached about possibly running for Congress;[16] and after several politically active, relatively rumor-free years Simms's name surfaced twice as a candidate for the presidency of South Carolina College, first in 1851 as successor to William C. Preston, and again in 1857 as successor to Charles Francis McCay (when A. B. Longstreet was offered the position).[17]

One of the most devastating political mistakes ever made by Simms came in 1856. Vexed by political defeat and disappointment and irked by the frustrating conclusion to his editorship of the *Southern Quarterly Review* (see chapter 7), he passionately and unwisely plunged into a tumultuous lecture tour of the North amid one of the most turbulent periods of North-South relations.[18] Although the inflammatory speech by Massachusetts Senator Charles Sumner in a May 1856 Senate debate over Kansas was the primary instigator of the worsened state of affairs between North and South, Simms had already written to Northern friends a month earlier that he was contemplating "a course of lectures at the North this winter" (*L*, III, 424; see also *L*, III, 425). Well before Sumner's tirade attacking South Carolina Senator

Andrew Pickens Butler and impugning the role of South Carolina in the Revolutionary War, Simms had expressed the intent to hold at least one lecture in the North "to establish better relations between North & South" and explained to Boston publisher James T. Fields that he designed "one or two Lectures touching the scenery, the society, habits manners, of the South, especially for your people . . ." (*L*, III, 429).

Thus the ill-fated Northern lecture tour of 1856 was not originally conceived of as a response to Sumner's condemnation of South Carolina, but as a friendly public-spirited mission to create better understanding between two widely divergent parts of the Union. The Sumner-Butler imbroglio, heightened by the caning of Sumner by South Carolina Representative Preston S. Brooks, almost certainly altered Simms's attitude toward what he had hoped to accomplish with his lectures: though his purpose was still educational, his outlook changed from one of kindly benevolence intent upon instructing with charm to one of righteous indignation set upon redeeming the honor of South Carolina and South Carolinians in a hostile environment. He changed, in short, from peaceful missionary representing only himself, to belligerent aggressor charged with righting a wrong done to his state and his people. Simms's letter of September 7, 1856, to Hammond reveals that political leaders in South Carolina looked to him to be their spokesman in this heated controversy:

> Butler and Evans[19] are flooding me with the attacks of the Northern Press on South Carolina. Butler says "I have no time to answer them. It is the business of the Historian." But his blunderings have provoked them, and he is one of the victims in all the attacks. In brief he wants me to take up the cudgels and fight his battles. It is a pretty thing that one has fed all his life at the treasury bowls, who is still feeding—who is chosen for this very sort of warfare—should call upon me to do the business, whom he & his fraternity have always contrived to keep without feed at all. (*L*, III, 446–47)

The bitter, defiant tone of this letter reveals the state of mind of Gilmore Simms just before he trudged North "to take up the cudgels and fight [the] battles" of his fellow citizens, an action that succeeded only in making a bad situation worse. One would hope that Hammond, at least, had advised his good friend against throwing himself into a no-win foray with high personal risk; although Simms's espoused intent, "to disabuse the public of the North of many mistaken impressions which do us wrong" (*L*, III, 454), reveals his crusading purpose, and perhaps Hammond, like Simms, felt that Northern cities (especially New York) would give the Southerner a fair hearing out of respect for his stature. At any rate, Hammond waited until after the disastrous experiences (fully documented in Shillingsburg's valuable article) in almost every Northern city in which Simms gave his lecture entitled "South Carolina in the Revolution," to express his dismay. Writing bluntly to Simms of his folly, Hammond charged: "… you have gone North at a somewhat critical time for *you* and martyred yourself for So Ca, who will not even buy your books & for Brooks whose course could at best be only *excused.* … What Demon possessed you, mon ami, to do this?" (*L,* III, 465n).

The most significant and far-reaching effect of this episode, which caused Simms to lose credibility with the Northern audience that had provided the greatest number of readers of his books, may have been, as Shillingsburg suggests, to poison his reputation in the North for the remainder of his life.[20] Simms himself was particularly sensitive to what he felt was unjustified criticism by Southerners of his performance in their behalf, as his testy and defensive letter of December 1856 to M. C. M. Hammond illustrates: "I am somewhat surprised that any body should accuse me of whining over my disappointments at the North. … I have assurances from every hand, (South Carolina almost entirely excepted) that my course has been approved and honoured, as manly and justly sensitive" (*L,* II, 473–74). In one sense, at least, Simms may have profited from his "rebuff at the North," as James Henry Hammond cynically put it: "From what I can see [it] is likely to be fine Southern Capital and yield you a good per cent" (*L,* III, 466n). Hammond's prediction probably helped to prompt Simms, almost immediately upon his return to South Carolina, to schedule a lecture tour in the South to replace his aborted Northern itinerary. Not only was he desirous of recouping some of his financial loss, but in his new lecture entitled "Antagonisms of the Social Moral. North and South," based upon his recent experiences in the North, he was intent upon "warning Southerners about … hostility … previously unimagined" (Shillingsburg, p. 190).[21]

Though Simms's political goals, whether as lecturer or would-be senator or ambassador, always exceeded his reach, a fact he had difficulty accepting, it should be recognized that Simms eventually did reduce, if not entirely relinquish, his political ambitions. And it was his good friend, James Henry Hammond, who was instrumental in Simms's facing at last the reality of his political frustration. Simms at times listened to Hammond when he turned deaf ears to other friends, for he and Hammond were kindred spirits. Like Simms, Hammond also felt the ambivalence of love and hostility toward his native state. He, too, believed that the finer qualities of his intellect and character went unappreciated by the philistines in Charleston and elsewhere in

South Carolina; and he, too, held that no matter how hard and unselfishly he labored, he could never win complete acceptance in the aristocratic state of his birth. Hammond was no more consistent than Simms was in his varying viewpoints, no more constant in his varying moods. Whenever the doughty owner of Silver Bluff plantation perceived that Simms was needed politically, or envisioned an opportunity for Simms to broaden his geographical and intellectual horizons, Hammond contradicted his own advice to Simms that he give up politics and concentrate on literature, that he give up dreams of New York and Europe and concentrate on South Carolina. Hammond's open and frank discussions with the proprietor of Woodlands plantation rose above "the hobgoblin of small minds"—their very inconsistency bespoke candor—and Simms was moved by Hammond as he was moved by no one else. In a letter of October 11, 1851, Hammond, apparently responding to Simms, posed the questions—"... what personal causes have prevented your elevation? Shall I tell you?"—and then proceeded with an elaborate and detailed answer:

> You want the art of concealing your superiority. Even though you may not intend or desire it, you make it palpable to every one you come in contact with. The very men who would join you heartily in admiring & crying you up, if you exhibited it only on stated occasions, are outraged when you thrust it in their faces & will conspire with others similarly aggrieved to put you down. Now although at the North or elsewhere this may be tolerated in a visitor may you not apprehend that once permanently settled among them they will also resent it, & more fiercely even than your countrymen. If so I should prefer, were I you to remain here, & kick & cuff & trample on the poor devils ... as you have hitherto done. There is no small satisfaction in doing it after all, though one must expect to pay for it. (*L*, III, 142n)

Simms's increasing awareness of the soundness of Hammond's advice is reflected in his correspondence in the late 1850s. Hammond never ceased speaking to Simms the truth as he saw it at any given moment: on February 7, 1858, for instance, he wrote to Simms with the counsel not to "dabble in anything unworthy of" posterity (*L*, IV, 42–43n); then three months later (in a letter of April 3, 1858) Hammond advised Simms that "you are the *very man*" (*L*, IV, 50n) to represent South Carolina in the U.S. Senate. Simms's response to the latter suggestion demonstrates that he may have finally come to grips with his political aspirations: "What you say touching myself in connection with a certain office, is simply a proof of your friendly judgment. In our country I am regarded simply as a Poet & Novelist, & even in these capacities they know not exactly where to rank me." Because the public "would as soon think of making a statesman out of whipt syllabub as out of a Poet," Simms retorted, "I long since gave up the idea of being any thing in the Body Politic. I am too old now for the necessary training, and this in connection with the fact that nothing can come of the suggestion, is sufficient for us, whatever my convictions, or yours in my favour, to keep us from any exposure of them" (April 12, 1858; *L*, IV, 50). A month later—on May 8, 1858—Simms reiterated to Hammond that "you [should] take no part in the nomination" of a successor to Senator Josiah James Evans, who died in office: "It would only do you harm ... and any inclination towards myself ... would be quite useless" (*L*, IV, 53). "I am speaking honestly, my dear Hammond," Simms concluded, "for whatever my political ambition might have been, it is very fairly burnt out ..." (*L*, IV, 54).

Jon L. Wakelyn's full-length study of Simms's political career (a longer book than has yet been devoted to Simms as a literary figure) maintains that "[p]olitics was Simms's career" and that literature to the Charlestonian was always subordinate to politics (p. 82, passim). While it is one thing to say that Simms was the most politically astute man of letters of his time, it is quite another to claim that Simms's main thrust, his chief ambition, was political power and prestige and that he used literature primarily as a means to political ends. The truth is just the reverse: although Simms threw weight behind political causes he believed in, he never dropped his primary goal of attaining literary eminence. Possessed of a keen political sense, Simms learned that his stature as literary celebrity gave credence to his ideas on almost any subject, and he was never reluctant to speak his mind or use his influence. But to assert that Simms's writings simply "reflected his interest in public service and important political issues" is a serious distortion of a lifelong passionate commitment to literature.

But why did Simms persist in his pursuit of a sinecure—preferably a prestigious one—that would enable him to be writer, gentleman, and public servant simultaneously? Why was he so slow to heed the advice of James H. Hammond (and doubtlessly others) that he concentrate upon a single great work rather than spread thin his abundant talents? There is no simple answer to these questions. Simms was a remarkably versatile man, as Hammond frequently pointed out, capable of distinguishing himself in many different fields; he was never too busy, or too committed, to take on a new task when the proper appeal was made to him, and he sincerely and earnestly believed that he was capable of accomplishing whatever he attempted. Furthermore, Simms believed, rightfully, that he could undertake many things simultaneously. His early sense of alienation and rejection caused him to seek praise and appreciation and to place a high value upon prestige and status. He had full confidence in his ability: his only doubts were whether others perceived and appreciated his capability. Thus, Simms was reluctant to be viewed, by even his most intimate friends, as a status seeker; his usual posture—whether his interest be in a diplomatic appointment abroad, in a place in Congress, or in the presidency of South Carolina College—was that others were urging him for the position and that he himself had simply acquiesced in their efforts. In short, he wished the position to be offered him without his seeming to seek it, and his early disappointments merely served to increase the desire for appropriate recognition of his talents and abilities. Although he never ceased to work assiduously for literary fame, his obsession to be and to be perceived as the perfect gentleman had priority at times above his longing for literary eminence. Now that he was a member of the South Carolina planter class, he had his place in a well-ordered society to which he became increasingly loyal; but he was disappointed that Woodlands did not provide the financial independence—the monetary cushion—to enable him and his family to live the luxurious life he associated with that status.

What Simms desired remained for him an unrealistic dream: he wished to combine the life of Southern gentleman, eminent author, and distinguished diplomat. Simms was sagacious enough to discern the difficulties inherent in playing these three roles concurrently, even without Hammond's admonition that he concentrate his energies on one activity; he knew that what he wanted posed problems, but perhaps he convinced himself that his multiple-ambition was not impossible for a man with his talents and his capacity for doing many things well simultaneously. With characteristic ambivalence, Simms never centered upon his greatest love, literature, to the exclusion of what he took to be his role as gentleman planter and responsible public servant. Students of belles-lettres, however, should be thankful that neither politics nor plantation ever supplanted literature as his highest priority.[22]

# VII

# Spokesman for the South

## *The Responsibilities and Frustrations of an Editor*

If William Gilmore Simms expended energy needlessly in chasing political rainbows, he spent far more time and effort in another pursuit, partly literary but inimical to his highest literary aspirations. Has ever an editor of magazines been accorded the laurel of literary greatness? Simms knew the answer, but, as with politics, magazines he could not leave alone. By 1842, when he turned again to magazine editing after an interruption of some nine years, much had happened on the national scene to intensify the South's growing distrust of and antagonism toward the North. Antislavery propaganda such as *Walker's Appeal* (1829), William Lloyd Garrison's *Liberator* (1831–1865), and Theodore Dwight Weld's influential books, *Emancipation in the West Indies* (1838) and *American Slavery as It Is* (1839), coupled with the Abolitionists' uncompromising attitude, increased resentment in the slaveholding South. White Southerners bitterly remembered the bloody Nat Turner Insurrection in Southampton County, Virginia, in August 1831, which they thought had been incited by the *Liberator*. As a result, the idea of abolishing slavery—which still held some favor in the South as late as 1828—was viewed by 1840 with contempt and alarm by Southern leaders, who claimed to see political and economic motives behind Northerners' loud demands for emancipation.[1]

Now fully allied with the Southern planter aristocracy, Simms in the 1840s and 1850s came increasingly to regard the "new" industrial North as a threat to the social traditions and the economic prosperity of the South, and consequently his interests became more pronouncedly sectional. As a man of letters, however, Simms retained a national outlook: he was still a determined advocate of a distinctively American literature and an equally determined opponent of British dominance of American literary thought, and his magazines still expressed faith in the people of the North even while objecting to abolitionism. "There is too much good sense and patriotic feeling among the broad masses of intelligent freemen ... to permit them to listen ... to the wild fanaticism of the spawn of foreign purlieus. ..."[2]

In many ways, however, it is incorrect to say Simms shared the sentiments of his section. In 1832, when he had defended the Union, he had been in the minority; in 1842, when he was a stout advocate of state and sectional rights, he was again outside the South Carolina political establishment, headed by Calhoun, which shied away from confrontational tactics. Simms managed to separate his political from his literary views rather successfully, however, and in the 1840s and 1850s he still urged the development of a national literature, though he now stressed the contribution of each region to that literature.

In nine of the years between 1842 and 1854 Gilmore Simms served as editor of three Charleston literary magazines:[3] the *Magnolia: or Southern Appalachian* (1842–1843); the *Southern and Western Monthly Magazine and Review* (1849–1854); and the *Southern Quarterly Review* (1849–1854). These were among the most influential journals published in the South; but none truly "succeeded" because in a sense, as Simms well knew, they were doomed from the start. All three of these magazines exemplified (1) the difficulties which faced a Southern literary journal and (2) the motives that prompted Simms to devote time and energy to the seemingly hopeless task of editor.

Simms's connection with the *Magnolia* differs greatly from his relationships with the *Album* and the *Southern Literary Gazette.* With the earlier two magazines he had been one of the actual founders, one of a group of young men who had enthusiastically launched an editorial ship of their own making, a goodwill ship which, they felt, could hardly fail to win the support of a select clientele. But when P. C. Pendleton approached him in the spring of 1842 to discuss the possibility of his editing the *Magnolia,* Simms found himself in a bargaining position. He was then a noted author whose name on the title page would increase the prestige of almost any magazine in America.

If Simms enjoyed such prestige as a novelist, what, then, induced him to return to magazine editing? Certainly his experiences with the *Album* and the *Southern Literary Gazette* had made him fully aware of the problems with which the editor of any Southern periodical must contend. In fact, when late in 1840 Pendleton moved the *Southern Ladies' Book* from Macon to Savannah and changed its title to the *Magnolia: or Southern Monthly,* Simms wrote a long letter to the editor in which he grimly spoke of the "almost certain fate which awaits" any Southern magazine. "When, something like a year ago, you solicited my aid," Simms began, "it was with a degree of indifference ... that I yielded to your wishes," not because "I was unfriendly to your purpose," but because "I had no faith in the project then; and ... I have very little more faith in it now." Simms's long experience "in the making of Southern Magazines" thoroughly familiarized him with "the usual story of confident hope and bold assurance with which they commonly begin." This confidence rapidly erodes when the "overtasked" editor discovers that he cannot depend upon contributors who, because of professional commitments, can write for him only "at moments of leisure"; yet he is compelled to wait for and then publish their submissions whether "good, bad or indifferent." This drain on the editor "enfeebles his imagination and exhausts his intellect," and his position "becomes one of pain, disquiet and the most unintermited [*sic*] mental drudgery." Yet other problems plague the journal: the collection of subscription fees "over an extensive tract of interior country ... are realized too slowly for the current expenses"; the printer, "who is seldom a capitalist," succumbs to "the pressure of pecuniary difficulties" and issues the magazine irregularly "on villianous [*sic*] paper"; as a result, subscribers "naturally reject the work," and the "general dissatisfaction" of all parties—"the editor being among the first"—"soon leads to the early abandonment of an attempt in which nothing has been realized but discredit, annoyance, and expense."[4]

If Simms no longer possessed his youthful confidence in the willingness of the South to support a magazine devoted to the promotion of its native art and literature, he nevertheless remained convinced that such a magazine was badly needed. Indeed, he felt that only through such a magazine could the South be awakened from its mental lethargy. The realization that the periodical was the best medium through which to serve his section's literature was more than anything else responsible for his decision to accept the editorship of the *Magnolia* when it was moved to Charleston in July 1842.[5] This point is made clear in a July 1842 letter in which Simms thanked Benjamin F. Perry for "the warm interest you express in the fortunes of the *Magnolia*." Reminding his friend of the "inert moral nature of our people" and the "too commanding influences of mere political intellect," Simms indicated that "a sign of improvement in this respect" had led him to consent once again to give his "name & help to a Southern periodical." Simms stressed: "I believe, not only that such a work is now wanted, but that it is almost the only means for stimulating into literary exercise the people of a country so sparsely settled as is ours" (*L*, I, 315–16).

There were additional reasons for Simms's return to magazine editing. Despite his great popularity as a novelist, he was still not free of financial worries. The lack of an international copyright law not only prevented him from profiting from the English reprintings of his novels, but also made American publishers unwilling to pay high prices (or often anything) for original manuscripts. In a letter of August 16, 1841, to his friend James H. Hammond, Simms complained bitterly of this situation: "There are very few American writers who ever get anything [for their books]. ... The publishers are very costive—the sales are terribly diminished within the last few years." He pointed out that "Irving now writes almost wholly for magazines and Cooper & myself are almost the only persons whose novels are printed—certainly, we are almost the only persons who hope to get anything for them. From England we get nothing" (*L*, I, 271).

If, as Simms contended, novel writing was less profitable in 1841 than it had been in the 1830s, perhaps part of the blame can be attributed to the phenomenal growth of the magazine as the reading medium of the American people.[6] On the other hand the enormous increase in the number of periodicals also provided American authors with a new market for their wares; the liberal prices offered to contributors by *Graham's* and *Godey's*, to quote N. P. Willis, "burst on author-land ... like a sunrise without a dawn";[7] and by 1842 many writers looked to the magazines as their best and in many instances their only source of income.[8] The monthly magazines, which in large part were replacing the quarterly reviews, were diverging more and more from British models and relying more upon fiction from native writers. Simms himself had never ceased to write for the literary journals, even during the 1830s and early 1840s when he was achieving prominence as a novelist. Between 1833 and 1841 he had contributed to no fewer than fourteen magazines.[9] Although Simms probably received nothing more than mental satisfaction for his services in behalf of the Southern journals, he doubtless expected (and received) material compensation for his contributions to the Northern magazines which could and sometimes did pay their leading contributors well.

Nevertheless, despite all his efforts, Simms in 1842 was a debtor, not a creditor.[10] Because "tasks of literary labor" no longer gave him "sufficient occupation" (*L*, I, 290), and because, as we have seen, his decision to enter politics was cut short by the death of his youngest child, what could have been more natural than for Simms—who in a decade devoted almost exclusively to belles-lettres had won fame but very little fortune—to turn once again to magazine editing, which at least provided the possibility (however uncertain) of an income and which, even more important, gave him the opportunity to renew in print his crusade for Southern literature. And because of Simms's reputation as the South's most distinguished man of letters, Pendleton was probably willing to promise him rather handsome pay for his services as editor.[11] Thus it was that Gilmore Simms, who in December 1840 had accurately forecast the doom of the *Magnolia,* nevertheless agreed some eighteen months later to shoulder the responsibility for its editing.

In the "Literary Circular" reprinted on the back cover of the opening number of the new series, Burges & James, the publishers, and Pendleton, who was to continue as agent, expressed confidence in the future of the "new" *Magnolia* and announced specific plans for improvement: "… the MAGNOLIA … has taken permanent root. … Its subscribers are increasing daily, the typographical garments will soon be as flowing and beautiful as the best among its contemporaries; and among the fine intellects assembled and secured … may be enumerated many of the most accomplished names of which the South can boast." The circular noted that the "Editorial duties will chiefly devolve upon Mr. W. GILMORE SIMMS, whose services we have secured to a greater degree than before. The Editorial Bureau will be entirely surrendered to his control, and his general supervision of the work is hereafter certain. …" Burges & James, moreover, pledged "large improvements" for the *Magnolia,* the "general plan of [which] will resemble that of the Southern Literary Messenger,—a journal confessedly among the neatest in this or any other country. …"[12]

Despite the enthusiasm and optimism of the proprietors, Simms himself seems to have realized from the beginning that only hard work and careful planning could make the *Magnolia* the magazine he wanted it to be. In the initial number he acknowledged that "Specious promises … will do little in gaining subscribers. … The 'Magnolia,' unless by its fruits, cannot hope to evade the decree … to be 'cut down and cast into the fire.'"[13] Apparently fully aware of the difficult nature of his assignment, then, Simms entered upon the editorship of the *Magnolia* (now subtitled the "Southern Appalachian") with his usual gusto. He immediately wrote such friends as Lawson, Perry, Hammond, and Joel R. Poinsett, asking them to pledge their support and to try to win contributors and subscribers. Others among "the fine intellects assembled and secured" were A. B. Longstreet, William A. Caruthers, Thomas Holley Chivers, Charles Fenno Hoffman, John Neal, Richard Henry Wilde, George Frederick Holmes, Mary E. Lee, Alexander B. Meek, and Simms's old friend of the *Southern Literary Gazette* days, James W. Simmons. These "accomplished names" gave the *Magnolia* an air of dignity which hitherto had been lacking; the prestige of the magazine became such that it began to rival that of the *Southern Literary Messenger* (then edited by Thomas W. White and Matthew F. Maury), which had long reigned supreme among Southern literary journals. The *Chicora,* for instance, remarked that the *Magnolia* "sustains itself excellently, in contrast with the periodicals of the day, and must continue to do so while Simms's pen flourishes over so many of its pages" (I [September 1842], 79). Simms himself claimed that in the South the *Magnolia* had "no competitor in public estimation" (*L,* I, 326).

In several ways, the *Magnolia* of 1842–1843 was in fact superior to the *Messenger* of the same period, which it closely resembled both in appearance and in content, for, as Burges & James had indicated, the *Magnolia* admittedly was modeled upon the older periodical. Despite the fact that the proposed "large improvements" in the "typographic air and costume" of the *Magnolia* were never carried out, in format the two magazines were almost identical: each contained "not less than 64 large super royal pages" per number,[14] with similar typography. Though both magazines were supposedly literary journals, both leaned more toward informative essays than toward belletristic writing, perhaps because of the South's predilection for statesmanship and oratory. The opening article of either magazine was almost always a "scholarly" discussion of some political, economic, social, or literary problem, much like a typical quarterly review article. The ratio of essays to fiction in both the *Magnolia* and the *Messenger* was roughly three to one; in addition each magazine usually contained one or two translations, had poems scattered throughout, and reserved a department at the end for book reviews. It was particularly in the latter department that the *Magnolia* during Simms's editorship excelled the *Southern Literary Messenger*: Simms's criticisms were almost always vigorous and bold, and sometimes distinguished; the critical notices in the *Messenger* were far below the level which Poe had attained for that magazine in 1835–1836. The *Magnolia*'s poetry, though sentimental and didactic, was for the most part equal to that of the *Messenger,* and the long-winded discussions of contemporary problems in both magazines seem equally dull and pompous today. In belles-lettres the *Magnolia* appears to have held its own; certainly the *Messenger* of 1842–1843 contained nothing of as much interest as Longstreet's new series of "Georgia Scenes" or Simms's "Castle Dismal."

Under Simms the *Magnolia* seems to have become less concerned with literature that merely entertains and more concerned with literature that provokes thought. Simms doubtless realized that in the minds of Southern gentlemen knowledge rather than pleasure was the primary object of reading, and he furthermore saw that the survival of his magazine depended upon the patronage of men as well as women. Though throughout his career he fought bravely and steadfastly for the advancement of Southern literature per se, he was realistic enough to recognize that historical and critical writings were also important in the development of a literary culture—and practical-minded enough to understand that the first requisite for a magazine's success was to satisfy its readers' tastes. The "manly tone"[15] of the new series of the *Magnolia*—a magazine which had had its start as a "ladies' book"—may be attributed to the influence of Simms, who was too much of a realist to have much sympathy with the rising tide of sentimentality that was flooding America with magazines and literature especially designed for women readers.[16] By the 1840s Simms probably shared the view of the Young Americans, who scoffed at the inane writing in the women's periodicals,[17] and of the critic in the *Harbinger* who exclaimed, "Heaven protect us from such a literature!" (III [August 8, 1846], 138). It must be remembered, however, that Simms himself had helped establish two magazines intended primarily for ladies, and certainly he never lost sight of the fact that America's reading audience was composed largely of women.[18]

Simms's own words best reveal his editorial policy in the *Magnolia.* In writing to classical scholar George Frederick Holmes in July 1842, he observed: "I would encourage you in reference to the classical papers. That on the Attic tragedy will no doubt commend itself to us & our readers. It is important, however, that your learning should be digested well. Magazine writing to be successful must exhibit fruits rather than processes" (*L,* I, 317).[19] Later on in the same letter appears a revealing comment on the reason why most of the *Magnolia*'s articles are unsigned: "I am of opinion that nothing discourages young writers so much as to have their articles placed in immediate juxtaposition with the *Star* contributors." Simms explained that in leaving readers "to guess out the authorship, a new sort of interest is awakened in their minds, and a young writer stands a fair chance of having justice done him. . . ." The practice of publishing contributions anonymously, however, was far from unique with the *Magnolia;* Simms was here following the policy of many of the better-known Northern and British quarterlies—the *North American Review,* the *Edinburgh Review,* and the *Quarterly Review,* for instance, never published the names of contributors.[20]

The letter to Holmes contains yet another comment on editorial policy. Simms wrote: "We can scarcely afford to pay for translations. We should not object to have them where they are particularly racy,—as would be the case with Rabelais—perhaps, *too* racy—but of that you must be the guardian." The editor added that for "accepted translations we can only pay one dollar per page ($1). You might send us a few pages of very choice passages" (*L*, I, 318). Simms probably felt that translations hardly fitted into his plan to encourage original writings by native authors. Nevertheless, that he was willing to pay anything at all for them seems to indicate that the chief contributors to the *Magnolia* did not labor entirely without compensation. In a letter of August 22, 1842, to James Lawson, Simms remarked, however, that his magazine "cannot yet pay anything that would compensate. It pays only a few persons, & the sum is purely nominal. To some $1.00 & to others $2 per page" (*L*, I, 322).

When one compares these rates with those of *Graham's, Godey's,* or the *Knickerbocker,* which ordinarily paid several times more,[21] it is not hard to understand why Simms was unable to attract the better-known Northern magazinists, who must have written for the *Magnolia,* as some of them occasionally did, only for friendship's sake. In fact, Simms's policy of publishing contributions unsigned may have been based on weakness; unable to secure a corps of contributors as notable as those of *Graham's* or *Godey's,* he perhaps did not wish to publicize the fact by listing his own. Included among the contributors to *Graham's* in 1842, for example, were Longfellow, Lowell, Benjamin, Chivers, Fay, Mrs. Stephens, Cooper, Seba Smith, Mrs. Osgood, Charles Fenno Hoffman, Richard Henry Dana, Bryant, Griswold, Tuckerman, Simms himself, and of course Poe. The *Magnolia,* which was probably unsurpassed in the South, fell far short of being the best literary magazine in the United States partly because it lacked the money to compete for the services of outstanding authors. Neither, of course, was the *Magnolia* able to afford engravings, which were particularly featured in *Graham's* and *Godey's.* And, given that the *Magnolia* targeted a sparsely settled, predominantly rural region, it never achieved a large enough subscriber list to break free of crippling budgetary constraints. To Simms's credit it may be said that he did remarkably well with what he had.

Simms apparently disagreed with Pendleton on the advisability of printing long articles or stories according to the "English plan."[22] He requested that his contributors not write articles that required serial publication: "we shall always give place and preference to those performances, which are unique and *publishable* entire." And although he wished to encourage young writers, he made it clear that they must not be impatient in making demands for space and attention. "When they grow famous," he observed, "they can command their own terms. In the meantime they must work hard, take up as little space as possible, finish up well, and wait patiently for the call." He added, however, that he would never be guilty of the "editorial barbarity" of "subjecting to a ridicule ... the immature performances of young beginners."[23] Perhaps

Simms's unhappy experience in criticizing rejected contributions to the *Album* helped to bring him to this conviction.

Not once during his editorship of the *Magnolia* did Simms cease his fight for Southern literature. In fact, so often was the literature of the South discussed in the pages of the *Magnolia* that to avoid duplication and preserve space, Simms felt compelled to reject a letter on that subject by John Tomlin, the literary-minded postmaster of Jackson, Tennessee. He agreed with Tomlin that "the South had been and remained in literary bondage but Southern pride would prompt the region to contribute its share to the erection of a national literature."[24]

In fact, the greatest satisfaction that Simms received from editing the *Magnolia,* as he stated many times, was the conviction that as editor of a Southern magazine he was playing a leading role in the development of Southern letters. "I am happy to say to you," he wrote to George Frederick Holmes, "that the highest compliment which I have had paid to me for some time past, results from the conviction, (now very clear) that in assuming the conduct of the *Magnolia,* I am rapidly accumulating about me, & in the cause of Southern Literature, a really able array of highly endowed and well educated men, who, without such an organ & an editor in whom they have confidence, would go to rust in our wilderness" (July 27, 1842; *L,* I, 318).[25]

There can be no doubt that Simms was doing much to encourage the young writers of the South. Contributions for the *Magnolia* poured in at such a rate that Simms was forced to use a finer type in order to accommodate as many contributors as possible[26]—and even then he received complaints from correspondents whose offerings had been found unacceptable. The editor used these complaints as a springboard for one of the most enlightening discussions of the difficulties of editorial management:

> We sometimes get a captious letter from a correspondent complaining of our limits. He cannot get his ideas ... in such narrow boundaries as we prescribe in our pages. Four to eight pages are not enough for such profound workers. ... The truth is, we give too much room. A bold, nervous writer, who speaks to the point,—who is not wordy and diffuse—will not want so much; and for any other, we take it, that even less room would be better for the popularity and success of our periodical.
>
> Others of our correspondents complain of the delay in the publication of their favours. But this must always be the case where the contributors are so numerous. Some must wait, and we always give a preference to such articles as are of passing and pressing interest. In this matter we have no partialities. ... We congratulate ourselves on the variety and abundance of our contributors,

and will strive to pacify them all in turn,—but our magazine has its limits, and we have our laws. We cannot expand the one, nor violate the other.[27]

Simms, like most magazine editors of his day, felt that it was his right (and duty) to revise or to "improve" any manuscript submitted to him for publication. Although this practice enabled the *Magnolia* to "save" many a contribution that otherwise would have been discarded, at times Simms stirred resentment by exercising his prerogative to make use of a correspondent's work in whatever way he thought best. Unfortunately, at least once the contributor whose ire was aroused was one of Simms's best friends, James Lawson. In a letter of October 28, 1842, Simms casually informed Lawson, "... I have availed myself of the permission so frankly accorded me, of making such alterations as my judgment counselled" (*L,* I, 325) in a poem and in an essay on mesmerism recently submitted by the New York Scotsman.[28] When Lawson indicated that he was displeased with the use made of his material, Simms was sincerely grieved at his friend's anger but staunchly defended his action as editor: "I conscientiously thought, and think, that in making the small corrections which I did, I was in fact bestowing the labor of the file which my friend in his hurry ... had not been able himself to bestow,—and this too, with his express sanction. ..." He informed Lawson that "you are not exempt from the fate of most authors, in being profoundly ignorant of your best performances" (*L,* I, 331). A man of Simms's impetuosity lacked the tactfulness and the sensitivity necessary for the editor who wishes to appease all readers and correspondents.[29] Since, however, Simms and Lawson enjoyed an unusually intimate and candid relationship, Simms was probably justified in this case in thinking candor his best policy.

Simms, always a sought after and willing speaker, had a particularly crowded itinerary late in 1842. A speaking engagement at Tuscaloosa, Alabama,[30] coupled with administrative responsibilities at Woodlands plantation, made it necessary for him to spend the better part of November and December away from Charleston, and consequently the December and January numbers of the *Magnolia* were hastily put together. Simms was disturbed to find frequent typographical errors in the two numbers; in one case, however, he bluntly stated that "the fault is rather with the author, or amanuensis, than the printer. Let the author but meet the publishers half way, and neither of them will have reason to complain hereafter."[31] Perhaps the fact that he was an extremely busy and harassed man accounts for the change in attitude toward the work of the printers; it will be remembered that some twenty months earlier he himself had bitterly complained of the same kind of printing errors for which he here blamed the author. Simms concluded this note to his readers by saying: "In a month or two, he [the editor] hopes to devote himself wholly to the work that he may not lie upon any reproach, of neglect, either of the taste of the public, or of its own interests."

To all outward appearances the *Magnolia* was thriving. Widely praised by critics,[32] the magazine added further to its subscription list if not to its income by absorbing the *Chicora: or Messenger of the South,*[33] another Charleston literary journal, which had failed after thirteen weekly numbers. Simms, pleased with the addition of new subscribers, looked upon the merger as a step in the right direction; in fact, he was very much encouraged by the progress the *Magnolia* was making, as indicated by his remark to Lawson in the late fall of 1842: "The Magnolia promises to do well, comparatively speaking—as well, perhaps, as a Southern Magazine can do. ... certain of the Northern journals pronounce favorably upon our merits, and by many it is called the ablest in the Union. At home, in the South, I believe we have no competitor in public estimation" (*L,* I, 326).

At the close of 1842, then, the *Magnolia* was generally recognized as a magazine of high caliber and higher promise. The proprietors began with enthusiasm and hopefulness the year that was to mark the death of their journal; as late as February 1843 they issued a statement congratulating "themselves and the public with the assurance, that it [the *Magnolia*] is now permanently established. ..." (n.s., II, 144). Yet the following month came public acknowledgment of the magazine's precarious financial standing. On the back cover of the March number Pendleton issued a long explanation of the reasons for the *Magnolia*'s eventual bankruptcy:

> My present embarrassment has not been occasioned by the want of subscribers, but by their withholding what was due. ... There is ... more than sufficient money due, if paid in, to cancel my liabilities. It may be asked, why we do not take the steps that others do to collect their dues. It must be remembered that they are in sums of five, ten and fifteen dollars, scattered over a district of more than a thousand miles in length and breadth. And suppose an agent were sent to make personal application for them, (as has in many instances been done) it would take a year of industrious travel to see near all, and when he arrives at the residences of subscribers, he will probably find one-half or one-third absent. The inutility is at once apparent, and the amount of success and indebtedness will not warrant the great expense necessary. ...

The proprietors of the *Magnolia* were confronted with one of the problems that Simms had foreseen long before assuming the editorship: the lack of a satisfactory method of collecting fees in a sparsely settled country with poor transportation facilities. And it was perhaps this need for better means of communication, rather than solely an unwillingness on the part of Southerners to pay for their magazines, that accounts mostly for the difficulties which nearly all Southern periodicals encountered in getting their subscribers to settle their debts. It is true, however, that embittered editors, seeing their magazines die apparently because the reading public refused to pay its honest debts, were more likely to place the blame upon the character of the Southern people than upon any mechanical or geographical handicap.[34] In any case, one wonders why Southern magazines did not demand payment in advance. The answer perhaps is that Southern readers were not willing to risk money on proposed magazines and that the magazines needed subscribers too urgently to attempt to dictate terms.

The brief announcement in May 1843 that "With the forthcoming, or June, issue of the Magnolia, Mr. Simms withdraws from its Editorial management" (p. 336) clearly indicated that the *Magnolia,* despite its rising reputation as one of the South's leading periodicals, was to follow in the footsteps of many another magazine of the Old South. It is ironic that on the same page an editorial appears in which Simms ("to prevent misconception") stated, "... there is but one editor of the Magnolia, whose responsibility extends to every thing published as original in the Editorial Bureau." Hereafter, he added, "any article admitted into the Editorial department, and not by the Editor, will carry with it the full signature, or the initials, of the proper author." This statement of future editorial policy by an outgoing editor seems to indicate that the decision to sever connections with the *Magnolia* was made at the last minute—after the contents for the May number had been prepared.

Simms's resignation, then, apparently came as a shock to the readers of the *Magnolia,* who no doubt had underrated the urgency of Pendleton's plea. Benjamin F. Perry perhaps summed up the feelings of many readers when on May 18 he wrote to Simms: "Why is this? You have taken the work and given it character and ability. Hundreds have taken an interest in it because you were the Editor." Perry emphasized that "for the honor and pride of Southern Literature," the *Magnolia* "ought to be continued, but without your aid I am afraid the work must fall" (*L,* I, 351n).

Simms's reply to his friend's inquiry is particularly illuminating in that it gives both the real and the apparent reasons for his withdrawal from the editorship, which came only "after calm consideration." "Under the existing conditions of the proprietorship the work cannot possibly continue long," Simms declared, "and I am unwilling that it should perish in my hands. The proprietors are squabbling among themselves and are accordingly either doing nothing for the magazine or positively injuring it. . . . This will suffice to make you comprehend the case & my motive for withdrawing from the Editorial *fauteuil.*" In the way of further explanation Simms added: "Burges proposes to yield it up to Pendleton entirely on the 1st of July. Pendleton has proposed to me to conduct it for him, but as he already owes me several hundred dollars and I am quite too poor to work for nothing, I have declined. My own opinion is that if Burges gives it up, it will stop for I very much doubt if the money credit of P. is sufficient to secure him a printer" (May 26, 1843; *L,* I, 351).

Simms's surmise proved correct, for the once proud *Magnolia* died with its very next number—that of June 1843. And it is interesting that Simms attributed the failure of the *Magnolia* not to the lack of public support but to the incompetence of one of its proprietors. From the beginning the editor had looked upon his work with the *Magnolia* as a personal sacrifice to ensure his geographical section a literary organ of its own. If indeed Pendleton did owe him "several hundred dollars," Simms must have realized for some time that the proprietor would never be able to pay him properly for his services. This loss he had been willing to accept as long as the future of magazine seemed promising, as long as he could contribute to the cause of Southern literature. But when it became apparent that Pendleton was also heavily in debt to others and that the *Magnolia* was certain to go under because of this indebtedness, Simms could see no reason to allow his name to be associated with a failure for which he was not responsible.[35]

Simms, moreover, had never been completely happy in his work as editor of the *Magnolia.* It will be remembered that he had apparently debated long and hard before agreeing to re-enter the "Editorial *fauteuil.*" And only five months after his acceptance—long before the true financial status of Pendleton was revealed—Simms had already indicated that he was tiring of his editorial duties. In a letter of November 22, 1842, to Perry, he had complained of "the multiplicity of my Editorial labors": "It is grievously uphill, that labor" (*L,* I, 333). By April 6, 1843, he had almost made up his mind to resign, as his letter of that date to Lawson reveals: "I have half resolved to abdicate my editorial *fauteuil.* The situation is irksome to me. I lose my sense of freedom in it, and the kind of labor is disagreeable to me, fatiguing yet not likely to enhance my fame" (*L,* I, 346).

It is apparent, too, that Simms never was able (or perhaps never was willing) to devote his full time to the *Magnolia.* At the same time that he served as its editor, he also was delivering public lectures, helping his father-in-law conduct the affairs of the plantation, arranging for the publication of *The Yemassee* and *The Damsel of Darien* in England, and working on at least two other books, *Donna Florida* and the companion piece to his history of South Carolina, *The Geography of South Carolina.* But the amount of work Simms was capable of turning out is remarkable—certainly in one respect the *Magnolia* of 1842–1843 never suffered from neglect on its editor's part, as his sixty-odd contributions well attest. In the brief span of one year, Simms had brought the *Magnolia* from comparative obscurity to a respected position among the better magazines of the United States. Yet he saw his labors go to waste, partly because of the incompetence of the proprietors and partly because of the difficulties which confronted any Southern periodical—difficulties which Simms himself had been among the first to point out.

Although the *Magnolia: or Southern Appalachian* is a good, representative literary magazine of the Old South,[36] to the student of American literature it is more than that. As the literary organ of a significant writer during one of the most productive periods in his career, it contains poems, essays, and reviews by the editor, many of which have been hitherto unattributed.[37]

Since Simms was usually steadfast in his policy of publishing contributions anonymously, it is often exceedingly difficult to determine the authors of individual articles, despite the fact that frequently the names of contributors were listed on the inside front cover. As a rule, however, poems were signed by initials or pseudonyms, and thus many authors who otherwise would have to remain anonymous can be identified. Then, too, occasionally a prose contribution by an important writer was signed by name, although the editor's own work was presented anonymously or over one of his numerous pen names.[38]

The bulk of Simms's writings in the two volumes of the *Magnolia* which he edited consists of poetry and criticism; oddly enough, only two works of prose fiction—"The Pirates and Palatines: A Legend of North-Carolina" and "Annihilation: A Romance of the Night"—can safely be attributed to him. Forty-seven poems (or fifty installments of poetry) can be identified as his; four long articles—"Our Relations with Great Britain," "Cooper: His Genius and Writings," "Bulwer's Genius and Writings," and "Tecumseh—A Poem"—definitely belong to him, and at least two others probably do;[39] and the "Editorial Bureau," comprising a total of some 130 pages, is almost entirely his. The latter contains not only book reviews and statements of editorial policy, but discussions of subjects as widely diverse as "Lunatic Asylum" and "Apostolical Succession."

Of the forty-seven Simms poems included in the *Magnolia: or Southern Appalachian*, twenty-three appear with no signature and the remaining twenty-four with pseudonyms.[40] With the exception of "M. E. S.," which is a carry-over from the *Album*, and "S.," which had appeared in both the *Album* and the *Southern Literary Gazette,* the pen names in the *Magnolia* had not been used in the earlier magazines.[41] "Childe Hazard" and "Delta" were to be used again in the *Southern and Western Monthly Magazine and Review* three years later.

Probably the best of the poems by Simms were unsigned. A few of them, "Dark-eyed Maid of Edisto," "The Maid of the Congaree," "Ask me no more for Song," and "The Traveller's Rest," display skill if not genius. Other poems of merit by the editor include "Oh! Linger Yet Awhile," "Beauty in the Shade," "Sonnet—by the Swanannoa," and "Song—Meet me when Stars." One suspects, however, that many of the poems Simms published in the *Magnolia* were unmarketable pieces which he wished to put into print—on the record, so to speak. Nevertheless, a large number of them were republished, often in revised or expanded form.[42]

Perhaps the most significant thing about the poetry by Simms in the *Magnolia*—and certainly the thing of most importance to the student of American literature—is that much of it is regional in sentiment and in setting. Whereas most of his poetry in the *Album* and the *Southern Literary Gazette* had dealt with classical or conventional subjects, Simms wrote poems for the *Magnolia* that are distinctly Southern in subject matter—"Well, Sang a Blue-Eyed Damsel," "The Maid of the Congaree," "Dark-eyed Maid of Edisto," "Dorchester," "Sonnet—by the Swanannoa," "The Texian Hunter to his Bride," and "The Traveller's Rest," to name a few. It is to be regretted that Simms did not more often make use of Southern folklore in his poems; perhaps its use would have led him to break away from the stilted style of his "conventional" poetry. Nevertheless, though Simms cannot be said to occupy a place among Southern poets corresponding to Whittier's place as an early "local colorist" among New England poets, he was perhaps the first important Southern man of letters to write poetry describing his native surroundings.

The only leading articles in the new series of the *Magnolia* that definitely can be ascribed to Simms are the two critical essays on Cooper and Bulwer. Simms's criticism of Cooper, coming as it did at a time when the latter was distrusted and misunderstood by the American public, is, on the whole, an admirable piece of writing,[43] displaying the perceptiveness, the hard-headedness, and the open-mindedness that made Simms at his best one of the better critics in nineteenth-century America—and at the same time revealing some of the impulsiveness and strong prejudice that was his chief weakness as a critic.

When Simms resigned the editorship of the *Magnolia* in June 1843, he apparently had had enough of magazine editing. He had complained: "... the kind of labor is disagreeable to me, fatiguing yet not likely to enhance my fame" (*L*, I, 346). Nevertheless, he was sorely disappointed that his efforts to establish a permanent literary journal in the South had proved unsuccessful. Though he attempted other things, he could not keep away from magazines, and scarcely more than a year after leaving the *Magnolia*, he was already discussing plans which led to the establishment of the *Southern and Western Monthly Magazine and Review* in 1845.

But the process was gradual. In March 1844 Simms wrote George Frederick Holmes that "a periodical of my own … just now is out of the question" (*L*, I, 412), yet five months later plans for a new magazine were beginning to crystallize. "Burges & James talk of establishing a Politico Literary Magazine, of which they wish me to be Editor," Simms informed Holmes in a letter of August 12. "They will begin in the fall. We shall see"(*L*, I, 430). By the middle of November, though the new magazine still existed only on paper, Simms apparently had committed himself to its editorship. "It is highly probable," he wrote Evert A. Duyckinck, "that I am shortly to have a magazine of my own. The publishers of the Magnolia and 'Orion'[44] have made me overtures for such a work to supply the place of these." Since the salary of the editor was to come primarily "from the profits of the work," in the beginning the journal would not be able to pay contributors, whom Simms hoped "to find among personal friends" willing to make "the same sacrifice that I do, in consideration of the same objects that I have in view" (*L*, I, 439).

This agreement must have looked particularly attractive to Simms: he was promised "half the profits" (*L*, I, 436) of the projected journal, yet he was not to be held financially responsible in the event of its failure; "… I am a share holder without the risks" (*L*, I, 440), he explained to Duyckinck in announcing his acceptance of the editorship. But it was not primarily the lure of financial reward that drew Simms back to the editor's chair. "My chief motive for consenting to this editorship," he wrote on to George Frederick Holmes, "is based upon our previous conversations, & the mutual desire we entertained to establish a manly & proper organ of literature & criticism in the South" (*L*, I, 442).

Apparently Simms was given free rein to make what he could of the magazine, and he knew that its success would depend largely upon his ability to secure well-known contributors. He could not afford to pay for contributions, but, as he intimated to Duyckinck, he had confidence that his literary friends would offer their services free of charge until the new journal was solidly established. Among those whom Simms counted on for help were Evert A. Duyckinck, James Lawson, William Cullen Bryant, Cornelius Mathews, Joel

Tyler Headley, J. L. H. McCracken, Edwin Forrest, and Catherine Sinclair Forrest in the North, and George F. Holmes, Benjamin Franklin Perry, Alexander Meek, James H. Hammond, and others in the South. Simms well knew, as he wrote Lawson in mid-November 1844, that unless he could enlist the aid of these friends, "the brunt will chiefly fall upon myself." He added, however: "I shall not shrink from it, and hope to make the magazine a first rate one . . ." (*L*, I, 436). Simms later expressed confidence to Holmes that "we can make the Magazine, if we try, one of the best of the day" (*L*, I, 442).

On January 15, 1845, Simms was able to write James Lawson that the "first number of the New Magazine will appear today." Although Simms stressed that "It is scarcely a fair specimen," he added, "You will find it fair, however, in comparison with such of our contemporaries as I have seen for January" (*L*, II, 13). Leading off the "Editorial Bureau" in the opening number of the *Southern and Western Monthly Magazine and Review* was the story of the birth of the "new Magnolia" (as Simms liked to call it) and a statement of the new magazine's editorial policy, which was to be strikingly like that of the old:

> Frequent applications to the present publishers [Burges & James], for the restoration of the Magnolia Magazine, and a conviction on their part that a work so well sustained by public favor should not have been allowed to perish, persuades them to make amends for whatever of the reproach may properly belong to them, by the establishment of a new journal as nearly on the plan of the old as possible. They have accordingly persuaded the Editor of that work to return to this *fauteuil,* and he in turn has succeeded in persuading to a resumption of their tasks, the greater number of his old contributors. To these, new names are to be added, from various parts of the country, from whose co-operation the happiest variety may be expected in the pages of the new Magazine. This, though differing in name from the former, will maintain a not dissimilar character. The endeavor will be made to impart to it *a more decided political complexion* [my emphasis] than was borne by the Magnolia, and, if possible, to impress upon it more of those sectional aspects, South and West, which need development quite as much as advocacy. (*SWMMR,* I [January 1845], 67)

The inclusion of *Western* in the title of the new magazine suggests that Simms and the publishers wanted to create an alliance between the South Atlantic states and the inland border states. In the 1840s there was much rivalry between the South and the North for the political support of the West—and the statement that the *Southern and Western* was to have "a more decided political complexion than was borne by the Magnolia" probably came as a consequence of that political rivalry. The word *Review* probably was added to the title to emphasize the fact that the new magazine was to contain more than fiction and poetry;[45] like the *Southern Quarterly Review,* its Charleston competitor, it was to include discussions of social and political ideas in the form of reviews of important books. Strangely, however, in practice the *Southern and Western* was, if anything, less "political" than the *Magnolia;* its proportion of political articles was much lower and it contained a correspondingly higher proportion of fiction. Nevertheless, in framework the two magazines were almost identical: both of them were devoted largely to prose articles interspersed with poems, with a section at the end reserved for Simms's "Editorial Bureau."[46]

As editor of the *Southern and Western Monthly Magazine and Review,* then, Simms was bearing the banner of the South and West in taking a defiant stand against Northern literary dominance. He pointed out that "[w]hile millions are sent away annually to recipients north of the Potomac, what is brought to us may be expressed by hundreds." In addressing "particularly ... the people of the South and West," however, the new journal did not mean to exclude readers from other geographical regions. "Our work simply proposes that justice should be done to the mind which fills our region," the editor explained, "to the development of which ... our Magazine will be honestly directed" (*SWMMR,* I [January 1845], 67–68). In this, then, Simms's fourth attempt to found a literary magazine in the South, the keynote was the same as always: the promotion of Southern letters.

But the remarkable thing about this new venture is that both the editor and the publishers—all old hands at magazine publishing in the South—were willing to invest their time and money in the establishment of another literary journal when all historical precedent showed that they would not succeed. These men were not blind to the fate of their predecessors, yet were nevertheless willing to take another chance. Perhaps they felt that now for the first time they had achieved the proper combination: an influential editor, progressive publishers, well-known contributors. At any rate, the announcement on the back cover of the second (February) number of the *Southern and Western* reveals something of the resourcefulness and determination of the publishers. Promising "to increase the number of its pages, the interest and value of its contents, and to adorn its several numbers ... with fine steel portraits," Burges & James stated that they "confidently believed" in the success of their magazine, "placed under well known literary auspices, and conducted with a true Southern spirit, at a time when, from North-Carolina, to Louisiana, there is not ... a periodical of the sort."

Perhaps, however, it was in the long editorial entitled "Southern Periodical Literature" that Simms gave clearest expression to what he expected to encounter and what he hoped to accomplish as editor of the *Southern and*

*Western.* The pessimistic but determined tone reflected the mind of a man prepared to make a last stand for a cause in which he deeply believed:

> To us it matters little in what periodical they [Southern writers] write, so that it be a Southern periodical,—so that they contribute to elevate and provoke the domestic genius. … Our humble efforts are devoted to this object almost wholly. … Let our readers take this thing to heart. Let them remember that the experiments now making in behalf of our literature in the South and West, are probably the last attempts that will be made. (*SWMMR,* I [May 1845], 363–64)

Here Simms was saying again what he had said many times already: though he expected no reward for his efforts, he nevertheless was willing to give his time and energy to the direction of a Southern literary journal in hope that he might somehow awaken in his people the spark necessary for the creation of a literature that was distinctly American because it was distinctly Southern.

It will be remembered that Simms had been fearful that the hastily prepared opening numbers of the *Southern and Western* would not do credit to him or to the magazine. Perhaps the harshest criticism of the initial number was written by Charles F. Briggs, then editor of the *Broadway Journal.* Briggs ridiculed Simms's leading article, "Americanism in Literature," and took the new magazine to task for pretending to be an organ for Southern writers while in reality giving priority to contributions from Northern authors.[47] Later, however, under Poe's influence, the *Broadway Journal* became one of Simms's staunchest supporters—and to such an extent that both Poe and the journal were charged with Simms favoritism by Simms's first biographer.

In general, however, even from the start, the *Southern and Western* was applauded by critics. *Godey's,* for instance, said of the opening numbers: "We are pleased with every feature of this new literary enterprise. The papers … all are brought up to standard of literary excellence, such as the editor's high reputation for ability and taste requires … the whole affair has a stamp of nationality which we decidedly approve."[48] The *New York Morning News,* which on March 7, 1845, had published a favorable notice of the February number of the *Southern and Western,* had particular praise for Simms's own work in the March issue of the new magazine.[49] In fact, some of the most ardent support of Simms and his magazine came from New York, perhaps because of his many friends among New York writers and critics. Duyckinck, for instance, probably wrote the review in the *Weekly Mirror* of May 3, 1845: "This magazine is always satisfactory. Its editor has many strings to his bow. … It is the most natural and desirable thing … that such a writer should have his own magazine, if only to relieve his study and his mind of the masses of valuable matter which from time to time accumulate." In the *Weekly News* of May 24 a critic (perhaps again Duyckinck) voiced even higher praise for the Southern magazine: "... there is no periodical of the kind in the country better worthy of support for the substance and variety of its contents, and none that surpass the force and originality of its views."

When, with the June number, the first half-yearly volume of the *Southern and Western* was completed, the editor and the publishers took the opportunity to make a public statement as to the standing of their magazine. Despite the general approval of their work by literary critics, the sponsors admitted in an "Advertisement" printed on the inside back cover that the *Southern and Western* "is not the work we designed, nor exactly the work we could wish; but time must be allowed us. ..." Even more important to the success of the magazine, however, was a "smile of encouragement. ... As nothing is more discouraging to him who toils in the fields of art and literature, than the conviction that he dwells in an unfriendly atmosphere. ..."

This announcement is typical of the appeals which were periodically issued by magazines of the Old South requesting financial and moral support. In fact, it is so typical that it can hardly be taken as indicative either of success or of failure. Simms once remarked that three thousand subscribers "would amply sustain" a Southern literary journal;[50] backed by former subscribers to both the *Magnolia* and the *Orion,* by this time the *Southern and Western* must have reached a circulation of some two thousand within ten Southern states.[51] Months earlier, when the magazine circulated only fifteen hundred copies, Simms—in a letter of February 11, 1845, to E. A. Duyckinck—had stated that it was "of no small moment in making up the opinion of the Southern Country" (*L*, II, 29).

Also in the June 1845 number was a notice requesting correspondents who "persist in addressing the Editor in person ... to couple this piece of consideration with another—by paying the postage of their favors. ..." Pointedly but tactfully, then, Simms made it clear that he had neither the leisure nor the wealth for time-and-money-consuming correspondence with disgruntled or thoughtless contributors.

On a whole, however, Simms's relationships with his contributors were cordial. As a harassed editor, he looked upon good writers as valuable assets and cultivated them almost to the point of flattery. But seldom did Simms's business sense becloud his critical eye: he did not allow his need for contributions to distort his judgment of their actual value. And when he could be frank without fear of offending, he tactfully suggested that the contributor try something else—as in the case of his good friend, James H. Hammond. After describing Hammond's "verses to Caroline" as being "as smoothly turned as if you had frequently practiced at the lathe" and promising them "an early place" in the magazine, Simms bluntly added: "But stick to the prose and do more of it" (*L*, II, 63).

By one means or another Simms was able to gather about him a small but fairly capable group of Southern writers, including most of those who had written for the *Magnolia* and several important additions—namely, E. A. Duyckinck and William Alfred Jones (from the North) as well as Caroline Lee Hentz and W. C. Richards. In addition, James M. Legaré, a neglected poet whose earliest published writings had appeared anonymously in the *Magnolia*,[52] added four contributions to the *Southern and Western*, perhaps his first publications under his own name. Legaré has been ranked by Curtis Carroll Davis "below only Poe, Lanier, and Timrod in the history of Southern verse."[53] The twenty-two-year-old Legaré was probably the best of the young contributors Simms introduced to the reading public.

But diligently as Simms worked to secure and encourage contributors, the burden of filling the *Southern and Western*'s seventy-odd pages each month still rested heavily on his own shoulders. It is doubtful if any other editor of importance wrote so voluminously for his own magazine as did Simms. If one compares him as editor of the *Southern and Western* with Poe as editor of *Graham's* or even Lowell as editor of the ill-fated *Pioneer*, one finds that whereas Simms was writing some forty pages for each issue, Poe and Lowell were printing only three or four choice selections. The difference, of course, was that both Poe and Lowell, with money to back them,[54] were able to secure as contributors some of America's best-known writers. Simms, on the other hand, could afford to pay his best contributors only a nominal sum and thus could induce major authors to write for his journal only as a gesture of friendship. One wonders how successful Simms, with his wide connections and his capacity for hard work, would have been if he had had the opportunity to edit a magazine with sound financial backing and a large circulation. Despite his assertion that "My magazine does not employ much of my time," the *Southern and Western* was sapping valuable creative energy; disappointed in his political hopes, worried about the health of his family,[55] and vexed with editorial labors, he must have desired the peace of mind and the leisure advocated by Hammond for the composition of a great work.

Nevertheless, depressed as Simms was, the *Southern and Western* continued to win critical plaudits. For instance, the *New York Morning News* of August 23, 1845, had the following to say of the August number:

> The criticism of this magazine is always elaborately executed with thought and suggestion. The industry of the editor is sustained by his philosophic habits of

> mind and liberal studies. In tone and character this Southern monthly is far in advance of the popular periodical literature of the day.

And a few days later the *Broadway Journal,* then edited by Poe, likewise termed the August number of the magazine "capital" and remarked that "it contains several of the finest kind of Magazine papers, and is as ably edited as any journal of its species in America—if not more ably edited than any" (II [August 30, 1845], 121).

Perhaps it was while associating with publishers and literary men in New York during the late summer and early fall of 1845[56] that Simms definitely decided to give up the editorial chair. This decision probably was influenced by a desire to spend more time writing books and less writing articles. He must have realized that if he were to receive pay for what he wrote, he would have to relinquish his Southern editorship and send his work to Northern publishers and editors.[57] Certainly Simms returned home from the North with his head full of publishing ventures; his letters reveal that during the last two and one-half months of 1845 he was to work in one way or another on six separate manuscripts to be published in book form. On October 28, less than three weeks after his return to South Carolina, Simms broke the news to Duyckinck that he was "withdraw[ing] from the Editorial Chair" of the *Southern and Western* and that the magazine (to be consolidated with the *Southern Literary Messenger*) would be published "hereafter simultaneously in Richmond & Charleston." Simms added that he had consented "to edit the work here till the close of the year" because so doing enabled him still "to give to Southern opinion that tone & character which it is so desirable for the independence of the intellectual character of the country that it should possess" (*L*, II, 110).[58]

In "A Word from the Chair" in the November issue of the *Southern and Western* (II, 343), Simms—before announcing his resignation as editor—painted a realistic picture of the mental and physical drudgery with which the magazine had afflicted him. He began by thanking his contributors for "so much literary material from other than our own" that had enabled him to enjoy a "two months vacation": "The numbers of our journal for September, October and the present month, owe little or nothing to our industry beyond ... the Editorial Bureau.[59] We have thus been enabled ... to snatch a brief respite from the daily drudgery of making provision for the month. ..." He then reiterated what he had often said before—that the South, as an agricultural section without intellectual stimulus, had fallen into a mental lethargy from which it needed to be rudely awakened. This awakening could come about only when the South learned to honor and to believe in its own men of genius: "They have the creative and endowing resources—the various powers of the imagination—in singularly high degree. … We have but to insist upon their exercise … we have been sending forth prophets daily into other lands, without having learned to honor them at home" (*SWMMR,* II, 343–44).

As if to drive home the point that the South failed to appreciate or encourage the efforts of its literary men, Simms next announced his withdrawal as editor with the December number. The *Southern and Western,* he explained, "has not answered our expectations," takes time away from "independent individual labors," and compensates "neither in money nor other reward." Probably "the last time" he would ever commit himself to provoking the South "into intellectual and literary exertions of her own," Simms proclaimed that "[t]o this endeavor" he nonetheless had "brought zeal and industry, if nothing more" (*SWMMR,* II, 344–45). He concluded with a long appeal to the people of his section, deploring the public inertia that made the conduct of a Southern magazine the most hopeless of tasks and at the same time emphasizing the importance and value of those magazines to an agricultural community. "Who will succeed us in our editorial seat" or "whether the publishers will continue to publish is unknown," Simms wrote, "and this is the greater misfortune." South Carolina alone, he stressed, should provide the three thousand subscribers needed "amply [to] sustain a Magazine and compensate the publishers" in "a sparsely settled country" in which the "monthly periodical would seem almost the only form of publication, which could, by any possibility, reach the homes and improve the hearts of our people" (*SWMMR,* II, 345–46).

Thus disillusioned but still determined, Simms closed another chapter in his editorial career.[60] Probably he was convinced that this was to be the final chapter, that he would never again occupy an editorial chair: but so he had thought before and yet on each occasion had been induced to make one more effort to fulfill his ambition as editor—the establishment of a first-class Southern literary journal that would help to encourage and to develop the literature of his section and his country. And once again—only four years later—Simms was to make yet another attempt. As editor of the *Southern Quarterly Review,* Simms was to work faithfully and zealously for the Southern cause, especially in politics, but after five years of toil he once more gave up in despair, again defeated in his primary objective.

In 1849 with his acceptance of the editorship of the *Southern Quarterly,* Simms admitted to his old friend, James Hammond: "I am conscious of many deficiencies as an Editor, and were I as scrupulous a person as yourself, with such impossible standards, I should have nothing to do with it. I am not a thoroughbred scholar. …" (*L*, II, 488). Despite these misgivings about his qualifications as an editor, Simms had already done more in the behalf of Southern letters than had any other editor of the Old South. Certainly he had fulfilled one ambition: by "giving a certain impetus to the thought and the will of the *genus* [*sic*] *loci*," he had achieved "a some thing" which in the future "shall be not wholly unlike fame!" (*SWMMR*, I [May 1845], 364).

Long before accepting its editorship in April 1849, Simms had been closely connected with the *Southern Quarterly Review*, established in New Orleans in 1842 by D. K. Whitaker and moved to Charleston the following year. In 1843, well before his tenure as editor of the *Southern and Western*, Simms had been approached by Whitaker, as revealed in a statement by the novelist in September of that year: "I am offered the charge of [the *Southern Quarterly Review*] for the ensuing year, and though I have not yet acceded to the offer, & am not likely to do so, I have yet *carte blanche*, and will probably contribute one or more articles to each of its numbers" (*L*, I, 369–70). By October 1843 Simms had consented "to lend all the assistance I can" to the Charleston quarterly (*L*, I, 370).

One of the reasons Simms was not eager to take full responsibility for the *Southern Quarterly* was his skepticism about Whitaker, whom he described in 1843 as "a dull man and frequently blunders" (*L*, I, 385).[61] But since Whitaker had "the sense to submit to counsel … in securing some good contributors" (*L*, I, 385), Simms apparently was willing to make an agreement to contribute regularly to the *Quarterly*. A. B. Meek, the literary-minded Alabama lawyer and judge who was always quick to encourage Simms's support of Southern magazines, rejoiced to learn of Simms's connection with the quarterly: "I am truly glad to hear that you have become connected with the So. Review. The work wants such aid, & we want such a work" (*L*, I, 370n).

As always, after committing himself to a task, Simms addressed it with vigor. One of his virtues as an editor was his willingness to seek important contributors, and he wasted no time in asking his literary and political friends to help the *Southern Quarterly Review* in any way possible. Simms realized that Southerners sometimes looked for praise from Northerners as Americans in general looked to British praise; thus in his letter of October 31, 1843, to Lawson, he asked the New Yorker's aid in persuading Bryant to "say something kindly of it [the *Southern Quarterly*] in the Post" (*L*, I, 383). Not yet content, on the following day Simms addressed the appeal directly to Bryant: "If you can say anything conscientiously (as I trust you can) in favor of the work, you will oblige me by doing so" (*L*, I, 385). In his reply—not written until February 9, 1844—Bryant explained that the *Southern Quarterly Review* was almost impossible to procure in New York. "I shall look out for it hereafter,"

Bryant wrote, "and get hold of it whenever I can, but it is astonishing how torpid the agents for it are here at the north" (*L*, I, 384n). Even the better Southern magazines, it seems, were little known, and even less available, to Northern readers.

Yet before he received Bryant's discouraging message, Simms's enthusiasm for the *Southern Quarterly* had cooled, probably because of a clash with Whitaker, and the prolific Charlestonian had pledged his support to another Southern magazine, the *Southern Literary Messenger*, whose editor, Benjamin B. Minor, he found more to his liking. "I care not what Southern Journal succeeds," he explained to George Frederick Holmes, "so that it deserves to do so" (January 26, 1844; *L*, I, 400). Although Simms was never able to come to an agreement with Whitaker and apparently fulfilled his commitments to the *Quarterly* only through a sense of duty, that magazine nevertheless continued to try to obtain his services. Sometime in April 1844 he received a proposal from Silas Howe, general agent for the *Southern Quarterly Review*, to edit the July number, but there is no indication that he accepted.[62]

Simms may well have concluded that a quarterly was not the best way to promote a Southern literature.[63] He was in any case more interested in creative writing than in reviews of books published chiefly in England or in the North. Probably the fact that he was considering founding another monthly magazine of his own partly accounts for his coolness toward the *Southern Quarterly*. In January 1844 he had written George Frederick Holmes, "... if I am to write for nothing I should [at] least exercise this benevolent disposition in reference to my own kindred; and ... my essays would cost me no more in a new Magnolia than in the Quarterly" (*L*, I, 400).[64] But Simms continued a tenuous relationship with the *Quarterly* throughout the remainder of the 1840s, writing occasionally for it, but more frequently voicing vexation with Whitaker, as in his letter of November 13, 1845, to E. A. Duyckinck: "As for the Southern Quarterly, I am thinking to curse & quit. The Editor is disposed to cheat me out of my wage" (*L*, II, 119). When Whitaker resigned in February 1847 to be replaced by J. Milton Clapp, Simms temporarily rejoiced. "The *South. Quarterly Review* has just fallen into tolerably good hands,—nay, as the times go, into very good hands," he wrote to Duyckinck on February 25, "Its present editor is Mr. J. M. Clapp, late Editor of the Charleston Mercury. ... I shall probably write frequently for it myself. ..." (*L*, II, 271–72). He attempted to interest Duyckinck in contributing to the *Quarterly* in July 1847 ("The compensation is $1.00 a page. The publishers are sound but costive, sound perhaps, because they are costive" [*L*, II, 336]); and by November 1848 he was considering becoming the editor of the review[65] which for five years he had considered outmoded. By the following February, he announced in a letter to Lawson that "I have just accepted the Editorship of the Southern Review under circumstances of particular compliment" (*L*, II, 475). Exactly what the "circumstances of particular compliment" were to induce Simms to take up the editorial *fauteuil* again with the April 1849 issue can only be surmised, but the newly appointed editor confessed to James H. Hammond with the candor that marked their relationship: "I am not sure that I *considered* the question of Editorship with a due regard to the *pros and cons;* but I have made it a rule in life never to reject *certain* employment, when it promises compensation and is congenial to my tastes & habits" (*L*, II, 487–88).

Simms's editorship of the *Southern Quarterly Review* was marked by a curious blend of cynicism and idealism. On March 15, 1849, he confessed in a letter to George Frederick Holmes that "the Review has been so shockingly mismanaged that all I can hope to do at present is to keep it alive. … It owes me probably quite as much money as it owes you; and my fear is that the debt is a hopeless one. … And this is my experience of almost every Mag. & Review in the United States!" (*L*, II, 494). Nevertheless, Simms urged Holmes to continue writing for the *Southern Quarterly* despite its nonpayment for past contributions. Simms advised his friend not to "let your anger for the past prevent your accumulations for the future." He promised that "while I am Editor," no article submitted by Holmes would be published "until the money was payed for it." This combination of skepticism and persuasiveness by the newly appointed editor enabled the quarterly to retain the best of its old contributors and indeed to attract important new ones. On April 27, 1849, Simms wrote to B. F. Perry that "[w]e … have already secured such an array of good Southern Contributors & able men—real thinkers & good writers—that it will discredit no man to work for the journal" (*L*, II, 507).

Simms's plan in 1849 was to stress the political importance of the *Southern Quarterly Review* to the South as a whole. Though he privately expressed reservations about the nonliterary, untimely nature of the review, in mid-March 1849 he wrote convincingly to one of his new contributors, Nathaniel Beverley Tucker, about the *Southern Quarterly*'s raison d'être: "As an organ of opinion and education at home, and for all the Southern States … the Southern Quarterly is one of those agencies in a wholesome and necessary work, which those who entertain its objects, should not suffer to perish or to lose its influence" (*L*, II, 496).[66] Simms's motivations as editor of the *Southern Quarterly Review* were nearly identical, then, to those that made politics and public service almost irresistible to him. More than his editorship of any other journal, his tenure at the helm of the *Southern Quarterly* drew him away from the literary into the political, with aims almost inseparable from those which made him ambitious for public office. Whereas his previous editorships, particularly those of the *Magnolia* and the *Southern and Western,* had been largely geared toward encouragement of American and Southern literature, this editorship was designed primarily to advance Southern political thought.

In emphasizing the *Southern* and the *political* direction of the *Quarterly,* Simms recognized the importance of establishing a high intellectual tone for the magazine through the careful selection of contributors who were by his standards "real thinkers & good writers." It is much to his credit that he maintained a commitment to creative literature even as he effectively battled for political causes he deeply believed in. Rather than compromise his standards as editor, Simms the writer would frequently overtax his own talents and energies to keep his journal filled[67]—a sacrificial practice he followed throughout his editorial career. But the *Southern Quarterly Review* profited from his editorship and, indeed, was unrivaled as the most influential magazine in the South, reaching at its apex a subscription list of more than two thousand. This success is even more remarkable in light of the fact that during his five years as its editor, Simms worked harder than ever before at other tasks—including the political maneuvering already elaborated upon, the management of escalating agricultural and financial responsibilities at Woodlands (to be discussed in chapter 9), and the composition of a steady stream of literary manuscripts (to be discussed in chapter 8).

However, Simms was never without reservations about both the nature and the format of the *Southern Quarterly Review.* In a letter of April 5, 1849, to N. B. Tucker he lamented the "vulgar notion that reviews are merely grave & learned things." "To be witty or playful," he continued, "or to employ other forms of Art than … the grave essay upon a printed book" was considered "exceedingly undignified." Simms confided to Tucker his desire "to go aside from the beaten track at times," to "put forth a story [rather] than a critique" (*L,* II, 499–500)—but in actuality as editor he seldom deviated from the traditional format. In another letter to Tucker, Simms wished that the *SQR* were "like Blackwood a monthly instead of a Quarterly Journal" because of the monthly's "greater susceptibili[ti]es, and more frequent utterance," but he quickly explained that "[t]his matter has been already under discussion" and that the "proprietors prefer the Quarterly form" (*L,* II, 506). Simms's preference for a timely literary journal over a largely political quarterly review is attested to by his having established four of the former and none of the latter. In the light of Simms's acquiescence to the conditions of the *Southern Quarterly Review* in becoming its editor, his comments to Tucker might have been self-serving diplomatic blandishments to a desirable contributor rather than legitimate criticisms.

With or without reservations by its editor, the *Southern Quarterly* met with both the acclaim he had hoped for and the financial difficulty he had feared. Few people in America understood the magazine business better than William Gilmore Simms, and his letter of May 8, 1849, to Lewis Reeve Gibbes is particularly illuminating:

> I fully concur [Simms wrote] with you that periodical Literature, to be valuable, must be paid for, & as soon as the South. Quarterly is able to pay, I shall insist (if its conduct remains with me) upon giving ample remuneration for every published article. Even now, the Publishers authorize me to say that they ... will pay at the rate of $1. per printed page. This is a sorry trifle, it is true; but it is the same which is paid by the North American, and much more than *is paid* by 7 in 8 of the periodicals of the country. Few of them pay any thing, unless the Lady's magazines. ... But most of them deal only in promises. I have lost $5,000 by them, and know them all—In taking charge of the South. Rev. I am doing so at loss—with the probability of losing all my labor. But it is the only organ of letters in the South, & I am willing to incur the ... risks. ... (*L*, II, 514–15)

Because of his knowledge and experience, as well as his wide reputation, Simms was given latitude as editor of the *Southern Quarterly* that his Charleston publisher, James S. Burges,[68] would have granted no one else. Thus, with competitive prices promised by his publisher and with much good will stored to his own credit, Simms succeeded in gathering "a steady and sterling corps of contributors" (*L*, II, 541) who appealed to the *Quarterly*'s targeted audience, Southern intellectuals who in Simms's words "read too little" (*L*, II, 525).

Despite the fact that his publishers sometimes reneged on their promised compensation, Simms justifiably boasted that "I have brought into the field many whom it will not discredit our best writers to commune with," and quietly asserted that with "good pecuniary footing ... I should be able to make it whatever we desire" (*L*, II, 538). Simms as editor also had the unpleasant responsibility of explaining to contributors proprietorial shortcomings other than financial; it must have been particularly irksome to him to write to Beverley Tucker the following: "I am exceedingly mortified to see the Errata you furnish. ... the Review has been badly managed & ... we are now by degrees endeavoring to correct past mistakes." Burges's "feeble health," the editor expounded, "make[s] him almost incapable of those tasks which belong properly to him"—in this instance proofreading. "My own eyes have made me reluctant to undertake this duty," Simms apologized; but "It will be my care to do something toward ensuring you a correct press hereafter" (*L*, II, 539). Though Simms belittled his editorial capacities to his close friends,[69] who questioned his wisdom in committing himself to such unprofitable drudgery,[70] the truth is that he had few peers among nineteenth-century American editors.

But fortunately for his ambitions as a creative writer (if not for his pocketbook), Simms's tenure as editor of the *Southern Quarterly* was destined to end after five years of frustration and accomplishment because of the magazine's proprietors' inability (or unwillingness) to meet his financial demands—or even to pay his agreed-upon salary. As early as September 5, 1849, Simms had admitted to his confidant, Hammond, increasing annoyance with the menial everyday tasks in keeping the *Southern Quarterly* going: "Its correspondence has become a sufficient duty, by itself, for an ordinary man, and the accumulation of letters ... keeps me scrawling & scribbling through the day, in vain seeking to lessen the pile before me" (*L*, II, 547). The following January Simms wrote to his old New York friend, James Lawson, that the *Quarterly*'s "publisher is greatly in arrears to me" (*L*, III, 5); and his correspondence during the early 1850s is filled with references to the poor financial and managerial conditions slowly submerging the substantive worth of the *Southern Quarterly Review.* Upon the death of Burges—insolvent and owing Simms "8 or 900 dollars" (*L*, III, 31)—the new publishers, Walker and Richards, promised immediate improvements,[71] few of which materialized.

Simms's vast knowledge of the mechanics as well as the principles of magazine publishing is revealed in his letters, one of the most noteworthy of which reads in part:

> It is a mistake to suppose that more than one in a dozen of the periodicals of the country pay their contributors. Few of them pay but the Editors of the Ladies Magazines, and these pay for Tales & Sketches,—seldom for Criticism. The North American pays a dollar a page, to *one or two contributors only;* the rest are amateurs. The S. Lit. Messenger, Knickerbocker, Whig Magazine, Literary World, none of these pay, except very occasionally & then only to a single favourite contributor whom they make drudge for it. The South. Review does precisely what is done by all. In isolated cases & under peculiar circumstances, a single contributor gets a draft for 20 or 30 dollars & this never exceeds one to a number. In fact, so wretched is the patronage, so slow do our planters pay up their bills, so reluctantly—so apt are they to withdraw when dunned,—that the Publishers can do no better. If they pay expenses, under

> the most narrow economy, they do all that can be done. I should be glad to pay for every thing that we publish, and to publish nothing but what we pay for, but the desire is idle. I am compelled to use all my economy, not to outrage them. … (*L*, III, 113–14)

A hastily scribbled note to John Pendleton Kennedy in 1851 suggests Simms's increasing intolerance: "The business of the Review, as incessant as that of a Grist Mill, keeps me costive, and almost churlish …" (*L*, III, 122); but even deeper disillusionment is revealed in his reference to the "vain & fruitless" labors "in trying to build up a literature or even a periodical in the South": "I am sick of the labor—drawing water in a sieve …" (*L*, III, 131), and in his statement of May 1853 to James Lawson: "I need not say how little time is left me for thinking and living. I do not live. I grub, and grub is my portion—my reward" (*L*, III, 232). The final breaking point came in mid-July 1853 when Simms, according to his letter to G. F. Holmes, gave notice to his publishers (now Walker and Burke) that "with this year my Editorship terminates unless I am regularly paid, though it be at the pittance of $1,000 only which they have hitherto professed their willingness to allow" (III, 245). Partly, perhaps, because Simms at least temporarily contemplated assuming the editorship of the *Charleston Evening News,* in partnership with Richard Yeadon, at an optimum income of "$5,000 per annum,"[72] he later increased his salary demands to the *Southern Quarterly:* "I have communicated to the publishers my resolve to do no more unless I am paid $1,500 per ann. & punctually" (*L*, III, 255).

At this time Simms received strong editorial support from both the *Charleston Courier* and the *Charleston Mercury* and encouragement from Hammond in a personal note. Hammond wrote him that the owners of the *Review* "must comply with your terms or give it up" because "[n]o one else can keep it on its legs at all for a single year." In Hammond's pungent words, the *Southern Quarterly* "is now certainly the best in America & not much if at all inferior to any in England, & if the damned Southern people will not sustain it they deserve to lose it & go to the devil as they are going at rail road speed any how" (*L*, III, 255n). Earlier, on July 13, the *Courier* had praised "the versatile and accomplished Simms" in a long-winded commendation of the *Southern Quarterly Review.* On July 22 the *Mercury,* after reporting his tendered resignation, spoke tellingly in behalf of Simms, who "has always been inadequately repaid for his editorial, to speak of no other public services to the South—and, during his conduct of the Review, there have been entire years in which he has received little or no compensation. …" The *Mercury* further reported that, under the circumstances, "it is a great injustice to expect him to continue labors, which are so entirely of a public nature, and undertaken in behalf of the community, at his own expense."

With the purchase of the *Southern Quarterly Review* in November 1853 by Charles Mortimer, a Virginian whom Simms described as "pushing & stedfast" (*L*, III, 273), the embattled editor seemed closer to having his salary ultimatum answered favorably, but such was not to be. Exactly what occurred between publisher and editor is unknown, but on May 5, 1854, Simms wrote to E. A. Duyckinck that he was "preparing to abandon" the *Southern Quarterly*, whose "new publisher" was "stupidly pragmatical and meddlesome" and "impossible to get on with" (*L*, III, 298). A week later Simms announced in a letter to B. F. Perry: "I withdraw from the Editorship with the publication of the July issue, being literally pushed out of the chair, when it promises to be profitable. The new publisher claims to reject and to publish what articles he thinks proper without regard to me, and on such terms I am forced to abandon" (*L*, III, 299). Though Simms was persuaded to edit the October 1854 number and did not unequivocally end his relationship with the *Southern Quarterly Review* and Mortimer until December 1854 (when Mortimer announced the journal's removal from Charleston to Baltimore), by the beginning of 1855 Simms had finally freed himself from the debilitating drain of "drawing water in a sieve" as editor of a doomed magazine. As he was wont to do, he had invested invaluable time and energy in a largely political, nonliterary project for the good of the Southern cause, but of insignificant benefit to his personal ambition for eminence as a writer. Praise he received, but, oh, how ephemeral! Witness the "obituary" for the *Southern Quarterly Review* published in the *Charleston Mercury* of January 31, 1855:

> Mr. Simms, the accomplished Editor, whose signal efforts to sustain the work, had won for him the highest approbation of the public, has been compelled to abandon his labors under circumstances, discreditable to the judgment and good sense of the proprietor. ... The Southern Review is dead. The periodical that now goes on under its name is a nondescript work, which we regard with distrust. ...

The most serious question raised by Simms's futile efforts in politics and in magazine editing is, why? Why would a man of good sense, good name, enormous talent, and growing reputation seemingly fritter away precious creative energy on projects which even if successful would lead him not to the mountaintop but only to the foothills? What had happened to his vision, his world view, his burning ambition to achieve the "Rome [that] lay beyond ... attainable, yet unattained"?[73] He was not afraid of hard work, difficult decisions, or physical pain: but did he possess the self-discipline to resist the temptations of public life and concentrate upon the primary goal of his life? He was a versatile man to whom most verbal accomplishments came easily; but was Simms the writer *consumed* with ambition to be the best, as he had claimed as a young man?

# VIII Nonetheless the Author

The challenge was issued to William Gilmore Simms numerous times during the two decades that James Henry Hammond served as his closest confidant. "[U]ntil you [have] accomplished the Great Work I have so often proposed to you," Hammond (in a characteristic letter of August 2, 1852) urged his literary friend to block everything else "out of your sight entirely." "My dear Simms," he continued, "this is *the* work to be done & you are *the* Man to do it. It will require, with even your facility for acquiring & re-producing five years of exclusive devotion. Can't it be managed to secure to you & for the world that much of your time? Do think of it seriously" (*L*, III, 194n). On this occasion Simms responded to Hammond's exhortation as he was wont to do: first he thanked the fellow South Carolinian for "affectionate solicitude in my interest & my fame"; then he asserted "the necessity of toiling on, as I do now" simply as "the means of staving off necessities" (*L*, III, 193–94). Though his marriage to Chevillette Roach had made Simms wealthy in land and property, he incurred "large pecuniary obligations" in maintaining "myself & family in the degree of comfort which they at present enjoy & to which they are accustomed" (*L*, III, 194). Pride in station and responsibility to family both weighed heavily upon Simms: he could not accept the one without the other. To live the good life at Woodlands, to uphold the aristocratic family tradition of genteel hospitality—nay, even to supply the creature comforts—cost more than the plantation provided.

Because the political sinecure Simms avidly sought always eluded him, his most accessible means of supplementing his income was editing magazines or delivering public lectures, activities respectable in themselves through which he could also support causes he deeply believed in. He could work long and he could work hard; and he could complain bitterly about his "drudgeries" and his lack of appreciation by the public; but what he could never do was knowingly shirk responsibility—personal or professional. In a hectic, harried life, he somehow found time for his family—to be a good provider, father, and husband;[1] what is truly remarkable, however, is that amidst almost continual distraction, he nonetheless managed to find time for his lifelong love, the craft of writing.

In the eighteen years between 1842 and 1860—a period during which he experienced anything but the "years of exclusive devotion" advocated by Hammond—Simms still produced no fewer than forty-two books, fourteen of them major works of fiction. He accomplished this feat not because he focused upon a "Great Work," but because he had the perseverance to continue to write seriously even as he seemingly engaged in activities counterproductive to literary eminence. Simms earnestly believed in his ability to work on many projects simultaneously, and during this time span he substantiated his theory through an extraordinary record of sustained creative energy. Simms himself never articulated the philosophical basis for his belief that his mind was sharpened, not dulled—refreshed, not fatigued—by constant exercise in diverse mental activities. But sixty years after Simms's death, it is interesting to note, Winston Churchill did express in clear terms a philosophy of intellectual self-renewal which suggests that the creative work patterns of the nineteenth-century American novelist and the twentieth-century British statesman were roughly the same:

> Change is the master key. A man can wear out a particular part of his mind by continually using it and tiring it, just in the same way he can wear out the elbows of his coat. There is, however, this difference between the living cells of the brain and inanimate articles: one cannot mend the frayed elbows of a coat by rubbing the sleeves or the shoulders; but the tired parts of the mind can be rested and strengthened, not merely by rest, but by using other parts.[2]

Churchill's observation illuminates the principle of restorative creativity that enabled Simms to rotate such diverse activities as political planning and enterprise, journalistic editing and management, and historical and belletristic writing without appreciable loss of intellectual energy or commitment. Indeed, these cerebral interchanges might even have functioned as a stimulus to his creative process. Churchill's statement helps to explain how Simms—after enduring decades of seemingly debilitating mental drudgery—could still possess the creative spark to produce in the last years of his life perhaps his most imaginative works of fiction. It also explains why Hammond's well-intentioned, apparently sound advice to Simms—that the author devote five years exclusively to his "Great Work"—might not have been valid in Simms's case. Churchill's theory that the mind can be refreshed and strengthened "not merely by rest but by using other parts" suggests why it is inappropriate to measure Simms's commitment to literary accomplishment by the exclusivity of his devotion to belles-lettres.

Yet it is true that after the publication of three major novels in a fifteen-month period in 1840–41, Simms did not immediately display another burst of creative power. Early in 1842, however, he did complete a project upon which he had done substantial work (and had expected to complete) in 1841:[3] *Beauchampe: or the Kentucky Tragedy. A Tale of Passion,* published in two volumes in Philadelphia by Lea & Blanchard. Simms took the idea for *Beauchampe* from an actual murder case in Kentucky in the 1820s—one which had attracted wide notoriety and had stirred the literary imagination of Poe, Thomas Holley Chivers, and Charles Fenno Hoffman as well as that of Simms.[4] The historical data for the revenge slaying of Warham Sharpe, seducer and betrayer of Margaret Cooper, by her strong-minded young husband, Beauchampe, provided Simms a ready-made "dyed in blood" plot apparently perfectly tailored for his bold-spirited Border Romance series. As was his custom in the series, Simms decided to publish anonymously (i.e., "by the author of 'Richard Hurdis,' 'Border Beagles,' etc."), presumably for the "particular purpose" (he explained to B. F. Perry) of "the bedevilment of the small tribe of underling critics, who are sagacious enough to detect a man's style in his sneeze, and his talent in a whisper" (*L*, I, 316). Despite Simms's contention to the contrary, the ruse misled few, if any, reviewers, who for the most part were thoroughly informed concerning the authorship of *Richard Hurdis* and *Border Beagles.* Perhaps the factual basis for Simms's fictional portrayal of immorality and savagery on the Southwestern frontier stifled his imagination, as was claimed by Poe (see below); but Simms's inability to imbue the sensational "true" story with a sense of realism is puzzling after his relative success with similar material in the earlier Border Romances. The strength of Simms's Kentucky Tragedy—particularly in its final revised and expanded form[5]—lies in the multidimensional portrayal of the self-centered village beauty, Margaret Cooper, who stands out as one of his most believable heroines. Margaret Cooper is a complex and compelling being: memorable not only for the warmth of her passion but for the coolness of her manipulative skill in denying Beauchampe until after he had vowed to fulfill her obsessive desire for vengeance against her past seducer.

Probably the most significant contemporary review of *Beauchampe* was written by Poe, already familiar with the Kentucky Tragedy through his own abortive use of it in *Politan.* In the May 1842 number of *Graham's Magazine* Poe said of Simms's new novel:

> The events upon which this novel is based are but too real. No more thrilling, no more romantic tragedy did ever the brain of poet conceive than was the tragedy of Sharpe and Beauchampe. We are not sure that the author of "Border-Beagles" has done right in the selection of his theme. Too little has been left for invention. We are sure, however, that the theme is skilfully handled. The author of 'Richard Hurdis' is one among the best of our native novelists—pure, bold, vigorous, original. (XX, 300)

Among other reviews of *Beauchampe* (and they were relatively few in number),[6] perhaps the only one worthy of consideration appeared in the *Greenville Mountaineer* for May 27, 1842, apparently the work of Benjamin F. Perry. It reads in part:

> … the well-known and popular author of 'Richard Hurdis' has put forth a Novel of surpassing and wonderful ability. … The reality of the story would seem to surpass the fiction of the novelist. But it has been handled with a master hand. … This story will rank with any of Bulwers, and is destined to be regarded as the very first of American novels. There is in it a power, a depth of thought, a delineation of character and a thrilling interest, which are rarely equalled and never surpassed. (*L*, I, 315n)

Simms was appreciative of these strong words of praise; "… I sincerely thank you for the compliments," he acknowledged in his letter of July 14, 1842, to Perry, which has particular significance because it contains an insightful passage concerning the author's "*stans pede in uno*" habits of composition (see below).

After the publication of *Beauchampe,* Simms busied himself for several years with editing and politicking and relatively small literary projects, producing in 1843 only *The Social Principle: The True Source of National Prominence: An Oration* (first delivered at the University of Alabama in Tuscaloosa on December 13, 1842, when he was awarded an LL.D. degree); *The Geography of South Carolina* (a companion piece to his earlier *The History of South Carolina*); and *Donna Florida: A Tale,* a slim volume of poetry imitative of Byron.[7] These books elicited little interest and cost their author little labor, being at best occasional pieces or resurrections of earlier efforts. Simms published no fiction during the year, but there is evidence that he was breaking ground and laying the foundation for several major works: during a twelve-month period beginning in November 1844, he brought out in book form two important novelettes, *Castle Dismal* and *Helen Halsey,* and his best collection of short stories, *The Wigwam and the Cabin.* Before assessing the significance of these works, however, perhaps one should attempt to clear up a possible misunderstanding.

A question frequently raised is why did Simms—for a nine-year period following *Beauchampe*—produce no major full-length novels? Why, in his only long novel between *Beauchampe* and *Katharine Walton* (1851), did he turn away from his forte—America's struggle for self-identity—to write again on a foreign topic?[8] Why, when he did choose to cover familiar American themes, did he select to write novelettes, short stories, essays, biographies, and poems rather than continue the trend toward success-tested two-volume novels? Despite this apparent error in literary judgment, Simms's imagination did not lie dormant during this period, for he produced in it some of the best writing of his career, albeit none of it in the field of the full-length novel. In short, he did not cease being highly productive, he did not desert familiar American themes, and his concentration on genres other than the novel probably represents his recognition of major changes in American publishing practices rather than a conscious decision to forsake the form through which his reputation had been achieved.

The Panic of 1837, with which a gradual collapse of the national economy began, had devastated the book market by 1843, particularly the sale of the once fashionable, yet costly, two-volume novel. Taking advantage of the absence of an international copyright, the advent of new and rapid printing techniques, and the availability of inexpensively manufactured paper, American publishers for their very survival resorted to "cheap books," paperbound reprints of popular British authors sold at ridiculously low prices, sometimes as low as six cents each. Simms was among the first of American writers to acknowledge the reality of the situation, as a letter of 1841 (partially quoted in chapter 7) reveals:

> Do not ... suppose that it is easy to get ... a work published or that ... writings are now profitable. ... There are very few American writers who ever get anything. [Joseph Holt] Ingraham could scarcely at this time get a novel published at all—certainly he could hope to get nothing for it. The publishers are very costive—the sales are terribly diminished within the last few years. You will perceive that Irving now writes almost wholly for magazines and Cooper & myself are almost the only persons whose novels are printed—certainly, we are almost the only persons who hope to get anything for them. From England we get nothing. In this country an Edition now instead of 4 or 5,000 copies, is scarce 2,000. (*L,* I, 271)

Simms's early and accurate perception of what was happening in the publishing industry almost inevitably influenced his choice of genre during the middle and late 1840s, though it did not affect his long-range commitment to writing novels on American historical themes.

Certainly with the exception of *Count Julian* and his ill-advised (yet often reprinted) biography of Francis Marion,[9] there was no falloff in the quality of his published works beginning in 1844. He first focused upon "Castle Dismal," one of several excellent stories of his to appear in the *Magnolia* in 1842, deciding in late 1843 to make it "a small vol. of 150 pages or thereabout" (*L*, I, 369). *Castle Dismal: or, The Bachelor's Christmas* (New York: Burgess, Stringer, 1844), which won the immediate admiration of no less acute a critic than Poe,[10] showed Simms in a vein in which he at times excelled—the supernatural story of manners. Even more laudatory than Poe's was the review written by Evert A. Duyckinck for the *New York Morning News* of November 9, 1844:

> If it be any merit in a ghost-story to arrest the reader's attention at the first moment of perusal, and hold it fixed page after page, chapter after chapter, through one hour, two hours to the fitting time of midnight till candle and story go out together, then is Castle Dismal one of the best ghost stories we ever read. The story is well told by Mr. Simms, an adept in this species of narrative. We question whether there is anywhere a better manager in the construction of a tale, who can take such simple unexaggerated material and make so much of it. ... Simms still relies upon character and passion and literally takes the reader by storm by the downright force and reality of his action.

Despite its praise by contemporaries like Poe and Duyckinck, *Castle Dismal*, like much of Simms's best work, has been neglected by present-day scholars and critics. It deserves a better fate: in establishing atmosphere, tone, and mood it is superb; setting and characterization deftly contribute to "the willing suspension of disbelief" essential in protraying the supernatural. As late as 1863 Simms listed *Castle Dismal* as one of his favorite works, one of those he sought to have republished.[11]

The publication of *Castle Dismal* was closely followed by that of another Simms novelette, *Helen Halsey: or, The Swamp State of Conelachita. A Tale of the Borders*, also issued in New York by Burgess, Stringer. Simms first mentioned "Ellen Halsey, or my Wife against my Will" in a June 12, 1843, letter to James Lawson; at that time the author was proposing it to Harper & Brothers as part of "a collection of Tales of the South" (*L*, I, 353–54). By the end of September Simms informed Lawson that the "nearly ready" manuscript of "'Helen Halsey ...' a Border Story—a tale of Mississippi" should best be considered a separate publication, a companion piece to *Castle Dismal* (*L*, I, 369). With his friend Lawson as his New York agent, Simms attempted to play one publisher against another, Benjamin against Harper (see *L*, I, 381, 390), an unsuccessful manipulation which led to Lawson's offering *Helen Halsey* (as well as *Castle Dismal*) to Burgess, Stringer,[12] the eventual publisher. But the new "Border Story" did not appear until January 1845, two months after *Castle Dismal.* Simms was annoyed that Stringer had not published *Helen Halsey* earlier—before *Castle Dismal*—for upon the latter's publication, he wrote Lawson: "I am sorry that Burgess & Stringer put forth this story first, for I think 'Helen Halsey' much the best, and they promised otherwise" (*L,* I, 436).

Perhaps because of the timing—that is, one book almost immediately following another, both by the same author and publisher—*Helen Halsey* was not reviewed so widely or so favorably as was *Castle Dismal.* A brief notice of "this most attractive and thrilling romance by our talented townsman" appeared in the *Charleston Southern Patriot* of January 2, 1845; and, before its date of publication, Duyckinck anticipated *Helen Halsey*'s arrival by recapitulating its plot for the benefit of future readers (*New York Morning News,* November 29, 1844). Despite the fact that no major journal, Northern or Southern, singled out *Helen Halsey* for critique,[13] Simms reported to E. A. Duyckinck that "Here, in Carolina" the book had "sold well" and that "here the favorable opinions of many of our best men console me" (*L,* II, 20). Simms always had a special fondness for *Helen Halsey;* in late June 1844 he had written Lawson that his new "Border Story" "is very superior" to *Count Julian* (a comparison not necessarily indicative of high praise), and added: "Indeed, as a rapid and truthful domestic story I think it one of my most successful performances. Besides, its style is, I am disposed to believe, particularly good" (*L,* I, 420).

*Helen Halsey,* it is interesting to note, follows a trend in Simms's Border Romances to highlight marital conflict as well as physical violence in frontier life. Like *Beauchampe* and *Confession* immediately before it in the series, *Helen Halsey* is a "tale of passion" in which the heroine is exploited and victimized in a domestic situation from which there is no escape. The teen-aged daughter of a well-meaning but weak father who collaborates in crime with the outlaw gang ruled by his vicious and vindictive brother, Helen Halsey is forced by her uncle into marriage with her lover, who has followed her into the brotherhood's swamp hideout in Conelachita (presumably Louisiana). The purpose of the marriage, performed by a corrupt Episcopal priest who is a member of the gang, is to ensure the loyalty of the couple and prevent their return to civilization, where they might disclose the bandits' operations and whereabouts. Thus, though happy to be married to each other, Henry Meadors (the first-person narrator and protagonist) and "his outlaw's daughter-bride" are virtual prisoners of the gang, and during their attempted escape, Helen is killed by her own uncle. *Helen Halsey's* strengths lie in its fast-moving, action-filled narration; its vivid imagery in the descriptions of the lush, dense swampland wilderness; and its especially detailed portrayal of the modus operandi of the criminal network that indeed had ruthlessly dominated much of the Southwestern frontier in the early nineteenth century. That the organization included rough, profane women who actively participated in assault and robbery; and that the Bud Halsey brotherhood possessed an in-kind chaplain to conduct weddings, funerals, and other "Christian" services for its membership were particularly dramatic revelations for readers of the day and constituted new and innovative subject matter for the American novel.

Perhaps the best-drawn character in the short novel is Mowbray, the intellectual, aristocratic, resentful, egotistical Episcopal divine who had deserted his wife, child, and church to pursue a life of dissipation and crime, first in New Orleans and then in the swamp kingdom. Simms's self-centered priest—who preaches more effectively after sinning, eventually confesses and repents of his hypocrisy, and dies in a willful act of penitence asking for God's mercy and forgiveness—anticipates Hawthorne's Dimmesdale by five years. Since it is known that Hawthorne read (and reviewed) Simms's *Views and Reviews* in 1846, the question arises if he could also have taken mental note of *Helen Halsey*, published only a few months earlier. Probably there was no direct influence; despite parallels in the behavior of Mowbray and Dimmesdale, each is his own character, the creation of the individual author. In any case Simms's characterization of Mowbray, perhaps the first basically sympathetic portrayal of an introspective, unsaintly priest in the American novel, is striking enough to stand on its own merits.

Though Simms stated to Rufus Griswold that "running through all these works [Border Romances]" is "a strong penchant to moral and mental analysis" (*L*, II, 225), this characterization is more applicable to *Confession*, *Beauchampe*, and *Helen Halsey* than to *Guy Rivers*, *Richard Hurdis*, and *Border Beagles*, the three novels that began the series. On the other hand, Simms's assertion that all the *Guy Rivers* "family" are "distinguished by great activity of plot, vehement & passionate personality, and pictures & sketches of border character & border scenery, in which I claim to be equally true & natural" (*L*, II, 225) more accurately describes the opening trio of Border Romances than the later three. *Confession* and *Helen Halsey* in particular have psychological qualities in common with Simms's "moral imaginative" fiction—self-confessional tales related in first person in the vein of *Martin Faber* and "Carl Werner."

Almost simultaneously with the publication of *Helen Halsey* in New York, another book with the Simms stamp appeared on the Charleston literary scene—*The Charleston Book: A Miscellany in Prose and Verse,* published in Charleston in January 1845 by Samuel Hart. *The Charleston Book* is aptly named: it is a volume of poetry and essays written by Charlestonians and collected (though anonymously) by Charleston's only nationally known author—primarily for the reading pleasure of a small elite audience of fellow Carolinians. Beginning in the late 1830s, America was deluged with anthologies representing the best writing by citizens of various individual cities, and Charleston naturally judged its literati capable of producing books competitive with those from New York, Boston, Baltimore, or Philadelphia. Actually, the idea for such a volume had originated as early as 1841, for in August of that year Simms had first mentioned the project in a letter to James Lawson: "You will see from the within prospectus[14] that they are about to do something for the honor of my old city. The publisher sends me a few prospectuses with the request that I will circulate them. … He will make a very fair book of it" (*L,* I, 266–67). The prospectus's statement that *The Charleston Book* "will be put to press as soon as an adequate number of subscribers is obtained, but not before" accounts for the volume's belated appearance more than three years after it had been announced. *The Charleston Book* has little literary value other than as a historical barometer of literary taste and talent in an aristocratic old city of the Old South. Louis D. Rubin, Jr., has found particular significance in the fact that

> an author such as Simms … would expend so much time and labor on a project such as this, which could scarcely benefit either his literary reputation or be of political gain. …
>
> What Simms craved most of all was to be recognized and honored as an outstanding man of letters, a distinguished literary personage in a city-state (as was often said) in which literature, culture, and learning were strongly allied with wealth and position.[15]

*The Charleston Book* reveals a literary man's love for the city of his nativity, a love generous enough to induce him to work in its behalf without foreseeable profit to himself.

Clearly the most important book published by Simms in 1845, however, was the two-volume edition of his short stories entitled *The Wigwam and the Cabin.*[16] This remarkable work represents Simms at his very best; with it he returns to the material of the Southwestern frontier that he knew so well, a frontier whose vernacular, courage, humor, violence, injustice, and beauty are vividly brought to life through the strokes of his pen.

Apparently the idea of collecting the choice of his border stories into a single title first struck Simms in mid-1843, shortly after he relinquished the editorship of the *Magnolia.* In June of that year Simms wrote to his New York agent about activities he was considering "[s]ince throwing aside the Magazine":

> I wish you to propose to [Harper & Brothers] a collection of Tales of the South; making such a book as Fay's at the same price. Two of the Tales are long—some of them have been published. The following list includes most of them. 1. Ellen Halsey, or my Wife against my Will; 2. Castle Dismal, or the Bachelor's Christmas, 3. Barnacle Sam, or the Edisto Raftsman. 4. The Last Wager, or the Gamester of the Mississippi, 5. Murder will out; a Ghost story; The Arm Chair of Tustenuggee, a Legend of the Catawba. 7. The Lazy Crow, a Story of the Cornfield, &c. This will afford some idea of the contents & their variety. Ellen Halsey will of itself make over 100 pages. Castle Dismal, another hundred. The rest will average 50, or 60. I am willing that they should try the experiment with a cheap edition, sharing half the profits. See & confer with them about it, that I may make any preparations before I go north, which I hope to do sometime in August[17] . . . . (*L,* I, 353–54)

Four months later Simms, still hopeful that Harper & Brothers would be his publisher, now visualized *Castle Dismal* and *Helen Halsey* as separate books, and referred to the short-story volume as "Murder Will Out, and other Tales." Noting, however, that "I half repent" of any "arrangement" with Harpers, he instructed Lawson: "unless they are willing to proceed at once, or if they show any reluctance, let the MS. be withdrawn" (*L,* I, 376). By March 1844, still without publisher, Simms was suggesting to Lawson that he "[a]sk Stringer[18] how he would relish to publish a series in the 12 mo. form at 12 1/2 cents each, of 'Tales of the South' by myself on shares?" (*L,* I, 410). Having received no commitment after seven months, Simms urged Lawson to "try and negotiate the volume of Tales" with Stringer "on the same terms" as *Castle Dismal* and *Helen Halsey* (*L,* I, 437). By this time Simms had hit upon "The Wigwam and the Cabin" as a title for the book, which he now apparently visualized as a companion volume to "Tales of the South"—the one concentrating on the frontier, the other on the plantation or the city.[19]

Simms's persistence in seeking a publisher for a collection of his short fiction[20] finally was rewarded when he concentrated his efforts on Wiley and Putnam, a New York publisher with a special interest in Americana. Wiley and Putnam's "Library of American Books" was edited by a Simms admirer, Evert A. Duyckinck; and by March 1845 Simms was corresponding with Duyckinck about the possibility of including "Tales of the South" in the project (*L,* II, 43–44). Duyckinck quickly became Simms's advocate, and after exchange of frequent letters during a short time span, the New York editor and the Woodlands novelist agreed upon the publication not only of a book of Simms's short stories but also a book of his essays.[21] By June 1845 Simms was asking Lawson to serve as his agent to cement the arrangement: "I have had a letter from Duyckinck suggesting one or more volumes of Tales for Wiley & Putnam's Library. I have referred him to you to make the arrangement. I may say to you that I would not have you stickle about the terms. Let him have the matter pretty much his own way. I have never labored much after money ..." (*L*, II, 71). During Simms's visit to New York in August 1845, author and editor (and perhaps agent) were able to work out final details of publication,[22] and in October *The Wigwam and the Cabin*, First Series, came from the press, shortly followed in February 1846 by the Second Series (also dated 1845, see note 16). In mid-October 1845 Simms, back in Charleston, wrote to Duyckinck, "They tell me that the Wigwam is selling here," though he complained that "no copies for the Editors have been received" (*L*, II, 108).

Despite this slowness in getting review copies into the hands of Charleston reviewers, the New York press carried critiques of *The Wigwam and the Cabin*, First Series, almost simultaneously with the book's publication, an indication that advance copies had been effectively distributed in the metropolitan area. Probably the most famous is the review of *The Wigwam and the Cabin* written by Poe for the *Broadway Journal* for October 4, 1845. It reads in part:

> This is one of the most interesting of the Library [of American Books] yet published—and decidedly the most American of the American books. ... In a recent number of our Journal[23] we spoke of Mr. Simms as "the best novelist which this country has, upon the whole, produced;" and this is our deliberate opinion. We take into consideration, of course, as well the amount of what he has written, as the talent he has displayed;—he is the Lopez de Vega of American writers of fiction. His merits lie among the major and his defects among the minor morals of literature. His earlier works of length, such as "The Partisan," were disfigured by many inaccuracies of style, and especially by the prevalence of the merely repulsive, where the horrible was the object—but in invention, in vigor, in movement, in the power of exciting interest, and in the artistical management of his themes, he has surpassed, we think, any of his countrymen:—that is to say, he has surpassed any of them in the aggregate of these high qualities. (II, 190)

It does not call in question Poe's integrity to point out that, because his own *Tales* (1845) was included in the series, Poe may have been favorably inclined toward Putnam and Wiley's Library of American Books. Duyckinck, of course, as editor of the Library, would have made every effort to have each volume fairly reviewed, and almost certainly he was responsible not only for Poe's getting an early review copy of Simms's book, but also for Simms's receiving an advance copy of Poe's.[24] Duyckinck's providing Poe and Simms each the opportunity to review the other has left posterity a rarity: concurrent critiques of one another by the two premier short-story writers of the era. Since both Poe and Simms scoffed at critics who indiscriminately praised mediocrity, each was zealous in pointing out defect as well as merit in the other's work; but keen appreciation of superior literary talent is nonetheless apparent in their respective commentaries.

Poe, of course, was not the only contemporary critic to admire Simms's achievement in *The Wigwam and the Cabin.* The *New York Evening Mirror,* in the earliest known review, on September 29, 1845, began the chorus of approbation with high, if not unmitigated, praise for the writer and the work at hand:

> After Mr. Simms' Tales of the wild West, stories of daring adventure, stormy passions, dark deeds, and startling fortunes, have been eagerly perused by his countrymen, and highly praised in Europe, there seems little left to say on this, their appearance in a new and very attractive dress. The opening novelette, 'Murder will out,' was pronounced by the London critics, the best ghost-story of modern times, so thrilling is its interest, and so natural and striking its development. Others of the stories are perhaps not inferior to this in merit of various kinds. An air of reality pervades them all; and though we may wish that this had permitted the exclusion of certain touches of coarseness, we must allow it to be a great merit, and one which would plead for greater blemishes.

*Godey's* quickly followed with an even more laudatory appraisal of the "collection of stories by the great novelist of the South," terming it "among the best of Simms' productions," with "more nerve and not less beauty and grace than his larger works" (XXI [December 1845], 271).

Nor was enthusiastic response lacking from British critics, in whom Simms expressed a particular interest because of their influence on "American purchasers."[25] From across the Atlantic highly favorable reviews of *The Wigwam and the Cabin,* First Series, appeared in the *New Monthly Magazine* (LXXV [December 1845], 499): "The life of the planter, the squatter, the Indian, and the negro, of the bold and hardy pioneer, and of the vigorous yeoman are given with a truthfulness that leaves the namby-pamby imitations, extolled as Cooper-like in this country, far, far in the back-ground"; and in the *Critic* (n.s., II [November 22, 1845], 605): "... written with a flowing pen, never at a loss for words, and seldom for ideas. ... The pictures of border life are very vividly drawn; there is flesh and blood in the personages who figure in them." When the Second Series came out shortly afterwards both these journals again contained admiring notices: the *New Monthly Magazine* (LXXVI [March 1846], 377–78) observed that "the tales of 'The Wigwam and the Cabin' ... are full of profound and startling interest"; the *Critic* (n.s., III [February 7, 1846], 149) called Simms's stories "faithful pictures of American life. ... Occasionally we light upon passages of really fine writing, full of eloquence and the descriptions of scenery are often extremely vivid. ..." Other noteworthy reviews appeared in the *Mirror of Literature, Amusement, and Instruction,* which in citing Simms's "rough vigour" singled out "Caloya; or, The Loves of the Driver" as "a gem," and added, "We never read a better story ..." (n.s., IX [May 23, 1846], 334); and in *Tait's Edinburgh Magazine,* which paid tribute to *The Wigwam and the Cabin* for its "very considerable merit, and even originality" (XII [April 1846], 267). Perhaps the only British journals to find serious fault with Simms's collection of short fiction were the *Spectator,* which, noting the book's "peculiarity, that its matter is American," objected that the "subjects are not pleasing," that "the treatment, though vigorous, is coarse," and that "the author leans too much to the physical and the extravagant" (XIX [February 21, 1846], 186–87); and *Blackwood's,* which objected that Simms's stories "seem to be neither good nor bad;—it would be a waste of time to cast about for the exact epithet that should characterize them" (LXII [November 1847], 574).

An episode revealing Simms's acute sensibility to what he perceived as unjustified slights to his work, reputation, or person occurred shortly after the publication of *The Wigwam and the Cabin.* The controversy began when the *New York Evening Mirror* (which earlier had commended Simms's new book) ran on October 6, 1845, an article labeled "Poe-lemical" which took exception to what it considered Poe's excessive praise of Simms in his *Broadway Journal* critique two days earlier:

> ... it is above the power of any single critic—or of all the critics in the country combined, to convince the world that William Gilmore Simms is a better novelist than Cooper, or Brockden Brown. He is certainly less known and read at home and abroad. We doubt if the copy-right of all Mr. Simms's collected works would bring as good a price in America or England, as the "Norman Leslie" of Fay, or the "Sketch Book" of Irving.

Simms's private response was immediate and furious. In his letter of October 19 to E. A. Duyckinck he noted that "the dirty fellows of the Mirror have been carping at my books & sneering at Poe for affecting them" and added:

> It is sufficient to denote the sort of critic with which one has to deal, when we find him not convassing the merits of an author, but insinuating his want of popularity—his inferior sales &c. As for Fay,—let these people go to H & B. and ascertain how many copies of the Yemassee & Norman Leslie have respectively been sold,[26] including all the editions—ask—but the thing is of a piece with the wretched & base creatures who conduct that print,—which, I suspect seizes upon the suggestion of that other dirty crawling creeping creature, Clarke, in the Knickerbocker to insinuate deficient popularity, when I know, and all the publishers know, and the public—South of the Potomac at least know—that my popularity was perhaps never greater than at this very moment. (*L*, II, 106–7)

Lewis Gaylord Clark (the "Clarke" in Simms's derisive reference), editor of the *Knickerbocker,* had already been engaged in a long battle of words with Simms, Duyckinck, Lawson, and Cornelius Mathews, an argument which had begun in 1841 when Clark had ridiculed the series of articles Simms had written on "Southern Literature" for the *Magnolia.*[27] In its October 1845 number the *Knickerbocker*—presumably in the person of Clark—belittled Simms as "a very voluminous author, now in the decadence of a limited sectional reputation" (XXVI, 378).

Though Northern periodicals were by and large staunch in their admiration of Simms's newest volume of fiction, the *Knickerbocker* and the *Evening Mirror* were not alone in their lack of appreciation. In a hostile critique ostensibly reviewing *The Wigwam and the Cabin* and other works by Simms, the *North American Review* for October 1846 found little to its liking in the South Carolinian. The reviewer, Cornelius C. Felton, condescendingly characterized Simms as a writer who labors "under a heavy load of words" in "endeavoring to give … an American fit" to "the cast-off garments of the British novelists" (LXIII, 357). Somewhat surprisingly, however, after having disparaged Simms in "Poe-lemical," the *New York Evening Mirror* of February 5, 1846, issued a third commentary on *The Wigwam and the Cabin*—apparently written by William A. Jones—which was highly laudatory of both the volume and its author. Jones also had words of praise for Simms and *The Wigwam and the Cabin* in his short piece entitled "Tales of the South and West" in the *U.S. Democratic Review* for June 1846: "His narrative is clear, racy, natural, constructed with practised art, (Mr. Simms has at least as much judgment as invention) and strongly American" (XVIII, 471–74). And Poe himself, partly in response to "Poe-lemical," revised and expanded his earlier review of *The*

*Wigwam and the Cabin* for publication in the *Broadway Journal* for January 1846; there Poe reiterated his high opinion of Simms's short fiction, particularly "Grayling," and repeated his earlier assertion that among American writers Simms was unsurpassed "in the aggregate of higher excellences of fiction" (XXXII, 41–42).

*The Wigwam and the Cabin* is a memorable book, notable not only for the "higher excellences" of the thirteen stories which make up its contents, but also for the dedicatory essay to "Nash Roach, Esq., of South Carolina" which Simms wrote for the reissue of the volume published by Redfield in 1856.[28] It is interesting that, for the original 1845 edition, Simms had been content simply to inscribe the volume to his father-in-law, without comment, but by 1856 he felt the need to elaborate upon both his practice and his purpose. The resulting statement of what constitutes realism and nationalism in literature is indeed remarkable for its time:

> One word for the material of these legends. It is local, sectional—and to be *national* in literature, one must needs be *sectional.* No one mind can fully or fairly illustrate the characteristics of any great country; and he who shall depict *one section* faithfully, has made his proper and sufficient contribution to the great work of *national* illustration. I can answer for it, confidently, that these legends represent, in large degree, the border history of the south. I can speak with confidence of the general truthfulness of its treatment. I have seen the life—have *lived* it—and much of my material is the planter, the squatter, the Indian, and the negro—the bold and hardy pioneer, the vigorous yeoman—these are the subjects. (pp. 4–5)

Although consideration of the overall significance and quality of Simms's fiction is reserved for the final chapter, every story in *The Wigwam and the Cabin* merits discussion. Simms in 1845 was close to being at the height of his narrative powers: sure of his craft, bold in his concept, confident of his theory. Each story selected in 1845 for inclusion in *The Wigwam and the Cabin* bore in part, in combination, or in entirety the earmarks of Simms's best writing: descriptive power, narrative skill, vernacular style, comic realism, controlled use of folklore and supernatural—and nearly all dealt with the familiar theme of life on the frontier.

The much-admired ghost story, "Grayling; or 'Murder Will Out,'" has a strong imaginative appeal, as indicated earlier, yet there are other, more skillfully handled tales of the supernatural in the collection. Six of the stories involve an unnatural, if not a supernatural, event, and the most effective center upon the portrayal of Indian character or tradition. In such tales as "The

Arm-Chair of Tustenuggee. A Tradition of the Catawba," "Jocassee. A Cherokee Legend," and "Lucas de Ayllon," the character of the Indian is depicted in a manner that allows the supernatural to be well knit into the fabric of his thinking. The reader is carried along by the event because it is "natural," for example, that Conattee, who has unfortunately seated himself in the armchair of Tustenuggee, must suffer the consequence of imprisonment by an overgrowth of bark—a beautiful, yet humorous rendering of Indian legend. In "Jocassee" the supernatural core episode centers around the belief of the warrior, Nagoochie, that the buck he is unable to kill is an enchanted spirit which leads him to the beautiful Jocassee. Simms does not betray Indian tradition by saving Nagoochie from death. Although one's sympathies are with Nagoochie, he is nevertheless scalped by his enemy, the brother of Jocassee, and Simms's touch of realism is effective. "Lucas de Ayllon" offers yet another example of Simms's extraordinary skill in handling legends dealing with the life and attributes of the Indian. Combahee's awaiting the enemies of Chiquola so that by burning their bones she might warm the limbs of Chiquola (drowned by their treachery) does not strike the reader as gratuitous sensationalism, but rather appears fully integrated into the depiction of Indian temperament and tradition.

Perhaps the most artistically satisfying tale in the whole impressive collection, however, is "The Two Camps. A Legend of the Old North State," in which Simms achieves unity of tone and effect by employing a single vessel of consciousness whose credibility the reader never questions. Once Simms has provided the historical background and introduced the "hale and lusty, but white-headed" frontiersman, Daniel Nelson (who "unfolds from his own budget of experience a rare chronicle"), the entire legend of ubiquitous spiritual mediums on the rugged "southern borders of North Carolina" (pp. 39–40) is put into the quizzical, picturesque dialect of the backwoods. Simms handles skillfully the delicate task of securing willing suspension of belief, crucial to the plausibility of Nelson's two visions of a hostile Indian camp. On the other hand, the least successful of the half dozen stories in *The Wigwam and the Cabin* that deal in some way with the supernatural is "The Last Wager; or, The Gamester of the Mississippi," in which Simms is not successful in his attempts to cast a certain unnatural tone over the story. In his introductory chapter the author emphasizes "the *naturalness*" of his story "of life as it is, or with life as it is shown … as … probable," and he obviously draws the material for his "strange narrative of frontier life" from "circumstances … picked up, when, a lad of eighteen, I first wandered over the then dreary and dangerous wastes of the Mississippi border … the great Yazoo wilderness" (pp. 71, 74). But in this story which "hangs" upon *"a pack of ordinary playing cards ... nailed"* to the wall (p. 76), he fails to achieve the sense of reality of his best fiction. The melodramatic suicide of the "gentleman" gambler, Eckhardt, serves to clinch the too-apparent lesson that gambling does not pay. But "The Last Wager" does have moments of strength, as in the striking introduction of Rachel Herder:

> I could see that she carried herself well, sat her horse upright like a sort of queen, and when the old man offered to take her off, yielded herself to him with a slow but graceful stateliness, not unlike that of a young cedar bending to the wind. (p. 99)

In the seven stories in *The Wigwam and the Cabin* which neither embody nor reflect the miraculous, the supernatural, or the preternatural, Simms displays admirable versatility in subject, tone, and purpose. Three titles particularly stand out: "The Giant's Coffin; or, The Feud of Holt and Houston. A Tale of Reedy River," set in 1766 in "the beautiful district of Greenville, in South Carolina"; "Sergeant Barnacle; or, The Raftsman of the Edisto," set "just five years before the Revolution" in "the pretty little settlement of Orangeburg, in South Carolina"; and "Those Old Lunes! or, Which is the Madman?" set in the very recent past "on the very borders of Mississippi." But except for being border or frontier narratives, the stories have little in common other than their singular excellence. In "The Giant's Coffin," the character of Peter Acker, the abused, embittered, and deformed epileptic, emerges with a vividness that makes the tale one of the best in the series. His twisted childlike mentality and the morbidity of his resentment are graphically revealed, yet he is sympathetically treated in one of Simms's most penetrating psychological studies. Acker's instinctive cunning enables him to entrap his abuser and the object of his revenge, the outlaw John Houston, in the "Giant's Coffin" on the banks of Reedy River, there to die a slow but certain death as flood waters rise. Simms pinpoints the effect superbly in the casual conversation between the epileptic and Arthur Holt, who knows not the fate of their common enemy:

> "The river is rising fast, Peter," was the remark of Arthur Holt as he caught a glimpse of the swollen stream as it foamed along its way.
>
> "Yes!" said the other, with a sort of hiccough, by which he suppressed emotions which he did not venture to declare: "Yes! I reckon 'twon't be many hours afore it fills the 'Coffin.'"
>
> "If it keeps on at this rate," returned the other, "one hour will be enough to do that."
>
> "Only one, you think?"

> Another hiccough of the Epileptic appropriately finished the dialogue. (pp. 270–71)

"Sergeant Barnacle" also focuses upon a violent murder, and once again Simms effectively presents the psychology of a fanatic. The author achieves an overtone of meaning in the fanaticism of Barnacle Sam which seems to be lacking in the other stories, where the reader's mind is held to a single line of thought and action. In "Sergeant Barnacle" there is a disjunction between what Sam thinks he is doing and the meaning of what he does. He believes that he is chosen of God to avenge Margaret's death by killing Wilson Hurst, who had jilted her; in achieving his end, he is of course committing murder. In the concluding episode, in which the "somewhat celebrated" Irish judge "of curious humour, and many eccentricities" (p. 311) comically reasons to a reversal of the court's decision that Sam was insane at the time of the killing, Simms has the deft touch of the ironic satirist. Frontier justice prevailed; "and Barnacle Sam went his way, perfectly satisfied as to the removal of all stain from his sanity of mind" (p. 312).

Simms seems to attempt so little in "Those Old Lunes!" that it might be easily misjudged. Yet Simms's humor emerges in his tongue-in-cheek treatment of the fickleness of young men and women. Emmelina and Susannah are beautiful and talented, as are most of his young heroines, but their flirtatious and capricious behavior, a clear departure from maidenly purity and modesty, distinguishes the tale. Clever, too, is the twist by which their flightiness is revealed: the disclosure that Colonel Nelson and the lunatic Archy Dargan are one and the same. Simms often achieves greater unity of plot and development when he speaks from the point of view of one of his characters; such is the case in "Those Old Lunes!" where the attitude of the whimsical young suitor permeates the narration.

The other selections in *The Wigwam and the Cabin* can be dealt with briefly. The impact of "Caloya; or, The Loves of the Driver" has been discussed earlier. The character of Mingo, the black driver whose lustfulness is fully captured, is drawn with some complexity; and the portrayal of the corrupted Indian, Richard Knuckles, compresses the mixture of indolence and pride in the Native American who is left detached from his tribe and tradition and yet not absorbed into white civilization. "Oakatibbe; or, The Choctaw Sampson," though interesting because of its depiction of a tragic Indian character, is an example of Simms's having expanded a text, in this case "Indian Sketch" (1828), his earliest successful fictional treatment of the Indian in the Southern backwoods, into a much longer piece, still powerful, but less effective as a narrative.[29] "The Lazy Crow" is a tale in which Simms does not fully exploit the rich possibilities of the subject he is treating, the psychology of superstition. Probably the weakest of the thirteen stories in *The Wigwam and the Cabin* is "The Snake of the Cabin," whose characters seem to fall into only two categories, scoundrels like Edward Stanton or paragons like Robert Anderson and Ellen Ramsey. An exception is another driver, the loyal and forthright Abram, who in the anticlimactic ending kills the confidence man Stanton for his attempts to incite slaves to insurrection for his own personal gain. But all things taken into account, with the exception of Hawthorne's *Twice Told Tales* and Poe's *Tales,* Simms's *The Wigwam and the Cabin* has no match among collections of short fiction by a single American author published by or before 1845.

Besides *The Wigwam and the Cabin* the other Simms book published by Wiley and Putnam in 1845 (though not issued until around May 1846) was an important collection of literary and historical essays entitled *Views and Reviews in American Literature, History and Fiction.* Like *The Wigwam and the Cabin, Views and Reviews* was published in both New York and London and was issued in both First Series and Second Series. Simms as a literary theorist and critic has been all but ignored by serious American scholarship, but C. Hugh Holman, recognizing *Views and Reviews* as "an important document in American literary and cultural history," snatched the collection from complete oblivion by editing and publishing the First Series in the John Harvard Library of the Belknap Press of Harvard University Press in 1962.[30] Included in this original series of *Views and Reviews* are "Americanism in Literature," "The Epochs and Events of American History," "Literature and Art Among the American Aborigines," and "The Writings of James Fenimore Cooper" as well as articles of lesser importance on "Daniel Boon; the First Hunter of Kentucky" and "Cortes and the Conquest of Mexico." The Second Series, apparently hastily thrown together and generally inferior to the first, was not widely reviewed; it is interesting to note, however, that "The Humourous in American and British Literature, the various writings of Cornelius Mathews, and others" helped fuel the controversy between Simms and the *Knickerbocker.*[31]

An interesting side issue is associated with the publication and the reception of *Views and Reviews,* particularly the First Series. There is evidence to support the contention by Perry Miller[32] that Evert Duyckinck was motivated by literary politics in deciding to include Simms's essays in the Library of American Books. By 1845 the hostility between nationalist-leaning, democratically inclined Young America (the New York circle of writers of which Duyckinck was the spiritual leader and of which Simms was in effect the spokesman for the South) and the conservative Whig group headed by the editors of the *Knickerbocker* and the *North American Review* had come to a boil—primarily over the issue of a national literature. What more effective way, then, to broadcast the ideals of Young America, Duyckinck must have reasoned, than to have it done in a volume of essays by the writer recognized nationally as the strongest and most consistent advocate of Americanism in literature? That the lead essay bore the title "Americanism in Literature" appeared to make *Views and Reviews* the perfect sounding board for Young American ideas. Such literary politics helps to account for the surprisingly intense critical heat generated by Simms's assertiveness on behalf of the national cause he championed.

Leading the frontal attack by the Whigs on Simms and his concept of a native American literature was the prestigious *North American Review.* In the review article (previously cited) dealing with Wiley and Putnam's entire Library of American Books, Eliot Professor Cornelius C. Felton of Harvard delighted in sarcastically taunting Simms, "a writer of great pretensions and some local reputation," and his views. Simms's essays, Felton asserted, "breathe an extravagant nationality, equally at war with good taste and generous progress in liberal culture" (LXIII [October 1846], 357–81). The *Knickerbocker,* it should be noted, stated its agreement (in its "Editor's Table" for November 1846) with the tenor and purpose of Felton's attack. But the voice of Young America was also to be heard: *Yankee Doodle* (edited by Cornelius Mathews) predictably called Felton to task for his "dry sticks," "sappless sentences," and "tame flatulency ... which has never been surpassed"; and exclaimed of "the nincompoup reviewer [with] asses' ears": "Why, *Yankee* is ashamed to strike his axe into such a meat-block as that reviewer's head" (I [October 24, 1846], 33). Evert Duyckinck's *Literary World,* on the other hand, was restrained in its denunciation of Simms's critics, but lavish in its praise for Simms and his values: "Mr. Simms is truly American. The subjects of this collection, from Americanism, the first paper, to the last, are purely American" (II [October 23, 1847], 282).

The intensity of feeling on this issue is foreboding (and the yet-to-be-discussed North/South juxtaposition of belief surprising)—but unmistakable evidence that American cultural nationalism was indeed an inflammatory topic came with entry into the controversy by editors from across the Atlantic. In its number for November 1847 *Blackwood's* contained a strongly negative review of both *The Wigwam and the Cabin* and *Views and Reviews,* stating that the latter volume demonstrates "in every page that [Simms] has quite liberated himself from all those fetters and prejudices which, in Europe, go under the name of truth and common sense" (LXII, 574–80). The

*Knickerbocker,* angered by accusations that its harsh treatment of Simms was based upon personal prejudice, asserted that "we now find our opinions fully confirmed on the other side of the water" by reviewers "uninfluenced by personal bias" (XXI [January 1848], 68–71). The *Boston Morning Post* for November 29, 1847, was not sympathetic with Simms's call for a distinctive national literature, adding: "It is a pity that some of these gentlemen should not produce a work which would serve to show what this singular 'American literature' really is. One look at such a model would be more convincing than the perusal of scores of essays." The *Knickerbocker* gleefully reprinted the *Morning Post* review in its number for December 1847, with comment that it "hits the nail on the head": "It was thought for some time that we could have no 'American Literature' unless our writers infused a large proportion of Indian character into all their works; so that we come to have aboriginal ingredients in all our intellectual food" (XXX, 556).

But by far the most significant single review of *Views and Reviews* was written by Nathaniel Hawthorne, a fellow Young American and a fellow contributor to Wiley and Putnam's Library of American Books. This remarkable piece of criticism, the only known commentary on Simms by Hawthorne, was published in the *Salem Advertiser* of May 2, 1846, shortly after the publication of the First Series of *Views and Reviews:*

> This work ... is made up of able review-articles, chiefly on historical subjects, and a series of picturesque and highly ornamented lectures on "American History, as suited to the purposes of Art."—These are all creditable to the author, and scarcely inferior, in our judgment, to the best of such productions, whether on this or the other side of the Atlantic. Mr. Simms is a man of vigorous and cultivated mind—a writer of well-trained ability—but not, as we feel most sensibly in his best passages, a man of genius. This is especially discernible in the series of lectures above alluded to; they abound in brilliant paragraphs, and appear to bring out, as by a skillfully applied varnish, all the lights and shades that lie upon the surface of our history; but yet, we cannot help feeling that the real treasures of his subject have escaped the author's notice. The themes suggested by him, viewed as he views them, would produce nothing but historical novels, cast in the same worn mould that has been in use these thirty years, and which it is time to break up and fling away. To be the prophet of Art requires almost as high a gift as to be a fulfiller of the prophecy. Mr. Simms has not this gift; he possesses nothing of the magic touch that should cause new intellectual and moral shapes to spring up in the reader's mind, peopling with varied life what had hitherto been a barren waste. He can merely elaborate what is already familiar. His style, we think, is one which, in a higher or lower degree of finish, is proper to men of his literary stamp. It is

> composed of very good words, exceedingly well put together; but, instead of being imbued and identified with his subject, it spreads itself over it like an incrustation.[33]

Hawthorne's sensitivity to the shortcomings of Simms's genius and to the limitations of his vision enables the astute New Englander to put into perspective the strengths and weaknesses of his Southern counterpart. Genius versus near genius is always an overmatch; and although in 1846 Hawthorne's major novels were as yet unwritten (whereas at least ten by Simms had been nationally recognized and generally acclaimed) the Salem review leaves little doubt that a superior mind has stood in judgment of another less superior. With *The Scarlet Letter* not yet even in process, Hawthorne nonetheless had a prophetic understanding of the artistry and imagination essential to the great American novel. Before demonstrating with *The Scarlet Letter* in 1850 the "high gift" of "fulfiller," Hawthorne in 1846 gave evidence of the "almost as high a gift" of "prophet of Art." Recognition of the superiority of Hawthorne's genius in no way detracts from our perception that Simms in the mid-1840s held generally clearsighted views on the need for a distinctively American literature and its purpose.

The debate over national literature set off in part by the publication of *Views and Reviews* was not marked, as perhaps would be expected, by a significant North-South alignment. In the years following 1845 there was little or no controversy over Simms's contention that sectional literature was a prerequisite for national literature; that the literature of the South and West, as well as the literature of the North, was integral to the creation of American letters. Though Simms derided Southern dependence on the North equally as much as American subservience to Europe, the debate in the 1840s centered almost entirely upon whether or not a national literature free from foreign influence was desirable.

Almost as many Northern editors and writers supported Simms's thesis as opposed it; the question in 1846 or 1847, simply put, was international *versus* national, not North *versus* South. In the middle 1840s the North in general did not perceive Southern sectionalism to be a threat; demands by Southerners for intellectual parity were viewed to be provincial, perhaps, but not ominous. Unfortunately, as has been witnessed, a rational separation of sectional from national feelings was no longer possible at the time of Simms's ill-fated Northern lecture tour in 1856.

Yet another interesting by-product of the New York literary wars was Simms's sharpened perception of the need for an international copyright. Among the earliest of America's professional authors to recognize the damage to American letters by literary piracy on both sides of the Atlantic, Simms's affiliation with the Author's Club of New York[34] motivated the versatile South Carolinian to take action—to begin putting his arguments into print, with a series of letters on "International Copyright Law," published in the *Southern Literary Messenger* throughout 1844.[35] Simms also took up the issue in his private correspondence with literary friends and acquaintances; for instance, on April 10, 1844, he had the following comments on the subject in a letter to James Fenimore Cooper:

> I have been throwing out some essays in the form of Letters, on the subject of our Copyright Law. I have no hope that Congress will do any thing in the matter. There are some stupid prejudices to be overcome. The notion of the half-witted fellows from the West is that this is a favor to the English. My object has been to show rather that the great benefit enures to ourselves, and that the chief good of the measure will be to emancipate us from the dictation of British mind. But the real difficulty is in the indifference of the people to the whole subject, and Congress is a body that dares not act, until it has previously been instructed by popular legislation. All our legislation is done by the newspapers. (*L*, V, 380)

Simms was perhaps the prime mover in the vigorous but unsuccessful national campaign to get Congress to pass an international copyright law (an act which did not occur until 1891). Although Bryant and Duyckinck, in particular among New York area writers, were highly active in the copyright movement, no other author spoke and wrote as much as Simms did in its behalf; and, indeed, there is evidence that Simms participated in drafting "the memorial to Congress" (a copy of which is dated "Woodlands, March 1 [1844]")[36] beginning, "The undersigned, men of Letters and citizens of the United States, interested in many ways in the cause of Literature, petition your honorable bodies for the passage of a law for the proper regulation of the copy-right of books." This whole episode—Simms's movements crucial to the cause of American letters—demonstrates the Southerner's strong commitment to the profession he had chosen as a youth in Charleston. It is significant that Simms strove for betterment of the profession as a whole as well as for personal eminence within the profession.

Intermixed with Simms's two major prose efforts with Wiley and Putnam—*The Wigwam and the Cabin* and *Views and Reviews*—were two poetic endeavors of less import, each placed with a Southern publisher: *Grouped Thoughts and Scattered Fancies. A Collection of Sonnets* (Richmond: Wm. Macfarlane, 1845) and *Areytos; or, Songs of the South* (Charleston: John Russell, 1846). In turning again to his earliest love, poetry, Simms first pulled together a group of miscellaneous sonnets for installments in the *Southern Literary Messenger* in 1844 and 1845. Subsequently, in October 1845, Simms reported that *Grouped Thoughts* was being printed for circulation—by Macfarlane, printer of the *Messenger.* This modest volume, not widely reviewed as a result partly of its limited distribution, nevertheless won favorable recognition from William Cullen Bryant, who in the *New York Evening Post* for May 23, 1846, noted that *Grouped Thoughts and Scattered Fancies* contains "some of the best verses of the author. Their tone is manly, and the expression free, bold and vigorous." In commenting on *Grouped Thoughts* in a letter to Duyckinck, Simms indicated his strong predilection for the sonnets he had carefully selected for the volume—"I am vain to think [they] are the best collection of sonnets ever printed in America" (*L,* II, 111). Simms's high regard for this little work of unpretentious origin—the author himself had arranged that it "not be published, but merely circulated" (*L,* II, 111)—is surprising; why had Simms not sought, for instance, to have the volume issued by an established New York publisher who would have assured wider circulation? The answer probably is that Simms, knowledgeable of the condition of the publishing industry in 1845, correctly surmised that no cost-conscious American publisher, however reputable, would undertake an edition of his sonnets at a time when, because of the absence of copyright laws, pirated reprints of noted European writers offered "cheap literature" competition. Whatever the reason for Simms's decision to have *Grouped Thoughts* "merely circulated" in 1845, recognition is very slowly dawning that Simms as a poet has merit—that the collection of sonnets he acclaimed in his correspondence does, after all these years, warrant serious consideration.[37]

Whereas in *Grouped Thoughts and Scattered Fancies* Simms had selected the best from his private repertoire of more than 160 mainly classical or traditional sonnets, in *Areytos* he chose to concentrate upon subject matter rather than form, and most of the poems deal with Southern scenes and settings. Perhaps for this reason, there is more striking originality, more verve and buoyancy, in *Areytos* than in *Grouped Thoughts,* though quality of performance in both volumes is inconsistent. Among the best poems in *Areytos* on Southern or Southwestern themes—Simms's forte in poetry as well as in fiction—are "The Texian Hunter," "Maid of Congaree," "Indian Serenade," "The South—The Sunny South," "Well, Sang a Blue-Eyed Damsel," "Dark-Eyed Maid of Edisto," "Farewell to Ashley," "Congaree Boat Horn by Moonlight," and "To the Mountains." In describing his purpose in *Areytos* in 1846, Simms stated:

> The object of these poems is not simply to associate the sentiment with a local habitation & a name, but to invest with an atmosphere of fancy. ...

> These[38] will all be found to embody equally the supposed warmth of a Southern temperament with the refining fancies which assumed to have distinguished the loves of a Sidney & Bayard. (*L*, II, 223)

Perhaps because John Russell was a more experienced publisher of belles-lettres than William Macfarlane (not a publisher at all, according to Simms), *Areytos* from the beginning attracted more and better reviews than *Grouped Thoughts.* Probably the most notable of these reviews are the highly favorable one in *Godey's Lady's Book* of June 1846 and the brief but discriminating one written by Poe for "Marginalia" in the *Democratic Review* for July 1846. The former reads in part:

> Rich in the beautiful imagery of the South, these songs seem to breathe the soft spirit of the land. ... There is also a vein of patriotic as well as of tender love running through the compositions—the true, loyal feelings of the American heart, which will make them favorites with all who love their country. We have not space to point out particular favourites in this collection; many deserve to be set to music,[39] if they have not already been so. (XXXII, 285)

Poe's review is less effusive, but no less complimentary. "I fully agree with Simms," Poe wrote, "... that the Provençal troubadour had, in his melodious vocabulary, no title more appropriate than the Cuban 'Areytos' for a collection of tender or passionate songs—such as we have here." Expressing appreciation of many "natural and forcible" passages and "exceedingly spirited" verses, Poe nevertheless singled out his favorite in the collection: "Altogether I prefer ... 'Indian Serenade' to any of Mr. Simms' poems. ... Mr. Simms is, beyond doubt, one of our most original writers" (XIX, 31–32).

The years 1845–1849 saw Simms, mesmerized temporarily with the idea that he could compete with America's best poets, produce no fewer than seven volumes of poetry—*Grouped Thoughts* in 1845, *Areytos* in 1846, and five others in 1848–1849 alone. But before the publication in 1848 of his next book of poems, *Lays of the Palmetto,* Simms diverted his energy to biography, producing *The Life of Captain John Smith* (published in New York in late 1846 by Geo. F. Cooledge & Brother) and *The Life of the Chevalier Bayard* (published in New York in 1847 by Harper & Brothers). One wonders if Simms was distracted from his long-term goal—portrayal of American historical themes in fiction and, to a lesser extent, in verse—by a review in *De Bow's Review* which lamented the author's preoccupation with poetry at the expense of history (I [March 1846], 287). About this time, too, Simms received another typical letter from Hammond exhorting him "to make choice of one walk in literature or politics if you prefer it—& devote your whole energies to some mighty work ..." (*L*, II, 247n–248n). Whatever motivated him—bad advice, too much advice, the need for diversity—Simms, unmindful of his literary reputation, expended valuable creative energy on conventional biographies now scarcely worthy of inclusion in his canon. Simms's special fondness for history—particularly the lives of heroic men—outweighed his better literary judgment in 1846 and 1847, just as it had in 1844 when he devoted endless hours to his now all-but-forgotten *The Life of Francis Marion.*

If a case were to be made, however, for Simms as a biographer of literary quality, his interestingly written portrait of the Chevalier Bayard might provide the substance. The almost childlike delight in the daring exploits of the honorable and courageous Chevalier breathes life into the fast-moving narrative, which seldom seems forced, almost never drags, and occasionally flows with the natural ease of Simms's best fiction. Though not for the sophisticated, discriminating reader, *Bayard,* in the words of Trent (usually reticent in praise of Simms's work), "reads smoothly, ... treats of interesting men and times in an easy and acceptable way, ... makes no pretence of being a work of erudition. If Simms had always used such simple English ... , he would have to-day a much higher rank as a writer" (p. 139). Critics contemporaneous with Simms also noted *Bayard*'s readability. According to the *Literary World* Simms's biography "appears to have been a labor of love," and its narrative "obviously arranged with judicious care" (II [January 29, 1848], 628–31). Bryant, reviewing *The Life of the Chevalier Bayard* for the *New York Evening Post* of February 2, 1848, had praise not only for the book, but in particular for Simms's skill in writing dramatic biography. Simms's letter of February 11, 1848, to Duyckinck contains an interesting self-comment on the author's technique: "I am glad you like Bayard. I was afraid of it at this season of blood & thunder. The temptations to episodical matter were numerous, but to indulge in them would have impaired the continued interest of the biography—that *wholeness* which a biographer must no more lose sight of than a dramatist" (*L*, II, 396). And, finally, a historian of American biography with a high regard for both *Marion* and *Smith* nevertheless considered *Bayard* best of Simms's "lives."[40] That Simms, who at one time had proposed writing lives of Thomas Sumter and Paul Jones,[41] eventually dropped all plans for further biography, suggests his overdue, hard-earned realization that literary immortality rests upon belles-lettres, not history or biography.

His taste for biography surfeited, then, by the end of 1847, William Gilmore Simms—still biding time to plunge headlong again into the writing of novels and novelettes—returned once more to his passion for poetry. First, he concentrated upon editing and explicating his first love, Shakespeare, bringing out *A Supplement to the Plays of William Shakspeare* (New York: George F. Cooledge, 1848), an edition which cost him "[m]ore than two months constant labour" (*L*, II, 403). Then, in rapid succession he came out with five slender volumes of verse: *Lays of the Palmetto: A Tribute to the South Carolina Regiment, in the War with Mexico* (Charleston: John Russell, 1848); *Charleston, and Her Satirists; A Scribblement* (Charleston: James S. Burges, 1848); *Atalantis; a Story of the Sea* (Philadelphia: Carey & Hart, 1848 [1849]); *The Cassique of Accabee. A Tale of Ashley River. With Other Pieces* (Charleston: John Russell, 1849);[42] and *Sabbath Lyrics; or, Songs from Scriptures* (Charleston: Walker and James, 1849). The sum total of these five books is fewer than 450 pages of miscellaneous poems; yet they nevertheless had an impact, particularly upon Charleston, and they helped to advance Simms's growing reputation as a creditable poet.

*Lays of the Palmetto* and *Charleston, and Her Satirists,* both paper-wrapped pamphlet-sized volumes published for local audiences, reflect Simms's feeling that "as a poet, he should voice the sentiments of his community."[43] In the former Simms was speaking as laureate for South Carolinians welcoming home the Palmetto regiment from the Mexican War; the latter was a playful "local satire" prepared (in Simms's own words) "at the request of some Gentlemen of Charleston:—the people of that goodly city being greatly outraged at a spiteful pamphlet[44] which purported to be from the pen of a Yankee woman, who revenged herself on the community by a lampoon" (*L*, II, 504). Simms admitted to dashing off *Charleston, and Her Satirists* "*stans pede in uno,*—almost without alteration,—at some three sittings" (*L*, II, 466).

*Atalantis* represents a more serious effort than the chauvinistic *Lays* or the intentionally trivial *Charleston, and Her Satirists.* A revised and expanded edition of *Atalantis* (1832), *Atalantis* (1848) includes in addition to the title piece thirty-two other poems. According to Simms, "Atalantis" itself had been "entirely rewritten and improved in many respects" (*L*, I, 244). Many of the other poems constituting the second half of the volume under the heading "The Eye and the Wing; Poems Chiefly Imaginative" had appeared in the *Southern Literary Messenger* in 1846 and 1847. Bryant, reviewing *Atalantis* in the *New York Evening Post* of October 6, 1848, particularly approved of Simms's revisions for the second edition: "The poem of Atalantis has been revised and amended by the author, who, we are glad to see, has pruned away nothing of the splendor of the imagery and wild adventures among the wastes and islets and in the depths of the ocean, which made this poem worthy to be placed among the most magnificent of the narratives of supernatural agency. The traces of a mature and vigorous mind are seen in the changes which have been made." Another of Simms's coterie of Northern literary friends, E. A. Duyckinck, must have disappointed the Southerner, however, with his brief, only mildly favorable review of *Atalantis* in which he spoke of Simms's "poetical faculty in something more than ordinary degree" (*Literary World*, IV [May 19, 1849], 434). A letter to Lawson, though written partly tongue-in-cheek, reveals Simms's characteristic testiness.

> I am almost cut off from all my sources of information in New York. You have failed me as a correspondent … , Duyckinck has failed me &c. The latter has not only failed me, as a Correspondent, but seems to have failed me entirely as a friend. His notice of Atalantis seems to have been a painstaking effort to say as little & speak as coldly as possible. (*L*, II, 533)

Probably the most enthusiastic, least discriminating review of *Atalantis*—one which must have assuaged Simms's ego as much as Duyckinck's review later offended it—appeared in the *Charleston Courier* of April 10, 1849. Signed "G. E. W.," this local notice began, "Indefatigable Simms! we hail thee with pleasure," and closed with the statement that Simms's poems "ought to be in every library … he ranks almost as high as any living American poet."

Never long between books, "Indefatigable Simms" followed the new *Atalantis* with yet another volume of poetry, *The Cassique of Accabee* (1849), again a collection of poems previously published, although the title piece is so greatly expanded that it really constitutes a new work. The book title suggests that Simms is returning to the Southern or Southwestern frontier for his subject matter, but in reality only "The Cassique of Accabee" itself is clearly Southern backwoods in theme or tone,[45] and many of the volume's other pieces deal with traditional topics like "Inscription for Thermopylae," "Heads of the Poets," "Attica," and "Heart Essential to Genius." Though not on the whole an impressive anthology, *The Cassique of Accabee* nevertheless attracted fairly wide attention from the contemporary press. By far the most penetrating and thought-provoking notice was written by Duyckinck, whose acuity here in analyzing Simms's strengths and defects rivals that of Hawthorne and Poe:

> … there is one author in the southern country, one professional author, … who is always first thought of whenever the literature of that section is considered. There is no writer of the country who, for his years, has done so much work, and who has been so inadequately rewarded, in just and fair-dealing criticism, as Mr. Simms. He has labored in almost all the spheres of composition; not always with equal judgment and success: failing in many trials, but fairly maintaining through the average of his works proper standards. …

> No writer whom we can at present call to mind, has suffered so severely from the miscarriages he has made, or has been so little estimated by what he has produced of real and permanent excellence. It is not that he has done too little, but that he has done too much. No man can deny that Mr. Simms is a poet; and yet no man in the country has sent before the world so much verse of doubtful character. That he is a prose-writer of first excellence, no one who has given a proper consideration to his various writings, would venture to doubt; and yet, in mere wilfulness it would seem, he is constantly sending to the press productions far below what must be his own standards of taste, and which cannot secure his own deliberate approval. In a word, Mr. Simms has trifled desperately with his own talents and reputation. ... One week we have a brace of volumes in customary cloth-blinding from the Harpers, the next a crimson-colored pamphlet of poems in small quarto, from Putnam, then a brown 18 mo. printed in the far south of Carolina, a couple of historical octavos, and so on through all the forms and varieties of paper, print, and binding. (*Literary World,* VI [January 26, 1850], 80–81)

Duyckinck, it seems, had joined Hammond in admonishing Simms for over-extending himself with minor work "far below ... his own standards"; for, in short, "trifl[ing] desperately with his own talents and reputation." Like Hammond, Duyckinck recognized Simms's versatility and accomplishments of "permanent excellence"; yet both chided the author—Hammond privately, Duyckinck publicly—for his apparent unwillingness to concentrate his enormous talent upon what Hammond called "a Great Work." Both friends were seemingly giving Simms much-needed sound advice, but in his own stubborn way he chose to ignore it, perhaps because he understood (as they did not) that spontaneous creativity sparked by exuberance and fire—not conscious, meticulous reworking of a text—was his special gift.

Be that as it may, Simms continued "sending to the press" volumes that did nothing to enhance his standing as a major author. Following *The Cassique of Accabee* in 1849 was yet another book of verse, *Sabbath Lyrics*—his fifth in two years, and once again of uneven quality, or "doubtful character," as Duyckinck had put it. *Sabbath Lyrics* (probably the volume Duyckinck described as "a brown 18 mo. printed in the far south of Carolina") consists primarily of poems Simms had previously published under the same title in *Godey's* in 1848 and 1849;[46] consequently, it cost Simms little effort to collect them for what was intended to be a Christmas "giftbook."[47] In a letter of December 24, 1849, Simms himself made light of his latest effort, referring to it as a "slight" volume consisting "of versions from & paraphrases of various passages in Scripture, chiefly from Isaiah, & some original things of serious character. I call it Sabbath Lyrics, a *brochure* of 72 pages" (*L,* II, 580). As might be expected, the Charleston press was generous in its praise both of the book and of its author, as illustrated by comments in the *Charleston Courier* of December 31, 1849: "It is hardly necessary to speak of the contents of the work, rather than to say it contains short Poems, on religious subjects, from the pen of W. Gilmore Simms, to insure its general perusal."

Another "slight volume" referred to by Simms is a prose work entitled *Father Abbot, or, the Home Tourist; A Medley* (Charleston: Miller & Browne, 1849)—a work of little literary significance per se, but of interest to the Simms scholar for its insight into the sometimes pungent, unconventional wisdom of its author. The essays in *Father Abbot* had been published anonymously in the *Charleston Mercury* under the title "The Home Tourist" beginning in September 1849; and in October of that year Simms explained his partly political intent to good friend and confidant J. H. Hammond: "The articles to the Mercury had an object beyond what was apparent on the surface. It is not improbable that they contributed to the nomination to Congress.[48] I have been applied to put them in pamphlet or book form ..." (*L*, II, 565). In *Father Abbot* Simms used the framework of a dictionary of wise sayings to express with overstated humor political and philosophical views that he and Hammond fervently held, and privately discussed, but only now dared to utter publicly. Hammond was immensely pleased, as indicated in his letter of February 1, 1850: "I have read Father Abbot & charge you flatly with stealing a great deal of my thunder. How & where I cant specify & in fact much of it I don't think I have ever given light (or lightening) to. ... On the whole it is a capital thing & among your best productions. ... It will be read with pleasure fifty years or more hence" (*L*, II, 565n).

Having used the years 1846–49 primarily for poetry, biography, and—finally—satirical essays with social and political purposes (scarcely a period of high literary accomplishment), at the beginning of 1850 William Gilmore Simms hardly seemed poised to unleash another of his sustained waves of creative energy. But the 1850s saw Simms return vigorously and imaginatively to the genre, the setting, and the theme by and through which he had first won national literary acclaim two decades earlier: between 1850 and 1859 Simms produced no fewer than ten major works of fiction with American (i.e., Southern) settings and dealing with American (i.e., Southern) experience and history. Perhaps the Churchillian principle of restorative creativity helps to account for Simms's outburst of fictional fire after four years of almost everything except books of fiction. But a gap in *book* publication in a particular genre does not necessarily mean an author is not at work in that genre; and in this case—since Simms continued to publish short fiction in periodicals at a fairly consistent if not rapid pace[49]—the years 1846–49 perhaps might be looked upon as an incubation period for the volumes of fiction soon to emerge.

The first evidence of Simms's return to high creativity came with an impressive, perhaps unique book that until very recently had been almost completely ignored since the author's death: *The Lily and the Totem, or, The Huguenots in Florida* (New York: Baker & Scribner, 1850). As early as April 1845 Simms had mentioned in a letter to Duyckinck the possibility of "an original Romance of Florida ... , the scheme of which is in my head" (*L*, II, 55); but apparently the proposed publisher, Wiley & Putnam, demonstrated insufficient interest, a situation Simms found difficult to accept, as his continued correspondence with Duyckinck reveals.[50] By July 1848—finally having given up on Wiley & Putnam as a potential publisher—Simms turned to another New York friend, James Lawson, with the message that "I am in hopes next month to complete my Huguenots, & at the close of September to look in upon you ..." (*L*, II, 414–15). The next month Simms in Charleston wrote Lawson that he was "drudging ... to get ready to visit you": "I ... am on my Huguenots in Florida ... writing 30 or 40 pages (letter sheet) per day, and feel perfectly prostrate by night" (*L*, II, 438). It was not until April 1850, however, that Simms remarked to Lawson: "I have in press of Baker & Scribner 'The Lily & the Totem, or the Huguenots of Florida'—Semi Historical ..." (*L*, III, 36), and it was June before Simms informed him that the book would "come out in August" (*L*, III, 49). It must have given Simms some small pleasure to state to Duyckinck, in a letter of September 11, 1850, "You will have seen before this reaches you, the 'Lily & the Totem,'" and to remind Duyckinck, with whom Simms was becoming disenchanted, that it "was to have been one of your W & P. Series of American Books" (*L*, III, 60).

*The Lily and the Totem*, dedicated by Simms to James Henry Hammond,[51] met with almost universal approval from the contemporary press, but it was not until 1988 that it was recognized and defined as "a new genre, which we may term *fictional history*."[52] First, however, let it be recorded that *The Lily and the Totem* was, in Simms's words, "considerably praised" (*L*, II, 79), by such Northern journals as the *Literary World*, the *Democratic Review, Harper's New Monthly Magazine, Sartain's*, and *Holden's Dollar Magazine* as well as by Southern periodicals like *De Bow's Review* and the *Richmond Examiner*. Perhaps the reviewer in the *Literary World* best captures the spirit of the consistently favorable notices: "The interest is awakened by raising the tone of history, warming it with the hues of fancy, and making it dramatic by the continued exercise of art. And it is with pleasure we commend it as a production which abundantly increases the fame of its author. It is by such efforts ... that Mr. Simms will best answer the demands of a reading public, and keep always fresh the admiration of his countrymen" (VII [September 7, 1850], 189–90). It is interesting, in the light of the strong sectional hostilities of the late 1850s, that the *Literary World* acclaimed Simms's choice of subject—the Huguenots in Florida—as a relief from the overexposed traditional theme, the Puritans in Massachusetts. The title of the book apparently puzzled some of Simms's contemporaries; the author took the opportunity to clarify its meaning to one of them, M. C. M. Hammond, in a letter of December 1850: "Strange, my dear fellow, that the meaning of the title should be a mystery to you! Strange that you should have tortured your ingenuity to so little purpose in finding it out! The Lily is the French badge, the Totem the Indian! Thank you for your praise of the work" (*L*, III, 82).

Twentieth-century recognition of *The Lily and the Totem* was almost nonexistent until Nicholas G. Meriwether's recent analysis of the book pointed out the striking originality of Simms's technique in dramatizing and personifying history. In his "Epistle Dedicatory" to Hammond (which serves as the introduction to the book) Simms had stated that his intent in *The Lily and the Totem* is something different from that of the traditional historical romance:

> Where the author, in this species of writing, has employed history, usually, as a mere loop, upon which to hang his lively fancies and audacious inventions ... I have been content to reverse the process, making fiction simply tributary, and always subordinate to the fact. I have been studious to preserve all the vital details of the event, as embodied in the record, and have only ventured my own "graffings" upon it in those portions of the history which exhibited a certain baldness in the details, and seemed to demand the helping agency of art. In thus interweaving the history with the fiction, I have been solicitous always ... to preserve the general integrity of the record from which I draw my materials .... My labor has been not to make, but to perfect, a history; not to invent facts, but to trace them out to seemingly inevitable results. ... I have been at no such pains to disguise the chronicle, as will prevent the reader from separating,—should he desire to do so,—the *certain* from the *conjectural;* and yet, I trust, that I succeeded in so linking the two together, as to prevent the lines of junction from obtruding themselves offensively upon his consciousness.

"It is by raising the tone of history," Simms concluded, "rather than by the actual violation of recorded facts, that I have endeavored to awaken interest" (pp. iv–v).

Accepting the author's own explanation of his purpose and technique and closely monitoring his practice throughout the book, Meriwether concluded that Simms indeed had succeeded in creating a new genre—*fictional history* as opposed to *historical fiction.*[53] Whereas in Simms's historical romances, the protagonists are fictional, in *The Lily and the Totem* all characters are historical figures whose actions must be based upon the broad outlines of history. Simms's gift in making those historical characters come to life depends upon his creation of fictional dialogues and episodes, an imaginative process designed to illustrate and expand upon the hard facts of history. Three characters in particular stand out for their robustness and vitality—Guernache, Le Genre, and Monaletta, Guernache's sensuous wife; and several chapters—among them "The Legend of Guernache," "The Conspiracy of Le Genre," and "The Sedition at La Caroline,"—move with the powerful narrative sweep of his best novels. There are weaknesses in *The Lily and the Totem:* some key characters—D'Erlach, for instance—are flat and uninteresting; transitions between chapters are sometimes awkward and cumbersome; and Simms's prose is too frequently turgid and bombastic, rather than sprightly and spare. But the book overall has remarkable vitality and readability, with stunning examples of realism in the graphic descriptions of the cruelty and violence of the Indians and the French; in the humanistic portrayal of the Indian; in the satirical treatment of pagan and Catholic religion; and in the relatively frank disclosure of human sexuality and passion. *The Lily and the Totem* is not Simms's masterpiece; but its power and originality cannot be denied. As the one and only example of fictional history—in Simms's or presumably any other writer's repertoire—*The Lily and the Totem* is among those neglected books whose reexamination can only lead to greater recognition of the stature of its author.

*The Lily and the Totem* is not, however, the only unusual work published by Simms in September 1850: on September 10 printer Edward C. Councell issued in Charleston a curious little book entitled *Flirtation at the Moultrie House,* Simms's only attempt at fiction in epistolary form. A light farcical comedy of manners gently satirizing fashionable Charleston society, *Flirtation* purports to be (in the words of the title page) "a Series of Letters, from Miss Georgiana Appleby, To Her Friends in Georgia, Showing the Doings At the Moultrie House, and the Events Which Took Place at the Grand Costume Ball, On the 29th August, 1850; With Other Letters." The advertisement to *Flirtation at the Moultrie House* claims that the "publisher happened upon these curious epistles in a strange manner. They were found, in a small reticule, near Steam Boat Ferry Wharf, on last Saturday night, by one of the imps of the printing office. … we print from the originals;—they are all to be seen at the office of the publisher."[54] Not only is *Flirtation* of interest because it represents a type of fiction almost wholly different from that characteristically associated with the prolific South Carolinian; it displays a levity and a deftness of satiric touch that make it entertaining reading even today. For contemporary Charleston wags *Flirtation* must have been a sparkling conversation piece. That Simms had no higher aspirations for this clever farce is suggested by his never acknowledging its authorship (or even mentioning its name) in his correspondence or elsewhere.

But for some time Simms had been contemplating focusing his energy again on a traditional novel dealing with his most traditional subject, the American Revolution in South Carolina. Not since the publication of *The Kinsmen* in 1841 had he produced anything for the Revolutionary War series that had won him early national recognition; and not since his ill-advised *Count Julian* in 1845 had he undertaken a full-length novel of any kind. After years of experimentation with different forms and subjects, the decision to return to his forte indicates, then, that Simms still fostered his dream of creating an American prose epic—a series of novels with high purpose on a lofty theme, America's heroic struggle for freedom and independence. The epic process, originated in 1835 (but left in suspension for almost a decade), was again resumed; and four major novels—*Katharine Walton* (1851), *The Sword and the Distaff* (1852), *The Forayers* (1855), and *Eutaw* (1856) appeared within six years—in effect rounding out the Revolutionary Romances series begun with *The Partisan*.[55]

First mention by Simms that he was at work on an as-yet-unnamed novel occurs in a letter of September 5, 1849, to Lawson: "I have partly agreed with Godey for a novel in *Series*" (*L*, II, 551). It is not clear whether the novel in mind was *Vasconselos* or *Katharine Walton* because Simms apparently offered the former to *Godey's* (it was rejected) before submitting *Katharine Walton*. The latter, according to Simms's correspondence, was contracted "to commence with January [1850]"; and by November 24, 1849, the author had "sent him [Godey] seven chapters already" (*L*, II, 570).[56] A month later Simms routinely reported that "Ten chapters are already written" (*L*, II, 582), again an indication that to begin serial publication with only a partially completed manuscript was a common publishing practice of the time. The looseness of the author's contractual understanding with his publisher is revealed by the fact that, even after the publication of two installments of *Katharine Walton*, Simms confessed to Godey: "I cannot say that I exactly comprehend the arrangement you propose to make in the continued publication of K. W. It will suffice, however, if I so provide you with matter as to enable you to execute what you design. I propose this week to send you three or four more chapters. I have drawn upon you for *two* instalments on K. W. in favor of J. Russell—Eighty dollars …" (*L*, III, 22). Because it lays bare the annoying circumstances under which Simms too frequently was required to write, Simms's letter to Godey of late March 1850 warrants examination at some length:

> My dear Godey.
>
> You confound me. I returned pages 148 & 149 within a day or two after I recieved them. If not recieved, as a matter of course I shall have to rewrite them; but in order to do this, I shall need the pages immediately preceding & immediately succeeding them. If then, by the time that you recieve this, they shall not have come to hand, be pleased to send me the folios 147 & 150—I shall then, as soon as possible, provide you with the missing pages. Up to this period, I have sent you the sheets up to the 20th chapter inclusive, numbering 226 pages. I have endeavoured to keep ahead of you, and hope still to do so if there be no farther mishaps by the mail. …
>
> Yours truly,
> W. Gilmore Simms
>
> I learn that K. W. takes well in Charleston. (*L*, III, 22–23)

Despite the frustrations and pressures of serial publication (further abetted by the uncertainty of the mails), Simms finished writing *Katharine Walton* by mid-September 1850 (*L*, III, 60); and upon the publication of the final periodical installment in December, he proceeded to use the printed version in *Godey's* as fair copy in seeking a book publisher. Within several months the novelist reached an agreement with Abraham Hart of Philadelphia for *Katharine Walton* to be published in book form, as Simms's letter of March 28, 1851, to Hart reveals: "I send you by the same mail with this 32 printed chapters of Katherine Walton. The residue shall be sent next week" (*L*, III, 104). Simms added with reference to the book's subtitle, "If you prefer to call it 'The Rebel of Dorchester,' I am satisfied."[57]

In late August or early September A. Hart published *Katharine Walton: or, The Rebel of Dorchester. An Historical Romance of the Revolution in Carolina,* and the book was greeted by generally favorable reviews and even more impressive sales, the "whole Edition" being "sold off in ten days" (*L*, III, 145).[58] Perhaps the most enthusiastic of the early reviews appeared in the *Literary World* of September 27, 1851: "Mr. Simms has thoroughly acquainted himself with the history and traditions of his own peculiar sphere, and that in the most minute manner. In 'Katharine Walton' his scenes are true to the life, the incidents, whether in the greenwood or the drawing-room, real occurrences ..." (IX, 244–45). The *Charleston Courier* of September 11 predicted "an extensive popularity" for "this volume" from "the pen of our talented fellow citizen, Wm. Gilmore Simms, Esq. ... ," a review apparently unseen by Simms, who complained in a letter to M. C. M. Hammond that, despite its popularity abroad, "[t]he work not noticed in the Charleston or S. C. papers" (*L*, III, 145).[59] Fuller, more extensive critiques followed the 1854 publication of a "new and revised edition" by Redfield, for which Simms produced an important introductory essay.

In a letter of February 16, 1850, to E. A. Duyckinck, Simms offered an explanation of the role of the new novel:

> It is one of a trilogy devoted to the illustration of Revolutionary History in South Carolina, the two first being "The Partisan" and "Mellichampe." Each of these works is independent of its fellow, but the progress of the action (Historical) is uniform and consistent through the whole bringing down events from the Siege & Fall of Charleston, to the virtual close of the conflict in the famous battle of Eutaw. (*L*, III, 19)

Simms's commentary to Duyckinck accurately reveals his concept of the Revolution as an American epic, but his claim that each novel "is independent of its fellow," though true, may be misleading in that *Katharine Walton* is actually a sequel to *The Partisan,* carrying over important characters and beginning at the exact point at which the latter leaves off.

Later—in the introduction to the Redfield edition—Simms expanded upon a major difference between *Katharine Walton* and the earlier two novels: "While 'The Partisan,' and 'Mellichampe,' occupied ground in the interior, scenes at the head of the Ashley and along the Santee and Wateree, 'Katharine Walton' brings us to the city; and a large proportion of the work, and much of its interest, will be found to consist in the delineation of the social world of Charleston, during the Revolutionary period" (p. 3). By concentrating upon Charleston as its scene of action, *Katharine Walton* possesses greater unity and cohesiveness than the other novels in the trilogy. Simms's powers of description are at their apex in his portrayal of the manners, morals, and mores—as well as the charm and sensuous beauty—of his native city. With the social and political intrigues of British-occupied Charleston as its unifying center, *Katharine Walton* is relatively free of the awkward shifts in action and setting that plague much of Simms's work; and his vivid characterizations of both historical and fictional figures are essential to his dramatization of the diplomatic and military battle for control of Charleston. The spunky and witty title character herself is the most appealing of Simms's nubile young heroines, too frequently unconvincing exemplars of beauty and piety. Deserving to be considered among the best of Simms's novels, *Katharine Walton* has a sense of structure and place—a wholeness of purpose—perhaps unmatched by the other Revolutionary Romances. Simms himself seems to have recognized his basic achievement in *Katharine Walton,* calling it "the most *symmetrical* & *truthful* of all my Revolutionary novels" (*L,* VI, 120).

In addition to *Katharine Walton,* the year 1851 saw the prolific Charlestonian —presumably while directing most of his thought and energy to the next novel in the Revolutionary series—add two other publications to his growing canon. One of these was a rare excursion into poetic drama, a little book (actually a pamphlet) issued in Richmond by John R. Thompson entitled *Norman Maurice; or, The Man of the People. An American Drama,* after first having appeared serially in the *Southern Literary Messenger* in six installments, April through August 1851.

The composition of "*the Tragedy,*" as Simms liked to call *Norman Maurice,* had begun as early as July 1847 (*L,* II, 341), and from the beginning he had visualized it as "the play for [Edwin] Forrest" (*L,* II, 346), the famous New York actor whom Simms knew, admired, and hoped would play the leading role. On September 23, 1847, Simms wrote Lawson in some detail of his hopes and expectations for "the tragedy" now "finished":

> Four acts have been sent to Forrest, and the fifth needs only to be copied out. For the thing now that it is done, I can say nothing. I liked it as I wrote, but have ceased to judge of it now. I leave that for him & you to say. I presume he'll give you a glimpse of it, and I trust 'twill like him. I have drawn the hero with F. himself in my eye—a portrait which I hope will not displease him. My notion is that if he likes it, it will tend very much to make the audience identify him with it mentally & politically. *But, nous verrons.* The fifth act, I shall probably copy out in another week. I was in hopes to have heard from him touching the first acts before I wrote the last three; but not a word. Had he written his suggestions, I might have altered as I wrote. Now, he must make his own amendments. If he don't like it, I will elaborate & publish for the benefit of the fraternity. I confess myself very anxious to hear from him. (*L,* II, 350)

This letter is significant in that once again we get insight into Simms's philosophy as well as his habits of composition. A later letter to Lawson, after the author had heard from Forrest "that the thing does not suit him," presumably because the blank verse dialogue was not "carefully elaborated," reveals Simms's mild irritation that Forrest had not recognized his intent of writing "a *domestic* drama," a "good *acting* piece," for which "a style … not greatly elevated above that of ordinary conversation" had been "deliberately determined on" (*L*, III, 356). Though reluctant to drop hope that Forrest perform the play written for him,[60] Simms eventually settled for having it published as a thin paperback finally hitting the literary market in December 1851 with its author still maneuvering for a stage production, either in Charleston or in St. Louis, the drama's setting.[61]

Despite Simms's lack of success in getting *Norman Maurice* performed, its printed version (whether in its form as a *Messenger* serial or as a separate book) attracted considerable notice, including several highly laudatory reviews. Rufus W. Griswold, writing in *International Magazine,* called it "in many respects an admirable play—bold, simple, and yet striking in conception, and wrought out with a general fitness and force of incident and style that should secure it … immediate and very eminent success on the stage. There has never been acted an *American* play of equal merit" (IV [October 1, 1851], 412). It was Griswold's review, no doubt, that prompted Simms to remark on October 11, 1851: "My drama of Norman Maurice is pronounced at the North the best ever published in America. In S. C. no notice of it at all" (*L*, III, 145–46). Later, however, the *Charleston Mercury* corrected this local deficiency by rendering praise for *Norman Maurice* in its December 5, 1851, issue: "There is great merit in this play of Mr. Simms, and it has been largely acknowledged. The dialogue is lively and often intense, and the verse has that unfettered movement which can only be the result of careful study and practice." Joining in the chorus of approbation were *Harper's New Monthly Magazine: "Norman Maurice* … can not fail to add to the high literary reputation of its distinguished author … marked by an idiomatic simplicity that reminds one of the golden age of dramatic writing" (IV [January 1852], 274); *Literary World:* "In Norman Maurice we have a noble ideal of many of the best qualities in our nature: trust, bravery, eloquence, address. … Scattered all over the piece are gems of poetic illustration, moralizing, and philosophy …" (IX [September 20, 1851], 223); and *Godey's:* "… a play of great merit and power …" (XLIV [February 1852], 167). Later, the *Southern Literary Gazette,* in issuing a supplement including Act I of *Norman Maurice,* commented: "That 'Norman Maurice' is an able play, and eminently fitted for the stage, is but a moiety of the praise which is its due. … we know none of its equal among American plays" (n.s., I [June 19, 1852], 52). And in 1854 when *Norman Maurice* was republished in the two-volume Redfield edition of Simms's *Poems Descriptive, Dramatic, Legendary and Contemplative,*[62] a reviewer in *Graham's* singled it out as "our favorite": "The smiting energy of the style, and the direct reference of the plot and characterization to contemporary American politics, have given it a wider circulation than the other poems collected in these volumes" (XLIV [May 1854], 546).

In their letters Simms's correspondents were no less lavish in praise for *Norman Maurice* than were the critics in print. James H. Hammond, never reluctant to deliver candid, frank criticism, wrote his author friend, "In a word I think it your best production. There is more true poetry & more genuine sentiment in it than in anything you have written, & the dramatic interest is completely sustained throughout" (*L*, III, 146n). In a letter of April 10, 1852, Thomas Holley Chivers made a similar observation: "I … find it the best thing that *I* have ever seen of yours—in fact, I am now puzzled to know why you should ever have worn out your faculties in writing Novels. … You have shown in this Play that you are not unacquainted with the *true Dramatic Style* …" (*L*, III, 169n). If there is reason to question Hammond's literary judgment and Chivers's literary motive[63] in these private comments, Simms himself held *Norman Maurice* in comparatively high esteem among his works, never departing from his early sentiment that, given fair opportunity, the play would "make a hit" (*L*, II, 364).

What Simms attempted to accomplish in *Norman Maurice* may have been impossible. In 1851 his combination of vernacular dialogue and what has been termed "bald" Elizabethan blank verse was a theatrical experiment in advance of its time; and his portrayal of Norman Maurice as the loyal, brave, honest, articulate "man of the people" who championed the Constitution addressed a political problem certain to polarize readers. In his study of Simms as a dramatist, Charles S. Watson pointed out that the "political purpose" of *Norman Maurice* "was to support the extension of slavery west of Missouri into the territory won by the Mexican War and to attack the well-known senator from Missouri, Thomas Hart Benton."[64] Indeed, in his otherwise laudatory review, Griswold had considered "one of the chief faults" of *Norman Maurice* to be its use "in the present time" of a plot involving "the election of a senator from Missouri," because "the history of Missouri politics is so familiar that no illusion in the case is possible" (*International Magazine,* IV [October 1, 1851], 412). This timely relevance might, in itself, be regarded a strength rather than a weakness, at least by modern standards, but in drawing the character "Colonel Ben" Ferguson, an opportunistic politician without principle or honor, in direct satire of Missouri's incumbent senator, "Colonel" Thomas Hart Benton, Simms was certain to antagonize Benton's adherents. In modeling his title character upon Forrest (who in actuality had voiced sentiments almost identical to those uttered in the play by Norman Maurice), Simms was on safer and sounder ground: Norman Maurice was in Simms's mind a symbol of the trust and honor that a democracy had a right to expect in the representatives of its people.

Simms created Norman Maurice for Edwin Forrest; but it is also true that Simms's concept of Maurice is strongly autobiographical. In the play Simms has Maurice, a Philadelphian, move west to Missouri; just as Simms, a Charlestonian, had contemplated a move west to Mississippi, largely for the reasons that motivate his fictional hero. Maurice—like Simms—could say of his fellow citizens:

> I know the people—
> Love them—would make them mine! I have ambition
> To serve them in high places, and do battle
> With the arch-tyrannies. . . .

When Clarice asks Maurice, "could you not serve them *here*?" he responds (again in a fashion reminiscent of Simms):

> *Maurice.* No! No!
> *Clarice* Wherefore not?—
> And oh! they need some saviour here, methinks!
> *Maurice.* Ay! They do need! But I am one of them,—
> Sprung from themselves—have neither friends nor fortune,
> And will not stoop, entreating as for favor,
> . . . In the West,
> There is a simpler and a hardier nature,
> That proves men's values, not by wealth and title,
> But mind and manhood. (*Norman Maurice,* p. 28)

Glorification of the West and an unwillingness to "stoop" to serve are Simms's characteristics as well as those of Norman Maurice. And when the author has Maurice reply to those who approach him about being a candidate for the Senate from Missouri:

> You, sirs, may make me
> A senator, but not a candidate (p. 77)

these sentiments are identical to those expressed by Simms when he was first approached about running for the South Carolina House of Representatives.[65] That one has a duty to serve when called upon—but no responsibility to seek office—is a democratic ideal Simms consistently held throughout his lifetime.

Simms's commitment to serve when called accounts for his other publication in 1851—*The City of the Silent: A Poem,* issued in mid-February in pamphlet form from the press of Walker & James in Charleston.[66] On November 12, 1850, Simms explained the circumstances of the composition of the poem:

> ... just as I was packing up for removal from the City to the plantation, with the bouyant hope that I should be able to give at least a week to deer & turkey hunting, I am appealed to to prepare a poem for the opening of a great public cemetery near Charleston—a task which I found it impossible to evade. My sporting week has been accordingly devoted to this labor. (*L*, III, 73)

A week later, on November 19, 1850, Simms delivered "The City of the Silent" as the dedicatory poem at the consecration of Magnolia Cemetery. The five-hundred-line ceremonial poem was widely reviewed, both North and South,[67] and its Charleston printing was quickly bought up: Simms reported to Duyckinck in March 1851 that the Walker & James "edition of 500 Copies is nearly exhausted" (*L*, III, 96–97). Probably no other week's work brought Simms comparable reward in good will, as the *Charleston Sun*'s day-after account of his reading at the dedication illustrates:

> As a conclusion to the interesting services of the occasion, Wm. Gilmore Simms, a writer of whom South Carolina should be proud— and indeed the only professional author at the South—delivered a Poem, who [*sic*] we at once set down as one of the best, perhaps the very best, he has ever penned. It was a lengthy production, but the interest was sustained to a remarkable degree, as the unflagging interest of the audience evinced.

The year 1852 dawned with William Gilmore Simms in the midst of one of the most productive creative surges in his career. Already the author of fifty books of varying purpose and quality, during 1852 he published four important volumes: three major works of fiction (including the most highly acclaimed novel in the Revolutionary War series) and another historic drama. In chronological order, the new titles by Simms appearing on the literary scene during the twelve-month period are *The Golden Christmas: A Chronicle of St. John's Berkeley. Compiled from the Notes of a Briefless Barrister* (Charleston: Walker & Richards, 1852), a novelette of social manners; *As Good as a Comedy: or, The Tennessean's Story* (Philadelphia: A. Hart, 1852), a short humorous novel, published anonymously; *The Sword and the Distaff; or, "Fair, Fat and Forty," A Story of the South, at the Close of the Revolution* (Charleston: Walker & Richards, 1852), an inspired full-length novel presumably rounding out the Revolutionary Romances; and finally *Michael Bonham: or, The Fall of Bexar. A Tale of Texas* (Richmond: Jno. R. Thompson, 1852), also published anonymously, Simms's last attempt as a dramatist.

It is not known precisely when Simms began the writing of *The Golden Christmas*, but he must have started sometime in 1851, because before being published in book form, the story had already appeared in three weekly supplements to the *Southern Literary Gazette* dated January 10, January 24, and February 10, 1852, respectively. The book publication on February 17, 1852—obviously prearranged by Walker & Richards, also the publishers of the *Gazette*—attracted little critical notice and apparently even smaller sales.[68] Perhaps the best review of Simms's slim volume was in the *Literary World* for March 10, 1852: "A Southern Christmas is, it is well known, a season of great hilarity, and its genial scenes both of indoor and out, high and low life, are full of the vigor and animation we are always sure of having from Mr. Simms" (X, 206). *Harper's New Monthly Magazine* for May 1852 was less complimentary, calling *The Golden Christmas* "a slight story," and charging that "In its execution, it is more careless than the usual writings of the author" (IV, 853).

Despite its lackluster reviews and poor sales, *The Golden Christmas* is one of Simms's better efforts—perhaps his best at social satire in a comedy of manners. The setting is Charleston and the South Carolina low country, and Simms was never more finely attuned to the peculiarities of class, speech, custom, and tradition that constitute the distinctive charm of his home region. Like "Maize in Milk" and *Castle Dismal, The Golden Christmas* is a centerpiece portrait of Christmas in the Old South, and it glories in presenting the sounds, tastes, smells, and other indoor and outdoor pleasures of the most festive season of the year. In addition *The Golden Christmas* is a fascinating study of the social and ethnic distinctions that separated Charleston's two ruling classes. Manly and overbearing, Major Marmaduke Bulmer, enamored of his sturdy English stock, and sharp-tongued and aristocratic Madame Agnes-Theresa Girardin, a French Huguenot proud of her "blue blood," are at the outset equally prejudiced and disdainful in their views of each other. As representatives of their respective classes, Major Bulmer, "the Carolina gentleman of the old school" (p. 29), and Madame Girardin, the tall, gaunt gentlewoman convinced that "some secret virtue in her blood ... made her very unlike, and superior to other people" (pp. 16–17), are eventually brought to mutual respect and understanding, graciously giving their blessing to the union of Bulmer's son, Ned, with Girardin's granddaughter, Paula Bonneau. The narrator-protagonist, Dick Cooper—"an English cross upon a Huguenot stock" who thus "seem[ed] not to have inherited any prejudice of race from either the English or French side of the house" (pp. 17–18)—greatly assisted in bringing the two rival factions together, in the course of winning for himself the hand of Beatrice Mazyck, the Charleston beauty initially selected by Major Bulmer as the prize match for his reluctant son. The plot unrolls quickly and the descriptive passages are vivid and sensuous, but, most significant of all, *The Golden Christmas* captures—with wit and good humor, yet with admirable objectivity—the nuances, the distinguishing characteristics, the strengths and weaknesses, of Southern society at its most sophisticated and gracious level.

*As Good as a Comedy,* Simms's second publication in 1852, shows the multi-talented humorist in yet another vein, the vernacular comic novel of the Southwestern frontier. The germ for the new book can be traced all the way back to 1839, when Simms—apparently with a humorous native tale like *As Good as a Comedy* in mind—wrote to Edward L. Carey, his Philadelphia publisher: "It may be that in a month or two, I will require you to break ground for another, new, anonymous author, in an entirely new field" (*L,* VI, 17). Another six years passed before Simms, in a letter to Lawson, revealed that he had not dropped the idea: "Ask Stringer [New York publisher] how he would like a story with the title 'A Dead Shot, or as Good as a Comedy'—a thing of 150 pages to be written" (*L,* II, 84). Again in 1845, in his essay entitled "The Humorous in American and British Literature" Simms demonstrated his continuing interest in the comic oral tradition of the South, particularly as exemplified in books like Longstreet's *Georgia Scenes* (1835). The "thing ... to be written" that Simms mentioned to Lawson was slow in coming; but the reasons are not difficult to comprehend. Though attracted to the idea of doing something different, Simms knew that his hard-earned reputation came from his full-length historical novels, and he (rightfully) gave them priority over an experiment with the short comic novel. Accordingly, to reduce the risk to his reputation, Simms—when he eventually finished *As Good as a Comedy* and hit upon A. Hart as the publisher—insisted that the work be issued anonymously.

"Be particular in maintaining the secret of the anonymous book," Simms urged Hart in a letter of March 1851, "as it enters a field which I had but partially before attempted" (*L,* III, 105). Simms persisted in expressing concern that his authorship of *As Good as a Comedy* not be revealed, suggesting to Hart that *Katharine Walton* and the comic novel "be confided to different printers, or they may discover the identity of scribblement & scribbler" (*L,* VI, 116). Finally, only two months before the date of publication, Simms wrote his publisher in some detail about his desire for anonymity: "It is an experiment in a path which I never pursued before, and I am disposed to think that, in our country, the better course is to be anonymous as often and as long as possible." The author believed that "in their passion for change & novelty," American readers "soon tire of familiar names"; and consequently "a reputation is seldom long the guarantee for circulation" (*L,* VI, 121–22).

Thus it was with caution that Simms entered a genre for which he was superbly endowed and in which he learned to excel. Published as an entry in A. Hart's series, "The Library of Humorous American Works," *As Good as a Comedy* was generally hailed as a significant contribution to native American humor. For instance, the *Literary World* for March 27, 1852, stated:

> As Good as a Comedy is a rather boastful title for the book of an unknown author, and yet never was promise more faithfully fulfilled. The publishers have given us many amusing books in their humorous library, but the last is worth all the others. ... it is ... the most faithful and amusing description of the bright side of Georgia Life that we have yet seen. ... one of the most truly amusing and thoroughly American books that we have met with. (X, 223)

Other critics joined with the *Literary World* in recognizing a bright "new" talent. *Godey's,* for June 1852, asserted that "the author ... in many respects, and in many of his descriptions, is quite equal to Dickens in some of his very best efforts" (XLIV, 515). The *Southern Literary Gazette* for June 19, 1852, claimed "the humor" of *As Good as a Comedy* "absolutely irresistible" (n.s., I, 291). "The author of this book is modest ..." the *Democratic Review* for May 1852 stated. "We assure him he is more humorous than he appears to believe he is, and much more than several who make large pretensions to that honored name, 'Humorist.' This book will please and is worthy of reading ..." (n.s., I, 479). Only *Norton's Literary Gazette* of May 15, 1852, added a sour note to the chorus: "If the book be regarded as a picture of life in Georgia, we should much prefer living somewhere else" (II, 89).

Even James Henry Hammond, who frequently chided Simms for writing "too much beyond all question" and warned him against "dilut[ing] yourself to such a degree that Posterity will not take the trouble to analyze you," nevertheless had words of praise for *As Good as a Comedy:* "... excellent. ... admirably drawn ..." (*L,* III, 178n). Simms himself must have been pleased that his experiment in humor was completed without mishap—indeed was accomplished with some distinction. The versatile writer had tested his abilities in a new genre and had discovered that he had the strength to compete in it successfully. Later—although he never gave backwoods humor, or any humor per se, a high priority—he was to return to the genre for some of his best writing. As an author Simms had matured, with knowledge of his powers and weaknesses and with the capability to pace himself creatively, without forfeiting his long-range goal of recording in fiction America's heroic struggle for national identity. He knew how to renew his energy and to fire his creativity for his major task by diverting his imagination into alternate (sometimes nonliterary) pursuits. But, it is important to note, portrayal of America was consistently his theme—though the medium, the intent, and the scope might vary.

Thus, in a very real sense the writing of *The Golden Christmas* and *As Good as a Comedy* rekindled Simms's genius for what some consider his *magnum opus, The Sword and the Distaff*—or, preferably, *Woodcraft or Hawks above the Dovecote,* the title Simms gave it for the revised edition issued by Redfield in 1854 and by which it is now known. With all the powers of the mature novelist, in *Woodcraft* Simms focuses upon the subject, the setting, and the characters he knew best: the close of the Revolutionary War in low-country South Carolina, peopled with historic and fictional characters that carry over from the earlier novels in the series. The fifth of the Revolutionary Romances to be written, *Woodcraft* is the last in the series of eight in its historical context. It probably represents the turning point, the climax, of Simms's career as a novelist.

Simms's first acknowledgment in his correspondence that he was at work on *Woodcraft* came on September 27, 1851, when he remarked to Abraham Hart, publisher of both *Katharine Walton* and *As Good as a Comedy:* "I have more than half written, a novel entitled 'Fair, Fat, & Forty; or the Sword and the Distaff.' It was begun, as a nouvellette … , but has run out to a reasonable sized novel." Before asking Hart, "Shall I send it you when finished … ?" Simms described the intent of the in-progress novel: "It takes up the scene and action at the close of the revolutionary war in S. C., showing the fortunes, in love, of an old soldier, with broken fortunes, whose military occupation, like that of Othello, is gone" (*L,* VI, 118). For whatever reason, A. Hart did not become the publisher of Simms's newest novel, because in December 1851 (a month earlier than Simms had predicted the manuscript would be ready for transmittal), the *Southern Literary Gazette* announced the forthcoming publication of *The Sword and the Distaff* in a series of semimonthly supplements. Once again, serial publication seems to have begun before the author had finished the writing, for on August 18, 1852—well after the serialization of *The Sword and the Distaff* had begun—Simms remarked in a letter to Hammond: "I have just got through one of my labours, the novel called The Sword & Distaff …" (*L,* III, 193). The first supplement containing *The Sword and the Distaff* appeared February 1852, the last supplement coming out in November 1852. The novel in book form, also published by the publishers of the *Gazette,* Walker & Richards, came from the press in late September—that is, before the serial publication was completed. This situation helps to account for the many "petty blemishes of which you should be ashamed" found in the novel by Simms's critical friend, Hammond (*L,* III, 243n). In addition to the "monstrosities in Sword & Distaff" (Simms's term) which Hammond found in the first printing, Simms himself had serious reservations about the management and marketing skills of Walker & Richards. On November 24, 1852, the novelist complained to Hammond: "... these miserable dolts in Charleston have been reprinting some of my old works & procured from me one or two new ones. Such has been their management that they have printed the books without arranging for their circulation. They have neither sought nor established agencies, & cannot sell the best book in the world" (*L*, III, 212).

Despite these real technical shortcomings, the unusual quality of the novel itself was almost immediately recognized. The first known review of *Woodcraft* (or *The Sword and the Distaff* as it was then termed), in the *Literary World* for December 4, 1852, is a worthy piece of literary criticism:

> In Mr. Simms's new novel, we recognize many of the characters of his "Katharine Walton," ... yet between the two works, there is but little similarity. In "Katharine Walton" the author introduced with an unsparing hand, so many anecdotes of the revolutionary times in Charleston, that although interesting ... they marred the vitality of the author into a super-abundance of drawing-room small talk, and scenes of city life, which certainly are not his forte.
>
> Mr. Simms requires breathing room and space for action. In the stirring scenes of wild-wood life, the ambush, the surprise, the bush fight, the campfire, and the break-neck hunt, he is pre-eminent. In his descriptions of the rough hewn; and the half published specimens of backwoods humanity, and in his rendering of droll vernacular, he is perfect. His negroes are living and breathing specimens of human ebony, filled with the same queer conceits, and speaking with the very tongues of the genuine article. It is evident that he has looked much at life with an humorist's eye, from the windows of a plantation cottage, that he has many a time and oft followed hound and deer through forest and thicket, and over river and swamp in the mad excitement of the chase, and that the love of the free air of heaven, and the passion for the wild sports of the greenwood thus imbibed, make imparted truth, freshness, and life to his pen-drawn pictures.
>
> In the "Sword and Distaff" Mr. Simms has given his fancy fair play in its own proper field. ... (XI, 358–59)

No other review of *The Sword and the Distaff* was as extensive as the *Literary World*'s, nor was the book widely noticed, giving substance to Simms's charge that his publishers were deficient in "arranging for ... circulation."[69] The novelist was wrong, however, in his remark to Hammond that "My last Book, 'The Sword & Distaff' has not been named by a single

Carolina Press" (*L,* III, 222). The *Charleston Courier* of October 21, 1852, had been both enthusiastic and generous in its reception of the new novel "from the polished pen of that talented and elegant writer, William Gilmore Simms, Esq.," observing that "In all his writings Mr. Simms draws most successfully from actual scenes and circumstances, and casts over them, with a master's hand, that atmosphere from the realms of the ideal. ..."[70]

It is in *Woodcraft* that Simms most fully develops Porgy, the gallant, corpulent, witty philosopher-soldier-epicure who is one of the most memorable characters in all of American literature. And Porgy is more than matched, in intelligence and diplomatic skill if not in wit and appetite, by his courageous, independent-minded, pleasantly plump neighbor and plantation owner, the widow Eveleigh, Simms's most attractive mature female character. These two figures dominate an impressive book filled with interesting characters, beautiful descriptive passages capturing the sensuousness of the South Carolina low country that Simms knew so well, and the kind of virile humor and vernacular wit that only Simms at his best could create. In addition, as James Meriwether has convincingly pointed out, *Woodcraft* is permeated by a serious theme that unifies the seemingly disparate elements of the novel: "the process of the evolution, growth, and progress of a society and a culture from their crude beginnings."[71]

For a book of well-earned distinction to be regarded as primarily or even partially a propagandistic device is regrettable, but there are those who have seen *Woodcraft* as Simms's response to abolitionism—more specifically, to Harriet Beecher Stowe's *Uncle Tom's Cabin.*[72] That Simms had "more than half written" *Woodcraft* at the time of *Uncle Tom's Cabin*'s publication in book form in March 1852 casts doubt upon a theory that, at best, has little relevance to the merits of Simms's novel. Admirers of Simms's literary achievement in *Woodcraft* concur with Meriwether[73] in believing that Simms's observation to Hammond about the novel's being "probably as good an answer to Mrs. Stowe as has been published" (*L,* III, 222–23) has been misread: rather than a statement of the book's purpose or intent, Simms's subsequent remark to a close friend seems only a side comment on its possible effect.[74]

With the completion of *Woodcraft* Simms had enlarged upon his epic story of America's battle for freedom and self-identity. But before proceeding further, he sought the diversion of an interesting but less arduous task, thereby perhaps entering into what was for him a natural cycle for restoring creativity. With the recent critical (if not theatrical) success of *Norman Maurice* in mind, why not—he must have asked—turn to drama once again, on a patriotic theme, with an eye to stage production? And because some risk would be involved—in a new venture by a well-known novelist in a relatively new field—Simms may have sought to minimize that chance by again publishing the work anonymously (as he had done with *As Good as a Comedy*). In any case *Michael Bonham,* "a tale of Texas," in five acts, "By a Southron," came forth in Richmond in July 1852 from the press of John R. Thompson, publisher of the *Southern Literary Messenger* and *Norman Maurice.*

As a result Simms accomplished in 1852 almost exactly what he had contemplated doing as early as 1843. In November 1843 he had first mentioned the *Michael Bonham* idea to James Lawson—"what think you of a melodrama which I have been projecting as an experiment, for the Charleston Theatre—the scene in Texas—the subject the fall of the Alamo &c" (*L,* I, 387). Shortly thereafter Simms wrote his New York friend in more detail: "By the way, I am preparing a melodrama for Forbes [William C. Forbes, manager of Charleston Theatre, 1842 to 1847]. … It is founded upon the conquest of the Alamo by the Texans & the subsequent battle of San Jacinto. … I am writing it just to see if I can accomplish the action of a drama. I hope to conclude it this week. Say nothing on the subject" (*L,* I, 388). Simms's interest in Texas was timely, for at that very time—the winter of 1843–1844—the U.S. Senate was debating the annexation of Texas as a new slave state, and Simms, as a member of the South Carolina legislature in 1844, enthusiastically advocated expansion of the United States into Texas.[75] For another eight months Simms continued off and on to write Lawson on the subject, always excitedly, it seems—suggestive again of Simms's practice of creative growth and self-renewal by allowing his imagination free play with random projects—and he theorized that his "very Texan drama" would "make a rumpus, be sure, if ever it reaches light upon the stage" (*L,* II, 23–24). Finally despairing of ever having Forbes produce the play, in October 1851 Simms dusted off the manuscript of *Michael Bonham* and, remembering what he had done with *Norman Maurice,* sent it to Thompson, first to be published serially in the *Southern Literary Messenger*[76] and afterwards in book form.

In its printed version *Michael Bonham* is known to have attracted but a single review. *Godey's* for April 1853 commented upon its appearance in a brief notice: "The author has chosen to present this tale of Texas … in the form of a drama, in which there are many scenes of a stirring character, and many specimens of wit, love, and valor in prose and poetry" (XLVI, 375). Yet, when Simms finally arranged to have his melodrama performed at Charleston Theatre, on March 26, 27, and 28, 1855, it was, in his words, "brought out with great success" (*L,* III, 372). Caught up in the spirit of the occasion—the proceeds of one performance would benefit the "Ladies Calhoun Monument Association"—both the *Charleston Mercury* and the *Charleston Courier* of March 27 glowed with extravagant praise for the melodrama whose hero and whose author were both South Carolinians.[77] Only the *Evening News* of the same date, while complimentary, pointed out flaws in plot and characterization.

*Michael Bonham*, however, is little more than a diversionary potboiler which failed both artistically and financially. In the headnote to the printed copy, Simms admitted to taking "some liberties with the historical facts" in the presentation "originally prepared with a view to performance"; but, he added, "the history will suffer little from my freedoms, while, I believe, the story gains by them" (p. 3). Unfortunately, neither calling the hero of the siege of San Antonio Michael Bonham (rather than James Butler Bonham) nor adding a *Romeo-and-Juliet*-type of romance between Bonham and Olivia, daughter of the Governor of Bexar, can rescue a melodrama so implausible that it matters little whether it be fact or fiction. In comparison with *Norman Maurice*, which despite faults is both powerful and moving, *Michael Bonham* seems artificial and contrived. It is ironic that political considerations may have prevented Simms's best drama from being performed, despite his strong efforts; whereas his weakest—probably for political reasons—was produced and applauded in his native city.

*Michael Bonham* was to be Simms's last book-length attempt at drama, the genre in which he least excelled, though his interest in theater continued until his death.[78] With 1852 and its four publications behind him, in January 1853 Simms directed his thoughts primarily toward bringing out a collected edition of his poetry and preparing for press an "anonymous novel" begun four years earlier. The results were *Poems Descriptive, Dramatic, Legendary and Contemplative*, 2 vols. (New York: Redfield, 1853), Simms's most important collection of poetry, and *Vasconselos. A Romance of the New World* (New York: Redfield, 1853). As early as June 1851 Simms had indicated a desire to have his poetry collected. "My poetry has been published in all cases, simply that I might put myself *on record*," he wrote to Hammond. "When I can get $500 to spare, I will publish a complete collection of my verse, that the record may be ample, and all my material gatherable at a glance" (*L*, III, 127–28).

Two months later he had arranged for such a collection to be published by John Russell, Charleston publisher, proprietor of Russell's Book Shop, and the host for frequent gatherings of Charleston's literati, headed by Simms. The prospectus of the proposed edition was issued by Russell on August 9, 1851:

> PROSPECTUS.—The subscriber, having made arrangements to publish by subscription, a complete collection of the POETICAL WRITINGS of W. GILLMORE [*sic*] SIMMS, Esq., in two volumes, 12 mo., containing from three to four hundred pages. ... The works of Mr. Simms recommend themselves

> peculiarly to the South, as illustrating its history—its traditions and legends—its scenery and its sentiments; and the frequent demand for a collection of his metrical writings, leaves the Publisher no doubt that the design of the proposed edition will meet the warm approbation of the Southern public. It will be delivered to subscribers at $3 per copy.[79]

In October 1851 Simms wrote to a friend concerning Russell's proposed edition: "I do not expect profit from the thing; but now that it is announced, my pride is concerned in carrying it through, and I am anxious also that Russell should sustain no loss. Yet I fear it" (*L*, III, 145). Simms's fear was well founded, for the list of subscriptions grew discouragingly slowly, causing J. H. Hammond again to complain of "the indifference of the South to her own literary men" (*L*, III, 145n). The Charleston man of letters nevertheless worked hard in his own behalf, and, in a January 1852 letter soliciting B. F. Perry's support, he again emphasized that profit was not his goal: "*I seek only to put myself fully on record for the future.* I regard my career as pretty well over, and wish now to revise and make myself as worthy as possible in the eyes of future criticism" (*L*, III, 155). Simms still had hopes for the success of Russell's subscriber plan as late as February 1852 when he wrote James Chesnut, Jr.,[80] that if money "had been my object, I should publish at the North. But in truth, this is one of the phases by which we are to secure home independence" (*L*, III, 158).

A year later, however, though publication of the collected edition was now assured, it was, after all, to be published "at the North"—by J. S. Redfield of New York, not by John Russell of Charleston. One can only assume that subscriptions to Russell's edition continued to lag, and that finally, to save embarrassment to all concerned, Simms was able to work out an agreement with Redfield not only to publish his poetical works, but a series of his prose works as well.[81]

Though *Poems Descriptive, Dramatic, Legendary and Contemplative* contains no new work by Simms, but rather a selection by the author of those of his old poems that he liked best, it is not true that the edition cost him little effort. On the contrary, Simms concerned himself painstakingly with correcting and revising the texts, "again putting the lie to the view that as a Southerner he was cavalier about such matters."[82] Simms's greatest accomplishment lay in the novel, for that medium lent itself best to his master subject, the panoramic portrayal of America's history and development. But if it can be said that every aspiring writer is a poet before he is a novelist, this saying certainly applies to Simms. The Charlestonian never ceased looking upon himself as serious poet; and at times he fancied, "... I shall someday assert a better rank in verse than I now do in prose ..." (*L,* III, 190). More specifically, with regard to *Poems Descriptive, Dramatic, Legendary and Contemplative,* Simms candidly confessed to Duyckinck his high regard for his own poetry: "I flatter myself that my poetical works exhibit the highest phase of the Imaginative faculty which this country has yet exhibited, and the most philosophical in connection with it. This sounds to you very egotistical, perhaps, but I am now 47 years old, and do not fear to say to a friend what I think of my own labour." The poet expressed desire to put himself "on record for future judgment" rather than to concern himself with catering to the "vulgar taste" of "the hurrying mob." "Still," he granted, "I do not question that even by contemporaries, the larger claims which I make will be temporarily accorded" (*L,* III, 261–62).

That some "contemporaries" recognized Simms's "larger claims" as a poet had already been indicated in 1851 by James Warley Miles's essay[83] on Simms in which he proclaimed the magnitude of Simms's poetic achievement:

> The vigor and originality of expression, the fervor and richness of imagination, the fulness of thought, the command of language, the power and wide range of conception, united with the softer graces of deep and truthful sentiment, and of musical rhythm, which distinguish "Atalantis," will also be found in greater or less degree, to characterize all of the poetry of its author. ... (*SLM,* XVII, 289)

Calling Simms "The National Poet of the Southern Land," Miles praised him for his "keen and fresh perception of nature," his union of "high imaginative powers" and "metaphysical thought," and his "manliness of tone"; Miles nevertheless concluded that Simms possessed "the power to accomplish vastly more that he has performed" (pp. 289–91). Upon reading Miles's critique, James Henry Hammond wrote to Simms, "... you ought now to feel sure that your poetry will survive to after times, if you had any doubts before. And as you live for fame, that ought to satisfy you & put an end to your restlessness & grumbling" (*L,* III, 127n).

Specific reviews of *Poems Descriptive, Dramatic, Legendary and Contemplative* (which though dated 1853 may not have been actually issued until January 1854) appeared January 7 in the *Charleston Weekly News;* January 12 in the *Charleston Mercury;* February 9 in the *Charleston Courier;* and April 4 in the *Richmond Semi-Weekly Examiner.* All of these notices were favorable, but the one written by George Frederick Holmes for the *Semi-Weekly Examiner* was by far the most elaborate. Holmes, in a long review, stated that "the tone of the pieces preserved in these volumes, prove him

[Simms] to be impregnated with the spirit of song. ... Mr. Simms writes easily, because he writes naturally, and is guiltless of undue limitation except in his earliest presses. He ... frequently approximates to the classic grace as well as to the calm severity of the Spenserian age." In conclusion Holmes emphasized the national quality of Simms's poetry: "Mr. Simms is truly an American poet—much more so than his more belauded northern brethren. English subjects are not re-galvanized by his pen. ... He selects his themes for himself, from the diversified scenes and incidents of American nature and life."

The other book by Simms published by Redfield with an 1853 imprint was the flawed, but interesting novel, *Vasconselos.* Simms had actually begun "a romance of Florida, the period, the invasion of De Soto" in 1848 (*L,* II, 406), and presumably upon its completion, he submitted the work in 1849 to *Godey's* for consideration for serial publication. Sarah J. Hale, one of the editors of *Godey's,* objected to what she considered the novel's excessive passion and violence, prompting an enlightening response from Simms:

> I trust you do not think so lightly, either of my good sense, or of my philosophy, as to suppose that I could feel offended at objections so gently, dispassionately and amicably expressed as those in your letter. I can readily concieve, in your situation, and with such responsibilities upon you, the propriety of your objections. In fact, I sent you on the first five chapters of "Vasconselos" promptly, in order that you might seasonably determine upon their suitableness for your pages. Of an intense and passionate temperament myself, delighting in deep tragedy, and the sternest provocations to the passions, I have learned to distrust my own judgment in such matters, and gladly give ear to the suggestions of a more deliberate method and a calmer mood. I do not think that Vasconselos would ever be considered an immoral story. It is one of dark & terrible imaginings & will, I think, prove one of the wildest interest and the most intense powers. It is a tale of crime, but not of voluptuousness, and none of the scenes would have embodied an argument for, or an inducement to sensuality. On the contrary, crime, as in the Holy Scriptures, would be shown, almost entirely, in its griefs, its glooms, and its terrible penalties. So much for my defence of my story *per se.* (*L,* II, 560)

In closing this letter (rich in insight into the fastidiousness of mid-nineteenth-century American reading taste) Simms declared: "But I do not argue for [*Vasconselos*'s] appropriateness to a publication which, like yours, appeals so intensively to the more delicate sensibilities of your sex. I cheerfully accept your decision, and will endeavour to supply its place, with another to which, I pledge you, no exception can possibly be taken."[84]

Simms next attempted to interest Abraham Hart, the publisher of *Katharine*

*Walton* (1851), in *Vasconselos.* "I have had for some time on hand an Historical Romance, founded upon the expedition of De Soto for the Conquest of Florida," Simms wrote Hart in May 1851. "It is a tale of War and Intense Passion, which, I fancy, if wrought out as I design it, would prove the most interesting of all my romances." Although he had submitted at least portions of *Vasconselos* to *Godey's* for publication more than eighteen months earlier, Simms indicated to Hart that the manuscript was not yet complete: "It is about one third written, and has been for some time lying by me; but if encouraged, I should resume the story & press it forward to conclusion" (*L,* VI, 117–18). Four months later, Simms reminded Hart of the availability of *Vasconselos:* "... let me hear also in respect to the romance which I told you of, and, which, as in the case of Richard Hurdis, I would put forth as from a new hand" (*L,* VI, 119); but ultimately the Philadelphia publisher rejected the idea of publishing the work.

Without a publisher for his "romance of Florida," Simms put the manuscript aside until January 1853 when, in making arrangements for Redfield to publish his collected poetry, he also sent to Henry Panton "the first 15 Chapters" of *Vasconselos* for possible immediate publication as an "anonymous novel" (*L,* III, 224). An agreement to publish *Vasconselos* was struck; and in June Simms again wrote Panton, informing him that in an accompanying packet "you will find seven chapters of Vasconselos, 28 to 34 inclusive. I shall condense the residue as much as possible, but will not be able to compress within your limits as all that remains will be the action and incidents which are unavoidable from what is already written. You must do the best with it. ..." (*L,* VI, 139). Later, in October, Simms informed Hammond: "My Poetical Writings 2 vols. will be out shortly. New Editions of the Yemassee & the Partisan are in the press, and there is another thing, of which you wot, that will come under your notice before long" (*L,* III, 255–56). *Vasconselos,* with its subtitle now "A Romance of the New World," came off the press sometime between December 15 and the end of the year. In accordance with Simms's wishes, the book's author was listed as "Frank Cooper," a pseudonym suggested by Redfield himself.[85]

Although some of Simms's works fared well when his authorship was not revealed, *Vasconselos* as a new work by an unknown writer attracted relatively little attention. *Godey's* (which because of Simms's earlier submission to Mrs. Hale may have recognized the work) reviewed the novel in March 1854 in generally favorable terms, stating that "This is a powerfully written romance. ... The style is energetic, and the incidents and the plot, though the latter is not altogether agreeable to our taste, are full of the spirit of the age and of the characters represented" (XLVIII, 274). *Graham's,* in its February 1854 number, praised *Vasconselos* for the "tropical exuberance" of its style, "evincing that the author completely realized the period and the time which he attempts to represent. ... It has the ingredients of a fine romance" (XLIV, 236). The writer of a very brief notice in the *Southern Quarterly Review,* of which Simms was editor at the time, professed not to have read *Vasconselos,* nor to know its author (n.s., IX [April 1854], 549)—a tactic perhaps designed to cover Simms's anonymity. Among Simms's friends who knew him to be the author was James Henry Hammond, who, as always, had definite views of the strengths and weaknesses of his literary colleague's work. Of *Vasconselos* he wrote: "I think it among the best if not the *very best one* of all your novels. But you know I am more exacting with you ... than with any other writers & your faults are more conspicuous & more grating to me. ... I think you might with little trouble have improved Vasconselos materially good as it is" (*L,* III, 256n).

*Vasconselos* does suffer from awkward, contrived shifts in action and point of view and from wordy, diffuse syntax, part of which might be attributed to its lengthy and piecemeal composition. Simms himself commented on difficulties in the writing of *Vasconselos:* "The romance of 'Vasconselos' was begun, and a score of chapters written, several years ago, when the subject was set aside, to give place to other performances of more passing claim, though scarcely of more absolute attraction." Yet he denied the negative impact of these distractions, claiming that he had resumed the work "with as much eagerness as it had been originally begun"; and insisting that the "romantic history" of the subject "had lost none of its beauty in my eyes, and none of its hold on my imagination" (*Vasconselos,* p. iv). And indeed his judgment that the subject had lost none of its hold on his imagination is verified by the magnificent sweep of the closing twenty-one chapters presumably written in "hot haste" between January and October 1853, after the novel's acceptance by Redfield.

The first 357 pages and the first twenty-nine chapters of *Vasconselos* deal exclusively with activities in Havana, Cuba, that provide the background for Hernando De Soto's invasion of Florida in 1539. The technique of thus setting the stage for rapid, dramatic action once the Spaniards' landing on Floridian soil has taken place is reminiscent of Melville's preparation for the symbolic closing pursuit of Moby Dick. By chapter 30 Simms has introduced all the major historical and fictional characters important in the attempted conquest and, in addition to establishing the prescribed love complications, has traced the political, social, and financial motivations for the invasion of Florida.

In doing so, Simms also revealed the hostility and mistrust between the ruling Spanish, led by De Soto, governor general of Cuba, and the minority Portuguese, represented by the title character, Philip de Vasconselos, and his brother, Andres.

Vasconselos, opposed by the villainous Don Balthazar in his hopes to marry the beautiful and wealthy Olivia de Alvaro, Balthazar's niece, is also discriminated against by De Soto, who refuses to recognize and reward Vasconselos's military prowess, partly because of jealousy and partly because of prejudice against the Portuguese. When shocked by his apparent, inadvertent discovery of a seemingly incestuous relationship between Don Balthazar and the abused and exploited Olivia, Vasconselos—despite being assigned a rank far below his merits—volunteers to fight with De Soto's raiders. He is charged subsequently with treason against Spain and officially dishonored by De Soto for his role in warning the Cofachiqui of the Europeans' cruel plan of exploitation of the very Indians who had generously received the invading expedition. Vasconselos, branded a traitor by the Spaniards, then befriends and becomes one with the heroic Cofachiqui. Under Vasconselos's heady and knowledgeable leadership, the Cofachiqui combine with neighboring tribes to battle De Soto in guerrilla warfare that gradually moves westward. Finally reaching the Mississippi River after heavy fighting in which his forces suffer painful losses in inflicting even more massive casualties on the valiant Native Americans, De Soto becomes ill, dies, and is buried there. His attempted conquest thus ends, without victory or treasure. Vasconselos's rejection of the Spanish and his bonding with the Indians is consummated by his marriage to the queen of the Cofachiqui, Coçalla, one of Simms's most effectively drawn female characters. It is ironic that *Vasconselos,* the book in which Simms identifies with the tragic fate of the North American Indian with greater compassion and understanding than in any other work, is not included in discussions of his treatment of the Indian, for it would further substantiate Simms's reputation for just and accurate portrayal of the Native American.

Despite its weaknesses, *Vasconselos* has imaginative appeal, displays power and movement, and significantly enhances our knowledge and understanding of the history of pre-colonial America, the portrait of which he had begun in *The Lily and the Totem.* Indeed *Vasconselos* and *The Lily and the Totem* prepare the way for *The Yemassee* and *The Cassique of Kiawah* in the same way that the two colonial romances anticipate the Revolutionary Romances, and the Revolutionary Romances in turn anticipate the Border Romances. In short, without *Vasconselos* Simms's epic vision of America would be less broad and inclusive; with it, his panorama of America in fiction is complete.

Another interesting, relatively unknown volume of fiction was brought out by Simms in 1853: *Marie de Berniere: A Tale of the Crescent City* (Philadelphia: Lippincott, Grambo, and Co.), a collection of short novels including "The Maroon" and "Maize in Milk" in addition to the title piece. (Two years later Lippincott, Grambo, and Company brought out an identical edition under a different title: *The Maroon: A Legend of the Caribbees, and Other Tales.*) As was the case with *Poems Descriptive, Dramatic, Legendary and Contemplative,* the *Marie de Berniere* volume consisted of work previously published.[86] Just as Simms at age forty-seven was thinking about getting himself "on the record" as a poet, he had similar thoughts about other genres as well. In June 1853 he wrote to Hammond: "... I am collecting my scattered novellettes and tales. You have probably seen 'Marie de Berniere &c.' This will be followed up by other vols. of similar material"; not incidentally, he added that the efforts would also "yield me a little money" (*L,* III, 240–41).

*Marie de Berniere* was not widely noticed, but those reviewers it did attract were unanimous in affirming its worth. "Logan," in the *Literary World* for May 28, 1853, wrote, "It is unnecessary to say these tales are good, exhibiting all the force of Simms's animated style, with local truthfulness of scene and characters. Nowhere else may we find so good a picture of life in New Orleans as in Marie de Berniere—its author has seen and appreciated everything. It is novel too; for society there is not as we cold Northerners can comprehend it without long familiarity ..." (XII, 447). *Harper's New Monthly Magazine,* in a brief notice in its July 1853 number, admired *Marie de Berniere*'s "highly-wrought portraitures of Southern character" (VII, 282), and *Godey's* for August 1853 had an even shorter notice (XLVII, 180). Paul Hamilton Hayne, reviewing *Marie de Berniere* in the *Charleston Weekly News* for May 21, 1853, asserted that the volume includes "some of the best of the author's minor tales," especially "The Maroon" and "Maize in Milk," both "highly meritori ous" (n.s., III, 3). Three days later the *Charleston Courier* stated: "The tales are all marked by the most felicitous traits and characteristics of the well known author, who would have been one of the most popular of our novelists, and the most generally read in the South, had he not lived in that section himself."

Yet another kind of literary collection came forth from Simms in 1853. *Egeria: or, Voices of Thought and Counsel, for the Woods and Wayside,* described by Simms as "a vol. of Laconics," was published in June or July "in handsome style" by E. H. Butler of Philadelphia (*L,* III, 241); and its chief importance today is the insight it offers into Simms's basic philosophy—his rugged individualism, his faith and self-reliance, his traditional moral values. Simms had first thought of collecting his own epigrams as early as 1846,[87] but he was not able to get such a collection published in book form until 1853, the same year he also succeeded in publishing editions of his poetry and his short novels, respectively. While *Egeria* should not be considered a major effort on Simms's part—in his letters he referred to it as "a nice little gift book of social morals" (*L*, III, 71) and "a small specimen of laconics" (*L*, III, 19)—the author took special pride in his ability to articulate aphorisms. "They are carefully elaborated, and ... are fruits of study & experience," he wrote to E. A. Duyckinck. "I flatter myself that they will pass muster with the critics in other spheres beyond our own" (*L*, III, 19); and, as Simms had predicted, the little book fared well both with contemporary critics and readers, being favorably reviewed in such journals as the *Southern Literary Messenger, Harper's New Monthly Magazine, Putnam's, Godey's,* and the *Literary World.* The last named stated in its August 27, 1853, number:

> Mr. Simms has, by his achievements in history, poetry, fiction, criticism—as an orator, journalist, playwright—attained a position among the honored names of his country. ... Self-reliance, industry, literature as a study, have been his means of education in the development of a generous nature. These are the proved qualities which give value to a book of thoughts like that before us. A maxim *per se* may be of considerable value; it is of far greater when we read it as the index and secret of a noble life. (XIII, 69)

The year 1853—on the whole a productive literary period for Simms—also marked the publication (under the pseudonym, "a Southron") of *South-Carolina in the Revolutionary War: Being a Reply to Certain Misrepresentations and Mistakes of Recent Writers, in Relation to the Course and Conduct of this State,* issued in Charleston both by Walker and James and by Courtenay. As we have already seen,[88] Simms used this document (containing essays originally entitled "South Carolina in the Revolution" and "The Siege of Charleston in the American Revolution") as the basis for his 1856 lecture answering Northern critics of South Carolina's role in the Revolution.

Toward the middle of 1853 James Henry Hammond wrote his author friend expressing the hope that all Simms's "new works & new editions prove profitable" and suggesting that he "use the knife freely" in making revisions (*L*, III, 242n). In putting together his only book of 1854—another "new edition"—Simms would have been wise to follow the politician's advice, for *Southward Ho! A Spell of Sunshine* (New York: Redfield) is a collection of previously published stories badly in need of editorial cutting and pruning. In *Southward Ho!* Simms attempted to hang disparate tales and sketches on the Chaucerian framework of storytellers on a common journey—in this case a sea voyage from New York to Charleston. Mainly espousing the "Southron" point of view, *Southward Ho!* contains observations on the people, politics, and geography of the various states along the eastern seaboard, but also as far west as Texas and Missouri. It is interesting to note that the first-person narrator, a Charlestonian, considered "the bay and harbor of New York" to be "fine and noble," disagreeing with Cooper, who "was clearly in error" in denying "that it could be called a beautiful one" (p. 15). Despite the derisive skepticism of the traveler from New York ("a genuine Manhattan—a lively rattlepate of good taste and good manners"), Charleston naturally was venerated by the narrator: "… I should just as soon, for the comfort of the thing, take up my abode … in the venerable city watered by the Ashley and the Cooper, as in any other region of the world" (pp. 4, 5). Perhaps the narrator's most prophetic proclamations, however, concerned "the mountain ranges of the Carolinas and Georgia," which in time "will be the fashionable midsummer resort of all the people north of the Hudson," who "will go thither in search of health, coolness, pure air, and the picturesque" (p. 8). In another vein, in providing philosophical background for "Legend of Missouri; or, The Captive of the Pawnee," the tale told by the "bibulous *raconteur*" from Alabama, Simms—noted for his sensitive and well-balanced portrayal of the Indian—made a commentary that was historically accurate in its reflection of the attitudes of the day, if seemingly unsympathetic:

> There are certain races who are employed evidently as the pioneers for a superior people—who seem to have no mission of performance,—only one of preparation,—and who simply keep the earth, a sort of rude possession, of which they make no use, yeilding [*sic*] it, by an inevitable necessity, to the conquering people, so soon as they appear. Our red men seem to have belonged to this category. Their modes of life more inconsistent with length of tenure; and even had the white man never appeared, their duration must have still been short. They would have preyed upon one another, tribe against tribe, in compliance with necessity, until all were destroyed. … (p. 404)

Though in some ways visionary, *Southward Ho!* is nevertheless a mediocre book, a collection of stories and tales far inferior to those in *The Wigwam and the Cabin.* Only one story stands apart. "The Bride of Hate; or, The Passage of a Night," a "dark and gloomy" legend related by "an intelligent German of the party" (p. 181), is one of Simms's better constructed tales, with a consistent point of view, almost no digressions, an artistic beginning, a perfectly anticipated and logically motivated ending—all written, however, in a cold and lifeless prose that leaves the story flat and colorless despite its mechanical correctness.[89]

Simms's recognition that *Southward Ho!* was not of major consequence is suggested by his offhand comment in a letter to Duyckinck: "Have you read 'Southward Ho!' & how does it take? It ought to be a good book for the traveller & for the Holidays" (*L,* III, 340). Recognition by at least one reviewer (*Putnam's,* V [February 1855], 213) that *Southward Ho!* contained no new work by its author may help account for the fact that the volume was not widely or enthusiastically greeted outside the South. Two notices of interest, however, are those written by fellow Southern authors, John Esten Cooke and Paul Hamilton Hayne. Writing in the *Southern Literary Messenger* for January 1855, Cooke observed that

> the best criticism of this entertaining volume would be the simple declaration that every thing about it is *Southern.* It is scarcely necessary, however, to tell the readers of the Messenger that this is the character of Mr. Simms' *last* volume;—his first and all which followed it have brimmed ... with the warmest, strongest and most enthusiastic devotion to the land of the South. ... (XXI, 63)

The review credited to Hayne, who was literary editor at the time, appeared in the *Charleston Evening News* of November 30, 1854. It has words of praise for *Southward Ho!* as "a very entertaining collection of miscellanies" written in Simms's "happiest vein," and concludes: "The activity of the author's mind is marvellous, and its versatility no less so."

In 1853–1854 when the concept of "New Editions" of Simms was being debated, the idea of a "new" enlarged *Beauchampe* must also have occurred to the author. That a new edition of his frontier tragedy was on Simms's mind during his August 1854 visit to New York is suggested by an editorial reference to James Hall, the author of *Legends of the West,* to whom Simms was to dedicate his expanded treatment of the sensational Kentucky murder case.[90] By February 1855 Simms was "exceedingly busy" (*L,* III, 366) on revisions of his works, including *Beauchampe,* endeavors which were largely completed by the end of the month, when he explained in some detail to Duyckinck:

> I have revised and sent to Redfield the copy of Richard Hurdis, Border Beagles, Guy Rivers, and—*Charlemont.* This last work is the first half of the novel of "Beauchampe." I found that the story, when revised, would make 700 pages of our print, and it happens fortunately that the Chronicle of Charlemont is complete in itself—Beauchampe being the sequel. I have divided it accordingly into two works, the one closing fully where the other begins. Beauchampe involves a new *Dram. Pers.* and the chief character himself is new. This will give us two separate, though connected works, one of about 400 the other 300 pages. "Beauchampe" the sequel will be prepared & ready in the course of a few weeks. (*L,* III, 368)

As a result, then, of this extensive revision, two new novels replaced the original novel of two volumes: that is, *Charlemont or the Pride of the Village. A Tale of Kentucky* (New York: Redfield, 1856) substantially supplanted the first volume of the 1842 *Beauchampe*, and *Beauchampe or the Kentucky Tragedy. A Sequel to Charlemont* (New York: Redfield, 1856) was the expanded version of the original second volume. The two-novel sequence represents a significant improvement over the 1842 two-volume novel: Simms concentrated upon developing more fully his already powerful portrayal of Margaret Cooper, whose proud defiance and almost savage vindictiveness[91] is gradually softened if never replaced by her growing realization that her love for her husband has outgrown her lust for revenge. Forget the flaws in structure, the too frequent authorial intrusions, the melodramatic rendering of the double suicide at the end; the *Charlemont-Beauchampe* sequence is engrossing reading partly because of its swift-moving narrative, but most of all because of the unforgettable characterization of Margaret Cooper (Anna Cooke) Beauchampe. Simms has painted a striking portrait of a proud, ambitious, talented woman determined to break out "from that province of humiliation to which the sex has been circumscribed from the moment of recorded history." For 1856 this is a bold statement of women's rights, and Simms's further contention that "the great object of attainment," woman's "full development as a responsible being," was dependent "upon herself, and upon self-education"[92] should not be lost upon twentieth-century readers. In the novel itself Simms significantly has Margaret Cooper ask herself a rhetorical question protesting the lack of opportunities for her sex: "Is it true that there is no field for woman's genius? Is it true that, of all this great country, there is no one region where the wisdom and inspiration of woman can compel faith and find tribute?" (*Beauchampe*, p. 37) And in an authorial aside near the conclusion of *Beauchampe*, Simms expostulates in outrage at society's neglect of women's rights:

> And what protection did society afford to Margaret Cooper, and what redress for injury? ... Give us, say I, Kentucky practice, like that of Beauchampe, as a social law, rather than that which prevails in some of our pattern cities, where women are, in three fourths the number of instances, the victims—violated, mangled, murdered—where men are criminals—and where (Heaven kindly having withdrawn the sense of shame) there is no guilty—at least none brave enough or manly enough to bring the guilty to punishment! (p. 342)

Such statements demonstrate that Simms, though still a product of his day, was surprisingly progressive in his view toward women, particularly in his protest against their exploitation by men and their limited access to intellectual opportunity. That the author should choose the backwoods setting of a border state for his strongest expression of women's rights is surprising only in the sense that according to Simms, "frontier justice" was perhaps less discriminatory toward females than were the customs and laws of civilized society.

For the most part the reviews of *Charlemont* and *Beauchampe* were enthusiastic. The *New York Evening Post* for April 9, 1856, reported that *Charlemont* "is worked up with the author's usual skill, and the materials used in its composition impart a realness ... not a common characteristic of works of fiction"; of *Beauchampe* the *Post* remarked in the same review: "The dénouement is powerfully described, and might seem to transcend the limits of probability, but that the main incidents are authenticated beyond doubt. ..." *Graham's* for May 1856 called *Charlemont* "An exciting story, written in Mr. Simms's best style of narration and characterization" (XLVIII, 467). *Godey's* for June 1856 referred to the Kentucky Tragedy sequence as "two of the most effective novels of an American author whose distinguished merits are now universally acknowledged" (LII, 563). In Charleston the *Mercury* of March 25 said of *Charlemont:* "This is one of Mr. Simms's novels in which he has adhered most closely to historical fact." The local commentator noted the "great power" of the "true story that, in its day, agitated the whole West in its terrible interest." Paul Hamilton Hayne, reviewing *Charlemont* in *Russell's* for June 1857 named it "one of the very best" of "Simms' series of 'Border novels'" (I, 251). Attesting to the popularity of *Charlemont* with readers, the *United States Democratic Review* for April 1856 cited "infallible statistics" that "the works of Mr. Simms are in more general demand among the romance-reading public than the works of any other author whatever. They possess the great elements of popularity—a graphic style and great fertility of incidents" (n.s., VI, 343–44).

With the last of his trivial books, *Southward Ho!,* behind him, Simms was able to find time during 1854–1855 (as we have seen) to recast his Kentucky Tragedy. But in early 1855 he was about to enter a four-year period marked not by the exuberance and the surging creative force of the young Simms, but rather by an artistic imagination tempered and refined by maturity and experience. Chastened by defeat, frustrated by disappointment, yet determined to toil on, Simms appeared at the apex of his powers—confident that ultimately posterity would recognize his efforts and his accomplishments. He no longer had doubts about his subject: the American quest for identity and fulfillment was his theme, providing his plot; and the South was his place, providing his setting. Simms's newfound commitment to write for posterity, attempting primarily to please himself and resisting conformity to specifications to please his audience, is indicated in his advice to John Esten Cooke in 1855: "If I could pretend to a right to advise you as a literary man, I should say never undertake to write to order if you would write with any *pleasure* to yourself. The *profit* is quite another thing. Write for your own pleasure while you can & not for the pleasure of the Public" (*L*, III, 364).

Simms first mentioned that he was at work (or about to begin work) "upon the new revolutionary romance of 'Eutaw'" in November 1854 (*L*, III, 333). Two months later he reported that despite "a world of work accumulated. ... my book clamors to me from a host of characters, half made up, that demand full development" (*L*, III, 361). Though Simms had always contemplated bringing his Revolutionary War series up through the historic battle of Eutaw,[93] he did not determine until February 1855 (when he was "about one half" through the writing), that his "next Revolutionary novel" would be entitled "'The Forayers; or, The Raid of the Dog-Days: A Tale of the Revolution'" (*L*, III, 362) rather than "Eutaw" as originally designated. (What this decision meant, of course, was that Simms now counted upon writing at least one more novel to carry the action through Eutaw and complete the series.) The writing of *The Forayers* was "suspended" several times,[94] and once, in April 1855, as Simms approached its conclusion, he confessed to E. A. Duyckinck that he was "half disposed to fling it aside" because "publishing reports are so bad" (*L*, III, 381). But this posture was merely Simms's rhetoric to a friend serving as conduit to his New York publisher, Redfield, because by July he had completed the manuscript and the novel was published in November 1855.

By standards of the time, *The Forayers* was an immediate success. Even apart from contemporary reviews, Simms himself felt especially good about the novel, expressing not only pleasure in its quality but also confidence in his ability to maintain his high level of creativity in its sequel, which was now to be called *Eutaw*. In a December 1855 letter to a friend, an unusually sanguine Simms seemed almost to glow with the knowledge that he had performed well and with the self-assurance that he would continue to do so:

> Of "The Forayers" at the North [Simms began], I hear almost nothing. My friends here, Gen. Hammond, Paul Hayne, Jamison & others, pronounce it my best story, and (they say) the best of the American romances of any body. You will smile at my repeating this, yet there is so much in the book that I find pleasure in, that I am only too happy to believe that it has touched our pleasant public just in the place where I meant that it should hit. I am afraid you have not read it. I wish you to find it a bold, brave, masculine story; frank, ardent,

vigorous; faithful to humanity, yet as faithful to the ideals which should crown humanity. But, you smile again at my egotism, and I will not vex your sense of the proprieties. Only read it, and let me hear from you. I could wish to see any notices of it which rise to the rank of criticism—a thing, just now, very rare in our periodicals as in our newspapers. The book I hold to be fresh and original, and the characterization as truthful as forcible. It is at once a novel of society & a romance. "Eutaw" will, I trust and believe fully sustain it, & perhaps, exhibit and excite a more concentrative interest. (*L*, III, 411–12)

The *Charleston Mercury* of November 10, 1855, enthusiastically greeted *The Forayers* almost as the "new novel by Mr. Simms" rolled from the press: "It is told with great spirit, and we doubt if any of the author's many stirring narratives can be preferred to this in their variety and truthfulness of delineation. As an illustrator of history, we know of no novelist who has dealt so faithfully with his as Mr. Simms." A month later, John Reuben Thompson, writing in the *Southern Literary Messenger* (XXI [December 1855], 764), hailed "the deeply interesting Revolutionary fictions of our great Southern novelist" as the most "faithful and vivid history of the early days of the Republic" and added—"we are glad to find the unbroken series presented to the public in so excellent and acceptable a form." Though lagging behind the Southern reviewers, both *Graham's* and *Godey's* contained favorable notices of *The Forayers* early in 1856. *Graham's* for January had the following commentary: "Another of Mr. Simms' revolutionary romances, evincing his usual power in realizing the character, manners and events of the old time, and full of striking adventures racily narrated. For conveying vivid pictures of the war in the South, during the Revolutionary struggles, the series of volumes to which this work belongs, may be said to be unmatched in our literature" (XLVIII, 83). The *Godey's* review—appearing in the February 1856 number—was equally complimentary:

With many of its author's productions in this line, "The Foragers"[*sic*] has South Carolina for its scene, and the romantic and historic incidents of South Carolina partisan warfare, during the Revolution, for its theme. It was our opinion that Mr. Simms had exhausted the subject of Southern revolutionary romance; but that we were mistaken is sufficiently proved by the freshness and originality of the present exciting volume, to which we can only object that it ends so abruptly and unsatisfactorily—or, rather, does not end at all. A sequel is promised, however, in the forthcoming romance of "Eutaw," for which we shall endeavor to wait with patience, but not without anxiety. (LII, 181–82)

Simms had originally thought in terms of portraying the battle of Eutaw in "the new revolutionary romance" he had begun in 1854 (the novel ultimately entitled *The Forayers*). *Eutaw: A Sequel to the Forayers; or, The Raid of the Dog-Days* (New York: Redfield, 1856), then, was in a sense not a new venture but the extension and completion of a scheme which kept expanding in the author's fertile imagination. Before the actual publication of *The Forayers,* Simms wrote E. A. Duyckinck of literary plans that would keep him "busy enough to remain home all winter": "I have my novel of 'Eutaw' to execute, and am meditating another book on the Revolution, to be called 'King's Mountain,' which I should like to achieve this winter also" (October 13, 1855; *L,* III, 405)—an ambitious plan the latter part of which never materialized, perhaps because the declining health of Nash Roach, his father-in-law, necessitated Simms's assumption of the day-to-day management of Woodlands. In a candid letter to Duyckinck dated December 18, 1855, Simms frankly outlined his problems at home:

> I am at this time, & have for a while, been troubled domestically. My good old father-in-law is sinking under his infirmities & his mind & body are in such condition that I am required to give more heed to the affairs of the plantation than hitherto. This subtracts from my literary hours, and compels me to do a little more work at night than I relish and am accustomed to. I rarely go to bed before 1 or 2 in the morning, and 3 has sometimes found me up. (*L,* III, 410)

If these domestic and financial troubles deprived Simms of time to undertake the King's Mountain project, his literary pertinacity permitted no curtailment of effort on *Eutaw.* "My night work has been 'Eutaw' mostly, of which I have half done at least," he added in his letter to Duyckinck. "It is probable that I shall have it all ready for the press in January, and I hope to forward to Redfield what is done before this month closes." On the penultimate day of 1855 the author (confident that *The Forayers* was a success and that Eutaw would "fully sustain it") informed his New York friend: "I have been driving hard at Eutaw, and have 25 chapters ready …" (*L,* III, 411). By the following April 19, the day on which *Eutaw* was issued from the Redfield press, Simms was exultant in his eagerness to have Duyckinck read and "report on both" the new novel and *The Forayers* (*L,* III, 425). With the completion of his two-novel sequence on "The Raid of the Dog-Days" (i.e., the battle of Eutaw Springs in September 1781, which ended British domination of South Carolina) Simms had filled the chronological gap in his Revolutionary War series between *The Scout* (whose action ends with the British withdrawal at Ninety-Six in June 1781) and *Woodcraft* (which begins with the British evacuation of Charleston in December 1782). Thus—though in 1867 he was to publish, in serial form, *Joscelyn,* dealing with the early Revolutionary period in Georgia and South Carolina in 1775—in actuality, with the appearance of

*Eutaw* in 1856, Simms had finished, after seven volumes and twenty-one years, the most comprehensive saga of the American Revolution in our literary history. This achievement alone assures his immortality.

The earliest review of *Eutaw* appeared only four days after its publication, in the *Charleston Mercury* of April 23, 1856—a favorable notice which must have fulfilled even Simms's high expectations. "In the truthfulness, vigor and learning with which he has illustrated the history of South Carolina, Mr. Simms stands alone among American writers of fiction," the reviewer proclaimed. "His chain of historical novels which 'Eutaw' completes will be to after generations the history of South Carolina, in the same degree that the historical plays of Shakespeare are the history of England for the period they embrace." But because Simms sought national as well as local recognition, the review of *Eutaw* in *Godey's* for July 1856 was perhaps even more appeasing to his ego:

> The numerous admirers of Mr. Simms' Revolutionary Tales will find in "Eutaw" a rich literary treat. The incidents are abundant and startling, but natural, and seemingly necessary to the full development of the plot which is intricate and well sustained to the last. In depicting the characters of "Hurricane Nell" and "Dick of Tophet," our author has exhibited a spirit and skill that scarcely fail to rank him among the best of American novelists. (LIII, 84)[95]

Among Simms's friends and acquaintances, James Henry Hammond (as was his wont) was quickest to read and to respond to his colleague's latest effort. On May 11, 1856, Hammond wrote Simms a detailed personal analysis of *Eutaw.*

> I got Eutaw some 10 days ago ... but have had so much company since that I did not finish it until last night. I believe I did not skip a line save a few paragraphs now & then of the dialogues between Nell & Mat Floyd, & between Inglehardt & Travis in wh[ich] I saw the same things were to be said over which had been already repeated often enough for me. "Eutaw" is not exactly what I wished as the *conclusion* of "The Forayers." It does not wholly sustain the thrill & sparkle of that grand Romance. But as a work of art, of analysis, of profound & truthful reflections & discriminations, & unceasing interest—to me at least—it is superior. It exhibits more genius & more culture. Nell Floyd is a new creation almost for which you are more indebted to Spiritualism, than to Meg Merrilies, Effie Deans, & all of that sort whom you have compounded into one, & Americanized & Spiritualized to re-produce Nelly. Yet Hell-Fire Dick is fully as original & not much less interesting[.] I don't think you ever

> dreamed of Bunyan in your conception or until he turned out from your culture, what fruit growers would call a successful *'seedling'*—having parentage of course but differing in the most essential qualities from the Old Stock. (*L*, III, 425n)

Hammond was astute in recognizing that much of the strength and vitality of *Eutaw* lay in the development of two of Simms's most interesting characters, Ellen Floyd, better known as Harricane Nell, and Joel Andrews, usually referred to as Hell-Fire Dick or Dick of Tophet. Though Hell-Fire Dick had made an impressive appearance in *The Forayers* as a hard-hearted, foul-mouthed, yet incredibly courageous ruffian whose cunning and avariciousness made him a successful looter under Tory protection, it was not until *Eutaw* that Simms concentrated upon revealing, in a brilliant characterization, the curious intermixture of good and evil in a hardened criminal who from birth had been harshly denied almost all of life's privileges. Hell-Fire Dick's recognition that "all this difference" between himself and "all these rich people" could be traced to "edication" starts a gradual amelioration of his character. "When we consider, boys," he muses to his fellow outlaws, "that books hev in 'em all the thinking and writing of the wise people that hev lived ever sence the world begun, it stands to reason that them that kin read has a chaince over anything we kin ever hev." At the end of the "rough commentaries" with his roguish comrades that lasted "through half the night," Hell-Fire Dick has a new understanding of the cause of his lowly status in life: "Yes, it's the book-larning — the book-larning! It comes to me like a flash. And now I tell you, fellows, that I'd jest freely give a leg or an airm, ef I could only jest spell out the letters, to onderstand 'em, in the meanest leetle book that ever was put in print" (p. 190). Thus motivated, Hell-Fire Dick approaches the widow Mrs. Avinger with unwonted kindness, requesting from her "one of your books there." The volume which she gives him, a copy of *Pilgrim's Progress*[96] (originally a gift to her ten-year-old son, who had been brutally murdered by Andrews in a drunken frenzy), so fascinates the ruffian that he goes to great length to have portions of it read to him for his almost childlike enjoyment and amazement. Hell-Fire Dick is not miracuously converted by his partial understanding of the book's message concerning the burdensome nature of sin, but he is humanized to such an extent that he displays some compassion and sense of responsibility in his dealings with young Henry Travis—qualities hitherto unsuspected in the makeup of the renegade outlaw. The "lingering seeds of humanity" which had lain "long dormant" in Dick of Tophet, however, did not cause Simms to spare him a violent end. In his final confrontation with Willie Sinclair, the lifelong plunderer more than met his match; the "quick as lightning" stroke of Sinclair's "terrible broadsword" "smote through the wrist" of the outlaw and "rushed, deep, down, into the neck of the victim, almost severing the head from the body. He sank without a groan! A moment of quivering muscle, and all was over!" (pp. 551, 556). It is this kind of graphic realism that shocked the proprieties of even some of Simms's admirers in his own day; but it is the author's willingness to lay bare repugnant details as well as depict glorious generalities that helps make him an important harbinger of the twentieth-century Southern novel.

Unlike Hell-Fire Dick, Harricane Nelly Floyd makes her debut as a Simmsian character in *Eutaw.* Though by no means the protagonist in the novel, Ellen Floyd so fully captures the imagination that she dominates the scenes in which she appears and must be considered perhaps the most intriguing of all Simms's fictional females: Hammond may well have been right in judging her Simms's most strikingly original "new creation." Like most of Hemingway's heroines she is proud, defiant, rebellious, independent and daring in spirit, lithe and athletic in body, and unconventional of thought; she also cuts her hair short and dresses and rides like a male. Yet she is sensitive to beauty, keen of wit and intellect, and possessed of great physical charm as well as an intuitive spiritual sense that gives her a rare psychic power. She is scorned or feared by conventional men, distrusted and misjudged by conventional women, yet loved and respected by those capable of insight into her courage, unselfishness, and wisdom. Her unceasing, inspired efforts to save her half brother, Mat, from the life of crime which eventually led him to the hanging death she had foreseen for him in one of her prophetic visions constitute a compelling subplot to the stirring account of the battle of Eutaw Springs which serves as the main plot. Simms's own strong interest in spiritualism—an interest encouraged and fostered by Hammond[97]—is certainly apparent (as Hammond was quick to see) in the creation of Nelly Floyd.

In appraising the work of his fellow Carolinian, Hammond developed a process (much appreciated and admired by Simms) that became almost habitual in their long and frequent correspondence: Hammond the statesman customarily combined stinging criticism of minutiae (to establish objectivity) with abundant recognition of overall worth (to demonstrate appreciation of substance), both in advance of (and perhaps in preparation for) unsolicited counsel to Simms for the future. After the publication of *Eutaw* Hammond—ever concerned with Simms's literary stature—had surprising advice which he knew in the giving would not be heeded:

> If I were you I would now cease to write novels. You can't better these last & may never again do so well. Your fame might safely repose on these if all the others were destroyed. But you will go on I know. For money you will say, if not for fame. No; from habit—just like the habit of fighting. You would grow woefull or what is worse utterly morbid, if the people & the press were to cease talking about you for 6 months, & for fear they may, you intend to continue to '*provocato*' them. . . . (*L*, III, 425n)

There is no reason to doubt Hammond's sincerity in advising Simms to "cease to write novels," for he had long urged him to conserve energy and concentrate on poetry; nor, in light of his awareness of Simms's stubborn determination and volatile discontent, is there reason to question the accuracy of his prediction that his novelist friend would "grow woefull or what is worse utterly morbid" if he ceased to struggle at his chosen craft. At age fifty, Simms was as determined as ever "not [to] slumber while Rome lay beyond," to toil on in pursuit of the literary eminence that he felt was "attainable, yet unattained."[98]

His next project, then, was a major one. At age eighteen, or thereabouts, young Gilmore Simms, according to his own recollection, had written "10 or a dozen chapters of a novel called 'Oyster Point' founded on the early History of Charleston, which was built upon 'Oyster Point,'" a fragment which he retained in his possession with the thought that he would "probably revise & work [it] out some future day" (*L*, I, 285–86). This juvenile effort was the germ for what became perhaps his best novel, *The Cassique of Kiawah*, not completed and published until 1859—thirty-five years after its conception. Though Simms contemplated turning again to the "Oyster Point" idea in 1845, he apparently looked upon it as a new project rather than as a revival of an old one, for he wrote to Duyckinck, "I have in preparation a new romance in two vols, entitled 'The Cassique, a Tale of Ashley River—' time somewhere about 1685" (*L*, II, 81); for whatever reason, however, Simms did not begin earnest work on "The Cassique" until twelve years later, when on July 25, 1857, he informed James Lawson, "I have just laid the keel of a new romance" (*L*, III, 504).

But Simms was overwhelmed with domestic difficulties[99] in 1857 to such an extent that in late December he confided to Duyckinck: "And my novel half finished & stereotyped, has not been touched for two months. I shall soon resume it, but shall probably have to write chiefly at night, & after a good days work done" (*L*, III, 520). More than a year later, however, still plagued by "duties of the plantation" which "tear me away from the desk, very much against my will," Simms complained, "I am doing nothing in my own vocation," and lamented that the novel "in press" remained "not quite finished" (January 14, 1859; *L,* IV, 108–9). Indeed, it was not until May that Simms could write to his old friend and confidant, James Henry Hammond, that he had finally "shaken off the tedious burden of a novel which had been lingering too long on my hands, in consequence of my troubles & toils" (*L,* IV, 152). *The Cassique of Kiawah: A Colonial Romance,* dedicated to Simms's good friend, William Porcher Miles, was actually released from the New York press of Redfield on May 21, 1859.

*The Cassique of Kiawah,* coming as it did at a crucial time in Simms's career, was widely reviewed and almost universally praised. Though there were earlier, highly favorable reviews, perhaps the one written by F. M. Hubbard for the *North American Review* of October 1859 best exemplified the general tenor of respect that must have been particularly gratifying to the ambitious, hard-working author:

> Since the demise of Cooper [in 1851] there is no one who can be reckoned his [Simms's] superior among American novelists. … With skill in portraiture is combined a constant onward movement in the action of the piece, and passions vehement and tender are so blended with changing scenes and interests that he who has once been engaged in its perusal will hardly feel disposed to lay the book aside until he has read it to its close. (LXXXIX, 559–61)[100]

Another prominent Northern journal that accorded Simms top rank among American novelists and *The Cassique of Kiawah* high marks among his works was *Godey's,* which stated in its August 1859 number:

> Our readers already know full well in what high estimate we hold the author of this volume. In that high estimation, moreover, we are sustained by popular sentiment. Since Cooper, there has been no novelist equal to Simms in the delineation of early American life, manners, and incidents. We need scarcely say that this latest production of our favorite is not at all unworthy of his fame and genius. (LIX, 180)

Not to be outdone in its praise of Simms, the *New York Leader* of May 28, 1859, also called the Southerner the best living American novelist and, ranking *The Cassique of Kiawah* second among his works only to *The Yemassee,* recognized its many literary merits, especially in characterization: "We are inclined to consider Zulieme Calvert the most admirable female character ever drawn by the author."[101]

Below the Mason-Dixon line the chorus of acceptance and recognition was no less flattering. Probably no other review of *The Cassique of Kiawah* meant more to Simms than the one every Charlestonian would have read in *Russell's* for June 1859: "Were this tale to be Mr. Simms' last, we scarcely think it would be possible for him to produce a work which more fittingly closes, in a high artistic sense, the brilliant series of Carolina Novels. All of the author's characteristic powers of invention, narrative, dramatic effect and picturesque tradition, are happily combined in this story" (V, 287). Also in Charleston, the *Mercury* (of which Simms served as book editor) found some fault with *Cassique*, objecting to its "strong expressions and ideas in regard to the social intercourse of the sexes" and pointing out crudities of style, but nevertheless found the novel "of much dramatic power" and "of great vigor and attraction" (June 7, 1859); in Columbia the *Courant* ran a much longer review, unstinted in its praise for Simms and his new book (June 9, 1859). In Richmond the *Southern Literary Messenger*, which in May 1859 carried a laudatory essay on Simms's Revolutionary Romances, followed up in its June number with a favorable review of *The Cassique of Kiawah*, stating that the sterling quality of the new book fully upheld the journal's high estimate of the author a month earlier (XXVIII, 476). As far south and west as New Orleans, *De Bow's Review* for July 1859 unabashedly reviewed *Cassique* without yet having read it, but was nevertheless confident of the novel's success because of Simms's stature and because the new work "is conceived to be the best of his novels" (XXVII, 123). Without exception, then, the reception of *The Cassique of Kiawah* by professional reviewers was approving and enthusiastic.

But what did amateur critic James H. Hammond think of the latest effort of his compatriot—a novel Simms never would have written had he followed Hammond's advice? Surely Hammond had an opinion, and just as surely he gave his literary friend the benefit of it, following the pattern of mixing small faultfinding with extensive praise. "I have read your last novel," Hammond stated in a letter of June 11, 1859. "As a mere Romance it does not equal the two preceding [*The Forayers* and *Eutaw*]. Yet even as a Romance it has passages surpassing any in them. But taking the performance altogether it is perhaps superior in genius & ability to any thing you have done in prose." Then comes the mild reprimand, playfully done: "You nodded some times & some times had a drop too much, & one of your most important scenes was to *my conception* a dead failure" (*L*, IV, 152n).[102] Hammond's affectionate accusation that Simms sometimes dozed, and sometimes drank a mite too much, presumably while laboring in the early morning hours on the *Cassique* manuscript, is evidence of the warmth and the candor of the friendship between the two men. Both men unburdened themselves to each other emotionally and intellectually, always with good humor, in a truly remarkable relationship.

Is *Cassique* "superior in genius & ability" to any other Simms novel? Anne M. Blythe, in her recent essay on the subject, makes a convincing case that it is—

> the best characters and scenes in *Cassique* are exceptional, perhaps unique. They are painted in colors so vivid and with such a confident and practiced hand that the result is a work in which the highly exciting and realistic narrative movement is enhanced by what may be Simms's finest achievement in description and imagery.[103]

Certainly *The Cassique of Kiawah,* more clearly than any other book by Simms, is the work of a master craftsman: it possesses in abundance all of Simms's magnificent powers of landscape description and fast-moving, hard-hitting narration; it has the humor, satire, and realism of Simms's best stories of manners, particularly in its portrait of the corruption and greed, as well as the charm and sophistication, of late seventeenth-century Charleston society; its characterization is unusually effective and realistic, including one of Simms's best-drawn female characters, Zulieme Calvert, who in sensuousness and lush vitality is challenged only by Maria de Pacheo, the *femme fatale* of "The Maroon," to whom she bears striking resemblances; its sympathetic and knowledgeable treatment of Indian life and character in colonial America surpasses even that in the more heralded *The Yemassee;* and, last but by no means least, its magnificent opening scene sets the tone and atmosphere sustained throughout the novel, the quiet elegant majesty of the wilderness contrasting with the loud bloodthirsty violence of civilized man—Simms, as well as Thoreau, deserves recognition as one of the first true naturalists and environmentalists in American literature.[104]

With the publication of *The Cassique of Kiawah,* Simms closed out with a flourish an eighteen-year period which, despite its abundance of strife, disappointment, and sorrow, left him recognized North and South as his region's most eminent man of letters and—with surprisingly little debate—as the nation's best (or at least best-known) novelist. The latter recognition is particularly significant despite the fact that it was possible only because Cooper's death in 1851 had left Simms unchallenged in popularity and because the superior genius of Hawthorne and Melville had not yet been perceived and accepted. Simms's national standing in 1859 is remarkable: it means that the literary reputation of the ebullient novelist from South Carolina had weathered the fiasco of his Northern lecture tour of 1856—had, thus far at least, escaped being decimated by the political crossfire soon to bring the nation to bloody civil war. At the end of 1859 the literary reputation of William Gilmore

Simms was high—and deservedly so. Since 1842 he had produced no fewer than forty books, increasing his career total to sixty-two. But, more important, in the previous eighteen years he had brought to a point of logical completion two series of novels dealing with two of the most significant sequences of events in American history: the seven-volume Revolutionary War series, depicting America's struggle for independence; and the series of seven Border Romances, charting the early nineteenth-century movement of the frontier from the Appalachians to the Mississippi. In addition, he had written a book of short stories, *The Wigwam and the Cabin,* containing some of America's finest short fiction to date; he had published a collection of his poetry, *Poems Descriptive, Dramatic, Legendary and Contemplative,* of sufficient quality to warrant him serious consideration as a major poet; he had authored two series of critical, social, and political essays of remarkable foresight and acuity; and in *Vasconselos* and in *The Cassique of Kiawah* he had contributed to his already impressive study of the Indian in America, the best and most complete fictional treatment by a nineteenth-century American author. James Henry Hammond was correct when he told Simms in 1856: "Your fame might safely repose on these if all the others were destroyed." And by 1859 Simms had added *The Cassique of Kiawah.* His fame was—or indeed should have been—secure.

# IX Personal Matters

Apart from politics, magazines, and books the years 1842–1859 were important to William Gilmore Simms in a personal sense. A keenly felt sense of family and place was central to Simms's concept of the full life, and his commitment to wife, children, and home became increasingly apparent as he grew older. Chevillette Simms proved to be an almost ideal match for her older, more imaginative but traditional husband. Loyal and loving, she was exceedingly proud of his accomplishments, yet remained disarmingly modest and unassuming herself, despite the high place in South Carolina society accorded her as heiress to magnificent Woodlands plantation. Though never robust of health, she nonetheless bore fourteen children (ten between 1842 and 1860), only five of whom survived her. As an affectionate mother and a doting wife, she was the soft, yet pivotal figure in the family circle that enveloped the Scotch-Irish novelist with love and responsibility, happiness and sorrow, satisfaction and frustration during the eighteen-year period under scrutiny in this chapter.

By 1842 Chevillette Simms had already given birth to three children—all girls—only one of whom, Mary Derrille, had lived as long as twelve months.[1] In April 1842, as Simms's letter to James Lawson reveals, this young daughter upon whom both parents lavished their love was suddenly and unexpectedly stricken by scarlet fever and died:

> I have just borne to the grave [Simms wrote his old friend on May 3] my dear young child, Mary Derrille, the last of three by my present wife; and her distress and my own may be readily conjectured in part at least, by all of you. You

> have been fortunate, and I trust, will continue to be, in raising yours, that they may honor & soothe your years. In this respect, my hope rests on one only, my dear Augusta. Our little girl was nearly three years old, very sweet, very gentle, and as I fondly fancied very smart. In full health, fat and promising, she was seized with scarlet fever which ended fatally in three days. (*L*, I, 306)

Mary Derrille's demise contributed greatly to Simms's melancholy, not only causing him to withdraw immediately from his campaign for the South Carolina legislature, but also confirming in him a belief that he had held since early childhood. In a candid letter to James H. Hammond in which Simms admitted to being "almost wholly baffled and broken up" by "the dire calamity" of his daughter's death, the author revealed a deep-seated conviction:

> One thing is very certain to me. I have been always, from my first consciousness, . . . a marked man—set aside and very much distinguished by the scourge. That I feel deeply, you can readily conceive from what you know of my temperament,—that I can endure manfully, should also be conjectured of one who has been so frequently subjected to the hand of punishment. (*L*, I, 304)

Simms's indomitable courage and will to "endure manfully" were to be tested severely during the remainder of his life, never more so than in the years during and after the Civil War. The acceptance by Simms of both predestination and stoicism is reinforced by another passage in this letter of April 30, 1842: "These successive strokes of Providence, I am sufficiently a Christian to believe,[2] are intended for some great end,—perhaps some benefit" (*L*, I, 304). While Simms saw himself as sufficiently "a Christian" and held membership in St. Paul's Episcopal Church, Charleston,[3] he was certainly not a traditional Christian. Like the Romantics, he believed that the woods rather than the church was the most sacred place for reverent worship. Somewhat a freethinker, he was at times critical of organized religion—disliked its hypocrisy and pomp. In 1856 he wrote that "my own mind stubbornly opposed every creed of every Christian Church extant. I rejected the Old Testament as a religious authority altogether, & satisfied myself that the New was, however true and good, & wise & pure in many things, a wonderfully corrupt narrative" (*L*, III, 431; see also *L*, II, 385). At one point he was almost deistic (or Unitarian) in denying Christ's divinity and the Bible's authenticity as the direct word of God. But he was traditional in his own commitment to Christian ideals and in his desire to have his family live in accord with them—to have faith in God; to seek the sanction and blessing of the church for memorable events like births, christenings, weddings, and deaths; and, most of all, to be grateful for the world's blessings, individual and general.

In mid-1842 Gilmore and Chevillette Simms, after almost six years of marriage, were left without a child of their own. Augusta, Simms's fourteen-year-old daughter by his first marriage, remained a special favorite of her father and had developed a loving relationship with her twenty-four-year-old stepmother, looking upon her as an intimate older sister. "Dear Augusta" helped to sustain the hope of her father and her young stepmother in their time of sorrow, and as a result the family became a close, tight circle. Augusta, of course, could not fill Chevillette's desire to have a child of her own, nor Gilmore Simms's wish for progeny by his second wife. But the "benefit" Simms had foreseen as emanating from repeated personal tragedy came in the form of increased familial resiliency and interdependence.

The successive deaths of three daughters within fewer than five years also served to confirm Simms's already solid reliance upon religion for support and solace. This religiosity is nowhere better demonstrated than in a long letter Simms wrote James Lawson on August 22, little more than four months after Mary Derrille's decease:

> I give you joy of your newborn treasure. Believe me, all your cares sink into nothingness in comparison with this blessing which God has bestowed upon you & your dear young wife. You should not repine for an instant, but with a humble delight you should look constantly to the Great Father who has so unreluctantly and without recalling any of his gifts, conferred upon you so many and exquisite ones. Let me commend to you frequent prayer, at morning, when you rise; at night, ere you lie down; and that you inspirit your little family, one and all, with this necessary & becoming duty. To humble yourself in the sight of God, is to be lifted in your own consciousness. Try it, teach it, and you will find the good of it. "The world is too much with us." Prove that you feel this, in an occasional service which approximates you to another & a higher one. In religion, my friend, is the only truth, and the only consolation. ... Every day, leaving me more alone & destitute on Earth,[4] warns me of the necessity of seeking to regain the beloved ones in a more secure dwelling place where Death comes not.—I have perfect faith that the mercy of God, will reconcile us to our condition, nor make it too painful for endurance. ... Be righteous. You are naturally a good man, with few or no evil passions, & none violent. It needs with you but moderate exertion, to be a Christian. Be so. Make the effort, and make your children so likewise. (*L*, I, 320–21)

There can be no doubt that Simms, always a God-fearing if not outwardly religious man, was sincere in this fervent outpouring to a friend; nor can there be doubt that he practiced what he preached, that he attempted to "inspirit" his own family, "one and all," with the "necessary & becoming duty" of frequent prayer. But never before or after did he lecture so pointedly to friend or family the importance of religion as "the only truth, and the only consolation." Doubtless his own recent harrowing experiences were still troubling him and he sought inner solace by externalizing his religious convictions. Knowing his man, Lawson would have understood Simms's need and would not have been offended by what some would have considered a patronizing tone.

But a more direct way—physical as well as spiritual—to fulfill a family need was also in progress. In a postscript to his letter to Lawson, Simms added: "If you write to me, *within three weeks*, address me at 'Flat Rock, North Carolina,'[5] whither my wife has gone for her health"—"for her health" being a euphemism for Chevillette's pregnancy. Slightly less than seven months later, on March 16, 1843, Chevillette Simms gave birth to a baby boy, whom she and the proud father gave the name William Gilmore Simms, Jr. "My wife has again made me a father," Simms wrote to Lawson on April 6, 1843, "and this time of a son, a fine fat large flourishing fellow, promising well for the future if God who gave will suffer us to retain him. Mother & child I rejoice to say are both doing well ..." (*L*, I, 345).

The father's sense of joy in his firstborn son was tempered by anxiety that he, too, might be struck down like his three sisters. Young "Gilly"—described by Simms as "very fat, and promising, and they say grows more & more like me every day"—was christened in June at St. Paul's Episcopal Church in Charleston (using a christening robe, lace cap, and silver cup still in the possession of the family), with the only regretful note being that Lawson could not be present "to be Godfather" (*L*, I, 355). Simms's concern for his son's health was registered in another letter to Lawson, in late July 1843, just before departing for his annual summer visit to the North: "I leave home ... with some anxiety. You know we have a little boy—a fine strong & promising little fellow—the largest of our children. But our Carolina summer is always perilous to children, and he has just gone through a little bout of sickness—the forerunner as we think of teething—always a period of trial to infants. At all events, it is idle to let our fancies run wild seeking occasions of apprehension. We & ours are in the hands of God" (*L*, I, 363–64). Five-month-old Gilly did recover but not before throwing another scare into his thrice-stricken parents' hearts, as Simms's August letter from Boston to Lawson in New York demonstrates:

> The contents of [a letter from Chevillette] have made me tremble. Our dear child has been very ill with the influenza, so seriously ill that all my wife's fears were awakened for the result. With God's mercy he is now better, and I trust

> will keep so. But the event will hasten my return. *You* can have no idea of the anxieties of a father who has mourned the loss of three out of four dear children. God grant, my friend, that you may always escape an experience so dreadful. (*L*, I, 364)

Upon his return home to Charleston, however, Simms faced yet another crisis, finding "my wife an invalid, and the whole family seriously needing my assistance" (*L*, I, 366). "The varioloid is among us," Simms explained in his letter of September 16 to Lawson, "and my wife is at this time grievously bespotted with it." Though Chevillette "look[ed] very badly" and Augusta complained "of the usual symptoms" of the disease, Simms admitted to Lawson that his "great apprehension" was "for the infant," still convalescing from his bout with influenza. Simms's stoic philosophy and strong moral will are made manifest by his family's actions in the face of possible calamity. Relating to Lawson the decision to allow young Gilly ("quite well" and "recently vaccinated") to nurse despite his mother's illness, Simms explained that "to separate him just now by weaning from the mother might be to incur worse dangers."

> One source of consolation [he added] is in the fact that the present type of the disease is a very mild one, &—God's will be done. My losses & sufferings have made me something of a fatalist. To send off any of the family not already sickened, would be the policy of many, but in the present instance such a measure would probably be too late for benefit, and apart from this, I prefer teaching to my family that they must be true to one another. It is very well for friends & relations to keep aloof from the household where infectious disease prevails, but not so for its own members. The lesson usually taught is one of a grievous selfishness that is not only very shameful in itself, but ultimately very unprofitable. The poisonous chalice comes commended, & justified, to the lips of the recreant hereafter.

Simms's own fatherless childhood—lacking in direction and support, particularly in crises—probably assisted in determining his own role as head of family: strongly didactic in his relationships with his children, he attempted to instill in them a sense of self-worth based upon integrity, trust, courage, and acceptance of responsibility. Warm, loving, genial, and jovial as a father, he was looked up to as the unquestioned leader in all family matters. His goal was to lead by precept and performance, to provide moral and intellectual guidance to his progeny—all within a liberal Christian framework, tinged as we have seen with fatalistic stoicism. Simms, like Henry James's John Marcher, felt that he was "a marked man—set aside and … distinguished by the scourge"; but unlike Marcher, Simms—far from being paralyzed or incapacitated by premonition of doom—struggled harder than ever to live a full life of aspiration and achievement. Simms could face and endure tragedy "manfully," as he did time and again throughout his life—but fortunately the illnesses which struck his family in 1843 led to full recovery, not tragedy. In this instance at least, the father's philosophy—his pedagogical emphasis that in crucial situations members of the family "must be true to one another"—was vindicated.

Part of Simms's concept of family was that normal living was to be maintained as much as possible even in periods of turmoil. It was this belief that enabled the writer to continue the work at hand no matter how distressing or distracting a personal situation might be. Thus it should be no surprise that the long awaited visit to Woodlands by William Cullen Bryant came during the last days of Chevillette's pregnancy, and that indeed young Gilly was born during the Northern poet's stay at the plantation.

Bryant and Simms had first met in 1832, during the Southerner's initial trip to the North, and the two men and their families became friends—to such an extent that the Simmses frequently visited the Bryants at Great Barrington, Massachusetts, Mrs. Bryant's home, and Augusta returned there for schooling in order to have Bryant's daughter, Fanny, as an everyday companion. As early as 1841 Simms had issued an invitation to the Bryants to visit Woodlands, in a letter rich in its revelations of family associations and of Simms's love of the low-country landscape, which he described vividly and graphically. This long letter, the earliest of the extant correspondence between two major men of letters, reads in toto:

Woodlands, near Midway P. O.
South Carolina, Jan. 10

My dear Sir,

Though I could have preferred that you should have sent Fanny as your *avant Courier*, yet, as that could not be, I rejoice in the partial promise which you give me that you will yourself come and see me in the spring. I trust that you may then be persuaded to bring her, and if practicable, all your family—the "dam and all her little ones." You will, I am sure, feel the benefit of such a trip for years to come, and your Muse, though she may need no such stimulus, will busy herself along the roadside in a manner equally pleasant to yourself and profitable to the public. I assure you that we have some refreshing novelties at that season which will bring you singular renovation and delight after a long winter of contracting cold. Our country lies too level for much that is imposing in scenery, but the delicate varieties of forest green, the richness of our woods, their deep & early bloom, and the fragrance with which they make the very atmosphere blossom, will, I fancy awaken you to a more encouraging memory of youthful hopes & dreams than could result easily from any contemplation, however pleasant, of the familiar objects. There are no inequalities of rocks & valley, in the country which we occupy, to strike the eye & startle the imagination, such as your native land everywhere presents,—but a mystery seems to clothe the dense & tangled masses of forest, that lie sleeping around you. You will look, naturally, to see the brown deer emerging from the thicket: and sometimes fancy, in the flitting of some sudden shadow, that the old Indian is taking his round among the graves which hide the bones of his family. But—all this, to you is very much like *gammon.* Come and you will make it for yourself, and to suit yourself. I think you can safely steal off for a month and cheat the public & the paper—to compensate a wider public—and a more grateful one, in the sequel. You must remember that our spring is much earlier than with you. You might find her awaiting you, here, so early as February. Toward the middle of March you certainly will. April is a very pleasant month with us,—a shade warmer, perhaps, than your May. We generally remain on our plantation until the 25th of this latter month. We have at present with us Miss Kellogg[6] of Gt. Barrington & Miss Sherwood[7] of your city. I think it not likely that Mr. G.[8] will be tempted to come out to Carolina just about the time when you might fancy it the most pleasant for your trip. Believe me, nothing would give me more real satisfaction than to grasp your hand in our backwoods, and guide you through some of their intricacies. My wife joins me in presenting our best regards to Mrs. Bryant and Miss Fanny. Mr. Roach (my father in law) begs me to repeat to you the pleasure he would have in seeing you with us. He fancies that our Southern woods yield the most glorious glimpses in springtime and autumn of all the world beside, and he next, & naturally, concludes, that, when you ever see them,—you will find some very efficient mode of making the public familiar with their beauties also. To this, let me add that we have very little other sight seeing. Our country is without palaces or public works of much importance. An agricultural country leaves few monuments but moral ones. Our people are scattered. Our villages small & infrequent, and a private interview with nature, in her season of greatest caprice, is all that I can promise you beyond the sincere welcome of friends. But both of these you are sure of in coming to Woodlands.

Yrs Ever with great regards
W. Gilmore Simms
(*L*, I, 213–15)

After the Bryants' visit—delayed until March 1843 when they stayed three or four days in Charleston and three weeks at Woodlands—Simms expressed disappointment that "wretched weather," "the condition of family," and other factors conspired to curtail activities during the Northern poet's first trip to South Carolina. But in his letter of April 6, 1843, to James Lawson, Simms nevertheless painted a very convivial picture of associations past, present, and future between himself and the two New Yorkers:

> [Bryant] promises us a visit next season, when I hope it will suit you to come out with him. Seated in my wigwam[9] over a bottle of Hock, I assure you that neither of us regretted anything more than your absence. The wish was frequently & fervently expressed that you could be present. We could both of us at the moment 'have better spared a better man'. The scene so reminded us of old times in N. Y. I shall certainly look for you next season whether he comes out or not. "What! shall there be no more cakes and ale?" (*L*, I, 346)

Despite Simms's misgivings, Bryant seemed to enjoy his firsthand view of a South Carolina plantation, as well as his renewed friendship with the novelist and his family. He recorded his positive observation of Woodlands in letters later published in Evert and George Duyckinck's *Cyclopaedia of American Literature*,[10] and to Simms himself he remarked: "I remember my visit to the South as one of the pleasantest periods of my life. It gratified a strong curiosity, which I had always felt in regard to that region and it left with me a favorable impression and a most friendly recollection of its inhabitants."[11]

Simms and Bryant remained friends until the former's death, despite a tenseness of relations during the Civil War years; but Bryant never supplanted longtime confidant James Lawson as the Southerner's favorite among his New York intimates. In fact, Simms family oral archives maintain that Lawson and Simms "from the first moment they saw each other, they were as brothers"; that through Lawson's influence Simms adapted so readily to the New York lifestyle, he "was as much a New Yorker as he was a Charlestonian" (*MCSO*, IV, V). But, as we have seen, even Lawson and Simms were temporarily estranged in 1842 over what Lawson considered Simms's "butchery" of a letter on mesmerism which the Scotsman had submitted for publication in *Magnolia*.[12] Simms dealt fairly but bluntly with his friend's anger; on November 17, 1842, he wrote Lawson "But that you are evidently distressed by the circumstances of self and family, I should be utterly at a loss to account for the style and expression of a portion of your last letter. ... I trust, my dear Lawson, when you look into it, at a moment of greater calm, you will do me justice, and recall those hasty and unkind expressions which, I sincerely believe, you will come to regret" (*L*, I, 330–31). In early January 1843 Simms pleaded with Lawson again, "We have been too long friends, through good &

ill report, to fall out about trifles" (*L,* I, 338). Even as late as June 1843 Simms was still seeking his friend's good faith:

> ... were I not disposed to make every allowance for your troubles and your indolence, I should long since have given you up, as totally untrue to your friendship, so far as their epistolary duties are concerned. ... My friend, you should be more true to your friendships. You shall not often find a friend so indulgent as myself,—so willing to forget your neglect, in consideration of what I know to be your real goodness and excellence of heart & character. (*L,* I, 352–53)

Simms's patience and loyalty resulted in the continuation, and even the strengthening, of the friendship between the two men—though Simms periodically (and characteristically) grumbled about Lawson's continued negligence as a letter writer. Few if any men wrote so frequently and so copiously as Simms; but it was his commitment and his candor—rather than his verbal facility—that enabled the Southern man of letters to establish and maintain intimate friendships with persons as diverse as his business-minded Scottish colleague from New York and his fire-eating confederate from South Carolina, James Henry Hammond.

Hammond's relationship with Simms was different from Lawson's in several important aspects. As young men Simms and Lawson had courted together during Simms's annual visits to New York, and from the beginning their friendship was more largely personal than literary or political, though Lawson was interested in both literature and politics, and indeed served as the Southerner's literary agent in New York. But in his letters to Lawson Simms did not discuss either literature or politics in as much depth as he did in his letters to Hammond, probably because Lawson—a "rascally correspondent" with a "diabolical infirmity of not writing"—provided less provocation than did the verbose and opinionated Hammond, perhaps Simms's only correspondent to match him in the frequency and copiousness of letter writing. Simms's frank and gossipy letters to Lawson were rich in details of family, finances, publishing, and literati in general—subjects which compelled the interest of both the New Yorker and the Charlestonian. But Lawson, seven years older than Simms, was after all an outsider to the close South Carolina circle to which both Simms and Hammond, almost exact contemporaries, belonged. Though as young men, Hammond, as editor of a Nullification newspaper, and Simms, as editor of a Union paper, had held opposite views, as they grew older they were drawn closer and closer together not only by their natural affinities for each other, but also by their strikingly similar opinions of politics and literature, on which both were remarkably well informed. Furthermore, both patriots (a word which fits Hammond better than Simms) deeply loved and were intensely loyal to their native state; but each at times felt neglected, unappreciated, or even abused by South Carolina citizenry, and their mutual dissatisfaction became a common cause. During the 1840s and 1850s Simms of Woodlands and Hammond of Silver Bluff exchanged views on almost every subject imaginable, though Hammond's political aspirations and Simms's literary ambitions provided fodder for most of their correspondence, with both men holding strong views—not always but usually in harmony—and demonstrating little reticence in unburdening themselves or providing counsel to each other. In the period 1842–1859 Hammond and Simms were confidants par excellence; and the personal tragedy that almost terminated Hammond's political career served only to strengthen Simms's loyalty to his lifelong friend.

The scandal associated with Hammond, well documented in three books published in the 1980s,[13] broke while Hammond was serving as governor of South Carolina in 1843; unfortunately for Hammond's reputation and political aspirations it involved accusations from his brother-in-law, Wade Hampton, scion of the prominent South Carolina family, that Hammond had sexually exploited Hampton's teen-aged daughter Catherine, a niece of Hammond. Though the episode never was publicly exposed in print, the infuriated Hampton made no secret of his contempt for Hammond and did everything in his power to ruin him politically. The whisper campaign against Hammond became even more vehement in 1846 when Hammond unsuccessfully made his first bid for a United States Senate seat, losing almost certainly because of the vicious opposition of Hampton, who even at the cost of his young daughter's reputation openly sought revenge against his brother-in-law for his sexual misconduct with a family member. After Hammond's defeat was announced, Simms—who must have known full details from private conversations with Hammond—wrote his tarnished friend a straightforward letter. Simms candidly informed Hammond that at first he questioned the former governor's decision to run for the Senate: "I might have been scared from it by the threats of your enemies, and by my own conviction that you had some atonement to make." But the bid served a useful purpose, Simms continued, because "It will not be possible for Hampton and his friends to commit a second time the monstrous blunder … which … subjected themselves to an exposure than which nothing could be more unhappy." Simms added, "… what the outer world conjectured was no doubt much more ugly than the truth," and consoled his plantation neighbor that he "had suffered the worst." Simms assured him that "Your friends have been encouraged and strengthened. They will stick to you" (*L*, II, 235–36).[14]

What is significant is that Simms was tolerant of the fallibility and indiscretions of a trusted friend. Despite Hammond's public scandal and private tribulation, Simms never wavered in loyalty and respect. As a realist he did not expect even his best friends always to be exemplary, accepting imperfection in others better than most people did. As Simms himself put it years later in a letter to Paul Hamilton Hayne, "I always find some excuse in my own heart, for what seems the shortcoming of my friend" (*L*, V, 303).

Though never as close to Simms as was his older brother, Marcus Claudius Marcellus ("M. C. M.") Hammond also enjoyed a cordial relationship with the man of letters. Seven years younger than James Henry (and eight years younger than Simms), M. C. M. Hammond, also a planter with wide interests, fought in the Mexican War and was credited with heroism, and, at Simms's urging, wrote frequently on agricultural, military, and Mexican matters, mostly for magazines edited by Simms. In many ways Simms served as arbiter between the two strong-willed brothers, who were noted for their violent quarrels. Simms's love for both Hammonds is attested to his naming a son for them—for "the General [James H] first as an old & true friend," Simms wrote teasingly to the younger Hammond; "you second as a young friend but one whom I hold no less true. … I take for granted that if any thing should happen to me, you will both give the boy the benefit of your good, and withhold from him the knowledge of your evil."[15]

After the birth of his namesake son, Simms had for the first time the satisfying experience of having both a daughter and a son (though the daughter, of course, was from his earlier marriage). Young Gilly quickly became the center of attention, a great favorite of his teen-aged half sister as well as his not-yet-thirty-year-old mother; and he was of course the delight of his proud, energetic father, now almost forty. Yet Augusta, as always, remained a major concern; Simms fretted about her "gradually declining" health, and wrote to Lawson in June 1845 that he was sending her North for "a brief rest with you and then … to Great Barrington, the climate of which would be less likely to debilitate and oppress her than that of the city." He added: "You who know what this child was to me, for so many weary years of privation and loneliness, can readily understand my present anxieties" (*L*, II, 82–83). Yet, even as he was making summer arrangements to help restore Augusta's health, Simms announced to Lawson "the expected *accouchement* of my wife." Chevillette gave birth, on schedule, to another baby girl, Valerie Govan Simms—on August 10, 1845, before her son Gilmore, Jr., was thirty months old, and while her stepdaughter was still convalescing in Great Barrington. Simms's jocular note to Lawson, on August 11, reveals both his intimacy with the Lawsons and his enjoyment of his enlarged family: "My wife presented me last night ... with a very fine daughter, at about a quarter to 11. She is thought to be the largest child we have had at birth, is very fat, and they all affirm, more like me than all the preceding children. Of course, this being the case, *she is decidedly the best looking of all.*" Then Simms added: "This last half sentence is written particularly for the benefit of your wife. Gilmore is in finer health and finer appearance now than I have ever seen him, and his mother is doing, in the ordinary phrase, quite as well as can be expected" (*L*, II, 100).

But Simms the family man was not long without worry: Chevillette, "quite thin and looking not so well" (*L*, II, 103), was slow to recover from childbirth, and their newest daughter, despite Simms's happy prognosis at her birth, was described a year later as "still puny ... very fretful, and frequently feverish" (*L*, II, 181) and was quickly stricken down. September 1846 was a particularly disastrous month for the Simmses: first, on the thirteenth frail Chevillette Simms bore yet another daughter, her fifth, who was named Mary Lawson; then, on the twenty-first her fourth daughter, Valerie, died of illness at the age of fourteen months. In a particularly moving letter to Lawson, on September 22, 1846, Simms made telling comments on both events:

> God has again stricken us with his anger, and we are again mourners. I committed to the grave yesterday our dear little girl Valerie, who has been suffering more or less all the summer. Her sufferings ceased on Sunday night. ... To us, this dispensation is particularly severe ... because it seems to show that our misfortunes of this sort are not lessened in their repetition. When we reflect that this is the fourth dear child whom we have been required to surrender to the giver in a comparatively short space of time, the heart shrinks with terror from what would seem to be a peculiar and unrelenting destiny. We ask of our secret terrors where and when this destiny will forego its demands. ... Keep us in your thoughts and prayers.
>
> I wrote you on the birth of our little Mary Lawson, and apprised you that we had called the little one after your wife.[16] It is thus that God compels us to thank his bounty even while he makes us feel his severity. If he takes away, he gives. He blesses even while he punishes. The infant is a very fine and very hearty one—looking, they tell me, very much like me. The mother is not so well as we could wish. She has been thinner than usual, for some time past,—and is too averse to exercise to be healthy. We shall try and amend it this winter. (*L*, II, 185–86)

Simms's stoicism—his acceptance that he has been singled out for "the scourge"—is likewise revealed in a letter expressing growing concern for the welfare of his wife. "You will have heard before this," Simms wrote E. A. Duyckinck, "of the scourge to which we have been subjected in our little family. I have learned to endure perhaps too stubbornly, but my poor wife suffers at once from actual pain, as from her privation" (*L,* II, 189). Significantly, however, again in recounting his personal tribulations, Simms closed the litany with an avowal: "Then, however, God willing, to determined labor." Work and tragedy were intertwined throughout his career.

But repeated trauma, particularly that afflicting Chevillette, caused even the strong will of Simms to waver occasionally. It is important to note that it was personal tragedy, not a lack of literary success that contributed most to Simms's malcontent in 1846. In a memorable letter written scarcely a month after the birth of Mary Lawson Simms, the author confided to James Lawson: "She (my wife) is very puny and feeble—looks wretchedly, and has broken inconceivably within the past year. Sorrow and frequent breeding are the causes of her prostration. We have had enough, as you know, to overthrow any spirit less stubborn than my own. But mine is not wholly unshaken." Simms then admitted, "The truth is my dear Lawson, I have become greatly discontent. Carolina has been a region of tombs for me, and my worldly prosperity is by no means such as to make me desire to continue here." The letter writer's next statement is significant, particularly in the light of later events: "Mr. Roach's affairs do not prosper [not "*My* affairs do not prosper"], and I seriously deliberate upon the propriety of transferring myself, family or not, to Philadelphia or New York" (*L,* II, 195–96).

About this time Simms became involved in an unfortunate controversy that did nothing to restore his peace of mind and, but for the judicial intervention of Benjamin F. Perry, might actually have threatened his life. That Simms was innocent of wrongdoing in the episode in which he was challenged for having ostensibly offended the sensitivities of a handicapped woman adds an ironic note to the regrettable incident. It all began with a review by Simms in the *Southern Literary Messenger* in which he questioned the historical accuracy of a defense of the notorious Tory, "Bloody Bill" Cunningham.[17] Material for the attempted vindication of Cunningham had been provided by a kinswoman, Ann Pamela Cunningham, crippled since childhood. Miss Cunningham took umbrage at Simms's questioning of her findings; and in early November 1846 her brother John, an attorney, felt compelled to challenge Simms to a duel, a challenge Simms could not honorably refuse. Perry, a friend of both Simms and Cunningham, agreed to serve as Simms's second if the duel should take place, but to his everlasting credit he worked to convince Cunningham that Simms was not guilty of having slandered his sister and had indeed conducted himself with restraint and honor from the very beginning. Thus a possibly fatal duel was averted. But, acccording to family tradition, the affair had gone far enough that Simms, who (in the words of his granddaughter) "was not a good shot," had "made his will and prepared for death" (*MCSO*, VI).

Shortly after receiving the challenge from Cunningham, Simms gave vent on November 17, 1846, to particularly hostile feelings in a heavily despondent letter to his South Carolina confidant, James Henry Hammond. Because 1846 seems to be the year in which Simms's morale was at its lowest ebb, this letter bears quoting in some detail:

> I am in a sad state of mental depression. My family afflictions rather increase than end. While I had one child dying in my arms, my wife was bringing forth another. From this confinement she has never recovered, and her condition now is such as to alarm us all. I myself am physically a sufferer, with something [like] pleurisy, or a severe attack of rheumatism which looks like it. I have been for two days and nights in great suffering and write now, with several umschlags (as the Germans have it) wet linen swathings around my body. … I have had losses in pecuniary matters, & but for the condition of my wife I should be tempted, repudiated as I am here, to clear out, and try my fortune wholly in literature either in the North or Europe. (*L*, II, 208)

Several factors, then—the death of Valerie and the almost simultaneous birth of Mary Lawson (with Chevillette's accompanying debilitation); the embarrassment of his political defeat for the South Carolina House of Representatives; the increased pressure of financial losses at Woodlands—all combined in the fall of 1846 to bring Simms to a desperate state. Only two days after writing Hammond, Simms reiterated his anguish in a letter to Lawson: "I am, I confess, still greatly troubled—my children dying—my wife an invalid—business unproductive—capital diminishing, and I—feeling that I am not working as I should be, in my proper sphere, in my true employments" (*L*, II, 212).

Realistically there was little chance that Simms would desert South Carolina—his commitments to family and place were too strong; his potential enjoyment of his role as gentleman-planter-author at Woodlands too great (with no equivalent opportunity apparent elsewhere); his pride in person too secure. But in late 1846, at age forty-one, jolted with personal sorrows and worries, Simms—still with his career as professional author foremost in mind—raised again questions concerning the wisdom of remaining in South Carolina.

Discussing all opportunities—as well as all problems—candidly with intimates like Lawson and Hammond helped Simms to strengthen his inner resolve; and it is significant that his impulses to leave South Carolina were in part predicated upon his ambition as a writer. In this period of doubt and turmoil, one alternative never seriously considered by Simms was to forget literature and concentrate solely upon other, more profitable means of earning a living. Simms was willing to forsake belles-lettres neither for fortune nor for family. He seems to have recognized that his life's work lay in achievement at his chosen craft.

But it is nevertheless true that in late 1846 the novelist burned with the anxiety of a husband whose spouse was being ravaged by the trauma of "frequent breeding" and by the inconsolable frustration of repeated losses of her offspring. The thought of sustained abstinence or contraception as a safeguard to Chevillette's health apparently never occurred to her self-centered spouse, whose lack of thoughtfulness on her behalf stands out almost as much as his egoistic perception of himself as a frustrated, unappreciated artist. His career came first, it is clear, though he did not intend that his wife and children suffer any consequence for his willful pursuance of his own goals. Such egocentricity was as important to Simms's ambitions as a writer as was his unshakeable commitment, because, as he noted, any spirit "less stubborn" than his own would have been devastated by the pattern of birth and death, hope and sorrow, that had plagued his family in the past five years. And Chevillette Simms—though deceptively tough for one so seemingly fragile—in her weakened state leaned upon her husband for moral as well as physical strength, inevitably sapping some of his energy in her emotional dependence. Simms acknowledged this drain on his creativity: "I am continuing my drudgery of the desk at home, but scarcely to my satisfaction. My wife's condition disturbs my mood too greatly to leave me free to the utter forgetfulness of self which proper literary work requires" (*L*, II, 233). "[M]y wife [is] in very bad health," he wrote despondently, "and I myself very much dissatisfied ..." (*L*, II, 237).

In addition to concern about Chevillette, Simms, we have observed, was becoming increasingly uneasy about his father-in-law's management of Woodlands. In a dejected, almost rebellious mood he wrote to Lawson: "The management of our planting affairs is such as to dispirit me utterly, and but for the health of my family, I should certainly leave them for the daily drudgery of business in N. Y. or Phil. Here I run to waste, and feel myself a weed" (*L*, II, 239). At almost the same time, in December 1846, Simms also confided to Hammond "the almost impossible of my condition," registering dissatisfaction with his relationship with Nash Roach with regard both to

Chevillette and to Woodlands. "My wife is an invalid," he related—"breeding every year—is an only child—her father advanced in life—unwilling that she should leave home even for a week's visit,—and I too have learned to be a nurse— ... and subdue my self to something of the drudge." But "[t]o leave my family," Simms asserted, "is not easy—to separate my wife from her father in this situation would be scarce humane—" Though fortified "with a good capital, as well mine as his," the novelist yet noted, "—I am compelled to see it ... is not well administered—certainly not profitably" (*L*, II, 247).

Though publicly and privately (except in veiled references occasionally to Lawson and Hammond) Simms expressed nothing but admiration and respect for his father-in-law, certain questions do arise concerning relations between Nash Roach and his son-in-law, in addition to their apparent disagreement over the author's desire for a foreign post (chapter 6). Upon the marriage of his only daughter to the brilliant young widower-novelist, Roach generously made one of his twin plantations available to the newlyweds as their country estate and offered the residence on Smith Street to them for use as their Charleston house. But ten years later both of these valuable pieces of real estate—Woodlands and the Smith Street house—were still in Nash Roach's name. It is possible that some of Simms's misgivings in 1846 resulted from the fact that, though he and his family enjoyed all the benefits of living at Woodlands, he was legally no more than a resident at the plantation. Why had Nash Roach not conveyed the vast estate—and consequently the management thereof—to his daughter and son-in-law? Simms indeed may have been slightly offended that—though he was fully committed in every other way to the plantation and apparently had invested some of his own capital in it—he had no legal authority in its business affairs. And despite the fact that he felt those affairs "not well administered," he was reluctant—because of his sensitivity to the feelings of both his father-in-law and his wife—to broach the subject with either of them, for fear he would appear ungrateful or disloyal. Eventually ownership of Woodlands did pass into Simms's hands, but only after the deaths of both Nash Roach in 1858 and Chevillette Roach Simms in 1863. In the meantime, the author's uneasiness about the condition of his family and his finances continued.

In 1847 William Gilmore Simms was forty-one years old, nearing the height of his powers—well established as South Carolina's most distinguished man of letters, noted far and wide as a gifted orator and a brilliant conversationalist. He was known to almost every South Carolinian of intellectual inclination and looked upon with awe and reverence by the aspiring young writers, one of whom was Paul Hamilton Hayne. In later life the poet remembered the charm and excitement of his first impressions of the fellow South Carolinian who was to become his friend and mentor. There are many accounts of Simms's impressiveness as a person—as speaker, conversationalist, raconteur, confidant, ally—but none so rich in meaning and substance as the one written by Hayne:

> *In the midsummer of the year 1847 I chanced to be one of a large audience assembled in the Charleston theater.*
>
> *It was the period of our war with Mexico, and the whole country was agitated and unsettled. For what special purpose this meeting had been summoned I can not now remember. The stage, I know, was crowded with local celebrities, noted editors, politicians, and lawyers, together with a few distinguished publicists and legislators from other Southern States. There was the usual flow of feeling sacred to these occasions through every variety of mental spout. When the last orator, having pumped up and set afloat some magnificent platitude about the American eagle screaming over the Halls of the Montezumas, he seemed to be so overpowered by his own elocution that he stammered, paused, convulsively recovered himself for a moment, and then came to a dead stop, before taking the advice, loudly uttered, by some free citizen, "Sit down old boy! don't you know that you are 'played out'?"*
>
> *A curious hush followed, and some persons had risen as if to depart, when there was a cry, at first somewhat faint, but rapidly taken up, until it became earnest, even vociferous, for Simms, Gilmore Simms! I felt a thrill of excitement and delighted expectation, for like most lads of any fancy or taste for reading I reverenced literary genius, and having already been fascinated by some of Simms' novels, I had long desired to see the author. He now came forward with a slow, stately step, under the full blaze of the chandeliers, a man in the prime of life, tall, vigorous, and symmetrically formed. His head was a noble one, with a conspicuously high forehead, finely developed in the regions of ideality, and set upon broad shoulders in haughty, leonine grace.*
>
> *Under strangely mobile eyebrows flashed a pair of bluish-gray eyes, keen and bright as steel. His mouth, slightly prominent, especially in the upper lip, was a wonderfully firm mouth, only less determined, in fact, than the massive jaw and chin which might have been molded out of iron.*
>
> *An impressive personality, likely to catch and hold one's observation any where, he paused near the footlights, rapidly glanced about him for an instant, and then began his speech with a bold, startling paradox.*
>
> *Every body's attention was sharply arrested, and to the end of his address as closely retained.*
>
> *An extraordinary speaker, certainly. For some time his manner was measured and deliberate; but once plunged* in medias res *he became passionately eager. His gesticulation was frequent, unrestrained, now and then almost grotesquely*

*emphatic. Indeed, in this respect, he resembled an orator of some one of the Latin races, Italian, Spanish, or Portuguese. For an Anglo-Norman, or even an Anglo-Celt, he might have been considered theatrical.*

*Really, it was not so. This manner was rightly his own, being the outward, unpremeditated expression of a fervent temperament, of hot, honest blood, and a buoyant, indomitable nature, which sustained him subsequently under trials of no common power and persistent bitterness.*

*His peroration I vividly recall. It was a scathing rebuke of the selfish, time-serving politicians and influential leaders of the press who sacrificed to personal and party ends the interests of their people and the dignity of their country.*

*I would it were possible to recover and reproduce those fiery words, and to launch them, like a thunderbolt, at the miserable, dwarfed Machiavellis of to-day, to whom consistency is an abstraction and honor but an antiquated myth!*

*(...)*

*[Simms] gathered around him, through the forces of sympathy and genius, a number of ambitious young men, who enjoyed his conversation, deferred to his judgment, and regarded him in literary matters as a guide, philosopher, and friend!*

*With us he could unbend, could dispense with conventional restraints, which he detested, and be as untrammeled socially as intellectually.*

*A sort of informal club was instituted, of which he was made president. Often during the summer months, when he resided in the city, we met at each other's houses, and after discussing a vast variety of topics would close the evening with a* petite souper, *which no man enjoyed more, within reasonable bounds, than the creator of the philosophical "Porgy."*

*Then it was, with a bowl of punch before him, brewed after the old Carolina fashion, in due proportions of "the strong, sweet, and sour," that Simms shone in his lighter moods. Of wit, that bright, keen, rapier-like faculty, which too frequently wounds while it flashes, he possessed, in my opinion, but little; yet his humor —bold, bluff, and masculine — with a touch of satirical innuendo and sly sarcasm, was genuine and irrepressible.*

*Few men have ever comprehended human nature more thoroughly, and he could not refrain from caricaturing its weaknesses, although there was never a drop of venom in his heart.*

*Simms, too, was somewhat of a mimic, had an odd kind of histrionic ability, and could, therefore, give effect to many a story which* per se *may not have seemed remarkable. As to his store of anecdotes, historical, traditional, and social, "their name was legion."*

*(...)*

*[Simms's mother] died when he was a child, [his father] removed to the West, whither he seems to have desired, at a later period, that his son should follow him. "Had I done so," Simms used to say, "I would have made my fortune."*

*"How?" I inquired.*

> *"By the law, to be sure! With due resolution I should have overcome my native* goodness *and bashfulness sufficiently to succeed in what old McIntyre, of Inchkeith (after the decision of an important case against him), was pleased to call 'the devil's trade.'"*
>
> *(...)*
>
> *In the substantial brick house at "Woodlands," I remember particularly one apartment on the groundfloor, devoted to the author's use, his* sanctum sanctorum, *whence all but a few sympathetic friends were excluded. Shelves rising from floor to ceiling groaned under the weight of books. Chairs for comfort, not show, and convenient lounges abounded.*
>
> *For a whole morning have I sat in that pleasant library, a book before me, but watching ever now and then the tall, erect figure at the desk, and the quick steady passage for hours of the indomitable pen across page after page — a pen that rarely paused to erase, correct, or modify. At last, when the eternal scratch, scratch became a trifle irritating, and this exhaustless labor a reproach to one's semi-idleness, Simms would suddenly turn, exclaiming, "Near dinner time, my boy; come, let's take a modest appetizer in the shape of sherry and bitters."*
>
> *At dinner he talked a great deal, joked, jested, and punned, like a school-boy freed from his tasks; or, if a graver theme arose, he would often declaim a little too dogmatically and persistently, perhaps, to please those who liked to have a chance of wagging their own tongues occasionally. At such periods it was impossible to edge in the most modest of "caveats." Still, Simms could be a charming host, and was,* au fond, *thoroughly genial and kind-hearted. His dictatorial manner, to some extent, originated, I have thought, in the circumstances of his early life.*
>
> *(...)*
>
> *"Woodlands" might justly have been called "Hospitality Hall." It was ever open, not merely to friends and neighbors, but to all visitors from abroad in any way worthy of attention.*[18]

The Simms family's visit to the mountains of North and South Carolina in the fall of 1847—the same trip that provided the novelist rich material for some of his best fiction written years later—seemed to do much to restore the health of Chevillette Simms. In late September Simms wrote Lawson a cheery and newsy letter from Spartanburg praising its climate and scenery: "No healthier region in the world, few prettier, and a more persuasive climate, for August & Sept. could not be found" (*L*, II, 351). As the physical health of Chevillette continued to improve,[19] so did the health of her husband. Simms's buoyancy of spirit—his innate ability to rebound from sorrow or depression—is nowhere better revealed than in a letter to Lawson in March 1848: "... I have yet every reason to be satisfied—when I think calmly,—with what the bounty of Heaven has done for me" (*L*, II, 402). Simms's 1848 correspondence to Lawson, in fact, is crammed with pictures of happy family life too vivid and too revealing to ignore. One letter with particular wit and humor offers insight into living habits at Woodlands:

> I am not sure that I have suffered quite so much this season as usual from my usual complaint of low spirits. ... Tell your wife that in all probability I owe this degree of relief to the habit of segar smoking which I began under *her auspices.* I ascribe to this habit the fact that I am also considerably reduced in flesh. I fancy that I have lost 10 or 15 pounds since I left New York and I now regularly smoke at least *one* segar *per diem*—and, when in company, two or more. Augusta, I believe, wrote Lady Lyde a week or two ago. My wife often speaks of *her,*—and Mr. Roach as frequently of *you.* You are invariably a subject of reference whenever we have any fine fish or game. Gilmore ... is spelling his way through three or more letters, and beginning to read to his Mama. He is a rough colt of a fellow—forever in the woods or fields—now planting in the garden with his Grandpa, or now in the cotton fields with the negroes. He has a bed to himself in the garden which is filled with salad, radishes &c. He is very strong though not very active—shy and bashful *like his father,* but, also like his father gentle and amiable. Mary Lawson is one of the liveliest and most laughing things in this world—seldom cries and is quite obedient *except when she wills* it otherwise, and then, *like her namesake,* she is for having every thing her own way. She prattles now a good many words. She is short and stout, is full of life and health, and has never given us an hour's uneasiness since she was weaned. All of us are doing well physically.—I mention these details that you may learn how, in like manner, to inform us of your flock in turn. (*L*, II, 406–7)

Matters had so completely returned to normal with the Simms family, in fact, that sexual relations between husband and wife—temporarily suspended while Chevillette was convalescing from the shock of too frequent births and deaths—also were resumed; with the predictable result that in mid-July Simms waggishly (but also proudly) announced—"my wife is unequivocally 'as women wish to be &c'" (*L*, II, 415).[20]

But before Chevillette Simms was due to give birth, for the seventh time in twelve years of marriage, her husband's attention was distracted by the illness of Augusta. Since Augusta, now twenty years old, was a great favorite of the Lawsons, who had known her almost since birth, Simms once again decided to send her North to escape "the oppressive heat" of the Carolina summer (*L*, II, 430). Perhaps Augusta suffered from mental and emotional exhaustion as much as from physical infirmity, because under the care of the Lawsons, she quickly recovered. Simms's letter to Lawson in late August 1848 expressed relief at Augusta's "improvement," which he attributed largely to "tenderness and affection ... at the hands of yourself & wife" (*L*, II, 438). Simms, in a rare outburst of affection, added, "... I know no method of showing you both how deeply I feel your kindness and attachment, & how fondly I long for the opportunity to prove that my affections are not less plentiful than yours & hers."

Although Simms had seemed almost cavalier in announcing the seventh pregnancy of his long-suffering, yet compliant wife, he expressed deep "anxiety" about her as the time for her "confinement" approached. "The affair is altogether full of disquiets," he wrote the Lawsons. "The last childbirth brought her almost to the grave" (*L*, II, 456). Later, Simms's account of the birth of Chevillette Eliza Simms on December 13, 1848, registers more relief than joy:

> We have just had the narrowest escape in the world [Simms wrote Lawson]. My wife and self left Woodlands for Charleston on Monday last, and she was taken with pains of labor in the car. She had miscalculated her time, and events were anticipated by something like three weeks. We sent for the Physician that night, and on the next the child was born—another girl—a fine fat hearty little fellow, with lungs of the most ample dimensions. Mother and child, I rejoice to say, are, thus far, both doing well, and I am relieved of the worst anxiety. (*L*, II, 461)

The year 1848 thus closed with the Simmses "all doing well." In an after-Christmas letter to the Lawsons, the virile and hard-working novelist painted a generally positive picture of life in the family: "My wife is more vigorous than usual and the infant thrives. Mary Lawson chirps about the house with an ever restless foot and tongue, and in a visit to the plantation, where I ate my Christmas dinner, I found Augusta and Gilmore in good health and spirits" (*L*, II, 468).

Although no one ever replaced James Lawson and James Henry Hammond as Simms's two chief correspondents, the year 1849 added another to Simms's "sacred circle" of intellectual Southern friends holding similar views about the literature, economics, politics, and philosophy of their region. Even if Simms's letters to Lawson are by far the most personal that he wrote, the novelist nevertheless acknowledged that discussions of politics with his New York friend posed difficulties. "At all events let us tell nothing of these matters," Simms wrote on February 5, 1849. "There is so much self complaisance and insolence in the speech of most Northern men when they address the South that the least said's the better" (*L*, II, 475). With Hammond, of course, no such caution was needed—nor was it with another highly articulate

Southerner, Nathaniel Beverley Tucker, with whom Simms struck up a correspondence in March 1849. Tucker, writer of fiction and professor of law at the College of William and Mary, and Simms, twenty-two years his junior, knew each other by reputation before 1849, but when (at Hammond's suggestion) the latter approached the Virginian about being a contributor to the *Southern Quarterly Review*, the two immediately became fast friends and confidants on all things Southern. Tucker's response to Simms's initial letter was in the Carolinian's words "so warm, its sentiment so frank and Southern, that it made its way at once to my heart" (*L*, II, 498). The intimate friendship and correspondence between two Southern gentleman planters-turned-intellectual lasted until Tucker's death, on August 26, 1851;[21] and afterward Simms's memory cherished the unusual loving quality of their relationship. "I once wrote a letter to old B. Tucker," Simms noted in 1859, "... and closed it with 'Yours *lovingly*.' I forget what were the exact terms of the old man's response, but it showed that his heart was touched by the use of a word which men employ femininely only,—and in their dealings with women" (*L*, IV, 164).

In addition to Hammond and Tucker, the other members of Simms's "sacred circle" were George Frederick Holmes, a transplanted Englishman who lived in Orangeburg, South Carolina, before, like Tucker, becoming a professor at William and Mary, and Edmund Ruffin, a forward-looking Virginia agriculturist with a strong penchant for reforming his profession. According to Drew Faust, these five men

> all believed that their innate genius had exiled them from society. This common sense of alienation provided a basis for intense personal friendship that evolved into ... a network of mutual emotional and intellectual support. In letters and visits, they explored their common plight and defined a common purpose: to reform the South to make a place for their particular talents.[22]

The literary-minded Holmes, whom Simms got to know well when the young Englishman (from British Guiana) was teaching school in Orangeburg, only a few miles away from Woodlands, was much closer to the novelist than was Ruffin, though the avant-garde theories of the astute, single-minded agriculturist were much admired by Simms the planter. Simms helped Holmes get his post at William and Mary, encouraged the younger man's literary proclivities, and several times tried unsuccessfully to secure for him a position at South Carolina College. Holmes's affection and high regard for his mentor are best revealed in his verbal portrait of "the kindly nature and genial humanities of the author": "... he is free from the pedantry and affectations of literary seclusion, and is a hearty, healthy, generous and full-formed man. The jovial, good temper and exuberant *bonhommie* of his intercourse with his friends, secure their esteem and affection, and add to his diversified talents a brighter luster than intellectual splendor could alone bestow."[23] Simms's early assessment of Holmes, succinctly stated in an 1846 letter of recommendation, remained essentially unchanged during their lifelong friendship: "He is a Gentleman of moral & character, an industrious student of rare industry and of powers of expression & acquisition quite as remarkable" (*L*, II, 193).

Unlike Simms's relationships with Hammond, Tucker, and Holmes—all men with literary pretensions of some degree—the main tie that brought Simms and Ruffin together was the science of agriculture. Actually every one of the "sacred circle" was interested in agriculture—how could a Southern gentleman planter not be?—but Simms had made himself well informed about agricultural research and correctly looked upon Ruffin as an innovative expert in the field. For example, in June 1853, Simms as editor urged Hammond (also highly knowledgeable in agronomy) to "do a good thing for me, for Ruffin & the State" (*L*, III, 239) by writing for the *Southern Quarterly Review* an article based on Ruffin's well-informed *An Essay on Calcareous Manures.* There is, however, no evidence of extensive correspondence between Simms and Ruffin—as there was between Simms and the other members of "the Brotherhood of the Quill."

Simms and his intellectual companions all had in common antiquarian interests and expensive tastes. In fact, one of the mysteries associated with Simms, puzzling even to this day to his descendants, is how the "born antiquarian" author managed to find money to support his passionate love of fine books, exquisite art, elegant music, fine pieces of furniture and silver, and rare wine and whiskey. At Woodlands he not only built a magnificent personal library of some "12,000 volumes" (*L*, IV, 215), including unique or scarce Revolutionary War documents and manuscripts of inestimable value; he also maintained a collection of some sixty-five paintings by artists like Thomas Sully and Benjamin West; in addition, both in Charleston and at Woodlands, he was famous for his "musical evenings," to which he invited distinguished guests as well as his own family members, including the slaves; and his fondness for the finest liquors—Jamaica rum, Madeira wine, and Monongahela or Scotch whiskey—was legion among his colleagues, literary, social, and political. One of the motivations for Simms's strong desire for a foreign diplomatic appointment was, as we have seen, the opportunity to live the life of a gentleman abroad. One suspects that Simms (who "just seemed to want the fine things") came by his valuable artistic, historic, literary, and aesthetic possessions largely from in-kind payment for services rendered (like reviews of thousands of books) or through the exchange of gifts, rather than by the outlay of cash, always scarce even during the best years at the plantation or on the literary market (*MCSO*, III, IV, V).

Life in the family at Woodlands and Charleston remained relatively stable throughout the late 1840s and early 1850s. While en route to Cuba, Bryant again visited Woodlands briefly late in March 1849, after which Simms wrote that he wished the poet could "have passed a week with us to the gratification of most of your senses. Birds, blossoms, breezes, all in finest condition—acknowledging by play and scent, the acutest sense of life and enjoyment" (*L*, II, 509). Simms's pride in South Carolina—particularly in Woodlands—is also manifest in his frequent letters to Lawson recounting "the enjoyments of the most singular health" (*L*, II, 533) by the various members of the Simms household. In late November 1849 the novelist was deeply moved when he learned that the Lawsons were naming their newborn son William Gilmore Simms Lawson, though he adopted the pretense that the "combination of W.G.S.L." was "quite too long and unwieldy." Simms closed the discussion with the affectionate statement that "my wife and daughter join with the warm feeling of persons who feel from over long and precious ties, that we already constitute a portion of your family." And, as was usually the case, he added a playful aside to his favorite spouse of a friend: "Tell Lyde, I look forward to our conference with great anxiety. It is so long—it seems an age—since I have seen her. Has she forgiven my manifold offenses" (*L*, II, 569–70).

Simms's feeling that he and his family had been "spared & blessed" (*L*, III, 5) continued throughout 1850 and 1851, though characteristically he had moments when he felt "hurried—not well—nervous, weary & dissatisfied" (*L*, III, 14). Nothing demonstrates his alternating moods of frivolity and sarcasm better than the tongue-in-cheek letter Simms wrote to James Lawson on April 25, 1851: "Well,—you were among the last men in the world whom I should have suspected of forgetting old friends as you become fortunate," the writer chided. "And how does all this prosperity affect your wife? Does she share in your forgetfulness. Does she ever ask you when you last received a letter from me." Simms then asked if the New Yorker ever admitted to Lady Lyde that "it is fully six months since I have written to Simms, and my last was six lines on a quarter sheet of paper *promising to write soon.*" Furthermore, the letter continues, Simms had "recieved ... kindly for your sake," a friend of Lawson's visiting South Carolina, entertaining him royally for a week at Woodlands. The visitor "expressed himself greatly satisfied and pleased," Simms related, "and we were pleased too, as we thought it would please you." On the other hand, when Chevillette's "very worthy young kinsman," Edward Roach, visited New York for the first time, Lawson failed to give him a reciprocal welcome. Simms's words dramatize his pretended shock and astonishment at the misunderstanding:

> My wife said—"Mr. Lawson will treat him kindly for my sake." I gave him a letter to you. You appointed to call for him to take him to dine or sup with you—*and never came*! My wife was confounded. What does yours say? "Was that done like Cassius"—like a gentle Scotchman I mean.—Fat and Fortune have evidently spoiled one of the best fellows in the world. You have clearly abandoned me to my fate! My wife says so! Is your wife to blame. Has she utterly lost all the love she had for me. Let me know. I can forgive you, for you are fat & need forgiveness—but she has no such excuse. (*L*, III, 110–11)

Simms closed the letter—which could have been written with impunity only by one intimate friend to another—"though forgotten we do not forget and still feel for you and Yours as lovingly as Ever. Simms."

Although at the time Chevillette was pregnant with her eighth child, it is interesting that her husband made no mention of the fact in his bantering letter to Lawson (unless the statement "we are all tolerably well" be taken as a sly allusion). Six and a half months later, on November 9, 1851, Sydney Roach Simms, "a promising little fellow enough," was born; but in the language of the father, the infant's mother "has been very ill,—has very severely suffered,—and still lies very feeble, very nigh exhausted" (*L*, III, 151). Chevillette Simms, giving birth again after a lapse of almost three years—the longest period between children thus far in her marriage—proved strong in constitution despite her frail appearance, and by August 1852 she seems to have regained her health.

But "the scourge" was soon to strike the Simmses again. In late April 1853 Chevillette (as related by her husband) "was prematurely brought to bed and delivered a dead child" (*L*, III, 228), a son who was to have been named Beverley Hammond Simms. "For this mischance she can in no way account," Simms added in describing the event to Lawson. "She has suffered neither from accident nor fright. … Last Friday week we left the plantation for the city. Her calculation was that she might look forward to at least three weeks of rest before accouchement. She was seized with the pains of labour on the ensuing Monday and was delivered before nurse or Physician could arrive. Fortunately, thus far, no ill consequences have ensued to herself. Though greatly alarmed, she has borne it well, and is doing as well now as could be expected. …" Thus, the unrelenting statistic of five deaths among nine children hung above Gilmore and Chevillette Simms like a dark, threatening cloud, casting a somber shadow across their family life for months and years to come. Though assiduous in his literary labor, Simms himself entered into a period of depression, feeling unappreciated and unrewarded in South Carolina, yet trapped by family obligations. In a gloomy letter of July 15, 1853, Simms again lamented: "... my wife is an only child; her father is in declining health & years; she cannot leave him, and I cannot separate from her and my children, except for a brief period. I am thus compelled to remain here, in my stable, when I ought to be speeding over the track" (*L*, III, 245). Simms's repeated use of the phrase "drawing water in a sieve" vividly describes the sense of emptiness he experienced periodically throughout the 1850s. Dread of new visitations of "the scourge" was so strong in the family that Simms canceled a much-looked-forward-to visit to New York in 1854 because of the "alarming accounts of the prevalence of Smallpox" there. "I have no apprehensions," Simms explained to Lawson in a letter written while en route, "but if I were to venture to N. Y. and contract & carry home the disease, I certainly never could excuse myself were our children to suffer" (*L*, III, 283).

It is important to note that though tragedy and despondency intermittently battered and bruised Simms throughout his life, they never overwhelmed him—a fact recognized by the perceptive Hammond. In expressing admiration for his friend's "bold heart," the politician succinctly stated in 1854: "I envy you your youthful spirit of enterprise, which neither time nor injustice has subdued ..." (*L*, III, 285n). And Chevillette Simms—the loyal, dutiful wife always—whose love for her husband was so unquestioning and unwavering that it never occurred to her children to do otherwise than worship their father—came close, in her own gentle way, to matching his courage and determination. Sorrow and physical pain were commonplace with her—she who had lost five children—but she took great pride and satisfaction in her family, with its recognized patriarch.

And such it was that on or about July 17, 1854, Chevillette Roach Simms gave birth to her tenth child, a son bestowed with the name, Beverley Hammond Simms, that had been intended for her ninth. For the first time the family of William Gilmore and Chevillette Simms included more living boys—Beverley Hammond, Sydney Roach, and Gilmore, Jr.—than girls—Chevillette Eliza and Mary Lawson—with Augusta from Simms's first marriage rounding out a family of eight. But once again the threat of death was soon to plague the Simmses, this time in the form of the yellow-fever epidemic that devastated Charleston and the South Carolina low country in the late summer and fall of 1854. On November 9 Simms wrote to E. A. Duyckinck, "When I tell you that two of my daughters have just recovered from the Yellow Fever, and that my eldest son is now in bed with it, you will readily concieve that I have neither had time nor mood for any thing" (*L,* III, 327). But in this instance the novelist and his family were to escape the scourge: on November 15 Simms reported to Duyckinck, "My boy is well again, and up to this moment, all my children are doing well. Laus deo!" (*L,* III, 329).

On the first day of 1856 Simms gave an interesting account of his domestic life in a long letter to William Cullen Bryant:

> My family—I have now six children living (of eleven) 3 sons & as many daughters, are all well; my wife & self still enjoy tolerable health; but my old father-in-law, breaks rapidly, and is now a mere wreck of himself—feeble, purposeless, inactive—with mind & body equally decayed. I am now compelled to give as much heed to the plantation as to my books—a duty which greatly distracts me in my own. Every thing, in short, is suggestive of the propriety of being at peace with the world, & more particularly with oneself, which, I take it, is the first real step towards being at peace with God. (*L,* III, 416)

This passage accurately reflects the mind of Simms in 1856—proud, realistic, acrid, stoic, peaceful—a curious almost contradictory combination of qualities. The year professionally given prominence by the publication of *Eutaw* was highlighted in his personal life by the birth of yet another son, on September 1, in the midst of Simms's preparations for his disastrous Northern lecture tour later in the fall. Once again a letter to Lawson—written on September 7—is the most vivid and revealing account of a major family event:

> ... we have passed a crisis, always one of doubt and anxiety in all well regulated families. My wife's accouchement has taken place, and she has added another specimen of the Boy genus to my menagerie; a stout, hearty little fellow, of a calm dignified placid bearing & look, who only yells under proper provocation, and when his porridge is too long in preparation. My quiver now, to use Biblical phraseology is tolerably full of arrows. Four boys and three girls ought to be enough to garrison any small fortress such as ours, particularly when they have for commissary no more adroit person than a Poet. As chef de commissariat I can feelingly assure you that I am sometimes at my wits ends, where to forage. But it grieves me little. My faith is so strong, that I should never doubt, if God should send me a dozen more, that he would also provide quails and manna. ... The mother, & the newcomer are both doing well. We name the latter *Govan Singleton,* Govan being the maiden name of his mother's mother—and Singleton of mine. (*L,* III, 444)

In fairness to Simms, whose relationship with Chevillette seemed at times marked more by polite consideration and formal courtesy than by passionate caring and unselfish love, it should be pointed out that his dealings with children, his own and others, were remarkably flexible and relaxed—lenient for those times and decidedly jovial. In fact, according to oral history of the family, Simms was so permissive with his progeny and those of his guests that autocratic friends like James Henry Hammond and David F. Jamison disapproved of the writer's easy discipline. Two anecdotes help to illustrate these points. Once, for instance, on a visit to Woodlands Hammond was shocked that Simms "had allowed Mary Lawson to come up with an opinion in the middle of an erudite conversation," purportedly occasioning the author to retort, "Would you rather that she be a fool or act like a fool?" (*MCSO,* III). Tradition has it that Simms the father did not shield his children intellectually; treating them almost as adults, he wanted them to meet all his guests and enter into their activities: "he let them have the most amazing run of the place and with all of his company" (*MCSO,* III). A particularly telling anecdote involves Sarah Aldrich (1846–1928), oldest daughter of Simms's old friend and neighbor, Judge A. P. Aldrich. Once while Sarah was the guest of her close companion, Mary Lawson Simms, at a time when each must have been thirteen or fourteen years old, her thoughts were not surprisingly more upon curling hair than upon intellectual matters (though later she "grew to be a semi-literary person"). Given the run of Simms's study, Sarah and Mary Lawson had earlier browsed among his books and joined in the conversation concerning what the novelist was then reading and writing. Then, in the inimitable language of Mary C. Simms Oliphant—

> time came to go to bed and Sarah didn't have any paper to put her hair in, so she ran down to Simms's study and there lying on [his desk] were these queer looking sheets with Simms's handwriting on them. It didn't mean anything in the world to her, and she grabbed them up and tore them into strips to put up her hair, only to find Simms exploding: "Where is the story that I've been working on all day?" (*MCSO,* III)

That visitors to Woodlands frequently brought their children with them is indicative of the open hospitality with which the families of guests were received. In addition to the visits from the children of South Carolina families like the Aldriches, it will be remembered that the sons and daughters of Northerners like the Lawsons and the Bryants became intimate friends particularly of Gilmore, Jr., Augusta, and Mary Lawson, and the exchange of visits became a common occurrence. Though Simms of course was never guilty of mistreating any of his progeny, his partiality toward his first daughter, his namesake son, and his daughter named for "Lady Lyde" clearly stands out—as does his fondness for "Lady Lyde's" own daughter Mary and for Aldrich's son, Alfred Proctor, Jr., with whom young Gilly was to serve side by side during the Civil War. If the father's advice to Gilly at times seemed overbearing and sometimes condescending, he treated his favored daughters with a lighter touch and generally a more sympathetic, if not more loving attitude. One gets the impression that Simms, who at every opportunity boasted of the academic and other accomplishments of Gilmore, Jr., nevertheless was disappointed that his son did not possess the intellectual prowess and the leadership qualities he would have cherished in his namesake. Augusta, perhaps more aggressive and assertive than any of Chevillette's children, was "the guiding spirit of the whole family," the one who particularly idolized her father and who "really raised the younger children" as her stepmother's surrogate.[24] But, clearly in the eyes of the family, "the one he [Simms] loved the most was Mary Lawson"—the namesake of the woman "who must have been a charmer," whom Simms was believed to have courted in New York, and whom "it was amazing that Simms didn't marry" (*MCSO,* V). Said to resemble her father more than any other of his children, Mary Lawson Simms, pretty, vivacious, and intellectual, eventually replaced Augusta as the novelist's traveling companion.

Throughout 1856 and 1857 Simms's correspondence is permeated with references to the poor health of Nash Roach and to the sorry state of affairs at Woodlands. For example, in 1856 Simms observed that his father-in-law was "almost hors de combat" and that the "business" of Woodlands was "horribly mismanaged and still more horribly neglected" (*L,* III, 453). In late 1857 the novelist-planter, noting "the situation of my wife's father, who is a paralytic, & is frequently subject to *turns* which threaten to carry him off," grumbled that "the business of the plantation … is enough to employ all my thoughts and time." Because of the senior Roach's ineptitude (and his refusal to relinquish the reins of authority) Woodlands had fallen into "utter dilapidation," causing great consternation and requiring "a degree of energy which will make every muscle tell, every wheel go, every engine work …" (*L,* III, 519).

Most of Simms's resentment at not being legal head of Woodlands was probably alleviated at the time of Roach's death on February 28, 1858. The will of Nash Roach,[25] probated in Charleston on March 23, named Simms "sole Executor of this my last Will and Testament" in which (after two small bequests to nieces) all his real and personal estate was left "to my beloved Daughter Chevillette Eliza Simms Wife of William Gilmore Simms." The will continued, "Should my son-in-law the said William Gilmore Simms survive his said Wife Chevillette Eliza Simms then from and after her death I bequeath all the rest and residue unto the said William Gilmore Simms for and during the term of his natural Life." It is interesting that Roach, though naming Simms executor—certainly an indication of trust—took every precaution to protect his daughter during her lifetime, stipulating not only that the estate was "for her sole separate use and benefit," but also that it was "not to be subject in any manner to the debts contracts or engagements of her present or any future husband." And in leaving the estate to Simms upon Chevillette's death, the will specified that after the demise of Simms "the rest and residue" go to "their eldest son who shall be then living"—thus denying Simms the option of leaving the property to anyone other than Gilmore, Jr. (or the next son in line in event of Gilly's prior decease). Though Simms may have felt some pique at Nash Roach's refusal even in death to entrust his entire estate directly to his son-in-law, the novelist could scarcely take offense at the old man's thoughtfulness in assuring first and foremost his only daughter's well-being and at the same time providing full benefits to her husband and their first male offspring.

Simms's letters for the remainder of 1858 and 1859 suggest some lingering bitterness toward his father-in-law, though he was too loyal to articulate his feelings. In writing Hammond on May 8, 1858, for instance, Simms referred to Roach only obliquely, reporting that "My Cotton is very promising ... and if things continue as they promise, I shall be able to wipe off all scores of my old father in law" (*L*, IV, 54). On June 26 he again wrote to Hammond: "Cotton doing well. I have 270 acres planted against Mr. Roach's 150—and with the same force. I begin to see where all the error has been" (*L*, IV, 73). Throughout 1859 references to Roach as "my predecessor" were common, such as in a letter to Hammond on January 10: "My crop though doubling those of my predecessor, and exceeding this year that of the last, is yet only half a crop, far short of my expectations" (*L*, IV, 106). Again, on January 14, Simms wrote in a letter to Duyckinck: "I have not been as successful as I anticipated; though I have doubled the crops of my worthy Predecessor" (*L*, IV, 108).[26] In a long letter to John Esten Cooke, on January 29, 1859, Simms went into some detail describing his problems in assuming responsibility for Woodlands. "The business of the plantation devolved wholly upon me last year," he wrote, "and I have to restore and repair a neglected and half-dilapidated establishment." Without money to retire existing debts, Simms stated that he needed "extraordinary energies" and "some good fortune" in order "to put things *rectus in curia*." He added: "I do not despair, but I am harassed and wearied ... doing a thousand things such as appertain to a large Southern plantation." As a result, Simms related, "you may readily concieve the little I have been able to do in letters" (*L*, IV, 115).

What is apparent is that Simm's early self-assessment "I would not be content if I could" applies to aspects of his life other than the literary. A wealthy man by all the standards of his time, living the life of the Southern planter-gentleman he so much identified with and enjoying the fruits of a beautiful estate, Simms nevertheless felt (and more than occasionally expressed) dissatisfaction with his lot. But, it is essential to record, his discontent did not affect his commitment to, nor his capacity for, work so long as that work involved something—literature, the Southern cause, or Woodlands—that he deeply believed in.

Despite the writer's new responsibilities, life in the Simms household at Woodlands went on after the death of Nash Roach much as it had before. Within two weeks of her father's demise Chevillette Simms gave birth to her twelfth child, a girl named Harriet Myddleton, born on March 14, 1858. Simms himself, perhaps because of the close proximity of his father-in-law's death and his newest daughter's birth, displayed more irritation than pleasure in late March in mentioning (without further identification) "a series of family afflictions and annoyances" (*L,* IV, 39). Some three months later, Simms referred to the new member of the family for the first time in his correspondence: "Did I tell you," he wrote to Lawson's daughter, Mary, on July 10, "... that she [Chevillette] had added the twelfth to her list, in a fine little girl whom we call Hattie (Harriett) Myddleton. With the exception of Govan and my wife herself, we are all pretty well" (*L,* IV, 74). In the same letter Simms mentioned a new situation that pleased him, the engagement of Augusta—now thirty—to "one of my wife's cousins, Edward Roach, a very excellent young man, who depends for his resources upon his own exertions; but he is one of the most moral, prudent and industrious young men, who will give her the best securities of happiness. The affair will probably take place in October, or there abouts" (*L,* IV, 76).

But before Augusta's wedding could take place, the "crowning calamity" of Simms's life was to hit—the deaths from yellow fever of his two middle sons on the same day, September 22, 1858. In a letter to James Henry Hammond two days later, the agonized words of the grief-stricken father are unforgettable:

> Oh! dear Hammond, weep for me! I am crushed to earth. I have buried in one grave, within twelve hours of each other, my two brave beautiful boys, Sydney, & your little namesake, Beverley Hammond, two as noble little fellows as ever lived. It was a dreadful struggle of 12 days with one, and nine with the other. It is a terrible stroke of fate, leaving us almost desolate. I feel heart broken, hope crushed and altogether wretched. I can write no more. God's bless-

ing upon you and yours. Weep for me and mine, dear friend, for I know that your sensibilities are keen enough to feel for the great agonies of mine.

Yours ever faithfully even now.
W. Gilmore Simms
(*L*, IV, 93–94)

In his reply Hammond wrote: "I do weep with my dear Simms & for you in this crowning calamity of your life. ... God help you to bear up" (*L*, IV, 94n).[27]

*Bear up* Simms did, of course, as he always had and always would in time of duress and tragedy. The wedding of Augusta was postponed because of "the terrible afflictions in our family," but a small ceremony with "no company" (*L*, IV, 101) took place on December 29 between the twenty-one-year-old nephew of Nash Roach and the oldest daughter of William Gilmore Simms, ten years his senior. Despite its inauspicious beginning, from all accounts their marriage was as stable as Simms had predicted it would be, and the novelist father and his courageous wife could count blessings among sorrows as 1858 came to a close.

A brief but significant letter by Simms in 1859 calls to mind an anecdote concerning his irrepressible penchant for mimicry. According to family legend, the Simms children had known for some time that their literary father had somehow given offense to members of the distinguished Middleton family at a dinner party at elegant Middleton Place, near Charleston; but the reason remained a mystery. In writing on November 2, 1859, to Williams Middleton, grandson of the signer of the Declaration of Independence, Arthur Middleton, the ebullient author—whether purposely, slyly, or inadvertently—slipped in a comment that gives a clue to the cause of the society-minded Middletons' embarrassment. "It is just possible," Simms wrote (one would like to think) tongue-in-cheek, "that, if you keep in Charleston this winter, I shall look in upon you for a single hour, in my character as a backwoodsman" (*L*, VI, 208). As Hayne acknowledged, Simms "could not refrain from caricaturing," and among his descendants there is no doubt that the novelist from Woodlands (who would "never just tell a story, he was acting it") had dramatized his "backwoodsman" character for the guests at Middleton Place (*MCSO*, II).

It was also in 1859 that in a letter to young Mary Lawson (with whom he had struck up a correspondence because "I seldom or never hear from Lawson") Simms gave a proud description of his namesake son, who was then attending King's Mountain Military School in Yorkville: "He is growing a very tall & stout fellow, will probably overtop his father by several inches, is modest and industrious—was at the head of his section of sixty five, and has a first rate report from his commandant." Recounting his son's activities, Simms affirmed, "He shoots, rides, runs and wrestles with any of his mates & is full of what the British call 'pluck'. Will hold his own promptly, and suffers no insult, or indignity; yet, withal is as docile to proper authority as I would have him" (*L,* IV, 112). An outdoorsman who enjoyed riding, hunting, and fishing, the father revealed his own sense of values in the traits which he admired most in his son and heir—manliness, modesty, courage, courtesy, and independent spirit. But Simms the family man, taking pride in and comfort from his brood, still suffered from the calamitous event of the previous year: "My boys! My boys!" he wrote to E. A. Duyckinck on January 29—"Ah! my friend, we who have so much in our children, how it lacerates all the fibers of life when they are torn from us. You have felt it all! But I—I have buried 7 children, and at every burial, how many strings of earth were severed. I have a larger family in heaven than on earth!" (*L,* IV, 113).

But what of Simms's relationship with Chevillette? In all his accounts of family tragedy, he nearly always spoke in first person only: "*My* boys," "*I* have buried 7 children," "*I* have a larger family in heaven," etc. Does this self-centered point of view indicate a lack of sensitivity toward the emotional needs of a loyal and apparently totally devoted wife? Does the fact that Simms never seemed to call Chevillette by any designation other than "my wife" signify a lack of respect for her as an individual? Contrast this attitude toward his spouse with his frequent romantic use of "Lady Lyde" in referring to Mary Eliza Lawson, for whom Simms had an open adoration. Interestingly enough, Simms's most enlightened concept of the role of woman can be seen in his advice to Lady Lyde's daughter, Mary, bespeaking of his view of the proper accomplishments of young women. In his letter of February 28, 1859, Simms—taking responsibility as Mary's mentor—counseled her to develop both the practical (the sewing machine) and the beautiful (the habit of reading)—the domestic and the intellectual. In stressing the importance of intellectuality and independence in woman, Simms was ahead of his time in his attitude toward women. But in his view of the utilitarian role of his spouse—whom he cherished, but apparently never desperately fell in love with—he reverted to the more traditional, centuries-old concept of woman as the bearer and caretaker of children. Simms honored, trusted, and assumed responsibility for his wife; she in turn venerated him, doing him full obeisance, striving in every way to please him, and expecting for herself nothing more than he was capable of providing. The evidence suggests that she from the beginning found Simms romantic and exciting, and if he never fully reciprocated, she gave no indication that her expectations were disappointed. According to family tradition, Chevillette Roach fulfilled the feminine ideal of the day—by instinct and training she loved with an unselfish love, always ready to serve her lord and protector.

No better evidence of the relationship between William Gilmore Simms and Chevillette Eliza Roach can be found than in the fact that, after the loss of seven of their children, wife Chevillette gave her husband their thirteenth child only ten months after the double loss of sons in a single day. After being "threatened with premature labour," Chevillette Simms, in the telling words of her husband, "added another son to my stock" on July 27, 1859 (*L*, IV, 169, 170). This son, Simms wrote to J. H. Hammond, would be called Sydney Hammond, in honor of "the two noble little boys I lost last summer." He added: "My wife, though fragile is doing well, better than I expected. She was so feeble that I was greatly apprehensive about her until the event terminated favorably" (*L*, IV, 172).

Indeed, near the close of 1859 William Gilmore Simms may have been as afflicted physically as his continually pregnant wife. In mid-September he complained in a letter to M. C. M. Hammond: "I am well *prima facie;* but I suffer from strictures across the forehead; from frequent and severe discharges of blood—piles—from the sedentariness of my habits, &c. My legs fail me. I walk but little—*can* walk but little. Get soon tired" (*L*, IV, 176). On the same day, September 18, Simms also wrote to J. H. Hammond a gloomy letter that reveals signs of fatigue and weakness of body and spirit. "My wife brought me another boy last month," Simms stated (apparently forgetting that he had already written his friend on the subject) and then added—"an event which added to my anxieties & kept me fettered. She is very feeble" (*L*, IV, 177). In a late November letter, to Porcher Miles, Simms bluntly remarked: "I am an invalid, and almost abstain from writing, doing just as little as I can. My head is troubled with symptoms that make me apprehensive, & my liver is out of order. I am under a cloud; worried & wearied . . ." (*L*, IV, 180). In December Simms wrote to John Esten Cooke, "I am still uneasy of brain & anxious of thought, & sad at heart, & wearied with troubles, & full of cares, and fevered by *vigilia*." And to this letter the exhausted and exasperated novelist added a postscript: "I wrote this at four o'clock this morning by an imperfect candlelight, & did not observe that I was using a sheet of common MS. paper. I could not sleep, got up, went into my study, & wrote to you" (*L*, IV, 181–82).

Though he accomplished much professionally, the period 1842–1859 was for Simms a time of many personal disappointments, sorrows, worries, and tragedies. Notwithstanding, it was also, on a personal basis, a time for strengthening friendships and building family ties. What is truly remarkable is that throughout this emotionally turbulent period Simms managed to produce, on a consistent basis, not only children but literature worthy of the name.

PART FOUR

# Against the Wind

(1860–1870)

# X The Years of Secession and War

The year 1860 dawned with William Gilmore Simms, at age fifty-three, ranked high among living American novelists, but feeling weighed down with personal problems: "I am sick, suffering, despondent, doubtful in hope, wearied with toil, mortified with defeat & disappointment—and good for nothing!" (*L*, IV, 188). He had produced in the 1850s alone eighteen books, including five major full-length novels and four significant volumes of shorter fiction, as well as his best collection of poetry. Nevertheless, he had been buffeted by personal sorrow, political disappointment, and financial worries to such an extent that even he recognized that his ailments were psychological as well as physical. "… I am now broken down," he explained to William Porcher Miles on January 18; "labouring under a degree of mental frustration, if not physical disease, which involves the utmost danger from any hard work, or close application, or unusual excitement" (*L*, IV, 185). Thus Simms declined an invitation to deliver in Washington, D.C., the oration inaugurating the equestrian statue of George Washington by Clark Mills, an opportunity he would "eagerly … have leapt at … in other days!"[1] It is possible that Simms was already in the early throes of cancer, apart from (and yet a part of) his depression, a condition consistent with the assertion "… I am an invalid threatened with a disease which forbids that I should undertake any protracted labor, or encounter any unusual excitement" (*L*, IV, 190).[2] As always, however, Simms's will to "endure manfully" prevailed over perceived and real problems, and he persisted with his lifework.

But South Carolina in early 1860 burned with political thoughts pointed toward the National Democratic Convention to be held in late April in Charleston, where among other things the issue of secession would be confronted. In keeping, however, with Simms's belief in the maintenance of normal family life whatever the situation, the hospitality of Woodlands was opened to James Lawson and two of his daughters for a protracted visit beginning in late January. Gilmore and Chevillette Simms greeted their New York friends warmly and treated them graciously[3] during their stay, but the state of mind of the master of the manor is revealed in his brief note to John Esten Cooke: "My house is full—my heart heavy—my head light. I cannot think, or write just now ..." (*L*, IV, 191). The timing of the Lawsons' visit was in no way propitious, for during their stay at Woodlands two-year-old Hattie Simms became seriously ill, hovering near death for several days; and before James Lawson and daughters Kate and Mary could complete their planned Southern itinerary, they were called back to New York by the severe illness of young William Gilmore Simms Lawson, namesake of the author, who died on March 6, 1860. Simms wrote to Lawson five days later: "Oh! my poor friend, how our hearts bleed for you all. Your dear, noble little Boy—so sweet, so promising, so full of pleasant ways—so precious in a thousand ways! Ah! God be merciful to you, my friend & to your poor wife, & to your dear children all, and strengthen you to bear such a blow as you had never felt before!" (*L*, IV, 205).

Misfortune in yet another form was to strike the Simmses soon thereafter. On or about April 27, 1860—while sessions of the National Democratic Convention were in progress—Simms's "wigwam" in Charleston, the brick residence on Smith Street left to Chevillette in Nash Roach's will, was burned almost to the ground. "You will see by the enclosed," Simms wrote to Lawson, "that I am still the victim of destiny. My house and furniture destroyed—some 5 to $6000 dollars. No insurance" (*L*, IV, 219). Adding that he had "no means to rebuild," Simms asserted, "I go to town by the next train, to sell out, if I can do no better."

But, always a Southern nationalist, Simms was admittedly preoccupied—before and after the Charleston convention—with the political issues at hand: the role of South Carolina among the Southern states and the role of the South in the Union. From Simms's point of view the convention itself was a failure, deciding nothing, but rejecting Southern initiatives to such an extent that most delegates from eight Southern states—Alabama, Arkansas, Florida, Georgia, Louisiana, Mississippi, South Carolina, and Texas—walked out, leaving all issues unresolved. Before the Democrats could convene again, in June in Baltimore, to name Stephen A. Douglas (strongly opposed by the South) as its presidential nominee, the Republican party on May 18 had caused consternation throughout the South by nominating Abraham Lincoln for the presidency. With neither party choosing a candidate satisfactory to the South, the region faced a political dilemma; and more strongly than ever cries for secession reverberated in the halls of capitols of the slave states.

Though Simms's role in orchestrating Southern strategy seems exaggerated by Wakelyn,[4] there can be no doubt that the novelist strongly advocated secession and wrote persuasive letters attempting to mold the opinions of J. H. Hammond, who despite his personal difficulties had finally become U.S. Senator in 1857, and William Porcher Miles, who had been elected to Congress in the same year. To Hammond Simms wrote that "the popular momentum" for secession "would … not … be withstood" and that "the death of the National parties" would cause Georgia (and other Southern states) to "go like an avalanche." It was a blessing, Simms added, that "the triumph of Lincoln was so complete as to leave all national parties hopeless of resuscitation. All will be right" (*L*, IV, 283). The novelist, certain of secession, urged Miles to consider running for the governorship of South Carolina because "the Executive now, of S. C. will be quite another sort of thing from what it has been. It will be, for a time at least, the Presidency of a new Republic …" (*L*, IV, 263). Perhaps Simms's letter of November 13, 1860, to James Lawson, complaining that "Black Republicanism … would run riot over the land" and "crush your conservatives & crush us," helps to measure the depth of his feeling on the tensions that divided the nation:

> We (S.C.) will secede. So will Geo. and so all the Cotton States—in succession. … We cannot wait—must not wait—will not wait one moment longer than we can help. There are overt acts enough, & the election of Lincoln is conclusive. … If the South submits, the Black Republicans are confirmed in their power, their predictions, their supremacy. … (*L*, IV, 265)

A week later Simms wrote Lawson again: "The popular momentum grows every hour, and at such a pace, that Unionism is dead and Conservative Politicians dare not open their mouths. It is here a perfect landsturm, and … there is no heeding the torrent. The Cotton States cannot now arrest themselves if they would" (*L*, IV, 267–68).

It is ironic, perhaps, that Simms tried to persuade his Northern colleague that "there will be no war. A war would destroy the whole confederacy of the North, & make that of the South supreme" (*L*, IV, 268). "Come yourself," Simms coaxed. "Settle here alongside of me, as a Cotton Planter. … I will get or give you a farm. …" It is doubly ironic that at this very time Simms should also invite Lawson's son Jimmy to visit Woodlands: "… be sure to send Jimmy as soon as you & he please, & you can spare him. I will take care of him; and he shall see what a free world is ours, and how much better calculated to make a man of him than yours!" (*L,* IV, 269).

Young James Lawson, a friend of Gilmore Simms, Jr., accepted the invitation, arriving in South Carolina scarcely two weeks before the Ordinance of Secession was unanimously adopted in Charleston on December 20. South Carolina's decision to secede thus became official while a Northern youth, Jimmy Lawson, was a guest at the home of a Southern youth, Gilly Simms—and while the fathers of the two young friends were exchanging letters about the course of the nation as well as the future safety of their sons. Two days before the Ordinance was signed, Simms had written Lawson that "Jimmy wins favor wherever he goes. He is considered, a fine young fellow, and while mannish is modest." His own son, Simms reported, "is eager to volunteer to take the forts. But our policy is to shed no blood" (*L,* IV, 310). Later, on the last day of December, Simms was less optimistic about averting war, advising the worried father in New York about Jimmy's possible risk in returning North: "… I have *ordered* him, if there be any fighting on the Seaboard, 'do you come back to *me.*' … It is to you much more important that the boy should be safe, than that he should be in a hurry to get home. He is safe with me, and under my counsel. We are on the eve of war, and our boys are not to be kept bridled much longer" (*L,* IV, 313). Later in the same letter Simms—predicting that "War is inevitable!"—disclosed his own anguish, particularly as the father of a seventeen-year-old son: "I am a small volcano in a canebrake: ready to boil over & burst …" in frustration, particularly over the quandary facing young Gilmore, "anxious to volunteer" and "fight like the devil, if I will let him." But, the father exclaimed, "*I* cannot afford it. He is the last hope of the family. … Sooner than he shall enter into the fray, I will go myself!"

What in Simms's mind ensured the inevitability of war was the misunderstanding between President James Buchanan and Gov. Francis W. Pickens of South Carolina concerning the status of Fort Sumter in Charleston Harbor, then occupied by federal troops.[5] Simms's last letter of 1860 gave the following advice to William Porcher Miles concerning the Union seizure of Fort Sumter: "You must either starve out or smoke out the garrison. You should certainly not suffer them to mount a cannon; but by incessant cannonade, from the landside, wear them out. … Do not attempt *escalade,* until all other means have failed" (*L,* IV, 315). Simms closed out the letter—and 1860—with the memorable lines: "I am … like a bear with a sore head, & chained to the stake.

I chafe, and roar & rage, but can do nothing. Do not be rash, but, do not let this old city forget her *prestige*. Charleston is worth all New England."

Simms's letters in January 1861 demonstrate that, among other accomplishments, the novelist was a knowledgeable military tactician.[6] In copious detail, and with surprising acumen, Simms wrote lengthy letters to Porcher Miles and David Flavel Jamison surveying the best strategies for the defense of Charleston Harbor[7]—all to no avail since Union forces there remained intact until the famous battle which opened the Civil War three months later. In February the seceded states—South Carolina, Georgia, Louisiana, Alabama, Florida, and Mississippi—met in Montgomery, Alabama, to form the Confederate States of America and elect Jefferson Davis as its president. At the time Simms still had some small hope that war could be averted, but remained defiant in the face of what he considered Northern aggression. "We crave peace," Simms stated in a letter of February 19, 1861, to James Lawson. "But we prepare for the war that is threatened & in which the North will more effectually cut its own throat than it has ever done yet ..." (*L*, IV, 326–27). In the event of war, the Southern strategy, Simms continued, would be to "declare our ports *free* to Europe & shut them to the North," making "Yankee commerce ... the prey of Yankee Privateers." But "If we are let to go in peace," Simms maintained, "we shall not discriminate against the North, and our trade will still be accessible to her industry & enterprise."

The Confederate States of America was strengthened on March 2, 1861, by the admission of Texas, setting up what Simms recognized as rival factions for leadership of the South. "On one hand," Simms wrote Miles, "Virginia, Maryland, Kentucky, Tennessee, North Carolina & Missouri" (*L*, IV, 331), *versus* the "Cotton States" led by South Carolina. Simms was concerned lest South Carolina's alignment with the cotton states alienate her from matriarchal Virginia and other states of the upper—or border—South: but he was equally disquieted by the possibility of Virginia rather than South Carolina assuming hegemony in the South. President Lincoln's immediate mobilization of troops, however, following Gen. P. G. T. Beauregard's attack on Fort Sumter on April 12, 1861, stopped the quibbling among the Southern states; and Virginia, North Carolina, Tennessee, and Arkansas joined the Confederacy in rapid succession, bringing its total constituency to eleven.

Even before Fort Sumter, young William Gilmore Simms, Jr., had volunteered (with the entire cadet corps of the Citadel Academy) for the Confederate army, despite his father's original misgivings.[8] On March 3, 1861, Simms wrote Lawson denoting Gilly's change of status as South Carolina prepared itself for eventualities: "But while making ourselves ready, nobody desires war, and we see no necessity for it. We reluct at bloodshed. Nothing but invasion will bring us to it ..." (*L*, IV, 340). Typical of Simms, however, who believed in preserving harmonious family life especially in times of discord, the novelist closed his long letter to his New York friend with a prideful account of the natural and architectural virtues of Woodlands. First, Simms boasted that "We are in the enjoyment of May weather" in March: "All our trees are blossoming, and a return of cold & frost, would lose us all our fruit. But you & Mary & Kate & all, should see our woods now, while putting on their morning glories." Next, he expressed the desire that Lawson could see the improvements in the buildings and landscaping at Woodlands. "I have altered my portals so that I have made my old brick steps as handsome an entrance as any in the state," he stated. Demonstrating his knowledgeable interest in design, the author explained his procedure: "I have rough cast them [the portals], cemented the whole flight, introduced an open balustrade at the front, along the first platform; have painted & whitewashed and added my corridor and the new library building," the latter constituting a single large room, thirty by twenty-two feet. "The corridor, connecting it with the main dwelling covers 20 x 12," he added, "with four arches in front; and cemented floor." To help his friend visualize these renovations, Simms drew a sketch of the "new" Woodlands (see Figure 1), with the explanation that he had not "regarded the

*(Figure 1)*

relative proportions," only seeking to give "some idea of the general plan which contemplates a corresponding wing & corridor on the opposite side." The author's pride, both in the already magnificent homestead and in the creative way in which he was bettering it, shows in his description to his friend: "The main dwelling is 50 feet front, the corridor 20, the library building 22, thus covering a front of 92 feet"; with the addition of "the opposite wing," contemplated in the near future, "the whole front will be 184 feet." For landscaping, Simms added, "We have set in front of the house some fine shrub trees—the English laurel, the Italian & other cedars & a variety besides," as well as "numerous roses & flowers." With the help of gifts from neighbors—

one being James H. Hammond—Simms also planted "fruit & shrub trees, and … 1000 grapes Catawba & Warren, and shall set out (D. V.) another 1000 in a week." The author-planter closed with an expression of "Love to all. God bless you" (*L*, IV, 340–41).

These sentiments—in the same letter in which he spoke bitterly of "the heads of those who would not suffer us to be at peace in the Confederacy [Union], nor have us at peace when we withdrew from it" and warned his Northern friend of the South's willingness, if provoked, to "let loose all our tigers, & carry the attack into the enemy's country"—are a remarkable demonstration of man's capacity to juxtapose aggressive thoughts of war and peaceful visions of domestic fulfillment. The irony, of course, is that the Woodlands of Simms's fondest dreams should eventually become a target and a victim of the belligerence he dreaded yet confronted.

Could Simms's vigorous commitment to literature possibly survive in an atmosphere where the author—already weakened by physical debility and emotional exhaustion—felt physically, intellectually, and morally threatened at every turn? Perhaps even his newly directed energy to transform his estate at Woodlands into unmatched magnificence was the result of his inability to channel his creativity into literary production. Certainly his despondent letter to Miles in January 1860 reveals the symptoms of a burned-out writer: "I have heart for nothing. I am resigned to obscurity, & can struggle no more. … You may judge of the terrible depression that weighs me down, when you hear that I have ceased to work" (*L*, IV, 187).[9] Three weeks later Simms, admitting that he was "getting old and weak," was still "in a momentary paroxysm of despair" (*L*, IV, 193). "I trust it will not last," he said to Porcher Miles. "I am trying not only to do, but to do cheerfully." What he was trying to do cheerfully was to bring out the previously mentioned "new collection of poems" which, he stated, "I mean to dedicate … to James, your brother" and which he now described as "a volume containing a selection from my fugitive pieces, song & sonnet, the growings of thirty years." This, then, was not a fresh creative effort (Simms was too mentally and physically debilitated for a spontaneous burst of creativity as of old), but a reworking of earlier artistic efforts. "I can still toil," Simms asserted, "and begin once more to cherish a feeble little nursling Hope." The result was to be Simms's last volume of poetry—in the author's words "the revision of my fugitive poems" (*L*, IV, 200)—bearing the title *Simms's Poems Areytos or Songs and Ballads of the South With Other Poems* and published in Charleston in December 1860 by Russell & Jones. But Simms did not pretend, even to himself, that *Areytos* was a major accomplishment. The Southern man of letters admitted that recently he had "been able to do very little else" than make a minimal contribution to Appleton's *New*

*American Cyclopaedia.* "My health," he explained, "especially that of my head, has been such as to make me avoid all possible mental strain." Consequently, Simms remarked, "this winter I have undertaken no literary labour for which I was not pledged & which I could possibly avoid"—the "revising for the press my occasional poetry of 20 years or more" (*L*, IV, 223) apparently not constituting an exception.

But the difficulty Simms had in getting this volume published lends support to his perception that he was being unjustly treated. Originally *Simms's Poems Areytos* was to have been brought out by Simms's regular publisher, Redfield, but as sectional animosity grew, particularly after the secession of South Carolina, the New York publisher exploited the situation, withholding from its mainstay Southern author royalties it owed him and refusing to publish the book, even after Simms had paid to have it stereotyped.[10] Thus it was that a small edition of *Areytos* was issued in Charleston, and none in New York; "What a commentary upon the way I am treated by all these men ..." was Simms's assessment in a November letter to Lawson (*L*, IV, 261).

Nor was the Charleston native pleased with his own state's reaction to his works in 1860, particularly its cool reception to the revised edition of *The History of South Carolina* issued simultaneously in New York and Charleston by Redfield and by Russell & Jones, respectively, in January. The chief evidence Simms gave Porcher Miles in support of his "In S.C. I am repudiated" statement was the shoddy treatment the Palmetto state gave his "entirely rewritten" history which had "fallen dead from the press." "Hardly a newspaper in the state has noticed it,"[11] he protested; and while the state legislature made "an appropriation for Laborde's Hist. of the College,"[12] not a member moved "the adoption of my Hist. in the schools"—despite the author's contention that "I have suffered nothing ... to escape me" in making the book essential "to the public man, as to the pupil." His efforts in their behalf, Simms averred, were "wasted upon a people who have seemingly deliberatedly decreed that, so far as my living is to depend upon their favor, I shall die!" (*L*, IV, 186–87).

Simms's depressed state of mind, his acute sense of not being appreciated, obviously magnified any slight, real or perceived, as national hostilities came to a boil in 1860–1861. He often complained of his treatment by South Carolina in letters to fellow South Carolinians like Hammond and Miles; but his loyalty to his home state never permitted him to voice the same sentiments to his Northern correspondents, even one so intimate as James Lawson. Particularly in the months leading up to secession and war, in writing his friends at the North Simms vigorously defended South Carolina's every action and painted favorable pictures of the quality of plantation life, even as he lamented to Hammond and Miles the state's inefficient leadership and its people's financial hardships. Candor in all matters was his creed with Southern intimates; as hostile feelings increased between North and South, in the early 1860s Simms as a loyal Southerner adhered to a creed of staunchly defending his region in communications with even his best friends north of the Mason-Dixon line.

Amidst all this emotional turmoil, it is small wonder that Simms had little time or taste for sustained literary endeavor. That he went through with the revisions of *Simms's Poems Areytos* and *The History of South Carolina* is evidence of toil under adverse circumstances—toil, but not inspiration. The only original creative work Simms undertook during the 1860–1865 period was a pre–Revolutionary War novel first conceived of in 1858, worked upon intermittently in the early 1860s, but not completed until 1866, and published the following year as *Joscelyn; A Tale of the Revolution.*

Apart from literature and Woodlands, his new artistic interest, Simms concentrated his thoughts on secession, a new independent South, and war. Yet even in long, largely political letters to fellow Charlestonian William Porcher Miles, who on February 12, 1861, had been appointed chairman of the committee on military affairs of the Congress of the Confederate States, Simms forgot neither literature nor architectural landscape. For instance, in writing to Miles on the subject of the ideal Southern nation, Simms opened with the exhortation, "Do not forget the interests of Literature in the formation of the new Government" (*L*, IV, 329). In March, after having immersed himself in "building & planting" at Woodlands, Simms wanted the Confederate congressman, whom he greatly admired, to see the estate firsthand: "You have never been at Woodlands. Come now. You may never, otherwise, see me again. I am sinking into the sere & yellow leaf, & have grown in the last two years, as grey as a badger. You will hardly know me" (*L*, IV, 345). Miles was not the only friend whom Simms wished would see Woodlands in all its glory; he also issued a nostalgic invitation to his New York friends, the Lawsons: "You must certainly come, & bring Lyde, to see Woodlands. I trust, unless burnt up, that I shall have things in proper trim to show her ladyship. The new library is completed; but will not hold all my books. I shall still have to keep some 2000 in the outer building. We shall have peace some day, and you shall come" (*L*, IV, 350).

But mainly Simms's correspondence in 1861 was overloaded with long discussions of political and military strategy, as, for instance, in his letter of March 7 to Miles. "Well! Mr. Lincoln has spoken! And we are to have war,"

Simms asseverated. "Let us not *declare* it. Hostilities may exist without war. Let us simply meet the issues as they arise." In Charleston, according to the writer, "they are daily expecting the struggle. I know nothing precise, but from what I hear, a few days will probably confirm these anticipations. God be with our people" (*L*, IV, 344).

Then, as was his wont, Simms proceeded to outline in specific detail plans to help with the defense of Charleston, on which subject[13] he had sent many letters to Gen. David Flavel Jamison, president of the Secession Convention and secretary of war in Gov. Francis Wilkinson Pickens's Executive Council. Simms's overladen words and accompanying illustrations reveal his obsession with the topic:

> I have been writing my counsels, night after night to Jamison, and am now engaged in trying to make a new, simple, cheap, & facile adaptation of the sword bayonet to the old musket. I have made the model, & expect a smith tomorrow to see if he can work my plan into ship shape. I find that Jamison has adopted my suggestion of using ranging timber with facings of R. R. iron for batteries; but I am not satisfied with the shape of the battery, nor with the manner in which the iron is laid on. The shape of the battery (profile) is this:
>
> 
>
> It presents too long a plane surface to a plunging fire. Besides the rails are not spiked down. I counselled that they should be spiked, but loosely, so as to allow some working of the rail under the shocks of shot or shell. My plan would have presented this profile:
>
> 
> 
>
> so that no shell or shot could strike without glancing upwards & over, or, if sticking in front, beneath the angle, then recoiling into the sands, below. And I would have had the structure solid, filled up with sand. (*L*, IV, 344)

It is uncommon that a literary man should have the knowledge, interest, and mechanical aptitude in military tactics demonstrated in this letter, which also serves to indicate the degree of his commitment to the Southern cause. With his region, his family, his *Weltanschauung* threatened, Simms became more decidedly than ever a patriot, and no demands weighed more heavily upon him than service to his state. That his military suggestions to Miles and Jamison were ignored, however, caused Simms grief, as he candidly pointed out in his letter of April 2, 1861, to the congressman: "... one feels a little sore that there should be no record of a patriotism & a devotion to his country, which has left him little time or thought for any thing else, ever since the moment of secession ..." (*L*, IV, 355).

Many of Simms's thoughts were with young Gilmore Simms, Jr., who after volunteering in February or March was allowed to remain on reserve duty at the Citadel, where (in Simms's words) he "has his knapsack ready, and is eager to get a crack at the enemy" (*L*, IV, 353). The proud parent, in writing Lawson, stated that "He is now about 6 feet high, some 2 inches taller than his father I fancy, or nearly so." Though Simms could not have known in advance of Gen. P. G. T. Beauregard's plans to demand the surrender of Fort Sumter by Union troops, on April 12 he was in Charleston, perhaps to see Gilly at the Citadel, and by chance "witnessed the bombardment of Fort Sumter" (*L*, IV, 355). Simms was naturally pleased with "the expulsion of the enemy from the sacred soil of Carolina";[14] but, after asking again in a letter to Miles to "be excused for writing on military subjects," he registered "natural solicitude ... for the safety of the good old city, & the brave young cause," and expressed concern lest the "principles" he had urged be once more ignored (*L*, IV, 357). Try as he might to remain aloof, to leave military matters to those in command, Simms could not refrain from expressing strongly held theories (again with illustrations) about the proper course of action in defense of Charleston and the South. But he closed his letter of April 17, 1861, to Miles with a disarming statement of friendship: "... I have Monongahela, hog & hominy & a loving welcome. Say this to any of your friends. ... Today, my dear Miles, I am 55! But my grey beard is 65. I have grown very old in 2 years. God bless you, my friend" (*L*, IV, 360).

But though "the position of the country, & of our State, keeps me dreadfully anxious" (*L*, IV, 361), primarily because (Simms felt) appropriate leadership was lacking, the novelist-turned-patriot had domestic worries as well. As he had explained early in 1860, "With a family so large as mine, I am rarely free from apprehension for my children. ... I have lost so many that the sickness, of one of my children now, is a Terror. I see behind the door a grim shadow casting a deadly dart" (*L*, IV, 216). Thus, when illness plagued his children in the summer of 1861, Simms once again faced Terror at close hand: "My House for the last 2 months has been something of a Hospital," he wrote Hammond on June 14, 1861; "I have had three children down, seriously, with Bilious remittent, in one case running into typhoid. They are now better, but my anxiety & suffering have been great, & I now tremblingly watch against relapse" (*L*, IV, 366). The three children were Chevillette, Hattie, and Sydney Hammond, and though the two girls continued to improve, the relapse Simms feared struck down two-year-old Sydney Hammond three weeks later, on or about July 2, 1861.[15] But Simms had scarcely "buried another son" (*L*, IV, 371) before his only remaining son received the call to report for active duty, on or about November 7, 1861, the same day Union forces attacked and captured Port Royal on the South Carolina coast. The letter of William Gilmore Simms to his namesake son and heir is memorable enough to be quoted in full:

Woodlands, Thursday Afternoon.
[November 7, 1861]

You had better, my dear Son, get a belt and pocket of leather, for your revolver, and not burden yourself with carrying the box. It will not be necessary to you. If you have enough of bullets, even the bullet mould & all the appurtenances of powder flask &c. may be left with the box. The same flask from which you load your musket, will afford you powder for your pistol. But as in the musket you may probably use cartridges, then carry the powder flask of the pistol. But be sure & strip yourself of all unnecessary incumbrances, which the Romans called *Impedimenta.* Be as lightly armed as you can. It would be better that I should provide you with moulded bullets than that you should carry mould & lead with you. Leave box, mould & all that sort of thing with your sister. Advise me, as soon as you can, of your whereabouts & the mode of reaching you, in the event of our desiring to send you any thing. See that your provision for clothing is warm & sufficient. Leave every thing that you do not need, with your sister; and remember that nobody is more light-hearted than he who has fewest cares, whether of brain or body. Your bowie knife may be very useful. You are to remember that you are to defend your mother country, & your natural mother, from a hoard of mercenaries & plunderers, and you will make your teeth meet in the flesh. The less you fear for yourself, the more your security. 'He who would save his life, the same shall lose it!' This is a biblical warning against that lack of firmness, that overcaution, always trembling at consequences, & calculating chances, which was the infirmity of Hamlet, and which is fatal to all heroism. And this audacity & courage are not inconsistent with the utmost prudence and circumspection. All generalship, in fact, is so much military prudence, as reconciles valour with judgment & wisdom. Mere inconsiderate rage is not so much valour as blindness, ignorance, presumption & insanity. Obey orders, do your duty faithfully & cheerfully & patiently, and wait your time, & watch your time, and keep your head so, that where your leader may falter, you shall be able to keep him up, counsel him on, & where he falls, take the lead yourself. A strong will, a brave heart & clear head, in the moment of danger, these constitute the essentials of heroism. Let nothing, at any time, divert your mind, from the immediate duty which is before you. This is *first* & therefore *over* all. It will be time enough tomorrow for other matters. But I will not bore you with laws and maxims. Be a man, my son, faithful & firm, and put yourself in God's keeping. All that the love & confidence of parents can do for you will be done. Yourself, with God's aid, must do the rest. We are in his hands, all of us! Pray to him. It will not lessen your strength & courage to do so, even on the abyss of battle! We are all well except your father. I am suffering from neuralgia in the head, from ear ache, and tooth ache, all at once. The latter will probably compel me to visit the city on Monday next, & I may go to the Mills House or Charleston Hotel. I trust you have the dressing case by this time. Better take out of it a single razor, get it *set* by the Barber, take a small box of the ointment & the Brush & leave the case with your sister. It would only encumber you. A mere pinch of the ointment is put upon the face, and the brush, wet with water is then applied briskly. In laying the razor to cheek or chin, let it be as flat as possible. It will then cut the beard better, and will be less likely to cut the skin. Besides, it will keep the razor longer from being dulled.—The news which reaches us is exciting without being satisfactory. I have for six months predicted the attempt of the enemy on Beaufort, with a formidable force, with which they would expect to make Beaufort a base of operations, against Charleston & Savannah equally. I expected them in September. What our troops will need is numerous small steamers & boats so as to have ready access from one island to another. What I fear is the cutting off of small bodies on isolated spots. We require, now, that we have made the issue on the sea islands where the naval force of the enemy can be employed, to sustain our batteries against launches landing infantry & light troops. Any small bodies landing, we can cut off. To concentrate our troops in sufficient bodies against a formidable force will be more difficult, and, in the end, in all probability, we may be reduced to a guerilla warfare along the main fronting the sea islands. Write when you get a chance. God be with you, my son,

Your father
W. G. S.
(*L*, IV, 378–80)

Combining practical and philosophical advice, this calm, almost matter-of-fact letter must have been calculated by the father to have a steadying influence upon the son. Certainly, by intention, it reveals none of the terrible anxiety the father must have felt at the time.

Though Simms had written Lawson in late August that "We are really in the enjoyment of abundance" and "I could feed all your family a year and never feel it," the head of Woodlands plantation exaggerated conditions to his Northern friend in making his case for "the independence of the South."[16] (*L*, IV, 372, 374). To his Southern confidant, James Henry Hammond, he admitted that though not "exactly a pauper ... I need some succour," and asked his planter neighbor for assistance in obtaining food and other supplies scarce because "the troops [have] consumed every thing" (*L*, IV, 382–83). By this time, it must have been evident to any objective observer that the drain on the South's supply system could only worsen as the war progressed. Simms, like many another Southron, however, attributed the South's difficulties to "the incompetence of those parties who at present have our destinies in charge"[17] (*L*, IV, 390–91) rather than to the superiority of the populous North in economics and transportation; and like others of his cast, he held out hope that Great Britain would "seize upon the ground of quarrel which this outrage offers her": "I should not be surprised to find her at war with the U.S. in less than 3 weeks" (*L*, IV, 388).

But before the year 1861 had ended,[18] Simms's "scourge" would afflict him personally again. On December 22 Simms reported to Miles that Harriet Myddleton Simms, "My beautiful little girl, your Goddaughter was seized 2 days ago with Scarlet Fever" (*L*, IV, 390). Though at the time "the worst seems to be over ... and the Drs. declare her improving," young Hattie—not yet four and perhaps never fully recovered from her bout with illness during the summer—died on Christmas Day. Simms gave a vivid account in a long letter to Porcher Miles written January 15, 1862:

> Alas! yes, my dear Miles,
>
> Our chief guest, on Christmas Day, was Death. He found his way, without warning, and tore away our precious little one. ... I, who have so frequently been made to groan and shudder, at his coming, am not a whit better prepared to meet him now. ... No sooner have new tendrils closed over the old wounds, than they are rent away, and the scars reopen, & the old hurt bleeds fresh. This child was very sweet & dear to us. ... And, in herself, she was so surpassingly lovely. You can have no idea how tall she had grown, & how beautifully. Her form was perfectly developed; her face very fine & her forehead & whole head were cast in a mould of peculiar intellectual strength and beauty! Alas! Alas!

Then, Simms continued, "scarcely had we laid her in the grave before I was again made to shudder with the most awful terrors": Govan, one year older than Hattie, "was taken down with the same loathsome & cruel disease." In his case, Simms reported, "God has been merciful ... & the boy has been spared," but the effect on William Gilmore and Chevillette Simms was devastating, as is graphically revealed by the writer in an intensely autobiographical passage:

> ... you can well concieve my own & the agonies of his poor mother. Ah! my friend, to think that of 14 children, we have now buried nine! ... Five are yet left us, but for how long—how long? I have no longer any sense of security. My days & nights teem with apprehension. I wake from fearful dreams. I walk musing with my fears & terrors. It affects my health, my happiness, my habits, my performances. I no longer read or write with satisfaction, or success. Briefly, my dear friend, I am under these successive shocks, growing feebler, rapidly aging, and shudder with a continued sense of winter at my hearth.

Nor could the inveterate writer of more than thirty years' experience now find solace in the practice of his craft. "My occupation utterly gone, in this wretched state of war & confusion," he continued, "I have no refuge in my wonted employments." Simms reiterated that "Could I go to work, as of old, having a motive, I might escape from much of the domestic thought." But with publishers and readers only hungry for political material and with his desks "already filled with MS.S.," he asked: "Why add to the number—the mass—when, I so frequently feel like giving these to the flames?" He closed this extraordinary outburst to a friend and compatriot with the admission, "My will is not strong enough, even in obedience to the calls of my mind, to engage in new labours which are so wholly motiveless" (*L*, IV, 393–94).

It is of course not surprising that even a disciplined author like Simms had difficulty in practicing his craft in 1862. Not only were the distractions of war ever around him, with his only son waiting for action in the Confederate army, but Simms—accurate in his observation that writing was now "motiveless" in the sense of profit making—was particularly disillusioned by the loss of his copyrights, which, he wrote Miles, "are all confiscated at the North" (*L*, IV, 398). Later, in a letter to Richard Yeadon, Simms placed the value of his confiscated copyrights and plates at "some $25,000—the whole earnings of my life, save my library. I realized annually from my copyrights, from $1200 to $1800." With "'Othello's occupation's gone!' and Cotton ... not to be sold" (*L*, IV, 399), Simms had lost his best sources of income, with family and plantation needs increasing by the day. Simms could only meekly express to Miles the hope, "When Peace is won, we shall then, no doubt, be enabled to effect an International Copyright" (*L*, IV, 398). But even in this dire situation ("... while the grass groweth, the steed starveth" was his observation), Simms nevertheless felt a surge of creativity amid his hopelessness. "My brain is seething with some new conceptions," he reported to Miles, and again put the question, "but surrounded with MS.S. as I am, I ask himself why add to the mass? I can now publish nothing." Despite Simms's ambivalence, his statement

> I propose a work to open all my revolutionary series, with the very dawn of the Revolution in S.C. It will need to be a work of very great painstaking. (*L*, IV, 398)

suggests a resolve that may have been fulfilled had not tragedy struck again on March 29, 1862.

On that date Woodlands burned—and with it a little more of Simms's *joie de vivre* (if not his pride and hope). The account of the fire written by David Flavel Jamison for the *Charleston Courier* of March 31 is graphic:

> I have just returned from witnessing a scene of ruin that has impressed me more painfully than any ... within my recollection. The fine residence of W. Gilmore Simms, Esq, ... now presents the sad spectacle of an informed mass of brick and rubbish, with the gaunt chimneys, standing out against the noble oaks of the still beautiful grounds. ... it was a saddening sight to behold the old homestead, where a liberal and almost lavish hospitality had been dispensed for thirty years, incapable of longer affording shelter to its generous owner.
>
> How the accident occurred, one can only conjecture. About three o'clock, this morning, the inmates of the house were awaked by a bright light, which proceeded from the burning roof. ... After it was discovered, the progress of the flames was rapid and irresistible. The negroes of the plantation promptly assembled on the alarm, and, under the cool and judicious direction of the owner, worked actively, faithfully and devotedly, and saved much of the furniture, though in a damaged condition. A number of handsome paintings were lost, and among them was a beautiful head of a peasant girl, painted for Mr. Simms by Sully, and which probably owed its fate to its not being framed, as the servants, in removing most of the other pictures, in the same room, esteemed of little value a painting without a gilded frame.
>
> Fortunately, by extraordinary perseverance and good management, the fine library, containing some eight or ten thousand volumes ... was saved, with its contents; only some hundred and fifty or two hundred volumes, scattered in different rooms of the mansion, were consumed with it.
>
> This is a heavy blow to a most estimable and distinguished man, especially in such times as these, when, even to the affluent and prosperous, it would be difficult to replace the loss. This is the third house that Mr. Simms has lost by fire. Within the last two years his town house was destroyed, which drove him from your city, and now his last place of refuge is gone from the same cause. (*L*, IV, 399)

Simms himself, writing a letter to William Porcher Miles dated "Woodlands in Ruins, April 10," demonstrated his usual stoic will: "Truly, I am pursued by a hungry fate! But I will not succumb. It may crush, but shall not subject me, no more than Yankeedom shall subject our country" (*L*, IV, 400). In an even stronger statement in a letter of the same day to J. H. Hammond, Simms assessed the "Fate [that] has pursued me for more than 30 years" and resolved that "if the Fate smites, the God strengthens." Even "under this severe calamity," he averred, "I have lost none of my energy & courage, though I may have lost some of my cheerfulness & elasticity" (*L*, IV, 403). The author was fortunate in that "all my M.S.S. and nearly all my library" were saved, a fact he attributed to the newly built wing to house his books and papers. Had these been lost, Simms related, "the blow would have been insupportable. As it is, I mean to die with harness on my back" (*L*, IV, 400).

That he survived the fire with his life Simms attributed to "the most eager zeal & most perfect devotion" of his slaves at Woodlands. "*That* fact, my dear H.," Simms related to James Henry Hammond, "is to me full of consolation." The novelist described his escape as "tacit proof" that "there was no lack of love for their master" on the part of his slaves, who rescued him "from an upper window" only minutes before the structure "came crashing down, with the fall almost literally of a thousand brick" (*L*, IV, 403–4). There were still other factors associated with the burning of Woodlands that must have provided solace for Simms. Friends, neighbors, and citizens in general responded to the disaster almost as a matter of patriotism, raising funds and providing materials for the at least partial restoration of the home of the state's most distinguished author. In a postscript to his April 10 letter to Hammond, Simms himself gave one account of the immediate generosity of a neighboring farmer—"one of the Jenningses[19] of Edisto river—a mill owner"—who offered the novelist the lumber to rebuild Woodlands—"all that you want," Simms quoted him as saying, "and you shall *not* pay me." The genuinely moved writer could only ask of Hammond, "Was not this handsome?" (*L*, IV, 405). In addition, in late June 1862 a group of South Carolinians headed by Hammond, John Dickson Bruns, William Gregg, and probably Miles and Jamison and others presented Simms with a donation of $3,600 "to aid in rebuilding your hospitable and honored homestead."[20] Simms wrote a long letter of acceptance, dated June 27 and published in both the *Mercury* and the *Courier* of July 8, 1862, in which he stated, "A sympathy so warm, ready and generous—a movement so spontaneous and unsolicited—touches me deeply, and lifts me greatly above the sense of privation and discomfort" (*L*, IV, 409–10).

Woodlands, then, was restored, at least partially,[21] in time, in the words of Simms, to provide "a shelter for my family, before the winter" (*L*, IV, 418). But before the rebuilding could be accomplished, the resolute will of the anxious father and husband was tested yet again. First, Gilmore Simms, Jr., contracted typhoid fever while serving as 3rd. sergeant in "The Cadet Company" of the 6th regiment of South Carolina Cavalry; on October 28, 1862, Simms wrote Hammond that his "eldest son has been lying dangerously ill" from the disease "contracted in camp" sometime in September (*L*, IV, 414). Young Gilmore's illness had come at a particularly crucial time in the family life of his parents, for when he arrived home from camp, requiring constant nursing, his mother was nearing the end of her fourteenth pregnancy. Simms reported that Chevillette watched her stricken son "day & night ... , never once leaving his bedside, till she was taken in labour." Another son was born to William Gilmore and Chevillette Simms on October 20, 1862, when his delicate, fragile mother was nearly forty-five years of age. The new son was named Charles Carroll Simms, in honor of the Charleston attorney who befriended the father when he was an unknown, yet aspiring young writer. The year 1862, then, closed with some joy and much relief; in his last known letter of the year, probably written in December, Simms summed up with a characteristic understatement: "How has our poor little State suffered in this war!" Then, also characteristically, he added, still with a flicker of hope: "Nothing but independence can compensate us for all; and this is a boon so precious, so necessary to our children and their children, that we must needs stifle our moans" (*L*, IV, 419).

In truly remarkable fashion, however, the resilient Simms began the new year with ideas about literature, if not with expectations of accomplishment. Writing on January 10, 1863, to John Reuben Thompson, assistant secretary of the Commonwealth of Virginia, sometime author and former editor of *Southern Literary Messenger*, Simms requested assistance in finding a Southern publisher for "a series of my minor tales or novels"[22] on the assumption that they "would be good selling books especially now, & for reading in camp and along the highways" (*L*, IV, 420). Admitting that "I have done little or nothing in literature for two years" and that "I have almost forgotten how to write," Simms nevertheless confirmed: "I am now trying to do something—working up an old story for the Illustrated News, but the work is uphill entirely." Simms confided to his fellow writer that he needed "leisure, repose & my wonted conveniences for composition": "I need not say to you, also, how much a man of my excitable temperament may be kept from his tasks by the condition of the Country. It will need a year of peace to bring me back to that calm of mood which Literature demands" (*L*, IV, 421).

The "old story" that Simms referred to is "Paddy McGann; or, The Demon of the Stump," which indeed did appear in the *Southern Illustrated News*, in sixteen installments, beginning February 14 and running through May 30, 1863.[23] In "working up" a manuscript probably begun in the 1840s or 1850s Simms retained the concept of a tall tale told in the vernacular of an Irish raftsman—successfully used in both "Sergeant Barnacle: The Boatman's Revenge: A Tale of the Edisto" (1845) and "Ephraim Bartlett, the Edisto Raftsman" (1852); but updating the time to the present, he directed his sharpest satire toward the cupidity and pretentiousness of the pseudo-intellectual North. "Paddy McGann," however, is much more than partisan political satire; in choosing "an original, a natural man" as his title character, Simms even before Mark Twain demonstrates that integrity, wonder, and wisdom are prerogatives of the backwoodsman all too often lost with the veneer of civilization. The short novel abounds in wit, humor, and irony as well as satire. Its pointed barbs at the North probably prevented its being read and appreciated in 1863 by a nationwide audience in a time of escalating sectional hostility; but with all its bawdiness and robustness "Paddy McGann" (as we shall see in chapter 12) embodies Simms's visionary concept of the frontier as the cradle for art and the precursor for civilization; and, as such, occupies a central place in his canon.

What becomes clear is that, even with his own declining health and the distractions of war and familial and personal anxieties, the overriding reason Simms did not write books during the 1860–65 period was the difficulty (almost the impossibility) of finding a publisher. With Redfield and his other Northern publishers no longer available to him, Simms lamented as never before the scarceness as well as the ineptitude of Southern publishers, who, he remarked more than once, did not distinguish between *publishing* and *printing* and knew almost nothing about merchandising. That Simms—cut off as he was from the publishing centers of the North—nevertheless kept contemplating and proposing literary projects is a testimonial to his commitment to his craft. For instance, in addition to his unsuccessful attempt to secure a book publisher for a series of his earlier fiction, Simms in March 1863 expressed to Cornelius Kollock, a literary-minded physician living in Cheraw, an interest in setting "a short novel" in "Cheraw, and the Pee Dee Country" if Kollock would assist in making the author "secure of my ground, my facts, &c" (*L*, IV, 423)—another idea that failed to materialize.

But Simms kept his literary options as open as the times and circumstances permitted. After June 1863 he and fellow South Carolina poet Paul Hamilton Hayne became frequent correspondents, exchanging views on social, economic, and political issues as well as literature, the first love of both men. In late June Simms counseled the poet "to settle on a small farm in our middle country" rather than to "persist in living at such enormous charges in poor & obscure up-country villages" like Aiken, where "you are out of the pale of civilization"—and presumably too far from Woodlands for the frequent exchange of visits. What Simms had to say about the advantages of living in his adopted region of South Carolina is interesting and enlightening (particularly when one remembers the omnipresent background of war). In all his travels, Simms related, he had never discovered a region with "so great a degree of health, comfort, profit & pleasure, as in this beautifully wooded middle country" of South Carolina. Barnwell District abounds in "delicious spots. ... *pleasanter* than Aiken—less hot, better wooded—better water—and cheap,—not at the *fancy* prices which make Aiken one of the dearest places in the state." Simms advised the younger writer to "Think over what I tell you," for "Ours is far the better region for the enjoyment of the *dolce far niente,* the great luxury of a Poet, when the sacred vapours are dissipated from his brain" (*L,* IV, 429–30). Not all of Simms's letters to Hayne, of course, attempted to persuade South Carolina's best-known poet to move into the neighborhood of South Carolina's best-known novelist. Somewhat surprisingly in time of war, their correspondence was mainly concerned with literary matters—techniques and theories of poetry; the poetic functions of Fancy, Imagination, Passion, and Thought; the purpose of analytical literary criticism.[24] When Simms did discuss war developments with Hayne, his tone was not nearly so ebullient or confident as it had been in earlier letters to Northerner Lawson, or even to Southerners Hammond and Miles. His new apprehensions in 1863 about the welfare and safety of citizen, city, and state are clearly visible in his letter written on July 29, 1863: "our poor old city," Simms confided, "is seriously menaced"; "[o]ur people" exhibit a "singular" apprehensiveness "not creditable to their manhood & resolve"; and "doubt & despondency among the citizens" are a cause of "great concern" (*L,* IV, 435–36). Simms's anxiety is particularly apparent when he turned the discussion directly from war to its indirect effect on literature and family. "... [M]y heart is too full of anxiety," he wrote, "to suffer me to write, and though I have contract for some $200 worth of prose,[25] I find myself unable to divert my thought from the crisis in which the country trembles in suspense." Simms indicated the seeming futility of his continued literary efforts: "What I write is in a spasm—a single burst of passion—hope, or scorn, or rage or exultation. If, where you are, you can abstract your mind from the present, & throw into the far land of the past, or poesy, do so for your own relief. I cannot!" Though the novelist had recently "sent the last instalments of ... 'Arnold'[26] to the 'Magnolia,'" he found "the business of revision … a drudgery," and was disgusted by "the horrible corruptions & blunders of the press." Perhaps even more depressing to Simms were his worries about members of his family: "I have had a child [probably Govan] very sick with worm fever, & my wife has been suffering severely with neuralgia in the face. They are now better—but who can be well, while this terrible war lasts, and while so many we love are in danger."

Though Simms had registered concern about the health of Chevillette, he was in no way prepared for what happened next. Her death on September 10, 1863, was the shock of his life: "I was struck down by the heaviest bolt of all that ever shattered my roof-tree" (*L*, IV, 437), he wrote to Paul Hamilton Hayne. Simms's letter dated September 23 went on to describe the author's physical and emotional reaction to the sudden death (probably of acute appendicitis) of the woman who loved him selflessly and for whom his own deep love was never fully realized until her demise:

> I was, I think, insane. I neither slept nor ate for four days and nights. Fever seized me, and I should have gone mad but for the administration of timely opiates. I am once more on my legs, but very weak. Today, is the first that I have given to the desk, and this I could do only in snatches of brief period. I move about the house & try to see to things. But every thing seems blank, & waste, & very cheerless. I am alone! Alone! For near 30 years, I had one companion in whose perfect fidelity, I felt sure. To her I could go, and say, 'I suffer!'—or, 'I am glad,' always satisfied that she would partake the feeling with me, whatever its character. Your eulogy [27] is not mere varnish & gilding. She was all that you describe,—a dutiful wife, a devoted mother, and the most guileless of women. Ah! God! And I am lone! (*L*, IV, 437–38)

Self-centered even in this tribute to his deceased wife, Simms probably cared for Chevillette as much as he was capable of lovingly giving himself to any woman whom he found "dutiful," "devoted," and "guileless," rather than exciting or intriguing in a passionate romantic sense. Simms's egoism made it difficult for him to empathize with the psyche of another person; his expectations of himself were high, in personal as well as literary terms, and he expected others to appreciate his intellectual and moral leadership. Chevillette subordinated her wishes to his, a role for which both instinct and tradition equipped her well. Simms honored and respected and cherished his wife; she in turn gave her whole life to him. She was never more than an important part of his life, the centerpiece of which was his literary career, his ambition to achieve excellence and fame. A strong family man, it is true that he placed more value on Chevillette as the mother of his children than as his lover and companion; true, that is, until her death shocked him as nothing before had ever affected him. If during her life he had taken her too much for granted, as an accompaniment to the Woodlands estate of which he was justly proud, upon her demise he suddenly realized both the intricacy of his love for her and the depth of his dependency upon her. Recognition that he had undervalued Chevillette led him to question whether he had valued other things too highly. In his intense confessional letter to Hayne, Simms seemed to renounce ambition as an ill-advised addiction. "We live too much for the world, my dear Paul," Simms said immediately after attesting to the virtues of his now almost hallowed deceased wife. "It is a poor affair. This ambitious struggle after greatness, is a vanity. Our sole justification must lie in the will & wish to *do,* irrespective of the profit and the loss." In this reflective and chastened mood, Simms admitted to being "much older—much feebler" and spoke of Hayne as "the younger brother of his guild" who would seek honors in the future. In an intensely personal poem entitled "What's Left" written about this time, Simms's stoic admission that "The soul once reft of loving light, / Must make its weary way alone" (*SP,* p. 242) is indicative of his painful reconciliation to Chevillette's death.

Though Simms's sorrow at the loss of his wife of thirty years was real and long lasting, his disenchantment with the struggle to achieve was not. Three weeks later, in a letter of October 15, 1863, to John Reuben Thompson, Simms reiterated the "terrible shock of my great calamity—so totally unexpected, & for which none of us was prepared." Yet the novelist then resolved "to throw the work of resistance upon my mind, & ... to address myself to some literary labour." Despite "the bolt from a clear sky" that had dazed him, the Woodlands planter and man of letters pledged once again "to divert the mind to the regions of the ideal" (*L,* IV, 438–39)—to assert "the will to *do,* irrespective of the profit and the loss." The courage and commitment that Simms showed at this time was to be tested yet further.

In late 1863 his illness was probably more severe than even he, with his usual candor, was prepared to acknowledge. On October 20 he wrote Francis Peyre Porcher that "I am up again, but very feeble. In order to change air & scene, & attend to some business, I visited the city a week ago, & could scarcely lift myself in & out of the cars. I could not walk 200 yards without exhaustion; and I recuperate slowly" (*L,* IV, 440). Once again, however, Simms stated his will to prevail: "I am very desolate; but duty to my children & to my own mind, finds my will to do, unimpaired; and I propose, as soon as possible, to subject my mind to some continuous task." Personal events had almost blocked out Simms's preoccupation with the war, but he closed his letter to Porcher with the following observation concerning the fate of Charleston: "The military & people are of opinion, that it may be partially destroyed but not taken" (*L*, IV, 441).

The war came closer than ever to Simms in 1864. In February his namesake son, still only twenty years old, saw his first combat in the battle of St. John's, acquitting himself well and escaping without injury.[28] Though Simms wrote several friends in 1864 that the war would "end this year," his information was based on the faulty information that Confederate troops were defeating Union forces on the battlegrounds of Virginia, the site to which his son was transferred in May as a member of the South Carolina Cavalry. Less than a month later, young Simms was wounded in the battle of Trevilians on June 12, 1864, as described in his only known extant letter to his father:

> The Battle took place at Trevillion's Depot about eight miles from Gordonsville & lasted two days. I was wounded on Sunday the 12th the last day of the fight. I was struck three times in as many seconds, one ball breaking my finger while in the act of firing on my gun. Another passed through Alfred Aldrich's shoulder and struck me full in the breast but glanced off inflicting only a scratch and another grazed my jugular vein raising a knot on my neck. Alfred A. is badly though not seriously wounded. We have all been sent to Charlottesville and have been well treated.
>
> I am going to send this note with some men who are going to walk to the James river about 15 miles from this place and then go to Richmond by canal. All communication with the south has been cut. It is possible not to be able to come home or write until the cars begin to run. Do not be at all uneasy about me as my wound is quite slight and my ... health is good. Our Brigade had to bare the brunt of the fight unsupported for two hours and we lost very heavily. Gen. Butler was delighted with the conduct of our Regiment and complimented Capt. Humphrey's [troops?] particularly. Gen. Hampton said that the Yankee cavalry had never before met with such a defeat. We are now in hot pursuit of Sheridan and the remnant of his force.
>
> Give my love to Sister, the girls and kiss the children for me.
>
> Your affec. Son
> W. G. Simms, Jr.[29]

On or about June 20 the elder Simms wrote a letter to his daughter Augusta (now Mrs. Edward Roach, living in Charleston on Society Street) informing her of the report that Gilmore had been "wounded seriously" because at the time he had heard nothing directly from his soldier son (*L*, IV, 457). Fortunately, though Gilmore barely escaped with his life, his wound in his own words was actually "quite slight."

A family reminiscence involving the Civil War duty of Gilmore Simms, Jr., and his close friends Robert and Alfred Aldrich is worth relating. According to this tradition, Simms had entrusted to Jupiter, the slave who (as was wont in the Confederate army) accompanied young Gilmore to war, the responsibility of assuring the safe return of the three youths after the fighting had ended. Simms, it will be remembered, had exhorted Gilly to have a "strong will, a brave heart & clear head, in the moment of danger"; in recognition of his responsibility, however, Jupiter sent the young soldiers off to their first combat with the following cautionary advice: "Now, boys, you just remember this: You've got to be *brave*, but you ain't got to be *too* brave" (*MCSO*, I, III). In that very battle—presumably at Trevilians—Gilmore Simms and Alfred Aldrich were wounded by the same bullet, but the three friends and Jupiter all survived the war. The anecdote reveals not only Simms's concern for his son, but also his recognition of Jupiter's admirable personal qualities and confidence in him as a responsible, trustworthy individual.

Another of Simms's psychic experiences occurred at about this time, as recorded in the oral history preserved by his descendants. This anecdote, which was a favorite of Mary C. Simms Oliphant, also centers around Gilly's war wound and his subsequent attempt to come home to South Carolina from Virginia. Presumably weak and feverish, the returning soldier collapsed somewhere near Chester, South Carolina, and fell unconscious in a creek, from which he was carried by other Confederates to the nearest military hospital, in Chester. That night, according to family memoirs, Simms dreamed that his son was dying; and the next morning he received confirmation from military authorities that Gilmore, Jr., had sunk into a coma and was not expected to live. Simms rushed to Chester by wagon ("the only way he could get there"), and upon arrival was told that his son's only chance of survival lay in his being aroused from his comatose state. Mrs. Oliphant's words vividly describe this most "notable experience" of Simms's "magnetic power":

> So he walked to the bed and he grabbed his son's hand and dug his nails deep into the boy's wrist, and he ordered him: "Now, son, you speak to me." And [Gilly] opened his eyes and said, "Father," and turned over and went to sleep. (*MCSO*, I)

This story stands out as "one of our favorite tales" among those handed down through three generations of the Simms family because it reveals the almost hypnotic effect attributed to the author by his children and grandchildren.

Around the first of August 1864, presumably after the experience just related, Simms assured a friend that his son was rapidly improving. Not until

Gilly's full recovery did Simms reveal some fatherly irritation with his "desultory & purposeless mode of life"; in a letter of November 14 Simms wrote his now recuperated son, "It was painful to me to witness in you, the irritable & feverish restlessness which marked all your movements while here—the impatience of the uniform—the fidgetting & nervous desire for change of scene, place & action—all of which, if indulged, must lead to a frivilous [*sic*] future—unsettled, unmethodical, without aim or purpose, beyond the mercurial impulse of the moment" (*L*, IV, 467–68)—hardly words of cheer for a returned war hero. But, like many another father before and after him, Simms must have felt the obligation to give his well-meaning but apparently misguided son the benefit of advice: "Begin to be an earnest man—earnest of aim,—concentrative of effort—your eye fixed on your purpose, and all your powers concentrated in the one direction for its attainment." The letter includes detailed instructions which may strike the twentieth-century reader as humorous, or petty:

> When you write, write on both sides of your paper, & send a half sheet rather [than] a whole sheet but half written, and when you send off two letters on the same day, one to me and another to the girls, put in one envelope. We judge of great things by small. —Paper is 25/100 per sheet. Each letter postage is 10/100. Why—when we have so little money, waste 100 per cent, on every letter that you write.

But its moral instruction not only reflects nineteenth-century thinking but also appears to embody Simms's own personal philosophy:

> If you do not economize your resources you will not economize your powers. In wasting the one you betray characteristics which will make you waste the other. ... Nor is it for the sake of money that I would have you economize; but because in the waste of money it becomes the melancholy agency for the dissipation of your best mental & moral qualities. This dissipation of money is a process, for the dissipation of time, & thought & performance.

Happy, then, with the physical safety (if not the mental and emotional state) of his now motherless eldest son returned from war, Simms was not so fortunate in the outcomes of two other important personal relationships. In August Charleston was again afflicted with an epidemic of yellow fever, and among the dreaded disease's victims was Simms's "poor & long tried friend," David Flavel Jamison, struck down on September 14, 1864 (*L*, IV, 462). Less than two months later, an even closer friend, James Henry Hammond, who for some time lay "dangerously ill, & with some very bad symptoms" (*L*, IV, 469), died on November 13. No man meant more to Simms than the brilliant, talented, if erratic Hammond, to whom Simms had written during the summer before his death: "Were you as rarely good as you are rarely endowed, you would be one of the most perfect men living. It is your passions, your impetuous & too frequently stubborn will, that neutralizes some of your noblest gifts" (*L*, IV, 458). A week after Hammond's death, Simms movingly testified in a letter to Edward Spann Hammond, son of the deceased, "my most confidential friend for near twenty five years." The author avowed that "Never were thoughts more intimate than his & mine," that he and Hammond had "few or no secrets from each other," and that they "took few steps in life without mutual consultation." Simms had "perfect confidence" in Hammond, and "I believe he had in me." Noting the "something kindred in our intellectual nature," Simms asserted that his appreciation of Hammond's genius—"its grasp—its subtlety—its superiority of aim"—was unmatched. "And most deeply did I sympathize with him," Simms proclaimed, "under that denial of his aim ... which, permitted, I verily believe he would have lived ... for far higher triumphs even than those which he achieved" (*L*, IV, 469–70).

Thus, within a period of fourteen months in 1863–1864 Simms had lost his two most cherished intimacies: that with his wife, his closest and only female confidante, and that with his best friend in all of South Carolina, his closest male confidant (with the possible exception of James Lawson, still a trusted friend, but now distanced by the war). In addition, he had a son wounded in action and had yet another valued friend die of yellow fever. Afflicted physically and psychologically, Simms—even without the personal burdens—was increasingly despondent over the course of the war itself. In writing Paul Hamilton Hayne (who with the death of Hammond was his best-attuned correspondent) on September 29, 1864, Simms expressed perhaps his most pessimistic assessment of the South's prospects for victory, conceding the possibility that "... we shall die by inches like the tail of a snake. Imbecility in office, civil & military, is tolling on the young life of our country, our youth, to unproductive peril & sure destruction. We are made daily to sup on horrors" (*L*, IV, 463).

But in two eerily prophetic letters of November 20 and 21, 1864, Simms anticipated even greater disaster. In the first of these, to young Edward Hammond, Simms presaged the downfall of South Carolina (with dire consequences to himself) and eventually of the South as a whole—"if Sherman had the requisite audacity—it did not need Genius," the novelist projected, "he would achieve the greatest of his successes, by turning his back on the enemy in his rear, & march boldly forward towards the Atlantic coast." Stating his fear that "such is his purpose," Simms asked: "If so,—what have we to oppose him? I dare not look upon the prospect before us. It may become necessary for you, for me, & all to prepare as we can, for the overrunning of Carolina! All's very dark ..." (*L*, IV, 471). In his letter of the next day to Hayne, Simms cast his prediction in a succinct aside—"pay me a visit sometime during the winter,—i.e. if Sherman does not smoke us out of our domain" (*L*, IV, 472). But even the prescient Simms could hardly have foreseen the specific consequences of Sherman's vicious and victorious drive through South Carolina: on February 17, 1865, a defenseless Columbia was burned with Simms an eyewitness; a few days later, apparently at the hands of Union stragglers, an even more defenseless Woodlands was burned (for the second time in less than three years)—fulfilling Simms's foreboding.

Ironically, Simms had attempted to lessen the impact of Sherman's impending invasion by evacuating his family from Woodlands to Columbia.[30] By January 24, 1865, most of the Simms children—with enough "*provision for all mine & Mr. Isaacs family* for one year" (*L*, IV, 478)—were housed in Columbia in the "obscure dwelling" of the George E. Isaacses—described by the novelist as "humble but excellent people, who are connected by marriage with my eldest daughter" (*L*, IV, 483–84). Simms himself, before leaving Woodlands, made an effort to box up manuscripts and books to bring with him to Columbia; but apparently because of their bulk and the lack of adequate transportation the books had to be left behind. It is not known for certain that Gilly and Augusta were with their father, Mary Lawson, young Chevillette, Govan, and Charles Carroll in the city when Sherman's troops entered Columbia on the morning of February 17, but by nightfall the author had witnessed much uncontrolled destruction of a surrendered city. Simms's graphic account, *Sack and Destruction of the City of Columbia, S.C. to Which Is Added a List of Property Destroyed,* was published in book form in the summer of 1865 after first having appeared in slightly different form in the *Columbia Phoenix*[31] during March and April. Simms's presence in the city and credibility as a historian lend substance to his depiction of the chaos that prevailed in the surrender of the civilian government of Columbia to the military command under Sherman. The fire which demolished the city after one day of Union occupation was attributed by Sherman to causes beyond his control; but Simms—shocked that the military commander did not take responsibility for events transpiring under his command—viewed the tragedy differently. "We have seen, with surprise," Simms wrote, "some attempts, to account for the destruction of Columbia by ascribing it to accident, to the drunkenness of straggling parties, to our negroes, and, indeed, to any but the proper cause." After citing the reasons for such accounts: "It is evidently the design of these writers … to relieve General Sherman and his army from the imputation," Simms continued with unmistakable irony:

> If it could be shown that one-half of the army were not actually engaged in firing the houses in twenty places at once, while the other half were not quiet spectators, indifferently looking on, there might be some shrewdness in this suggestion. If it could be shown that the whiskey found its way out of stores and cellars, grappled with the soldiers and poured itself down their throats, then they are relieved of responsibility. If it can be proved that the negroes were not terrified by the presence of these soldiers, in such large numbers, and did not … on the night of fire, skulk away into their cabins, lying quite low, and keeping as dark as possible, we might listen to this suggestion, and perhaps admit its plausibility. But why did the soldiers prevent the firemen from extinguishing the fire as they strove to do? Why did they cut loose the hose as soon as it was brought into the streets? Why did they not assist in extinguishing the flames? Why, with twenty thousand men encamped in the streets, did they suffer the stragglers to succeed in a work of such extent? Why did they suffer the men to break into the stores and drink the liquor whenever it was found? And what shall we say to the universal plundering, which was a part of the object attained through means of fire? Why, above all, did they, with their guards massed at every corner, suffer the negroes to do this work? Those questions answered, it will be seen that all these suggestions are sheer nonsense.[32]

Simms's account of this low point in the fateful history of South Carolina's capitol city during the Civil War is an important and impressive document, recognized by James Kibler as "among Simms's best works" for its graphic description and its "stark and powerful prose style."[33]

Because he was in Columbia, falsely assuming it a safer place for his family, Simms did not witness the second burning of Woodlands, which—like Columbia—was destroyed under controversial circumstances. In fact, as late as March 6—probably at least two weeks after his plantation had been demolished—Simms apparently did not know precisely the fate of Woodlands, as his letter to B. F. Perry reveals: "I am here [Columbia], perforce, in a sort of durance, with my little family, & cannot, for the present, get away; & know not the fate or state of my plantation. Several reports lead me to apprehend that my house & every thing has been destroyed" (*L,* IV, 484). As Simms painfully discovered soon afterwards, the reports were all too true; the most detailed account appeared in the *Columbia Phoenix* of April 12, 1865, apparently written by the novelist himself, based upon a letter by Mrs. Hopson Pinckney, in whose care he had left Woodlands when he went to Columbia:

> When the enemy reached the neighborhood, Mrs. P.[inckney] addressed a letter to Gen. [Francis Preston] Blair, requesting protection for the dwelling and library, and suggesting the enormity of the crime which could destroy books, especially such a collection—some ten thousand volumes—made with great care, during a period of forty years, and constituting, perhaps, the most valuable library, to a literary man, to be found in the Confederacy. Before an answer could be received to this application, bands of stragglers had penetrated the house and begun the work of robbery. The trunks and bureaus were at once broken open. In the midst of this scene, the guard sent by Gen. Blair made its appearance, and relieved the house of plunderers. The General himself, with Gen. [Oliver Otis] Howard and other officers, visited the estate, and spent some time in the examination of the library. They took away a collection of maps, including Mills' Atlas of South Carolina, and perhaps a few other volumes. They also carried off a couple of double barrelled guns and a rifle; but nothing besides of any importance, and their deportment was courteous and becoming. They left a sufficient guard behind them, and the building was saved while this guard remained on the premises. But, with their departure, frequent attempts to burn the house at night were made, and the ladies became so much alarmed and wearied with night watching, that they fled, and sought refuge for themselves and family at the neighboring hamlet of Midway. With their departure, the fellows succeeded in their design. The house, a very extensive, newly built one, and only partially finished, but with six habitable rooms, besides the library, was fired at four several quarters, and when the flames were discovered by the servants, at day break, they had reached a degree of height and intensity which made all efforts impossible to save. The library … was the first to burn. Not a volume was saved. (*L*, IV, 484–85n)

That the war and its ensuing hardships engendered a climate of confusion and resentment is illustrated by the rumors that surfaced casting suspicion alike upon the loyalty of slaves and upon the forthrightness of Union officials. Like Columbia, Woodlands was not destroyed by official military action, and innuendos that the flames had been ignited by plantation slaves were bolstered by denials of wrongdoing by Northern generals. In this tense atmosphere Simms's body servant, Isaac Nimmons, was both praised for heroism in his efforts to save valuable property from the fire and also accused of the crime of setting the blaze—an accusation of which he was eventually exonerated. Simms, who prided himself upon his good relationship with the slaves at Woodlands, occasionally wavered in his faith in their loyalty,[34] but ultimately laid the full responsibility for the burning of Woodlands upon stragglers from General Sherman's army.

Though Simms's losses at Woodlands were extensive,[35] it was the plundering of his library and books that hurt most. "[M]y Library!" he lamented in writing E. A. Duyckinck of the "destruction of my house and plantation, by your army under Sherman": "You can form, from what you know, a sufficient idea of the value of the collection which numbered some 10,700 vols." (*L*, IV, 501). Simms's anguish was, if anything, even stronger in his outcry to James Lawson: "My books! My books! My heart is ready to break when I think of them" (*L*, IV, 501).

But more ignominious, if not more painful, to Simms than the loss of his library was the reduction of his family to almost abject poverty. Always a pragmatist Simms painted a grim but realistic picture of the circumstances in which he and his children found themselves at the end of the war. In his June 13, 1865, letter to James Lawson, Simms starkly observed that he was "temporarily destitute, without money to spare to telegraph you," that he and some of his family were literally "sleeping in a garret" in Columbia, and that other family members, seeking refuge in "the little village of Bamberg," had "barely bread enough to support life." Existing on "a small pittance weekly" from editing the "newly started" *Columbia Phoenix*[36] (which, he added, "does not yet pay"), Simms recounted the various disasters which he had encountered—leaving him homeless, penniless, but thankful that "By the blessings of the Good God" his wounded and "dangerously ill" son had been spared and that he himself was able to "see to my duties here & my other children" (*L*, IV, 499). In the *Phoenix* and elsewhere he published a handful of poems dealing with the devastating loss of Woodlands and giving voice to his harrowing struggle with despair before resolution took hold. Though in the conventionally patriotic "'Ay De Mi, Alhama!'" (composed while Simms was "strolling among my ruins"), the poet seems mawkish and sentimental,[37] for the most part the tone of these lyrics is controlled yet highly personal, as in the lines, "The bitter road of exile must be ours, / Oh! desolate children!—We must leave the home—" from "Among the Ruins"; and in

> Ever a voice is pleading at my heart,
>   With mournful pleading, ever soft and low,
> Yet deep as with an ocean's overflow,
> "Depart! depart! Why wilt thou not depart?["]

from "The Voice of Memory in Exile, from a Home in Ashes."[38]

It is significant that Lee's surrender to Grant officially ending the war on April 9, 1865, seemed to have little impact upon Simms and shell-shocked South Carolina in general. Still reeling from the devastation of Sherman's march through their state, South Carolinians had seen their own phase of the war end in February, and from that time they were numbed into the agonizing acceptance of the inevitability of defeat. In Simms's case, it is to the credit of the man that after the war he was not too proud to call for assistance from Northern friends like Lawson—his only friends in a position to help. In the letter cited above, Simms frankly asked: "Can you help me to any [money]? You are aware that I have rarely taxed my friends for help of this nature, & nothing but the direct necessity compels me to call upon them now. I wish to borrow from you $500." Lawson—and probably Duyckinck among "a couple of friends at the North"—responded quickly to Simms's request, sending "timely assistance" (*L*, IV, 512),[39] which alleviated some of the needs of the stricken writer and his family; but even while literally still in the ashes of ruin the stalwart Simms began to make plans to rebuild his future. Almost immediately, recognizing the possibility that with the end of hostilities Northern publishing centers might no longer be closed to him, Simms requested Lawson "to see the Brothers Harper, who will probably help me in consideration of past & future writings" (*L*, IV, 499–500). "I have two or three articles[40] on hand," Simms continued, "suitable for their monthly and which I deem very good. These, I will revise in a few days, & forward by the next opportunity. You need hardly assure them, for they know me almost as well as you do, that I will faithfully work out the debt according to my best ability."[41] The resilient Simms, redoubtable in his ability to rebound, assured both Lawson and Duyckinck that he was not seeking charity, that his intent was to resume his career as writer. To Lawson he stated: "My health is good, my strength unabated and my mind, I think, in its best condition, at once vigorous & mature" (*L*, IV, 500).

Specific plans for specific projects, however, still met with obstacles. The South Carolinian's letter of September 9, 1865, to Duyckinck is important in that it demonstrates the novelist's almost desperate efforts to "resume [his] profession" despite disadvantageous circumstances:

> A few months ago, I had a volume in press here. The advent of Sherman was fatal to its publication. The book was considered a good book & so pronounced in your journal. It is entitled "Tom Nettles; or, As Good as a Comedy." You will probably remember the story. … I propose that Mr. Widdleton should republish it, in connection with another tale, though with this one title, uniform with my other books. It will probably help the sale of the others. I have other materials which will be used in other volumes, & it is important to him that the works should be uniformly published. I do not see that in his advertisement, he has announced either the History of South Carolina, or the Cassique of Kiawah. Of these two works, the History will always sell in the South, & the Cassique is one of my most interesting romances.

Though Simms seemed predominantly interested in getting new editions of old writings back into circulation, he also announced plans "to proceed to the plantation & prepare a new romance ... which I think I can make equal to any thing I have yet done." The intended "new" work was to deal with "Pirate life & practice"—a subject Simms had "long desired to work up into a standard romance" (*L*, IV, 518–19). Once again, however, Simms's rededication to literature did not pay immediate dividends; he succeeded in getting no books published in 1865, though at his death he left a manuscript of 173 pages entitled "The Brothers of the Coast," apparently his contemplated novel on pirate life. His lack of success in finding a publisher interested in bringing out his work drew from Simms a bitter comment. "But you, by this time, know of what materials Publishers are made," Simms wrote to Henry Dawson on October 2. "After five years of interval, in which I never recieved a copper, the present publisher of my works [Widdleton] sends me $100. Such a result might well discourage the author from ever again putting pen to paper. It is clear to me that I shall need to adopt some better system for dealing with such people. Living in affluence hitherto, I have been very easy with my publishers, & have *not* regarded the money profits from my writings. It is now a necessity with me that I should do so" (*L*, IV, 524–25).

His words to Duyckinck were also quietly confident: "My hair & beard are quite white, and I am verging on 60, but I am healthy, comparatively vigorous, & with my children present ever to my eyes, I feel that I have many years of good work in me yet ..." (*L*, IV, 503). The commitment "to resume my profession" was repeated in a letter to a South Carolina friend: "... if my right hand has not lost all its cunning, I trust to extort from Fortune ... an adequate means of living decently to the end of the chapter" (*L*, IV, 513). Most inspirational of all, however, was Simms's statement in August 1865 that his brain was "seething ... with fresh conceptions," sparking him to the belief that he "could do better things in letters than ... ever ... before." During "loving mood[s] of meditation" these crisp images suddenly became as "familiar to the eye, as they have been to the mind" (*L*, IV, 515–16).

Niggardly or exploitative publishers notwithstanding, Simms's commitment to literature and his will to write remained strong—a fact truly remarkable in that, despite his proclamations of good health, Simms in 1865 was suffering severe periodic pain, probably afflicted with the cancer of the colon that eventually took his life. As early as January 9, 1865, in a letter to Governor Andrew Gordon Magrath requesting exemption from military service,[42] Simms had testified that "For 30 years I have suffered from hemorrhoids which were duly & greatly increased under circumstances of fatigue, exposure and excitement," perhaps explaining why he found standing to write more comfortable than sitting. "Even now," he continued, "when I have little blood for waste, cold, exposure fatigue, uneasiness, or unusual excitements, occasion copious discharges of blood, which leave me for a time utterly exhausted" (*L*, IV, 475–76). A comment in his letter to his son on January 16 when Simms was working feverishly to pack up valuables at Woodlands for shipment to Columbia is the key to understanding Simms's mastery of physical pain: "I did not break down … till the work was done" (*L*, IV, 480). Simms's endurance of pain—mental and emotional as well as physical—was never more tested than in 1865. But just as he was concerned as a father that Gilmore, Jr., "begin to do for and develop yourself, & the resources within you" (*L*, IV, 521), Simms recognized the same need in himself. Though impoverished and incapacitated, Simms could and would exert himself; as a result, at the end of 1865 his will to survive—indeed, his will to create—was alive and healthy.

# XI "The Strength to Endure"

In one of the original writings William Gilmore Simms managed to get published during the last five years of his life, Leonard Voltmeier, an iron-willed intellectual of courage and commitment who has suffered through adversity's sharpest pangs, proudly proclaims: "I have the strength to endure. I *have* endured!"[1] Voltmeier in many ways personified Simms. In the tragic years before his death the author, like the character, possessed the will to endure hardship, misunderstanding, and pain with courage and dignity. Simms had always prided himself on his will—"I can endure manfully," he had said to Hammond in 1842. But never before was his valor so sorely tested—his "strength to endure" so thoroughly challenged—as during the aftermath of the Civil War.

Remarkable though it was, Simms's valor, without the will to write, without a commitment to literature, would have contributed nothing to his status as writer, however much it increased his stature as man. His valiant efforts throughout 1866 "to resume [his] profession" generated no appreciable momentum, but, *mirabile dictu,* late in 1867, despite incapacitating illness, his creativity seemed to explode into one of those marvelous surges that periodically marked his career. And even if the final four years of his life did not see the publication of any books, his best work of these terminal years (much of it buried in obscure periodicals or left in manuscript at his death) approximates that of 1833–1836, 1838–1841, or 1853–1856. What in addition to poor health makes Simms's postwar literary accomplishments surprising is that no editorial task promising even meagre compensation was too menial for the poverty-stricken author. During all this time he remained the faithful and attentive father of six motherless children, kept up a steady correspondence with friends old and new, and continued as a recognized spokesman for his region's lost cause and its hopes for the future.

Before the close of 1865 Simms had undertaken an assignment that for almost six months proved a drain on his creative energy without putting much money in his pocketbook—the associate editorship (along with Henry Timrod) of the *Charleston Daily South Carolinian.*[2] After publishing a variety of editorials, book reviews, poems, short stories, and prose articles in the newspaper, Simms severed connections with it in May 1866 when it was moved from Charleston to Columbia, its original seat of publication (*L,* IV, 560). Still finding it necessary to grub for finances, he then formed an alliance with the *Charleston Courier,* writing for it not only book reviews but also a section called "New York Correspondence," letters he sent to the newspaper from New York during his visit there during July–September 1866.

A more significant editing assignment for Simms in 1866 was a collection of "Southern Poetry of the War," whose forthcoming publication was announced in the *Daily South Carolinian* of December 15, 1865. In February 1866 New York publisher Charles Benjamin Richardson proposed publishing the edition under terms not totally satisfactory to Simms—an offer Simms nevertheless accepted, "needing money as I do" (*L,* IV, 536). The response to Simms's request for manuscripts for the anthology was so large that he wrote a potential contributor in late February, "It is at present impossible for me to say what I have and what I might wish to have, especially as it is impossible for me to know what things may be scattered over the country ..." (*L,* IV, 538). Taking seriously the concept of putting together a reputable anthology of war poems written by Southerners, Simms wrote Duyckinck that the "book will be quite creditable. There will be a very large mass from which to select. ... I find the demand for these things very considerable" (*L,* IV, 540). In a later letter to Duyckinck he added: "I am very rapidly accumulating the war poetry of the South. It comes in to me daily, and much of it will take high rank" (*L,* IV, 542). "The Poetry of the South, during the war," he observed in April, "will possess (I think) a much higher character, than any thing that has yet been published" (*L,* IV, 549). Using his personal relationships with, and wide knowledge of, Southern poets to great advantage, Simms was not content with publishing simply the best random selections sent to him; he recruited poems from the well-known writers, from various regions of the South, attempting to recognize the region's cultural and geographic diversity. Finally, during his visit to New York in the summer of 1866, the editor wrote his son back home at Woodlands: "My volume of the War Poems, is now in the hands of the printers ..." (*L*, IV, 581); he had found, however, "little to encourage me in the literary prospect," adding the following commentary:

> The hands of the Publishers are full of Books, & the public demand for them seems to be lessened, except in regard to books of a certain class, such chiefly as have originated in the war. As a matter of course, Southern books on this frightful subject, have a more limited demand, and one written & published under such embarrasments, that a truly Southern man who is patriotic & honest, cannot readily write them.

*War Poetry of the South* (New York: Richardson, 1866) was issued in November, attracting generally favorable reviews throughout the South.[3] An exception was the notice appearing in the *New Orleans Crescent Monthly*, which charged Simms with showing "too much Palmetto partiality" and having "too great a sympathy for mediocrity in verse" (II [January 1867], 77–78). For what it purported to be, a volume reflecting the sentiments and the talents of poets of the Confederacy, *War Poetry* succeeded in fulfilling Simms's ambition that it be the best anthology of its kind. It embodies creditable editing, performed for money however small and for a cause however lost.[4]

Perhaps the floundering postwar resumption of his literary career persuaded Simms to return to a once-discarded manuscript dealing with his favorite topic, the American Revolution. As early as 1858 the author had visualized writing a final book for the Revolutionary Romances series—a novel to be set in Augusta, Georgia, in pre-revolutionary times, making it chronologically the first in his epic-like portrayal of America's battle for independence.[5] Simms had been discouraged in that effort when an Augusta newspaper attacked him with "ridiculous & malignant innuendoes" charging him with prejudice against Georgia: "Now, if this is to be the sort of treatment which I am to anticipate," he wrote to Hammond, "I will write no book about Georgia. I can plant my story any where else" (*L*, IV, 83–84). Dropping the idea for two years, Simms picked it up again in the summer of 1860, referring to his intent "to prepare a new romance, for which the material has been already collected & in some measure digested" (*L*, IV, 223). Apparently, however, because "there is no policy in publishing just now," he set aside the project again in November 1860 (*L*, IV, 275), not to return to it again for almost six years.

During his visit to the North during the summer of 1866, Simms wrote E. A. Duyckinck that "my object is to make such arrangments for permanent writing as will enable me to return to Woodlands, in the autumn, with full &

regular employment on hand to exercise my pen all the winter." The novelist proposed "to concentrate ... on a romance, and on 'My Life and Times, an Autobiography, and a History'" (*L,* IV, 577). The "romance" was the long-delayed Revolutionary novel set in Augusta—and concentrate upon it Simms did. The proposed autobiography, on the other hand, failed to materialize; indeed there is no evidence that Simms ever worked on it. But work on *Joscelyn; A Tale of the Revolution* (as it was ultimately titled) moved rapidly; in October 1866 Simms remarked in a letter to Paul Hamilton Hayne: "I am cudgelling my brains at a new romance, the first scene of which opens at the Sand Hills of Augusta. I have done some 120 pages—and hope by the close of the week to have done 150 more!" (*L,* IV, 614). In November Simms reported to Duyckinck that he had written "some 250 pp. MS. on a new revolutionary romance called 'Joscelyn'" and that it was "to be put forth serially" (*L,* IV, 618), arrangements having been made for it to appear in the New York monthly, the *Old Guard,* beginning in January 1867.[6]

Simms's letters make clear that, as was customary with serial publication of a novel, the first chapters of *Joscelyn* were put into print before the final chapters were written. To ensure uninterrupted progress of the sequel once begun, the *Old Guard* specifically required that Simms provide a substantial portion of manuscript in December. Thus "in order to secure a respite of a week at Christmas," Simms wrote, "I had to grapple with my tasks almost immediately upon my return" (*L,* IV, 622–23) from New York. On December 13, 1866, he informed E. A. Duyckinck, "You may judge with what earnestness I must have worked (with what *success,* I can say nothing) when I tell you that I have despatched to the Publishers 24 chapters, making some 550 pp. MS." (*L,* IV, 623–24). The painstaking process of writing *Joscelyn* under pressure of continual deadlines took its toll on the author. "Absorbed, indeed, almost wholly in labours of the desk, writing, on the average, 20 to 40 pages of MS. per day, I have no *fingers* left ... ," he stated in a letter of December 20 to William Hawkins Ferris. "I find this concentration of thought & eye upon the one subject, with so little chance for relief, a severe strain upon the mind, but the work must be done. My brain is occasionally very foggy under the pressure" (*L,* IV, 626–27).

Shortly after the publication of the opening installment of *Joscelyn* in the January 1867 *Old Guard,* Simms queried Duyckinck: "Have you seen Joscelyn? If so, tell me how you like the opening chapters" (*L,* V, 8). Not satisfied to have the work published only as a serial, the novelist requested the New York critic's aid in spurring William J. Widdleton (who, using the Redfield plates, had reprinted the seven Revolutionary Romances in 1864[7]) into publishing

*Joscelyn* in book form; for, Simms added, "I shall need shortly to make or seek arrangements elsewhere, should his efforts fail me" (*L*, V, 9). As the year wore on, the constant drain on Simms's energy of meeting *Old Guard* deadlines and simultaneously seeking a book publisher dulled the author's creativity. "Joscelyn drags heavily," he confided to Paul Hamilton Hayne in April 1867. "I have written nothing on it for some time, being considerably ahead of the Magazine" (*L*, V, 41). Later, in June, he wrote James Lawson: "I have been much drudging & am overworked, especially as I work to so little profit" (*L*, V, 63). Finally, in December, Simms thought (wrongly) that Widdleton had agreed to a "new edition of my writings" which was to begin with "my Revolutionary Romance of *Joscelyn*" (*L*, V, 181). Disappointed again in his expectations Simms must have been deeply discouraged; but, despite acknowledging fatalistically that "Literature does not compensate" (*L*, V, 43), he met discouragement with renewed commitment to continue writing.

Though Simms planned to rework *Joscelyn* for its publication as book, he was not displeased with it in its serialized form, holding it "to be among the most excellent of my prose writings" (*L*, V, 181). Certainly, as his initial post-war creative effort, composed under the most trying of circumstances, *Joscelyn* is remarkably good, a worthy addition to the Revolutionary Romances series. As such, though written last, it should—for historical chronology—be read first, centering as it does on the pre-Revolution civil conflict between Loyalists and Whigs in South Carolina and Georgia in the last six months of 1775.

As Stephen Meats has convincingly argued, Simms's seven Revolutionary War novels written prior to *Joscelyn* picture the Revolution in South Carolina as "principally a civil war from beginning to end"; but not until his eighth "tale of the Revolution" does the novelist from Woodlands focus upon "the origins of this partisan conflict."[8] Certainly nowhere else in American literature does one find a more accurate or more striking portrayal of the intense conflicts in interest and in loyalty that divided neighbors and families in backwoods Georgia and South Carolina when in 1775 the question of a nation independent of Great Britain was raised. With the historian only slightly concealed in the novelist, Simms uses both historical figures and fictional characters in a dramatic but plausible rendering of the emotional and physical violence that erupted in the two states.

Always faithful to the spirit of history—sprinkling his narrative with actual characters and events—Simms draws in-depth portraits of South Carolina orator William Henry Drayton, influential leader of the revolutionary forces, and Georgia renegade Thomas Browne, hot-headed, iron-willed Scotsman fiercely loyal to the crown. But the main interest centers upon three fictitious families, one living in Augusta, Georgia, and the other two just across the Savannah River in South Carolina (at Beech Island, home of Simms's close friend, James H. Hammond). The Dunbars, aristocratic Georgians of Scottish descent, were British sympathizers, with the domineering, patrician father permitting no dissent from his indecisive son, Walter, or his independent-minded daughter, Annie. Walter, handsome, well educated, and weak, is ruled over not only by Malcolm Dunbar, his well-drawn father, but also by his betrothed from South Carolina, Angelica Kirkland, a "vain and foolish" bosomy heroine of great beauty and vindictive nature. Angelica contrasts with her older sister Grace—mature, responsible, plain-faced—just as Walter Dunbar does with the novel's title character, country schoolteacher and lawyer Stephen Joscelyn, a free-thinking intellectual overly sensitive to the handicap of a crippled leg. Not only is Joscelyn, like Dunbar, enamoured with Angelica—and stung by her thoughtless, child-like capriciousness—but the two men are also brought into conflict with one another after a misunderstanding created by Angelica's self-centered spite. The strong-minded South Carolinian with the malformed body *versus* the weak-willed Georgian with the noble bearing is only part of the conflict. Stephen Joscelyn, a great horseman despite his deformity, and a natural leader, is a captain of cavalry for the nationalists; Walter Dunbar, well meaning and chivalrous and ready to die for principle, is the duped puppet of a loyalist father. Though Simms's sympathies clearly lie with the revolutionaries, the effectiveness of *Joscelyn* rests largely upon the author's ability to present with sensitive insight the conflicting loyalties of the Dunbar family. Not only Malcolm and Walter Dunbar, but also even the audacious, unrelentingly dogmatic loyalist Thomas Browne are drawn with compassion and empathy.

Even before the serial publication of *Joscelyn* was complete, Simms was planning another major fictional effort—the novel eventually to be entitled *Voltmeier*—beginning negotiations in September 1867 with John Y. Slater, editor and proprietor of the *Southern Home Journal.*[9] By the end of the year Slater and Simms tentatively agreed to terms, for the *Southern Home Journal* of January 4, 1868, announced that "Wm. Gilmore Simms is ... writing a serial for the Southern Home Journal"—an arrangement which Simms, smarting from past relationships with publishers, gingerly acknowledged in a letter to Duyckinck: "I am about to commence a story for which I am to get $600—if I am ever paid; I have been a loser some $300 since I left New York, writing for periodicals;[10] and now doubt all of them" (*L*, V, 106). A month later Simms recorded that he had written "500 pages MS. note paper" of the "serial for the

Southern Home Journal" (*L*, V, 114); but, although the publishers thus far "have behaved properly," the author nevertheless feared that "my experience will end in disappointment," because "these papers are gotten up mostly by mere Bohemians, who contrive ... like maggots ... to eat up the brains of authors" (*L*, V, 114–15). Despite his misgivings Simms continued hard at work on his manuscript, completing 640 pages by early May, leaving "about 360 more to write between this & July" (*L*, V, 126). A week later he noted: "I write with difficulty, with heart sore, head heavy, brain dull," and with considerable foresight he observed: "I am overtasked & badly paid. These periodicals are great delusions" (*L*, V, 130). Simms's apprehensions had increased by June 12, 1868, when he wrote from Charleston to Gilmore, Jr., at Woodlands: "... I am uneasy at not hearing from the Baltimore publisher, who has failed to acknowledge the reciept of the last 155 pages of MS. sent him, and does not as yet respond to my call for a money instalment" (*L*, V, 138–39). On the last day of June he complained to Duyckinck that he could not "get one cent of remittance" from his publisher. Finally, Simms's worst suspicions of Slater became reality; on July 25, 1868, the author wrote in desperation to Duyckinck that the periodical "for which I have been writing for five months, & to which I had sent on 650 pp. of MS. for which I was to recieve $600 (which MS. its editors approved) the moment I called for a remittance, voided the contract, and, for the present, I am absolutely *hors de combat*—almost penniless" (*L*, V, 153).

Fortunately, perhaps, for Simms, he was able to find another publisher for the serialization of *Voltmeier:* Orville James Victor, who was in the process of establishing in New York a new weekly, the *Illuminated Western World*, and whom Simms had first met in New York in 1858 or 1859, when the latter edited the *Cosmopolitan Art Journal.* Upon hearing of the plans for the *Illuminated Western World*, the Southern novelist wrote Victor in October 1868, proposing *Voltmeier* to him "for Seven Hundred Dollars," half to be paid "on the sheets already in your hands," and the remainder "on delivery of the completed MS." (*L*, V, 166). Victor eventually accepted the offer; and though annoyed that the *Southern Home Journal*'s breach of contract had delayed publication, Simms must have been pleased that he had apparently negotiated a better financial arrangement with a magazine of better prospects.[11] With publication now assured, Simms returned to his manuscript with vigor. "I am approaching the close of my Mountain Romance of 'Voltmeier' which is to be published serially," he wrote to E. A. Duyckinck in December 1868, "and which is, as I think, one of the most remarkable books I have ever written" (*L*, V, 181). The day after Christmas found Simms "putting the finishing strokes" to his latest "Border Romance" (*L*, V, 190); and in its number dated January 9, 1869, the

*Illuminated Western World* announced its good fortune "in securing a romance of striking characteristics from the pen of William Gilmore Simms, the well-known writer. ... This last work from his hand is so new, so full of vigor, so entirely original in conception, character, and circumstance, that we are impatient to lay it before our readers ... (I, 4). At mid-January Simms "sent off by Express ... to N. Y. 800 pages of MS." (*L*, V, 195), and *Voltmeier* began appearing in the *Illuminated Western World* on March 6, running weekly through the issue of August 28, 1869.

As a serial *Voltmeier* could not be expected to attract much critical notice—and apparently attracted none. It is ironic that its first critical appraisal came in 1969 (rather than 1869), when Donald Davidson introduced *Voltmeier* to twentieth-century readers as the opening volume in the proposed Centennial Edition of Simms—the novel's first publication in book form.[12] Despite its numerous flaws, many attributable to the circumstances under which it was written and originally printed, Davidson, recognizing its value, stated in his introduction that *Voltmeier* "is likely to leave a strong impression even upon a modern reader" (p. xvi).

Simms himself recognized the potential of the hastily prepared, unwieldy manuscript he submitted to Victor in mid-January 1869. In noting that "*Voltmeier* considerably exceeds in the number of pages my own estimate [1255 rather than 1000]," the author nevertheless cautioned the editor against abridging it without "great tenderness." "Try, on the contrary," he suggested, "the experiment on your readers, of an art-romance—a something which passes above the sensational, into the psychological & largely imaginative; subordinating and using the passions without suffering their domination." Not one to be modest, Simms continued: "I think you will find enough in 'Voltmeier' of the sensational; enough for pictorial illustration on a bold scale for the most gluttonous of your readers; but much besides for that higher class to which ... you seem to appeal" (*L*, V, 197).

Perhaps some of the novel's flaws can be attributed to Victor rather than to Simms. In his excellent essay Davidson theorizes that Victor's refusal to follow Simms's advice in cutting the long manuscript accounts for the most glaring discrepancy in *Voltmeier:* its failure "to clear up the mystery" why the amulet given to Fergus Wallace ("greatly emphasized at the beginning") disappears from the narrative without explanation. In the words of Davidson, Simms "would hardly have been guilty of *that* omission. He must have intended for the amulet to carry dramatic weight" in the meeting of the novel's two heroes, Fergus and Voltmeier (p. xxvi). Davidson's conjecture is credible, even though there is no extant record that Simms indeed objected to Victor's excision of parts of his manuscript. Furthermore, the author may well have failed to read carefully the printed version in the agonizing last months of his life. However, despite the troublesome unaccountable disappearance of the conspicuously introduced amulet, despite the even more annoying extravagant use of exclamations and exclamation points (both of which could have been the result of the vagaries of serial publication, injudicious editing and erratic printing), *Voltmeier* deserves reading for its narrative power and pictorial quality.

Certainly the mountains of western North Carolina have never been more thoughtfully and caringly described than in the words of Voltmeier, as he sought to impart to his apprentice nephew a keen appreciation of their magnificence:

> "Now,—look around you, Fergus!" and, stopping his horse on one of the commanding eminences of the mountains, he waved his hand with a great sweep at the grand amphitheatre which opened before their eyes, and exclaimed:
>
> "Here, Fergus, you behold an imperial group,—world giants—each a crowned head, such as the world rarely beholds; stationed, as it were, as guardians over the loveliest empire of vale and dale, grove, thicket, and waterfall, that was ever sung by the poet, or accorded to the dreams and fancies of art or fiction. At the same moment you behold no less than five beautiful cascades glittering in the sun, and each wearing its rainbow crown, trembling with its weight of gems; diamonds encrusted with all the beautiful and various dyes that sunbeam ever manufactured from the clouds in heaven. Look, my son—gaze your fill, and if you feel with a poet's feeling, your raptures will keep you dumb!" (p. 178)

There is much, much more—but this passage captures the exuberance—almost ecstasy—of Simms's response to the grandeur of the Blue Ridge Mountains, described by Voltmeier as "the Helvetia of our country." Though Simms frequently and fervently exalted the alluring beauty of the luxuriant South Carolina low country, he almost equally apotheosized the wild appeal of the rugged mountainous regions of the Carolinas. The low country was his home and workplace; the upcountry his vacationland and source of rejuvenation and inspiration—and his love of both is manifest in his writing.

Simms's penchant for fast-moving suspenseful action is admirably suited for the telling of Voltmeier's stirring legend based in part upon an actual counterfeiting case in North Carolina in the early nineteenth century.[13] Allen Twitty himself—the accused but never convicted counterfeiter, whose sensational trials attracted wide attention in North Carolina between 1805 and 1815—was, like the character Voltmeier, a highly respected member of a prominent family noted for public service. Simms's knowledge of Twitty—acquired during the author's 1847 visit to the Appalachians[14]—doubtless influenced but did not dominate the author's imaginative creation of Voltmeier, the philosophical German intellectual, and his alias, Bierstadt, the black-clad masked criminal who masterminded large-scale counterfeiting as well as the robbery of governmental supplies and money. The clash between Voltmeier/Bierstadt and Gorham, the grasping "Black Dog" who is determined to supplant the former as leader of the gang, leads inevitably to the powerful climax of the novel, the scene in which protagonist and antagonist lock in battle on a steep precipice and fall together to their death. Simms's choice of words in describing Voltmeier's emblematic death is reminiscent of Melville's memorable closing to *Moby-Dick:* "Two arms for a moment appeared above the waters, one hand still grasping a knife, and striking wildly; the other thrown up in air, and grasping vaguely, as if seeking for some support, and then all disappeared" (p. 424). The demise of Old Grizzly (as Voltmeier was known) represents the end of an era in which powerful men of intellectual and physical superiority could and did dominate the frontier. Throughout *Voltmeier* the fictive world created by Simms is marked by alternating patterns of trust and betrayal, malevolence and beneficence, bravery and cowardice, needless violence and reasoned restraints—a world in which the only hope for justice and peace of mind lay in the will of man to think clearly and act bravely.

In addition, the novel conveys Simms's concept of the American frontier: a wild, uncultivated region, caught in conflict between good and evil and torn by moral, social, and environmental forces, in the gradual yet violent process of becoming civilized. The future of the country was dependent upon the success of that process; and educated men like young Fergus Wallace represented the nation's hope that the civilization of the frontier could occur without the ravaging of its environment or the exploitation of its people. In the hands of intelligent, knowledgeable, and caring frontiersmen like Fergus, the sanctity of both natural and human rights would be preserved; and yet with all his sensitivity and concern, Fergus seems disarmingly susceptible to human error—pride, rashness, jealousy, qualities which render him one of Simms's most believable young heroes.

The heroine of *Voltmeier,* Mignon Voltmeier, is less effectively drawn than Fergus Wallace, but nevertheless is an interesting figure with pluck enough to defy her loving yet overbearing father when she suspects him of dealing unfairly with her lover. Among the minor characters, all the ruffians—Brown Peters, Swipes, Mother Moggs—characteristically speak, think, and act in ways consistent with Simms's realistic bent. And Gorham, the rebellious, greedy recreant obsessed with uncovering Voltmeier's secret, is given ample motivation for his vindictive actions. Early parental abuse and an instinctive hatred of authority feed his ambition for power and wealth and justify in his eyes his desire for revenge.

But Simms's most masterful creation in *Voltmeier* is the title character. Whereas Fergus Wallace represents what is best among American frontiersmen, Leonard Voltmeier is a compelling figure cloaked in ambiguity, possessing qualities that make him capable of both the best and the worst—safeguarding some principles and protecting certain individuals while exploiting and destroying others. Caught in a web of contending forces, he is at once a protector of good and a doer of evil; a builder and a spoiler; a man of principle and an opportunist; a believer and a questioner. He is Simms's Ahab, a moody, god-like, intellectual, poetical, mettlesome, stubborn, obsessive, self-destructive, honorable yet dishonored man with magnetic and prophetic powers beyond other humans. Voltmeier's iron will—his insistence upon his mind's ability to withstand the cruelest cuts of fate—were traits that the author, who himself faced terrible adversity during the period of the work's genesis, had very much in mind—and had every reason to try to exemplify. Just as in 1862 Simms had insisted, "... I will not succumb. ... [Fate] may crush, but shall not subject me"[15]—Voltmeier asserts: "I have still *my mind.* Over *that* ye have no power. *There,* I am still sovereign. *There,* I defy ye; and, no matter what the fate, I am still its master. Ye may crush, but ye can not subdue." The credo enunciated at the end of Voltmeier's defiant soliloquy also may well have been Simms's own: "The soul must brave the dark, even as it faces the light!" (p. 213).

During 1869 Simms brought out serially yet another novel which, like *Voltmeier,* was set in the mountains of North Carolina and likewise drew heavily upon the annotations the author made during his 1847 visit to the region.[16] Like *Joscelyn* in 1867, *The Cub of the Panther* in 1869 was published serially in twelve monthly installments (January–December) in the *Old Guard,* the New York journal edited by Charles Chauncey Burr. Simms's first mention "of a new Border story, designed for one of the periodicals" came in October 1868 when the novelist was "engaged" in "some three different romances"(*L,* V, 170, 171).[17] A few days later Simms "sent off 100 pages of MS. all written since I reached Woodlands" (*L,* V, 173)—a reference either to *Voltmeier* or *Cub,* since he was at work on both at that time. By mid-November the novelist had "written, on two different books, nearly 500 pp." (*L,* V, 176); and by the first of December "nearly a thousand pages MS." (*L,* V, 177). On Christmas Day 1868 the author characterized *The Cub of the Panther* as "a *short* romance, poor pay, poor preachee" (*L*, V, 189), with its first installment now "in the hands of the Publishers" (*L*, V, 185). Later Simms admitted to "writing for what the backwoodsmen call 'a dead horse'"—meaning that he should "have eaten up fully" all the publishers "*advances* of money" before completing the manuscripts of either *Voltmeier* or *Cub*.

More nearly a potboiler in Simms's eyes than *Voltmeier*, *The Cub of the Panther* held a relatively low priority with the impoverished, hard-working author. Although *Voltmeier* began publication two months after *Cub*, Simms finished writing the former in January 1869, while merely keeping "pace with ... the Printers" for *The Cub of the Panther* (*L*, V, 185). Though "almost disabled with Rheumatism," the harassed writer continued to work "very hard" even while lamenting that "I am not in good condition & need rest" (*L*, V, 196). "I do not now write for fame or notoriety or the love of it," Simms confessed in March 1869, "but simply to procure the wherewithal of life for my children ..." (*L*, V, 213). Nevertheless, despite writing only for subsistence, Simms took pride in his work even under dire circumstances. While maintaining a decided preference for *Voltmeier*, he professed to "think well of both ... of my new romances," and expressed hope that "one or both" might be issued "in book form" (*L*, V, 223)—a hope not fulfilled. In December 1869 the novelist asserted that *The Cub of the Panther* was "quite a readable romance & out of the beaten track" (*L*, V, 279)—deserving wider circulation than the *Old Guard* had been able to give it.

The germ for *The Cub of the Panther* is contained in a vivid notation in Simms's 1847 Appalachian notebook: "Green's wife's story of the male panther—The appetite of the beast for women in pregnancy &c—Horrid story of his eating one in this situation & of the discovery of her remains by her husband." That Simms combined folklore, raw border life, and colorful vernacular of hunters in a hastily written "mountain legend" suggests both the strengths and the weaknesses of *Cub*. The story lacks unity and balance—partly because two of its manuscript chapters were omitted in the serial publication[18]—but even with allowance for trying circumstances, *The Cub of the Panther* suffers in comparison with Simms's better work. Nevertheless, the author recognized that it contains raw material with strong literary appeal.

Simms's rising opinion of *Cub* is indicative of his growing conviction—especially prevalent in the last year of his life—that his "out of the beaten track" writing had worth. During the final harrowing months of his terminal illness, Simms turned at least four times to fresh native materials impressed upon his memory during his 1847 visit to the mountains of North and South Carolina. In addition to the two "mountain legends," *Voltmeier* and *The Cub of the Panther*, the embattled author completed writing two backwoods dialect tales of exceptional merit, "How Sharp Snaffles Got His Capital and Wife" and "'Bald-Head Bill Bauldy,' and How He Went Through the Flurriday Campaign!—A Legend of the Hunter's Camp." In yet another vein of humor he composed "The Humours of the Manager," an ironic sketch reflecting his life-long fascination with theater. The latter three, all left in manuscript at Simms's death, rank among the author's higher accomplishments—and in a genre he had been reluctant to take seriously until after the war. Correctly gauging that traditional Southern historical novels held little appeal to postbellum Northern publishers and readers, Simms resorted to humor and dialect (for which he had a remarkable ear), focusing upon common folk of the South and Southwest. He read the market astutely and he performed well; but neither his insight nor his efforts were of much avail against the wind of his time.

What is remarkable is that Simms continued to think, talk, and write literature even as he was slowly dying of cancer in 1869–70. In his "Sonnet,—Exhaustion" two years earlier Simms had confessed,

> I am so weary, wounded, scant of breath,
> So dispossessed of Hope. So comfortless,
> That sometimes, in the dread of this duress,
> I half persuade myself to fly to death;
> (*SP*, p. 254)

Yet his spirit always rebounded: "But evermore springs up the generous Faith," the poem continues, "... and the life renews." Notwithstanding his unflinching resolve, "after a continued strain of literary labour pursued ... without the pause of a single day," he finally "broke down" physically (*L*, V, 221). Even then the writer still "contrived to work, after a fashion," completing *The Cub of the Panther* and "taking notes for a third romance" (*L*, V, 221–22) that never materialized. Simms must have labored on will power alone, keeping "busy with unprofitable work" between "frequent intervals of suffering & depression" (*L*, V, 225). A long letter addressed to his children on July 3, 1869, evidenced his mental anguish as well as physical debility. "My humiliation is ... great that I can do so little for you at present," he wrote apologetically. "I am almost too feeble for any prolonged effort, at the desk or any where else" (*L*, V, 230).

Despite his precarious health Simms made his usual pilgrimage to the North in the summer of 1869, vainly seeking publishers interested in original manuscripts or reprints of earlier works. But, as he wrote to his son-in-law from New York on July 29, "I have made no progress here, have done nothing in the way of business, and hardly see any distance before me. ... Books do not sell, and the complaint of the lack of money is almost as great here, as it is with you in Charleston" (*L,* V, 233). Later, in writing his children from Yonkers, Simms admitted to a wasted summer: "I have been very ill, my dear Children, and am still suffering. ... As a matter of course, I have done no work. My whole summer has been consumed in suffering. ..." Because of severe financial worries Simms had wanted to go to New York to "do what little work I can. But that is doubtfull. I am still so feeble & my stomach so weak at present" (*L,* V, 246–47). Slightly more than a week later, the author doggedly reasserted his will to "struggle on, working & hoping to the last." He preferred "dying in the harness," which he considered "a more grateful process" than either "going out like the snuff of a candle" or "expiring by degrees like the tail of a snake whose head has been hammered" (*L,* V, 249). In October, ready to return to South Carolina, the destitute Simms faced the embarrassment of having to borrow from Lawson sufficient funds to pay for what was to be his final voyage from New York to Charleston (*L,* V, 250–51).

There can be little doubt that Simms knew that death was near. Back in Charleston, in a letter of November 8, 1869, in which he spoke lightly of "the humble hospitalities of 13 Society Street—i.e. a good cigar and a stoup of Bourbon," the courageous novelist addressed his friend Lawson frankly: "... I fear my malady is complicated with an affection of the kidneys, the serious character of which complication need not be dilated upon. ... My own opinion is that it may be mitigated, my sufferings alleviated, but that the case is incurable" (*L,* V, 259–60). Simms saw the irony of his situation: unlike the snake whose body still writhes though its head was dead, he possessed a brain that "still seethes with thought" (*L,* V, 262) though his body lacked strength even to sit. "... I cannot sit to write for more than a brief period at a time," he wrote on to E. A. Duyckinck. "My whole abdominal region suffers, & there is a continued soreness at all times in the lower part of the bowels ..." (*L,* V, 270). Then, as one literary man to another, Simms cited "a wild Arabian tale of a living head that delivered oracles while joined to a dead or petrified body":

> I sometimes think of that story, while I am talking here to some one or other of my circles,—talking oracularly too, as some of them think,—with no failure of voice or memory; but reminded of my mortality when I forget my pain & seek to rise & illustrate my thought by action. It is then that the body pulls me down from my perch. Terrible, that a man's brains should be at the mercy of his bowels.

Throughout the remainder of 1869 and the opening months of 1870,

Simms was like the old warrior "resolved to fall in the heat of the battle, with all my armour on" (*L*, V, 279). Though every physical exertion pained him, he delighted in working "the small mine of intellect which I possess, so long as it shall yield me what shall weave a golden thought, or silvery fancy." He put forth every effort to get his affairs in order. He gave agricultural, financial, managerial, and moral advice to his namesake son, a son of good heart and limited endowment over whom the father fretted and whom he loved with a father's love. He continued against all odds to try to market his literary wares—manuscripts, revised reprints, library holdings—to publishers and book dealers. He maintained an active correspondence with other writers and editors, with Paul Hamilton Hayne becoming his particular favorite. His frequent letters to Hayne abound in literary small talk, intermixed with serious thoughts on the nature of life, death, family, and art. Beyond love of family, Simms wrote Hayne on December 22, 1869, "life has few objects for me,—but these suffice to make me desire that I may be permitted to die in harness, spurs at my heels, lance in rest, and in the heat of a desperate charge. This sinking into the lean & slippered pantaloon, dealing in old saws and drowsy proverbs does not suit my taste. I am for action to the last for all life is so much warfare against sin, the Devil, and Tom Walker" (*L*, V, 285–86). In a realistic self-appraisal on January 2, 1870, the steadily declining novelist had stoic words for the younger poet: "I am now nothing, & can do nothing. I am rapidly passing from a stage, where you young men are to succeed me, doing what you can. God grant that you be more successful than I have been" (*L*, V, 290). But the literary spark was slow to burn out even in a Simms so ill that he could "only sit for a brief space at the desk" (*L*, V, 292); in rejecting a suggestion by Duyckinck that he write his memoirs, Simms replied: "... invention is, even now, an easier exercise than the challenge of memory. ... I prefer, like the swan, to die singing" (*L*, V, 294).

Simms's deterioration was now relentless. Near the end of March 1870 he reported that "I can no longer sit up to write. My back begins to ache, and my body to writhe" (*L*, V, 304). To William Cullen Bryant, the novelist noted that "My health has been somewhat improving in the last two weeks" (*L*, V, 309), but the recovery was partial and short-lived. In mid-April he reported to Duyckinck that "dysentery keeps me in a constant state of uneasiness & subjects me to frequent pain"; and a week later he wrote his son, "I am feeling badly, having been compelled to take one of my powerful pills last night. I am now beginning to writhe under the gripings" (*L*, V, 310).

Yet even in the throes of terminal cancer Simms took solace in literature and literary people. In an almost radiant passage to Bryant, he exulted: "My people honour me, and the young men gather around me with proofs of love and reverence, ... it is one of my great consolations that our young men come & minister to me, with the reverence which they can no longer yield to better abler men." Simms's comments on Bryant's *The Iliad* reveal that he was a lover of literature and a literary critic to the last. "Thanks for the 1st. Homer," he remarked. "I have been reading in it without pause, ever since recieved, & last night regretfully closed the 12th. Book. I am delighted with it." Simms praised Bryant for his translation's "manly simplicity," "directness of aim," and "good, stout, manly English heroic blank verse" (*L*, V, 308, 309).

Simms's strength to endure as well as his commitment to art is manifested in his accepting an invitation to address the Agricultural and Horticultural Association in Charleston on May 3, 1870. Though "too wretchedly feeble for the assertion of will or the exercise of faculty" Simms nevertheless wrote his namesake son: "it is incumbent upon me to prepare my address for the Floricultural Society. I am now writing it, tho' in pain" (*L*, V, 310). Thus the afflicted writer literally rose from his sickbed to write "The Sense of the Beautiful," and then to deliver it, perhaps the most moving address of his career. The next day Simms wrote with pride and pleasure to James Lawson: "I enclose you a copy of my address delivered last night ... to a large & brilliant audience. I was quite feeble, & exhausted from delivery, but contrived, by *sheer will* [italics mine] to hold out & hold forth to the last" (*L*, V, 313). Simms's achievement was confirmed by the May 4 *Charleston Daily Courier*. Calling the statewide meeting "the most important Convention in the State since the close of the war," the newspaper published in its entirety "The Sense of the Beautiful," "listened to with marked attention by the large crowd ... and ... warmly applauded."[19]

Simms lived only another thirty-nine days. During that time he first proposed to take a "trip by the Steamer to Florida" to recuperate (*L*, V, 313), but decided instead to "run up to Woodlands" to visit with his children there (*L*, V, 314). Therefore, leaving the house in which he was to die—Augusta's home at 13 Society Street—Simms went from Charleston on May 7 to spend a fortnight at the plantation which had been his life. Even in the last stage of his illness, Gilmore Simms maintained his letter writing[20] and retained his sense of humor: "This morning ... I am headachy & have swallowed a bottle of Congress Water, cork & all!" he wrote William Ferris on May 4 (*L*, V, 314). On May 17, in his last letter from Woodlands, Simms routinely informed his son-in-law in Charleston of the current state of his health—"suffering a good deal last night, I rose & swallowed one of Geddings' powerful pills"—and gave a fuller account of conditions at Woodlands:

> ... for the last 36 hours it has been warm & sultry. In the sun monstrous hot. The drouth continues still. There has been no rain for nearly 5 weeks. Of course nothing can be planted and nothing comes up, while, if these hot days continue, without long and refreshing rains every thing will burn up. We have seen few people. (*L*, V, 318)

After additional comments on agricultural and family matters, the novelist closed with the promise that "before coming down [to Charleston], I will try to pick up a few dozen fresh eggs; but it is almost too warm to trust any that you buy. Love to Augusta and the children. Best regards to the girls. Believe me Ever Your affec. father W. Gilmore Simms" (*L*, V, 319).

Shortly after writing this almost casual letter, Simms returned to Charleston on Saturday, May 21, with his health slightly improved. Two days later, he was suddenly struck again with a paroxysm—of the kind with which he had become all too familiar. The last of his more than seventeen hundred known letters—this final one addressed to William H. Ferris—was written in Charleston on May 27, 1870:

> I spent a couple of weeks very gratefully at Woodlands, and felt quite a physical improvement there; came to the city last Saturday, was quite well that day & Sunday, but Sunday night had one of my atrocious paroxysms & have been suffering ever since. For two successive nights I never slept a wink. I am better today—i.e. easier;—but I am still under the action of medicine & quite feeble. All are well save myself. I write simply to tell you that I still live. God bless you & yours.
>
> W. Gilmore Simms
>
> (*L*, VI, 279)

On June 11, 1870, William Gilmore Simms died in the home of his eldest daughter at 13 Society Street in Charleston, the city of his birth.[21]

## *Last Respects*

Without exaggeration it can be stated that Simms's death brought forth a chorus of grief and praise, almost as if recognition of his life of solid accomplishment was now a mandate, both local and national. Two days after his death both the *Charleston Courier* and the *Charleston News* carried long, laudatory accounts of Simms's life and achievements—but with differences in tone and fervor. The *News* of June 13 carried a largely straightforward, five-column obituary headed, "Wm Gilmore Simms. Death of the Great South Carolina Novelist. His Life Character and Writings," with only one emotional outpouring in the opening paragraph:

> The bells of St. Michael's tolled yesterday—the solemn notes conveying to the whole city the mournful tidings of the death of him who was the ornament and the pride of the State he loved so well.

The *Courier* of the same date was less restrained and more personalized, indicating a deep sense of loss for Simms the man as well as Simms the author not only in an obituary entitled "Hon. Wm. Gilmore Simms, LL.D.," but also in a black-bordered editorial on "Death of Wm. Gilmore Simms." The editorial begins and concludes in the following manner:

> Perhaps there was not a single heart in our city, yesterday, which did not realize with what an apposite beauty, with what a graceful comeliness, and how deservedly rendered, was the offering, as from the turrets of old St. Michael's the plaintive chimes pealed forth their requiem for the gifted Simms!
>
> For who had been more filially true to the ancient heir-looms o'er which in sacred guard, their sonorous chant, has kept watch and ward? Who, with the loving tenderness of son for mother, had with more pious zeal, more unremitting devotedness, delved in the rich archives of that mother's honored past, and made to glow with the burnish of his pen, the wealth and glories of her storied long ago?
>
> Mr. Simms' whole life has been one of public contribution. Unaided, with nothing but his own great endowments, his own high promptings, self-educated and self-reliant, he has wrought out a name for himself, in History, Poetry, Imaginative Literature, Criticism, and the broad realm of letters, which, while it rears for him a monument enviable and enduring, reflects its lustre upon the city and State, of whose treasured records he was at once the expounder and adorner. Without any of those important aids which spring from wealth, family-connexion, and those auxiliaries which, though adventitious, are yet so potent, Mr. Simms qualified himself thoroughly for his work, and with his own right arm, unsealed the oracles, conserved with more than Delphine hedge—proving and earning his title in the great temple of intellect, as Prophet, and Priest and Master.
>
> In the fullness and freshness of our grief, we feel how inadequate must be any tribute we can render to our departed friend! We desire only to commingle our sorrows, and to share in the sympathies, which everywhere throughout the State, we feel, will outpour themselves, as the sad tidings are announced, that one, who has done so much, so honorably, and so usefully, for the common

> good, and in promotion of the laudable pride of our people, is gone from us, FOREVER!

The *Courier*'s obituary reveals equal pride in Simms as a native South Carolinian:

> Though the fame and achievments [*sic*] of this gentleman were reflected upon the whole South, who claimed him as one of the most distinguished of her sons, yet he was eminently a South Carolinian by birth, education and feeling.
>
> No man was more warmly attached to his native state, or defended, worked for, and served her more faithfully and constantly than he did. ...
>
> ... when we consider what he has accomplished, and the positive influence of his life, we have always ranked him among the first men which this state has produced; for his characteristics, the order of his mind and the nature of his avocations are rarely found associated. Abroad he was by far the most widely known of the literary men of the South.

Yet another Charleston newspaper paid final tribute to Simms as follows:

> The Death of William Gilmore Simms.
>
> —
>
> South Carolina has lost a great man—one who earned a just distinction in every walk of literary life; who never faltered in his devotion to the land which gave him birth; whose pious care and masterly genius made of the past history of the South a living, breathing reality; who caused the manners and customs, the men and the women, of the "good old times," to dwell with us again in the melodies of his verse and the romantic splendors of his prose.
>
> William Gilmore Simms, poet, historian and novelist, the veteran head of South Carolina literature, died in this city on Saturday last.
>
> To him the State and the whole South owe a debt of gratitude that cannot soon be paid. At least let him live in his works, and in the kind thoughts and grateful remembrance of the whole Southern people.[22]

Elsewhere in South Carolina Simms's death drew similar responses. The *Columbia Phoenix*, of which Simms had been the first editor, remarked that

> The Nestor of literature in the South is dead. A Carolinian, self-made and distinguished in the department of history, romance and poetry, is no more. And in him also the state has lost a citizen true and devoted. ... We unite in the respect and consideration due to the memory of this gifted son of Carolina.[23]

According to the *Georgetown Times,* Simms "contributed much towards perpetuating the history of our State, and lending to it a romance so charming to the young. Some of his poetry has been justly regarded of a high order, and entitles him to a prominent place among our American poets." Perhaps most significant of all, however, are the resolutions offered by Robert Aldrich and adopted by the widely publicized statewide Union Reform Convention assembled in Columbia on June 15, 1870:

> *Whereas,* Not only the State of Sout[h] Carolina, but the whole country, has received with profound sorrow the announcement of the death of our beloved and honored fellow-citizen, Wm. Gilmore Simms, who has illustrated in song and story every portion of our history; therefore,
>
> 1. *Resolved,* That this Convention mourn with manly grief the irreparable loss the State has sustained.
>
> 2. *Resolved,* That in his life-long works and labors which have so distinguished this great man, and which have reflected as much honor on his beloved State as on himself, he has merited the love and gratitude of his fellow-citizens.
>
> 3. *Resolved,* That the president of this convention be requested to convey to W. Gilmore Simms, Jr., the oldest son of his distinguished father, the heartfelt sympathies of this body with the children of the illustrious dead, whose loss they and we deplore.
>
> 4. *Resolved,* That the papers throughout the State be requested to publish this preamble and resolutions.[24]

Outside South Carolina, Simms's death seemed to unite the rest of the South in spontaneous tribute to the merits and achievements of the region's acknowledged literary leader and spokesman. Among the Southern newspapers and magazines writing highly favorable notices were the *New Orleans Times,* the *Mobile Register,* the *Atlanta Constitution,* the *Savannah Advertiser,* the *Montgomery Advertiser,* the *South Alabamian,* and the *Southern Farm Journal.* I have selected the "handsome tribute" by the *Atlanta Constitution* as most representative of these out-of-state reviews:

> Every man flatters himself that, had circumstances luckily combined, he, too, at some period of his career, might have been a Napoleon or a Washington. …
>
> Not so in the contemplation of the lives of poets, or the classical writers of ancient or modern times. For, while their works may delight and edify and elevate us … , we are loth to grant to them that need of affection and praise to which, as benefactors of their race, they are entitled. … It is only occasionally

> that the popular heart throbs in sorrow at the announcement of the death of a great literary man.

The death of Simms elicited praise from the Northern press noticeably less generous than that which came from the South. As might be anticipated because of his close ties with New York City, all four daily newspapers in that city immediately ran obituaries, on June 13, 1870, two days after Simms died. The longest and most laudatory appeared in the *New York World*, which closed as follows:

> He was undoubtedly the most esteemed of American historical novelists after Cooper. In personal character he was a genial, refined, and pleasant gentleman, frank and courteous in his manners, and blameless in his private life. Wherever he lived, there he had troops of friends, and among them not a few admirers who were wont to regard him with something of the same worship that was lavished by the neighbors of Gad's Hill upon the great novelist [Dickens], whose career and death were almost contemporaneous with those of the subject of this sketch.

The *Evening Post*, remarking that "the southern states have been deprived of their most prominent and versatile man of letters," added that "Mr. Simms will be remembered chiefly for his novels, several of which will take rank with the best American productions of their kind. . . ." The *New York Herald*, referring to Simms as the "well known and popular Southern novelist," had particular praise for *Martin Faber*, and closed with the following paragraph:

> As a novelist Mr. Simms belonged rather to the old school of romance writers than to the school of Dickins, of Collens [*sic*], or of Reade. His poetry was fair, nothing more. His lively humor, fascinating conversation, pleasing anecdotes made his company much sought after, and his death will be learned of with regret by many who knew and prized him for those *qualities of head and heart* which invariably make men respected, esteemed and loved.

The briefest and most subdued New York obituary appeared in the *Times*, which curiously closed with the statement, "A history and a geography of South Carolina are the most important of his contributions to the literature of national history."

Outside New York, the *Newark Evening Courier* ran an obituary largely copied from the longer and more laudatory one which had appeared in the *New York World*. The review in the *Pittsburgh Commercial* is interesting not only for the direct comparison between Simms's reputation in the South and his reputation in the North, but also for its testimony to the esteem—even enthusiasm—with which he was held in the South:

> Whoever in the days before the war made a journey through the South, must have noticed how extensively his works were diffused throughout that part of the country; the "region" was "full of his labor." The traveler ... may have been surprised to hear Mr. Simms spoken of as "an American Walter Scott in prose and verse;" may even have heard him preferred to the Scotchman both as a poet and a novelist. His books have also been read in the North, though with less enthusiasm, and some of them have been republished in England, and even praised by critics of renown.

As far west as Ohio, the *Cincinnati Enquirer,* observing that the "notable points" of Simms's novels "were thrilling interest in story, graphic delineation of character, historical truth, ... fidelity in ... narration ... and great purity of style," ended its obituary with expression of great regret, "the more so as we have no romance writer competent to take his place." The *American and United States Gazette,* while noting that "There is, perhaps, no American writer who has attempted such a variety of work," was more than sparing in its praise: "Some of his stories, particularly the Yemassee, the Partisan, Vasconselos and one or two others, are likely to live for some time, though none of his work is constructed with the care and detail necessary for permanence."

In summary, Simms's death brought forth a nationwide expression of grief: the longest, most laudatory, and most warmly personal tributes emanated, in descending order, from Charleston, the rest of South Carolina, and the rest of the South; with those from north of the Mason-Dixon line noticeably less eulogistic and fervent, but nevertheless still largely complimentary. This reaction to the demise of a distinguished Southerner and the South's greatest contemporary author is precisely what one would have anticipated. Reviews more guarded in praise and more restrained in tone emanated from the North; any other result only five years after the Civil War would have been surprising indeed. The response from the South—unabashedly emotional, effusively laudatory, and emphatic in their sense of loss—testifies to the love and the veneration bestowed upon Simms by the state he had so fervently loved, the region he had so ardently championed, and the city he chose to make his home.

## *The Idea for a Monument*

Perhaps the most significant tribute to Simms by Charleston remains to be noted. Three days after his death Charleston friends of William Gilmore Simms conceived the idea of erecting a monument in his honor. The *Charleston Daily Courier* of Wednesday, June 15, 1870, ran the following notice.

> A MONUMENT FOR DR. SIMMS.
>
> —
>
> Our own more Chaste Theocritus!
>
> Several of the friends and admirers of our late distinguished author, William Gillmore [*sic*] Simms, LL D., suggested to us yesterday, the propriety of erecting a monument to his memory. The debt of gratitude which South Carolina owes to Dr. Simms, her eloquent historian, graceful and versatile novelist, and elegant poet, is incalculable, and nothing short of immortality can repay it. Let him live forever in our hearts and our history. The Nestor of our literature, it is upon his beautiful and classic features that those who have enjoyed the pleasure of knowing Dr. Simms will instinctively look in thought when the term "Southern Literature" is mentioned; while the intellects and tastes of our yet unborn children will be shaped and cultivated by the majestic beauty of his prose and the lofty measure of his verse. Let the high appreciation of our State be expressed for his genius and noble contributions to her letters, in the hey-day and prime of his manly powers, in a structure worthy alike of herself and her illustrious son whom she would honor. In order that the work may progress with proper system and direction, let a meeting be called and the matter be put into the hands of a proper committee.

Exactly two weeks later, under the heading "A Monument for the Late William Gilmore Simms," the *Courier* announced a meeting in the Charleston Library "for the purpose of considering the propriety and practicability" of a Simms monument. On June 30, 1870, less than three weeks after the death of Simms, both the *Charleston Daily News* and the *Courier* headlined the meeting in which Charleston's "most prominent citizens" made the decision that "a suitable Monument ... be erected to the late WM. GILMORE SIMMS."

It is extraordinary after the death of an author for the city of birth under any conditions to move as quickly and decisively as Charleston did in commemorating its literary son—but it is truly extraordinary in a time of circumstances as dire as those faced by Charleston in the aftermath of the war. The city's almost immediate decision to honor its leading man of letters culminated nine years later with the unveiling of the bronze bust of Simms that looks out over his native city from its pedestal in White Point Garden at the tip of the historic Battery, across the harbor from Fort Sumter. The bust, the commissioned work of the nationally recognized New York artist, John Quincy Adams Ward, was undraped in an elaborate ceremony on the ninth anniversary of Simms's death, June 11, 1879. Among the twenty-seven testimonials to Simms printed in the event's program were tributes from James Lawson, W. H. Ferris, John Bockie, Henry Marford, T. Addison Richards, and Parke Godwin, all of New York; A. K. McClure, Philadelphia; J. Dickson Bruns, New Orleans; Arthur W. Austin, Robert Winthrop, and—probably most distinguished of all—Oliver Wendell Holmes, Boston; as well as South Carolina intimates like A. P. Aldrich and William Porcher Miles. In the knowledgeable main address W. D. Porter, chairman of the Simms Memorial Association and a personal acquaintance of Simms, concluded that "this grand bronze bust, mounted on a pedestal of South Carolina granite" perpetuates the community's "popular gratitude" to "our poet, novelist, historian and benefactor":

> … as it is the prerogative of genius with an easy prodigality to confer honor and renown upon a people, so it is the privilege, the pleasure, and the pride of a cultured people to give expression to their gratitude for such services in the most fitting and durable form that human art can devise.[25]

# Conclusion

*One hundred and twenty years after the death of the author, the ghost of Gilmore Simms paid me a visit and asked a difficult question: "Why have I been forgotten?" In reflecting upon his troubling query, I rephrased his inquiry but could not erase its lamenting tone from my memory. Simms's ghost is entitled to an answer.*

# XII The Measure of the Man

*"... a man greater than his works ..."*
*Paul Hamilton Hayne*

*"Yes, Hayne was right. The man Simms is worthy of all honor."*
*William Peterfield Trent*

*"For my epitaph—Here lies one, who after a reasonably long life, distinguished chiefly by unceasing labor, has left all his better works undone."*
*William Gilmore Simms*

The three quoted passages pose a problem for Simms's biographer. Though Paul Hamilton Hayne was the first commentator to categorize Simms as "a man greater than his works," the idea (perhaps initiated inadvertently by Simms himself in the suggested wording for his epitaph[1]) was not given permanence until William Peterfield Trent adopted it as a central theme for his influential book on Simms. The result has been that the "great" and "noble" man has been eulogized—and the "*emphatically ... not ... great*" author (Hayne's words) all but forgotten and relegated to quasi-obscurity. The image that has been created is as erroneous as it is unfortunate. Simms has received inordinate praise as one who "ceases to be a mere man and assumes proportions that are truly heroic,"[2] "a virile and upright spirit constitutionally incapable of fraud or meanness,"[3] and yet, as the preceding portrayal has revealed, he possessed more than a few human foibles and flaws in character. On the other hand, his works have been apologized for (his "genius *never had fair play*!" [*PHH*]) in an ante-bellum Southern society in which it was "impossible" to "produce a great artist"[4] rather than recognized for their worth. To a writer as ambitious as Simms—to whom literary eminence had been "the dream of my life, the unnamed inspiration of my boyhood—dearer than life"[5]—to be judged a great man, but a mediocre writer is to have failed. The question of fairness put aside, it is essential that misconceptions be erased, past judgments be reviewed, and evidence new and old be thoroughly examined before an accurate measure of Simms the man and Simms the author can be taken.

It is my purpose in this closing chapter to articulate what the accumulated record has already demonstrated: mainly that William Gilmore Simms was not a saint. He had weaknesses in character, blind spots in vision, and vagaries in temperament. In common with other human beings, he sometimes acknowledged his faults and transgressions and even occasionally apologized; but he was also known at times to insist upon his righteousness and benevolence even as he hid from himself and others his selfish motives. A compulsive aspect of his personality perhaps helps to account for some of his weaknesses. Simms felt a need, almost an obsession, to be in charge and his unusual verbal facility made it possible for him, by effective speaking or writing, to take control of situations through his ability to explain, interpret, clarify, or make plausible to others, who looked to him for leadership. At times, this compulsiveness led to the manipulation of the thoughts and actions of those around him. On the other hand, as a positive force this strong drive to explain, interpret, and control also accounts for his willingness to undertake difficult and tiresome tasks, whether they be editing a literary magazine; writing history, biography, and geography for the edification of his children; managing a large plantation; planning a political or military strategy; or, most important, completing a series of literary works on the American revolution and frontier. His compulsion to be active, to bring things together and to fruition, also helps to explain his feverish work habits, to explain why even when weak and dangerously ill in 1867, he could say with little complaint and a touch of pride, "I am writing from morning to night" (*L*, V, 26). His obsession to work, to be in control, accounts for why Simms, almost at death's door in 1870, would observe to his son, "When you can not work at one thing, d[o] so at another" (*L*, V, 291)—a statement in harmony with the principle of restorative creativity he himself exemplified.

Though unconditionally loved and revered for almost three decades by his wife, Simms was so self-centered, and so preoccupied with his own disappointments and frustrations, that he often failed to be thoughtful and considerate in his relationship with her. And though idolized by his children (who may have been also a little fearful of him), he displayed partiality in his actions and attitudes toward them, overloading his favorites with advice while almost ignoring the others, and quickly displaying displeasure and disappointment when any of them fell short of his expectations. In dealing with his elders, he was capable of resentment and mistrust even when their actions were proper, necessary, and justified; in social gatherings he had a tendency to monopolize conversation—appeared interested only in imparting information, not in being a good listener—and often offended the mild-mannered with his boorishness and conceit. Yet with all these human failings, he had many endearing and admirable personal qualities as well. In short, he was a complex, ambitious, headstrong, well-meaning, courageous, blunt, lovable, loyal, strongly biased, at times ebullient, often despondent, sometimes devious, but usually straightforward individual who was well worthy of respect, but hardly of hero-worship—a credible human being whose personal ambitions and arrogance occasionally overrode his sensitivity, gentleness of spirit, open-mindedness, and thoughtfulness of others. However, it is time that the "measure" of Simms be literary rather than biographical, for Simms the man was in essence Simms the literary man.

Thus I shall make a case for Simms as a writer. The time has come to acknowledge the magnitude of Simms's accomplishment as the only American author of the nineteenth century to envision, design, initiate, and consummate an epic portrayal of the development of our nation.

Alone among American novelists of the nineteenth century William Gilmore Simms perceived a national literary need and opportunity, sensed his capability to fulfill it, developed a plan to attain it, and lived to complete it. Simms had vision, commitment, intensity, and perseverance—ingredients without which sustained literary accomplishment of first magnitude is impossible. Relatively early in his career, in 1845, Simms articulated his mission for artistic fulfillment with precision and comprehensiveness, and throughout his life, despite the multiplicity of his activities, he remained constant to that mission, neither altering its formulation nor wavering in his commitment. A single work, "The Epochs and Events of American History, as Suited to the Purposes of Art in Fiction,"[6] consisting of a group of six essays, reveals Simms's acumen in identifying subjects of national significance and his skill in casting them in fictional form. Indeed, Simms's lifelong practice of using American history "for the purposes of art in fiction" is prefigured in the third article in "Epochs and Events," a prescient and farsighted overview entitled "The Four Periods of American History." In this imaginative essay Simms explained his ideas for "the illustration of ... national history" (p. 53)—a formula which he had used in writing some of his novels before 1845 and which was to provide him ready-made "national-theme" subjects for future volumes.

The first period of American history, in Simms's words, "should comprise the frequent and unsuccessful attempts at colonization in our country by the various peoples of Europe—the English, French, and Spaniard ... down to the permanent settlement of the English in Virginia" (p. 77). It is interesting that Simms should include the French and Spanish as shapers of American history and that he expressed interest in "discovery and exploration" by "whatever people." His recognition of non-English forces in North America anticipates both *The Lily and the Totem* (1850), Simms's experiment in fictional history which encompasses a series of "picturesque" sketches of the French Huguenot colonies in Florida in the 1560s, and *Vasconselos* (1853), the neglected novel which centers upon De Soto's Spanish expedition to Florida. Simms's understanding of the continental European background to American history is indicative of the sophistication of his world view; in the introductory essay "Epochs and Events" (in which he stressed "ductility" and "universality" among the "true uses of history") he derided the "sort of patriotism" that called for the American author to "confine himself exclusively to the boundaries of his own country" (p. 49). And conversely, he shunned the parochial view that stressed the role of Great Britain in the building of English-speaking America. As a writer Simms was once more in advance of his times in depicting the diverse national and cultural origins of sixteenth-century American society; he was the only American novelist of the century to recognize that the "singularly attractive" pre-colonial period of our history provided "magnificent" material for literature (*Vasconselos*, p. 4).

The second stage in Simms's conception of American history was the English colonial period, comprising the "progress of British settlement" down to "those aggressions upon popular liberties" preceding the revolution itself (p. 81). Long steeped in English history, as well as the history of his own state, Simms had already dealt with the story of the early settlement of Charleston in his successful second novel, *The Yemassee,* his epic portrayal of the tragic defeat of the heroic Yemassee Indians by gallant and courageous Carolinians under the leadership of Gov. Charles Craven. Almost twenty-five years later Simms returned to colonial South Carolina for what may well be his masterpiece. *The Cassique of Kiawah* is a sensitive and dramatic account of the

English settlers' bloody war with the first tribe of Carolina, the valiant Kiawah. Simms's colonial romances depict illustrious albeit inevitable victories by New World settlers over noble aborigines who are ultimately deprived of their rightful habitat. Together *Yemassee* and *Cassique* rank easily as America's premier works of fiction dealing with our colonial history.

A third division of American history, according to Simms, "would cover the preliminaries to the revolutionary war" and extend "through the war of the revolution" itself (pp. 83–84)—a field that particularly caught his imagination, just as he in turn captured its drama and excitement. Simms specified that by "preliminaries" he meant not only "the aggressions of the British parliament," but perhaps more important "the increasing power of the colonies" coupled with "their reluctance at being officered from abroad." The colonists' "sentiment of independence" grew in "feelings long ere it ripened into thought," long before "the popular will had conceived any certain desire of separation." Certainly his statement that "[f]or the merits of this period, in serving the purposes of art, we have but to refer you to the partisan conflict of the South" was made with reference to the success of *The Partisan, Mellichampe,* and *The Scout* and with knowledge of his intent to continue his series of Revolutionary Romances. Simms's characterization of the Revolution as "the wars of riflemen and cavalry, the sharp shooter and the hunter, and the terrible civil conflicts of whig and tory, which, for wild incident and daring ferocity, have been surpassed by no events in history" seems perfectly to describe the actions and emotions already depicted in his existing Revolutionary novels, and to be delineated again in *Katharine Walton, The Forayers,* and *Eutaw,* as well as in the pre- and post-revolutionary *Joscelyn* and *Woodcraft,* respectively. With the eight novels (which for a hundred years Simms critics from Trent to Wimsatt have almost unanimously considered his major accomplishment) Simms has given readers the most "comprehensive vision of an entire culture at bay"[7] found in the annals of American literature.

Simms's "fourth and last" period of American history begins after the Revolution and "bring[s] us to the present time" (p. 84)—that is, 1845. It includes, in the language of the author, "our transition experience from the colonial to the republican condition," and features "the progress of interior discovery and settlement." Encompassing the westward migration of the early nineteenth century, the period embraces

> our Indian wars, the settlement of Kentucky and Ohio, the acquisition of Louisiana and Florida, the war of 1812 with Great Britain; the conquest of Texas, and the final and complete conversion to the purposes of civilized man, of that wild tract that

## Simms's "Four Periods of American History" (1845)

| Period | Dates | Fictional Representations |
|---|---|---|
| First: "The first period should comprise the frequent and unsuccessful attempts at colonization in our country by the various peoples of Europe—the English, French, and Spaniard—from the first voyage of the Cabots, under Henry, the Seventh,—and should include all subsequent discovery and exploration by whatever people down to the permanent settlement of the English in Virginia." | c. 1497–c. 1607 | *Vasconselos* (1853): Spanish in Florida and Mississippi Valley, 1538–1542.<br>*The Lily and the Totem* (1850): French in Florida and Southeast, 1562–1570. |
| Second: "Our second period should comprise the history and progress of British settlement down to the accession of George the Third, and to the beginning of those aggressions upon the popular liberties in America, which ended in Revolutionary conflict." | c. 1608–1763 | *The Cassique of Kiawah* (1859): colonial South Carolina, 1684.<br>*The Yemassee* (1835): colonial South Carolina, 1715. |
| Third: "A third division would cover the preliminaries of the revolutionary war … through the war of the revolution. For the merits of this period, in serving the purposes of art, we have but to refer you to the partisan conflict in the South—the wars of riflemen and cavalry, the sharp shooter and the hunter, and the terrible conflicts of whig and tory, which for wild incident and daring ferocity, have been surpassed by no events in history." | 1764–1782 | *Joscelyn* (1867): Augusta, Georgia, and South Carolina backcountry, 1775.<br>*The Partisan* (1835): events of the summer of 1780 (Battle of Camden)<br>*Mellichampe* (1836): guerrilla warfare on Santee following the Battle of Camden.<br>*Katharine Walton* (1851): British occupation of Charleston, late 1780–1781.<br>*The Scout* (1841): May 1781 to the British evacuation of Ninety-Six, June 1781.<br>*The Forayers* (1855): events around Orangeburg before the Battle of Eutaw Springs. |

| Period | Dates | Fictional Representations |
|---|---|---|
| | | *Eutaw* (1856): Battle of Eutaw Springs in September 1781; British defeated in South Carolina<br>*Woodcraft* (1852): post-war problems after English evacuation in 1782. |
| Fourth: "A fourth and last period would bring us to the present time, include our transition experience from the colonial to republican condition, illustrate the progress of interior discovery and settlement, comprise our Indian wars, the settlement of Kentucky and Ohio, the acquisition of Louisiana and Florida, the war of 1812 with Great Britain; the conquest of Texas, and the final and complete conversion to the purposes of civilized man, of that vast wild tract, that<br>Boundless contiguity of shade, spreading away from Altamaha to the Rio Bravo!" | early to mid-19th century | [Border Romances and other frontier writings]<br>*Guy Rivers* (1834): Georgia<br>*Richard Hurdis* (1838): Alabama<br>*Border Beagles* (1840): Mississippi<br>*Confession* (1841): South Carolina, Alabama, Texas<br>*Charlemont* (1842): Kentucky<br>*Beauchampe* (1856): Kentucky<br>*Helen Halsey* (1845): Louisiana<br>*The Wigwam and the Cabin* (1845): frontier stories<br>**Norman Maurice* (1851): Missouri<br>**Michael Bonham* (1852): Texas<br>*As Good as a Comedy* (1852): Georgia<br>*Paddy McGann* (1863): South Carolina<br>*The Cub of the Panther* (1869): North Carolina<br>*Voltmeier* (1869): North Carolina<br>"Sharp Snaffles" (1870) and "Bald-Head Bill Bauldy" (1870): dialect tall tales<br><br>*poetic dramas |

> Boundless contiguity of shade,
> spreading away from Altamaha to the Rio Bravo![8]

It is noteworthy that as early as 1845 Simms had grasped the significance of the frontier in molding the mind and character of the American people and in fulfilling the materialistic and territorial aspirations of the young republic. Simms began writing of the violence and lawlessness of the frontier in his first full-length novel, *Guy Rivers,* set in the backwoods of Georgia about 1815. With *Guy Rivers* Simms introduced his Border Romances to the American reading public, and within the decade following its dramatic entry on the literary scene, he had produced no fewer than six other books dealing with the frontier: *Richard Hurdis* (set in Alabama), *Border Beagles* (Mississippi), *Confession* (South Carolina, Alabama, and Texas), *Charlemont* (Kentucky), *Helen Halsey* (Louisiana), and *The Wigwam and the Cabin* (frontier stories with various settings). Later—that is, after the publication of *Views and Reviews*—he was to complete the second volume of his Kentucky Tragedy, *Beauchampe;* write two poetic dramas set in border states, *Norman Maurice* (Missouri) and *Michael Bonham* (Texas); struggle to finish before his death two Appalachian frontier novels, *Voltmeier* and *The Cub of the Panther* (both set in western North Carolina); and compose four short novels (or long short stories) in the vein of Southwestern humor, three of them in dialect, for which Simms had an unusual gift.[9]

Simms's advantage in contemplating a series of diverse books variously illustrating "national history," "national consciousness," or "national themes" —an amorphous task to most eyes—was that he saw organic wholeness in the multiplicity of forces and influences shaping American history from its beginnings to his own times. As one fascinated by the symmetry of historical patterns, he could sight threads of unity in the complex cultural woof from which the fabric of a new nation was being woven. Thus, to Simms, his writings about ante-colonial America, the English colonies, the Revolutionary War, and the rampaging frontier were not isolated efforts, but part of a sustained, interconnected literary saga covering more than four hundred years. He traced the development of American national consciousness through four centuries in two dozen books which, taken together, form a powerful, intense, highly readable epic and constitute a unique national literary treasure.

Part of the debate over Simms's literary status centers around the longstanding question whether Simms should be considered a romanticist or a realist—for he undeniably possessed characteristics of both. The predominant view was offered by Trent (and his numerous followers), who believed that Simms's best work followed the romantic traditions of Scott and Cooper, and who abhorred the violence, the coarse humor, and the crudity—the "lack of nobility"—of the Border Romances and Simms's other frontier writings. In opposition was the concept of Parrington, who insisted that Simms was at his best when he shed the artificiality of chivalrous and idealistic romance and donned the unpretentiousness of plain-spoken realism intent upon depicting life as it really was, not as it should be. Simms himself added to the confusion, since on separate occasions he went on record with articulate, prescient statements in support of romanticism and realism, respectively. His early definition of *The Yemassee* as a "romance," not a "novel," and his accompanying contention that the romance was a modern prose epic, approximating "the poem" and "of loftier origin than the Novel," are his best-known enunciations of romantic theory. Yet his forthright letter in defense of "Caloya; or, The Loves of the Driver" and his forward-looking introduction to *The Wigwam and the Cabin* are substantial evocations of tenets of realism. On the one hand Simms advocated a "wild and wonderful" "*American* romance" which "does not confine itself to what is known, or even what is probable";[10] on the other he argued convincingly for the "right to call things by their proper names" in the depiction of "low life—very low life" if the writer "takes care to speak the truth, the whole truth, and nothing but the truth!" (*L*, I, 256, 257, 259). Simms further defined his view, stating with almost a tone of missionary zeal: "To be truthful, a true writer—an earnest man, full of his subject ... must lay it as bare as possible. He must roll up his sleeves to it, and not heed the blushes of the sophisticated damsel, who is shocked at the bare, brawny arms. Convention is always the foe to truth; and the literature of a country and the literary man thereof ... must stick to nature and scorn the small requisitions of little cliques and classes. They have higher responsibilities than those of fashion" (*L*, I, 263). The writer of these lines, it seems safe to say, was instinctively, and deliberately, a realist. That Simms—long before Henry James developed it as a principle of realism—understood the relationship between character and plot is made clear by his comment in *The Golden Christmas:* "The artist does not make events; they make themselves. They belong to the characterization. The author makes the character. If this be made to act consistently,—and this is the great necessity in all works of fiction,—events flow from its action necessarily, and one naturally evolves another, till the whole action is complete. Here is the whole secret of the novelist" (*GC*, p. 154). It is true that Simms was strongly drawn to the romantic novels of Scott which were steeped in tradition and history; yet anyone who has read Simms's works—his novels, his stories, his criticism, and, perhaps above all, his letters—must agree with Arlin Turner's observation that Simms "was surely a realist by both temperament and conviction."[11] Like Whitman a robust realist and yet romantic dreamer, Simms was exuberant, intuitive, multi-dimensional: he was more concerned about being candid than being consistent. Perhaps it would have been appropriate for him to argue, as Whitman did in 1855,

> Do I contradict myself?
> Very well then ... I contradict myself;
> I am large ... I contain multitudes.[12]

The crux is that Simms the writer defies classification. While not in itself inherently disadvantageous, in Simms's case it has hampered recognition of his stature. The problem is not that literary critics have followed Trent in believing that Simms was a traditional romanticist strongly imitative of Scott (for there is evidence, some supplied by Simms himself, to support the theory in part); the real predicament is rather that scholars have also tended to adopt Trent's bias against "the horrible and the revolting" and "the real and the natural" in Simms's writing and to accept his view that Simms novels lack the "nobility ... essential ... to permanence" (pp. 88–89). Such thinking serves, for instance, to highlight unduly the derivative aspects of even the preferred Revolutionary Romances, and, perhaps more significant, to deprecate the "bold" originality of much of his writing, the Border Romances in particular.

Even an important recent book on Simms is subject to this pervasive influence. Though Mary Ann Wimsatt notes that both Trent and Parrington misread Simms (Trent in viewing him as idealistic romancer corrupted by ethos, Parrington in perceiving him as realist thwarted by convention in society), she maintains with Trent that it is in the genre of romance that Simms's work will endure. Despite her recognition that "leading scholars of the twentieth century have taken their cue from Trent, and therefore Simms has suffered almost as much as if he had been left to languish in dignified neglect," she hardly supplies a corrective in several crucial areas, the most surprising being in her Trent-like assessment of the Border Romances: "Given the gore that embellishes the Murrell extravaganza, the wonder . . . is that they are not worse." This harsh judgment of the "extravagant and violent" in Simms's frontier novels seems strangely discordant in twentieth-century literary criticism, particularly when its premise echos even more Trentian tones:

> Unlike the patriotic histories about the Revolutionary War, it [the material for the Border Romances] is not lofty and idealistic, but vulgar, sensational, and cheap. It did not evoke in Simms a sense of moral urgency or patriotic pride,

> nor did it give him the same comprehensive vision ... that he found in the Revolutionary War material.[13]

Until Simms scholarship can abandon the erroneous and dichotomous supposition that Simms's writings must be either lofty and idealistic *or* "real and ... natural" (Trent's words), there can be no authentic appreciation of what the author with "roll[ed] up ... sleeves" accomplished in portraying the "vulgar, sensational, and cheap" along with the heroic, the noble, and the patriotic in writings that attempt (ahead of their time) to "call things by their proper names" and "lay it as bare as possible." Boldness is an earmark of Simms; and boldness exists in crime and betrayal as well as in honorable deeds and loyalty. Simms's robustness precludes no form of boldness that exists in life—or, as he would say, in "the border history of the south." Furthermore, as Donald Davidson and Thomas L. McHaney rightfully point out, Simms's Southern and Southwestern frontier is no less "national" and is much more nearly "the real thing" than Cooper's "romantic and decorous—and largely imaginary—frontier" five hundred miles to the North. Nevertheless, to most critics "Cooper's frontier is *the* American frontier"; they fail to "grasp the nature and meaning of the frontier in Southern life and history" because it does not "fit the pattern of ideas that they have inherited or acquired about the American frontier."[14] Furthermore, Simms's graphic depiction of the frontier is not limited to his Border Romances; indeed the case may be made that nearly all of his fiction, including the pre-colonial novels, the colonial novels, the Revolutionary Romances, and many of his short novels and stories, portray a frontier environment. In the words of Davidson,

> The field of Simms's fiction, if not its essential subject, is the frontier of the Lower South. At its farthest stretch of time, it is the frontier from the Spanish explorations of the sixteenth century up to the "flush times" of the eighteen-thirties when land-speculators and land-pirates were crowding into the newly opened Indian country of Georgia, Alabama, and Mississippi.

"Most important of all," Davidson continues, "the field of action" in Simms's Revolutionary War novels "is frontier South Carolina." Because the expulsion of the Indians did not occur until 1838, at the outbreak of the Revolution the frontier "as a social and cultural conditioning element" extended almost to "the gates of Charleston." Even the Southern plantation itself was "in principle and essence a frontier institution," for it not infrequently served as a headquarters to plan military strategy or as a fortress to help repel attack, as shown occasionally in Simms's novels. But since the frontier of the Lower South, especially South Carolina, is not known to

Americans generally, Davidson concludes, "in the same familiar way that the history of frontier Kentucky and Tennessee, the Ohio valley, and the trans-Mississippi West is known," Simms's novels dealing with frontier-like warfare in pre-colonial Florida and in colonial South Carolina have been "virtually lost to our historical consciousness."[15]

But it is clear that "the interaction between civilization and frontier" is Simms's "real subject";[16] it is the unifying principle of a career devoted largely to historical novels about the development of American identity from 1539 to 1862—from *Vasconselos: A Romance of the New World* to *Paddy McGann: The Demon of the Stump.* Simms provided the reader of his day and today with four centuries of comprehensive Americana, modes of thought and action in our growing consciousness as a nation, compressed into the contents of two dozen works of fiction with but a single broad, but clearly identifiable goal: an enlightened understanding of the history of civilization in America made vivid through fictional illustration. Put another way, Simms's underlying and continuing goal—in writing to please himself and his readers—was, in widest terms, to portray the development of America as a nation. His own statement to John R. Thompson in 1856 is particularly illuminating: "My novels aim at something more than the story. I am really, though indirectly, revising history … extending somewhat our usual province of His'l Rom." (*L,* III, 421). Later he reiterated that he was "seeking to open new clues to the student in [the] province" of historical understanding (*L,* III, 435). He succeeded to a degree that is unmatched by any of his contemporaries in productiveness and surpassed by only a few in the quality of his best work.

Simms's amazing productivity, in fact, leads to a question which in any assessment of Simms must eventually be answered. How does one measure the accomplishments of a literary man who, in the words of Parrington, "poured out his material copiously, lavishly, with overrunning measure," thus producing annually "an incredible amount of work,"[17] with a career output of eighty-two books, a total staggering enough for two or three ordinary professional men or women of letters. Though the great authors are best judged by their masterpieces, even a critic as elitist as Poe conceded that in calling Simms "the best novelist which this country has, upon the whole, produced," he had chosen to "take into consideration, of course, as well the amount of what he has written, as the talent he has displayed."[18] That a writer's productivity be taken into account in any determination of his literary rank is essential to the good reputation of Simms, for he admittedly wrote nothing to rival the truly great works of fiction of his era—no *The Scarlet Letter* or *Moby-Dick* or (at a slightly later time) *Huckleberry Finn.* But whereas Hawthorne finished at most five novels and Melville eleven, Simms had twenty-three "regular novels,"[19] perhaps fifteen of which should be considered major. Even Cooper's productivity does not compete with Simms's, for after 1827 with three novels of the Leatherstocking saga completed, Cooper the exponent of the frontier shifted largely to being Cooper the critic of American democracy.

But more than upon his amazing fecundity, Simms's reputation is dependent upon a certain willingness—displayed by critics of, say, Dickens, or Fielding, or Melville, or Dreiser, or Wolfe—to recognize strengths as "major" and blemishes as "minor." Poe's statement that Simms's "merits lie among the major and his defects among the minor morals of literature" exemplifies the critical position essential to the status of Simms as a major writer. No one has seriously questioned his possession of strong literary virtues, and Simms himself has freely acknowledged the presence of defects in even his best writings. In admitting to Beverley Tucker that his works were "wanting in symmetry and finish" and "grossly disfigured by errors of taste and judgement," Simms explained that he was pointing out his "crudenesses without endeavouring to excuse them." But, as in an earlier admission to Lawson of deficiency in his writings, Simms expressed hope that his friend "discover in them proofs of original force, native character, and some imagination" (*L*, II, 528, 504, 528).

Simms's strengths as a writer are both abundant and distinctive. As recognized by even his detractors, an "extraordinary gusto" permeates his writings, which in vigor, spontaneity, and robustness can compete with any body of fiction by a single author in pre-Civil War America. Among novelists of the time, it was Simms alone who (as Parrington astutely observed) captured much of Whitman's "largeness and coarseness" and "delight in the good things of earth" (p. 127). In addition, Simms's writings possess power, exuberance, intensity in a measure that anticipate Thomas Wolfe, another Southerner with boldness, impetuosity, and a sense of alienation and resentment. Donald Davidson was right in pointing to the oral, folk quality of Simms's best novels and tales. Simms can be appreciated to the fullest only if read aloud in order to reveal the rich cadences of his narrative style, best described as that of a marvelous storyteller who composes as rapidly as he thinks. Perhaps it is this inborn ability to communicate, this love of oral storytelling that gives a sense of reality to Simms's fiction; there is a presence in his best work that immediately grabs and holds the reader's attention and imagination. Simms himself—who found it easier to "invent a new story than to repair the defects of an old one"—recognized that when he forgot "himself in the excitement of the story" (*L*, II, 224–25), he wrote with his most effortless, free-flowing style. In describing his habit of composition, Simms more than once remarked that he wrote "*stans pede in uno*, goon like, literally, as fast as pen could fly over paper" (*L*, I, 316). On another occasion, he used a particularly vivid analogy to elucidate his everyday practice: "I ... write like steam, recklessly, perhaps thoughtlessly—can give ... no idea of the work" (*L*, I, 278); yet again, in a passage revealing remarkable self-awareness, he asserted: "I ... write usually as I talk; and as the world goes, am accounted a somewhat rude, blunt man" (*L*, VI, 27). Perhaps with the plea of Hammond (and other well-meaning advisors) in mind, Simms acknowledged that his "mode" of composition was "not very favorable to a work of permanent merit," but, he added significantly, it was "particularly suited to a temperament like mine" (*L*, I, 316).

Since the natural, seemingly careless writing habits of Simms have been widely assailed as being accountable for the lack of polish and refinement in his writings and yet also have been acclaimed as the source for the easy flow and raw power of his lusty, swift-moving prose at its best, the question of the effect of Simms's practices of composition upon the quality of his work needs to be resolved. Though assiduous efforts have been made to demonstrate that Simms revised his writing with more frequency and more effectiveness than commonly believed, the evidence suggests that he wrote his most memorable lines, passages, chapters, and books when he served almost involuntarily as the conduit through which his amazing creativity surged without restraint, almost without direction. This is not to say that Simms never improved a work when he revised it, for there are specific instances when he did; but these revisions were never enough to transform mediocre writing into excellent writing. In Simms's best work he lost himself in the heat of creativity; he wrote "like steam" or "as I talked," "as fast as pen could fly over paper" because he gave himself up to his inspiration. When he became conscious of observing literary proprieties, he tended to become awkward, stilted, pretentious, boringly conventional; when he "rolled up his sleeves" and spoke in natural language about the raw frontier he had experienced, he wrote visceral prose marked by a vernacular robustness and vibrancy not found in American letters before Mark Twain. Early in his career Simms detected that his "style was better" when his "feelings were aroused" (*L*, I, 162). He later observed, truthfully in his case, that "fame does not so much as follow polish & refinement as Genius—not so much grace and correct delineation as a bold adventurous thought" (*L*, I, 400). Whatever Simms did best, he did with passionate intensity, and if he burned himself out with one topic or with one endeavor, he turned to another, a lifelong practice which seemed to refresh his energy and restore his creativity.

Because "bold adventurous thought" was characteristic of Simms the man and writer, he naturally was attracted to aspects of human behavior other than the timid, the righteous, and the elegant. Though he depicted the civilized virtues of the drawing room and the plantation (sometimes very effectively in a vein of humorous, ironic satire) as well as the violence and lawlessness of the frontier, with his penchant for realism and his sense of dramatic awareness he was never reluctant to focus upon the sensational and the horrible with an intensity unusual for his time.[20] Early in his career Simms had written: "I certainly feel that, in bringing the vulgar and the vicious mind into exceeding activity in a story of the borders, I have done mankind no injustice." He was persuaded, he had added, that particularly during periods of war and hostility "vulgarity and crime must always preponderate—dreadfully preponderate" (*Mellichampe*, p. 6). Though Simms's unconventional use of graphic details in his treatment of murder, brutality, and other forms of violence revolted some critics and readers of his day and today, it is recognition of the existence of violence and disorder as a prominent strain in Southern life that inevitably links him to Faulkner, Warren, and Styron—a relationship noted only superficially, if at all, in the exhaustive studies of Southern literature as the preeminent representative of twentieth-century American letters. The roots of Faulkner and Warren are clearly found in Simms if one but makes the effort to read their fiction as emanating from a literary tradition rather than springing full-grown from previously unplowed Southern soil. And Simms's once controversial concept that an artist's role in a national literature is the faithful and meaningful protrayal of his own region is now accepted in the philosophy of composition of most "later Southern writers of fiction [who] write as though their theory was similar to that of Simms."[21] Simms's pivotal role as a kind of ancestral father to modern literature of the South cries for greater recognition.[22]

Though Simms never relinquished thought that his "frank, manly, honest" poetry might in posterity be accorded a place on "the 'specular mount' at which I aimed" (*L*, VI, 177), most of his contemporaries recognized that his forte was fiction, not poetry.[23] Simms's claim, however, that "my poetical works exhibit the highest phase of the imaginative faculty which this country has yet exhibited" has been given some credence by the recent thorough examination of his poetry by James Kibler, who finds Simms "directly at the center" of the English and American romantic tradition, "perhaps in a way unsurpassed by any of his American contemporaries."[24] In his poetry as well as in his fiction, Simms performed best when he could strip himself of pretension and pedantry and write simply and directly in sonorous vernacular language. Unfortunately, however, in much of his verse he is stiff, stilted, and artificial, rather than fluid and natural; too few times did he "lay it ... bare" in poetry as he did in prose, but an exception is his delightful "Ballad. The Big Belly," a classic example of the use of the dialect and the subject matter of folklore in poetry. When Simms concentrated on describing the peculiar beauty of the South Carolina low-country landscape or depicting the quaintness and charm of Indian legend or tradition in the lower South, he produced some strikingly original poetry. Among the most notable are "Dark-eyed Maid of Edisto," "The Maid of the Congaree," "Ask me no more for Song," "The Traveller's Rest," "Oh! Linger Yet Awhile," "Song—Meet Me When Stars," "Dorchester," "Chilhowee, the Indian Village," "Thlecathcka; or, The Broken Arrow," and the little known "Tzelica, a Tradition of the French Broad," the latter a particularly effective evocation of Simms's use of Indian legend in poetry. In a different vein are his autobiographical lyrics, one of the best of which is "The Two Upon the Hearth," and his artistic-philosophical poems such as "Sketches in Hellas," completed only a few months before his death. The excellence Simms attained as a poet is overshadowed by his achievement as a novelist, but he practiced the craft of writing poetry throughout his career and ever regarded himself as a poet of consequence. His place alongside Lanier, Timrod, and Hayne among leading poets in the Old South is secure; and his importance as a forerunner, rather than an imitative follower, in American romantic poetry is being increasingly urged, with an ultimate ranking somewhere between Bryant and Whittier not out of the question.

As a critic, Simms fares better than as a poet. During his career as editor of six literary journals he practiced the art of criticism with admirable consistency, judiciousness, discrimination, and foresight. His evaluations of his contemporaries—British and American—seem remarkably accurate and fair-minded when adjudged from the vantage point of more than a hundred years. His candid appraisals of Poe, Hawthorne, Cooper, Bryant, Irving, Kennedy, Holmes, Hayne, Timrod, Schoolcraft, Bird, Longfellow, and Lowell among Americans; and of Dickens, Thackeray, Browning, Tennyson, Goldsmith, Carlyle, Byron, Scott, Wordsworth, Bulwer, and De Quincey among the English; strike the modern reader as both lucid and penetrating. Simms's judgment of Melville was harsh and unsympathetic—he found *Moby-Dick* deserving of "a writ *de lunatico*" against both its "raving" "Mad Captain" and the author himself, for instance[25]—but such blind castigation was not unusual in estimates of Melville in 1852 and Simms's narrow-mindedness in this instance serves only to make his usual broad-mindedness and acuity stand out. Simms's thoughtful yet succinct definition of criticism—"justly to discriminate, firmly to establish, wisely to prescribe, and honestly to award—these are the true aims and duties of criticism"[26]—was not to him empty rhetoric. As editor and literary spokesman from 1825 to his death he worked assiduously to "merit the high and distinguished title of critic"[27] and to "elevate the standards of criticism to a proper level."[28] In addition, as a noted champion of national and sectional literature he was committed to a policy of encouraging writers on native themes and of disparaging mere imitators of popular or conventional European literature. His consistent observance of this policy did not mean that he indiscriminately puffed "Americanism" in literature and just as indiscriminately condemned everything stemming from foreign influences. Simms could (and did) encourage authors of national themes even when he conscientiously could not (and did not) praise them; likewise he could admire the excellence of American writings steeped in European traditions even while noting that they were of no aid in establishing a native literature. Though Simms's criticism is colored by his own firm beliefs, he made a point to single out both merits and defects in books that he reviewed, whether his over-all estimate was favorable or unfavorable. Everything considered, Simms, a critic of exceptionally high quality, was one of the most influential and judicious in all American literature before 1860.

As a dramatist Simms was of considerably less significance. Though he began writing drama early—he composed at fourteen a juvenile drama, "The Female Assassin,"—and at his death was trying to publish in book form his manuscript play dealing with Benedict Arnold, Simms wrote more effectively *about* drama than he wrote drama itself. Two lengthy short stories, *The Prima Donna* and "The Humours of the Manager," reflect his interest in theater, and the passages in *Border Beagles* dealing with Tom Horsey's theatrical adventures constitute some of his most effective humorous writing. But his only two truly serious efforts at play writing were neither dramatic nor critical successes. His attempt, however, to combine blank verse and vernacular speech in *Norman Maurice* is an interesting experiment in the genre in which he displayed least aptitude. That he also edited an edition of Shakespearean apocrypha manifests the strong influence of Shakespeare upon his own nondramatic and dramatic writing, as well as his lifelong addiction to the study of drama. And it should not be overlooked that *Norman Maurice* and *Michael Bonham* extend Simms's portrayal of the frontier to the trans-Mississippi West.

No literary man of his time wrote as many, as varied, or as interesting, informative, and entertaining letters as did Gilmore Simms. Whether one peruses them for the historical perspective of a fascinating and complicated period in American history or simply for the enjoyment they provide for connoisseurs of racy, readable prose, Simms's letters are priceless. After the death of Simms, John Esten Cooke tried to persuade Hayne to use Simms's "delightful" correspondence as the basis for a biography, "letting our noble old Southern Maestro paint himself, his own large generous character, his struggles, trials, successes, and all."[29] More than a century later a prominent literary scholar termed Simms's edited letters "the most important single document in the study of ante-bellum Southern cultural life," describing them as a "treasure-trove," "essential not only for matters involving Simms but almost anything having to do with Southern literature, intellectual and political life during those key years when fateful identity of the region was being established."[30] But the significance of Simms the letter writer is not limited to documentation or enlightenment of the South. Since Simms's circle of friends included Northern authors, critics, and publishers; since he visited the North frequently and commented thoughtfully and sometimes pungently on his impressions of the conditions of life there; and since his correspondence covers a wide range of American politics, economics, and philosophy as well as literature and publishing, his letters have national implications and importance. They are in effect a cornucopia of Americana—the most vital collection of its kind by a nineteeth-century man of letters.

In the introduction to Simms's *Stories and Tales* (1974), I suggested that the author's "strongest abilities lay in the short story."[31] Though Simms's highest *accomplishment* was in writing novels, his *abilities* were peculiarly adapted to short fiction, which benefited from his skill at swift-moving narrative more than did the slower-paced novel. During his career Simms wrote many sketches and tales as fillers for his magazines or as potboilers to provide ready cash; but these efforts do not properly belong to his canon any more than, say, Hawthorne's stories for children belong to the canon of the artistic New Englander. What is pertinent and consequential is that Simms produced enough extraordinary short fiction for five or six volumes of stories and novelettes of the first magnitude. *The Wigwam and the Cabin* alone contains thirteen stories ranging from Poe's favorite, "Grayling" to the controversial "Caloya; or, The Loves of the Driver," to a half dozen personal favorites: "The Two Camps," "The Arm-Chair of Tustenuggee," "The Giant's Coffin," "Sergeant Barnacle," "Those Old Lunes!" and "Lucas de Ayllon," each with distinctive excellences in the vein of Simms's border writings. In addition, Simms's companion pieces, "How Sharp Snaffles Got His Capital and Wife" and "Bald-Head Bill Bauldy," each told in dialect and each left unpublished at Simms's death, constitute perhaps the finest writing in the special genre of the tall tale in all of American literature. Another tale left in manuscript by the author, "The Humours of the Manager," though not of the calibre of "Snaffles" and "Bauldy," nevertheless is an impressive addition to Simms's humorous and satirical stories of manners, which also include the farcical *Flirtation at the Moultrie House.* Other titles of interest and significance are "Ephraim Bartlett," "Mesmerides in a Stage-Coach," "Indian Sketch," "The Unknown Masque," and "Geoffrey Rudel: A Pilgrim of Love." In Simms "moral imaginative" category fall such tales as "Confessions of a Murderer," "Carl Werner," and "The Bride of Hate."

Perhaps even more than in the short story,[32] however, Simms excelled in the writing of the short novel or novelette. In this category of "regularly planned ... novels in little" (*L*, III, 342) he produced no fewer than seven outstanding examples, beginning in 1833 with the appearance of *Martin Faber*, Simms's first short novel and his first psychological study in the confessional mode, and culminating in 1863 with the publication of *Paddy McGann*, whose ironic humor and biting satire make it one of the most telling of Simms's fictive works. In between *Faber* and *McGann* fall his extraordinary studies of contemporary Carolina life—*Castle Dismal*, "Maize in Milk," and *The Golden Christmas*, each depicting the Christmas season; his Poesque novella set in New Orleans, *Marie de Berniere*, somewhat anticipatory of Kate Chopin; and his artistically pleasing Spanish romance, "The Maroon" (originally subtitled "A Legend of the Caribees"), never published separately as a book as he had hoped. These "novels in little" offer such rich varieties of tone, mood, and substance and display such evidence of literary virtuosity that, combined with his accomplishments in the short story, they testify to Simms's mastery of all forms of fiction, not simply of the novel, in which his greatest achievement lies.

In summary, then, Simms is a *poet* of more power, originality, and versatility than had been recognized prior to the recent study placing him among the important writers of poetry before the Civil War. As a *literary critic* and spokesman for belles-lettres in general, Simms stands almost unchallenged as the most influential of his place and time; a discriminating and powerful, if sometimes biased and volatile force to the good of American and Southern letters, he occupied a position of such importance in the nation's literary circles that some called him the Samuel Johnson of his age. As a *writer of drama* (for which he held a poorly concealed lifelong passion), he is among the unsuccessful pioneers in a genre late to develop in America as a serious art form, but he displayed enough promise to prompt a distinguished literary historian of our time to conclude that if his efforts had been so channeled he would have been a significant playwright. Among our *literary letter writers* of the nineteenth century, Simms is unique in his importance to historians and literary scholars. His almost two thousand pieces of correspondence display many of the striking qualities—audacity, frankness, rebelliousness, exuberance, spontaneity, keen insight, and good humor—that characterize the man and his works. While it is remarkable that he accomplished so much in other literary fields—poetry, criticism, drama, letter writing—it is as a *writer of fiction,* and particularly as a *novelist,* that Simms leaves his most enduring mark. Within the narrative mode he adapted his talents superbly to the different and difficult tasks of writing the short story, the novelette, and the novel. Whether in short fiction or long, Simms has few peers among his contemporaries, whether gauged by the substantial worth of his work in each genre, or by the singular excellence of those efforts adjudged to his finest.

And most of all, Simms's fiction breathes with the vitality of the American frontier. The harsh, brutal frontier of Simms's experience and observation contrasts sharply with the idealized frontier of Cooper's imagination and reading. Realistic portrayal of the frontier is uniquely the power and the glory of Simms as an author. The frontier in Simms shifts from the Spanish and the French expeditions in Florida in the sixteenth century, to colonial and revolutionary times in South Carolina in the seventeenth and eighteenth centuries, to the land-rush settlements of the lower Mississippi valley in the first half of the nineteenth century. Such comprehensiveness of vision is found nowhere else in our national literature.

Yes, all things considered, Poe may well have been right in saying of Simms: "... in invention, in vigor, in movement, in the power of exciting interest, and in the artistical management of his themes, he has surpassed, we think, any of his countrymen:—that is to say, he has surpassed any of them in the aggregate of these high qualities."[33] Simms the man was worthy of respect, but Simms the author was greater. He deserves place as a major American writer.

Appendix I

# The Children of William Gilmore Simms

I am indebted to Mary Simms Oliphant Furman for her assistance in the preparation of this chart.

| | Date of Birth | Date of Death |
|---|---|---|
| *With* Anna Malcolm Giles Simms (c. 1808–1832; married October 19, 1826): | | |
| Anna Augusta Singleton Simms* | November 11, 1827 | January 18, 1898 |
| *With* Chevillette Eliza Roach Simms (c. 1817–1863; married November 15, 1836): | | |
| Virginia Singleton Simms | November 15, 1837 | October 10, 1838 |
| Mary Derrille Simms | September 6, 1839 | April 1842 |
| Agnes Simms | May 23, 1841 | May 28, 1841 |
| William Gilmore Simms, Jr.* | March 16, 1843 | October 15, 1912 |
| Valerie Govan Simms | August 10, 1845 | September 21, 1846 |
| Mary Lawson Simms* | September 13, 1846 | April 26, 1908 |
| Chevillette Eliza Simms* | December 13, 1848 | June 17, 1914 |
| Sydney Roach Simms | November 9, 1851 | September 22, 1858 |
| unnamed stillborn boy | April 25, 1853 | April 25, 1853 |
| Beverley Hammond Simms | July 17, 1854 | September 22, 1858 |

| | | |
|---|---|---|
| Govan Singleton Simms* | September 1, 1856 | July 7, 1891 |
| Harriet Myddleton Simms | March 14, 1858 | December 25, 1861 |
| Sydney Hammond Simms | July 27, 1859 | c. July 2, 1861 |
| Charles Carroll Simms* | October 20, 1862 | December 10, 1930 |

*Living at the time of Simms's death

Appendix II

# The Final Will of Nash Roach

Box 115

No 17 State of South Carolina

I Nash Roach of Charleston in the State of South Carolina, and Planter in Barnwell District in the State aforesaid, do hereby make publish and declare this my last Will and Testament in writing as follows

First I give and bequeath to my beloved niece Mary Govan Rivers Wife of C. M. Rivers five hundred Dollars to be securely invested for her sole use and benefit as if she were a feme sole and not to be subject in any manner what ever to the debts contracts or engagements of her present or any future Husband.

Second I give and bequeath unto my beloved niece Anna Washington Steele Two thousand Dollars to be safely and securely invested by my Executor hereinafter named for her sole use and benefit so that she may semi-annually receive the interest or income arising therefrom. And it is my Will that this Legacy be not subject in any manner what ever to the debts contracts or engagements of any husband she may have.

Third I hereby give devise and bequeath all the rest and residue of my real and personal Estate which I now have or which I may be seized and possessed of or entitled to at the time of my death together with all my choses in action of every every [*sic*] description unto my beloved Daughter Chevillette Eliza Simms Wife of William Gilmore Simms for her sole separate use and benefit not to be subject in any manner to the debts contracts or engagements of her present or any future Husband she may have so that she may receive the rents interest income and profits thereof as if she were a feme sole.

Fourth Should my son in Law the said William Gilmore Sims [*sic*] survive his said Wife Chevillette Eliza Simms then from and after her death I give devise and bequeath all the rest and residue aforesaid of my real and personal Estate aforesaid unto the said William Gilmore Simms for and during the term of his natural Life.

Fifth From and after the death of the Survivor of them the said William Gilmore Simms and Chevillette Eliza Simms I give devise and bequeath all the rest and residue aforesaid of my real and personal Estate unto their eldest son who shall be then living at the death of such survivor to him his heirs Executors Administrators and Assigns forever.

Sixth I hereby nominate and appoint the said William Gilmore Simms sole Executor of this my last Will and Testament hereby also revoking all former Wills by me at any time made.

IN WITNESS WHEREOF I have hereunto set my hand and Seal this twelfth day of July in the year of our Lord One thousand eight hundred and fifty five

N. Roach [Seal]

Signed Sealed published and declared by the said Nash Roach as his last Will and Testament in the presence of us who in his presence and at his request have hereunto set our names as Witnesses

Alfred H. Dunkin Chas. E. B. Flagg C. R. Brewster

Ex:GB Probate before George Buist Esq O. C. D. 23[d] day of March Anno Domini 1858. October 28[th] 1858 qualified Wm Gilmore Simms Sole Executor therein named

Appendix III

# Simms and International Copyright

In his letter of February 10, 1844, to George Frederick Holmes, Simms discussed the need for an international copyright law and referred to "the memorial to Congress" to which he had devoted time and energy. A copy of the memorial with the notation in pencil, "Woodlands, March 1," is in the collection of the Department of Archives and History, State of Alabama, Montgomery, Alabama:

*To the Senate and House of Representatives of the United States:*

The undersigned, Men of Letters and Citizens of the United States, interested in many ways in the cause of Literature, petition your honorable bodies of the passage of a law for the proper regulation of the copy-right of books. Having considered the matter in all its various aspects, and under all the light shed upon it by the repeated discussions of the last few years, they beg respectfully to represent,

That the tenure of literary property in this country is an anomaly among the tenures of every other kind of property, for which no good reason has been or can be assigned; which is unjust in the very nature of it, and extremely injurious in its practical operations.

That the author of a book is the sole and exclusive owner of it, as much as the farmer is of his land, or the merchant of his bale of goods; and that, whether he be a native of this country or of a foreign country, the Republic is bound, by the recognized morality of every enlightened and christian people, to guarantee and defend his property against invasion, as much as it is bound to protect the ordinary commodities of commerce.

That the American government, by denying to foreign authors the copy-right of their books, while it is grossly unjust towards them, inflicts an irreparable injury upon its own authors, by compelling them to enter the market under a system of the most disadvantageous competition; and thus fills the channels of circulation with an unpaid and often corrupt foreign literature, to the partial exclusion, if not to the entire extinction, of all sound and healthful native products.

That the reading of the American people does not, at this time, harmonize with their just desires, their wants and their institution.

That American authors who can best satisfy these, some of whom have grown gray in the honorable service of the country, and others entering upon what they hoped might be a useful career, will be and are crowded aside, not only from lack of remuneration, but from want of general sympathy in their pursuits, into other pursuits from which they cannot be recalled.

That the business of book publishing, which is one of vast public consequence, has become an irregular and uncertain traffic, discouraging to the employment of sound mercantile industry and skill.

That American authors, while they deprecate a merely dollar and cent discussion of this question,—as they desire, nothing more, the good will and affection of their countrymen, would at all times desire that books should be furnished to them at such rates as to secure the widest circulation and most general usefulness.

That a native literature may be said, without disparagement to other and more generally recognized branches of the public service, to be of at least as much national consequence as the navy, the army, the public beacons, and the establishment of public highways and means of intercommunication.

That experience, which has been long and ample, teaches us that there is no other rectifying influence of a sufficiently potent character to amend these evils and justify the good results hoped for, but the law now sought.

For these considerations, for every consideration of Right, of Honor and National Self-respect, your memorialists ask at your hands a bill to equalize all copy-rights, native and foreign, of books printed and published, originally or simultaneously, in this country and abroad. They ask this bill now, of the Congress now in session; and they ask instant and careful heed to their prayer, of the better and higher life of the Republic, not seen yet strong beyond account, for good or evil, impalpable to the eye, yet filling the future with shapes of apprehension or joy, as your honorable body may find it in you to determine.

Appendix IV

# Two Elegies in Charleston Periodicals

Additional evidence of Charleston's high regard for Simms at the time of his death are two elegies in his honor which appeared in Charleston periodicals shortly after his burial. The first, entitled "Monody. The Late Wm. Gilmore Simms," ran in the poetry section of the *Courier* of June 22, 1870:

He has gon[e] from earth, to where seraphs shall sing
  His welcome to bowers of bliss!
And the harps of the blest should joyously ring
  At his flight from a world like this!

Yes, he's gone to the home of the pure in heart,
  With spirits of light around him,
Where the glow of that glory shall ne'er depart,
  In which God's messenger found him.

Then l[a]ment not for one who so haply came
  To beam round our path sweet delight,
And ere earth could have sullied that manly frame,
  His soul sought its heavenly flight.

And yet aged chronicler! thou canst not die!
  For [a] chaste halo surrounds thee;
It is not your fate which demands a sigh,
  But that of the State that mourns thee.

IPSDEN.

The second, written by fellow poet F. O. Ticknor, was published in the new Charleston monthly, the *Rural Carolinian*, for August 1870:

AGAINST THE WIND!

Dedicated to Wm. Gilmore Simms, "Nestor."

Your big Balloon! Your Galleon,
Require the breeze abaft!
The silken sail, the silver spoon!—
The swan's down on the shaft!
And hit the ——— Devil, late or soon,
Whatever wind may waft.

But hail the head-wind singing through
Our canvas worn and white—
And hail the sea-song tingling to
Our wind-wire straining tight!
The keen, elastic springing through
The arched—unutterable blue—
*Against* the Devil and his crew,
To HEAVEN like a kite.

Appendix V

# The Writings of William Gilmore Simms Appearing in Book Form*

Works of fiction integral to Simms's portrayal of the development of America as a nation appear with boldface titles.

*Monody, on the Death of Gen. Charles Cotesworth Pinckney.* By A South-Carolinian. Charleston: Gray & Ellis, 1825.

*Lyrical and Other Poems.* By William G. Simms, Jun. Charleston: Ellis & Neufville, 1827.

*Early Lays.* By William G. Simms, Jun. Author of "Lyrical and Other Poems,"—"Monody on Pinckney," &c. Charleston: A. E. Miller, 1827. Dedication: To Charles R. Carroll, Esq.

*The Vision of Cortes, Cain, and Other Poems.* By W. Gilmore Simms, Jr. Charleston: James S. Burges, 1829. Dedication to James L. Petigru, Esq.

*The Tri-Color; or, The Three Days of Blood, in Paris. With Some Other Pieces.* London: Wigfall & Davis, 1830. [Charleston, S.C.: James S. Burges, 1831]

*Atalantis. A Story of the Sea: In Three Parts.* New York: J. & J. Harper, 1832. Dedication to Maynard D. Richardson, Esq.

*Martin Faber; The Story of a Criminal.* New York: J. & J. Harper, MDCCCXXXIII. Dedication to the author's daughter [Anna Augusta Simms].

*This list includes all first publications (regardless of brevity) issued separately in "book form" and all book-length publications, whether or not in "book form," issued during Simms's lifetime. The bibliographical information includes the title and the identification of the author as given on the title page.

*The Book of My Lady. A Melange.* By a Bachelor Knight. Philadelphia: Key & Biddle, 1833; Boston: Allen & Ticknor, 1833.

***Guy Rivers: A Tale of Georgia.*** By the author of "Martin Faber." New York: Harper & Brothers, 1834. Two volumes. Dedication to Charles R. Carroll, Esq.

***The Yemassee. A Romance of Carolina.*** By the author of "Guy Rivers," "Martin Faber," &c. New York: Harper & Brothers, 1835. Two volumes. Dedication to Samuel Henry Dickson, M.D.

***The Partisan: A Tale of the Revolution.*** By the author of "The Yemassee," "Guy Rivers," &c. New York: Harper & Brothers, 1835. Two volumes. Dedication to Richard Yeadon, Jr.

***Mellichampe. A Legend of the Santee.*** By the author of "The Yemassee," "Guy Rivers," &c. New York: Harper & Brothers, 1836. Two volumes. [No dedication; 1854 Redfield edition has dedication to Colonel M. C. M. Hammond.]

*Martin Faber, The Story of a Criminal; and Other Tales.* By the author of "The Yemassee," "Guy Rivers," "Mellichampe," &c. New York: Harper & Brothers, 1837. Two volumes. Dedication to the author's daughter [Anna Augusta Simms].

*Slavery in America, being a Brief Review of Miss Martineau on that subject.* By a South Carolinian. Richmond: Thomas W. White, 1838. Dedicated to the Hon. Delegates from South Carolina, in the Congress of the United States.

***Richard Hurdis; or, The Avenger of Blood. A Tale of Alabama.*** Philadelphia: E. L. Carey & A. Hart, 1838. Two volumes. Dedication to the Hon. John A. Grimball, of Mississippi.

*Pelayo: A Story of the Goth.* By the author of "Mellichampe," "The Yemassee," "Guy Rivers," "The Partisan," "Martin Faber," &c. New York: Harper & Brothers, 1838. Two volumes. Dedication to William Hayne Simmons.

*Carl Werner, An Imaginative Story; With other Tales of Imagination.* By the author of "The Yemassee," "Guy Rivers," "Mellichampe," &c. New York: George Adlard, 1838. Two volumes. Dedication to Prosper M. Wetmore.

*Southern Passages and Pictures.* By the author of "Atalantis," "The Yemassee," "Guy Rivers," "Carl Werner," &c. New York: George Adlard, MDCCCXXXIX. Dedication to William Cullen Bryant.

*The Damsel of Darien.* By the author of "The Yemassee," "Guy Rivers," "Mellichampe," &c. Philadelphia: Lea and Blanchard, 1839. Two volumes. Dedication to the Hon. James K. Paulding.

*The History of South Carolina, from its First European Discovery to its Erection into a Republic: with a Supplementary Chronicle of Events to the Present Time.* By William Gilmore Simms, Author of "The Yemassee," "The Partisan," "Damsel of Darien," &c. Charleston: S. Babcock & Co., 1840. Dedication to the Youth of South Carolina.

***Border Beagles; A Tale of Mississippi.*** By the author of "Richard Hurdis." Philadelphia: Carey and Hart, 1840. Two volumes. Dedication to M—— L——, of Alabama. [1855 Redfield edition has dedication to the Hon. John A. Campbell, of Alabama.]

***The Kinsmen: or The Black Riders of Congaree. A Tale.*** By the author of "The Partisan," "Mellichampe," "Guy Rivers," "The Yemassee," &c. Philadelphia: Lea & Blanchard, 1841. Two volumes. Dedication to Colonel William Drayton, of Philadelphia. Revised as *The Scout or The Black Riders of Congaree.* New York: Redfield, 1854. Two volumes. [Now known as *The Scout.*]

***Confession; or, The Blind Heart. A Domestic Story.*** By the author of "The Kinsmen," "The Yemassee," "Guy Rivers," etc. Philadelphia: Lea and Blanchard, 1841. Two volumes. Dedication to James W. Simmons.

*Beauchampe, or The Kentucky Tragedy. A Tale of Passion.* By the author of "Richard Hurdis," "Border Beagles," etc. Philadelphia: Lea and Blanchard, 1842. Two volumes. Dedication to the Hon. James Hall, of Cincinnati. [Later revised as *Charlemont* and *Beauchampe*: see under *Charlemont,* below.]

*The Social Principle: The True Source of National Permanence. An Oration, Delivered Before the Erosophic Society of the University of Alabama, at its Twelfth Anniversary, December 13, 1842.* By William Gilmore Simms, of South Carolina. Tuscaloosa: The [Erosophic] Society, 1843.

*The Geography of South Carolina: Being a Companion to the History of that State.* By William Gilmore Simms. Charleston: Babcock & Co., 1843. Dedication to Southern Teachers.

*Donna Florida. A Tale.* By the Author of "Atalantis," "Southern Passages and Pictures," &c. Charleston: Burges & James, 1843. Dedication to James Lawson, of New York.

*The Prima Donna: A Passage from City Life.* By W. G. Simms, author of "Guy Rivers," "The Yemassee," "Richard Hurdis," etc. Philadelphia: Louis A. Godey, 1844. No. 1 of Godey's Library of Elegant Literature.

*The Sources of American Independence. An Oration, on the Sixty-ninth Anniversary of American Independence; Delivered at Aiken, South-Carolina, before the Town Council and Citizens Thereof.* By W. Gilmore Simms. Aiken: Council, MD.CCC.XLIV.

*The Life of Francis Marion.* By W. Gilmore Simms. New York: Henry G. Langley, 1844.

*Castle Dismal: or, The Bachelor's Christmas. A Domestic Legend.* By the Author of "Guy Rivers," "The Yemassee," "Richard Hurdis," &c. New York: Burgess, Stringer & Co., 1844. Dedication to Richard Henry Wilde, of Georgia.

***Helen Halsey: or, The Swamp State of Conelachita. A Tale of the Borders.*** By W. Gilmore Simms, Author of "Richard Hurdis," "The Yemassee," "The Kinsmen," &c. New-York: Burgess, Stringer & Co., 1845. Dedication to Randell Hunt, Esq., of Louisiana.

*Grouped Thoughts and Scattered Fancies. A Collection of Sonnets.* By the Author of "Atalantis," "Southern Passages and Pictures," &c. Richmond, Va.: Wm. Macfarlane, 1845.

***The Wigwam and the Cabin.*** By the Author of "The Yemassee," "Guy Rivers," &c. New York: Wiley and Putnam, 1845. First and Second Series. Dedication to N. Roach, Esq.

*Count Julian; or, The Last Days of the Goth. A Historical Romance.* By the Author of "Guy Rivers," "The Yemassee," "The Damsel of Darien," "Richard Hurdis," "Border Beagles," "The Kinsmen," &c. Baltimore and New York: William Taylor, 1845. Dedication to the Hon. John P. Kennedy, of Baltimore, Maryland.

*Views and Reviews in American Literature, History and Fiction.* By the author of "The Yemassee," "Life of Marion," "History of South Carolina," "Richard Hurdis," &c., &c. New York: Wiley and Putnam, 1845. First and Second Series. Dedication to Professor E. Geddings, of the Medical College of South Carolina.

*Areytos: or, Songs of the South.* By W. Gilmore Simms, Author of "The Yemassee," "Confession," etc. Charleston: John Russell, MDCCCXLVI.

*The Life of Captain John Smith. The Founder of Virginia.* By W. Gilmore Simms. Author of "Life of Marion," "History of South Carolina," etc. New York: Geo. F. Cooledge and Brother [1846].

*The Life of the Chevalier Bayard; "The Good Knight," "Sans peur et sans reproche."* By W. Gilmore Simms. New York: Harper & Brothers, 1847. Dedication to John Izard Middleton, Esq., of South Carolina.

*Self-Development. An Oration Delivered Before the Literary Societies of Oglethorpe University, Georgia; November 10, 1847.* Milledgeville, Ga.: Thalian Society, 1847.

*Lays of the Palmetto: A Tribute to the South Carolina Regiment, in the War with Mexico.* By W. Gilmore Simms, Esq. Charleston, S.C.: John Russell, 1848.

*Charleston, and Her Satirists; A Scribblement.* By a City Bachelor. Charleston: James S. Burges, 1848. Two pamphlets [No. 1 and No. 2].

*The Cassique of Accabee. A Tale of Ashley River. With Other Pieces.* By William Gilmore Simms, Esq. Author of "Atalantis," "The Yemassee," etc. Charleston: John Russell, 1849. [Almost identical copies issued in New York with Geo. P. Putnam and Harper & Brothers imprints.]

*Father Abbot, or, the Home Tourist; A Medley.* By W. Gilmore Simms, Esq. Charleston, S.C.: Miller & Browne, 1849.

*Sabbath Lyrics; or, Songs from Scripture. A Christmas Gift of Love.* By W. Gilmore Simms. Charleston: Walker and James, MDCCCXLIX. Dedication to My Wife and The Mother of my Children [Chevillette Roach Simms].

***The Lily and the Totem, or, The Huguenots in Florida. A Series of Sketches, Picturesque***

***and Historical, of the Colonies of Coligni, in North America. 1562–1570.*** By the author of "The Yemassee," "Life of Marion," "Life of Bayard," etc. New York: Baker and Scribner, 1850. Dedication to the Hon. James H. Hammond, of South Carolina.

*Flirtation at the Moultrie House: In a Series of Letters, from Miss Georgiana Appleby, To Her Friends in Georgia, Showing the Doings At the Moultrie House, and the Events Which Took Place at the Grand Costume Ball, On the 29th August, 1850; With Other Letters.* Charleston: Edward C. Councell, 1850.

*The City of the Silent: A Poem.* By W. Gilmore Simms. Delivered at the Consecration of Magnolia Cemetery. November 19, 1850. Charleston: Walker & James, 1850 [1851].

***Katharine Walton: or, The Rebel of Dorchester. An Historical Romance of the Revolution in Carolina.*** By the author of "Richard Hurdis," "Border Beagles," "The Yemassee," "The Partisan," "Mellichampe," etc. Philadelphia: A. Hart, late Carey and Hart, 1851. [1854 Redfield edition dedicated to the Hon. Edward Frost.]

***Norman Maurice; or, The Man of the People. An American Drama.*** By W. Gilmore Simms, Author of "The Yemassee," &c. Richmond: Jno. R. Thompson, 1851. [1852 Walker & Richards edition dedicated to Henry Gourdin, Esq. of South Carolina.]

*The Golden Christmas: A Chronicle of St. John's, Berkeley. Compiled from the Notes of a Briefless Barrister.* By the author of "The Yemassee," "Guy Rivers," "Katharine Walton," etc. Charleston: Walker, Richards and Co., 1852.

***The Sword and the Distaff; or, "Fair, Fat and Forty," A Story of the South, at the Close of the Revolution.*** By the author of "The Partisan," "Mellichampe," "Katharine Walton," etc. Charleston: Walker, Richards & Co., 1852. Dedication to Joseph Johnson, M.D. Republished as *Woodcraft or Hawks about the Dovecote. A Story of the South at the Close of the Revolution.* New York: Redfield, 1854. [Now known as *Woodcraft.*]

***As Good as a Comedy: or, The Tennessean's Story.*** By an Editor. Philadelphia: A. Hart, late Carey & Hart, 1852. Dedication to Harry Placide.

***Michael Bonham: or, The Fall of Bexar. A Tale of Texas.*** By a Southron. Richmond: Jno. R. Thompson, 1852.

*South-Carolina in the Revolutionary War: Being a Reply to Certain Misrepresentations and Mistakes of Recent Writers, in Relation to the Course and Conduct of this State.* By a Southron. Charleston: Walker and James, 1853. Charleston: Courtenay, 1853.

*Marie de Berniere: A Tale of the Crescent City, Etc. Etc. Etc.* By W. Gilmore Simms, Author of "The Yemassee," "Richard Hurdis," "Guy Rivers," etc. Philadelphia: Lippincott, Grambo, and Co., 1853. Republished as *The Maroon; A Legend of the Caribbees, and Other Tales.* Philadelphia: Lippincott, Grambo & Co., 1855.

*Egeria: or, Voices of Thought and Counsel, for the Woods and Wayside.* By W. Gilmore Simms, Esq., Author of "Katharine Walton," etc. Philadelphia: E. H. Butler & Co., 1853.

***Vasconselos. A Romance of the New World.*** By Frank Cooper. New York: Redfield, 1853. Dedication to Dr. John W. Francis, of New York.

*Poems Descriptive, Dramatic, Legendary and Contemplative.* By William Gilmore Simms, Esq. New York: Redfield, 1853. Charleston, S.C.: John Russell, 1853. Two volumes.

*Southward Ho! A Spell of Sunshine.* By W. Gilmore Simms, Esq. Author of "The Yemassee"—"The Partisan"—"Mellichampe"—"Katharine Walton"—"The Scout"—"Woodcraft," etc. New York: Redfield, 1854.

***The Forayers or The Raid of the Dog-Days.*** By W. Gilmore Simms, Esq. Author of "The Partisan"—"Mellichampe"—"Katharine Walton"—"The Scout"—"Woodcraft"—"The Yemassee"—"Guy Rivers," etc. New York: Redfield, 1855. Dedication to Gen. D. F. Jamison, of Orangeburg, S.C.

***Eutaw A Sequel to The Forayers, or The Raid of the Dog-Days. A Tale of the Revolution.*** By W. Gilmore Simms, Esq. Author of "The Partisan"—"Mellichampe"—"Katharine Walton"—"The Forayers"—"The Scout"—"Woodcraft"—"Charlemont," etc. New York: Redfield, 1856. Dedication to the Hon. John Perkins, Jr., of Ashewood, Madison Parish, Louisiana.

***Charlemont or The Pride of the Village. A Tale of Kentucky.*** By W. Gilmore Simms, Esq. Author of "The Partisan"—"Mellichampe"—"Katharine Walton"—"The Forayers"—"The Scout"—"Woodcraft"—"Beauchampe," etc. New York: Redfield, 1856. Dedication to the Hon. James Hall, of Cincinnati.

***Beauchampe or The Kentucky Tragedy. A Sequel to Charlemont.*** By W. Gilmore Simms, Esq. Author of "The Partisan"—"Mellichampe"—"Katharine Walton"—"The Forayers"—"The Scout"—"Woodcraft"—"Guy Rivers," etc. New York: Redfield, 1856.

***The Cassique of Kiawah A Colonial Romance.*** By William Gilmore Simms, Esq. Author of "The Yemassee"—"The Partisan"—"Guy Rivers"—"Scout"—"Charlemont"—"Vasconselos"—etc., etc. New York: Redfield, 1859. Dedication to Hon. W. Porcher Miles, M.C.

*Simms's Poems Areytos or Songs and Ballads of the South With Other Poems.* By W. Gilmore Simms, Esq. Author of "The Yemassee," "The Cassique of Kiawah," "The Partisan," "Eutaw," "The Forayers," etc. Charleston, S.C.: Russell & Jones, 1860. Dedication to Professor James W. Miles, of South Carolina.

***Paddy McGann; or, The Demon of the Stump.*** By W. Gilmore Simms, author of "Richard Hurdis," "The Cassique of Kiawah," "Border Beagles," "The Yemassee," etc. *The Southern Illustrated News,* February 14–May 30, 1863.

*Sack and Destruction of the City of Columbia, S.C. to Which Is Added a List of Property Destroyed.* Columbia, S.C.: Power Press of Daily Phoenix, 1865.

***Joscelyn; A Tale of the Revolution.*** By W. Gilmore Simms, Esq. Author of "The Yemassee," "The Partizan" [*sic*], "The Cassique of Kiawah," &c. *The Old Guard,* V (January–December, 1867).

***Voltmeier, or The Mountain Men.*** By William Gilmore Simms. *Illuminated Western World,* VI (March 6–August 28, 1869).

***The Cub of the Panther; A Mountain Legend.*** By W. Gilmore Simms, Esq. *The Old Guard,* VII (January–December, 1869).

*The Sense of the Beautiful. An Address, Delivered by W. Gilmore Simms, before the Charleston County Agricultural and Horticultural Association (Now the Agricultural Society of South Carolina), May 3, 1870.* Charleston: The Society, 1870. [Simms rose from his sickbed to deliver this final address a month before his death.]

# Notes

## Chapter I

1. George C. Rogers, Jr., *Charleston in the Age of the Pinckneys* (Norman [1969]), p. 3.

2. See also William Gilmore Simms, "Charleston, the Palmetto City," *Harper's New Monthly Magazine,* XV (June 1857), 1–22.

3. Jay B. Hubbell, *The South in American Literature, 1607–1900* (Durham, 1954), p. 572.

4. A "William Simes" is listed as a passenger on the ship *Pennsylvania Farmer* which arrived in Charleston on January 6, 1773. Though "Simes" (or "Simmes" or "Syms") is an acceptable variant spelling of the family name, subsequent research confirms that this "Simes" could not have been the grandfather of the author. See Jean Stephenson, *Scotch-Irish Migration to South Carolina, 1772* (Strasburg, Va. [1971]), p. 72.

5. William Sims, Sr., and William Sims, Jr., were both given as heads of families, with the son living alone, and the father's family including his wife, three other females (at least two of whom were his daughters), his other three sons, and no slaves (*Heads of Families at the First Census of the United States Taken in the Year 1790: South Carolina* [Washington: Government Printing Office, 1908], p. 25). One daughter of William and Elisabeth Sims was named Jean (or Jane); another was Susan; the additional female may have been another daughter, or a white maid, since the family owned no slaves.

6. *Negrin's Directory and Almanac for the Year 1806: Containing Every Article of General Utility* (Charleston, S.C.: From J. J. Negrin's Press, No. 124, East Bay), p. 73.

7. See *Complete Index to South Carolina 1800 Census* [1973], p. 483.

8. See Gordon D. Simms, "The Long Search for the Grandparents of William Gilmore Simms" (unpublished manuscript [1978] in the author's possession).

9. *Directory for 1806,* loc. cit.; *Negrin's Directory for the Year 1807 ...* (Charleston, S.C.: From J. J. Negrin's Press, No. 106 Queen Street), pp. 100, 181. The issue is confused, not clarified, by the fact that the 1810 census of South Carolina includes a William Sims both in Lancaster and in Charleston. See *South Carolina 1810 Census Index* [1976], p. 79.

10. John Singleton had died in 1799. In the notice of his death the *City Gazette* of September 12, 1799, reported that "all who had the pleasure of his acquaintance" found him "a good and honest character, a fond father, and good husband." See Jeannie Heyward Register, compiler, "Marriage and Death Notices from the *City Gazette,*" *South Carolina Historical and Genealogical Magazine,* XXV (October 1924), 189.

11. In 1793 Thomas Singleton had signed an indenture with William and Elisabeth Sims authorizing Mrs. Sims to become a trader and dealer of merchandise. See Miscellaneous Records, Book EEE, South Carolina Archives, Order No. 11411. The Charleston directory of 1790 lists "Singleton Thomas [no occupation] 168 King-Street."

12. William Gilmore Simms, "Personal Memorabilia," Charles Carroll Simms Collection, South Caroliniana Library, University of South Carolina; hereinafter cited as *PM.* With the exception of some early partial citations by William P. Trent, this material has been previously unpublished.

13. The announcement also appeared in the *Charleston Courier* for June 2, 1804. See A. S. Salley, Jr., ed., *Marriage Notices in Charleston Courier, 1803–1808* (Columbia, S.C., 1919), p. 11. The Reverend James Malcomson, from the Belfast presbytery, moved to Charleston early in 1804 from Bethel Church, Williamsburg. He died of yellow fever later in the summer of 1804.

14. *The Letters of William Gilmore Simms,* ed. Mary C. Simms Oliphant, Alfred Taylor Odell, and T. C. Duncan Eaves, 5 vols. (Columbia, S.C., 1952–1956), I, 164. A sixth volume of *The Letters of William Gilmore Simms,* Supplement (1834–1870), ed. Oliphant and Eaves, was issued by the University of South Carolina Press in 1982. Hereinafter, citations from *Letters* will be designated *L,* followed by volume and page number within parentheses in the text.

15. John Singleton's widow had later married Jacob Gates, whom she had also apparently survived. The Charleston directories for 1813 and 1816 list "Gates, Mrs. (widow) King-st road" and "Gates, Jane, widow, e side king st. road," respectively.

16. Taped interview with Mary C. Simms Oliphant, June 20, 1978, Greenville, S.C. Between June 20, 1978, and May 11, 1979, I recorded twelve conversations with Simms's granddaughter in her home in Greenville; hereinafter cited as *MCSO,* I–XII.

17. For insight into the grandmother's influence, see *Donna Florida: A Tale* (Charleston: Burges & James, 1843), pp. 10, 12, passim.

18. *MCSO,* III.

19. Paul Hamilton Hayne, "Ante-Bellum Charleston," *Southern Bivouac,* I (October 1885), 261–62.

20. *MCSO,* V, VII.

21. In this context a quotation from a later novel is of significance. In *Border Beagles* (1840) the protagonist, Harry Vernon, advises the stage-struck Tom Horsey not to seek a career in drama in Mississippi or other border states: "I do not believe this story of theatrical establishments at Benton and other places. The country is unfit for, and unable to support them. A circus, now, would be more reasonable … I look upon the dramatic art as utterly foreign to such regions as the Yazoo. There is, as yet no settled population. The country is uncleared, and thoroughly wild; settled by squatters chiefly—without means, tastes, education, or sensibility; rude, rough people; a people peculiarly fitted for the conquest of savages and savage lands, but utterly incapable of appreciating an art so exquisite and intellectual as that of the legitimate drama. Go back, and if it be your resolute determination to seek for fame in the prosecution of your present purpose—which I would not counsel—seek it, then, where only it is to be found" (p. 159).

22. According to Simms's family history, the epigram on Jackson reads:

"Jackson is dead," cries noisy Fame;
But Truth replies, "That cannot be:
Jackson and Glory are the same,
Both born to immortality."

The other poem by the elder Simms that is recorded in family archives is an improvised barroom song: "I went to John Brown's and I sat myself down and I asked for a drink of gin tonic, but he wouldn't give me none, so I up the gun and I put a hole low through his body" (*MCSO,* I).

For an almost identical version of the "single epigrammatic verse" on Jackson, and for a slightly different account of Simms's father as "no small poet in the acceptation of those days," see Simms's letter of December 29, 1839, to James Lawson, in which he called his father "a discontented & forever wandering man" (*L,* I, 160).

23. *The Wigwam and the Cabin,* First Series (New York: Wiley & Putnam, 1845), p. 8; other citations to "Grayling" will be given by page number within parentheses in the text.

## Chapter II

1. [Jasper Adams], *A Historical Sketch of the College of Charleston, South Carolina,* first published in the *American Quarterly Register* [XII, 164–77 (1839)] n.p., n.d., p. 15; J. H. Easterby, *A History of the College of Charleston, Founded 1770* (Charleston, 1935), p. 62. Though Simms's tenure at the College of Charleston is attested to in the oral history of the family (*MCSO,* III, XII) and in the biographical sketch of Simms by Alexander S. Salley in *L,* I, lxiv, Simms himself never referred to his attendance at the

College in his extant private correspondence or published writings. Easterby's history does not list Simms in the "Alphabetical List of Students in the Grammar and English Schools, 1790–1836" (pp. 278ff.), although this omission in itself is not conclusive since the list contains no names for the years 1811 to 1823, the period during which Simms's enrollment would have occurred.

2. Evert A. Duyckinck, *National Portrait Gallery of Eminent Americans* (New York [1867?]), I, 513.

3. See also Simms's letter to Rufus Wilmot Griswold, June 20, 1841, in which he again summarized his juvenile writings (*L*, V, 356).

4. *MCSO*, VIII. The intimates of Simms in this informal club can not now be identified, but according to family tradition young Simms was depressed by the "tragedies of his boyhood where he lost one friend after another by death," including three "in close succession" (*MCSO*, III). Years later in 1839 in describing the loss of one of his children, Simms mentions "frequent afflictions of the kind from my own childhood" (*L*, I, 138), an apparent reference to these boyhood events.

The melancholy, erudite youth was much taken to wandering alone along the rivers and beaches near Charleston; and a vivid anecdote has it that once, when scolded by his grandmother for getting lost near Summerville, he responded by walking up and down the beaches in a reverie that lasted for hours (*MCSO*, III).

5. William Stanley Hoole, "Alabama and W. Gilmore Simms," *Alabama Review*, XVI (1963), 86. Hoole's research corrects the erroneous impression given by Simms's first biographer, William P. Trent, that Simms's *first* journey to the Southwest began with a sea voyage from Charleston to New Orleans. See William P. Trent, *William Gilmore Simms* (Boston and New York [1892]), pp. 14–15. Trent's reference to "some trouble with a mutinous crew" more properly applies to Simms's 1826 voyage from Charleston to New Orleans (discussed below). In "Flights to Florida, II," published in the *Charleston Courier* of March 5, 1867, Simms commented as follows on "my *first* voyage" at sea "forty years ago": "Never had man a more wretched time of it as a passenger. We were twenty-two days out, on a voyage from Charleston to New Orleans, with most miserable fare, and in most miserable weather. A succession of gales and calms; danger from water spouts; —six of them appeared before us in a single morning. We were short-handed; small-pock appeared on board; our steward died of it, and we buried him, off the Balize, a gale of wind blowing furiously all the while. We got off our course … and made a narrow escape from shipwreck; having been sucked in by the insidious currents of the Gulph, among the long reach of the Double-Headed Shot Keys." This account fits in every detail Simms's description in the *Album* of his 1826 voyage from Charleston to New Orleans. In January 1826 Simms would have been eighteen—much like the young narrator in Simms's "The Unknown Masque" who "at eighteen" paid his "first visit to the 'Crescent City'" in the "winter of 1825–26." Simms registered the impressions of his 1831 visit to New Orleans in "Notes of a Small Tourist—No. 10," published on May 17, 1831, in the *Charleston City Gazette*. Simms's statement, "New-Orleans has grown prodigiously … since 1825," seems to confirm the earlier, 1825 visit.

6. I am indebted to Professor Shillingsburg for an advance copy of her "The Senior

Simmses—Mississippi Unshrouded," forthcoming in *University of Mississippi Studies in English,* X (1992).

7. Simms recorded the experience, which took place near Tuscaloosa, in a lecture he gave in 1842 at the University of Alabama—an address later published as *The Social Principle: The True Source of National Permanence* (Tuscaloosa: The Erosophic Society, 1843).

8. First published in *Lyrical and Other Poems* (1827), "Writtten in Mississippi" is included in *Selected Poems of William Gilmore Simms,* ed. James Everett Kibler, Jr. (Athens, Ga. [1990]), pp. 8–9, 318–19. This collection is hereinafter cited as *SP.*

"The Grave in the Forest," an "extract from an unpublished narrative," appeared under the signature "By a Southron," in the 1853 issue of *The Odd Fellows' Offering.* (New York: Edward Walker); see *L,* III, 258n. For a discussion of *Vasconselos,* see chapter 8.

9. See above, chapter 1. Since, however, young Simms did visit the Southwest again in 1826, less than a year after the first journey, his confrontation with the elder Simms over Charleston could possibly have occurred at that time rather than in 1825. I choose the earlier time partly because of the establishment of his first literary magazine in Charleston in June 1825, just after his first trip, in keeping with his choice of a literary career. Whether 1825 or 1826, however, the effect on Simms's career is unchanged.

10. *MCSO,* IV. Legaré's praise for Simms's juvenile poem celebrating the Ashley River proved inspirational to the young poet, who as a boy had been fascinated by his walks along the Ashley where the Legaré estate was located. In Simms's own words, "I sang the Ashley, in heroics, a thousand lines, when I was a boy of seventeen—in heroics, by the way, which won the praise of Hugh Legaré, then one of our local literary oracles in Carolina. He loved the Ashley ... and, in his full, rotund manner, would say, 'Yes, sir, it deserves to be sung in high heroics. It is a noble and *poetical* river'" (cited in "Simms' Circle," *L,* I, cxx). Michael O'Brien, *A Character of Hugh Legaré* (Knoxville [1985]), contends, however, that although Legaré invited some young Charlestonians "to write, in the mode of himself," he "never reached out to the young William Gilmore Simms" (p. 51).

11. In the 1813 Charleston directory Giles is listed as state coroner at a King Street address; by 1819 he had become a grocer with a 19 Market Street address. See *A Directory of the City and District of Charleston ... for the Year 1813,* ed. Joseph Folker (Charleston, S.C.: Printed by B. M. Bounethear), p. 32; *The Directory and Stranger's Guide, for the City of Charleston ... For the Year 1819* (printed by A. E. Miller, 1819), p. 46.

12. Letter to John Esten Cooke, September 2, 1867, *L,* V, 85.

13. The opening number of the *Album* contains at least two writings that can be identified as Simms's—a poem entitled "Camp Meeting" and a piece of fiction called "The Robber—An Eastern Tale." Though Simms says that he published poems in the Charleston newspapers at age fifteen, these contributions have not been identified. In a recent article James E. Kibler identifies "Light Reading" from the July 27, 1824, *Charleston Courier* as Simms's "earliest prose work" ("Simms's First Published

Fiction," *Studies in Bibliography,* XLIV [1991], 377). Kibler (in an earlier work) also reveals that Simms had published a poem, "Sonnet—To My Books," when he was "16"—the pseudonym under which the sonnet appears. See James E. Kibler, Jr., *Pseudonymous Publications of William Gilmore Simms* (Athens, Ga. [1976]), p. 91, and *SP,* pp. 3, 314–15.

14. James E. Kibler, Jr., "*The Album* (1826): The Significance of the Recently Discovered Second Volume," *Studies in Bibliography,* XXXIX (1986), 66. Kibler's excellent article should be read in conjunction with John C. Guilds, "Simms's First Magazine: *The Album,*" *Studies in Bibliography,* VIII (1956), 169–83.

15. James E. Kibler, Jr., "The First Simms Letters: 'Letters from the West' (1826)," *Southern Literary Journal,* XIX (Spring 1987), 81.

16. "*The Album* (1826)," p. 70.

17. *Ibid.,* pp. 70–71.

18. The publisher and printer of the *Album* was the well-established firm of Gray & Ellis, 9 Broad Street, which probably accounts for the journal's ability to survive for almost twelve months without a sufficient number of paying subscribers (see *Album,* I, passim). More disappointing to Simms than the financial failure may have been the fact that his maiden editorial venture failed to receive mention in the contemporary Charleston press.

19. Kibler, "*The Album* (1826)," points out that Simms could not have been the journal's sole editor because he was "not in residence while most of Volume II issued from Charleston week after week" (p. 64). Kibler identifies William Allen (whom Simms recalled in his "Reminiscences of South Carolina," *XIX Century,* II [May 1870], 921–22) as "most probably a member of the editorial staff" (p. 65) as well as a regular contributor; he also speculates that James Wright Simmons (1790–1855), co-editor with Simms of the *Southern Literary Gazette* in 1828, "may have been a member of the editorial staff" (p. 65), and that publishers Gray and Ellis may have assisted editorially.

20. For a list of these contributions, see the original list in my "Simms's First Magazine" (pp. 180–83) and the supplemental list in Kibler's "*The Album* (1826)" (pp. 72–73).

21. For a discussion of *Martin Faber,* see chapter 4.

## Chapter III

1. A poem published in the *Charleston Courier,* September 5, 1826, bears the notation that it is included in *Lyrical and Other Poems* "now in press."

2. Simms was demonstrably fond of literary deception: see the discussions of *The Tri-Color* (below), *Flirtation at Moultrie House* (chapter 8), and "The Humours of the Manager" (chapter 11). In addition, as the young editor of the *Album* he invented a "celebrated saying of SYMS" for his use in making a point. See *Charleston Courier,* June 15, 1825. The chief evidence against Simms's having played a role in the "FLORIO"

review—whether actually written by him or somehow arranged for by him—is that Simms at least twice attributed it to James G. Brooks: see his letter of December 29, 1839, to James Lawson (*L*, I, 163); and his letter of December 6, 1846, to Rufus Griswold (*L*, II, 231). In both instances Simms, seemingly inordinately proud of the review, quoted from (or directly referred to) "Brooks" in support of the contention that he (Simms) was a major poet. Brooks (1801–1841), minor poet and editor, collaborated with his wife, Mary E. Brooks, in writing *The Rivals of Este, and Other Poems* (New York: J. and J. Harper, 1829), reviewed by Simms in *SLG*, I (August 1, 1829), 121–22. In 1827 James Brooks co-edited with James Lawson and John B. Skilman the *New York Morning Courier*. Brooks later moved to Winchester, Virginia, and became editor of the *Republican*. While acknowledging that "Florio" is a frequent Simms pseudonym, Kibler cautions that it "may easily mark another author's work, even in the periodicals Simms himself edited" (*Pseudonymous Publications*, pp. 9, 13n).

3. *MCSO*, II, III, VIII, XI. The eyewitness to this event of unspecified date in Summerville passed on her reminiscences to Simms's granddaughter many years later. The anecdote became a favorite among many others in the family archives relating to the author. According to unofficial family records, Simms had inherited a house in Summerville from his maternal grandfather, as well as two houses in Charleston, twenty-five slaves, and a large tract of land in Edgefield District, South Carolina (*MCSO*, VII). See also Alexander S. Salley, "William Gilmore Simms" *L*, I, lxi. If so, the description "small maternal property" (see above, chapter 1) hardly seems accurate, though it is true that the inheritance as reported above was not income-producing without skillful financial maneuvering. There are no records in Charleston or in Summerville to indicate the location of Simms's house in Summerville, assuming that he did own the residence in which he lived after his first marriage.

4. Kibler further speculates: "It is not unlikely that there was some 1827 bridge between *The Album, Or, Charleston Literary Gazette* of 1826 and *The Southern Literary Gazette* of 1828, particularly when one considers Simms's statement that he 'commenced editing' at 18 and 'continued to do so until I was 23,' in other words from 1824 to 1829. ... Although no issue of a Volume III is known, the strong possibility of its existence should not be discounted. For after all, it has taken over a century for Volume I to surface and a century and a half for Volume II" ("*The Album* [1826]," p. 63). Simmons (1790–1858) had the following publications to his credit in 1828: *Blue Beard* (Philadelphia, 1821); *Manfredi* (Philadelphia, 1821); *Julian* (n.p., n.d.); and *Valdemer; or, The Castle of the Cliff* (Philadelphia, 1822). His later writings include *De Montatt; or, The Abbey of St. Clair*, presented in the Charleston Theatre, February 2, 1843, and *The Greek Girl* (Boston, 1852). At one time Simmons was connected with the *New York Mirror*. Later he moved to Texas, became comptroller general and treasurer of the Republic of Texas, and worked for the *Galveston Banner*. He was the brother of Dr. William Hayne Simmons (1784–1870), likewise a friend of Simms.

5. See *Charleston Courier*, September 10, October 19, 1828; *City Gazette*, September 23, 1828. For a full account of the *Southern Literary Gazette*, see John C. Guilds, "William Gilmore Simms and the *Southern Literary Gazette*," *Studies in Bibliography*, XXI (1968), 59–92, and "The 'Lost' Number of the *Southern Literary Gazette*," *Studies in Bibliography*, XXII (1969), 266–73.

6. *SLG,* I, 192.

7. *SLG,* I (March 1829), 386.

8. See Guilds, "'Lost' Number," pp. 266–67. In 1968 (or 1969) James Kibler, then a graduate student at the University of South Carolina, discovered the November 1829 number among materials in the Kendall Collection of the South Caroliniana Library.

9. See Guilds, "Simms and the *SLG,*" pp. 88–91, and "'Lost' Number," p. 267.

10. "Advertisement to the Second Edition," *Martin Faber; The Story of a Criminal; and Other Tales,* 2 vols. (New York, 1837), I, xi–xii.

11. See Guilds, "'Lost' Number," pp. 268–71.

12. For discussion of the probable source of "Confessions of a Murderer," see my "Explanatory Introduction to 'Confessions of a Murderer,'" in *Stories and Tales* [vol. 5 of *The Centennial Edition of the Writings of William Gilmore Simms*], ed. John Caldwell Guilds (Columbia, 1974), pp. 563–64. Hereinafter citations of Simms's texts in *Stories and Tales* are given by page numbers within parentheses in the text of this biography; references to the Explanatory Introductions (or Notes) to the individual stories will be handled as above.

13. "Indian Sketch," *Stories and Tales,* pp. 2–3. "Indian Sketch" originally appeared in *Southern Literary Gazette,* I (November 1828), 142–49.

14. See Albert Keiser, *The Indian in American Literature* (New York, 1933), pp. 154ff. For even earlier evidence of Simms's sympathy for the Native American, see his poem "The Broken Arrow" (the date of composition of which was May 1825). This poem is included in *SP,* pp. 6–7, with extensive notes and commentary, pp. 316–18. For other studies of the Indian in American literature, see Louise K. Barnett, *The Ignoble Savage: American Literary Racism* (Westport, Conn., 1975); Roy Harvey Pearce, *Savagism and Civilization: A Study of the Indian and the American Mind,* rev. ed. (Baltimore, 1965).

15. The fact that Poe left Charleston on December 11, 1828, and that the December *Gazette* (in reality a combined December–January number) apparently was not issued until January 4 or 5, 1829, means, however, that Poe would not easily have come upon a copy unless he was a subscriber to the magazine. See William Stanley Hoole, "Poe in Charleston, S.C.," *American Literature,* VI (March 1934), 78–80; *Charleston Courier,* January 5, 1829.

16. See John C. Guilds, "Poe's 'MS. Found in a Bottle': A Possible Source," *Notes and Queries,* n.s., III (1956), 452. "A Picture of the Sea," which is unsigned in the *Gazette,* was later revised by Simms and published under his own name in the *Southern,* a magazine edited by his friend Alexander B. Meek. See "A Story of the Sea," *Southern,* I (June 1839), 329–35.

17. For example, in "The Cypress Swamp" appears the following sentence: "A heavy plunge from a bank to which we were approaching gave us the first indication of an approximation to an alligator of the largest class; while the phosphorescent qualities of the disturbed water, as it bubbled up from the interruption, flashed vividly and strangely upon our eyes" (n.s., I, 212). This passage was condensed and altered by

Simms to read in *The Partisan:* "Sometimes a phosphorescent gleam played over the stagnant pond, into which the terrapin plunged heavily at their approach ..." (*The Partisan,* Redfield edition, 1854, p. 67). Also compare the following statement from "The Cypress Swamp" with Porgy's fondness for terrapin stew (*The Partisan,* pp. 317ff.): "These terraqueous monsters [terrapins] make a most admirable condiment in the shape of a soup, of which at different times, we have liberally partaken" (n.s., I, 212).

18. See John C. Guilds, "The Literary Criticism of William Gilmore Simms," *South Carolina Review,* II (November 1969), 49–56; Edd Winfield Parks, *William Gilmore Simms As Literary Critic* (Athens, Ga., 1961).

19. There is no evidence of Simms ever composing other books of "Cain."

20. *The Poetry of William Gilmore Simms: An Introduction and Bibliography* (Columbia, S.C., 1979), pp. 50–51.

21. *Ibid.,* p. 16. In a more recent study Kibler maintains that the poet Simms "should be considered as directly at the center of the [romantic] tradition, perhaps in a way unsurpassed by any of his American contemporaries" ("Perceiver and Perceived: External Landscape as Mirror and Metaphor in Simms's Poetry," in John Caldwell Guilds, ed., *"Long Years of Neglect": The Work and Reputation of William Gilmore Simms* [Fayetteville and London, 1988], p. 121). In the introduction to *SP* Kibler reiterates that "a good case could be made" for Simms's "being the most richly diverse of all our American poets, old or new" (p. xiii).

22. This incident, though important, does not have the lasting significance given it by Trent (*Simms,* pp. 62–64) and by James A. B. Scherer ("William Gilmore Simms," *Library of Southern Literature,* ed. Edwin Anderson Alderman, Joel Chandler Harris, and Charles William Kent, 16 vols. [Atlanta, 1907], XI, 4795–96), both of whom overdramatize it as evidence of the hostility Simms encountered in Charleston throughout his life. The eyewitness account by A. P. Aldrich is reported in *MCSO,* VIII.

23. See, for instance, *Southern Literary Messenger,* IV (August 1828), 530.

24. As editor of the *City Gazette* Simms published in it a good deal of literature, including poems, essays, and book reviews from his own pen. See, for instance, the series of ten "Notes of Small Tourist," reprinted in *L,* I, 10–38.

25. Simms apparently at one time shared this house with his maternal grandmother, Jane Singleton Gates, and may have inherited it from her upon her death in 1830. As early as 1813 the Charleston directory lists "Gates Mrs. (widow) King-st road," and she continues to appear in Charleston directories intermittently under that or similar designation through 1825, after which time I have found no additional listings for her. But the 1829 directory which lists (under "Offices of Attorneys at Law") "Simms, W. G. jr. State, nearly opposite Unity alley" also lists (under "Residences ... of Charleston Neck") "Simms, William G. jr. east side King, between Ann and Mary"—a clear indication that Simms had lived at the residence before moving his offices there.

26. See Kibler, *Poetry Introduction,* pp. 62–63.

27. For instance, see the "Introduction" to the first volume of *SLG,* I, 1.

28. "Simms," *L,* I, lxvii.

29. Trent, pp. 68–69.

30. The "friend" probably was Charles Rivers Carroll, who also had taken care of Augusta at his plantation home at Clear Pond after the death of Anna Giles Simms (*MCSO,* VIII). Notwithstanding these precautions Augusta apparently became ill during her father's absence. On his first letter to Lawson upon his return to South Carolina, Simms reported, "My little girl is quite well & greatly improved ..." implying that he recently had cause for concern about her health. In the same letter, dated "Summerville, So. Ca. Oct 25 [1832]," Simms poetically described the beauty of his rural setting: "I write you from my own woods. The pines are bending with their monotonous chorus, in concert with the winds all around me. Summer still lingers, and her drapery of flowers & green leaves still carpets the ground and curtains the distance" (*L,* I, 41).

31. For a valuable study of Lawson, see Thomas L. McHaney, "An Early 19th-Century Literary Agent: James Lawson of New York," *Publications of the Bibliographical Society of America,* LXIV (Second Quarter, 1970), 177–92.

32. See *L,* V, 357.

33. Though *Atalantis* was reviewed more widely, both in North and in South, than any of Simms's earlier volumes, it was hardly either a bestseller or a critical success. See Kibler, *Poetry Introduction,* pp. 64–65.

34. The sale of the *City Gazette* to W. L. Poole took place on June 7, 1832.

## Chapter IV

1. The discussion of *Martin Faber* which begins here is almost identical to the account given in my "Explanatory Introduction to *Martin Faber,*" *Stories and Tales,* pp. 564–71.

2. See my "Textual Introduction to *Martin Faber,*" *Stories and Tales,* pp. 572–73.

3. See Guilds, "'Lost' Number," pp. 269–70.

4. J. V. Ridgely, *William Gilmore Simms* (New York [1962]), devoting some three paragraphs to *Martin Faber,* finds it a "foolish story" with "no intrinsic merit" and excludes it from serious consideration (pp. 43–44). Two earlier articles, Floyd H. Deen, "The Genesis of *Martin Faber* in *Caleb Williams,*" *Modern Language Notes,* LIX (May 1944), 315–17, and Edward Stone, "*Caleb Williams* and *Martin Faber*: A Contrast," *MLN,* LXII (November 1947), 480–83, debate the merits of Godwin as the source for Simms's book, with Stone defending Simms's "originality" and concluding that "it may seriously be doubted that Godwin's novel had any noticeable influence on the shaping of *Martin Faber*" (p. 483). Eugene Current-Garcia, "Simms's Short Stories: Art or Commercialism?" *Mississippi Quarterly,* XV (Spring 1962), 56–57, quickly dismisses

*Martin Faber* as "a fantastically implausible, self-confessed tale of murder and seduction, told by a typically Byronic figure ..." (p. 58). Worthy of note, however, is J. Wesley Thomas's excellent if brief discussion of the possible German influence on *Martin Faber,* correctly concluding that Schiller's *Der Verbrecher aus verlorener Ehre* was the probable inspiration ("The German Sources of William Gilmore Simms," *Anglo-German and American-German Crosscurrents,* I [1957], 139–40).

5. *Simms,* p. 83. Ludwig Lewisohn, "Books We Have Made," *News and Courier,* August 2, 1903, agrees with Trent. William Stanley Hoole, *A Check-List and Finding List of Charleston Periodicals, 1732–1864* (Durham, 1936), p. 35, lists Simms as the only editor. The publisher of the *Cosmopolitan* was William Estill of 212 King Street. For a fuller treatment, see John C. Guilds, "William Gilmore Simms and the *Cosmopolitan,*" *Georgia Historical Quarterly,* XLI (March 1957), 31–41, from which material for this discussion of the *Cosmopolitan* is drawn.

6. Guy A. Cardwell, Jr., "The Influence of Addison on Charleston Periodicals, 1795–1860," *Studies in Philology,* XXXV (July 1938), 467n. and J. Allen Morris, "The Stories of William Gilmore Simms," *American Literature,* XIV (March 1942), 20–35. Two of these stories—"Isabel of St. Augustine" and "The Outlaw's Daughter"—were later published as the work of "the late Edward Carroll" in the *Southern Literary Journal,* III (March 1838), 183–98, and IV (September 1838), 193–206, respectively. The third, "The White Horse: A Legend of Table Mountain," appeared under the name of Charles R. Carroll as "The Demon of Table Mountain" in *Chicora,* I (July 30, 1842), 25–26.

7. See J. Wesley Thomas, *Amerikanische Dichter und die deutsche Literatur* (Goslar [1950]), p. 78.

8. See Cardwell, "Charleston Periodicals," pp. 466–67. That Simms may have had the "Noctes Ambrosianae" in mind in determining the framework of the *Cosmopolitan* is suggested by the fact that he later considered including a Southern "Noctes" in the *Southern and Western Monthly Magazine and Review.* See his letter of December 30, 1844, to George Frederick Holmes, *L,* I, 449.

9. Trent states that Charleston was not treating Simms kindly—"for some time in 1833 he had attempted to start there a new publication somewhat after the order of 'Salmagundi,' and had dismally failed. This was 'The Cosmopolitan: an Occasional,' which seems not to have got beyond its first number [*sic*]" (*Simms,* p. 83).

10. Cardwell, "Charleston Periodicals," p. 467n, states that three issues of the *Cosmopolitan* are extant. A search through the Charleston newspapers turned up no mention of a third number, however, and the Charleston Library Society holds only the two numbers bound in a single volume.

11. Even the title *Cosmopolitan* might be taken to imply nonparticipation in local controversy.

12. *Dictionary of American Biography,* VII, 635–36. Grimké (1796–1834), a graduate of Yale and for a time the law partner of Robert Y. Hayne, was the brother of the wife of the abolitionist, Theodore Dwight Weld. The dedication to Grimké reads: "To

one-who, amidst the daily calls of a severe and arduous profession, still, with no less ability than enthusiasm, asserts the value and charms of science and letters, this little *melange* is most respectfully inscribed by THE AUTHORS."

13. For Simms's own comment, see *L*, I, 53.

14. Undated, but before July 19 because the *Courier* of that date quotes the *American* review.

15. "Dedicatory Epistle to Charles R. Carroll, Esq. of South Carolina," dated November 15, 1854, and published as the preface to the "new and revised" Redfield edition of *Guy Rivers* (New York, 1855), p. 10. In this paragraph all other quotations from this "Dedicatory Epistle" are indicated in the text page number[s] in parentheses.

16. *Guy Rivers* is set in the north Georgia region through which the Chestatee River flows. Simms's fictitious village of Chestatee, the setting for the novel, is modeled upon the gold-mining town of Auraria. See E. Merton Coulter, *Auraria: The Story of a Georgia Gold-Mining Town* (Athens, Ga. [1956]).

17. Trent, *Simms*, pp. 88–89.

18. *Simms*, p. 86.

19. See William Dean Howells, *Editor's Study*, ed. James W. Simpson (Troy, N.Y., 1983). p. 112.

20. The *New York Mirror* of August 2, 1834, announced that the author of the highly successful *Guy Rivers* was at work on another American novel (XII, 39).

21. *The Romantic Revolution in America, 1800–1860* (New York [1927]), pp. 131, 135; Vol. II of *Main Currents in American Thought*, 3 vols. (New York, 1927–30).

22. In a revised preface addressed "To Professor Samuel Henry Dickson, M.D., of South Carolina," *The Yemassee: A Romance of Carolina*, new and revised edition (New York, 1854), Simms modified his original statement, "The modern romance is a poem in every sense of the word," to read: "The Romance is of loftier origin than the Novel. It approximates the poem" (p. vi).

23. "The Influence of Scott and Cooper on Simms," *American Literature*, XXIII (May 1951), 203–18. For insightful recent studies of *The Yemassee*, see the chapter entitled "William Gilmore Simms: Writer and Hero" in Michael Kreyling, *Figures of the Hero in Southern Narrative* (Baton Rouge and London [1987]), pp. 42–47; Louis D. Rubin, Jr., *The Edge of the Swamp: A Study in the Literature and Society of the Old South* (Baton Rouge and London [1989]), pp. 103–26; and Louis D. Rubin, Jr., "The Romance of the Colonial Frontier: Simms, Cooper, the Indians, and the Wilderness," *American Letters and the Historical Consciousness: Essays in Honor of Lewis P. Simpson* (Baton Rouge and London [1987]), pp. 112–36.

24. *SQR*, XV (April 1849), 41–83.

25. In her interesting and stimulating study, *A Sacred Circle: The Dilemma of the Intellectual in the Old South, 1840–1860* (Baltimore and London, 1977), Drew Gilpin Faust explains why the Southern intellectual of whatever origin living in the South was

likely to hold these views. The intellectuals she concentrates upon in addition to Simms are Edmund Ruffin and Nathaniel Beverley Tucker, both from Virginia; George Frederick Holmes, an Englishman who lived in both South Carolina and Virginia; and James Henry Hammond of South Carolina.

26. In the opening paragraph of Chapter 6 Hector's remarks to Harrison reveal genuine concern, and a sense of personal responsibility unusual in the portrayal of a slave-master relationship are accounted for as follows: "Hector, though a slave, was a favourite, and his offices were rather those of the humble companion than of the servant" (p. 43).

27. For instance, even after there was "no longer the form of a battle array" among the Yemassee, "the negroes cleared the woods with their clubs, beating out the brains of those whom they overtook, almost without having any resistance offered them" (p. 374).

28. Not only criminals like Chorley, but also responsible white citizens like Dick Grimstead, Moll Granger, and even Gabriel Harrison display brutality while under the effects of war. After hurling Chinnabee "like a stone to the ground," the "fully aroused" Harrison stood before the now defenseless Indian and proclaimed, "Coosaw—thou are the last chief of thy people. The cunning serpent will die by the Coosah-moray-te, like the rest." To emphasize the tragedy of Chinnabee's "knife ... in ... heart" execution, the Indian's last words convey the sense that his death is actually an act of genocide; "Chinnabee is the last chief of the Coosaw—his people have gone—they wait for him with the cry of a bird. Let the pale-face strike. Ah ha!" (pp. 372–73).

29. *American Monthly Magazine,* I, n.s. (January 1836), 101–4. For other reviews of *The Partisan* in addition to Poe's discussion below, see *Graham's* XI (January 1836), 54; *Waldie's Select Circulating Library,* VI (December 15, 1835), 1–3—both of which are favorable.

30. *Cavalier of Old South Carolina: William Gilmore Simms's Captain Porgy* (Chapel Hill [1966]), p. 13. Hetherington, who confesses, "... I just happen to like Captain Porgy better than any other personage in American literature," calls Porgy "nothing less than the chief ornament and epitome—in fiction—of the old southern aristocracy" (p. viii). Hetherington further states: "The case of Simms and his Porgy is nearly unique, at least in American literature. Is there elsewhere a character, clearly its author's most inspired creation, appearing importantly in as many as six full-length novels, and by a writer of at least Simms's stature?" (p. 5). For a better balanced view, see Mary Ann Wimsatt, "Simms's Porgy, the Romance, and the Southern Revolutionary Militia," *Southern Humanities Review,* XIII (Winter 1979), 1–12.

31. See Hubbell, pp. 7–8, for an accurate account of the Virginia gentleman of Revolutionary times, a mold that Simms's Porgy fits.

32. The sequel to *The Partisan* referred to is *Mellichampe: A Legend of the Santee,* published by Harper & Brothers in 1836. For a discussion, see chapter 5.

33. See the letter of October 25, 1832, *L,* I, 42. John Street, located between Broadway and East River, was in the 1830s a highly fashionable neighborhood. Other 1832–1835 references by Simms to the courtships conducted with Lawson are found letters of

November 13 and 25, 1832; January 19, November 27, December 29, 1833; June 12, July 19, December 5, 1834; May 28, June 10, November 5 and 20, December 5, 1835.

34. In a letter of May 27, 1836, Simms gave another largely physical description of Chevillette to which he added that she "sings sweetly & plays upon piano and guitar" (*L*, I, 90). Two years after his marriage to Chevillette, it should be noted, Simms recorded the happiness he discovered in their loving relationship in a poetic tribute (entitled simply "Invocation") to his wife's "gentle nature." The opening stanza displays in conventional lines the traditional Romantic blending of idyllic love with nature:

Come, Chevillette, my own love, come with me,
No idle pomp, no bustling world, I seek;
Enough, if in the shadow of the tree,
I watch thy glistening eye and glowing cheek.
(*SP*, p. 103)

35. *MCSO*, I. Within the family Augusta was known as the "shining sword." Simms spoke of Augusta as being "very dear to me" (*L*, I, 247), "almost the only tie ... which bound me to life and society" (*L*, I, 249).

36. In addition to Simms's desire to clear up his debts before marrying, another circumstance that necessitated the postponement of the wedding between Gilmore Simms and Chevillette Roach was the recent death of her brother Govan, Nash Roach's only son. In 1833 Govan Roach had killed a close friend, John G. Adams, in a duel fought while both were students at the South Carolina College—a duel precipitated by an argument at the college supper table. Young Roach was wounded in the duel, and in addition suffered an emotional breakdown over the death of his friend. Though Govan Roach lived another two years after the duel, he never recovered from his physical and emotional wounds. The family later felt resentment toward prominent officials who had permitted the duel to take place (*MCSO*, V). See also *L*, I, 90 and 90n.

37. *MCSO*, I. See also "The Negroes at Woodlands," *L*, I, cli.

## Chapter V

1. The references to Hannibal having attained the summit of the Alps, with his ultimate goal of Rome still lying beyond, is expanded upon in the July 19, 1834, letter to Lawson: "The Alps may be passed but Rome's beyond them, and I shall not be satisfied short of a fine marble and permanent, not to say classically well-built residence in the Eternal City! So much for the love of fame, and human approbation, a terribly large development of which my head possesses" (*L*, I, 59).

2. When the revised edition was issued in 1854, Simms dedicated *Mellichampe*—"which has hitherto gone without a sponsor"—to M. C. M. Hammond. In 1839 Simms dedicated *Southern Passages and Pictures* to Bryant.

3. For a listing of known reviews of *Mellichampe*, see Keen Butterworth and James E. Kibler, Jr., eds., *William Gilmore Simms: A Reference Guide* (Boston [1980]), pp. 34–37.

4. See Stanley T. Williams, "Spanish Influences on the Fiction of William Gilmore Simms," *Hispanic Review,* XXI (July 1953), 221–28.

5. It is not certain why Simms writes "books" rather than "book." *Richard Hurdis* was the only work by Simms published by Carey & Hart in 1838, but the firm did publish *Border Beagles,* the sequel to *Richard Hurdis,* in 1840.

6. The literary histories of the American frontier display a surprising lacuna with regard to the contributions of Simms. See Edwin Fussell, *Frontier: American Literature and the American West* (Princeton, 1965); Richard Slotkin, *Regeneration Through Violence: The Mythology of the American Frontier* (Middletown, Conn., 1973); and Lucy Lockwood Hazard, *The Frontier in American Literature* (New York, 1927).

7. On August 20, 1837, Simms had written Lawson, "My publishers have just written me a doleful epistle. They are doing nothing, and doubtful when they shall do better" (*L,* I, 112).

8. See Simms's letter of August 20, 1837, to Lawson, in which he noted: "Bryant has been up at G. B. for a week. We have rambled together to the Mon. Mountain, Green River & c. and regretted you were not with us" (*L,* I, 112).

9. It is not certain whether Simms's first child by his second wife was born on the night of November 15 or in the morning of November 16. There is also some confusion about the wedding date of William Gilmore Simms and Chevillette Roach: the actual date is November 16, but the Simms family Bible records the date as November 15, 1836.

10. Nancy Kellogg of Massachusetts conducted with her two sisters "The Rose Cottage Seminary," a boarding school for girls in Great Barrington, which Augusta may have attended. According to family records, Nancy Kellogg visited Woodlands frequently and there served as Augusta's teacher.

11. As noted in *Letters,* "Miss Aldrich, recalling the incident in later years, obviously elaborated the tale as the telegraph was not in use in 1838" (*L,* I, 136n). Simms's letter of November 1838 to Lawson—the first after his return to Charleston from New York—makes clear that his passage had been by sea, not by "the earliest train." In 1856 Simms wrote that "Spiritualism as a philosophy is in more complete accordance with my own speculations, felt & pursued for 30 years, than any other system" (*L,* IV, 431).

12. "German Sources," pp. 132–33. Thomas expands upon the idea as follows: "'Carl Werner' is a Faustian story dealing with the strife between the principles of hate and love for a man's soul. ... Although the story obviously imitates the 'German manner,' it does not closely resemble any particular German tale. A possible source is suggested in the 'Advertisement' to the collection in which 'Carl Werner' appears: 'The first story in this collection is founded upon a passage from an ancient monkish legend, which the lover of antiquarian lore will most probably remember.' Simms's source may have been Hoffmann's *Die Elixiere des Teufels,* which had appeared in English translation early as 1824. ... The essentials of Simms's story—as the struggle between good and evil forces for a man's soul, the two *Doppelganger,* and the kindly priest—are all present in Hoffmann's story. The same elements, however, appear in Fouque's *Sintram,* a work which was also available to Simms in translation. The pact, which nearly causes the destruction of the hero, is, of course, reminiscent of the Faust legend" (pp. 132–33).

13. See Simms's letter of September 4, 1868, to Redfield, when in the last years of his life the author was still attempting to get the story republished (*L*, V, 157).

14. See Faust, *Sacred Circle*, p. 125; see also George Fredrickson, *The Black Image in the White Mind: The Debate on Afro-American Character and Destiny, 1817–1914* (New York, 1971).

15. See Simms's long letter of December 29, 1839, to James Lawson in which he summarized his life and literary accomplishments (*L*, I, 166).

16. Kibler, *Poetry Introduction*, p. 68; Kibler also clarifies the complicated publication history of *Southern Passages* (p. 66–67).

17. See his letters of January 3, 1839; March 30, 1839; July 7, 1839; and July 20, 1839 (*L*, I, 138–39, 140–42, 148–50, 150–52).

18. One particularly interesting review is the one written by Poe for *Burton's Gentleman's Magazine*, V (November 1839), in which he called *The Damsel of Darien* superior to *The Partisan*, greatly admired the "most meritorious" ballad "Indian Serenade," but objected to the book's bad taste and numerous "awkward or positively ungrammatical phrases" (pp. 283–85).

19. The first volume of fiction published in America to carry Simms's name on the title page was *Helen Halsey* (1845). The American edition of *The Wigwam and the Cabin* (also published in 1845) did not bear Simms's name, although some of the English and German editions of the work did. Beginning in 1841 some English editions of Simms's earlier fiction bore his name.

20. A reviewer in the *Southern Literary Journal*, in condemning the portrayal of criminal violence in Richard Hurdis, stated that the narrative was "dyed in blood" (n.s., IV [November 1838], 332–49).

21. *Guy Rivers* pictures Chub Williams, a five-foot dwarf, and *Richard Hurdis* sympathetically portrays Jane Pickett, a feeble-minded, yet attractive girl of fifteen who is the object of John Hurdis's lust.

22. See his letters to James Lawson of September 15, 1840 (*L*, I, 188); and September 28, 1840 (*L*, I, 191).

23. On February 20, 1841, Simms again mentioned to Lawson that *The Kinsmen* "is full of typographical errors" and explained why he had not read proofs: "I did not *get* the proofs [italics added]" (*L*, I, 231). The data suggest that an author's not having opportunity to read proof of his work was not an uncommon practice among American publishers of the time. Perhaps one of the reasons for Simms's customary summer trip to the North was to provide him an opportunity to proofread forthcoming publications.

24. An important difference between Lawson's and Hammond's criticisms, of course, is that Lawson made his public in print, whereas Hammond chose to keep his private in a letter to Simms. Furthermore, despite his objections, Hammond called *The Kinsmen* a "delightful" novel in which "the interest is well maintained throughout,

& there are many powerful & many piquant passages." Hammond also made the disarming statement: "But I am not a critic."

25. One of the admirers of Flora Middleton is Poe, who called her "an exquisite creation ... to be placed alongside of [G. P. R.] James's finest female characters" (*Graham's,* loc. cit.).

26. See Simms's letters of August 7 and 15, 1840, written to Lawson from Charleston (*L,* I, 181, 184). Simms apparently had in mind specifically the *Knickerbocker* and the *Democratic Review.*

27. For Clark's statement that Simms's story was among other "new communications" awaiting "the consideration which we have not as yet found leisure to award them," see "Editor's Table," *Knickerbocker,* XVI (October 1840), 368. Simms roared in his letter of October 25, 1840, to Lawson: "D——n his consideration!" (*L,* I, 193). The incident seems to have been the beginning of a feud between Clark and Simms that does little credit to either man. For fuller treatment, see John C. Guilds, "The Feud with the *Knickerbocker,*" Chapter 6 of *Simms as a Magazine Editor, 1825–1845: With Special Reference to His Contributions* (unpublished Duke University diss., 1954), pp. 175–81.

28. "Caloya; or, The Loves of the Driver" (the final title of the story as it appeared in *The Wigwam and the Cabin*) appeared in the *Magnolia* under the title "The Loves of the Driver; A Story of the Wigwam," III (May, June, July 1841), 222–29, 264–73, 317–24.

29. See *Magnolia,* III (June 1841), 286–87.

30. Parrington, *Romantic Revolution,* p. 126.

31. *Southern Literary Messenger,* IV (August 1838), 528.

32. According to Simms, *Confession* was "now in press" on October 13, 1841 (*L,* I, 281).

33. See Butterworth and Kibler, p. 50.

34. Trent, *Simms,* p. 123.

35. Ridgely, *Simms,* p. 85.

36. "Introduction," *L,* I, li.

37. "Werther on the Alabama Frontier: A Reinterpretation of Simms's *Confession,*" *Mississippi Quarterly,* XXI (Spring 1968), 130.

## Chapter VI

1. See Michael O'Brien and David Moltke-Hansen, eds., *Intellectual Life in Antebellum Charleston* (Knoxville [1986]). Much earlier, however, Jay B. Hubbell had made essentially the same point (*The South in American Literature,* pp. 70–71, 568–71).

2. Kibler, "*The Album* (1826)," p. 64.

3. Trent, *Simms*, p. 129. Hubbell's masterful commentary on Charleston in *The South in American Literature* pointed out, however, that Charlestonians read more, not less, than most Americans, Northern or Southern (p. 570).

4. One of the most descriptive accounts of Simms's speaking ability is the following: "Few persons who have heard Mr. Simms upon public occasions—who have listened to his sonorous voice, and the stormy music of his animated and rolling periods—will have any doubt upon the subject of his capacity for the law. His mind is eminently *judicial;* his career at the bar, or in politics, would, in all probability, have outshone his present fame as an author" (*Cosmopolitan Art Journal,* III [December 1859], 212–14). See also the comments of Benjamin F. Perry quoted below in this chapter.

5. The phrase *gentleman planter-turned-statesman* is intended to be broad enough to include "editor" and "lecturer" as well as "politician/diplomat" as used in this chapter.

6. The full title is *The Sources of American Independence. An Oration, on the Sixty-ninth Anniversary of American Independence; Delivered at Aiken, South Carolina, Before the Town Council and Citizens Thereof* (Aiken: Town Council, 1844).

7. In a letter of January 29, 1842, Simms had jokingly anticipated his role during Hammond's governorship: "Have you any counsel? Will you, in return, for taking yours so readily, make me one of your Privy Council when you arrive at the Chair of State. I shall try & look sage whenever a fool cometh" (*L,* I, 300).

8. In 1979 Simms's granddaughter, Mary C. Simms Oliphant, in a discussion of family history, emphasized that during Simms's time "no matter how distinguished you were, you were not a Southern gentleman unless you were a planter" (*MCSO,* VIII).

9. Under President Tyler, John C. Calhoun had served as secretary of state. Instead of reappointing him as expected, President Polk offered the powerful South Carolina statesman the ambassadorship to the Court of St. James, which Calhoun refused to accept.

10. *The Politics of a Literary Man: William Gilmore Simms* (Westport, Conn., 1973), p. 103.

11. See the *Mountaineer* for November 13, 1846, and the *South Carolinian* for November 28, 1846.

12. In a letter of October 20, 1847, to Hammond, Simms remarked: "I am greatly obliged to you for your thoughtful friendship in the matter of the foreign mission. I have never sought to disguise … , that such an appointment would be equally agreeable & serviceable to me" (*L,* II, 353).

13. See Simms's letter of November 22, 1847, to Hammond (*L,* II, 373).

14. Simms to Hammond, [c. January 2, 1848]; (*L,* II, 388).

15. Simms to Lawson, November 9 [1848]; (*L*, II, 451).

16. Simms to Lawson, November 24 [1849]; (*L*, II, 570).

17. See Simms's letters of October 31, 1851, and July 25, 1857 (*L*, II, 150, 505). In the 1857 letter to James Lawson, Simms remarked: "I have lately been offered the Presidency of a college, with $3,000, but must decline" (*L*, III, 505). Longstreet accepted the appointment as president of South Carolina College in November 1857.

18. For the best and most complete account, see Miriam J. Shillingsburg, "Simms's Failed Lecture Tour of 1856: The Mind of the North," *Long Years of Neglect*, pp. 183–201; for an earlier study, see Merrill G. Chrisopherson, "Simms's Northern Speaking Tour in 1856: A Tragedy," *Southern Speech Journal*, XXXVI (Winter 1970), 139–51.

19. Josiah James Evans served as South Carolina's junior senator from 1853 until his death in 1858. The inept senior senator, Butler, who bore the personal brunt of Sumner's attack, was elderly and in poor health. He died in office on May 15, 1857.

20. "Though Simms could not know it in 1856, attitudes in the press about his lectures would subsequently be applied also to his fiction" (Shillingsburg, p. 199).

21. Among the cities covered by his Southern lectures in 1857 were Washington, D.C., in early February; Baltimore, on February 10; Norfolk, on February 12, 13, 16; Petersburg, on February 18 and 19; Richmond, on February 24; Raleigh, on February 27, 28 and March 2, 3; Greensboro, on March 4, 6; and Augusta, c. April 15 or 16. The manuscript of "Antagonisms of the Social Moral. North and South," still unpublished, is housed in the Charles Carroll Simms Collection, South Caroliniana Library.

22. The impact of his inability or unwillingness to focus exclusively on literature and the question whether it did disservice to his achievement as writer will be discussed in the final chapter.

## Chapter VII

1. See Charles S. Sydnor, *The Development of Southern Sectionalism, 1819–1848* (Baton Rouge, La., 1948), pp. 222–48. A particularly enlightening explication of a scholarly Southerner's view that "slavery had been foisted upon the South by the traders and merchants of Europe and the North" appears in Michael O'Brien, *A Character of Hugh Legaré* (Knoxville [1985]), p. 163.

2. *Magnolia*, n.s., I (August 1842), 68–69. The writer blamed the British East India company for much of New England's antislavery sentiments.

3. Although the *Southern Quarterly Review* was much less literary and much more political in subject matter than the *Magnolia* or the *Southern and Western*, both of which featured original poetry and fiction, all three magazines can be classified as literary in the sense that good writing was emphasized and literary works and ideas were regularly reviewed.

4. *Magnolia,* III (January 1841), 1–3.

5. Early in 1842, when the *Magnolia* was still published in Savannah, Simms had agreed to lend support to Pendleton as co-editor.

6. Frank Luther Mott, *A History of American Magazines, 1741–1850* (New York and London, 1930) estimates that the number of American magazines increased from "less than a hundred" in 1825 to "about six hundred" in 1850 (pp. 341–42).

7. Quoted in Henry A. Beers, *Nathaniel Parker Willis* (Boston, 1885), p. 260. *Graham's* prices, which became a kind of standard, ranged from four to twelve dollars a page for prose, and from ten to fifty dollars for poems, with occasional much higher rates for famous contributors. See Mott, p. 506.

8. For a well-balanced account of the relative increase in importance of the periodical and the relative decrease in importance of the book as a means of livelihood for the professional writer, see the work of William Charvat, *Literary Publishing in America, 1790–1850* (Philadelphia, 1959); *The Profession of Authorship in America, 1800–1870: The Papers of William Charvat,* ed. Matthew J. Bruccoli ([Columbus] 1968); and "The People's Patronage," *Literary History of the United States,* ed. Robert E. Spiller and others (New York, 1948), 3 vols., I, 513–25.

9. These include *American Monthly Magazine, Godey's Lady's Book, Knickerbocker, Ladies' Companion, Democratic Review, Roberts' Semi-Monthly Magazine, Boston Notion,* and *New York Mirror* in the North; and *Southern Literary Messenger, Southern Rose, Southern Literary Journal, Family Companion and Ladies' Mirror, Southern Ladies' Book, Magnolia: or Southern Monthly,* and probably others in the South.

10. See his letter of August 16, 1841, to Hammond, in which Simms asserted: "I am not my own master. I am in debt" (*L,* I, 271).

11. Rufus Griswold was paid a thousand dollars a year as an editor of *Graham's* in 1842. Simms could hardly have demanded as much from a Southern periodical, but his close association with Northern editors, publishers, and writers probably kept him acquainted with what the more prosperous magazines were paying. There is no real evidence as to what salary Simms was offered. For a discussion of editors' pay, see Mott, pp. 512–13.

12. The circular is dated "Charleston, June, 1842," and is signed "P. C. PENDLETON, BURGES & JAMES, Proprietors."

13. *Magnolia,* n.s., I (July 1842), 63.

14. See the "Prospectus" in the back of each number of the *Southern Literary Messenger,* VIII (1842).

15. See "Literary Circular" reprinted on the back cover of *Magnolia,* n.s., I (July 1842), 63.

16. See Mott, pp. 348–54; Herbert Ross Brown, *The Sentimental Novel in America, 1789–1860* (Durham, N.C., 1940), passim.

17. See *Democratic Review,* XV (September 1844), 247. For further discussion of Young Americans, see chapter 8.

18. Mott, p. 351, points out that *Godey's Lady's Book* was probably the most popular and most influential magazine in mid-nineteenth-century America.

19. In August 1842 Simms expressed this same sentiment in his next letter to Holmes: "The papers on Athens & Greek literature will be acceptable, only do not encumber them with notes or learning. ... Magazine Literature requires *results,* not processes" (*L,* I, 319).

20. Even as late as 1857 the newly founded *Atlantic Monthly* did not at first give the names of authors of articles.

21. In 1851 as editor of the *Southern Quarterly Review,* however, Simms questioned whether magazines like the *Knickerbocker* were able to pay competitive prices.

22. As editor of the *Magnolia: or Southern Monthly* (as the magazine was called immediately before its move from Macon to Charleston in June 1842), P. C. Pendleton had put into effect what he termed "the English plan" of printing novels and other longer works in monthly installments. To inaugurate the new policy Pendleton was able to obtain William A. Caruthers' best novel, *The Knights of the Golden Horse-Shoe,* which appeared monthly January through October 1841.

23. *Magnolia,* n.s., I (August 1842), 128. Simms may have had in mind certain harsh reviews of his own books—Poe's of *The Partisan,* for example, for which he never fully forgave Poe.

24. *Magnolia,* n.s., I (September 1842), 200.

25. For another expression of the same idea, see *Magnolia,* n.s., I (August 1842), 128. Thomas Holley Chivers, Henry Rootes Jackson, Mary E. Lee, Alexander Means, Alexander B. Meek, Albert Pike, D. Henry Robinson, James Wright Simmons, Richard Henry Wilde, William A. Caruthers, Elizabeth Fries Ellet, J. Edward Henry, George Frederick Holmes, Benjamin F. Perry, John Tomlin, and A. B. Longstreet were perhaps the most notable Southern writers who contributed to the *Magnolia.* If Simms overrated this group, it nevertheless represented a nucleus of Southerners interested in the creation of a literature.

26. See *Magnolia,* n.s., I (September 1842), 200.

27. *Magnolia,* n.s., I (November 1842), 328.

28. For the essay, incorporated in the "Editorial Bureau," see *Magnolia,* n.s., I (November 1842), 324–27; for the poem, entitled "The Sainted Sister," see the same number, p. 310.

29. Once for instance, Simms unintentionally offended a contributor (Robert M. Charlton) while actually attempting to flatter him. See *Magnolia,* n.s., II (March 1843), 203 and Simms's undated letter to I. K. Tefft, *L,* I, 345.

30. Simms delivered an oration, *The Social Principle: The True Source of National*

*Permanence,* at the University of Alabama, December 13, 1842, at which time he was awarded an honorary LL.D. degree.

31. *Magnolia,* n.s., I (December 1842), 396.

32. *Graham's Magazine,* for instance, had praise for the *Magnolia* and said of its editor: "No man in the south is so well qualified for the office" (XXI [August 1842], 108). The *Orion* stated, "... this magazine has improved vastly since the accession of Mr. Simms to the editor's chair. ... The Magnolia appears to have found a genial soil in Charleston and bids to flourish well" (II [January 1843], 187).

33. See *Magnolia,* n.s., I (November 1842), 328.

34. Some years earlier, for example, Bartholomew R. Carroll, editor of the *Southern Literary Journal,* had been outspoken in charging the failure of his magazine to the negligence of its supporters, both subscribers and contributors. See *Southern Literary Journal,* n.s., IV (December 1838), 474–75.

35. Perhaps, too, the launching of the *Southern Quarterly Review* in 1842 had something to do with Simms's decision to give up the *Magnolia.* The *Quarterly* was moved to Charleston in January 1843.

36. It perhaps should be noted that all Southern magazines, in spite of their titles, were local and represented not the whole South but certain Southern states or regions of two or three states. The circulation of the *Magnolia* probably was limited chiefly to South Carolina and Georgia, although its contributors came from all sections.

37. See John C. Guilds, "Simms as Editor and Prophet: The Flowering and Early Death of the Southern *Magnolia,*" *Southern Literary Journal,* IV (Spring 1972), 69–92.

38. For the most complete listing of Simms's known pseudonyms, see James E. Kibler, Jr., *Pseudonymous Publications of William Gilmore Simms* (Athens, Ga., 1976).

39. "Our South-Western Writers, Part I. Mrs Caroline Lee Hentz," *Magnolia,* n.s., II (June 1843), 357–63, and "The Knickerbocker for April," *Magnolia,* n.s., I (August 1842), 109–14.

40. The pen names and the number of poems so signed are "Childe Hazard," eight; "Spiridion," six; "Pierre Vidal," four; "Wesley," two; "Delta" or "D," two; "M. E. S.," one; and "S.," one.

41. It should be added that one poem signed "Vidal" had appeared in the *Southern Literary Gazette.*

42. For instance, "Donna Florida," which appeared in the *Magnolia* in three installments, was expanded and published in book form in 1843.

43. Bryant called Simms's essay on Cooper "a critical essay of great depth and discrimination, to which I am not sure that any thing hitherto written on the subject is fully equal" (*Homes of American Authors* [New York, 1853], p. 262).

44. Despite the fact that William C. Richards, editor of the *Orion,* spoke rather derisively of Simms at times, Simms remained a faithful contributor to the magazine. In

the 1844 volume appeared his "The Moral Character of Hamlet" in four installments (March, April, May, and June) and "The Hermytte of Drowsiehedde" in two installments (July and August), in addition to "Ballad" signed "Claude" and probably other unsigned poems. Richards was also publisher of the *Orion,* which was issued from Penfield, Georgia, but was actually printed in New York until March 1844, when the business was shifted to Burges & James in Charleston.

For a somewhat fuller account of the *Southern and Western Monthly Magazine and Review* than can be adapted to this biography, see John C. Guilds, "Simms and the *Southern and Western,*" *South Carolina Journals and Journalists,* ed. James B. Meriwether (Columbia, S.C., 1975), pp. 45–59, from which much of the material of the following pages is drawn.

45. But whatever the reason for its choice, the cumbersome title came in for ridicule from word-economizer Edgar Allan Poe. In commentary on the news that the *Orion* was to be merged with a new magazine to be edited by Simms, Poe remarked in the *New York Evening Mirror:* "We must be permitted to doubt ... whether he [Simms] has been at all concerned in selecting the name of the new journal. The Southern and Western Monthly Magazine and Review is assuredly a speech if anything" (February 3, 1845; quoted in William Doyle Hull, II, "A Canon of the Critical Works of Edgar Allan Poe, with a study of Poe as Editor and Reviewer" [University of Virginia Ph.D. thesis, 1941], p. 466).

46. Actually, in format the two journals were quite dissimilar. Though both magazines normally contained seventy-two pages per issue, the pages of the *Magnolia* were larger than those of *SWMMR.* The *Magnolia* was printed in double columns; *SWMMR* was superior in typography: though the print for both magazines was the same size, that of *SWMMR* was clearer and more widely spaced.

47. See *Broadway Journal,* I (February 1, 1845), 77. Simms did not answer Briggs in print, but in his letter of March 15, 1844, to Duyckinck, he commented: "I see your Mr. Briggs does not like us. I mortally offended his *amour propre ...*" (*L,* II, 41–42).

48. *Godey's Lady's Book,* XXX (March 1845), 144. For another favorable review of the *Southern and Western* in *Godey's,* see the June 1845 number (XXX, 821).

49. *New York Morning News,* March 29, 1845. I am indebted to the late Mary C. Simms Oliphant for transcripts of the reviews from the *Morning News* and the *Weekly News.*

50. *SWMMR,* II (November 1845), 345–46.

51. The circulation of the *Southern and Western* was small in comparison with that of the more popular Northern magazines. *Graham's,* for instance, boasted a circulation of forty thousand in 1842 (See *Graham's,* XX [March 1842], 154), though the figure may be inaccurate. See Mott, p. 552. According to Herman E. Spivey, the *Knickerbocker*'s smallest circulation between 1835 and 1846 "had been about five thousand" ("Poe and Lewis Gaylord Clark," *PMLA,* LIV [December 1939], 1131).

52. See James E. Kibler, Jr., "Legaré's First Poems and His Early Career," *Southern Literary Journal,* VI (1973), 70–76.

53. "Poet, Painter and Inventor: Some Letters by James Mathewes Legaré, 1823–1859," *North Carolina Historical Review,* XXI (July 1944), 215. Davis has called *Orta-Undis* (1848), Legaré's only published book, "one of the better volumes of poetry to have appeared in the ante-bellum South" ("A Letter from the Muses: The Publication and Critical Reception of James M. Legaré's 'Orta-Undis, and Other Poems' [1848]," *North Carolina Historical Review,* XXVI [October 1949], 418). Legaré's poems, by title and date of publication in *SWMMR,* are "Miserere" (July 1845), "Quae Carior?" (December 1845), and "Toccoa" (November 1845); Legaré also published a prose piece, "Going to Texas," in the December 1845 number.

54. For a discussion of the unusual financial agreement Lowell and his partner, Robert Carter, made with their publishers, see Sculley Bradley, "Introduction," *The Pioneer: A Literary Magazine,* Scholars' Facsimiles & Reprints (New York, 1947), pp. ix–x. The *Pioneer* ceased publication after three numbers.

55. Two of Simms's children—Gilmore and Augusta—were in poor health, and Mrs. Simms was pregnant with Valerie Govan Simms, born August 10, 1845.

56. In the "Editorial Bureau" for November 1845, Simms wrote: "Our recent visit to the North necessarily took us frequently among publishers. With some few axes of our own to grind, we naturally looked a little among the doings of other workmen, co-laborers in letters and the arts" (*SWMMR,* II, 347).

57. See Simms's letter of December 24, 1847, to James Henry Hammond for an indication of the writer's dissatisfaction with his lot as a Southern man of letters (*L,* II, 385–96).

58. On the preceding day Simms had written Lawson: "I withdraw from the Magazine at the close of the present volume, and the work will be united with the Messenger. Minor has bought out our publishers. I have agreed to do his critical department" (*L,* II, 109). For the publishers' announcement of the sale of the *Southern and Western,* see the back cover of the November 1845 number. Notwithstanding his statements to the contrary, the work that Simms did for the *Southern and Western Literary Messenger and Review* (the unwieldy title was dropped in 1847) was apparently that of a contributor, not that of an editor.

59. Actually the October number is the only issue to which Simms apparently contributed nothing but the "Editorial Bureau." The following can be ascribed to the editor: September—"The Child Angel," "The Maiden's First Dream of Love," "Elodie—A Ballad," "Stanzas," "Bayard, the Chevalier," and "The Epochs and Events of American History ..."; November—"Kaatskill," "Come Out to Play," "Hast Thou a Song for Flower," and "The Huguenot Settlements in Florida: Stephen Le Genevois." Unquestionably Simms had these contributions prepared before he visited the North in late August, September, and early October 1845.

60. In the December 1845 *SWMMR* (the final issue) Simms gracefully bowed out as editor and wished the "new" *Southern and Western Literary Messenger and Review* every success: "It deserves our support, and will assert and sustain our interests" (II, 421).

61. Earlier, Simms said in a letter of November 22, 1842, to B. F. Perry: "... you were never more right than when you said I differ with the poetical criticism of the Quarterly. In truth *entre nous*, I regard it as very wretched & very ignorant in all its literary criticisms" (*L*, I, 334).

62. See Simms's letter to Holmes, April 17, 1844; *L*, I, 414.

63. On July 20, 1843, Simms had written G. F. Holmes: "Periodical literature, particularly that of the Reviews, is not very successful in the South, or even in America" (*L*, I, 362).

64. On March 29, 1844, Simms wrote Holmes that "Whitaker's case is hopeless. He is incorrigible. With the present number I cease writing for his work altogether" (*L*, I, 411)—a resolution which Simms did not follow.

65. On November 2, 1848, Simms remarked in a letter to Lawson: "Some talk of my going into Editorial harness, but mum" (*L*, II, 449).

66. Included in *SQR*'s "objects in politics" Simms listed "the promotion of Free Trade,—the maintenance of state Rights—the arrest of centralism,—and the assertion of our institutions, morally as well as socially."

67. For example, see his letter of March 2, 1851, to N. B. Tucker: "My Toils are incessant also. You need not be told that we can seldom rely upon the punctuality of amateur writers, and ... I am frequently compelled to turn in & write doggedly to fill out a number" (*L*, III, 94).

68. Burges was publisher of the *Quarterly* throughout Simms's first year as editor, but upon his death in April 1850, Walker and Richards (later to become Walker and Burke) became publishers. In January 1854 C. Mortimer replaced Walker and Burke as publisher.

69. See, for instance, his letter of c. February 25, 1849, to Hammond quoted above in this chapter.

70. On September 18, 1849, J. H. Hammond wrote to his brother, M. C. M. Hammond: "I feel greatly for [Simms], condemned to drudge, when he is qualified to soar ..." (*L*, II, 547n).

71. On April 13, 1850, Simms remarked to Holmes: "We commence a new series, & in excellent style, typographically" (*L*, II, 33). Later, on May 8, 1850, Simms wrote in more detail to Nathaniel Beverley Tucker; "The Review has passed into new hands, and the first number of a new series ... exhibits some improvement. There is still much to be done before any of us can be satisfied with it. The work needy; our planters pay slowly. ... We need a good proof reader in especial, and are making efforts to find the proper person. Hitherto, the Review has been kept up by occasional appropriation on the part of friends. Our hope hereafter, is to see it go alone. Of this, the prospect improves" (*L*, II, 39–40).

72. See Simms to J. H. Hammond, June 20, 1853; *L*, III, 239. Hammond had strongly advised Simms against sinking capital in either the *Southern Quarterly Review* or the

*Evening News:* "You must not quit it [*SQR*] if you can well avoid it—much less must you buy it or in my opinion the News" (Hammond to Simms, c. August 5, 1852; *L*, III, 239n).

73. See above, chapter 5.

## Chapter VIII

1. During the period between 1842 and 1859 Simms's family was marked by tragedy numerous times: the death of Mary Derrille Simms ("youngest of my two surviving children") in April 1842; the death of Valerie Simms, age thirteen months, on September 20, 1846; the loss of a stillborn son on April 25, 1853; the affliction of three Simms children in the yellow fever epidemic of October–November 1845 (all survived); the death of his father-in-law, Nash Roach, on February 28, 1858; and the deaths of Sydney Roach Simms and Beverley Hammond Simms, "my two brave beautiful boys," by yellow fever "within twelve hours of each other" on September 22, 1858. Between 1843 and 1859 eight children were born of the Simmses, and at the end of 1859 a total of six were still living—Augusta (born of his first wife), William Gilmore III, Chevillette, Govan Singleton, Harriet Myddleton, and Sydney Hammond, in chronological order by age. See "The Children of William Gilmore Simms," Appendix I.

2. *Painting as a Pastime* (New York [1965]), pp. 7–8.

3. See Simms's letters to James Lawson on August 16 and September 10, 1841, *L*, I, 267, 277–78. On October 31, 1841, Simms again wrote to Lawson: "I have been very busy on Beauchampe—writing myself half blind & not done yet" (*L*, I, 282).

4. Poe used the "Kentucky Tragedy" as the basis for *Politan: a Tragedy*, though he chose to set the blank verse drama in sixteenth-century Rome; Poe published selected scenes of *Politan* in the *Southern Literary Messenger* in 1835–36, but the work remained in manuscript until 1923, when Thomas Olive Mabbott prepared a scholarly edition. Chivers based his verse drama, *Conrad and Eudora* (1834), upon the sensational events; and Hoffman's novel, *Grayslaer* (1840), was yet another version. In the twentieth century Robert Penn Warren revived the saga in his acclaimed novel, *World Enough and Time* (1952), a rendering superior to the earlier versions, of which Simms's is the best. For additional information see Willard Jillson, "The Beauchampe-Sharp Tragedy in American Literature," *Register of Kentucky State Historical Society*, XXXVI (1938), 54–60; and W. B. Gates, "William Gilmore Simms and the Kentucky Tragedy," *American Literature*, XXXII (May 1960), 158–66. The most recent and most thorough study is William Goldhurst, "The New Revenge Tragedy: Comparative Treatments of the Beauchampe Case," *Southern Literary Journal*, XXII (Fall 1989), 117–27. Goldhurst calls Simms's treatment "the most intelligent, rounded, and interesting" (p. 127).

5. For a discussion of Simms's 1856 version of *Beauchampe*, see below in this chapter.

6. See, for instance, *New World*, IV (April 2, 1842), 224, and the *Charleston Mercury* for April 23, 1842, for brief but generally favorable notices. The *Mercury* cites unnamed

Northern critics who pronounce *Beauchampe* "too horrible ... tragic beyond the reach of sympathy" (p. 2).

7. *The Social Principle* was published in Tuscaloosa by the Erosophic Society of the University of Alabama; *The Geography of South Carolina* in Charleston by Babcock; and *Donna Florida* in Charleston by Burges & James.

8. *Count Julian; or, The Last Days of the Goth: A Historical Romance* was published in Baltimore and New York by William Taylor in 1845. Having conceived of the idea of a story "founded on the apostacy of Count Julian" when "I was 17–18" (see above, chapter 2), Simms had begun work on *Count Julian* again in 1838 or 1839, but the unfinished manuscript was lost for at least two years (see *L*, I, 142n) before Simms recovered it and decided to "bestir myself with the conclusion" (Simms to Lawson, January 6, 1845; *L*, II, 12). Simms dedicated the book to John Pendleton Kennedy, who graciously acknowledged the honor in a letter of March 18, 1846 (*L*, II, 159–60n). Willis Gaylord Clark, however, in a scathing review of *Count Julian,* sarcastically chided Simms for linking a worthy name to an unworthy book (*Knickerbocker,* XXVII [April 1846], 356–57).

An interesting anecdote, one of several concerned with the author's psychic experiences, centers on the "loss" of the *Count Julian* manuscript. According to family tradition, Simms was advised by a spiritual medium near the New York docks not to travel from New York to Charleston on a certain ship on which he had already booked passage. Simms consequently canceled his passage, but was unable to retrieve the manuscript. "The ship did go down off Cape Hatteras and *Count Julian* was washed up somewhere on the shores and was finally published" (*MCSO,* I). In 1841 Simms referred to the manuscript of *Count Julian* as "the work which was lost so long & has now only recently been restored to me" (*L*, I, 281).

9. *The Life of Francis Marion* (New York: Henry G. Langley, 1844) was rather widely (and at times favorably) reviewed; but, other than providing its author excellent background for his Revolutionary Romances, it has little literary value. It should be noted, however, that from a historical viewpoint, Simms as a biographer has received recognition. See Edward H. O'Neill, *A History of American Biography, 1800–1935* (Philadelphia, 1935), pp. 29–30, 54; J. W. Webb, "Simms as Biographer," *University of Mississippi Studies in English,* II (1961), 111–24; and Peter L. Shillingsburg, "The Uses of Sources in Simms's Biography of Francis Marion" (unpublished University of South Carolina master's thesis, 1967).

10. In his review of *The Wigwam and the Cabin* Poe has high praise for Simms as an author and lists *Castle Dismal* among his "best fictions" (*Broadway Journal,* II [October 4, 1845], 190–91). Trent was impressed that Poe "praised this story highly, and as its theme lay in Poe's own province, his opinion is entitled to carry much weight"; but Trent added—"a modern reader, however, might be inclined to set less store by the supernatural portions of the story than by the description of the old homestead from which it took its name" (p. 150).

11. See his letter of January 10, 1863, to John Reuben Thompson, *L*, IV, 420.

12. Simms to Lawson, February 15, 1844: "You are quite at liberty to dispose of the

other tale [*Helen Halsey*] at the same price [as *Castle Dismal*] to Stringer. My object is to get them off of my hands without positively giving them away" (*L*, I, 404). Apparently Simms received a hundred dollars apiece for the two books; on April 30, 1844, he stated to Lawson: "I should like to get my $100 for the latter" (*L*, I, 416–17).

13. Note, however, that Poe included *Helen Halsey* among Simms's "best fictions" in his famous review of *The Wigwam and the Cabin* in the *Broadway Journal* for October 4, 1845.

14. The PROSPECTUS, dated "Charleston, S. C. July 15, 1841," began, "SAMUEL HART, Sen. proposes to publish in Charleston, by subscription, 'THE CHARLESTON BOOK,'" and listed by name sixty-eight "of our citizens" who "form but a part of our list of Authors." For a modern reprint, see David Moltke-Hansen, "Introduction," *The Charleston Book: A Miscellany in Prose and Verse*, edited by William Gilmore Simms (Spartanburg, S.C., 1983).

15. "Simms, Charleston, and the Profession of Letters," *Long Years of Neglect*, p. 219. The quoted passage is repeated almost verbatim in Rubin's *The Edge of the Swamp*, pp. 88–89.

16. Though 1845 appears on the title page of both volumes of *The Wigwam and the Cabin* (called First Series and Second Series), the second volume was actually published in February 1846. The publisher was the New York firm of Wiley and Putnam.

17. *Helen Halsey* and *Castle Dismal*, we have seen, were published in 1844 and 1845, respectively, as separate books. The other five stories, however, were included in the first volume (series) of *The Wigwam and the Cabin.* Between 1838 and 1847 Harper & Brothers did not publish any book by Simms. The reference to "such a book as Fay's" is to Theodore S. Fay, *Hoboken: A Romance of New York*, 2 vols., published by Harper & Brothers in 1843.

18. New York publisher Burgess, Stringer—publisher of both *Castle Dismal* and *Helen Halsey.*

19. This original plan helps to explain why the picturesquely named *The Wigwam and the Cabin*—a perfect title for a book dealing with the frontier—contains some stories ("Grayling" perhaps being the most notable) for which the title does not seem entirely appropriate.

20. He continued to badger Lawson to persuade Burgess, Stringer to make a commitment. See, for instance, Simms's letters of November 19 [1844] and January 6 [1845] (*L*, I, 443; II, 12).

21. *Views and Reviews in American Literature, History and Fiction*—see the discussion below in this chapter.

22. See Simms's letters of June 8, June 25, August 7, and August 8, 1845, to Duyckinck (*L*, II, 74, 44–49, 96, 98); also his letter of June 27, 1845, to Lawson (*L*, II, 84).

23. See *Broadway Journal*, I (September 20, 1845), 168.

24. That Duyckinck had written Simms about the possibility of his reviewing Poe's

book is made manifest by Simms's response of June 25, 1845: "The Tales of Poe have not come to hand, though I have nos. 1 & 3 of the American Series. I have every disposition to do him justice" (*L*, II, 78). Simms's penetrating analysis of *Tales* appeared in the December 1845 number of *Southern and Western Monthly Magazine and Review*. In it Simms stated: "... we have read with delight the fine artistic stories of Mr. Edgar A. Poe,—a writer of rare imaginative excellence, great intensity of mood, and a singularly mathematic directness of purpose, and searching analysis, by which the moral and spiritual are evolved with a progress as symmetrical, and as metrical, and as duly dependent in their data and criteria, as any subject matter however inevitable, belonging to the fixed sciences. Certainly, nothing more original, of their kind, has ever been given to the American reader. Mr. Poe is a mystic, and rises constantly into an atmosphere which as continually loses him the sympathy of the unimaginative reader. But, with those who can go with him without scruple to the elevation to which his visions are summoned, and from which they may all be beheld, he is acknowledged master,—a Prospero, whose wand is one of wonderful properties. That he has faults are [*sic*] beyond question, and some very serious ones, but these are such only as will be insisted upon by those who regard mere popularity as the leading object of art and fiction" (II, 426–27).

25. Simms to Duyckinck, February 9 [1846]; *L*, II, 144–45.

26. Both the *Yemassee* and *Norman Leslie* were published by Harper and Brothers in 1835. In 1845 Theodore S. Fay (1807–1898) was an editor of the *Evening Mirror*.

27. See *Magnolia*, III (January 1841), 1; (February 1841), 69–74; and (April 1841), 189–90, reprinted in *L*, II, 196–208, 215–28, 236–40.

28. Though labeled a "new and revision edition," the 1856 reissue of *The Wigwam and the Cabin* used the original plates with no revisions whatsoever. Citations to *The Wigwam and the Cabin* are given by page numbers within parentheses or brackets in the text.

29. For a differing view, see Miriam J. Shillingsburg, "The Maturing of Simms's Short Fiction: The Example of 'Oakatibbe,'" *Mississippi Quarterly*, XXXVIII (Spring 1985), 99–117. That Simms himself was aware that his philosophical elaborations had not enhanced the slim narrative style of the original "Indian Sketch" is indicated by his comment to Sarah Drew Griffin: "I am sorry that Oakatibbe does not please you. ... You are aware that the story was meant to be a subservient to the argument" (*L*, VI, 36).

30. "Introduction," p. ix.

31. See *Knickerbocker*, XXVI (October 1845), 378; XXVII (March 1846), 273–74; XXVII (April 1846), 354–59. The starting point for the verbal hostilities was an article entitled "American Humor" (by William Alfred Jones) in the *Democratic Review* for September 1845 (XVII, 212–19), which took into account Simms's essay on Mathews as originally published in the *Southern Quarterly Review* for October 1844 (VI, 307–42).

32. *The Raven and the Whale* (New York, 1956), p. 154. For amplification of Simms's early viewpoints of the role of Southern letters in American literature, see John C.

Guilds, "Simms's Views on National and Sectional Literature, 1825–1845," *North Carolina Historical Review*, XXXIV (July 1957), 393–405.

33. Reprinted in Randall Stewart, "Hawthorne's Contributions to *The Salem Advertiser*," *American Literature*, V (January 1934), 327–41. Stewart points out that Hawthorne felt antipathy toward Simms perhaps greater than revealed in the review; in a manuscript note of April 30, 1846, he wrote: "I know well enough what I like, but am always at a loss to render a reason. Mr. Simms I do not like at all" (p. 330).

34. In a letter of October 27 [1843] to George Frederick Holmes, Simms explained, "The Author's Club has for its object to awaken the American public to the importance of a National Literature to the national morals and permanence,—and the attainment of a proper Copyright Law as one of the necessary agents in bringing about this awakening" (*L*, I, 378). Later, the Author's Club apparently changed its name to the Copyright Club, with William Cullen Bryant as its first president. See Simms's letter of February 10 [1844] to Holmes (*L*, I, 402). Most members of the Author's Club or Copyright Club were, like Simms, Loco Foco Democrats and Young Americans.

35. See *SLM*, X (January 1844), 7–17; (March 1844), 137–51; (June 1844), 340–49; (August 1844), 449–69.

36. This copy of the Memorial "*To the Senate and House of Representatives of the United States*" is preserved in the Department of Archives and History, state of Alabama. The Memorial, an important document in American cultural history, is reprinted in Appendix III.

37. The scholarly work on Simms's poetry by James E. Kibler, Jr., is largely responsible for this new awareness. His edition of Simms's poetry, published in 1990 by the University of Georgia Press, is an important contribution to American scholarship.

38. It is interesting that the specific poems Simms cites as illustrative of his "object"—"Hast Thou a Song for a Flower," "Beauty's Spring-Time," and "'Such, Oh! Beauty!'"—are not the best examples by modern standards of taste.

39. Simms's remark to James Lawson in a letter of May 15 [1846] reveals that he had read the *Godey's* review: "Did you get my Areytos? Will you marry any of them to immortal music?" (*L*, II, 162–63).

40. O'Neill, pp. 29–30, 54.

41. See Simms's letter of November 6 [1844] to George Frederick Holmes, *L*, I, 434–35. Although Simms was at first believed to be the author of *The Life of Nathanael Greene, Major-General in the Army of the Revolution* (New York: George F. Cooledge & Brother, 1849), in reality he merely edited for publication the biography of Greene written by W. P. Johnson. See Frederick Wagner, "Simms's Editing of *The Life of Nathanael Greene*," *Southern Literary Journal*, XI (Fall 1978), 40–43. Another "drudgery" that Simms undertook in 1847 was "the task of preparing an oration for the Literary Societies of Oglethorpe" (*L*, II, 352), which was published as *Self-Development. An Oration Delivered Before the Literary Societies of Oglethorpe University, Georgia; November 10, 1847* (Milledgeville, Ga.: Thalian Society, 1847). *Self-Development* was favorably reviewed in the *Charleston Mercury*, February 9, 1848. The

lecture itself received such "unqualified praise" that Hammond wrote Simms to "congratulate you sincerely on having won laurels in Georgia, where every thing Carolinian is viewed with such bitter prejudice" (*L*, II, 371n).

42. *The Cassique of Accabee* was also published in New York in 1849 by both Harper & Brothers and Geo. P. Putnam.

43. Kibler, *Poetry Introduction*, p. 77.

44. The work referred to is *Charleston: A Poem* by a Northern Lady (Charleston, 1848). On November 9 [1848] Simms wrote to James Lawson: "There are sundry satirical publications in regard to Charleston, in rhyme, of which I hope to obtain copies which I shall send you. They will afford some queer pictures of our venerable city" (*L*, II, 451).

45. In describing "The Cassique of Accabee" to Duyckinck in a letter of September 19 [1849], Simms stated, "It puts the Indian in a new and not unnatural light. The scene is one under our city's eye" (*L*, II, 558). A favorite of Simms, and perhaps the most successful poem in the collection, is "The Traveller's Rest" (earlier published in the *Magnolia* in 1842), which Simms called to Duyckinck's attention with the comment: "The vein, I think, is not a common one, yet distinguished by its simplicity" (*L*, II, 558).

46. "Sabbath Lyrics" appeared in *Godey's*, XXXVII (October–December 1848), 200, 307, 346; XXXVIII (June 1849), 376; XXXIX (August, October, December 1849), 127, 240, 375.

47. In a letter of February 16, 1850, to Duyckinck Simms explained his intent with *Sabbath Lyrics*. "It was put forth by a Charleston publisher as a sort of Christmas Gift—though, as usual with our publishers, it did not appear till a week or two after Christmas" (*L*, III, 18). Actually *Sabbath Lyrics* was issued by Walker and James on or before December 29, 1849, for an advertisement in the *Charleston Mercury* of that date listed the volume as just published and for sale—as a New Year's gift.

48. Earlier in the same letter Simms had queried Hammond: "How would you like to be in Congress, with me in the lower House? This *inter nos*. A caucus has recently been held in Charleston among *our* friends. In plain terms the movement is made by the solely powerful party, and I have been applied to to succeed or to supersede Holmes, as their nominee. I have consented promptly & frankly, telling them that the place would please me" (*L*, II, 563). Like most of Simms's political ambitions, this one, too, was frustrated. Isaac Edward Holmes (1796–1869), a Charlestonian, was elected to Congress in 1838 and served until 1850.

49. Though Simms published no fiction in periodicals in either 1846 or 1849, three important titles (among others of lesser quality) appeared in 1847 and 1848: "Maize in Milk" in *Godey's* and "The Maroon: A Legend of the Caribbee" in the *New York Illustrated Magazine*, both in 1847; and "The Voice of the Mute" in *Union Magazine* in 1848.

50. Throughout 1845 and 1846, and as late as March 1847, Simms maintained hope that Wiley and Putnam would follow up *The Wigwam and the Cabin* and *Views and*

*Reviews* in the Library of American Books with the publication of his "The Huguenots of Florida" (see *L,* II, 106, 111, 118, 143, 147, 164, 170–71, 199, 234, 273, 286).

51. Hammond wrote to Simms on September 30, 1850: "I appreciate most sensibly the kindness of your dedication to me. ... There are men who will abuse you & your work on that account *solely,* for I am getting to be awfully hated. ... It does not trouble me, but it will if my friends come to share it with me. I think my best chance of surviving in name to another generation is from this dedication & I therefore owe you all the gratitude that the thought of such a survivorship can excite in me" (*L,* III, 61n).

52. Nicholas G. Meriwether, "Simms's *The Lily and the Totem:* 'History for the Purposes of Art,'" *Long Years of Neglect,* p. 82. For an earlier brief recognition of the unusual merits of *The Lily and the Totem,* see John C. Guilds, "Simms's Use of History: Theory and Practice," *Mississippi Quarterly,* XXX (Fall 1977), 505–11, which, in surveying Simms's artistic theories and use of history in fiction, points to "a yet more important colonial-American work which has been almost totally neglected. ... *The Lily and the Totem, or the Huguenots in Florida* (1850), which successfully blends history and fiction and contains some of Simms's finest writing" (pp. 509–10).

53. In Meriwether's definition, *fictional history* and *historical fiction* both use "historical settings and facts to paint a convincing backdrop for the action and characters," but whereas historical fiction employs fictional main characters and fictional subplots, fictional history relies upon "history to provide the plot and characters" and "uses history in a different and more demanding fashion" (pp. 81–82).

54. For a detailed account of Simms's ingenious method of adding to the air of reality of *Flirtation at the Moultrie House,* see my explanatory and textual introductions and notes, *Stories and Tales,* pp. 779–85.

55. In 1867 Simms published "Joscelyn; A Tale of the Revolution" serially in *The Old Guard,* January through December. Though it was never published in book form during Simms's lifetime, *Joscelyn* was issued in 1975 by the University of South Carolina Press as an eighth volume in the Revolutionary War series.

56. The serial publication of *Katharine Walton* actually began in February (rather than January) 1850 and continued monthly in *Godey's* through December (XL, 107–18, 161–69, 243–51, 320–26, 397–411; XLI, 13–27, 89–100, 162–79, 205–19, 286–98, 332–52.

57. In *Godey's* the subtitle to *Katharine Walton* was "the Rebel's Daughter. A Tale of the Revolution."

58. See also Simms's letter of September 27 [1851] to Hart, in which he tells his publisher that "K. W. ... sells very well here" (*L,* VI, 119). On November 1, 1851, stated to Hart that "K. W. ... continues to sell here" (*L,* VI, 120). Still, despite a sold-out edition, *Katharine Walton* must have yielded small profit to its author. On January 5, 1852, Simms remarked in another letter to his publisher: "I fear that the profits must be small upon so small an edition of Kath. Walton at so small a price. Make it as much as you please & can, for the sake of the poor devil author. ..." (*L,* VI, 122).

59. Other brief notices of the first edition of *Katharine Walton* can be found in

*International Magazine* (IV [October 1, 1851], 416) and the *Southern Literary Gazette* (IV [October 4, 1851], 4).

60. See in particular Simms's letter of November 16 or 17, 1847, to Lawson, in which—after a long defense of the play's action and characters from criticisms made by Lawson and Forrest—the Charlestonian conceded that "Should Forrest determine to take the piece, I would cheerfully come on to N. York this winter and amend it as he might suggest" (*L*, II, 369).

61. Despite Simms's efforts *Norman Maurice* was never performed on stage. According to Trent, a Nashville actor named George K. Dickinson wrote to Simms in 1854 an enthusiastic letter about the prospects of staging *Norman Maurice* in St. Louis. But (to quote Trent) "although Dickinson filled an engagement at St. Louis during the Christmas holidays of 1854, and although the 'Missouri Republican' contained a glowing notice of Mr. Simms's new American play, which would shortly be produced at the People's Theater, the performance did not come off, and Dickinson's letters suddenly ceased" (p. 200). Dickinson is not among Simms's correspondents in the *Letters*, but apparently Trent had available material for which no record exists.

62. Though "New York, 1853" appears on the title page of this edition, it actually was not issued until 1854.

63. In a letter to Chivers on April 5, 1852, Simms had dealt harshly with the Georgia poet, stopping perhaps just short of accusing him of plagiarizing Poe: "Give him [Poe] up as a model and as a guide. ... It would keep you from sinking into the sin of mere imitation" (*L*, III, 170). In his response, Chivers first has high praise for *Norman Maurice* (perhaps to curry Simms's favor?); then he proceeded—patronizingly, it seems—to instruct Simms on principles of "Dramatic Composition": "The truth is, you seem to have a perfect *contempt* for what may be called the *Art of Composition;* but, let me tell you that this is the *glory of all Poetry* ..."(*L*, III, 169n).

64. *Antebellum Charleston Dramatists* (University, Ala. [1976]), p. 135.

65. See above, chapter 6.

66. Although the year 1850 appears on the title page of *The City of the Silent*, publication did not actually occur until February 1851.

67. Among the many notices of the publication of *The City of the Silent* were the following (nearly all favorable): *Charleston Mercury*, February 17, 1851; *Charleston Evening News*, February 21, 1851; *Southern Literary Gazette*, III (March 8, 1851); *Southern Literary Messenger*, XVII (April 1851), 256; *Harper's*, III (April 1, 1851), 36; *De Bow's*, X (April 1851), 483; *Sartain's*, VIII (May 1851), 347; and *Literary World*, VIII (August 1851), 95.

68. In a letter of November 24, 1852, to James Henry Hammond, Simms commented that *The Golden Christmas* "has not yet yielded me a cent" (*L*, III, 212). Evidence that the sale of *The Golden Christmas* was poor comes from the fact that copies of the volume were remaindered by William Gowans, New York City, in 1858 (see *L*, III, 213n).

69. Among the journals noticing the publication of *The Sword and the Distaff* are

*Arthur's Home Magazine,* II, (August 1853), 2; and *Godey's,* XLVII, (September 1853), 277. Though short, both of these reviews are favorable. On June 25, 1853, the *Literary World* contained a second review of *The Sword and the Distaff* (signed "LOGAN"), which concluded: "This book will sustain Mr. Simms's reputation" (XII, 516).

70. Nevertheless, it is surprising that *The Sword and the Distaff* was not widely reviewed by the "Carolina Press"—giving more credence to Simms's contention that his publisher was negligent in seeing that his books were circulated properly. It is noteworthy, too, that the revised edition issued by Redfield in 1854 (under the now standard title *Woodcraft*) did receive relatively wide notice, both North and South, despite the fact that a reissue two years after the original publication does not normally attract much attention.

71. "The Theme of Freedom in Simms's *Woodcraft,*" *Long Years of Neglect,* p. 23.

72. See Charles S. Watson, "Simms's Answer to *Uncle Tom's Cabin:* Criticism of the South in *Woodcraft,*" *Southern Literary Journal,* IX (Fall 1976), 78–90. See also Ridgely, *Simms,* p. 97, and "*Woodcraft:* Simms's First Answer to *Uncle Tom's Cabin,*" *American Literature,* XXXI (January 1960), 421–33; S. P. C. Duvall, "W. G. Simms's Review of Mrs. Stowe," *American Literature,* XXX (March 1958), 107–17; and Trent, pp. 174–75.

73. "The Theme of Freedom," pp. 29–30.

74. It should be noted, too, that Simms had originally defined the purpose of the novel in September 1851 in terms clearly having nothing to do with the slavery issue. In a review of Mary H. Eastman's *Aunt Phillis' Cabin; or, Southern Life as It Is* in the *Southern Quarterly Review* for April 1853, Simms expressed disapproval of books "designed as an answer to 'Uncle Tom's Cabin'" (n.s., VII, 523).

75. Simms's pro-Texas sentiment is also revealed in his novel, *Confession* (1841), in which one of the characters, Kingery, persuades the narrator-hero, Edward Clifford, to go to Texas with him, because the future of America lay in the west.

76. *Michael Bonham* appeared in *SLM,* XVIII (February, March, April, May, June 1852), 89–96, 145–49, 234–40, 296–304, 342–49.

77. Trent makes some ado about the fact that Simms, who did not attend the performances apparently because of illness within his family, was "chagrined" that the audience made "no call for the author" and quotes a letter from M. C. M. Hammond to Simms: "What author was ever called out in your goodly city? I never heard of one. The folks did not know the compliment,—they paid the very highest known to them, and quite unusual, too, that of encoring *scenes*! A song might do. But scenes! it is surely a *rara avis*" (quoted in *Simms,* pp. 216–17; original no longer extant). It is true that Simms had hoped for a benefit performance for the author; on March 27, 1855, in explaining to Duyckinck that he "had so little curiosity as not to visit the city on the occasion" of the performance, he added: "If they tender me a Benefit, However, I must be there—if only to get the money, of which I am in no small need" (*L,* III, 372). Simms's "Calhoun—An Ode," read on the night of the second performance, is included in his "Charleston, the Palmetto City," *Harper's New Monthly Magazine,* XV (June 1857), 1–22.

78. Note that at his death Simms left two manuscripts of his unpublished "The Humours of the Manager," an excellent comic account of episodes in the career of Charles Gilfert, manager of the Charleston Theatre.

After the Civil War, Simms published "Benedict Arnold: The Traitor. A Drama, in an Essay" in the *Magnolia Weekly,* I (May–August 1863), 165–67, 173–75, 186–87, 194–95, 202–3, 210–11, 218–19, 226–27, 234–35, 242–43, 250–51, 258–59. As early as 1845 Simms had included "Benedict Arnold as a subject for Fictitious story" among "The Epochs and Events of American History, as Suited to the Purpose of Art in Fiction" (*Views and Reviews,* I, 55–75). In her study of "The West Point Treason in American Drama, 1798–1891," Miriam J. Shillingsburg states that "in several ways Simms's play represents an interplay of history and art that remains of lasting interest" (*Educational Theatre Journal,* XXX [March 1978], 83). See also Shillingsburg's "Simms's Benedict Arnold: The Hero as Traitor," *Southern Studies,* XVII (Fall 1978), 273–89.

79. The prospectus was printed in full in the *Literary World,* IX (August 16, 1851), 131.

80. Chesnut (1815–1885), member of the South Carolina House of Representatives from Kershaw District, served as an aide to President Jefferson Davis during the Civil War. Toward the end of the war Chesnut, then a brigadier general, became commander of the reserves in South Carolina. His wife, Mary Boykin Chesnut (1823–1886), was the author of a now-famous diary covering most of the Civil War years; see C. Vann Woodward, ed., *Mary Chesnut's Civil War* (New Haven and London: Yale University Press [1981]).

81. For details of the arrangement, see Simms's letters of January 25 and June 10, 1853, to Henry Panton, brother-in-law of Evert A. Duyckinck and an associate in the Redfield publishing firm—*L,* III, 224–25 and VI, 138–40, respectively. In deciding to undertake publication of the collected edition of Simms's poetry, evidently Redfield also agreed to the publication of any new novels by Simms, as well as to the publication of new editions of Simms's previously published novels. That Russell cooperated with the new plan is made clear by Simms's statement to Panton that "Russell thinks the Revolutionary novels should be the ones to begin with" (*L,* VI, 139). With reference to *Poems* James E. Kibler, Jr., explains that, apparently to satisfy Russell, "copies bearing the Russell imprint were printed by Redfield to be distributed to those subscribers which Russell, Simms, and Friends had succeeded in procuring when the work was first planned" (*Poetry Introduction,* p. 96).

82. Kibler, *Poetry Introduction,* p. 96.

83. Miles's article, entitled "Southern Passages and Pictures," was published in the *Southern Literary Messenger,* XVII (May 1851), 289–96; it was reprinted in the *Southern Literary Gazette,* IV (July 5, 12, and 19, 1851).

84. After *Vasconselos*'s rejection, Simms substituted for it *Katharine Walton,* which (as we have seen) was published serially in *Godey's* in 1850.

85. Dedication, *Vasconselos: A Romance of the New World,* 2nd ed. (New York: Redfield, 1857), p. iii.

86. "Marie de Berniere; A Tale of the Crescent City" was published in *Arthur's Home*

*Gazette*, II (February 14, 21, 29, March 6, 13, 20, 27, 1852). The original of the story, "The Unknown Masque. A Sketch of the Crescent City," appeared in the *Southern and Western Monthly Magazine and Review*, I (April 1845), 262–69, and another version, "The Egyptian Masque; A Tale of the Crescent City," scheduled for serial publication in the *American Metropolitan Magazine*, ran only one installment in the February 1849 number (I, 69–73) before the magazine ceased to operate. See my "Textual Introduction," *Stories and Tales*, pp. 700–701. "The Maroon: A Legend of the Caribbees" was first published as a serial, in six installments, in the *New York Illustrated Magazine of Literature and Art*, III (January–June 1847), and was republished, with minor revisions, under the same title in the *Southern Literary Gazette*, III (May 4, 11, 18, 25, June 1, 8, 1850). For a complete account of the origins and textual variations in "The Maroon," see my "Textual Introduction," *Stories and Tales*, pp. 707–10. "Maize in Milk. A Christmas Story of the South" was first published in *Godey's Lady's Book*, XXXIV (February–May 1847). See my "Textual Introduction," *Stories and Tales*, pp. 763–64.

87. "Wayside Laconics" appeared periodically in the *Southern Patriot* in 1846 and 1847, at the end of which time Simms sought Rufus Griswold's assistance in locating a book publisher—an unsuccessful venture. See *L*, II, 316, 320. Before finally being published as a book in 1853, *Egeria* also appeared anonymously in installments in *Richards' Weekly Gazette* during 1849–1850. Among publishers Simms tried to interest in *Egeria* were Redfield and Appleton and Co. (see *L*, III, 177).

88. Shillingsburg, "Simms's Lecture Tour," p. 193. See above, chapter 6. "South Carolina in the Revolution" and "The Siege of Charleston in the American Revolution" were first published in the *Southern Quarterly Review*, XIV (July, October 1848), 37–77, 261–337.

89. "The Bride of Hate" had first appeared in *Godey's Lady's Book*, XXII (March 1841), 115–27, under the title "The Passage of a Night; or the Benefactress. A Tale." It is reprinted in *Stories and Tales*, pp. 137–71; see my "Explanatory and Textual Notes," pp. 681–84.

90. See *L*, III, 321. James Hall (1793–1868), editor, historian, and writer of tales, was at this time president of the Commercial Bank, Cincinnati, Ohio. In addition to *Legends of the West* (1853), Hall was the author of *Wilderness and the Warpath* (1846). The dedication of *Charlemont* reads as follows: "To the Hon. James Hall, of Cincinnati: As one of the Ablest of our Literary Pioneers; A Genuine Representative of the Great West; Whose Writings Equally Illustrate Her History and Genius: this story of 'Charlemont,' and its Sequel 'Beauchampe,' are respectively inscribed by Their Author. Woodlands, S.C., *December*, 1855." *Charlemont* and *Beauchampe* (the sequel) were brought out by Redfield, in its series of "New and Revised Editions of the Border Romances of the South." The 1842 edition of *Beauchampe* had also been dedicated to Hall.

91. In her first encounter with Orville Beauchampe, who declares himself "the slave of a passion" for her, Margaret Cooper (alias Anna Cooke) retorts, "I have my passion, perhaps, but surely love makes no part of it. ... Hate is my passion. ..." (*Beauchampe*, pp. 98, 102).

92. "Advertisement," *Charlemont*, p. 11.

93. It will be remembered that in writing *Katharine Walton*, thus completing *The Partisan-Mellichampe-Katharine Walton* trilogy, Simms had planned to carry the action through Eutaw.

94. See his letter of February 27, 1855, to Evert A. Duyckinck (*L*, III, 368).

95. *Arthur's Home Magazine*, VII (June 1856), 379, contains a short, favorable review of *Eutaw*, which is interesting because of its statement that Simms's literary reputation is higher in the North than in the South.

96. *Pilgrim's Progress* had been a favorite among books of Simms's reading as a youth.

97. For a long letter dealing with Simms's experiences with mediums in New York undertaken at Hammond's request, see *L*, III, 475–83.

98. See above, chapter 5.

99. See below, chapter 9.

100. *The North American Review* critique was reprinted in *Russell's*, VI (December 1859), 276–77.

101. The *Leader* review was reprinted in the *Charleston Mercury*, June 14, 1859.

102. Hammond added, half-facetiously, concerning the scene in question: "At least I think I could very greatly amend it. I wont tell you which because I think you *put yourself out* in it—(your ability not your genius which explains the failure)—& I should not be surprised to see some reviewer select it as the best passage" (*L*, IV, 152n).

103. "William Gilmore Simms's *The Cassique of Kiawah* and the Principles of His Art," *Long Years of Neglect*, pp. 37–59.

104. The plantation books at Woodlands reveal that Simms was not merely an extoller of beauty, nor experimental agriculturist, nor landscape architect though he was all of those. He was passionately interested in protecting the flora, the fauna, and the waterways of the South Carolina low country, and in this sense he was a true exponent of environmental integrity (*MCSO*, V, X). Also see James E. Kibler, Jr., "Simms as Naturalist: Lowcountry Landscape in his Revolutionary Novels," *Mississippi Quarterly*, XXXI (Fall 1978), 499–518; Annette Kolodny, "The Unchanging Landscape; The Pastoral Impulse in Simms's Revolutionary War Romances," *Southern Literary Journal*, V (Fall 1972), 46–67.

## Chapter IX

1. Virginia Singleton Simms—born on the first anniversary of her parents' wedding, November 15, 1837, died on October 10, 1838. The couple's second child, Agnes Simms, born May 23, 1841, survived only five days. For a list of Simms's children, see the chronological chart in Appendix I.

2. The reference to "strokes of Providence" is to the rapid successive deaths of the three daughters born to Simms and his second wife. Earlier in the letter Simms had written: "In the last three years death has annually assessed my little family, seizing on one or other dear treasure." See above, note 1. Simms was mistaken only in the timing of the three deaths, which occurred within four and a half years, not three.

3. See David Aiken's "Introduction" to a reprint of *The Cassique of Kiawah,* issued in 1989 by Magnolia Press, Gainesville, Georgia, p. vii.

4. In addition to the deaths of three daughters, Simms had recently received word "of the death of my uncle in Mississippi"—that is, James Simms, brother of Simms's father.

5. Evidencing both consideration for his wife and the closeness of his association with his daughter, Simms cared for Augusta, who "is in bed today with a slight attack" (*L,* I, 323) in Charleston before joining Chevillette in the mountains. Upon their return to Charleston, on October 7, 1842, Simms reported again to Lawson: "I have just returned from a trip to the mountains of North Carolina, whither I followed my wife who had gone thither in July for her health. She has returned with me, and with the exception of my father-in-law, we are all in good health" (*L,* I, 323). Particularly during the hot summer months, it was traditional, if circumstances permitted, for expectant wives of low-country South Carolina gentry to visit the cooler mountain regions of North Carolina.

6. Nancy Kellogg had been Augusta's teacher at "the Rose Cottage Seminary" in Great Barrington, became a friend of the family, and (according to Augusta's descendents) frequently visited Woodlands. For further information concerning the Kelloggs, see *L,* I, 130n.

7. Miss Sherwood of New York was a friend and relative of Nancy Kellogg.

8. Parke Godwin, an associate of Bryant at the *New York Evening Post,* married Fanny Bryant in 1842.

9. Simms referred to his residence in Charleston at 56 Smith Street as his "wigwam." Nash Roach put the Charleston town house at the disposal of his son-in-law and daughter immediately after their marriage in 1836.

10. *Cyclopaedia* was published in New York by Charles Scribner in 1856. For Bryant's letter describing a cornshucking by blacks at Woodlands and neighboring plantations, see Vol. II, p. 190.

11. February 9, 1844, original in South Caroliniana Library; quoted in *L,* I, 384–85n. Simms spoke of the warm reception Bryant received in the South in a letter of June 12, 1843: "Bryant made many friends in the South. The Gentlemanly quietness of his manner, his unobtrusiveness, please in the South. All who met, were pleased with him" (*L,* I, 355).

12. See above, chapter 7. In the "Editorial Bureau" of the *Magnolia,* n.s., I (November 1842), 324–27, Simms quoted extensively from a letter from a "friend in New York" in his own editorial analysis of the nationwide interest in mesmerism, a

subject which fascinated both men. Simms's "Mesmerides in a Stage-Coach" is an effective example of Simms's use of mesmerism as the subject for fiction. In April 1843 Simms related to Lawson, "Here in Charleston, every third man is a mesmerist" (*L*, I, 347).

13. See Drew Gilpin Faust, *James Henry Hammond and the Old South: A Design for Mastery* (Baton Rouge and London [1982]), pp. 241–54, 314–19, and passim; Carol Bleser, ed., *The Hammonds of Redcliffe* (New York and Oxford, 1981), pp. 9–12; Carol Bleser, ed. *Secret and Sacred: The Diaries of James Henry Hammond, a Southern Slaveholder* (New York and Oxford, 1988), pp. 171, 175, 269.

14. Hammond expressed great gratitude for the loyalty of his friends at this time, writing to Simms on December 8, 1846, "To you & all my dear Simms I feel as though I owed a life—a separate life to each. Such generous & abiding confidence in one who wrapped himself in mystery, while the *nobles* of the land denounced him in such unmeasured terms, is without parallel. It consoles—it compensates me a thousand fold for all that I have suffered. ... No man ever had such friends. ... God bless you" (*L*, II, 235n). Later, however, involved in additional controversy concerning accusations of sexual liaisons with female slaves, Hammond was deserted by his wife and wrote in his diary in 1852, "Friends I have none" (See Bleser, p. 12)—none, perhaps, other than Simms, with whom his extensive and intimate correspondence remained unabated until his death in 1864.

15. Quoted in "Simms' Circle," *L*, I, cxiii. For the details of birth of Sydney Hammond Simms, see below.

16. In the light of Simms's having once offended Lawson for paying too much attention to his wife, whom Simms greatly admired and was very much attracted to, it is somewhat surprising that a child of his should be named for "Lady Lyde." The naming, is, however, further evidence that the Simms-Lawson relationship was truly resilient and loving, with small wounds healing quickly.

17. For an account of the terroristic activities of Maj. William Cunningham (variously known as "Bloody Bill" or "Murdering Bill") in the Revolutionary War, see *Figures of the Revolution in South Carolina: An Anthology*, ed. Stephen Meats (Columbia, 1976), pp. 119–25. Simms's review of George Atkinson Ward's edition of the *Journal and Letters of the Late Samuel Curwen* (1845) appeared in the *Southern Literary Messenger* in 1846 in the form of five articles. The fourth and fifth, entitled "Biographical Sketch of the Career of Major William Cunningham, of South Carolina," *SLM*, XII (September, October 1846), 513–24, 577–86, offended Pamela Cunningham's *amour propre*. See Simms's letter of October 30, 1846, to Perry, in which he laboriously explained his position (*L*, II, 200–203); that the matter stuck in Simms's craw is evidenced by his bitter remarks on the continuing controversy in a letter of January 25, 1847, to James Henry Hammond (*L*, II, 258–60).

18. "Ante-Bellum Charleston," pp. 257–58, 261, 265–66.

19. In a playful letter of October 26, 1847, Simms reported to Lawson: "My wife weighs 118 [up six pounds in a month] and yr hbl servt. 170. But say nothing of the dimensions of the latter person, to that critical woman, your wife,—or I may lose

whatever small portions of her affections still remain to me" (*L*, II, 359–60). Near the end of November Simms noted that "My wife is hanging curtains" (*L*, II, 376)—another indication that her health was returning to normal.

20. The full quotation from John Home, *Douglas*, I, i, reads, "As women wish to be who love their lords." Simms's humor, which seems in questionable taste even in a letter to Lawson, expanded: "Our women, you are aware, do not love to be in this condition, and as a logical deduction, do not love their Lords." Earlier Simms had stated with obvious reference to Chevillette's pregnancy: "Here, I am likely to have *groaning* instead of smiling and scolding" (*L*, II, 415).

21. Simms was with Tucker in Virginia when the latter became "seriously indisposed" (*L*, III, 140) two weeks before he died. In "My Ways—Along the Highways and Byways," No. X, published in the *Charleston Evening News* (August 1851), Simms wrote of Tucker just before his death: "At seventy, bowed with years, and with a pride greatly mortified by the decrepitude of his native state,—he is still the 'old man eloquent,' full of originality in writing and conversation, a living record of all that was great and noble, in men and events, in the history of the Old Dominion, and still pouring forth, daily, from a most fluent and unembarrassed pen, the noblest appeals to the slumbering patriotism and virtues of his countrymen."

22. *Sacred Circle*, p. x.

23. *Richmond Semi-Weekly Examiner*, April 4, 1854.

24. Augusta Simms Roach, described by the family as "a militant" and "the defender of the faith," may have influenced Trent in the writing of his biography of Simms. In the words of Simms's granddaughter, on Trent's visit to Charleston "Augusta filled [him] with nothing but complaints of all the critics from Charleston up and down. And one thing that she would say, Simms was received far more enthusiastically in the North [than in Charleston]. You see, she stayed in the North a great deal and was very thick with those literary people up there. They made a lot of her. She was a very aggressive and attractive, commanding person ..." (*MCSO*, II).

25. Record of Wills, Vol. 48 (1856–1862), Probate Court, Charleston, South Carolina. The will is printed in its entirety in Appendix II.

26. On at least four other occasions in 1859, Simms made comparisons between his management of Woodlands and that of "my predecessor," always to the discredit of Nash Roach's administrative skills. See *L*, IV, 112, 115, 124, 141.

27. James Kibler's claim that "Clearly, art for Simms was not an escape from reality, but a way of facing it" (*SP*, p. xvi) is borne out by the fact that the author wrote at least three poems dealing directly or indirectly with his sons' untimely deaths. See "Ballad.—Come, Let us Discourse," "Ballad.—Oh! My Boys!" and "Sonnet.—To W. Porcher Miles" (*SP*, pp. 204–5, 205–6, 206).

## Chapter X

1. According to family history, Simms's financial status was the primary, yet unstated reason for his not accepting the invitation; in early 1860 he felt that "he couldn't afford the clothes or the trip for the occasion" (*MCSO*, III).

2. On February 5, 1860, in a letter to Porcher Miles, Simms admitted to being morbid, as accused by Miles: "But the morbidness has come from real ailments of mind & body, the one overworked disappointed, defeated, anxious almost to despairing, the other dyspeptic, and sore from other sources of annoyance. Brain & liver disordered ... my temperament no longer comes to my relief" (*L*, IV, 192).

3. See, for instance, Simms's letter of February 21, 1860, introducing Lawson to Joseph Henry as "a Scotch Gentleman of taste & education, of amiable manners & ingenuous character, whom I have known & valued for 30 years" (*L*, IV, 194).

4. See the chapter entitled "A Political Adviser to the Secession Movement" in *The Politics of a Literary Man*, pp. 214–52. Simms's most celebrated letter defending the Southern position was printed in the *Charleston Mercury* of January 17, 1861, though the letter itself, addressed to John Jacob Bockee, was dated December 12, 1860. The letter purports to answer a plea from Bockee that the South not destroy the "*blessed* Union"; it took Simms forty-two long paragraphs to elaborate with sarcasm the idea succinctly stated in his opening paragraph: "We have learned ... to value the Union, not according to the hopes of its beginning, but through the wrongs which now demand that we bring it to an early end" (*L*, IV, 287). Apparently in appreciation of his permission to print the letter, the *Mercury* sent Simms "5000 cigars & a barrel of Monongahela" (*L*, IV, 328).

5. For a full account of the events at Fort Sumter which precipitated the Civil War, see Charles E. Cauthen, *South Carolina Goes to War, 1860–1865* (Chapel Hill, 1950), pp. 92–101.

6. See W. G. Belser, "William Gilmore Simms: Fictionist as Military Historian" (Ph.D. thesis, St. John's University, 1977).

7. See Simms's letters of January 12 and 13, 1861, to Miles and his letter of January 15 to Jamison (*L*, IV, 316–18, 318–22, 322–25).

8. As late as February 19, 1861, the novelist, still hoping for peace, had said to his son's request "for a hand in the fight": "No! not till you are called," Simms wrote to Lawson. "He is only 17, and I wish him to get his growth and education" (*L*, IV, 326).

9. Earlier in the same letter Simms seemed utterly defeated in spirit and full of self-pity: "The very imagining proves the disease to be real, & in the most dangerous region, the Brain! I have been overworked; I have been unsuccessful all my life; my books fail to pay me; I am myself a failure! In S. C. I am repudiated" (*L*, IV, 186).

10. For a record of the publishing history of *Simms's Poems Areytos*, see Kibler, *Poetry Introduction*, pp. 101–4. Of the Simms-Redfield relationship, Kibler remarks that "the whole affair is revelatory of the quiet manner in which Northern business interest took advantage of a difficult situation" (p. 104).

11. The *Charleston Mercury*, February 7, 1860, reprinted a notice of *The History of South Carolina* from *De Bow's Review*, XXVIII (February 1860), 238.

12. Maximilian La Borde's *History of South Carolina College* was published in Columbia in 1859. La Borde was a professor of metaphysics at South Carolina College.

13. Simms also wrote many unsigned articles on "public affairs" for the *Charleston*

*Mercury* throughout 1861, though only those on the subject of seacoast defense can be identified. See his letter of February 19, 1861, to Lawson (*L*, IV, 327); and particularly his letter of November 18 to J. H. Hammond, in which he identified "Our Coast Defences" in the *Mercury* of November 13 as his "lost article" sent to the newspaper: "I wrote nearly all that they have published on this subject, for the last 8 months" (*L*, IV, 385).

14. After the Battle of Charleston Harbor Simms wrote an "Ode—Our City by the Sea" celebrating the valor of Confederate defenders: "To the brave old City, joy!" The poem was first published in the *Charleston Mercury*, June 22, 1865, and later in Simms's anthology, *War Poetry of the South* (1866). See *SP*, pp. 223–27.

15. Though Simms's family Bible and the family tombstone at Woodlands both give July 22, 1861, as the date of Sydney Hammond's death, this date is incorrect, for on July 4 he wrote to James Lawson, "We have lost our youngest son, the boy Sydney Hammond . . ." (*L*, IV, 369).

16. For example, Simms also informed Lawson that "we are prepared for a long war" and that "Every day of delay in the conflict strengthens us, & every man feels that our cause is just & that God is with us" (*L*, IV, 374).

17. In this letter of December 22, 1861, to Miles, Simms asserted: "Never was our poor State so sadly deficient in becoming & able men" (*L*, IV, 391). Gov. Francis Pickens's incompetence particularly attracted Simms's wrath: "Pickens is such an ass that he will drive away from him every decent counsellor," Simms had complained to Hammond on June 14 (*L*, IV, 366).

18. Simms's poem "The Close of the Year 1861" does not, as its title perhaps suggests, deal with specific events of the year, though its central theme, "whether man has the freedom to rise above circumstance" (as Kibler puts it), is appropriate for the hectic and uncertain times just before the outbreak of the Civil War. Simms actually conceived the germ of the poem as early as 1827. (See *SP*, pp. 215–20, 383–84).

19. This generous neighbor was John S. Jennings, for whom Simms wrote a short obituary for the *Charleston Daily South Carolinian* of January 10, 1866, in which he related the story of Jennings's civic-minded generosity following the first burning of Woodlands.

20. From an unsigned letter to Simms dated "Charleston, June 20, 1862" and published in the *Charleston Mercury* and the *Charleston Courier* of July 8, 1862, and reprinted in *L*, IV, 409n.

21. In his April 10, 1862, letter to Hammond, Simms wrote concerning Woodlands: "I am bracing myself to bear, and to repair. To restore is impossible. As you say, there are losses in such a calamity as can never be restored" (*L*, IV, 403). On January 10, 1863, Simms indicated in a letter to John R. Thompson that work on Woodlands was still going on: "I am now busy rebuilding it" (*L*, IV, 421).

22. The "minor tales or novels" Simms specifically mentioned are "Martin Faber, Castle Dismal, Helen Halsey, The Maroon, Marie de Berniere, &c" (*L*, IV, 420).

23. "Paddy McGann" was included with "As Good as a Comedy" as Volume III of

the Centennial Edition of *The Writings of William Gilmore Simms*, introductions and notes by Robert Bush (Columbia, S.C. [1972]). For an interesting commentary, see Linda E. McDaniel, "American Gods and Devils in Simms's *Paddy McGann*," *Long Years of Neglect*, pp. 60–75.

24. A good example is Simms's letter of July 4, 1863, to Hayne (see *L*, IV, 430–32).

25. Probably a reference to the novel set in the Pee Dee that Simms proposed, but apparently never completed.

26. See chapter 8, note 78.

27. A eulogy of Chevillette Roach Simms entitled "In Memoriam," perhaps written by Hayne, appeared in the *Charleston Mercury*, September 23, 1863, the day of Simms's letter.

28. See Simms's letter of c. February 15, 1864, to M. C. M. Hammond, *L*, IV, 443. On May 15, 1864, Simms wrote to John R. Thompson that his son "has behaved well in several small actions & is recommended for promotion" (*L*, IV, 453–54). Also on or about May 15 Simms reported that Gilmore "succeeded in capturing a des[er]t[er]" (*L*, IV, 455).

29. I am indebted to Mary Simms Oliphant Furman for a copy of this undated letter, originally transcribed by Mary C. Simms Oliphant and now in the possession of the family.

30. See, in this respect, his letter of December 27, 1864, to William Gilmore Simms, Jr., *L*, IV, 473.

31. Beginning with its opening number on March 21, 1865, Simms served as editor of the *Columbia Phoenix*, established by Julian A. Selby to replace the old *South Carolinian*, burned out with the rest of Columbia. In addition to writing for it the "Capture, Sack and Destruction of Columbia" Simms contributed frequent editorials, many of them stinging criticisms of Union occupation forces. In one instance, at least, Simms (in his own words) "was on the eve of being arrested for an article in the paper. The article of arrest was made out; but, cited to appear before the General in Command, I satisfied him that his arrest would be an error" (*L*, IV, 506). Selby was much more impressed than Simms by the incident, and recorded it in his memoirs written almost forty years later: In Selby's version Simms was taken into custody by a corporal and squad of soldiers, and summoned to "appear at once before the offended General":

> Entering the room where military law was being dispensed, Mr. Simms embraced the opportunity of a temporary lull in the proceedings, to request to be allowed to seat himself, as he was well advanced in years; and he was permitted so to do—an orderly quietly handing him a chair. ... Mr. G. [*sic*] was placed directly in front of the General, and the trial began. In a very short time the charge was dismissed, and Mr. S. was invited to partake of an elegant luncheon in an adjoining room. ... The General expressed himself ... the next day, to the effect that if Mr. S. was a specimen of the South Carolina gentleman, he would never enter into a tilt with one again. "He out-taled me, out-drank me, and very clearly and politely showed me that I lacked proper respect for the aged"

(*Memorabilia and Anecdotal Reminiscences of Columbia, South Carolina* [Columbia, 1905], pp. 24–25).

32. William Gilmore Simms, *Sack and Destruction of the City of Columbia, S.C.*, Second Edition, ed. A. S. Salley (Oglethorpe University Press, 1937), pp. 84–85. In writing Benjamin F. Perry on March 6, 1865, Simms observed: "Seven-eights of the best portions of Columbia have been destroyed. In fact, what remains unburnt are, almost exclusively, the suburban precincts. All is wreck, confusion & despair" (*L*, IV, 486).

33. *DLB 73*, p. 291.

34. See his letter to his son-in-law, Edward Roach, on June 25, 1865 (*L*, IV, 505n).

35. On June 13, 1865, in the first letter Simms wrote to James Lawson after Lee's surrender at Appomattox, the novelist, speculating that the New Yorker had yet to hear that "my house, newly rebuilt, has been destroyed by Sherman's army," enumerated his property losses for his friend—"my stables, carriage house, barns, gin house, machine and threshing houses; in short every building of any value; my mules, horses, cattle driven off & carried away, or butchered; my wagons, ploughs, implements, all destroyed ..." (*L*, IV, 498–99).

36. On May 15, 1865, the *Phoenix* had become the *Columbia Daily Phoenix;* on July 31 it became simply the *Daily Phoenix.* On August 12 Simms reported in a letter to a friend in South Carolina: "I am still conducting the Phoenix paper, which yields me a miserable stipend, hardly the wages of a Journeyman printer. I do not expect to retain the situation beyond the summer months" (*L*, IV, 512). By October 1, 1865, Simms could write Duyckinck with well-earned pride: "This day, I resign the Editorial chair of the Phoenix Newspaper. I created it, & have already made it the best organ of opinion in the state. In the end, it will be a fortune to its publisher" (*L*, IV, 522). See James E. Kibler, "Simms's Editorship of the Columbia *Phoenix* of 1865," *South Carolina Journals and Journalists*, pp. 61–75.

37. The final stanza reads as follows:

Tender and True, my Dixie Land!
Though faint and few, my Dixie Land!
We keep the Faith our Fathers knew,
For which they bled, in which we grew,
And at their graves our vows renew,—
For nought is lost of truth, where Faith keeps true,
Oh! Dixie Land! O! Dixie Land!

38. Of these three poems, all collected for the first time in *SP*, "The Voice of Memory in Exile, from a Home in Ashes" appeared in the *Phoenix* on April 19, 1865; "'Ay De Mi, Alhama!'" in the *Charleston Mercury*, January 11, 1867; and "Among the Ruins" in *Southern Society*, October 19, 1867. See *SP*, pp. 241, 252–53, 254–57. In the introduction to *SP* Kibler states of these and other Simms poems of this period: "While Simms's youthful Cavalier lyrics are charming and often memorable, his great lyric contribution came in his maturity, particularly in those poems which express love, grief, and loss" (p. xvi).

39. In his June 13 letter to Lawson, Simms had anticipated Lawson's continued friendship and willingness to help: "You have the will to succour me, I believe; I trust you have the ability also & that your family & fortune have suffered no loss in the terrible interval of time which has thrown an impassable chasm between us—impassable till now" (*L*, IV, 500).

40. These "two or three articles" cannot be identified; after Simms's death "How Sharp Snaffles Got His Capital and Wife" was published in *Harper's New Monthly Magazine* for October 1870 (XLI, 667–87). Although Simms customarily did not refer to poems as "articles," he did publish several poems in the *Columbia Daily Phoenix* in 1865 and the reference could possibly be to them. See *SP*, pp. 236–37, 238–40, 241, 241–42, 242–43, and 243–45.

41. In his letters to Duyckinck Simms made similar requests with regard to "Harper & Brothers" and "any other publishers whom you know, of liberal character." Simms also suggested to Duyckinck that a private subscription for "an illustrated octavo containing my complete poetical works" would greatly assist "the most partial reestablishment of my affairs" (*L*, IV, 502–3).

42. Simms's letter was in response to the request "that all free white men between the ages of sixteen and sixty shall be liable to military service" (*L*, IV, 475n).

## Chapter XI

1. *Voltmeier; or, The Mountain Men*, volume I of *The Centennial Writings of William Gilmore Simms*, ed. James B. Meriwether (Columbia, 1969), p. 212. All future references are given by page number within parentheses in the text. During Simms's lifetime *Voltmeier* was published serially in *The Illuminated Western World*, March–June 1869.

2. See Simms's letter of December 19, 1865, to E. A. Duyckinck: "... I do a daily amount of drudgery for my own & the good of the public ..." (*L*, IV, 527).

3. The earliest review of *War Poetry of the South* appeared in *Round Table*, IV (November 10, 1866), 244. Other notices (all laudatory) include the following: *Charleston Courier*, November 23, 1866; *Charleston Daily News*, November 27 and December 25, 1866; *Charleston Mercury*, November 29, 1866; *Southern Cultivator*, XXIV (November 1866), 273; *De Bow's Review*, n.s., III (February 1867), 219–20; *The Land We Love*, II (February 1867), 309, and III (May 1867), 71–74; and *Old Guard*, V (March 1867), 202–6.

4. Ever in search of the additional money needed to support himself and his family, Simms throughout 1866 wrote on a regular basis for both the *Charleston Courier* and the *Charleston Mercury*, though it is doubtful that either provided enough revenue to justify Simms's time and effort. Typical is the comment Simms wrote to son Gilmore in July: "My engagement with the 'Courier' affords me less money than I had hoped for" (*L*, IV, 581).

5. On March 27, 1858, Simms had written Harry Hammond, son of James H. Hammond, owner of Redcliffe, a plantation on Beech Island on the Savannah River, very near to Augusta: "You are at Redclyffe? It is possible that I may wish to visit Augusta sometime this spring or summer. I have a book to write the scene of which is in that precinct" (*L*, IV, 41). In another letter three months later Simms broached the subject again, writing to the senior Hammond that he wished "to spend at least one day or two in Augusta, in order to get from the Sandhills, a bird's eye view of the city & the environs, with somebody at my elbow to point out & describe localities" (*L*, IV, 72)—the purpose of which visit, he explained later: "I go to take the *coup d'oeil* of that precinct, with regard to a Revolutionary novel" (*L*, IV, 82).

6. "Joscelyn: A Tale of the Revolution," *Old Guard*, V (January–December 1867), 1–17, 91–103, 161–76, 241–60, 321–39, 401–21, 481–500, 561–76, 668–81, 731–45, 822–34, 897–935.

7. See A. S. Salley, ed., *Catalogue of the Salley Collection of the Works of Wm. Gilmore Simms* (Columbia, S.C., 1943), pp. 35, 39–42, 55, 75, 80–81, 92, 95.

8. "Introduction," *Joscelyn: A Tale of the Revolution*, vol. XVI of *Centennial Edition* (Columbia [1975]), pp. ix–x.

9. See Simms's letter of September 2, 1867, to John Esten Cooke, in which he asked Cooke's opinion of Slater and his journal, which was being published in Baltimore (*L*, V, 84).

10. For Simms's account of his experience of nonpayment with *Southern Society* and *Southern Opinion*, see his letter of March 13, 1868, to Charles E. A. Gayarré (*L*, V, 113–14).

11. Though Simms negotiated with Victor for seven hundred dollars (rather than six hundred dollars) in compensation, it is not certain that he actually received the higher figure. His letter of January 18, 1869, to Victor requesting payment of "the balance of Three Hundred Dollars" suggests that the total figure may have been lower than that proposed by the author (*L*, V, 197).

12. *Voltmeier; or, The Mountain Men*, vol. I of *Centennial Edition* (Columbia [1969]). Much data (as well as insight) for the introduction were furnished by Simms's granddaughter, Mary C. Simms Oliphant, co-editor of the volume; however, the actual text of the introduction was the work of Donald Davidson.

13. See Davidson, "Introduction," *Joscelyn*, p .xix.

14. In his 1847 notebook Simms commented on his visit to the "residence of Allen Twitty, the famous counterfeiter—his farm—his cave—& anecdotes of his career—his character—his *virtues*" (South Caroliniana Library; quoted in *Voltmeier*, p. 433).

15. See above, chapter 10.

16. Simms's 1847 journal is preserved in the Charles Carroll Simms Collection under the heading "Personal and Literary Memorials," South Caroliniana Library, University of South Carolina. A typescript of the journal is included in Miriam Jones

Shillingsburg, "An Edition of William Gilmore Simms's *The Cub of the Panther*" (Ph.D. thesis, University of South Carolina, 1969), pp. 108–33.

17. The third "romance" which Simms was "meditating" was apparently "on the Old French Wars, including Washington's early career & Braddocks defeat" (*L*, V, 171)—a work he seems never to have written.

18. Shillingsburg gives a detailed commentary on the possible reasons for and effect of the missing chapters in the introduction to her study of text of *The Cub of the Panther* (dissertation, pp. 13–16).

19. Clipping in the possession of the late Mary C. Simms Oliphant. I am grateful to Mrs. Oliphant for making available to me her large collection of newspaper clippings concerning her grandfather. These clippings are quoted from extensively in the section of the chapter that immediately follows.

20. During the final three weeks of his life Simms wrote at least six letters that are extant; he almost certainly wrote others.

21. Details of Simms's death include the following: At midday on June 9, 1870, Dr. Eli Geddings, the family physician and an old friend, visited Simms and pronounced that he could live only a short while longer. Nevertheless, in the words of Simms's granddaughter, "Nothing could make an impression upon the children that their father was not immortal (the word they use); they looked upon him in a spirit akin to reverence. They could not believe, think of life without him, and there he was a dying man, and everyone knew it, but the children never recognized he was dying" (*MCSO*, I). On the afternoon of June 9, according to Augusta, he "got up from bed & walked down stairs ... he was death struck then—the cold sweats of death rolls [*sic*] in strains from his face ... I never could imagine such wonderful force of will that kept him up longer than he would otherwise lasted." Perhaps the disbelief that their father was dying accounts for the fact that they (with the exception of Augusta) seem not to have been by his side during his final hours. The woman who served as his nurse at the end, Sallie F. Chapin, friend of the family, reported that Simms's last words on June 11 were, "Where is Gilmore. It will not be long." Simms died at five o'clock that afternoon. It was Mrs. Chapin who, in helping prepare his body for burial, noticed that Simms's fingers "refused to take any other position than their natural one, *drawn up as if to write*." The burial took place on June 13 in Magnolia Cemetery, the original tombstone inscribed simply "SIMMS." (Much of the above material comes from Hayne, "Ante-Bellum Charleston," p. 268; the originals of the Augusta Roach and the Sallie F. Chapin letters to Hayne are in the Hayne Papers.)

22. This clipping in the possession of Mary C. Simms Oliphant is undated and unidentified.

23. Reprinted in the *Charleston Daily Courier*, June 22, 1870.

24. Another undated and unidentified clipping in possession of Mary C. Simms Oliphant. For information about the Columbia convention "in favor of good and honest government," see the front-page story entitled "The Reform Movement" in the *Charleston Daily Courier*, Thursday, June 16, 1870; an editorial entitled "The Union

Reform Convention," *Charleston Daily Courier,* Friday, June 17, 1870; and John S. Reynolds, *Reconstruction in South Carolina, 1865–1877* (Columbia, S.C., 1905), p. 139.

25. *Ceremonies at the Unveiling of the Bronze Bust of William Gilmore Simms at White Point Garden, Charleston, S.C., June 11th, 1879,* reprinted from the pamphlet published originally by The News and Courier Book Presses, with a preface by Gail Morrison (Columbia, 1979), p. 31.

## Chapter XII

1. Simms's requested epitaph appears as the first lines of *PM.*

2. Trent, p. 332.

3. Hayne, "Ante-Bellum Charleston," p. 268. The passages by Hayne quoted earlier in this chapter come from an 1870 Hayne letter to Francis Peyre Porcher now in the Paul Hamilton Hayne Papers, South Caroliniana Library. The two letters to Porcher, dated July 9 and August 4, 1870, are hereinafter cited in the text as *PHH.* For an enlightening study of the complicated Hayne-Simms relationship, see Rayburn S. Moore, "Paul Hamilton Hayne and William Gilmore Simms: Friends, Colleagues and Members of the Guild," *Long Years of Neglect,* pp. 166–82.

4. Trent, p. 327.

5. Simms to Rufus W. Griswold, June 20, 1841 (original in South Caroliniana Library).

6. First delivered as a lecture in Savannah, Georgia, in March 1842, then published in the *Magnolia,* n.s., I, for July 1842 and later in the *Southern and Western Monthly Magazine and Review* in 1845 in six installments, "Epochs and Events" in its final version (the one here used) appeared in *Views and Reviews in American Literature, History and Fiction,* First Series (1845), pp. 32–127; page citations to this work are given within parentheses in the text.

7. See Mary Ann Wimsatt, *The Major Fiction of William Gilmore Simms: Cultural Traditions and Literary Form* (Baton Rouge and London [1989]), p. 100.

8. The quotation, "Boundless contiguity of shade," is from William Cowper, *The Task,* Book II, line 2. The Altamaha is a river in southeast Georgia which flows into the Atlantic; Rio Bravo is another name for Rio Grande, on the border of Texas and Mexico. The War of 1812 is the only listed aspect of American history that Simms did not treat in book-length fiction or drama.

9. *Paddy McGann,* "Sharp Snaffles," and "Bald-Head Bill Bauldy" (all told in dialect), and *As Good as a Comedy* (set in backwoods Georgia) are discussed elsewhere.

10. Preface, *The Yemassee,* new and rev. ed., p. 6.

11. "William Gilmore Simms in His Letters," *South Atlantic Quarterly, L,* III (July 1954), 412.

12. "Song of Myself," ll, 1314–16.

13. *Major Fiction,* pp. 263, 100–101.

14. Davidson, "Introduction," *L,* I, xxxviii; McHaney, "William Gilmore Simms," *The Chief Glory of Every People: Essays on Classic American Writers,* ed. Matthew J. Bruccoli (Carbondale and Edwardsville, Ill. [1973]), pp. 176–77.

15. "Introduction," pp. xxxvii–xl.

16. Ridgely, p. 67. Ridgely, however, fails to perceive that such interaction was effectively delineated in the Border Romances as well as in the Revolutionary novels.

17. *The Romantic Revolution in America,* p. 127.

18. *Broadway Journal,* II [1845], 190–91.

19. Exclusive of ten "novels in little" which include some of his best work.

20. Striking examples of Simms's earthy "unflinching" realism are recorded in McHaney's appreciative study, pp. 183–87.

21. Hubbell, p. 595.

22. Simms's place in the development of the novel of violence and the psychological novel in twentieth-century American literature also deserves further study.

23. John Esten Cooke, for instance, wrote: "I do not estimate Simms' poetry highly ..." (April 2, 1873, Oliphant Collection); Hayne commented that Simms's "prodigious faculty of verse-making, amounting to improvisation, led to great diffuseness, and a fatal neglect of the '*labor linae*' ... the lack of uniform artistic excellence is but too obvious" ("Ante-Bellum Charleston," p. 262).

24. "Perceiver and Perceived," p. 121.

25. *SQR,* n.s., V (January 1852), 262.

26. *Egeria,* p. 19.

27. *SLG,* n.s., I (September 1, 1829), 173.

28. *Magnolia,* IV (April 1842), 248.

29. Loc. cit.

30. Louis D. Rubin, Jr., to John C. Guilds, April 10, 1986, in possession of the author; published in *Long Years of Neglect,* p. xi.

31. *Stories and Tales,* p. xi.

32. It is worth noting that Poe, Hawthorne, and Simms were the only short-story writers included by discerning critic Evert A. Duyckinck in the "Library of American Books" which he edited for Wiley and Putnam in the 1840s.

33. *Broadway Journal,* II, 190–91. See above, p. 172.

# Index